The Routledge Companion to Strategic Human Resource Management

Combining up-to-date research, innovative content and practical perspectives, this book is the benchmark by which all other strategic HRM reference works should be measured. Leading figures from around the globe survey the current state of the discipline, while also introducing and exploring new, cutting edge themes in order to offer a comprehensive and authoritative overview of the field.

Section introductions and integrative critiques pull together the separate themes to provide cross-comparisons between chapters to create a cohesive and well-structured volume. Unlike other texts in this area, *The Routledge Companion to Strategic Human Resource Management* incorporates contributions from leading management and business writers in areas adjacent to human resource management, including strategy, innovation and organizational learning. These add fresh and challenging insights into HRM themes from key mainstream business and management thinking. Strategic HRM is thus enriched and extended by this volume.

Focusing on the interplay between theory and practice, this book is an essential resource for researchers and students studying human resource management and strategy.

John Storey is Professor of Management at the Open University Business School, UK. He regularly consults for public and private sector organizations and for UK government ministers. He is Chair of the IPA and has published many articles in refereed journals and authored several books in the field of HRM as well as other areas of management.

Patrick M. Wright is William J. Conaty GE Professor of Strategic Human Resources at Cornell University, USA. He has published widely in leading international journals and worked with a number of the world's leading firms in their efforts to align HR with business strategy.

Dave Ulrich is a Professor of Business at the Ross School of Business, University of Michigan, and a partner and co-founder of the RBL Group. He has published 15 books and consulted and done research with over half the Fortune 200 companies. He has been ranked by *Business Week* as the #1 management educator and listed in Forbes as one of the "world's top five" business coaches.

The Routledge Companion to Strategic Human Resource Management

Edited by
John Storey,
Patrick M. Wright
and Dave Ulrich

LONDON AND NEW YORK

First published 2009
by Routledge
2 Park Square, Milton Park, Abingdon, Oxon OX14 4RN

Simultaneously published in the USA and Canada
by Routledge
270 Madison Ave, New York, NY 10016

Routledge is an imprint of the Taylor & Francis Group, an informa business

© 2009 John Storey, Patrick M. Wright and Dave Ulrich

Typeset in Bembo by
Keystroke, 28 High Street, Tettenhall, Wolverhampton
Printed and bound in Great Britain by
MPG Books Ltd, Bodmin, Cornwall

British Library Cataloguing in Publication Data
A catalogue record for this book is available from the British Library

Library of Congress Cataloguing in Publication Data
The Routledge companion to strategic human resource management/[edited by]
John Storey, Patrick M. Wright, and Dave Ulrich.
 p. cm.
 Includes bibliographical references and index.
 1. Personnel management. 2. Strategic planning. I. Storey, John, 1947–
II. Wright, Patrick M. III. Ulrich, David, 1953–
HF5549.R638 2008
658.3'01—dc22   2008017371

ISBN10: 0–415–77204–4 (hbk)
ISBN10: 0–203–88901–0 (ebk)

ISBN13: 978–0–415–77204–4 (hbk)
ISBN13: 978–0–203–88901–5 (ebk)

Contents

List of Illustrations   ix
List of Contributors   xiii

Part 1: Introduction   1

1   Introduction   3
     John Storey, Dave Ulrich and Patrick M. Wright

Part 2: Analytical frameworks   15

2   Beyond HR: Extending the paradigm through a talent decision science   17
     John W. Boudreau and Peter M. Ramstad

3   The employment perspective in strategic HRM   40
     Paul Edwards

4   Critical perspectives on strategic HRM   52
     Mats Alvesson

Part 3: The external environment of SHRM   69

5   Foundations for understanding the legal environment of HRM in a
     global context   71
     Mark V. Roehling, Richard A. Posthuma and Stacy Hickox

6   New organizational structures and forms   90
     John Storey

7   Changing labour markets and the future of work   106
    David Coats

Part 4: The strategic role of HR   **123**

8   The knowledge underpinning HR strategy   125
    John Storey

9   The pursuit of HR's core purpose: The practical doing of strategic HRM   137
    Anthony J. Rucci

10 Managing strategic change   149
    David A. Buchanan

Part 5: The HR function   **165**

11 HR competencies that make a difference   167
    Wayne Brockbank and Dave Ulrich

12 The next evolution of the HR organization   182
    Dave Ulrich, Jon Younger and Wayne Brockbank

Part 6: Areas of practice   **205**

13 Recruitment and selection   209
    Christopher J. Collins and Rebecca R. Kehoe

14 Compensation   224
    Barry Gerhart

15 Strategic performance management: Issues and trends   245
    Manuel London and Edward M. Mone

16 Strategic training and development   262
    Raymond A. Noe and Michael J. Tews

17 Collaborative teams   285
    Lynda Gratton and Tamara J. Erickson

18 Employee engagement   299
    John Storey, Dave Ulrich, Theresa M. Welbourne and Patrick M. Wright

Part 7: The capability-building perspective   **317**

19 Leadership development and talent management   321
    David D. Hatch

20 Human resources, organizational resources, and capabilities   345
    Patrick M. Wright and Scott A. Snell

21 Options for human capital acquisition   357
    Mousumi Bhattacharya and Patrick M. Wright

Part 8: Changing contexts   **375**

22 The changing context for HR   377
    Tamara J. Erickson

23 Research at the intersection of Strategic Human Resource Management
    and entrepreneurship   390
    Janice C. Molloy, Judith W. Tansky and Robert L. Heneman

24 Identifying and developing Global Leaders   410
    Schon Beechler and Dennis Baltzley

Part 9: Regions   **433**

25 Managing human resources in India   435
    Pawan S. Budhwar

26 HRM in China   447
    Fang Lee Cooke

27 Managing human resources in Africa: Emergent market challenges   462
    Frank M. Horwitz

Part 10: Performance outcomes   **477**

28 HRM, the workforce, and the creation of economic value   479
    Richard W. Beatty

29 The effect of organizational change on managers' experience of their
    working lives   488
    Les Worrall and Cary L. Cooper

30 Linking human resource management and customer outcomes   502
    David E. Bowen and S. Douglas Pugh

    Index   519

Illustrations

Figures

2.1	DuPont return on equity model	24
2.2	Finance, marketing and talentship decision frameworks	25
2.3	Yield curves for automobile features: tires vs. interior design	35
5.1	Sources of law contributing to the legal environment of HRM in a global context	75
6.1	Mapping the forms of work coordination	93
7.1	Employment change in the UK labour market 1996–2006 (% share of total employment)	108
7.2	Occupational change in the UK 1984–2014 (% of all in employment)	110
8.1	Types of knowledge underpinning HR strategy	128
8.2	Complementary multiple pathways to HR strategy formulation	134
9.1	A simple idea about intangible value creation	143
10.1	HR change agent roles	151
11.1	Competency model for the HR value proposition	170
12.1	Alignment of business organization and HR organization	184
12.2	Overview of the HR organization	189
13.1	Alternative staffing system models	210
14.1	Dimensions of total rewards and total compensation	225
14.2	Pay-for-performance (PFP) programs, by level and type of performance measure	229
15.1	The performance management cycle	246
16.1	The strategic training and development process	263
18.1	The VOICE framework	304
18.2	Interactive effect of energy and engagement on individual employee performance	312
19.1	The right stuff	324
19.2	Highest leverage developmental experiences	334
19.3	The integrated talent management process	339

20.1	Complete value chain	350
20.2	Starbucks coffee	352
21.1	Options model for human capital acquisition	363
22.1	Shifts in retirement patterns	385
24.1	Information-processing model for leaders	419
24.2	Characteristics of Global Leaders	421
28.1	Leading the workforce management transition	482
28.2	The strategic context of workforce management systems	484
30.1	A model linking HRM practices and customer outcomes in services	503

Tables

9.1	HR's core purpose and strategic implications	139
10.1	Change agency roles	152
10.2	Political tactics	158
11.1	HR effectiveness in each competency category and the influence of each competency category on business performance	170
12.1	Functional HR, shared services, and dedicated HR	187
13.1	Components of alternative recruitment and staffing models	214
14.1	Average hourly labor costs for manufacturing production workers, by country 2005 (in equivalent US dollars)	228
15.1	Examples of seminal theories and research guiding performance management policies and programs	248
15.2	Example of strategic performance management relationships – an HR department and recruiting manager	250
15.3	Strategic performance management at GHT	257
15.4	Improvement in "compliance to deadlines" over time	258
15.5	Lessons learned from GHT	259
16.1	Tannenbaum's (2002) strategic learning imperatives	263
16.2	Intellectual capital indicators and sample measures	276
16.3	Examples of training and development measures used in SHRM research	278
19.1	Contrast between changing global business and a mature domestic business environment	327
19.2	Components of talent management	338
21.1	Comparison of financial, real, and human capital options	361
23.1	Founding conditions: typology of entrepreneurial enterprises	396
24.1	Differences between expatriate and global managers	413
24.2	Traditional and global mindsets	414
24.3	Competencies of the global executive	415
26.1	Employment statistics by ownership in urban and rural areas in China	449
26.2	Key characteristics of HRM in different ownership forms	450
29.1	The incidence of organizational change by type of organization (percentage of managers citing)	492
29.2	The effect of long working hours by level in the organization (percentage citing that working long hours has a negative effect)	495

29.3   The percentage of managers citing that they have "sometimes" or "often"
       experienced various ill-health symptoms   496
29.4   Percentage of managers agreeing with each statement   496
29.5   Correlations between physical and psychological health and stressors 497

Contributors

Mats Alvesson is Professor of Business Administration at the University of Lund, Sweden and Honorary Professor at University of Queensland Business School, Brisbane and at University of St Andrews. He has previously held positions in Montreal, Turku, Linköping, Stockholm and Gothenburg, and has been a visiting academic at the universities of Cambridge, Melbourne, Colorado and Oxford. He has published a large number of books on a variety of topics, including *Reflexive Methodology* (with Kaj Skoldberg, 2000), *Understanding Organizational Culture* (2002), *Understanding Gender and Organization* (with Yvonne Billing, second edition 2008), *Postmodernism and Social Research* (2002), *Studying Management Critically* (co-edited with Hugh Willmott, 2003), *Knowledge Work and Knowledge-intensive Firms* (2004) and *Changing Organizational Culture* (with Stefan Sveningsson, 2008). He is on the editorial board of *Academy of Management Review*, *Human Relations*, *Journal of Management Studies*, *Strategic Organization*, *Management Communication Quarterly* and *Organizational Research Methods*, and is a co-editor of *Organization*.

Dennis Baltzley is an Executive Director at Duke Corporate Education. He was formerly Global Head of Leadership Development for Royal Dutch Shell. Here he managed the Shell Learning staff and the Learning Centre in The Hague, Netherlands. He ran Shell's CEO-level development programs and managed a large portfolio of partners and programs for Shell. Prior to Shell, Dennis was a police officer, a human factors engineer, a psychologist, an HR director, and later managed the ten European offices of Personnel Decisions International, a consulting firm specializing in leadership development from their Geneva office.

Richard W. Beatty is Professor of Human Resource Management at Rutgers University and a Core Faculty member at the University of Michigan's Executive Education Center. He is Director, Executive Master's in Human Resource Leadership, Rutgers University; and Director, Executive Master's in Human Resource Leadership-Europe, Bocconi University, Milan, Italy, and Rutgers University. He received his BA from Hanover College, his MBA from Emory University, and his PhD in Human Resources and Organizational Behavior from Washington University. He has published several books and more than one hundred articles, and is an associate editor of Human Resource Management. He was president of the Society for Human Resource Management Foundation and received the society's book award, and twice won the research award from the Human Resource Planning Society. He is co-author of The Workforce Scorecard (2005), named as one of the top ten must-reads for HR leaders by Human Resource Executive.

Schon Beechler is Academic Director, Duke Corporate Education, and Director, Positive Leadership Programs in Executive Education, Stephen M. Ross School of Business, University of Michigan. She was previously associate professor at Columbia Business School and directed the Columbia Senior Executive Program. Professor Beechler has conducted research and published widely in the fields of global management, human resource management, and leadership. Her work has been published in leading academic journals, including the *Academy of Management Learning and Education Journal*, the *Academy of Management Review*, the *Journal of International Business Studies*, and *Human Resource Management*, as well as in book chapters and practitioner-oriented journals. She is past chair of the International Management Division, Academy of Management, and received her PhD in Business Administration and Sociology from the University of Michigan.

Mousumi Bhattacharya is Associate Professor of Management at the Charles F. Dolan School of Business, Fairfield University. She has a PhD in Management from Syracuse University (USA), an MBA from Jadavpur University (India), and a BA in Economics from Jadavpur University (India). Her research areas are flexibility of human resource systems and its components, strategic and operational flexibility of organizations, real options theory, and flexibility of people in different countries. Dr. Bhattacharya has published in *Journal of Management, Journal of Business Research*, and *International Journal of Human Resource Management*. She has presented her work in conferences organized by the Academy of Management and the Strategic Management Society. Dr. Bhattacharya teaches strategy, international business, and human resource management (HRM). She has worked for several years in HRM, management development and strategic planning as a manager for a Fortune 500 company in India.

John W. Boudreau is Research Director at the Center for Effective Organizations, and Professor of Management and Organization at the Marshall School of Business, University of Southern California. He is recognized worldwide for over twenty-five years of breakthrough research on links between human capital and competitive advantage. A Fellow of the National Academy of Human Resources, he has received scholarly contribution and research innovation awards from the Academy of Management. He consults and conducts research worldwide, with organizations as diverse as the Global 100, early-stage entrepreneurial companies, and the U.S. Navy. He is the co-author of *Beyond HR* and *Investing in People*, as well as over fifty scholarly articles and chapters.

David E. Bowen is the G. Robert & Katherine Herberger Chair in Global Management at the Thunderbird School of Global Management. His work focuses on HRM organizational behavior issues associated with delivering service quality. His book, *Winning the Service Game*, with Benjamin Schneider, has been published in five languages. He is a past recipient of the Scholarly Achievement Award from the Human Resource Division, Academy of Management, and the Best Paper Award, Academy of Management Perspectives.

Wayne Brockbank is Clinical Professor of Business at the Ross School of Business at the University of Michigan. He is a faculty director and core instructor of its Human Resource Executive Programs. Over the past eighteen years, these have been consistently rated as the best HR executive programs in the United States and Europe by *BusinessWeek* and *Fortune*. He is director of the Michigan Human Resource Executive Programs in Hong Kong, Dubai, Singapore, and India. His research focuses on links between HR practices and business strategy, high-value-added HR strategies, and implementing business strategy through people. He has published many academic and popular articles on these topics. He is the co-author with Dave Ulrich of *Competencies for the New HR* and the *Human Resource Value Proposition*. Among his clients have been General Electric, ICICI Bank (India), Harley-Davidson, Citicorp, Cisco, General Motors, Saudi Aramco, Texas Instruments, BP, Goldman Sachs, and Hewlett-Packard.

David A. Buchanan is Professor of Organizational Behaviour at Cranfield University School of Management. He holds a degree in business administration and another in organizational behaviour from Heriot-Watt and Edinburgh Universities respectively. He has also held positions in universities in Scotland, Canada and Australia. He is the author of numerous books, book chapters, and papers on various aspects of organizational behaviour. Research interests include the management of change, change agency, factors influencing the sustainability and spread of new working practices in healthcare, and the management experience and use of organization politics. Current projects include a study of links between corporate governance arrangements and performance in healthcare organizations.

Pawan S. Budhwar is Head of the Work and Organisational Psychology Group and a Professor of International HRM at Aston Business School. He received his PhD from Manchester Business School. His main research interests are in the fields of HRM, expatriation, and organization studies and call centers with a specific focus on India. He has published in journals like *Organizational Behaviour and Human Decision Processes*, *Organization Studies*, *Management International Review*, *Journal of World Business*, *Journal of Labor Research*, *International Journal of HRM*, *Journal of Organisational Behavior*, *Human Resource Management Journal* and *Thunderbird International Business Review*. He has authored, edited and co-edited books on HRM in developing countries, Asia-Pacific and the Middle-East. He is also the Senior Associate Editor of the *British Journal of Management*.

David Coats has been Associate Director (Policy) at The Work Foundation since February 2004. He is responsible for TWF's engagement with the public policy world, seeking to influence the national conversation about the world of work. David was a member of the Low Pay Commission from 2000 to 2004 and was appointed to the Central Arbitration Committee (the UK's industrial court) in 2005. He also serves on the National Stakeholder Council, advising the government on the implementation of the Work and Well-Being Strategy.

Christopher J. Collins is an Associate Professor of Human Resource Management in the ILR School at Cornell University. He earned his PhD in Organizational Behavior and Human Resources from the Robert H. Smith School of Business at the University of Maryland. Dr. Collins's research interests include strategic human resource management, the link between HR practices and knowledge creation and innovation, the role of leadership and HR practices in creating employee engagement, and employment brand equity. His research has appeared in the *Academy of Management Journal*, *Journal of Applied Psychology*, *Personnel Psychology*, *Human Resource Management Review*, *Human Performance*, and the *Journal of Business and Psychology*. Dr. Collins serves on the editorial review board of the *Academy of Management Journal* and as an ad hoc reviewer for the *Journal of Management* and the *Journal of Applied Psychology*. Dr. Collins is a member of the Academy of Management, the Strategic Management Society, and the Society for Industrial and Organizational Psychology.

Cary L. Cooper is Professor of Organizational Psychology and Health and Pro Vice Chancellor at Lancaster University. He is the author/editor of over 100 books, 300 scholarly articles and the Editor-in-Chief of the Blackwell Encyclopaedia of Management (thirteen volumes). He is also the Chair of the government's Sunningdale Institute, President of the British Association of Counselling and Psychology, past President of the British Academy of Management and a Fellow of the (US) Academy of Management.

Paul Edwards is Professor of Industrial Relations, Warwick Business School, University of Warwick. He is a Fellow of the British Academy and a former Senior Fellow in the UK's Advanced Institute of Management Research. He edited *Work, Employment and Society* for three years and is an Associate Editor of *Human Relations*. His research interests include the personnel policies and practices of multinational companies and the organization of work and employment in small firms. Recent books are, with Judy Wajcman, *The Politics of Working Life* (2005) and, co-edited with Marek Korczynski and Randy Hodson, *Social Theory at Work* (2006).

Tamara J. Erickson is a McKinsey Award-winning author and co-author of the book *Workforce Crisis: How to Beat the Coming Shortage of Skills and Talent* (2006), as well as *Retire Retirement: Career Strategies for the Boomer Generation* (2008). Her recent articles have appeared in *Harvard Business Review* and *MIT Sloan Management Review*. Her blog "Across the Ages" appears weekly on HBSP Online (http://discussionleader.hbsp.com/erickson/). She is also the co-author of *Third Generation R&D: Managing the Link to Corporate Strategy*, a widely accepted guide to making technology investments and managing innovative organizations. She is a former member of the Boards of Directors of PerkinElmer, Inc., and of Allergan, Inc. and is President of the Concours Institute, the research and education arm of BSG Alliance. Her publications also include "What It Means to Work Here," *Harvard Business Review*, March 2007, "Managing Middlescience," *Harvard Business Review*, March 2006, and "It's Time to Retire Retirement," *Harvard Business Review*, March 2004, which was winner of the McKinsey Award for the most significant HBR article of the year.

Barry Gerhart is Professor of Management and Human Resources and the Bruce R. Ellig Distinguished Chair in Pay and Organizational Effectiveness, School of Business, University of Wisconsin-Madison. His research interests include compensation, human resource strategy, international human resources, and employee movement. Professor Gerhart received his B.S. in Psychology from Bowling Green State University and his PhD in Industrial Relations from the University of Wisconsin-Madison. He serves on the editorial boards of the *Academy of Management Journal, Human Relations, Industrial and Labor Relations Review, International Journal of Human Resource Management, Journal of Management and Organization, Management Review,* and *Personnel Psychology*. Professor Gerhart is a past recipient of the Scholarly Achievement Award and of the International Human Resource Management Scholarly Research Award, both from the Human Resources Division, Academy of Management. He is also a Fellow of the American Psychological Association and of the Society for Industrial and Organizational Psychology.

Lynda Gratton is Professor of Management Practice at London Business School where she directs the schools programme "Human Resource Strategy in Transforming Companies." In 2007 she became a scholar of the Advanced Institute of Management and since then has directed a major study of innovation and teams. Her work has been published in the *Harvard Business Review*, the *Sloan Management Review* (where she received the award for the best paper of 2007), *The Economist* and *The Financial Times*. Lynda's latest book is *Hot Spots – why some teams workplaces and organisations buzz with energy and innovation – and others don't*.

David D. Hatch is a Consulting Partner with The RBL Group and co-founder and Managing Director of Center for Leadership Solutions LLC. He was formerly a senior vice president, Executive Development and Learning with Thomson Corporation where he was responsible for e-learning, performance and talent management systems, and the leadership development of Thomson's top 600 executives worldwide. He was previously vice president of Organization, Executive Development and Learning for IBM worldwide where he worked with Chairman Lou Gerstner to build and reshape IBM's worldwide executive resource systems. Prior to IBM he was with PepsiCo. for over eleven years during its greatest period of growth, serving for six years as the leader of PepsiCo.'s Organization and Management Development group worldwide.

Robert L. Heneman is Professor of Management and Human Resources in the Fisher College of Business at The Ohio State University. He received his PhD in Industrial and Labor Relations from Michigan State University. His research has been funded by the Society for Human Resource Management, Work in America Institute, AT&T Foundation, Ford Motor Company, American Compensation Association, State of Ohio and Kauffman Center for Entrepreneurial Leadership. Dr. Heneman is the author/editor of *Business-driven Compensation Policies*, *Human Resources Management in Virtual Organizations*, *Merit Pay*, *Staffing Organizations*, plus numerous articles and chapters. His research has been published in the *Academy of Management Journal*, *Personnel Psychology* and *Academy of Management Executive*.

Stacy Hickox is an Assistant Professor in the School of Labor and Industrial Relations at Michigan State University. As an attorney, she practiced in employment and labor law, including claims of discrimination, unemployment compensation, and wage and hour claims. Before coming to MSU, she practiced in disability law at Michigan Protection and Advocacy Service. Ms. Hickox also taught for several years at MSU's law school, including courses in employment law, disability law, and civil rights. She has written a book on the Americans with Disabilities Act and several law review articles on various employment law topics. Ms. Hickox attended the School of Industrial and Labor Relations at Cornell University and received her law degree from the University of Pennsylvania.

Frank M. Horwitz is Director of the Cranfield School of Management, University of Cranfield and Professor in Business Administration. He was formerly Director of the Graduate School of Business, University of Cape Town. He was a member of the Board of Governors of the Association of African Business Schools (AABS). He specializes in human resources management, organization change and industrial relations. Professor Horwitz has been Visiting Professor at the Rotterdam School of Management (RSM) Erasmus University in the Netherlands, Nanyang Business School in Singapore, and the Faculty of Management at the University of Calgary, Canada. He has some ten years' executive experience with AECI and ICI in England. His co-authored books include *Employment Equity and Affirmative Action: an International Comparison* and *Managing Human Resources in Africa*. He has presented invited papers at conferences in Australia, Belgium, Canada, Ireland, Israel, Italy, Japan, Korea, Mauritius, Singapore, USA, United Kingdom and Zimbabwe, and has lectured at universities in Canada, Hong Kong, Singapore and the United States. He is a board member of companies, has acted as a consultant in organizational change and human capital strategies for companies in Canada, Namibia and South Africa, and to the governments of Namibia, Singapore and South Africa.

He was also the Chair of the Commission investigating the effects of sub-contracting on the collective bargaining system in the building industry. He was on the national Council of the Industrial Relations Association (IRASA), was a (part-time) commissioner on the Commission for Conciliation, Mediation and Arbitration (CCMA), and was also on the Clothing Industry Bargaining Council Dispute Resolution Panel.

Rebecca R. Kehoe is a doctoral candidate in the Department of Human Resource Studies in the ILR School at Cornell University. Her research interests include strategic human resource management, equifinality in HR systems, organizational commitment, and diversity management in organizations. She is a member of the Academy of Management.

Fang Lee Cooke is Professor of HRM and Chinese Studies at Manchester Business School, University of Manchester. She received her PhD from the University of Manchester. Her research interests are in the area of human resource management (HRM), knowledge management and innovation, outsourcing, comparative studies of employment and HRM in Asian countries, Chinese outward FDI and Chinese diaspora. Fang has published extensively on HRM and employment studies in general and on China more specifically. She is the author of *HRM, Work and Employment in China* (2005), and *Competition, Strategy and Management in China* (2008).

Manuel London is Associate Dean of the College of Business, Director of the Center for Human Resource Management in the College of Business, and Professor of Management and Psychology at the State University of New York at Stony Brook. He received his PhD from the Ohio State University in industrial and organizational psychology. He taught at the University of Illinois at Champaign before moving to AT&T as a researcher and human resource manager. He joined Stony Brook in 1989. He has written extensively on the topics of 360-degree feedback, continuous learning, career dynamics, and management development. He is co-author with Marilyn London of *First Time Leaders of Small Groups: How to Create High-Performing Committees, Task Forces, Clubs, and Boards* (2007) and, with Valerie Sessa, *Continuous Learning: Individual, Group, and Organizational Perspectives* (2006).

Janice C. Molloy is an Assistant Professor of Human Resource Management in the School of Labor and Industrial Relations at Michigan State University. She received her PhD in Labor and Human Resources with a focus on business strategy from The Ohio State University. Her research focuses on bridging micro- and macro- human resource management, including human resource management in entrepreneurial settings.

Edward M. Mone has more than twenty-five years of experience in career, leadership, and organization change and development. He is currently Vice President for Organization Development at CA, Inc. He was previously vice president for organization development at Cablevision and director of people processes and systems at Booz Allen Hamilton, Inc. He was HR division manager for strategic planning and development at AT&T, where he also held a variety of human resource and organization development positions. He is an adjunct faculty member in the College of Business, State University of New York at Stony Brook. He holds an MA in counseling psychology, and has completed doctoral coursework in organizational psychology, as well as individual, team, and organization learning at Teachers College, Columbia University. He has co-authored and co-edited books, book chapters, and articles in the areas of human resources and organization development, including *HR to the Rescue: Case Studies of HR Solutions to Business Challenges* (1998) and *Fundamentals of Performance Management* (2003).

Raymond A. Noe is the Robert and Anne Hoyt Designated Professor of Management in the Department of Management and Human Resources at The Ohio State University. Professor Noe's teaching and research interests are in human resource management, organizational behavior, and training and development. He has published articles on training motivation, employee development, work and nonwork issues, mentoring, web-based recruiting, and team processes in the *Academy of Management Journal*, *Academy of Management Review*, *Journal of Applied Psychology*, *Journal of Vocational Behavior*, and *Personnel Psychology*. Professor Noe is currently on the editorial boards of *Journal of Applied Psychology*, *Personnel Psychology*, *Journal of Organizational Behavior*, and *Human Resource Management Review*. Professor Noe has authored three textbooks, *Fundamentals of Human Resource Management* (2nd ed.), *Human Resource Management: Gaining a Competitive Advantage* (6th ed.), and *Employee Training and Development* (4th ed.). He has received awards for his teaching and research excellence, including the Herbert G. Heneman Distinguished Teaching Award, the Ernest J. McCormick Award for Distinguished Early Career Contribution, election as a Fellow of the Society for Industrial and Organizational Psychology, and the American Society for Training & Development Research Award in 2001.

Richard A. Posthuma earned his Masters degree in Labor and Industrial Relations from Michigan State University in 1977, his JD (cum laude) from the Thomas M. Cooley Law School in 1992, and his PhD in Organizational Behavior and Human Resource Management from Purdue University in 1999. He is admitted to practice law in Michigan and the District of Columbia. He is certified by the Society for Human Resource Management as a Senior Professional in Human Resources (SPHR) and Global Professional in Human Resources (GPHR). He has more than fifteen years of professional work experience in labor relations, human resource management, risk management, and law. He has published numerous articles in leading journals on employee selection procedures, procedural justice, and legal issues in domestic and international settings.

S. Douglas Pugh is an Associate Professor of Management in the Belk College of Business at the University of North Carolina at Charlotte, and an Associate Professor in the interdisciplinary program in organizational science. Previously he was a faculty member at San Diego State University. He received his PhD degree in organizational behavior from Tulane University's A. B. Freeman School of Business. His research includes the study of organizational climate in service organizations and on the emotional labor demands of service work. He has published his research in outlets including the *Academy of Management Journal*, *Academy of Management Executive*, *Journal of Applied Psychology*, *Journal of Occupational and Organizational Psychology*, *Journal of Business Ethics*, and *Organizational Behavior and Human Decision Processes*.

Peter M. Ramstad is Vice President, Human Resources and Business Development of the Toro Company, a role that includes leadership of the human resources function. Formerly at Personnel Decisions International (PDI), a global leader in helping organizations build superior strategies that provide a competitive advantage, he also served as the firm's CFO for several years. Prior to joining PDI, he was a partner in the consulting division of McGladrey & Pullen and specialized in information technology and financial consultation. He has served as an executive education faculty member at several universities and is published in Harvard Business Review and other periodicals.

Mark V. Roehling is an Associate Professor in the School of Labor and Industrial Relations, Michigan State University. He received his law degree from the University of Michigan, and his PhD in Human Resource Management (HRM) from Michigan State University. Mark's work has appeared in leading academic journals (e.g., *Harvard Business Review*, *Personnel Psychology*, *Journal of Applied Psychology*), law journals (e.g., *Employee Relations Law Journal*, *Dispute Resolution Journal*), and the popular press (e.g., *The Wall Street Journal*, *New York Times*). Mark is on the editorial review boards of *Human Resource Management*, *Employee Rights and Responsibilities Journal* and the *International Journal of Conflict Management*. Prior to his doctoral training, Mark was a practicing attorney focusing on litigation and employment law matters.

Anthony J. Rucci is Senior Lecturer in the Department of Management at Ohio State University. He was an executive officer for twenty-five yeears with three international companies: Baxter International, Sears Roebuck and Co., and Cardinal Health. His roles have included global responsibility for corporate strategy and development, legal, human resources, information technology, quality and regulatory affairs, media and investor relations and corporate branding. He has been Chairman of the Board of Sears de Mexico and Dean of the College of Business at the University of Illinois at Chicago. He has published over twenty-five journal articles and book chapters, and has delivered over 125 invited keynote addresses at major conferences over the past ten years. He holds Bachelors, Masters and PhD degrees in organizational psychology from Bowling Green State University.

Scott A. Snell is Professor of Business Administration in the Leadership and Organization area at the University of Virginia. He is the author of over fifty publications in professional journals and edited texts and has co-authored three books: *Management: Leading and Collaborating in a Competitive World*, *Managing Human Resources*, and *Managing People and Knowledge in Professional Service Firms*. Professor Snell has worked with companies such as American Express, AstraZeneca, CIGNA, Deutsche Telekom, Shell, and the World Bank to address the alignment of human resource issues and strategic management. He was formerly professor and director of executive education at Cornell University's Center for Advanced Human Resource Studies.

John Storey is Professor of Human Resource Management at the Open University Business School and Chairman of the Involvement & Participation Association (IPA). He is an Elected Fellow of the British Academy of Management, a Fellow of the Higher Education Academy and a member of the UK Government's Leadership & Management Panel. He was Editor of the *Human Resource Management Journal* 1994–2000. He was the Principal Investigator on the ESRC project "Manager's Roles in the Evolution of Knowledge" which was part of the ESRC Programme on The Evolution of Business Knowledge; he is currently Principal Investigator on the three-year NHS-funded project on "Comparative Governance and Comparative Performance". His books include: *Developments in the Management of Human Resources*, *The Management of Innovation*, and *Leadership in Organizations*, and he co-authored *Managers of Innovation*. He has extensive consultancy experience at senior management and board level.

Judith W. Tansky is Senior Lecturer of Management and Human Resources in the Fisher College of Business at The Ohio State University. She earned her PhD in Labor and Human Resources from The Ohio State University and has conducted research in human resources in small business/entrepreneurial firms, employee development from both an organizational and individual perspective, career development, the contingent workforce, and reward systems. Her research has appeared in numerous professional journals, including *Entrepreneurship Theory and*

Practice, Human Resource Management Journal, Human Resource Development Quarterly, Canadian Journal of Administrative Sciences, and *The Labor Law Journal.*

Michael J. Tews is an Assistant Professor in the hospitality management program at Ohio State University. He earned his PhD from the Cornell University School of Hotel Administration and his M.S. from the London School of Economics and Political Science. His research focuses on employee selection, training and development, and retention in the context of service employees, and his work has appeared in outlets such as the *Journal of Hospitality and Tourism Research, Journal of Vocational Behavior, Organizational Research Methods,* and *Personnel Psychology.* Michael's research and consulting sponsors have included the American Hotel and Lodging Association, Concord Hospitality Enterprises, Rainforest Cafe, and Uno Chicago Grill.

Dave Ulrich is a Professor of Business at the Ross School of Management at the University of Michigan and a partner in the RBL Group (www.rbl.net). He has published over a dozen books and hundreds of articles on issues of leadership and HR. He has created award-winning databases and consulted in hundreds of companies. His work centers on defining and delivering value to internal and external stakeholders. He likes the pursuit of ideas with impact as he bridges theory and practice.

Theresa M. Welbourne is Adjunct Professor of Executive Education at the Ross School of Business, the University of Michigan. Prior to her adjunct work with Michigan, she was a full-time professor at the University of Michigan and at Cornell University. She is the founder, President, and CEO of eePulse, Inc., a technology and management research company delivering web-based leadership tools that transform real-time business information from employees into real-time results for organizations. With over twenty-five years in the HR field, her particular focus is on understanding how various human resource, communication, and leadership strategies can harness employee and customer energy to improve firm performance. Her research has been featured in popular publications such as *Inc. Magazine, Wall Street Journal, The Financial Times, Business Week, New York Times,* and *Entrepreneur Magazine.* Her work has been published in several books and in journals such as the *Academy of Management Journal, Journal of Management, Human Resource Planning, Journal of Organization Behavior, Compensation and Benefits Review, Journal of Applied Psychology,* and *Journal of High Technology Management Research.* She is the Editor-in-Chief of *Human Resource Management.*

Les Worrall is Professor of Strategic Analysis at Coventry University Business School, Coventry University. From 1998 to 2007 he was Associate Dean (Research) at the University of Wolverhampton Business School and Director of the Management Research Centre. From 2001 to 2004, he was Visiting Professor at the Manchester School of Management at UMIST and he has been actively involved with the British Academy of Management since 1998 where he became Chair of the Academy's Directors of Research Network in 2006. For the past ten years, Professor Worrall has been working with Professor Cary Cooper and the Chartered Management Institute on the "Quality of Working Life Project". The project, which has had multiple sponsors, has focused on monitoring the effect of organizational change on managers' physical and psychological well-being and exploring how the nature of managerial work is changing.

Patrick M. Wright is the William J. Conaty GE Professor of Strategic Human Resources in the School of Industrial and Labor Relations, Cornell University, and Senior Research Fellow in the School of Social Sciences at Tilburg University. He holds a BA in psychology from

Wheaton College, and an MBA and a PhD in Organizational Behavior/Human Resource Management from Michigan State University. Professor Wright teaches, conducts research, and consults in the area of Strategic Human Resource Management (SHRM), focusing particularly on how firms use people as a source of competitive advantage. He has published over sixty research articles, twenty chapters in books and edited volumes, co-authored a leading HRM textbook (now in its 6th edition), and co-authored or co-edited six books.

Jon Younger is a Principal of the RBL Group, and leads the firm's strategic HR practice. He was previously SVP and chief talent and learning officer for a leading financial services organization; prior to that he was a co-founder and managing director of the Novations Group. His work has appeared in the *Harvard Business Review*, *HRM Journal*, *HR Planning*, and the *Research and Technology Management Journal* among other publications, and he is a co-author of the forthcoming book *HR Competencies* with Dave Ulrich, Wayne Brockbank and others. His PhD is from the University of Toronto.

Part 1

Introduction

This first Part contains just one chapter. Written by the editors of the volume, it seeks to set the scene for the book as a whole. To do this it describes the background and identifies some of the central themes of the book.

Four themes in particular deserve special mention. First, that there is a growing demand for a bridge between theory, research and practice. The chapters in this volume seek to attend to this. Second, that there is an increasing realization that what goes on inside a firm affects what happens outside, and vice versa. The chapters in this book make the case for connecting HR issues inside the firm (e.g., employee commitment, policies, etc.) in ways which connect to the external world – suppliers, investors and customers. How things are done inside the organization shape the things that go on outside – and vice versa. A good example of this is the notion of 'employer brands'. A third theme is the need for HR to manage both at the micro- and macro-levels – for example, to actively manage individual talent and organization culture and form. The fourth theme is that HR must learn to manage both transactions (administrative, operational work of HR) as well as transformation (change, strategic and long-term work). These are often seen as two different types of operations. The operations require efficiency through technology; the strategic requires transformation through alignment and integration. One possible implication is that just as other functions have gone through separation (finance versus accounting, sales versus marketing, information for data centers versus decision making), so too HR may need to split.

Hence, there are a number of paradoxes to be confronted and they present considerable challenges to practitioners and researchers. There is a clear need here to bring theory and practice closer together. Theory offers conceptual roadmaps that explain why things happen. Research tests those relationships and offers evidence and data that confirm what happens. Practice built on theory is more likely to endure and to be effective. Theory built on practice passes a relevancy test. When HR theorists and HR professionals work together, both gain. This volume is an indicator of how this collaboration might be taken further.

Introduction

*John Storey, Dave Ulrich
and Patrick M. Wright*

Strategic Human Resource Management is concerned with the constellation of policies and practices relating to the interaction between people and organizations designed to enable an organization to achieve its purposes. As such, it is both a field of practice and a field of study. Although one might desire and assume this strong connection between the study and practice of strategic HR, in reality, there is often a considerable disconnect.

The gap between research into and application of HR has been described as a 'great divide' and even a 'chasm' (Rynes, 2007: 985). Indeed, such is the level of concern about this that in October 2007 the *Academy of Management Journal* devoted an Editor's Forum to a concerted exploration of the causes of this 'two-worlds' academic–practice divide. This *Routledge Companion to Strategic Human Resource Management* is designed to bridge research and practice. It does not speculate about why there may be a divide or propose what might be done about it; rather, it seeks to show how there is much of mutual relevance between current theory and practice. Practice anchors theory and theory informs practice. One without the other is incomplete. Theory without practice falls prey to abstract thinking that informs no one. Practice without theory leads to fads rather than sustained learning and improvement (Ulrich, 1998a).

The authors commissioned for this volume have much to say about both theory and practice. Most play in the field of practice as active consultants or managers but they are also academically grounded in the work they do. They observe, describe, explain, advocate, and reflect on how HR work is done. But at the same time, they rely on data and evidence-based research to shape practical recommendations; and they work to build theory that will explain and predict future practice. Even the more academically oriented authors sense the need for more authentic and effective links between theory and practice. They try to ground their ideas in reality, to test the impact of their observations, and to turn research into results. Thus, one of the key purposes of this book is to bridge the theory/practice divide.

We see four ways to begin to bridge research and practices, which we will cover in this introduction:

- the nature of SHRM and its link with performance;
- an examination of analytical frameworks;

- a review and analysis of current issues and key trends;
- implications for practical action.

Strategic HRM and performance outcomes

The fundamental underlying premise underpinning any serious discussion or action within HRM and SHRM is that a causal connection exists between HR practices and organizational performance (measured in various ways and against various outcome criteria). Without such an assumption, the only rationale for allocating time and effort in HR from a management point of view would be to comply with prevailing employment laws or to meet minimum operational requirements in hiring, firing and labour deployment and the like.

At the most basic level, scholars have sought to measure the statistical correlations between the existence of certain HR practices and a range of performance outcomes (Arthur, 1994; Delery & Doty, 1996; Guthrie, 2001; Huselid, 1995; Ichniowski et al., 1997). While such statistical relationships may be fairly crude measures and subject to all manner of caveats they provide a starting point to show the relevance of HR research.

Some observers declare themselves convinced that there is now an accumulated body of evidence that HR practices can be demonstrated to be connected with favourable measures of effectiveness (Becker & Huselid, 1998; Gerhart et al., 2000; Wright et al., 2005). While this body of work is widely cited as reliable at the generic level (though many caveats about reliability remain, such as single-respondent bias in the instruments used), even when associations are found and thus the case for HR is to this extent made, this leaves open questions about the intervening processes (Becker et al., 1997; Delery & Shaw, 2001; Lepak et al., 2003; Wright & Gardner, 2003). This is sometimes referred to as peering into the black box. The premise is that, in some shape or form, HR policies have an effect on HR practices and these in turn influence staff attitudes and behaviours which will, in turn again, impact on service offerings and customer perceptions of value.

Investments in HR may impact both individuals and organizations. At the individual, or human capital level, investing in HR practices may increase the competence or the commitment of the individual employee (Ulrich, 1998b; Wright et al., 1994; Wright & Snell, 1998). Competence is comprised of knowledge and skills including tacit knowledge as well as formal knowledge. This 'human capital' embedded in individuals can be enhanced through education, training and development, or an aligned compensation system. Individuals may become more competent in delivering an organization's financial or strategic goals (e.g., learning to do business in China). Commitment deals with engagement or application of knowledge to a particular condition or setting. Regardless of competence, individuals may be more or less committed to the extent that they dedicate their energy and attention to a particular set of goals. HR practices may focus and enhance how much individuals attend to a particular set of issues through staffing, compensation, or training.

Commitment deals with 'effort'. This has always been a point of focus for HR, labour relations and staff management of all kinds. Human capital is unique in the inherent variability with which it can be deployed. No matter how regulated the job, people tend to have degrees of *discretionary effort* which they can withhold or commit. As a result, a great deal of time has been spent in thinking about how managers can 'motivate' and how they can 'engage' workers so that they will be sufficiently committed to go the extra mile in their work. This attempt to win hearts and minds has long been core to HRM. Much recent discussion of the theme when applied to the application of effort towards organizational-wide rather than 'merely' task focus is based on the concept of 'organizational citizenship behaviour' (OCB). For example, it has been shown that High Performance HR practices can drive organizational citizenship behaviour which can in turn increase productivity and decrease labour turnover – when certain mediating variables are taken into account (Sun et al., 2007).

However, individuals do not usually work in a vacuum. They are surrounded by co-workers: peers, subordinates, and managers in their work group, as well as in other work groups across the organization. Often, the effectiveness of one's own contributions depends upon the network of relationships one has with others around the firm. The communications and trust with others form the basis for what is referred to as 'social capital' (Nahapiet & Ghoshal, 1999). This aspect was reflected in Robert Putnam's (2000) book *Bowling Alone* which lamented the decline of community in the USA. At the organizational level, this translates into an agenda based on shared sense of purpose and corporate citizenship. The concept is also closely entwined with that of 'trust'. The agenda on social capital necessarily extends beyond the workplace into the wider society and connects with issues of health, crime and social participation. Some in turn argue that the loosening of social ties is not unconnected with changes in polices and practices in the work domain (David Coats in this volume, Chapter 7).

As Nahapiet and Ghoshal (1998) have argued, competitive advantage can derive from a combination of social capital and human or intellectual capital. The latter term is used by Youndt et al. (2004) to denote the aggregation of all knowledge in an organization which can be leveraged for competitive advantage. The implication is that SHRM needs not only to tackle the resourcing and development of individual abilities, but in addition to attend to the fuller utilization and development of shared and *complementary capabilities* (Subramaniam & Youndt 2005). The relationship between HRM and the knowledge literature is still in its infancy. Further exploration of this relation is to be found in the chapter by John Storey in this volume (Chapter 6).

At an organization level, HR practices may be used to build organization capabilities (Ulrich & Smallwood, 2007). Organizations develop identities, often called cultures, social capital, or simply things the organization is known for and good at doing. When HR practices align to create and shape an organization's capabilities, the organization creates a unique identity that enables it to better research its strategy. Wal-Mart desires to be known for low prices, a distinct part of its strategy. When HR practices align to this identity, Wal-Mart is more able to sustain this organization capability. In this volume, the Wright and Snell chapter (Chapter 20) attempts to examine the links between HR, resources, capabilities, and dynamic capabilities.

Ultimately, HR builds both individual ability and organizational capability, human capital and social capital. When taken together, these individual (competence and commitment) and organizational (capability or social capital) outcomes concern cooperation and working together in a mutually dependent way to deliver positive outcomes. The examination of how HR links to these outcomes is addressed by a number of chapters in this volume, most notably in the study of the link between SHRM and financial outcomes by Beatty and Huselid (Chapter 28); the link with employee outcomes (Worrall and Cooper, Chapter 29) and the link with customer outcomes (Bowen and Pugh, Chapter 30). Arguably, the positive reinforcement between high-involvement practices and high performance could be even greater if corporate analysts and forecasters took into account the degree and efficacy of these practices. According to recent research, analysts tend to neglect such variables and indeed find access to relevant data difficult (Benson et al., 2006).

Even from these initial observations, it is evident that SHRM has to deal holistically with a range of variables. In dealing with the range of variables, theorists and practitioners have developed a number of analytical frameworks to guide thinking and decisions about the linkages between HR, strategy, and various individual and organizational outcomes. We turn to some of these frameworks next.

Analytical frameworks

Contemporary SHRM is the confluence between diverse streams of academic work. The field of HRM has various roots in economics, sociology, and psychology, and similarly SHRM has evolved as a somewhat multidisciplinary field of inquiry. Wright and McMahan (1992), in their analysis of theory in SHRM, identified economic, sociological, and psychological theories that have been used to explain HR practices. However, without question, theoretical developments in strategic management literature have been of special importance. The resource-based view of the firm has been especially influential (Barney, 1991; Pfeffer, 1994; Wright et al., 2001). The resource-based view focuses on the valuable and unique internal resources and capabilities that firms possess that enable them to outperform their competitors. Building on this framework, many early authors focused on the concept of 'human capital', or the talent pool, as having the potential to be sources of competitive advantage. Lepak and Snell (1999) specifically recognized that different human capital pools within the firm varied in terms of the value and uniqueness of their skills, and that these differences implied different HR systems to manage them. Moving another step forward in this vein, Boudreau and Ramstad contend that the part of HR focused on talent is ripe for upgrading into a more sophisticated 'Decision Science'. Their concept of decision science suggests that value and uniqueness of human capital can be measured, and that the measurement of such is critical to effective HR decision making. They discuss this framework in Chapter 2.

An additional set of analytical approaches tends to not only focus on how individuals perform but also on how organizations perform through the capabilities embedded in the organization itself. This is examined in this volume through chapters on building capabilities such as leadership, talent, capacity for change, culture, accountability, strategic clarity, customer service, efficiency, collaboration, or learning. For example, an approach to linking human capital to organizational outcomes focuses on the concept of knowledge management. Because a number of authors within the strategic management literature have suggested such ideas as the 'knowledge-based view of the firm' (Curado & Bontis, 2006; Quinn, 1992) and knowledge resides at least partially in the people of the firm, authors have begun to examine HR's role in knowledge management (Kang et al., 2007). Storey's chapter in this volume (Chapter 8) presents another approach to exploring the links between HR and knowledge.

Using these analytical frameworks, considerable and extensive analysis of the HR function itself may be done. This analysis covers the strategic reshaping and evolution of the HR function (Ulrich, Younger and Brockbank, Chapter 12) and the competencies required of HR professionals to deliver against increased expectations (Brockbank and Ulrich, Chapter 11).

While the preponderance of SHRM frameworks comes from links to the strategic management literature, it is important to note that such approaches are largely managerialistic in their orientation. They focus on managers as key decision makers in how to structure the work systems and HR practices to manage the workforce, and usually ignore constraints to such decision making. While useful, these frameworks often miss important constraints. Within the European tradition in particular, assumptions about managerial priorities cannot be assumed. The pluralist tradition which remains alert to multiple interests and stakeholders of which managers are but one, runs deep. Further, critical management which explores issues of power, conflict and institutional bias is more prevalent in Europe than in the USA, for example. A rather different analytical approach is illustrated by Paul Edwards's probing of the evolution of HR from traditional industrial relations (Chapter 3). The influence of critical theory and post-modernism is discussed in the chapter by Mats Alvesson (Chapter 4).

As previously discussed, the field of HR must attend to a number of different external forces, and a number of analytical frameworks have been proposed to help explain and explore the linkages between HR, strategy, and various outcomes. However, these often static models must be balanced and adapted to a changing set of issues and trends. It is to these trends that we now turn.

Current issues and key trends

The nature and purpose of strategic HRM does not stand still. It is honed and shaped by global, national and local currents and is thus ever-changing. Hence 'solutions' are time specific. These currents are multiple in nature and can be political, legal, economic, social and cultural. Key changes impacting massively on HRM include globalization, technological changes, migration and demographic changes, ownership structures, and customer expectations to name just the salient ones.

Globalization has undoubtedly been one of the major factors driving organizational change. As transportation has enabled the movements of goods and people more quickly and easily, companies have been able to expand their products and services into other markets. Early on, globalization required HR to understand how to manage people from different countries and geographies, but the work in each was largely the same. However, the recent advances in telecommunications have enabled the mass migration of work to whatever area of the globe provides the necessary skills to perform that work at the lowest cost. The phenomenon of 'globalization' takes numerous forms including off-shoring, relocation of headquarters, changes in corporate ownership, challenges of immigration, new strategic alliances, joint ventures, and other forms of cross-boundary working such as global teams, global sourcing, mass migration and so on.

Globalization deals both with how to create organizations that work across the world as well as how to design HR practices which work with the unique requirements of a particular country or region (Friedman, 2005; Palmisano, 2006). Each of these carries very significant implications for human resource management. A crucial one has been the way in which multinational firms have been able to move capital investment from location to location and thus put pressure on local managers and employees alike. Another HR dimension is the way in which HR inputs may be needed to build trust between inter-organizational teams that are supposed to collaborate (Williams, 2007). Globalization, most especially the need to develop a new breed of global leaders, is explored by Beechler and Baltzley (Chapter 24). The analysis of global trends is examined further in a series of chapters exploring developments in a range of rapidly developing economies. Chapter 25, by Budhwar, probes the nature of HR changes in India; Chapter 26, by Cooke, examines developments in China; and Horwitz (Chapter 27) assesses developments in South Africa.

The resulting degree of competition for jobs as a result of globalization has meant that the sophisticated 'commitment model' of HRM with its integrated package of high performance fuelled by high pay and benefits, excellent training, careful selection and the like has not been the only response from employers. Some employers, using global sourcing, have outsourced key jobs in a search for low-cost labour. In this vein companies have utilized short-term and temporary contracts, outsourced labour, low pay and insecure work. Rather than advocate the political or economic superiority of one approach, this volume discusses the trade-offs for each and helps make informed choices about alternative approaches to global labour management.

Thus, while an emphasis on investment in human capital along with the associated 'war for talent' has been a prominent feature along with an associated dramatic rise in salaries and bonuses for some sections of the workforce, at the same time there have been other trends moving in the reverse direction. Thus, some firms have sought to compete through the casualization of labour. Small-scale enterprises using the services of 'gangmasters' hire low-paid labour on conditions which amount to daily contracts. Large-scale migration into Europe and North America and, within Europe, large-scale movement from the new accession countries in the East to the more developed economies of the West has fuelled these practices. The idea of a global 'dual labour market' appears alive and flourishing.

As a result of such variety the discovery and identification of a single overall trend in HRM practice seems improbable. There are, however, a number of 'hot topics' which practising managers tell us they are keen to know more about. Four in particular tend to be ranked at the top:

- employee engagement;
- talent management;
- leadership;
- legal and regulative requirements.

The first three are interesting in that they share a strong emotional pull. They appeal to *feelings* and not just the rational mechanics of, say, performance management, reward mechanisms, or clarity of role definition. It is not only that managers instinctively tend to believe that emotions as well as intellect and rationality matter but there is also research to support the notion (Amabile & Kramer, 2007). Feelings of pride at work, sadness, fear, anger, warmth and so on have significance in relation to work performance. A further observation is that each of the three offers a fresh approach to related enduring themes such as commitment, change management, organizational culture management, the psychological contract and values. Taken together, these topics speak to the underlying strategic human resource management themes of winning hearts as well as hands and minds so that superior performance can be elicited. Chapters in this volume address these and related themes in some depth. For example, Storey, Ulrich, Welbourne and Wright tackle the idea of employee engagement directly in Chapter 18; Gratton and Erickson report on HR and innovative teams in Chapter 17.

The fourth in the list above is rather different. A concern with changes in the law and regulations is indicative of another facet of human resource management work. Senior managers here are expressing their anxiety to minimize exposure to risk by seeking to avoid breach of state requirements. A discussion of international variations in legal requirements is to be found in Chapter 5, by Roehling, Posthuma and Hickox.

An analysis of current issues and key trends also points up a number of other key social and economic changes. These include demographic shifts, including issues relating to age and retirement; and a significant increase in migration of labour across the globe. The creation of new trading blocks in a Europe of twenty-seven countries with its own hinterland of Eastern countries with fewer regulations and cheaper labour, is indicative of the importance of labour market issues. Chapter 7, by David Coats, probes the various economic and social aspects of changing labour markets. There are changes too in terms of technology. These kinds of developments are explored in the chapter by Gratton and Erickson (Chapter 17). New organizational forms and networks are assessed in Chapter 6, by Storey, while the related topic of enterprise, small businesses and entrepreneurship is examined in detail by Molly, Tansky and Heneman in Chapter 23.

One practical implication of the above summaries of positive links between HR inputs and organizational performance outcomes is that there would seem to be a sound case for more systematic development of HR professionals and other senior managers who shape the human capital elements of corporations and public sector organization. Recent research suggests that systematic programmes targeted at developing the competencies of HR professionals can have positive results (Quinn & Brockbank, 2006).

In the final section of this Introduction we turn to a set of practice-related proposals. Accordingly, in this part of the chapter we shift our tone from the normal academic–analytical to a more prescriptive mode. This is in line with our declared mission for this volume.

Practical action within a world of paradoxes

We do not pretend to predict the future, yet we must anticipate it. An executive recently said that a business that took twenty years to create could collapse in two years if it could not adapt quickly to unpredictable changes. Hence, there is a pressing need to attempt to anticipate the future so as to avoid being mired in the past. If HR professionals are to retain any presence in the future they must add value. Adding value means focusing less on what HR does and more on *what HR delivers* and to whom it delivers it. HR professionals have responsibility to help multiple stakeholders get value from the HR work they do. Employees should have a value proposition where those who deliver value get value back. Line managers should be assured that strategic plans are realized by having as much discipline about making strategy happen as crafting strategy. Customers should know that the firm will be organized so that customers buy products and services and increase customer share with targeted firms. Investors gain value from HR as they have confidence in future earnings as reflected in the price/earnings ratios which affect stock price. Communities are well served by HR as firms build reputations for social responsibility and service. As HR serves each of these stakeholders, they deliver value. The question is less the need to serve stakeholders, but how to do it.

In recent months, we have seen HR professionals who deliver the most value by managing paradoxes. Traditionally, HR is asked to do one thing (e.g., manage terms and conditions of work); now they are being asked simultaneously to do multiple things (manage terms and conditions of work, and create human capital for the future). Let us suggest three primary paradoxes that may shape how HR professionals can make a practical contribution in the near future.

Manage both the individual and the organization

HR professionals will need to manage both individual talent and organization culture. A trend in HR is to focus on an individual's ability, called talentship, workforce, or human capital. Many have focused lately on winning the war for talent. Managing talent means that steps are actively taken to ensure that employees are competent, committed, and contributing. Competence means that employees have the skills today and tomorrow required for business results. This means focusing on staffing, training, promoting, retaining, and outplacing employees. Commitment means that employees put in discretionary energy and are engaged to the firm. This shows up in commitment indices and productivity. Contribution, an emerging area for talent, means that employees find personal abundance at work. This means focusing on meaning, purpose, identity, and other disciplines that touch employees' hearts and souls.

But having great talent without teamwork makes people into all-star teams who do not work well together. The challenge ahead will be to build both individual ability and organizational capability. Organizational capability deals with the culture and organization as a whole. Culture deals with the identity of the firm. It focuses on how individual talent comes together in a common purpose to make the whole more than the parts. Culture makes *individuals* who can perform good events into *teams* who can create good patterns.

HR professionals must learn to manage both the person and the process. HR professionals who only play in the talent arena and avoid organizations may find great people who don't make others around them better. HR professionals who primarily look at organizations may have wonderful systems that lack the individual ability to win.

HR theorists and researchers need to conceptualize and study how individual and collective action can work together for the benefit of multiple stakeholders. HR professionals need to engage their line managers in conversations about how to improve both talent and culture.

Connect the inside and the outside

Historically, HR investments focus inside the organization on employees and line managers. For example, we frequently hear the words that a company wants to be the 'employer of choice'. Increasingly, HR needs to connect the inside and the outside, and change the image; we want to be the employer of choice *of employees our customers would choose*. This has implications for the movement on building on strengths. No one would disagree with the proposition that strengths matter, but HR professionals should learn to build on strengths *that strengthen others*. Leadership competency models should be guided by customer and investor expectations (Ulrich & Smallwood, 2007). Ulrich and Smallwood argue that the concept of the 'Leadership Brand' defines leadership from the outside/in. It starts with what customers want an organization to be known for (firm brand), then translates this external identity into internal employee actions and organization capabilities. If a targeted customer looked at your company's performance appraisal or training programme, would they see the behaviours and outcomes that increase customer and investor confidence in the future of the firm? If your company has a set of values (most often in practice created from the inside/out), then shift them to an outside/in focus. Take them to targeted or key customers and ask them: first, are these the values that matter most to you; second, how do we live the values in ways that are meaningful to you; third, when we live these values, would you be willing to buy more from us? Each of these examples connects traditionally internal HR practices to external customers and investors.

By connecting the inside to the outside, HR professionals contribute to management discussions with the ability to deliver real business value. Too often, HR professionals see their 'customers' only as employees inside the firm, not taking into account customers, investors, and communities in which the firm operates. HR professionals who think about value do so by understanding customers. One firm encouraged their HR generalists to spend a day a month in customer sales calls. HR professionals go with sales or account managers into customers' offices. At first, both the account manager and customer wondered what HR delivered. Then the customer learned that when HR could translate customer expectations into hiring, training, paying, and organizing work, customer needs were better met. Account managers were delighted to find longer term customer relationships rooted in the organization more than an individual person. And, HR professionals could re-assess their HR work and upgrade it with these principles in mind.

HR theory and research can and should work across internal and external boundaries, to show that what happens inside an organization has impact on what happens outside an organization. Bowen and Pugh (Chapter 30) offer insightful observations about how employee attitude is a lead indicator of customer attitude. HR professionals who link the inside to the outside become part of the management team focused on the business not just on HR. Too often HR professionals declare themselves partners just because they attend the management team meetings. If the primary HR contribution in management discussions remains focused on HR issues (labour policy, staffing, training, compensation), then HR is not fully contributing. When HR professionals link what they know to external stakeholders, sustainable value is created.

Deliver both transaction and transformation

Going forward, HR must learn to manage both transactions (administrative, operational work of HR) and transformation (change, strategic long-term work). These are often seen as two different types of operations. The operations require efficiency through technology; the strategic requires transformation through alignment and integration. Just as other functions have gone through separation (finance versus accounting, sales versus marketing, information for data centers versus decision making), so too HR may need to split in half.

Transaction-centered HR will be measured by the efficiency with which transactions occur. Technology may drive employee and administrative transactions to be increasingly done through e-HR systems, service centers or outsourcing. HR theory and practice about doing administrative work efficiently is rapidly emerging with most large global firms investing heavily in administrative support. In many cases, practice leads theory and large HR information systems may be set up but not meet expectations. Emerging theory and research in this area will tease out best practices in administrative support.

Transformational HR requires that HR professionals learn how to adapt HR investments to business success. The evolution of the HR function into centres of expertise, embedded HR, and operational HR (Ulrich, Younger and Brockbank, Chapter 12) offers a glimpse into how HR can organize to make transformation happen. As HR professionals master the competencies to transform their business, they will also contribute in ways that add value.

Clearly, these are not the *only* paradoxes on the horizon for HR practice and theory. As we envision the next generation of HR, we see a need for both theory and practice to address issues such as:

- defining accountability for HR work as both HR professionals and line managers;
- building strategic HR work that focuses on turning business strategies into results and doing HR strategic work that makes the function of HR operate in a more accountable and business like way;
- using HR practices to develop and engage people and using HR practices to drive business performance;
- ensuring that HR practices offer stability and continuity to an organization and at the same time enable the organization to adapt and change;
- shaping HR practices that give firms a global leverage and also a local responsiveness;
- using HR practices to ensure that all employees are treated equally and also using HR practices to demonstrate equity or differentiation among employees.

These and other paradoxes offer challenges for where theory and practice can come together. Theory offers conceptual roadmaps that explain why things happen. Research tests those relationships and offers evidence and data that confirm what happens. Practice built on theory endures. Theory built on practice passes a relevancy test. When HR theorists and HR professionals work together, both win. This volume is an indicator of how this bridge might be built.

References

Amabile, T. and Kramer, S. (2007). "Inner work life: understanding the sub-text of business performance." *Harvard Business Review* May: 72–83.

Arthur, J. B. (1994). "Effects of human resource systems on manufacturing performance and turnover." *Academy of Management Journal* 37(3): 670.

Barney, J. (1991). "Firm resources and sustained competitive advantage." *Journal of Management* 17(1): 99.

Becker, B. E. and Huselid, M. A. (1998). "High performance work systems and firm performance: A synthesis of research and managerial applications." *Research in Personnel and Human Resources Management* 16: 53–101.

Becker, B. E., Huselid, M. A., Pickus, P. S. and Spratt, M. F. (1997). "HR as a source of shareholder value: Research and recommendations." *Human Resource Management* 36(1): 39–47.

Benson, G., Young, S. et al. (2006). "High involvement work practices and analysts' forecasts of corporate earnings." *Human Resource Management* 45(4): 519–538.

Curado, C. and Bontis, N. (2006). "The knowledge-based view of the firm and its theoretical precursor." *International Journal of Learning and Intellectual Capital* 3(4): 367–381.

Delery, J. E. and Doty, D. H. (1996). "Modes of theorizing in strategic human resource management: Tests of universalistic, contingency and configurational performance predictions." *Academy of Management Journal* 39: 802–835.

Delery, J. E. and Shaw, J. D. (2001). "The strategic management of people in work organizations: Review, synthesis, and extension." In G. R. Ferris (ed.), *Research in Personnel and Human Resource Management* (vol. 20: 167–197). New York: JAI.

Friedman, T. (2005). *The World is Flat: A Brief History of the Twenty First Century*. New York: Farrar, Straus, & Gireaux.

Gerhart, B., Wright, P. M., McMahan, G. C. and Snell, S. A. (2000). "Measurement error in research on human resources and firm performance: How much error is there and how does it influence effect size estimates?" *Personnel Psychology* 53: 803–834.

Guthrie, J. (2001). "High Involvement work practices, turnover, and productivity: Evidence from New Zealand." *Academy of Management Journal* 44: 180–192.

Huselid, M. A. (1995). "The impact of human resource management practices on turnover, productivity, corporate financial performance." *Academy of Management Journal* 38: 635–672.

Ichniowski, C., Shaw, K. and Prennushi, G. (1997). "The effects of human resource management practices on productivity." *American Economic Review* 87: 291–313.

Kang, Sung-Choon, Morris, S. and Snell, S. A. (2007). "Relational archetypes, organizational learning, and value creation: Extending the human resource architecture." *Academy of Management Review* 32 (1): 236–256.

Lepak, D. P. and Snell, S. A. (1999). "The human resource architecture: Toward a theory of human capital development and allocation." *Academy of Management Review* 24(1): 31–48.

Lepak, D. P., Takeuchi, R. and Snell, S. A. (2003). "Employment flexibility and firm performance: Examining the moderating effects of employment mode, environmental dynamism, and technological intensity." *Journal of Management* 29(5): 681–705.

Nahapiet, J. and Ghoshal, S. (1998). "Social capital, intellectual capital and the organizational advantage." *Academy of Management Review* 23(2): 242–266.

Pfeffer, J. (1994). *Competitive Advantage Through People: Unleashing the Power of the Workforce*. Boston: Harvard Business School Press.

Putnam, R. D. (2000). *Bowling Alone: The Collapse and Revival of Community*. New York: Simon & Schuster.

Quinn, J. B. (1992). *Intelligent Enterprise*. New York: Free Press.

Quinn, R. T. and Brockbank, W. (2006). "The development of SHR professionals at BAE Systems." *Human Resource Management* 45(3): 477–494.

Rynes, S. (2007). "Editor's Foreword: Tackling the 'Great Divide' between research production and dissemination in human resource management." *Academy of Management Journal* 50: 985–986.

Subramaniam, M. and Youndt, M. A. (2005). "The influence of intellectual capital on the types of innovative capabilities." *Academy of Management Journal* 48(3): 450–63.

Sun, L.-Y., Aryee, S. et al. (2007). "High performance HR practices, citizenship behaviour and organizational performance: A relational perspective." *Academy of Management Journal* 50(3): 558–577.

Ulrich, D. (1998a). "Integrating practice and theory: Towards a more unified view of HR." In Patrick Wright, Lee Dyer, John Boudreau and George Milkovich (eds), *Research in Personnel and Human Resources Management*. Greenwich, CT: JAI Press.

Ulrich, D. (1998b). "Intellectual capital = competence × commitment". *Sloan Management Review* 39(2): 15–26.

Ulrich, D. and Smallwood, N. (2007). "Building a leadership brand." *Harvard Business Review* July–August.

Williams, M. (2007). "Building genuine trust through interpersonal emotion management: A threat regulation model of trust and collaboration across boundaries." *Academy of Management Review* 32(2): 595–621.

Wright, P. and Gardner, T. (2003). "Theoretical and empirical challenges in studying the HR practice–firm performance relationship." In D. Holman, T. D. Wall, C. Clegg, P. Sparrow and A. Howard (eds), *The New Workplace: A Guide to the Human Impact of Modern Working Practices* (pp. 311–330). Hoboken, NJ: John Wiley & Sons.

Wright, P. M. and McMahan, G. C. (1992). "Theoretical perspectives on strategic human resource management." *Journal of Management* 18: 295–320.

Wright, P. and Snell, S. (1998). "Toward a unifying framework for exploring fit and flexibility in strategic human resource management." *Academy of Management Review* 23(4): 756–772.

Wright, P., Dunford, B. and Snell, S. (2001). "Contributions of the resource based view of the firm to the field of strategic HRM: Convergence of two fields." *Journal of Management* 27: 701–721.

Wright, P. M., McMahan, G. C. and McWilliams, A. (1994). "Human resources as a source of sustained competitive advantage: A resource-based perspective." *International Journal of Human Resource Management* 5: 301–326.

Wright, P., Gardner, T., Moynihan, L. and Allen, M. (2005). "The HR–performance relationship: Examining causal direction." *Personnel Psychology* 58: 409–446.

Youndt, M. A., Subramaniam, M. and Snell, S. A. (2004). "Intellectual capital profiles: Examination of investments and returns." *Journal of Management Studies* 41(2): 335–361.

Part 2

Analytical frameworks

The chapters in this part of the volume are concerned with ways of looking at strategic human resource management. The practical actions which occur under this label can be approached from a number of perspectives. The chapters in this part indicate just how different these analytical approaches can be.

The chapter by John Boudreau and Peter Ramstad seeks to outline a forward-looking manifesto for the discipline. In seeking to trace the foundations for highly regarded disciplines such as finance and marketing, these authors argue they can be found in the decision science on which they are based. Likewise, for HR the secret is to locate the underlying decision science – in this case they contend it rests on a decision science of 'talentship'. This means that HR's essential contribution is to help organizations compete in the critical market for talent. This means attending to decisions made by managers and others outside the HR function itself. The other key aspect of this chapter is its clarification of the aspiration for a science of HR. This chapter serves as a manifesto which places certain HR issues as necessary elements of the work of organizational leaders even though they are outside the HR function – just as chief executives are expected to understand and act upon financial matters related to assets and liabilities. Boudreau and Ramstad envisage 'game-changing' effects resulting from the first-mover effects that will be created when their ambitious decision science approach is first adopted.

The chapter by Paul Edwards reveals and illustrates a markedly different analytical perspective. This chapter reinterprets HRM as essentially about the 'employment relationship'. This means attending to the multiple perspectives of employees and employers. As such it is inherently open-ended and needs to be alert to and able to handle competing and even contradictory principles. It means, for example, dealing with both conflict and cooperation. It means an understanding of the role of power in the relationship – and the way roles inscribe a (temporary) balance of power. There is even a methodological dimension to this perspective, Edwards suggests, characterized by a mixture of an holistic view and an approach which involves detailed empirical work. The case is made in this chapter that conventional forms of HRM would benefit from a greater openness to this employment or industrial relations tradition. Finally, as with other chapters in this volume, there is an emphasis on the way in which external forces such as the notion of 'Corporate Social Responsibility' impact on the internal world of HRM.

Mats Alvesson in Chapter 4 takes a critical perspective, where the term *critical* denotes perceived political and social limitations and neglect in HR theory. Thus, Alvesson explains how critical, in the sense he wants to use it, focuses on social phenomena from the perspective of the 'weaker' parties in society. Thus, as well as any functional outcomes from organizations there tend also to be other effects including the exercise of power, controlling effects and even 'disciplinary' effects. This kind of perspective thus incorporates analyses based on the work of Foucault and others which lead to a concern with themes such as the formation of subjectivity and identity.

2

Beyond HR

Extending the paradigm through a talent decision science

John W. Boudreau and Peter M. Ramstad

Introduction

Why are professional disciplines such as Finance and Marketing so powerful in the minds of organization leaders, yet the discipline of HR remains stubbornly associated with personnel administration or human resource practices and programs? In this chapter, we propose that the hallmark of strategic disciplines such as Marketing and Finance is the foundational "decision science" on which they are based. We argue that such a decision science is about to emerge in the arena of the talent market. This evolution echoes the way Finance emerged in the early twentieth century to guide decisions about how organizations compete for and with the resource of money, and as Marketing emerged around the 1950s to guide decisions about how organizations compete for and with the resources of customers and offerings. We have called this the "essential evolution."

History shows that as a resource becomes more pivotal to strategic success, more scarce, and more analytically tractable, a decision science for that resource emerges to redefine its market. These are precisely the conditions that characterize the talent market today, and that characterized the markets for money and customers/offerings in early eras.

This chapter will describe the foundational elements of a talent decision science, and illustrates how those elements will evolve, by comparing the talent market to examples of more mature markets. We will also describe how the decision science principles that support this essential evolution will redefine the future of talent management, HR strategy, and indeed organizational strategic success.

Why a "decision science?"

We began using the term *decision science* around 1999/2000 to capture the essence of the way the underlying paradigm for HR was evolving. Since then, its use has become increasingly common among HR executives, thought leaders, and academics. The 2005 book of essays by thought leaders on the future of HR co-published by the Society for Human Resource Management contains an entire section entitled "See HR as a Decision Science and Bring Discipline to It" (Lossey et al., 2005). This section includes not only a chapter from us that applies talentship concepts to the sustainable enterprise (Boudreau and Ramstad, 2005b), but also other chapters such as "Science Explodes Human Capital Mythology"; "Human Resource Accounting, Human Capital Management, and the Bottom Line"; "Improving Human Resources' Analytical Literacy"; and "The Dual Theory of Human Resource Management and Business Performance."

Yet there is no widely accepted definition of, or a methodology for, a talent decision science. For decades there has been a general science of decisions and decision making, producing insights about how decision makers behave and the factors that enhance and reduce their rationality and accuracy. Our concept of a decision science for talent draws on this research. As we shall see, the components of a decision science help define the necessary elements for improving talent decisions and the relevance of the HR profession.

Stubborn traditionalism in HR management

In 2005 an article appeared in *Fast Company* entitled "Why We Hate HR" (Hammonds, 2005). It chronicled many of the all-too-common symptoms of a profession that focuses on administrative activities, requires compliance with rules, demonstrates little logical connection to strategic value, and works diligently on functional programs and practices that have no clear connection to business goals. The article has received a lot of attention. In 2006 a Web search on the title produced over twelve thousand hits, and its author asserts that it got more response than any *Fast Company* article in the prior two years (compensation.blr.com, 2006).

What many people don't remember is that in 1981 there was a similar article in the *Harvard Business Review* entitled "Big Hat, No Cattle" (Skinner, 1981). The title referred to a "tall, well-dressed businessman" in the Dallas, Texas, airport "wearing a large and immaculate Stetson hat." Nearby, two middle-aged, sunburned men in faded jeans looked him up and down and said to each other, "Big hat, no cattle." The businessman dressed like a cattleman but really had no herd. The sunburned men were the real cattle ranchers, and they didn't need to prove it with a big hat. In 1981 HR had the executive title and the executive offices, and looked and dressed like other business leaders, but the article asserted that all too often there was no evidence of real contribution to business success.

It's the same story twenty-five years apart. As we'll see, this doesn't mean that the HR profession hasn't progressed. It has. It doesn't mean that business leaders don't want to compete better for and with talent and how it is organized. They do. It *does* suggest that after twenty-five years of admonishments that HR professionals become strategic business partners, and calls for business leaders to tap the potential in their people, organizations still have not produced the kind of change we would expect. There is an answer to this problem, but it is not to continue doing the same thing better, and it is not achieved by the HR function alone.

Evidence from many sources confirms that the HR profession has made many technical advances, but in many ways it has changed little. Perhaps the most vivid evidence comes from a unique survey done by the Center for Effective Organizations. Beginning in 1995, HR professionals were asked how much time they spent on strategic pursuits compared to administrative pursuits. They noted the time they remembered spending on various activities five to seven years ago, and then they noted the time they currently spend. Every year the responses suggested that HR professionals perceived a statistically significant shift toward more strategic activities. Yet, when we examine what HR leaders said were their actual activities, then in every survey since 1995 virtually the same percentages have been reproduced each time (Lawler et al., 2006).

Obviously, today's arsenal of HR activities is very different and more sophisticated than it was in the mid-1990s, and of course, HR professionals are doing different things and doing many things better. There are improved information systems, scorecards, benchmarks, outsourcing contracts, and competency models. Workforce plans can now track the headcount moving between jobs using computerized databases and forecasting algorithms. Selection testing is done through kiosks or online surveys. These are better versions of the same tools that HR has been using for decades, and they have made important differences in the efficiency and effectiveness of the HR function. Yet by their own reports, HR professionals' focus is still largely on administrative and service-related goals, not on strategic decisions. The Center for Effective Organizations data vividly reveal a profession that is getting better at the traditional paradigm— but as we shall see, the opportunities for breakthrough strategic successes lie in a new, extended paradigm.

Talentship: the new decision science

As we will see below, the lessons from marketing and finance tell us that the goal of a talent decision science would be to increase the organization's success by improving decisions that impact or depend on talent resources. We have coined the term *talentship* to describe the new decision science and to reflect the notion of stewardship of employee talent resources. Talentship is to "human resource management," as finance is to accounting, and as marketing is to sales. The talentship decision science provides a logic that connects human capital, organizational design, organizational effectiveness, and ultimately, strategic success.

We considered for some time what to call the resource that is the focus of the talentship decision science. Finance deals with the resource of money, marketing deals with the resources of customers and offerings. We will use the word *talent* to mean *the potential and realized capacities of individuals and groups and how they are organized, including those within the organization and those who might join the organization.*

The talent resource as we define it includes not just the talents that an organization currently tracks and manages, but all those talents that are potentially available and valuable, if only you knew about them. It includes not just the people you have and how they are organized but the people you could potentially engage and the organizing decisions you could make about them. In the future, this may even go well beyond traditional employment. For example, a trend called "crowdsourcing" involves tapping customers and outside experts who are not employees, to contribute to organizational objectives. News organizations tap viewers to send in photos or videos of breaking news. Consumer products organizations tap their customers to create imaginative video ads they can post to the company website. Online search companies send mapping kits to local residents of remote regions to create more detailed maps. This is not traditional employment, yet it is certainly competing for and with talent in creative ways. Thus, the talent resource must transcend even traditional ideas about employment.

Improving the decisions about this talent resource is the domain of talentship. The talent resource includes not only the abilities of individuals; it also includes their motivations and the opportunities they encounter. It includes concepts such as human capital and knowledge. The decision science of talentship includes a structure for improving decisions about how to enhance individual contributions, and also how to enhance the way individuals interact in formal and informal groups, organizational designs, structures, and so on. Talentship is concerned with improving decisions about the talents of people and how they organize and interact.

Distinctions between markets, decision sciences, and professional practices

If we want to understand how a profession becomes strategic, we can't do it by looking within the profession or by asking internal customers whether it is strategic. Neither the HR profession nor the training of HR's constituents has prepared them to define the necessary strategic requirements. History shows that we must begin where strategy is formed and enacted, in the *markets* where organizations compete and thrive.

Consider three markets vital to organizational success: the financial market, the customer/offering market, and the talent market. In the financial and customer/offering markets, there is a clear distinction between the professional practice that defines how organizations operate in the market and the decision science used to analyze and deploy the resources there. For example, there is a clear distinction between accounting (the professional practice) and finance (the decision science). Accounting is vital for management reporting and external requirements, while finance develops tools used to make decisions about appropriate debt structure, internal rate-of-return thresholds, and so forth. There is an equally clear distinction between the professional practice of sales and the decision science of marketing. Excellent sales practices and measures are vital, but they're very different from the tools used to make decisions about customer segmentation, market position, and the product portfolio.

Today the differences between accounting and finance are so clear that we seldom even consider them. The competencies to be a successful accountant are related to but are clearly distinct from those needed to make a successful financial executive (CFO, treasurer, etc.), and professional curricula reflect this. The industry itself has segmented this way—large accounting firms are very different from investment banking firms that focus on finance. Similarly, the competencies and activities of sales are clearly distinct from those of marketing.

This does not mean that the professional practice is merely administrative or less important. The decision science cannot exist without the professional practice; the professional practice must, in fact, precede the decision science. Few organizations survive with great marketing and ineffective sales, or with great finance and unprofessional accounting. Today the synergy between accounting and finance, or between sales and marketing, is so strong that it is easy to overlook how the decision sciences evolved from the professional practices and how they are both inextricably related yet distinct. Taking a closer look at this symbiotic relationship between the professional practice and the decision science reveals insights about the evolution of HR and the talent decision science that will change it.

Like finance and marketing, HR helps the firm operate within a critical market—in this case, the market for talent. Organizations cannot succeed in the financial and customer markets without both effective decisions and effective professional practices, but they are two very distinct elements. In the talent market, organizations will also increasingly compete through the synergy of effective decisions aligned with professional practices. When we see this distinction applied to HR and talent, we see that decision processes for competing in the talent market are less mature and refined than those used in the markets for money and customers/offerings. Yet, HR *professional practices* are often as mature as accounting and sales. Today the distinction between professional practices and effective decision systems is less clear in the talent market. Yet a clear understanding of this difference reveals the path for the coming evolution. Next, let us consider the power of combining *decisions* and *science*.

Decisions

Why focus on decisions? Service excellence alone cannot achieve strategic success through resources like money, talent and customers, because such decisions are integral and ongoing in the organization, not isolated within a single function or a particular yearly cycle. The majority of decisions that depend on or impact financial capital or customers are made by leaders and employees *outside the finance and marketing functions*. This is also true for talent decisions.

When we ask leaders inside or outside of HR to think of a decision that depended on or affected talent resources but in retrospect was not made well, even companies with best-in-class HR functions can describe numerous examples. The lessons from these examples are remarkably consistent. The talent decisions are *not* typically made by HR professionals. Poor talent decisions seldom have poor HR programs as the root cause. Rather, they were made by well-intentioned leaders outside of the HR profession, trying very diligently to be logical and strategic, but using poor talent decision models. So, they create unintended and unanticipated negative talent implications.

For example, one highly specialized high-tech firm made a decision to relocate to be closer to its key customer, one that accounted for well over 50 percent of revenues. The decision logic was that the organization could more efficiently and quickly serve this large customer by locating its operations closer. This is a talent decision being made with an operational efficiency logic. What was overlooked was that the key services required certain talent—several sophisticated and highly specialized experts. When the relocation requirement was announced, many of these essential experts left the organization, creating a disruption that was far more damaging to client relationships and the company's reputation than any possible benefits of proximity. The decision required integrating perspectives from finance, marketing, operations and talent. The financial, marketing and operational elements were logically considered, but the failure to accurately consider the talent implications undermined the intended benefits.

Several senior executives we have worked with have noted that HR strategies often reflect traditionally critical industry needs, such as "avoid employee strikes" in companies where unionized manufacturing is vital and where leaders often worked in labor relations before advancing to top HR roles. In many sales organizations the rallying cry is "reduce turnover" because turnover costs among top salespeople are so apparent. HR leaders point out that without a logical decision framework, such goals can become so prominent that they mask other significant organizational needs. It is not appropriate to do absolutely anything required to avoid a union strike, nor to spend indiscriminately to reduce turnover.

The greatest opportunity to improve decisions about talent and how it is organized is by improving those decisions that are made outside the HR function. Just as with decisions about financial and customer resources, talent decisions reside with executives, managers, supervisors, and employees. They make decisions that affect the talent over whom they are responsible, the talent they interact with, and their own personal human capital. Even in functional HR processes—such as succession planning, performance management, selection, and leadership development— potential improvements in effectiveness rely far more heavily on improving the competency and engagement of non-HR leaders than on anything that HR typically controls directly.

The relocation example is typical in that most significant business decisions impact multiple resources, so the objective should be to equip leaders with more comprehensive decision frameworks. It's not a matter of choosing between people versus profits, with the organization's financial controller arguing for profits and the HR leader acting as the employee advocate. Instead, the goal is a decision science that enables leaders to integrate talent resources with other vital resources. To be sure, this improves talent and organization decisions, but its ultimate goal is to improve strategic decisions more broadly.

Science

Why use the term *science*? Because the most successful professions have decision systems that follow scientific principles and that have a strong capacity to quickly incorporate new scientific knowledge into practical applications. Disciplines such as finance, marketing, and operations not only provide leaders with frameworks and concepts that describe how those resources affect strategic success; they also reflect the findings from universities, research centers, and scholarly journals. Their decision models are compatible with the language and structure of the scholarly science that supports them.

For example, in operations research there is often a very close connection between the technical tools used in industry and the scholarly research that informs them. In the arena of total quality management (TQM), the decision frameworks used by managers reflect fundamental logical elements—such as plan, do, check, and act—that translate into logical connections with such processes as inspection, maintenance, adjustment, and equipment replacement. This logic allows managers' decision models to be quickly informed by research on topics like statistical process control, control charts, and time-series statistical analysis. It also provides a context for researchers, who frame their research questions consistently with the logic and practical issues facing leaders who apply TQM (Schroeder et al., 2005).

With talent, the logical frameworks used by leaders often bear distressingly little similarity to the scholarly research in HR and human behavior at work (Colbert et al., 2005). This is regrettable because there is much that leaders can learn from scholarly findings and much that scholars can learn by better incorporating business leaders' insights into their research (Boudreau, 2003). Consider the contrast between the scientific approach to bond ratings in finance versus employee assessment practices in HR. Both strive to provide a valid and reliable measure of the future performance of an asset with some risk. A treasury department is expected to purchase information on scientifically rigorous bond ratings in its investment decisions. HR functions often cannot generate support for more scientific employee assessment investments (valid tests, interviews, assessment centers, surveys, etc.) because their constituents don't see the value. In fact, frameworks for comparing the costs of employment testing to their benefits have existed since the 1940s, but they are not widely used, in part because organizations' decision frameworks have few connections to the logical principles of these models (Cascio and Boudreau, 2008).

A decision science also approaches decisions through a scientific method, which means that questions are framed so that they are testable and falsifiable with data-based results. It means that the logic supporting the decision science is modified when new findings make old ideas obsolete. It means that the decision framework clearly translates new scientific findings into practical implications. This scientific method includes, but goes well beyond, a fact-based approach to HR. Many articles that carry the label of "decision science" are about improved analytics, measurement, or scorecards. Deeper measures and data are certainly an element of a decision science, as we will describe later, but much of the data being used by HR lack a logical framework required to advance either decisions or science.

A true decision science does more than just incorporate facts and measures. A decision science draws on and informs scientific study related to the resource. There is a vast array of research about human behavior at work, labor markets, and how organizations can better compete with and for talent and organization resources. Such disciplines as psychology, economics, sociology, organization theory, game theory, and even operations management and human physiology all contain potent research frameworks and findings. Unfortunately, the transfer of such findings into actual decisions is often woefully slow or nonexistent. Indeed, studies suggest that even HR professionals are often surprisingly unaware of findings that are routinely accepted by the HR academic research community (Colbert et al., 2005). A decision science connects research to the practical dilemmas facing decision makers in organizations. It also provides a means to apply research on talent and organization to other fields and to bring insights from other scientific fields (such as operations, strategy, marketing, etc.) to bear on talent decisions within organizations.

Components of a talent decision science

There are five important elements in a mature decision science:

- decision framework;
- management systems integration;
- shared mental model;
- data, measurement, and analysis;
- focus on optimization.

We will describe each component in detail below, but it is important to understand how they fit together. The decision framework is the logic that connects decisions about a resource and their ultimate effects on organizational success. It defines how decision makers should logically think about these connections. Without this logic, even the most elegant systems and measures can fail because decision makers simply do not know how to interpret the information they provide. The second element is the logic integrated into management systems. When a valid and consistent logic is embedded in management systems, they become powerful tools. Consider how powerfully the finance and accounting systems incorporate principles such as net present value or internal rate of return. The third element flows naturally from the first two. Valid and useful logic that is embedded in the management systems that decision makers use will cause decision makers to better understand and value the logical frameworks. They begin to develop shared mental models that define the vital connection points in their decisions about the resource. Organization leaders understand market segmentation so well, in part because the principles of market segmentation are seamlessly embedded in virtually every customer relationship management system. The fourth element of data, measurement and analysis is often the only way that HR leaders try to enhance decisions—giving leaders more numbers. Yet, as we can see, more data is hardly helpful without a shared and logical framework to understand it. In marketing and finance, the data and measures flow naturally from the shared logical models and thus are more easily understood and used. Finally, the fifth element, a focus on optimization, means that when the logic, systems and measures are well developed, it is not sufficient merely to maximize outcomes or describe activities. Organizations do not strive merely to maximize the capacity of every machine on an assembly line. Rather, they optimize capacity by balancing between machines, and focusing on bottlenecks. Organizations do not strive to maximize customer service for every market segment. Rather, they optimize customer service to reflect the strategic value of different market segments, providing greater service where it has the largest payoff.

Too often today, HR and talent systems focus either on describing the activities of the function, or on attempting to maximize outcomes everywhere. Typical examples are setting goals that every manager increase employee engagement, that every employee increase their learning, or that every position be populated with the best performers. None of these goals is likely to optimize. As we shall see below, one of the most important implications of a decision science for talent is that it will lead to frameworks that help organizations differentially increase learning, engagement, performance and other talent outcomes according to where they have the greatest strategic effect.

Decision framework

The decision framework defines the logical connection between the decisions about a resource and the organization's ultimate goals. It defines how the organization should think about the talent and organizational implications of business decisions in a common and consistent way. It provides the basis for evaluating and improving the decisions that involve the resource.

An effective decision framework provides a consistent logical model of the chain of causal connections divided into independent elements. The DuPont return on equity (ROE) model is a good illustration (Johnson, 1975). There is a goal—ROE—segmented into three elements (margin, asset productivity, and leverage), as shown in Figure 2.1.

ROE is a consistent and logical model that can be expressed as an algebraic formula. It also depicts the causal chain of capital:

$$\text{Equity} \rightarrow \text{Assets} \rightarrow \text{Sales} \rightarrow \text{Profits}$$

Starting at the denominator in the right corner of the model, the causal chain may be described as follows:

- Equity (investment) is used to acquire assets (the ratio of assets to equity is leverage).
- Assets are used to generate sales (the ratio of sales to assets is the asset productivity).
- Sales generate profits (the ratio of profits to sales is the margin).

There is a significant amount of independence between margin, asset productivity, and leverage. While there is almost never complete independence between the elements, a good decision framework will achieve as much as possible. Within the DuPont model, lowering the cost of goods sold could increase margins without affecting asset productivity or leverage. Increasing the accounts receivable could improve asset productivity without affecting margin or leverage. Finally, reducing equity by increasing debt could increase leverage without affecting asset productivity or operating margin. The same chain of causal connections can also be seen in the decision frameworks from marketing. While there can be many variations, a typical decision framework for marketing is:

Figure 2.1 DuPont return on equity model

Reprinted by permission of Harvard Business School Press, from *Beyond HR: The New Science of Human Capital* by John W. Boudreau and Peter M. Ramstad, Boston, 2007: 30.

Investments
↓
Mix (such as the "four Ps" of product, price, promotion, and placement)
↓
Targets (typically customer or market segments, such as males 18–25 years old)
↓
Lifetime Profits

The decision framework for talentship

The causal chain for talent and organization decisions may be described as:

Investments
↓ (Efficiency)
Program and Practices
↓ (Effectiveness)
Performance of Organization Elements and Talent Pools
↓ (Impact)
Organization's Sustainable Strategic Success

Figure 2.2 illustrates the causal logic of finance, marketing, and talentship that we have described. While the analogy is not perfectly precise, you can see that the underlying logic is similar. The point is not that the talentship logic maps perfectly against marketing and finance,

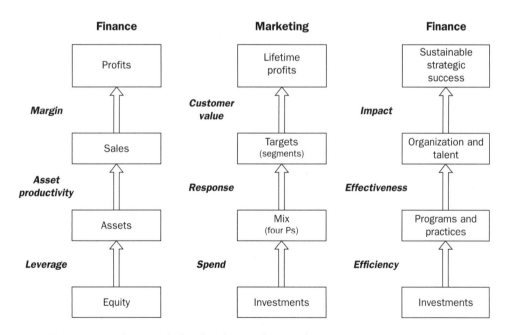

Figure 2.2 Finance, marketing and talentship decision frameworks

Source: Reprinted by permission of Harvard Business School Press from *Beyond HR: The New Science of Human Capital* by John W. Boudreau and Peter M. Ramstad, Boston, 2007: 31.

25

but rather that it is logically consistent with them. Resources are expended on activities or assets; those activities or assets produce changes in targets, such as sales, customers, and talent pools; those targets produce changes in financial outcomes or other sustainable strategic success factors.

The segments are also independent. You can spend the same amount to produce training activities (efficiency) and get far different results from the training programs and practices (effectiveness). Likewise, you can enhance skills to the same degree in different talent pools (effectiveness), but the outcomes achieved through the new skills can vary significantly. The same level of efficiency can produce different levels of effectiveness. The same level of effectiveness can produce significantly different impact. As we shall see, when organizations lack such a framework, they mistakenly consider only one part of the logical chain (such as squeezing HR budgets to produce more efficiency without considering effectiveness or impact), or they mistakenly assume that improving effectiveness improves impact (such as assuming that if employees have more training, the organization will compete better on its unique knowledge). This framework for organization and talent is called the "HC Bridge" framework, and refers to impact, effectiveness, and efficiency as "anchor points."

Traditional HR decision frameworks are often control systems

HR leaders' common first reaction to talentship and the need for a decision framework for HR is, "We already have many systems designed to help leaders outside HR make decisions, like salary structures and competency systems." Consider salary structures. Virtually everyone knows their salary grade, and employees and managers routinely use salary structures in their decisions about budgeting, headcount planning, merit pay, and other rewards. Because salary grades are often the only available framework for mapping the organization's talent resources, they can become the default framework for things such as signature authority, participation in leadership programs, parking space allocation, and many other decisions unrelated to the original purpose. The salary grade system certainly affects decisions, but it is not a decision framework in the way that we have defined it. It is an organizing framework for the delivery of an HR system, not a decision framework for the resource.

Competency systems that span an enterprise serve a similar purpose. When done well, they provide a common architecture for defining, measuring, and developing capabilities within an organization, including not only the requirements for a job but also the logical progression and important transition points between jobs. Such systems may be used to align key talent management systems, and individual measurement to help develop both individuals and the talent pool overall. Like salary grade structures, they are very important and useful, supporting both decisions and data analysis. Even well-developed versions of competency systems, however, do not provide necessary insight into important business questions such as the talent implications of alternative business models, organizational structures and design, competing talent market value propositions, and the value of HR investments.

Salary structures and competency systems are very similar to the organizing frameworks such as the "chart of accounts" in accounting that existed before the decision science of finance emerged.[1] The chart of accounts provides a classification system to organize large amounts of data, and it certainly improves the consistency of decisions. Like the chart of accounts, the salary grade system provides its primary value through systematic management control. It often creates more value in restraining excessive investment than in identifying areas where increased compensation would optimize organizational value. Competency models emerged more recently, to integrate and align HR services. When compensation and competency systems are integrated within a decision science framework, they become even more powerful and offer potentially greater impact on the organization, because they can be deployed in a more strategically relevant and integrated perspective.

Management systems integration

The next component of a decision science is the integration of its decision framework and key principles into the general management systems. When this is done well, decisions about different resources seamlessly support the overall organization and business processes. Decisions consider all the key resources, including talent, rather than focusing on resources in isolation. This integration also requires more alignment between the general business planning processes and functional planning processes, such as finance, marketing, information technology and talent. For example, planning for the finance and marketing functions is closely tied to planning for the overall organization.

A second important purpose of integrating a consistent and valid logic into management systems is that the logic is then routinely used and understood by leaders outside the functional area. Financial reporting and analysis systems reflect principles such as net present value and return on investment. Customer relationship management systems reflect principles such as market segmentation and lifetime customer profitability. Decision makers using these systems receive consistent reinforcement and encouragement to better understand the logical frameworks that underpin the decision sciences.

For example, financial frameworks are well integrated into general management systems in most organizations. In fact, one challenge to improving talent and organization decisions is that organizations often rely solely on financial management systems and lack well-developed decision systems for other important resources. For example, many organizations have strategic planning processes that focus on preparing the long-range financial plan, rather than on optimizing the overall strategic position across all resources, including talent. It is not so much that the finance function intentionally dominates but rather that its processes and frameworks are much more mature and integrated. The same integration is rarely apparent when it comes to the leadership capabilities that support the financial plan. Yet, those leadership capabilities may be far more pivotal to strategic success.

Which management systems must integrate the decision science?

Two types of management systems must be integrated with a mature decision science for organization and talent:

- Management systems outside the HR function, where talent issues should be considered and addressed, which include strategic planning, product line management, corporate development (e.g. mergers and acquisitions), operational budgeting, and capital budgeting.
- Talent management systems (often within the HR function) that must consider the strategic context of the organization, including workforce planning, staffing, development, performance management, compensation, and succession planning.

It is extremely difficult to change organizations merely by imposing new decision frameworks that compete with the familiar and useful management processes already in place. Too often, HR leaders roll out their new talent planning and decision systems as distinct and separate additions to existing processes. In our experience we've encountered workforce planning systems that have little commonality and integration with the long-range planning processes. HR leaders would often better serve the organization by improving the business planning process by integrating logical principles about talent decisions into existing systems, in partnership with other leaders, rather than deploying new and separate HR processes. When HR and talent planning processes are separate and distinct from the existing core management processes, they risk being less strategically effective.

Illustrating talent decision integration with capital budgeting

Let us illustrate how talent decision frameworks can integrate with management systems using the capital budgeting system, which is well refined in most organizations. A basic financial assumption is that higher returns carry higher risk. Yet, many of the potential risk factors in capital investments are linked to talent resources. One way that capital budgeting could be more integrated with talent decisions is to specifically identify the talent and organization risk factors associated with capital investments (availability and quality of leadership, degree of organizational change required, experience in the organization with the technology, etc.) and then set a higher required minimum return for investments that are higher risk due to organizational factors. Notice how this type of integration does not require leaders to learn a new leadership or talent system, but rather that it exploits the familiarity that leaders already have with the concept of risk, and embeds logical talent resource issues within that risk.

Integration requires aligning the timing of planning processes

Integration of talent and organization systems with management systems must also consider the sequence of planning processes. It is not unusual to encounter organizations where the talent planning process occurs long after the organizational planning process has concluded, and where the HR budget basically distributes the allotted budget for headcount or training. In some organizations HR planning couldn't possibly affect organizational strategic decisions because the HR planning process occurs *after* all the key strategic decisions are made. Even something as simple as adjusting the timing of the HR planning process so its results are available to the broader budgeting and planning process can significantly enhance integration and the resulting decision quality.

Leaders at Pepsi in the 1980s referred to decisions about hiring and training levels as the "human capex," meaning the human capital expenditure plan. They believed that organizations should treat the human capex process as equally important as the financial capex. As John Bronson, former senior vice president at Pepsi, recalls:

> One of the legacies of Andrall [Andy] Pearson at PepsiCo was the MRPA, the management resources planning audit. It was his audit of the talent of the organization. He was unabashed that it was his process, not HR's process, and not even the division presidents' process. He expected leaders to treat their human capex with the same importance as the more traditional financial capex. Andy believed that blue-chip companies required blue-chip players. He was relentless in driving the process through the PepsiCo organization. He was like a merchant banker reviewing a financing plan. If the business—unit CEO couldn't explain how the talent plan supported the growth, budget, and financial capex, not only would his plan be in jeopardy; he might lose his job. To Andy, if you didn't have a solid plan for how talent supported both superior business performance and growth, you weren't a serious contender for larger jobs.
>
> (Boudreau, 2006)

Integration requires professional consistency

A fundamental requirement for the kind of business leader accountability that PepsiCo achieved is a consistent decision framework that is aligned with functional and general management systems. HR is a less mature profession, so there is often less consistency in the decision models used within the profession when compared to more mature fields like finance. Here is one of our favorite discussion questions for business and HR leaders: suppose you asked ten controllers to address a specific financial challenge, and you asked ten HR professionals to address a specific organizational or talent challenge. Where would the responses be more consistent and aligned, among the controllers or among the HR professionals?

The answer is nearly always that there will be less consistency and alignment on the people issues than the financial ones. In addition, HR leaders' different backgrounds, experiences, and perspectives create wide variation in their responses. Often, there is significant misalignment between the guiding logic used by HR professionals at headquarters and those in the business units. Important areas such as performance management, motivation, rewards, learning, and the pipeline of talent are often presented through vastly different theories and logical frameworks. For example, when it comes to employee motivation, some may subscribe to the logic that emphasizes linking rewards to behaviors. Others may subscribe to a perspective that emphasizes creating systems that are perceived as fair. Still others may subscribe to an approach that emphasizes setting appropriately difficult and specific goals. Indeed, all of these approaches are valid, but none of them is valid by itself.

This is a symptom of HR functions operating without a common point of view. Without a consistent decision framework connecting the various elements of the talent management systems and decisions, HR professionals lack a consistent message to integrate their core systems, much less to affect the broader management systems outside the HR function. Thus, aligning internal HR systems, such as talent planning and HR functional planning, with a shared logical framework, is just as important as aligning systems outside of the HR profession with principles of talent markets.

Shared mental models

A successful decision science is used by organizational leaders as a natural part of their work. Its logic elements are a part of the mental models and mind-set of key decision makers inside and outside the profession. A very important obligation of professions with more mature decision sciences is to hold leaders *outside the profession* accountable for the quality of their decision models when it comes to the resource that is the domain of that profession. In a mature profession, all organizational leaders are expected to be conversationally competent in the basic principles of the decision framework. They are required to have the necessary skills and support from the profession to use the systems that require their direct involvement in decisions about the resource.

Shared financial mental models

For example, every organization leader must be conversant with principles from finance decision science, such as net present value and assets and liabilities. Likewise, they must be familiar with marketing decision science concepts, such as customer segments and product life cycles. The marketing and finance functions provide the minimum standards for leader competency, and they provide support and deeper professional capabilities when necessary, but all leaders know that they cannot abdicate the basic knowledge of finance and marketing principles to others. Leaders do not get to say, "I don't understand net present value, but that's just a finance concept that only accountants need to know."

As we noted above, these shared mental models are encouraged by the consistent use of professional logical frameworks within the systems that are routinely used by leaders outside the profession. For example, financial principles operate in management systems like budgeting, so leaders not only understand why they are important, but routinely use financial decision science concepts. When finance wants to improve leader competency, there is less resistance and more opportunity to improve decision making using those existing systems. It doesn't seem strange if marketing or finance suggest enhancements to the decision systems for general managers because those managers are already accustomed to systems that work with marketing and finance principles.

The importance of shared talent mental models

Today, individual leaders too often approach talent and organization decisions with vastly different mental models, divergent logical principles, and a focus on very different factors. Organizational leaders would never presume to adopt financial or marketing principles merely because they heard a compelling presentation, but their sources of talent principles are often adopted from sources as varied as the latest motivational speakers and high-profile executives to successful athletes and an occasional college professor. Such sources may well have valid information to offer, but in more mature professions the information is expected to be evaluated by the professional decision science, and incorporated into management systems before it earns widespread use. When leaders fail to see or understand a common set of principles, talent and organization management systems lack context and are seen as administrative or bureaucratic. As the talent and organization decision science matures, its principles will become more consistent and a more natural part of the mind-set of both line leaders and HR leaders, with the appropriate level of sophistication.

To achieve this goal, HR leaders will need to focus more on teaching than telling, a significant change. Finance and marketing are effective in part because their principles have been taught to business leaders in business school, followed up with executive development, and reinforced with real-world practice and career experiences in which leaders are usually coached by functional specialists. Even with very mature and strong staff functions within finance and marketing, the need for senior leaders with well-developed competencies in finance and marketing is seen as important. The emergence of the talentship decision science will very likely be supported by decision frameworks for talent and how it is organized, that will be consistently taught to organization leaders, becoming a natural part of their work and decisions.

Illustration of a motivation decision framework

When leaders are confronted with an issue involving operating cash flow, they do not attempt to invent a new measure of operating cash flow, nor do they insist that the accounting profession change their cash flow measures, so that the leader's results are stronger. It is well understand that a manager's approach to operating cash flow must be consistent with the professional standards of finance decision science.

Yet, when it comes to employee motivation, leaders often have vastly different guiding frameworks, and it is not unusual for leaders to ask HR professionals to adopt their particular motivation framework. Leaders will often say, "The employees in my unit are not performing well, so please create a new bonus incentive." Or, "I find the requirement that I rate employees on several facets of performance difficult, so let's just use one overall rating." Is cash flow really so much more important that leaders should be held to stringent standards for cash but be allowed to adopt vastly different standards for motivation?

In a mature decision science, the HR profession will be far more skilled at providing well-grounded logical frameworks for talent-related elements such as motivation. Moreover, the profession will require leaders outside of HR to become facile with these frameworks. Consider the required sophistication when it comes to motivation, for example. There are several prominent theories that describe well-supported elements of a complete solution to motivation issues (Pinder, 1998). Examples include:

- goals, that are appropriately challenging and clear;
- equity, that the motivation systems provide outcomes, processes and relationships that are perceived as fair and legitimate;
- needs, that rewards take the form of things that individuals value;
- valence-instrumentality-expectancy, that rewards are valued, seen as related to performance measures, and that individuals have confidence their efforts will produce performance outcomes;
- social influence, that group norms and perceptions affect how performance and rewards are valued and interpreted.

One can envision a future in which organization leaders are as routinely and carefully assessed for their ability to understand and apply these principles, as they would be for understanding and applying principles of operating cash flow, net present value, or customer segmentation.

Talentship decision frameworks are important within HR as well as outside HR

The need for a talentship mind-set is also vital for HR functional leaders. In our experience there are almost always some HR professionals in any organization who effectively understand, teach, and enhance decisions based on how talent connects to strategic success. These HR professionals typically admit that they learned to provide this kind of support in their own way, with little systematic instruction or development. One HR professional put it well: "This capability is critical to our future, but it doesn't scale because everyone does it and learns it differently."

A decision framework contributes to decision scale by developing, using, and teaching a consistent, logical point of view about how to connect talent resources to strategic success. A logical point of view provides a consistent script for an ongoing dialogue about talent and strategy, allowing more reliable and consistent diagnosis, analysis, and action on talent issues throughout the organization.

Data, measurement, and analysis

A mature decision science has data, measurement, and analysis aligned with its decision framework principles. These are refined and deployed throughout management systems, used by leaders who understand the principles, and supported by professionals who add insight and expertise. Today finance reflects this level of maturity almost everywhere. Marketing approaches this level of maturity, particularly in industries such as packaged consumer products and multilocation retail, where competitive dynamics hinge on marketing sophistication. For example, every leader at PepsiCo receives a daily report via email on their PDA (personal digital assistant) on product sales, broken down into very specific brands and customer segments.

These systems have evolved over decades, and today we hardly notice how well integrated financial measurement and analysis processes are with decision models. It seems to have always been that way. Today the ratios commonly measured in financial decisions and the structure of accounting statements link directly to the DuPont decision framework. Similarly, marketing decision frameworks provide the logical structure for customer relationship management and customer analysis systems, which use vast amounts of data mining and advanced analytics to produce competitive insights.[2]

In stark contrast, HR data, information, and measurement face a paradox today. Although there is increasing sophistication in technology, data availability, and the capacity to report and disseminate HR information, frustration increases when investments in HR data systems, scorecards, and integrated enterprise resource systems fail to create the strategic insights needed to drive organizational effectiveness. One reason for this paradox is that the technological advances have outpaced the fundamental logic connecting talent and organization decisions to strategic success (Boudreau and Ramstad, 2006; Boudreau and Ramstad, 2007, Chapter 9; Lawler et al., 2004). Major elements of marketing and finance are well over fifty years old, so those decision sciences were far more mature by the time technology advanced. The computer-enhanced systems could build on well-developed decision frameworks, integrated management systems, and shared mental models, making information technology much more valuable.

HR has not yet developed such a decision science and thus has no such decision framework to organize data and information technology. Thus, in HR, technology has found its greatest value in automating areas with more established organizing frameworks, such as payroll, but has not reached the level of impact in supporting more strategic decisions. For example, lacking a common logic regarding employee turnover, specific HR functions often create their own unique employee turnover classifications when installing a new software system. It's not surprising that even after years of using such systems, there remains too little insight into the factors that affect employee turnover, how it affects the organization, and what to do about it (Cascio and Boudreau, 2008). In contrast, operations management approaches inventory turnover with enterprise resource systems that adopt definitions and reporting protocols built on specific decision principles regarding inventory optimization.

As we have discussed before, HR measures exist mostly in areas where the accounting systems require information to control labor costs or monitor functional activity (Boudreau and Ramstad, 2003). Efficiency gets a lot of attention, but effectiveness and impact are often unmeasured. While there have been significant advances in applying analytics to the field of HR management—including high-level data analysis approaches like social network analysis and multivariate regression—such methods often suffer from the lack of a more comprehensive decision framework. For example, a statistical method from marketing, called "conjoint analysis," has been applied to employee survey data to see which work elements most significantly associate with employee engagement or turnover.[3] This provides insights into how HR programs might enhance those work elements, but it often fails to identify where engagement and retention matter most and why. Advanced analytics hold great promise for enhancing talent decisions, but it is often the logic, not the analytics, that creates the big breakthroughs.

A decision framework provides the logical structure to organizational data, measures, and analytics, and identifies gaps in existing measurement systems. Armed with such a decision science and framework, organizations can avoid investing in sophisticated data and analysis that fails to achieve its potential because the tools don't address the important questions.

Focus on optimization

The final pillar of a mature decision science is that its logic reveals how decisions can optimize the returns from a resource, rather than simply describing them or only partially maximizing them. A mature decision science reveals how to optimize results by balancing trade-offs instead of always assuming that more is better.

Optimization in finance: Focusing on investment returns not just profits

Finance provides a good illustration. Before the DuPont model (which marks the beginning of the decision science of finance), the goal was simply to maximize profits. Disproportionate amounts of capital were directed to businesses with large profits, often resulting in high margins but low return on capital. Instead of maximizing profits in isolation, the DuPont model strove to optimize profits by recognizing the constraints on financial capital resources (Johnson, 1975). As finance decision science matured, other factors were integrated. Financial decision models now not only maximize returns but use decision frameworks, such as portfolio theory, to optimize return in the context of risk and liquidity. Further refinements revealed how to balance liquidity in the broader strategy, by investing in ways that consider the range of future strategic options that investment might enable.

Optimization versus maximization in talent decisions

By contrast, many HR decisions often try to increase learning, engagement, or retention without limit or context. This is very different from optimizing a portfolio of HR practices against the organization's unique resource opportunity costs and constraints (Boudreau and Ramstad, 1999). For example, if more sales training increases product knowledge, which increases selling success, a less mature decision framework might apply training more broadly. Having proved the value of training by linking it to increased sales, the right decision seems to be to acquire more training. Several executives we have worked with have termed this the "peanut-butter" approach, because it spreads something equally across the entire organization.

In fact, considering the necessary investments (time, money, etc.) to achieve increased selling success through training, enhancing product knowledge from an already high level may be very expensive. The optimal solution might involve less product knowledge and more motivation, and thus less training and more incentives. The key point is that a mature decision science frames the question in terms of optimal solutions rather than just describing relationships or increasing one desired outcome out of context. Even when optimal decisions cannot be precisely defined, the logic that a focus on optimization provides will often lead to insights that are missed by a less comprehensive approach.

Distinguish average from marginal value

A core principle in optimization is the difference between average and marginal (or incremental) impact. Although something can be highly valuable, increasing or decreasing the amount of it may not have a big effect. For example, suppose an organization has a hundred sales representatives and total revenue of $50 million, making the average sales per sales representative $500,000. What is the optimal number of sales representatives? You can't tell from the average. Optimizing requires that you know the potential effects of increasing or decreasing the sales force. If the same $50 million in revenue could be generated by ninety representatives, then the marginal value of the last ten representatives would actually be zero. On the other hand, if these sales representatives were working to their capacity and there were available sales territories without adequate sales coverage, additional reps would create significant incremental sales.

A mature decision science clearly articulates the difference between resources or activities that provide high average value and those that provide high marginal value. We use the word *pivotal* to describe the marginal effect of resources, activities, and decisions. *Pivotal* captures the idea of a lever, where a small change at the fulcrum causes very large changes on the other end. Highly pivotal areas are those where a small change makes a big difference to strategy and value. A resource, decision, or activity can be highly valuable and important, even if it is not pivotal. For example, every machine on an assembly line is important because each machine contributes something unique to the production process. However, increasing the capacity of every machine is not pivotal. The marginal value of increased capacity is much higher in the machine that represents the bottleneck, or constraint. Some resources, decisions, or activities are both important (highly valuable on average) and pivotal (changes make a big difference).

Pivotal versus important in product design

Consider how two components of a car relate to a consumer's purchase decision: tires and interior design. Which adds more value on average? The tires. They are essential to the car's ability to move, and they impact both safety and performance. Yet tires generally do not influence purchase decisions, because safety standards guarantee that all tires will be very safe and reliable. Differences in interior features—impressive sound system, elegant upholstery, portable technology docks, number and location of cup holders—likely have far more effect on the consumer's buying decision. In terms of the overall value of an automobile, it cannot move without tires, but it can function without cup holders and an iPod dock. Interior features, however, clearly have a greater impact on the purchase decision. In our language, the tires are important, but the interior design is *pivotal*.

Figure 2.3 shows this example in the form of what we call a "performance yield curve." The performance yield curve for tires is much higher than for interior features, which reflects tires' importance. The yield curve for tires is relatively flat across a large range of performance levels, and it drops quickly on the left if tire performance falls below a certain level. Tires create tremendous value and are very important, but once they reach a certain level, increasing their performance does not add value to the consumer's purchasing decision. Yet, if they fall below the minimum standard (as happened with the Firestone tires on Ford SUVs, resulting in a massive recall in 2000), the result is very bad indeed. The key to optimizing tires against their effect on the initial purchase decision is to get them to standard, not significantly higher. Beyond this point the incremental cost of increasing tire performance exceeds the incremental value in customer purchases.

The marketing and finance decision sciences have sophisticated systems to exploit the distinction between marginal and average value. As marketing decision science evolved, the concept of segmentation was applied at multiple levels, including markets, customers within markets, products, and as we just discussed, product features within products. Conjoint analysis and other statistical tools use data from extensive consumer research to produce deep insights about the incremental value of features, which informs decisions about product designs. They carefully isolate those attributes (such as safe tires) that are core or expected (sometimes referred to as "table stakes") from those where differences drive perceptions of value (such as the interior design of a new car). Optimization requires investing based on the incremental contribution, not the average contribution. To do this, features must be segmented on their marginal value

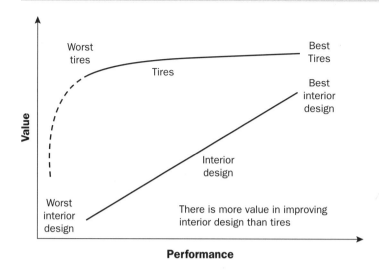

Figure 2.3 Yield curves for automobile features: tires vs. interior design

Source: Reprinted by permission of Harvard Business School Press from *Beyond HR: The New Science of Human Capital* by John W. Boudreau and Peter M. Ramstad, Boston, 2007: 41.

(pivotalness), not their average value (or importance). Failing to segment based on pivotalness often results in equal investments, even when the potential marginal return is significantly different.

Distinguishing what is pivotal from what is important in talent decisions

This seems fundamental, but it is frequently misapplied in organization and talent decisions. What we have called "talent segmentation" is still very rudimentary (Boudreau and Ramstad, 2005a). We see this in the frequent tendency of organizations to apply the same investments and activities across a wide range of jobs or talent pools. Examples include: "If stock options are good for executives, then they should be expanded to all employees" and "If it's important to increase attention given to our customers, then everyone should have thirty hours of training in customer awareness" and "If weeding out the bottom 10 percent of performers makes sense in our sales force, let's weed out the bottom 10 percent in every job."

Effective segmentation based on marginal value in talent and organization decisions helps answer questions such as "Where does my strategy require increasing the performance of our talent, or our organization?" The answer cannot be "everywhere," because that is cost prohibitive. The answer also cannot be "nowhere," because competitive advantage must have some source—one or more multi-incumbent roles, or talent pools, where superior talent quality makes a significant strategic difference. Lacking a decision science that guides this kind of talent segmentation, organizations typically invest too little in talent pools that are most pivotal and too much in talent pools that are important but far less pivotal. The idea that talent and organization decisions are vital to competitive advantage is a virtual truism today, as we noted earlier, yet the very essence of competitive advantage is finding unique and different ways to advance a particular value proposition, seize specific market opportunities, or leverage distinctive strategic resources. We have described how organizations including Boeing, Corning, Disney and Williams-Sonoma that have achieved this with talent, in ways that are consistent with the principles described here (Boudreau and Ramstad, 2007). Still, today's decisions about organization and talent are often made with an eye toward duplicating the practices of other successful companies, rather than in-depth internal analysis to find the appropriate investments for specific contexts. The absence of a decision science that distinguishes marginal from average value is a significant cause.

Segmentation in auto insurance

Segmentation based on marginal impact produced a competitive advantage for Allstate Insurance Company. Allstate (then a division of Sears) was one of the first companies to adjust rates based on age, auto usage, and claims history—a revolution at the time (Allstate, 2006). This easily described idea had massive implications for virtually all aspects of the auto insurance business. Allstate was able to extract much more value from the insurance market and provide much greater value to its customers by adjusting what it charged according to customer characteristics related to the probability of accidents and other factors. Allstate has continued its tradition of innovative differentiation in its pricing models by bringing in a variety of new factors that it now markets under the brand "Your Choice Auto Insurance," which is based on sophisticated pricing models. This changed the game from a product definition perspective by providing customers with a much wider variety of choices. Before, customers could choose their level of coverage and size of deductibles. Now they can customize policies on features such as accident forgiveness and what types of rewards they would like associated with good driving records.

Allstate's research revealed interesting and surprising patterns in auto safety among different consumer groups. A *BusinessWeek* item noted:

> For decades, Allstate had lumped customers into three main pricing categories, based on basic details such as a customer's age and place of residence. It now has more than 1,500 price levels. Agents used to simply refer to a manual to give customers a price; now they log on to a computer that uses complex algorithms to analyze 16 credit report variables, such as late payments and card balances, as well as data such as claims history for specific car models. Thus, [drivers who are safe bets] are rewarded, saving up to 20% over the old system, and high-risk drivers are penalized, paying up to 20% more. It has worked well enough that Allstate now applies it to other lines, such as homeowners' insurance.
>
> (Carter, 2005)

What are the implications for talent? Financial services organizations such as insurance, mortgage and credit-card companies have vastly increased the number of variations in their offerings. This has often meant that the traditional jobs of pricing products simply did not capture the new requirements of sophisticated statistical analysis of customers and markets, and actuarial savvy in setting and adjusting prices to fit demand and supply. One implication was the need to segment the talent market for insurance pricers. Traditionally, employees in the pricing jobs were facing only a few products that did not change very much. With the emergence of such highly segmented insurance products, it was necessary to distinguish traditional pricing capability from the capability to apply very deep mathematical, statistical and actuarial methods to continually adjust pricing based on customer and market data. Allstate now needed to create a new talent segment—pricers who could apply sophisticated mathematical algorithms. Indeed, this talent segment was so new that traditional job descriptions did not even describe it (Boudreau, forthcoming).

Thinking differently using decision science principles

A decision is an invitation to think differently. Historically, as decision sciences become embedded within organizations, natural synergies emerge across the five decision science elements. This creates tangible but very organic changes in the way business and HR leaders, employees, investors, and potential employees converse about a strategic resource. Consider the power of just three changes in the way your organization approaches its talent and organization decisions.

First, clearly distinguish between pivotalness and importance. This motivates a focus on the marginal value of talent decisions. It is as important to talent decisions as the distinction between the marginal and average value of advertising. It helps decision makers avoid getting lost in a sea of important initiatives and set priorities correctly.

Second, consistently use performance yield curves, to identify the nature of pivot-point slopes and shapes. Not only does this kind of discipline help identify where decisions should focus on achieving a standard versus improving performance, it also provides a way to think about the risks and returns to performance at different levels. It helps people avoid making decisions based on well-meaning but rudimentary rules such as "get the best person in every job."

Third, focus on optimization, not just maximization. This creates an environment in which trade-offs can be discussed with less of the emotion that usually prevents good decisions and often leads to decisions like "Let's just do the same thing for everyone to be fair." Optimization presumes that talent investments will be unequal but also creates a high standard for analyzing and communicating good reasons for such unequal investments.

Thus, even in the early stages of implementing a decision science, tangible changes occur in how talent and organizations are understood and made. History shows that it is from these small tangible steps that significant untapped strategic success flows.

Conclusion

When new decision sciences emerge, they typically present difficult changes in social, organizational, and personal traditions. Before the new logic is used by competitors, a failure to make decisions more optimally doesn't create any relative disadvantage, so less sophisticated decision systems still allow organizations to stay competitive. Before Allstate applied the decision science principle of customer segmentation and optimization, no one did any worse by following the old model. Yet first movers who apply a new decision science often create formidable competitive advantages. Once Allstate generated value by adopting a more sophisticated decision science, its competitors were at a disadvantage. Soon everyone began to realize the power of the new decision framework and tried to catch up.

We believe that HR, and the larger domain of organization and talent decisions, is at precisely this historical point. A few organizations are beginning to develop some elements of a more mature decision science. For example, at Corning, HR leaders who support key divisions use talent-focused strategy analysis during their annual strategy sessions. At the Hartford Financial Services Group, Inc., investments in HR programs are allocated in part based on where they will have the most pivotal effect (Farrell, 2004).

Still, because the effects are so isolated, there is not yet an urgent need to evolve. The vast majority of organizations can compete effectively, even while making more traditional talent and organization decisions. A new decision science, however, will emerge for talent, just as surely as it emerged for other resources. The first organizations to apply the new decision framework will achieve significant first-mover advantages, forcing others to react. In time we envision the talent decision science becoming as natural a part of management thinking as finance and marketing are today, but before that happens there are opportunities for game-changing strategic decisions by organizations that apply it first.

Acknowledgment

This chapter has been adapted by the authors with permission of Harvard Business School Press from *Beyond HR: The New Science of Human Capital* by John W. Boudreau and Peter M. Ramstad, Copyright © 2007 by the Harvard Business School Publishing Corporation; all rights reserved.

Notes

1 In accounting the *chart of accounts* is a listing of all the accounts in the general ledger, with each account accompanied by a reference number. Examples might include assigning numbers 1000–1999 to asset accounts, 2000–2999 to liability accounts, and 3000–3999 to equity accounts. Source: "Chart of Accounts," NetMBA, http://www.netmba.com/accounting/fin/accounts/chart/.
2 Customer relationship management (CRM) is a corporate-level strategy that focuses on creating and maintaining lasting relationships with customers. CRM enables organizations to better manage their customers through the introduction of reliable systems, processes, and procedures. Source: "Customer Relationship Management," *Wikipedia*, http://en.wikipedia.org/wiki/Customer_Relationship_Management.
3 Conjoint analysis is a tool that allows a subset of the possible combinations of product features to determine the relative importance of each feature in the purchasing decision. Source: "Conjoint Analysis," QuickMBA, http://www.quickmba.com/marketing/research/conjoint.

References

Allstate Corporation (2006) "Press Kit: History & Timeline 1930s," Allstate, http://www.allstate.com/Media/PressKit/PageRender.asp?page=1930s.htm.

Boudreau, J.W. (2003) "Strategic Knowledge Measurement and Management." In Susan E. Jackson, Michael A. Hitt, and Angelo S. DeNisi, eds, *Managing Knowledge for Sustained Competitive Advantage* (San Francisco: Jossey-Bass/Pfeiffer): 360–96.

Boudreau, J.W. (2006) *Interview of J.S. Bronson, former senior vice president of HR*, Pepsi, August.

Boudreau, J.W. (forthcoming) "Allstate's 'Good Hands' Approach to Talent Management." In Robert Silzer and Ben Dowell, eds, *Exceptional Leadership Talent Management* (New York: Jossey-Bass), Chapter 16.

Boudreau, J.W. and Peter M. Ramstad (1999) "Human Resource Metrics: Can Measures be Strategic?" In Patrick Wright et al., eds, *Research in Personnel and Human Resources Management*, Supplement 4, *Strategic Human Resources Management in the Twenty-First Century* (Stamford, CT: JAI Press): 75–98.

Boudreau, J.W. and Peter M. Ramstad (2003) "Tapping the Full Potential of HRIS: Shifting the HR Paradigm from Service Delivery to a Talent Decision Science." In PeopleSoft, *Heads Count: An Anthology for the Competitive Enterprise* (Pleasanton, CA: PeopleSoft): 69–88.

Boudreau, J.W. and Peter M. Ramstad (2005a) "Where's Your Pivotal Talent?" *Harvard Business Review*, April: 23–4.

Boudreau, J.W. and Peter M. Ramstad (2005b) "Talentship, Talent Segmentation, and Sustainability: A New HR Decision Science Paradigm for A New Strategy Definition." In Mike Lossey, Dave Ulrich, and

Sue Meisinger, eds, *The Future of Human Resource Management: 64 Thought Leaders Explore the Critical HR Issues of Today and Tomorrow* (New York: Wiley).

Boudreau, J.W. and Peter M. Ramstad (2006) "Talentship and Human Resource Measurement and Analysis: From ROI to Strategic Organizational Change," *Human Resource Planning Journal* 29, 1: 25–33.

Boudreau, J.W. and Peter M. Ramstad (2007) *Beyond HR: The New Science of Human Capital* (Boston: Harvard Business School Publishing).

Carter, A. (2005) "Telling the Risky from the Reliable," *BusinessWeek*, August 1, http://www.businessweek.com/magazine/content/05_31/b3945085_mz017.htm.

Cascio, Wayne F. and John W. Boudreau (2008) *Investing in People* (Upper Saddle River, NJ: Prentice-Hall).

Colbert, Amy E., Sara L. Rynes, and Kenneth G. Brown (2005) "Who Believes Us? Understanding Managers' Agreement with Human Resource Research Findings," *Journal of Applied Behavioral Science* 41, 3: 304–325.

Compensation.blr.com (2005) "Writer Defends 'Why We Hate HR' Article," November 29, http://compensation.blr.com/display.cfm/id/154876.

Farrell, L. (2004) "Turning HR Cost Reduction Into Opportunity at The Hartford." Presentation in *Beyond the Bottom Line* executive program. Center for Effective Organizations. April.

Hammonds, Keith H. (2005) "Why We Hate HR," *Fast Company*, August: 40–8.

Johnson, H.T. (1975) "Management Accounting in an Early Integrated Industrial: E. I. DuPont de Nemours Powder Company, 1903–1912," *Business History Review* 49, 2: 184–204.

Lawler III, Edward E., John W. Boudreau, and Susan Mohrman (2006) *Achieving Strategic Excellence* (Palo Alto, CA: Stanford University Press).

Lawler III, Edward E., Alec Levenson, and John W. Boudreau (2004) "HR Metrics and Analytics: Uses and Impacts," *Human Resource Planning Journal* 27, 4: 27–35.

Lossey, Mike, Dave Ulrich, and Sue Meisinger, eds. (2005) *The Future of Human Resource Management: 64 Thought Leaders Explore the Critical HR Issues of Today and Tomorrow* (New York: Wiley).

Pinder, Charles C. (1998) *Work Motivation in Organizational Behavior* (Upper Saddle River, NJ: Prentice-Hall).

Schroeder, Roger G., Kevin Linderman, and Dongli Zhang (2005) "Evolution of Quality: First Fifty Issues of *Production and Operations Management*," *Production and Operations Management* 14, 4: 468–81.

Skinner, Wickham (1981) "Big Hat, No Cattle: Managing Human Resources," *Harvard Business Review* 5: 106–14.

3

The employment relationship in strategic HRM

Paul Edwards

Any view of HRM – whether it treats the field as generically about all ways of managing employees or adopts a particular view of HRM as a distinct approach to management – must have a view of the relationship between manager and employee. This chapter argues, first, that HRM *necessarily* tends towards a rather narrow view and, second, that this narrowness constrains its ability to address the field adequately. Third, an 'industrial relations' (IR) view can correct these limitations. Fourth, however, both IR and HRM tend to focus on the internal dynamics of the employment relationship, and both need to address more fully the external forces that impinge on it. 'IR' will be used to characterize an analytical perspective, with the employment relationship being the object of empirical inquiry.[1]

The chapter proceeds as follows. First, an approach to the employment relationship within mainstream HRM is identified and criticized. This critique identifies the concept of the psychological contract as the most developed, but flawed, effort to see the relationship as an exchange between two parties. The IR perspective is then presented. In the third section, some ways in which this perspective corrects the HRM view are outlined. This is followed by a relatively 'optimistic' view of further developments around the context of the employment relationship and a more 'pessimistic' conclusion on the likelihood that HRM will accept the solution proffered.

The employment relationship in mainstream HRM

To sustain the first argument in detail would require extensive commentary, and I merely cite statements that assert it. I also focus on debate among UK scholars, for it is here that discussion of the meaning of HRM has been most extensive. There would appear to have been little discussion in the US HRM circles about the fundamental nature of the employment relationship. Thus when Kaufman (2004) offered an 'integrative theory' of HRM he did so in terms of largely taken-for-granted assumptions about what it is that HRM is managing – even though, in his other work, Kaufman (2007) lays out an IR view on this question.

Bach (2005: 4) comments that HRM focuses on management practice and 'tends to ignore employee interests'; HRM also limits itself to the individual firm. Sisson and Storey (2000: 7–10) identify a predominant pattern of rather uncritical, descriptive and prescriptive approaches in HRM and they embrace a view that sees the employment relationship as a social product. They say rather little, however, about its fundamental features and stress instead the context in which it is embedded. Bacon (2003: 84) summarizes the weaknesses of HRM:

> The emphasis upon the individual overlooks the collective aspects of employment and it is unnecessarily unitarist [that is, seeing the organization as having a single set of goals shared by all]; management choices are restrained by institutions and context; high commitment management is rare; and it lacks a theory of power and cannot explain who gets what.

The key mainstream response to these issues is to draw on analysis of the psychological contract. At least two books use this concept to address explicitly the employment relationship (Coyle-Shapiro et al. 2004; Sparrow and Cooper 2003) and it is deployed in the work of leading scholars, notably David Guest (2007).

The psychological contract: 1, the contract as socially embedded

The concept is arguably the most sophisticated of conventional approaches. Thus earlier accounts left themselves open to charges of taking a managerialist and prescriptive approach that was often unitarist (Legge 2005). The idea of the psychological contract, by contrast, speaks either of the perceptions of *both* parties in relation to mutual promises and obligations (Herriot and Pemberton 1997) or specifically of the *employee's* expectations (Rousseau 1990).

This approach rightly focuses on the famous 'black box' of HRM, the attitudes, expectations, and behaviour of workers themselves; the HR-performance literature for example needs to assume that HRM practices work through this particular mechanism if it is to have any convincing explanation of performance outcomes. There are also tantalizing suggestions that the psychological contract can entail conflict, for example, evidence summarized by Guest (2007: 133–5) that breaches of the contract occur on a very regular basis. The implication is clearly that managing HR is more than a technical exercise, but the contract is rendered as a narrow exchange process, and the 'technical' rapidly re-asserts itself.

The fundamental problem is that, as its name implies, the psychological contract is seen in individual terms. This leads to two kinds of issues. The first concerns the worker as an atomized unit: a fiction but a standard analytical device. Even such a person will approach a contract in the light of its social and historical context. 'A contract is not sufficient unto itself,' as Durkheim (1964: 215) famously put it. Even commercial contracts assume, first, the existence of a legal and social environment permitting the contract to be honoured; that is, they assume a set of institutions without which a contract is merely a piece of paper. A second feature is that contracts assume away what are essentially a series of problematical terms. For example, building contracts typically include a requirement to 'make good' a piece of work, but what this means can be understood only on the basis of extra-contractual understandings of the duty.

Individual employees' expectations are shaped by their understandings of what a 'job' is. A worker employed in the US as a check-out worker at a supermarket will have a clear image of what this job means, not only in terms of pay but also the kind of managerial control regime to which she is subject and what satisfactory behaviour entails. This is what the IR view means when it insists that the employment contract is indeterminate (Kelly 2004). Obligations cannot be specified exactly, and the employment contract is different from a commercial one because what workers provide is an ability to work rather than a concrete thing and because they do so under the authority of others. The indeterminacy is of course resolved in practice, in that a certain amount of work gets done. But this is the point: it is through the process of work that outcomes emerge, and the employment relationship is a living and shifting one whose meaning emerges in its day-to-day enactment. The approach through the psychological contract threatens to reproduce the old debate on 'orientations to work' which started from the assumption of fixed orientations and then had to admit that views of work are often inchoate and shifting. More developed views (summarized in Edwards and Wajcman 2005: 19–43) offer a much more sophisticated account that the psychological contracts literature might consider.

This perspective matters for two reasons. First, discussion of the psychological contract talks of delivering certain things to employees such as wages and job satisfaction. But expectations do not revolve around concrete, definable, sets of outcomes that employees can specify in advance. They are shifting, and the emphasis that is placed on different parts can change in unexpected ways. They also contain notions such as fairness which cannot be elaborated in purely contractual terms. Second, the indeterminacy of expectations also works from the managerial side: organizations provide all kinds of things to workers, and the messages that they convey are mixed and often conflicting.

The psychological contract: 2, collective norms

The second issue emerges once we relax the assumption of atomized individuals. It is notable that early use of the term 'psychological contract' by Argyris in 1960 referred to a collective relationship between a work group and its manager, but this idea was soon dropped (Taylor and Tekleab 2004: 254). Similarly, the concept of the norm of reciprocity, now widely used in the literature, was introduced at the same time by Gouldner (1960) in an explicitly collective and social context. For Gouldner, reciprocity involves rights and obligations and is a product of social structures. Recall Goulder's earlier celebrated work on industrial bureaucracy, which portrayed the complex web of social norms that workers developed and that managers challenged at their peril. Expectations were strongly social.

It might be thought that collective norms are a thing of the past, being based in strong work groups and working-class identities. But the fact of collective norms has been demonstrated in modern workplaces, even though their form of expression may have changed (Ackroyd and Thompson 1999). And even where workers are individualized, the norms under which they operate are social constructs, not purely explicit expectations. Studies repeatedly find that issues of control, power, and conflict continue to characterize the employment relationship, even in circumstances most favourable to unitary models including small management consultancies and firms practising 'knowledge management'. In other words, workers may approach jobs with certain expectations, which a contractual approach – psychological or of course economic in origin – takes as given. But why do workers expect what they expect?

The limitations of the psychological contract view are highlighted if we look in more detail at Guest's (2007) analysis, given that it sets out specifically to look at HRM from a worker's point of view. Several features stand out. First, there is no effort to draw on the substantial case study evidence of what workers actually do (on which, see Thompson and Harley 2007). Second, it acknowledges that 'organizational change is now so pervasive that sooner or later any deal [between manager and worker] is in trouble' (p. 133). This statement thus admits that apparent 'deals' are extremely fragile while at the same time – and like Sparrow and Cooper (2003) – making no effort to specify the conditions generating 'change' and tending to fall back on treating 'change' as a mere fact of life like the weather (see Grey (2005) for criticism). Third, it also admits that there has been work intensification, this time citing grounded evidence

(Green 2006) on the causes of this trend. It then uses this fact to argue that, because HR practices are rare, intensification cannot be 'attributed to HRM' (p. 140). This can only mean that intensification cannot be blamed on that variant of HRM which is rare, namely one using a wide set of high-commitment, high-involvement practices. It is plainly wholly consistent with 'low road' HRM. Moreover, there is evidence that high-involvement activities also entail work pressures (Edwards and Wajcman 2005: 123–41): the *general* rise in work intensity does not reflect such HRM, but where this HRM is practised, intensification can also occur, though here workers may well accept the result because of the countervailing benefits. Guest's conclusion on this point is that 'HRM is only associated with stress where management fails to meet its promises and obligations' (p. 140), which is like saying that sin occurs only where there are sinners. We might add that Guest sees 'satisfaction' as a lasting and fixed attribute, rather than asking 'satisfied with what, and in the light of what?' Job satisfaction surveys since the 1950s have shown that most workers are 'satisfied' most of the time. It may be true that those working under some regimes are more satisfied than others, which should not be surprising, but to conclude that there is happiness is rather overly optimistic. Other approaches have shown substantial unmet demand for more voice (Bryson and Freeman 2006; Freeman and Rogers 1999).

This leads to Guest's next argument, that trade unions are associated with low satisfaction, which he uses to dismiss the claim that HRM promotes a unitarist system that reduces employee voice. There is a curious slippage here, for whether or not union workers are dissatisfied says nothing about the voice that they enjoy. The association of unions with low satisfaction is not new, and a key possible explanation – that unionized workers simply expect more than others – has not been ruled out.

More generally, it surely is the case that HRM does promote a particular interpretation of the world. This may not be crudely unitarist: I would also agree with Guest's next point, that HRM is not a deceitful ideological ploy: workers are not cultural dopes. But ideologies and world views are much more subtle than deception. The 'change is inevitable' theme certainly seems to have persuaded Guest himself, and it is part of a set of discourses – about competition, globalization, and so on – that affect how people see the world and what they think they can do to change it. As HRM's many critics point out, there is much in HRM that is geared to managerially defined notions of performance (Legge 2005), as opposed to the recognition of competing definitions of what constitutes performance and of how it is to be attained.

Nature of the employment relationship

For an IR approach,

> 'human resources' are different from other resources because they cannot be separated from the people in whom they exist. The employment relationship is about organizing human resources in the light of the productive aims of the firm but also the aims of employees. It is necessarily open-ended, uncertain, and . . . a blend of inherently *contradictory* principles concerning control and consent.
>
> (Edwards 2003: 4, emphasis in original)

First, there is equal attention to the employer and the employee. HRM is necessarily about the management perspective whereas IR is not.

Second, the employment relationship is open-ended in that obligations cannot be specified in detail in advance. Now, this view has been adumbrated in several traditions including transaction cost economics, but these deal only with the uncertainties of any form of contracting where there is imperfect knowledge and terms cannot be laid down in advance. IR goes further, by locating this uncertainty in the fundamentals of the relationship.

This is the third element, an explanation of conflict and co-operation (note that this is an *explanation*, even though some IR scholars think that a focus on conflict is merely an assumption or a matter of personal emphasis (Edwards 1986)). The fundamentals of the employment relationship entail a double indeterminacy: from the side of the employer, there is a need to control (i.e. regulate, manage, discipline) workers but also to use workers' creative capacities constructively; workers wish to resist or to negotiate the terms of this control while also wishing to work effectively. Reasons for working effectively include instrumental ones, notably an interest in the continued survival of the firm, but also ones to do with personal satisfaction and pride in the work: studies repeatedly find that workers feel commitment to the job itself and enjoy a sense of achievement. The relationship is contradictory because it entails the working through of principles which pull in different directions. Conflict and co-operation are thus mutually entwined.

The employment relationship has an element of conflict at its heart. This is called a 'structured antagonism' (Edwards 1986) to distinguish conflict in the sense of an overt dispute from underlying principles. Managing the employment relationship is a process of dealing with inherently contradictory forces. Antagonism is built into the basis of the relationship, even though on a day-to-day level co-operation is also important. This idea is superior to that of a conflict of interest, for the latter has the problem of implying that the real or fundamental interests of capital and labour are opposed, which leads to a stark and readily dismissed view. A structured antagonism is a basic aspect of the employment relationship which shapes how day-to-day relations are handled but is not something which feeds directly into the interests of the parties. Firms have to find ways to continue to extract a surplus, and if they do not then both they and their workers will suffer. Balancing the needs of controlling workers and securing commitment rests ultimately on ensuring that a surplus continues to be generated. It may well be in workers' interests that it is indeed generated, but this should not disguise the fact that they are exploited.

Yet employment relationships do not entail a daily working out of first principles. How is this achieved? IR's answer – and the fourth element of the approach – is 'rules', as in a classic definition of the field as the 'study of the rules governing employment' (see Edwards 2003: 8). Rules tended to mean the formal rules of employment as laid down by law or in collective agreements. But IR research also gave great attention to more informal rules. These can be placed on a continuum. Some achieve quasi-formal recognition, as in the once-familiar concept of 'custom and practice', meaning established norms in a particular workplace over the conduct of work. A standard example would be leaving work early if tasks had been completed. Custom and practice can establish strong expectations about key aspects of work such as who has the right to allocate work and the dividing line between one job and the next. Other rules are much more informal understandings. But they remain social products that define how work is organized. They are produced continually, and they shift in the light of the activities of their authors and the external environment. In offices in the past, for example, it was often the tacit rule that secretaries acted as office wives. In the light of equal opportunities policies, such informal understandings of the respective rights of managers and secretaries have changed. The key analytical point here is that any work relationship has such unwritten expectations which are socially defined and reinforced. Students of the psychological contract who believe that a limitation of IR is its neglect of the informal are seriously misinformed.

Rules are ways to manage the conflict and co-operation that are inherent in the employment relationship. An IR approach does not deny the centrality of co-operation, and a 'unitary' view reflects part of reality. But we need to understand the nature of co-operation. It is true that workers, when asked whether a firm is like a football team or whether employers and workers are on opposite sides, often choose the former. An early study found that 67 per cent of a sample of manual workers agreed with the statement that 'teamwork means success and is to everyone's advantage'. But what does this mean? When asked whether they agreed with the team view 'because people have to work together to get things done' or because 'managers and men (sic) have the same interests in everything that matters', workers split about six to one in favour of the former (see Edwards 2003: 12). A unitary HRM view mistakes pragmatic accommodation for fundamentally shared goals and values.

Rules are social products in that they are negotiated, formally or informally, between managers and workers and they then become inscribed in norms and expectations: they exist over and above any preferences that individuals may have. Any workplace has a set of norms and expectations governing conduct. British IR used to give particular attention to the informal, reflecting the limited scope of formal collective agreements in that country. In many other countries, legal and collectively bargained rules played, and continue to play, a much greater role. HR and IR scholars accustomed to Anglo-Saxon practice are sometimes surprised to learn that in France, where trade union membership is probably even lower than it is in the USA, coverage by collective agreements continues to embrace around 90 per cent of the workforce. This idea has been given new impetus by the emergence of rules at several levels, which has given rise to the concept of multi-level governance. In Europe, this embraces EU-level directives on issues embracing working time and information and consultation, national-level laws, collective bargaining rules, and local practice and precedent. In the USA, courts in some states have developed case law that puts limits on the traditional doctrine of employment at will, while equal value and sexual harassment cases have also placed powerful constraints on the conduct of employment issues within the firm.

Fifth, HRM's lack of a view of power was noted above. It is true that IR texts have also lacked explicit attention to power. But the concept has run implicitly through the analysis (Edwards 2003: 10–13). Most obviously, power is deployed in overt disputes. But it may also be used to legitimize certain claims, as when a worker uses an existing rule to dispute a managerial demand. More broadly still, rules themselves inscribe a balance of power, which may reflect the result of some previous overt dispute or more tacit processes of compromise. Power is a resource. It can be seen in terms of 'power to' achieve goals and 'power over' others. A conventional view stresses the former, whereas some 'radical' views stressed the latter. In fact, the two interact. Consider, for example, a performance appraisal scheme. It may achieve some broadly shared objective such as greater transparency of the link between effort and reward. But it can also promote a particular vision of how an organization should function. And it may reflect purely sectional goals, such as the desire by one group of employees to monitor and control another more strictly. A perspective in terms of power can help to untangle these different elements (Edwards and Wajcman 2005: 116–23).

A final feature of IR is more methodological. Historically, there was an emphasis on a 'going to see' approach, often with little by way of formal theory or hypotheses. Despite the rise of large-scale surveys, the approach remains a substantial one, as illustrated by book-length studies of the conduct of employment relations as well as journal articles and edited collections. Though originally focusing on factory jobs, the approach has powerfully informed studies of service work and even management as well as recent innovations such as Total Quality Management (see Edwards 2005: 270–1).

A key feature of the approach is the desire to obtain a holistic picture of work experience. Methods typically include observation and unstructured interviews. This research illustrates the nature of contradictions in the employment relationship. Watson's picture of a group of managers, for example, is of people who felt commitment to their role as managers but also distance from and scepticism towards more senior company management; this was combined with similarly contradictory relations with workers, which turned on managers' own sense of distance and a belief in the need to control workers but also the view that change programmes could be made to work.

Correcting some weaknesses in HRM

What difference does it make to insist that the employment relationship is one of power and ambiguity and that it takes place on a particular terrain of 'political economy'?

First, HRM has a tendency to hubris. This is most marked in that part of the performance literature that claims to distil specific principles or even to calculate the financial returns from a set of practices (see Legge (2005) for criticism). Claims to find lasting answers to the management of firms often ring hollow, as the search for 'excellence' showed. The HRM debate has been marked by studies that try to rein in this exuberance by reporting limited and at best ambiguous achievement (e.g. Mabey et al. 1998) and by insisting on the importance of the human subject and the very narrow and instrumental view of the 'human' in HRM. Such work often builds on the idea of the employment relationship as contested and uncertain, and it constitutes a necessary corrective to excessive claims. It helps, moreover, to understand the reasons for common HRM puzzles such as why the returns on high performance systems are so uncertain. Once we move away from a view of HRM as constituting a set of levers that can be pulled to a more complex view of the politics of work, the uncertainties of claimed 'effects' can be grasped. Note, moreover, that even models of contingency and fit do not go far enough: they recognize that certain levers may work in only some circumstances, but they still assume that appropriate conditions of fit can be identified. A richer view suggests that any fit may be partial and uncertain, and that the degree of fit may be apparent only *ex post*.

Second, the above argument may seem to imply that there are no solutions. It is true that practice needs to be seen as more uncertain than the finding of clear answers, for if messages are necessarily mixed and HRM is about the management of contradictory forces then there can be none. An IR approach, moreover, insists on treating the employment relationship from the points of view of different parties: what may be a solution to one party may be a problem for another – and these parties need not be defined in 'management and worker' terms, as when actions by senior managers affect the job prospects of other managers. Yet ways of thinking about practice can readily be suggested. Sisson and Storey (2000) identified two key issues – balancing flexibility and security, and linking collective and individual approaches to workers – which they drew together around a third, the need for integration *within* HR activities and *between* HR and business strategy. They were proposing not concrete solutions, but ways of thinking through the dilemmas of managing people. They may have implied a sanguine view of integration, for it is not clear how one can achieve integration among competing and amorphous elements. But the central message was to be aware of the need to think whether one practice is consistent with another: a solution may not be possible, but thinking explicitly about the consequences of actions improves the process through which contradictions are managed.

Third, the uncertain nature of strategy can be addressed. Discussion of strategic HRM has turned on securing internal and external fit, as though these things are technical questions. Yet around the time that these debates were emerging, Hyman (1987) pointed to the different domains in which strategy might be practised and the fact that these are in contradiction with each other. He is often quoted for the argument that any strategy is a route to partial failure, which was certainly an important perception, but underlying this was a view of employment strategy as a contested process. The more recent development in the wider strategy literature of 'strategizing' perspectives also underlines the enacted and contested idea of strategy – as opposed to strategy as a clear 'thing' that can be laid down from the top. A continuing awareness of strategy as a resource with varying meanings for different groups can help HR practitioners to reflect on what they and other groups are trying to achieve.

Fourth, HRM can be linked to its social context. Take the issue of the skills and knowledge of workers. Looking at HRM as a managerial technique at the level of the firm can deal with such issues as systems of recruitment and training. It cannot ask why the firm has the skills pattern that it does. This is one of the problems of strategic integration: HR practice is 'integrated' with what the firm currently does, but it does not ask whether this is desirable in the longer term. The approach is, moreover, limited to the individual firm. But what of the pattern of skills at the level of the economy? This issue cannot be resolved through an approach that assumes that organizations identify the skills that they need and they are provided either by the market or by appropriate policy interventions to improve supply. HRM in its high-road variant places great emphasis on skills and knowledge, but the question of where skills come from, and how they are used, and why firms demand the skills that they do, requires a different level of analysis. This point leads to challenges to both HRM and IR.

Beyond IR and HRM?

The limitations of an IR approach are increasingly recognized (Ackers and Wilkinson 2003b). It tended to treat the worker as a category ('labour power') and found it hard to incorporate gender and ethnicity. The emphasis, in the definition given above, on the humanity of human resources also implies interest in such issues as ethics and human rights, but these scarcely featured in IR texts until very recently. In many respects, IR and HRM have both felt the need to become more open to ethics and 'social legitimacy' (Boxall and Purcell 2003). Influences from outside the workplace, notably the state, were perhaps easier to take into account but were still treated as largely exogenous.

In terms of method, too, the limitations of the case-study approach are easy to identify. It can be hard to establish the nature of events in any one case, because there is no specific hypothesis under test, explanations of patterns may be implicit rather than explicit, and some information may be absent (because the focus is the concrete experience of work, with managerial strategies and the external context appearing indirectly if at all). And generalizing from a case is difficult since it may be atypical in many respects. Some HRM researchers argue that case-study-based evidence is indeed unreliable, and often not a test of HRM at all (Guest 1999). Yet it cannot be dismissed so readily. First, much of it – for example, evidence on work intensification and tightening managerial control – is consistent with quantitative studies (Green 2006). Second, it has been possible to suggest causal accounts (Edwards 2005). It remains the case, however, that such accounts are often *post hoc* and plausible interpretations rather than clearly grounded and tested explanations.

These limitations are considerable, as rehearsed at length elsewhere (Ackers and Wilkinson 2003a). But they should not be fatal to IR as an intellectual project. If we look first at the range of issues directly addressed by IR and HRM, there is clear evidence that gender perspectives have increased their influence. Related to this, attention has turned to groups of workers outside the core remits of IR (those covered by collective bargaining) and HRM (workers who are in some way seen as key assets and who work for firms practising some kind of systematic HR policy). These groups include workers in small firms and those in low-paid and marginal jobs.

Turning, second, to the social and political context, international comparison has been transformed from a rather dull cataloguing of labour laws and collective bargaining arrangements to comparative research asking analytical questions about the nature of employment regimes. The 'varieties of capitalism' and 'national business systems' literatures have become well known, and they have stimulated research on how employment systems operate in different contexts. The fact that Rubery and Grimshaw (2003) have been able to produce a text synthesizing a range of knowledge is one measure of the success and maturity of this tradition.

There remains, however, a great deal more to be done within these traditions. One example will suffice (Edwards 2005: 272). A core focus of IR has long been the extent to which workers organize collectively and how they identify sets of interests and represent these interests to managements. A gender perspective has thrown substantial light on the gendered processes involved here. But the contribution to date has tended to stress the overall way in which relevant processes are gendered. The next step is to show just what gender 'does' in different circumstances: how far, for example, do men from one social background have distinct sets of gender-based resources (male solidarity and so on) that are different from those of men from different backgrounds? A further step would address how work experience acts to amplify or amend gender-based resources.

If this example is relevant to an IR approach, what does it say in HRM terms? One part of the answer is that there should be no distinction. If HRM is concerned with the employment relationship, then it needs to address the social structuring of work. But the question is pertinent because HRM has been about the management aspects of the relationship, and gender has been analysed in terms of equal opportunities practice and not more fundamentally in relation to workplace regimes and their social structuring. A broader view would see gender identities as part of the contested nature of the employment relationship.

We do not need here to lay out a detailed research agenda, but one overall point is key. Debate in HRM has tended to swing between some very general overall models, as reflected in the numerous textbook frameworks and diagrams, and concrete empirical research, usually undertaken within a positivist hypothesis-testing mode. Between these extremes lie, of course, a series of case studies but there are at least two issues around them: they address their own particular themes, so that they do not generalize into a research programme; and they often try to reveal the essential features of a practice, rather than showing the conditions under which it has some features rather than others. Once a set of core propositions about the employment relationship has been identified, it should be possible to proceed towards more nuanced questions about how the relationship works in different conditions. An earlier generation of IR workplace studies was able to show what kinds of rules existed in different circumstances and to offer implicitly causal accounts.

It should be possible to take these ideas and apply them in a new context. The task is more challenging than it used to be for at least two reasons. First, the subject of inquiry is more slippery than a set of rules that may have had at least a degree of concreteness in being expressed in understood custom and practice. Second, there is a need to take account of a wider set of causal influences. There is growing emphasis on the multiple levels that shape the employment relationship in a particular workplace and also the need to understand the workplace in different countries (Thompson 2003). But some means exist to put order on this empirical complexity.

Conclusions: will a critical view of the employment relationship develop?

We may conclude by asking whether the above view is likely to become the dominant one. I have argued that it has clear benefits, but institutional fields are defined by assumptions, past practice, norms, and interests as well as by what may be 'correct'. There are reasons to be doubtful. First, HRM is a management discourse that has its own logic that is hard to shift. Critiques have indeed been around for a long time (see Legge 2005) without markedly changing practice. Second, a rationalistic approach to human nature and a methodology driven by formal hypotheses fits current approaches to the doing of management research. Third, the obverse of the second point is that users of this approach can readily ask where a broader view takes us in terms of researchable questions. The broader view has in fact demonstrated its worth, in showing in detail how work is being reorganized and with what consequences; it also contains clear explanatory ideas (Edwards and Wajcman 2005: Chapters 2–6). Thus an approach that contrasts mainstream empirical inquiry with 'critical' studies – that question assumptions but do not, it is claimed, offer much with which to replace a conventional view except deconstruction – is no longer an accurate one, if it ever was. But research paradigms have their own momentum that is hard to shift. Finally, of course, HRM is a management phenomenon as well as an academic discourse. The more that its practitioners sell HRM as a contribution to corporate strategy and as a set of techniques, the more it will be locked into a technical and narrow conception. As Kaufman (2004: 334) among others points out, HRM has become a discourse that promotes the interests of its practitioners.

There are however – as in any practice riven by contradictions – alternative possibilities. A growing interest in stakeholder models of the firm and a willingness to engage with 'corporate social responsibility' suggest that some firms may be open to pluralist models of the enterprise. It may also be the case that a style of targets and performance measurement has run its course and that there will be a swing back towards allowing more creativity and autonomy. In laying out the 'core principle' of industrial relations, Kaufman (2007: 29) argues that

> free labor markets – without the balance, fairness, social protection and macroeconomic guidance offered by the institutions of industrial relations and the visible hand of state management – will necessarily create or perpetuate conditions that undermine their own effectiveness and survival.

This is of course an old Marxist argument: that capitalism unrestrained is self-destructive. It should be seen as a tendency and not an inevitable consequence, for capitalism has been very effective in re-inventing itself. It is nonetheless central: HRM functions in a contradictory world, and the practices that it promotes need underpinning through other mechanisms. In the words of Kaufman, to 'democratize and balance the market system' calls for expanded and reformed institutions, and an IR view can help us ask what those institutions might be and do.

It is indeed well established that management fashions run in cycles, from tight control to more 'human relations' styles and back again. Whether or not such cycles embrace a genuinely pluralist view of the enterprise is a more difficult question. HRM, even in its more 'empowering' mode, is essentially driven by management agendas, and managers are reluctant to give up power to others.

The answer is likely to depend not so much on debates within HRM and IR as on external forces. Corporate Social Responsibility, for example, reflected changes in the business environment and not a sudden conversion within firms to a new approach. In the employment field, labour laws have required firms to do all kinds of things that they might prefer to avoid. It is true that firms have been able to shape the nature of the response but nonetheless they have had to respond, for example, in the area of equal opportunities. Other influences come from the labour market and the demands that workers are able to make: limited labour supply can be a powerful motivator for firms, as when equal opportunities become promoted as a means to retain skills that are hard to replace. And customers can also put pressure on firms, as, for example, the many firms that stress that their call centres have not been outsourced and that they offer a personal service. Examples of changed practices are not hard to find; for example, firms have rushed to be seen to be family friendly. Such developments have often been patchy, and, in liberal market economies such as the US and the UK in particular, it is difficult to institutionalize them. They nonetheless illustrate what may occur.

HRM is, however, strongly embedded in teaching and practice. Whether or not a more reflective approach emerges is hard to say, but the results of concrete efforts to 'add value' have been at best very patchy. It may be that a different style will emerge. As Marx might not have said, 'HR managers have merely tried to change the world; the point, however, is to understand it'.

Note

1   To keep within word limits, referencing has been restricted. References and fuller discussion of analytical themes can be found elsewhere (Edwards 2003, 2005); empirical evidence is summarized in Edwards and Wajcman 2005.

References

Ackers, P. and A. Wilkinson (eds). 2003a. *Understanding Work and Employment*. Oxford: OUP.

Ackers, P. and A. Wilkinson. 2003b. 'Introduction'. In Ackers and Wilkinson 2003a.

Ackroyd, S. and P. Thompson. 1999. *Organizational Misbehaviour*. London: Sage.

Bach, S. 2005. 'Introduction'. In Bach (ed.), *Managing Human Resources*. Oxford: Blackwell.

Bacon, N. 2003. 'Human Resource Management and Industrial Relations'. In Ackers and Wilkinson, 2003a.

Boxall, P. and J. Purcell. 2003. *Strategy and Human Resource Management*. Basingstoke: Palgrave.

Boxall, P., J. Purcell and P. Wright (eds). 2007. *The Oxford Handbook of Human Resource Management*. Oxford: OUP.

Bryson, A. and R. B. Freeman. 2006. 'Worker Needs and Voice in the US and the UK'. National Bureau of Economic Research Working Paper 12310, June.

Coyle-Shapiro, J., L. M. Shore, M. S. Taylor and L. E. Tetrick (eds). 2004. *The Employment Relationship: Examining Psychological and Contextual Perspectives*. Oxford: OUP.

Durkheim, E. 1964. *The Division of Labor in Society*. Trans. George Simpson. London: Free Press.

Edwards, P. 1986. *Conflict at Work*. Oxford: Blackwell.

Edwards, P. 2003. 'The Employment Relationship and the Field of Industrial Relations'. In Edwards (ed.), *Industrial Relations*. 2nd edn. Oxford: Blackwell.

Edwards, P. 2005. 'The Challenging but Promising Future of Industrial Relations'. *Industrial Relations Journal*, 36: 264–82.

Edwards, P. and J. Wajcman. 2005. *The Politics of Working Life*. Oxford: OUP.

Freeman, R. B. and J. Rogers. 1999. *What Workers Want*. Ithaca: ILR Press.

Gouldner, A. W. 1960. 'The Norm of Reciprocity'. Reprinted in Gouldner, *For Sociology*. London: Allen Lane, 1973.

Green, F. 2006. *Demanding Work*. Princeton: Princeton UP.

Grey, C. 2005. *A Very Short, Fairly Interesting and Reasonably Cheap Book About Studying Organizations*. London: Sage.

Guest, D. E. 1999. 'Human Resource Management: the Workers' Verdict'. *Human Resource Management Journal*, 9 (3): 5–25.

Guest, D. E. 2007. 'HRM and the Worker: Towards a New Psychological Contract?' In Boxall et al. 2007.

Herriot, P. and C. Pemberton. 1997. 'Facilitating New Deals'. *Human Resource Management Journal*, 7 (1): 45–56.

Hyman, R. 1987. 'Strategy or Structure'. *Work, Employment and Society*, 1: 25–56.

Kaufman, B. E. 2004. 'Toward an Integrated Theory of Human Resource Management'. In Kaufman (ed.) *Theoretical Perspectives on Work and the Employment Relationship*. Champaign: IRRA.

Kaufman, B. E. 2007. 'The Core Principles and Fundamental Theorem of Industrial Relations'. *International Journal of Comparative Labour Law and Industrial Relations*, 23: 5–34.

Kelly, J. 2004. 'Industrial Relations Perspectives to the Employment Relationship'. In Coyle-Shapiro et al. 2004.

Legge, K. 2005. *Human Resource Management: Anniversary Edition*. Basingstoke: Palgrave.

Mabey, C., D. Skinner and T. Clark (eds). 1998. *Experiencing Human Resource Management*. London: Sage.

Rousseau, D. 1990. 'New Hire Perceptions of Their Own and Their Employer's Obligations'. *Journal of Organizational Behavior*, 11: 389–400.

Rubery, J. and D. Grimshaw. 2003. *The Organization of Employment*. Basingstoke: Palgrave.

Sisson, K. and J. Storey. 2000. *The Realities of Human Resource Management*. Buckingham: Open UP.

Sparrow, P. R. and C. L. Cooper. 2003. *The Employment Relationship*. London: Butterworth Heinemann.

Taylor, M. S. and A. G. Tekleab. 2004. 'Taking Stock of Psychological Contract Research'. In Coyle-Shapiro et al. 2004.

Thompson, P. 2003. 'Disconnected Capitalism'. *Work, Employment and Society*, 17: 359–78.

Thompson, P. and B. Harley. 2007. 'HRM and the Worker: Labor Process Perspectives'. In Boxall et al. 2007.

4

Critical perspectives
on strategic HRM

Mats Alvesson

Strategic HRM can be studied from a number of perspectives and with a number of different purposes in mind. The purpose of this chapter is to outline the nature and the implications of adopting a 'critical' perspective. It will describe and examine the nature of the different strands which constitute a critical approach. It will locate these within the wider field of critical management studies (CMS). The chapter will also point out some of the shortcomings within some of the critical approaches – thus constituting a critique of critique. In particular, the chapter demonstrates how some critiques suffer from similar shortcomings and lapses as found in the mainstream approaches. Drawing upon a detailed case study, the chapter sketches a more nuanced approach.

Like many other contemporary knowledge areas and occupations, HRM has been targeted for upgrading in the claims of its status, importance and impact in organizations and the economy over recent decades. Relabelling personnel management into HRM is one move. The increased interest in knowledge work and broad claims that the knowledge economy is on its way, calling for heavy investments in the competence of the personnel arguably fuel some interest in HRM (Newell et al., 2002; Storey & Quintas 2001). However, there is great variation in the opinions of the meaning and significance of the knowledge economy and work, where some argue that it is only a relatively small, although expanding, part of work that is characterized by high demands of advanced knowledge and intellectual or symbolic skills (Alvesson 2004; Thompson et al. 2001). It is also debatable whether all or most organizations in the knowledge-intensive sector are that interested in ambitious HRM. There is great variation, and many instances of, for example, competence development receiving little attention from management in consultancy firms (Fosstenløkken 2007).

HRM is, it is argued, a core strategic activity (e.g. Boxall & Steeneveld 1999; Lengnick-Hall & Lengnick-Hall 1988; Tichy et al. 1982: 47). HRM focuses on what can broadly be described as the human side of an enterprise: recruitment, training, staffing, career planning and development, compensation, and labour relations (Steffy & Grimes 1992). Strategic HRM is about how the employment relationships for all employees can be managed in such a way as to contribute optimally to the organization's goal achievement. Even stronger formulated, HRM is said to be 'a distinctive approach to employment management which seeks to achieve competitive advantage through the strategic development of a highly committed and capable workforce using an array of cultural, structural and personnel techniques' (Storey 2001: 6). HRM then becomes a huge area, including potentially 'everything' relating to people in organizations, perhaps also corporate culture, work organization and leadership. Many have pointed at the indeterminacy of HRM, both in terms of its novelty and uniqueness and about what it covers and means (Keegan & Boselie 2006; Keenoy 1999).

Common distinctions involve soft and hard HRM systems (Tyson 1995), or perhaps better labelled high- and low-commitment ones (Legge 2005; Watson 2004). Soft or high-commitment HRM is characterized by long-term relationships, caring and personal development. Hard or low-commitment HRM is characterized by exploitative and short-term relationships. It relates to the business-focused and calculative aspects of managing 'headcounts' in a rational way. The former emphasizes the human, the latter the resource part of HRM. Some critics play with the expression of 'inhuman resource management' (Steyaert & Janssens 1999). In some workplaces employees remain however treated more as a commodity (Legge 1999: 251; Palmer & Hardy 2000: 38). There are, as Watson (2004) points out, reasons not to overplay the soft/hard distinction, as no business can neglect the business-oriented and calculative view on the personnel, which is not to say that it can't blend with more long-term and development-oriented considerations.

The purpose of this chapter is to take a critical look at HRM, where 'critical' relates to political and social shortcomings, not only intra-academic critique for deviations from academic standards in terms of rigorous research, conceptual clarity and theory building. Of course, there are overlaps, e.g. on the theme of whether HRM advocates' claim is true that large-scale investments in people management produce at the same time better performance and better work conditions – a favorite topic for debates within HRM. Political and academic critique also sometimes go together in negative remarks about the theoretical standing of HRM. The HRM literature is often described in less than flattering terms by people monitoring it with regards to academic standards. There is a strong emphasis on what *should* be. The field seems more concerned with tools and techniques than explanation and understanding. Large parts of it are possibly too preoccupied with investigating and trying to prove that heavy investments in HRM pay off. The focus on the normative and descriptive means that the area is fairly a-theoretical and exhibits a shortage of rich and deep empirical studies (Schneider 1999; Steyaert & Janssens 1999). Critics argue that HRM literature, in particular in HRM journals, is 'narrow, techno-cratic and managerialist' and excludes broader concerns (Keegan & Boselie 2006: 1508).

This chapter reviews work drawing upon interpretive and critical perspectives in challenging the dominant functionalist, technicist and objectivist assumptions and research agenda dominating the field.

Critical perspectives

Compared with many other management subdisciplines, there is fairly little ambitious critical work within HRM. Some review authors do however give critical work a prominent place. Legge (2005) contrasts strategic HRM with a critical perspective studying work under allegedly soft or high-commitment HRM systems. Steyaert and Janssens (1999) refer to three versions of HRM research: designing theoretically based HRM tools, typically based on psychology theory; examining HRM practices and establishing links between HRM and performance; and critical reflections on the concept and its implementation (or the lack thereof).

The word 'critical' has, of course, a number of meanings. All research is, ideally, 'critical' in the sense that the research norm is an intolerance of loosely defined and used concepts, weak argumentation, speculative statements, erroneous conclusions, etc. But there are also 'stronger' versions of critical thinking. In this chapter, 'critical' is understood as the stimulation of a more extensive reflection upon established ideas, ideologies and institutions in order to achieve certain social outcomes. These include an intent to reduce repression, self-constraints and human suffering and even to help resistance to and emancipation from what is seen as an illegitimate form of domination. Critical research aims to stand on the weaker part's side when studying or commenting upon relations of dominance. Critical theory is referred to as a tradition of social science, including the Frankfurt School and related authors and lines of thought such as those of Foucault, critical poststructuralism, neo-Marxism, certain versions of feminism, etc. (For summary reviews of critical management studies (CMS), see Alvesson & Deetz 2000; Alvesson & Willmott 1996, 2003; Grey & Willmott 2005.)

'CMS' is a broad label, used in different ways and referring to somewhat varied constellations of approaches. CMS is interested in what is viewed as the negative or problematic aspects of organization and management, those associated with social domination and repression, and often hidden behind seemingly rational arrangements and good intentions.

Organizations do not merely contribute to people's needs through producing goods and services, but have many other implications for humans, nature and society, including the exercise of power, creating disciplinary effects on customers and subordinates but also on managers and professionals. According to Fournier and Grey (2000), trying to find a minimalistic characterization, CMS has the following features:

- non-performativity;
- denaturalization (constructivism);
- reflexivity.

Performativity is defined as being about means–ends calculation and has the 'aim to contribute to the effectiveness of managerial practice' (p. 17). By non-performativity they mean that CMS should not seek to develop theory that increases the efficiency of organizations. By de-naturalization, they mean that CMS should attempt to show how organizational realities are not natural, but are in fact a social construct. By reflexive, they mean that CMS should acknowledge power relations that are associated with knowledge claims. Their vision of critical management studies is of a field that seeks to simultaneously advance a critical politics (by rejecting performativity), a critical ontology (by arguing the social world is a construct), and a critical epistemology (by arguing that our knowledge about the social world is also a construct).

But this definition is controversial (Thompson 2004). Reflexivity and denaturalization characterize a lot of research, as does non-performativity. These are characteristic of many interpretivist researchers. It is also debatable whether CMS itself is characterized by this, as for many advocates of critical research the very purpose is to bring about social change, and the 'effective' triggering of emancipation or progress is a possible key ambition. But it is non-performative in the sense of giving priority to critical scrutiny over objectives and rejecting the priority of means–ends calculations. CMS takes these three listed features seriously. It has the ambition to contribute to political consciousness about social conditions and practices.

Another and more specific and stronger, although not inconsistent with the one suggested by Fournier and Grey, definition of CMS would be:

1. the critical questioning of ideologies, institutions, interests and identities (the 4 Is) that are assessed to be (i) dominant, (ii) harmful and (iii) underchallenged;
2. through negations, deconstructions, revoicing or defamiliarizations;

3. with the aim of inspiring social reform in the presumed interest of the majority and/or those non-privileged, as well as emancipation and/or resistance from ideologies, institutions and identities that tend to fix people into unreflectively arrived at and reproduced ideas, intentions and practices.

And, given the management context,

4. with some degree of appreciation of the constraints of the work and life situations of people (including managers) in the contemporary organizational world, e.g. that a legitimate purpose for organizations is the production of services and goods (Alvesson 2008).

Critical studies then:

offer counter images to those put forward in dominant discourse – drawing attention to hidden and less desirable aspects of HRM practices, offering alternative readings, giving voice to those marginalized, discriminated against or silenced, and offering innovative or insightful ways of interpreting employees' experiences of HRM.

(Keegan & Boselie 2006: 1508)

This chapter is based on these concerns, although the concept of being critical also covers somewhat broader terrain, including strong critique for the inclination for most HRM research to black-box HRM practices and processes.

Critical work on/in HRM

Critical HRM studies have been conducted within the following areas: 1. assumptions in mainstream HRM; 2. scrutiny of the link between HRM and performance; 3. ideology critique pointing at discrepancy rhetoric-reality; and 4. Foucauldian work on the forming of subjectivity. This will be reviewed and critically discussed in this section. I will then address 5. empirical studies on HRM policies and arrangements 'in practice' in the subsequent section.

Assumptions

HRM research is often accused of being managerialist, technocratic, positivist and lacking in reflexivity. One key aspect here is the idea that human beings are fixed subjects to be worked upon. An alternative assumption suggests that the individual is produced, rather than discovered, in HRM processes (Deetz 2003; Steffy & Grimes 1992; Townley 1993). HRM practices in this sense create what they allegedly discover. This is, as will be explored later, an idea that most critical work takes seriously.

The HRM literature is strongly dominated by the assumption that recruitment, assessment and development processes deal with people who have stable sets of skills and capacities, and that these characteristics are possible to investigate objectively and measure, thus making so-called job performance prediction possible (Steffy & Grimes 1992; Iles & Salaman 1995). An obvious counter-assumption is that people are more processual, context-dependent, hard to grasp and fix and generally not 'object-like', but make sense of their world, actively interpret it and act based on constructions of themselves and their intentions. These assumptions are common in highly different forms in interpretive and poststructural work but have put limited imprints on mainstream HRM, which consequently can appear naïve and old-fashioned for those who have considered alternative viewpoints.

Another assumption is that the important aspect of HRM is the resource element, i.e. a one-sided instrumentalization of people as 'assets'. This is not a neutral idea, and it hardly reflects a broadly shared interest or a superior rationality. Critics point out that the emphasis on performance means a normalization of managerialist and unitarist ideas and the neglect of ethical concerns and that employees may be affected in negative ways, including work intensification, job stress and insecurity (Keegan & Boselie 2006: 1508).

Critique of the HRM–P formula

Another common assumption is that there is a strong payoff from investments in HRM. The idea is that there is a success formula, meaning that if one gets a specific set of HRM practices in place performance and profit will follow. Examples of good HRM arrangements typically include:

- careful recruitment and selection;
- extensive use of communication;
- teamworking with flexible design;
- emphasis on training, learning and KM;
- empowerment;
- performance appraisal and performance-based reward systems.

Mainstream HRM researchers claim that company performance is positively affected by HRM practices (Guest 1999; Huselid 1995; MacDuffie 1995; Pfeffer 1994). One can refer to this as HRM–P studies. Of course, these results are very popular amongst HRM academics, consultants and practitioners – a welcome response to accusations of HRM being fluffy, ambiguous and of limited relevance for results. There is plenty of critique on the methodological difficulties of making such claims (see Legge 2005; Marchington & Grugulis 2000; Purcell 1999). There is, for example, variation as to which combinations of 'good' HRM practices or other characteristics are included in various studies (Legge 2001).

Even more profound is the critique that 'this research does not proceed beyond attempts to find an empirical association between HRM practices and organizational performance' (Hesketh & Fleetwood 2006: 679). The phenomena are in a black box, only input and output are registered and what is happening remains clouded in the dark. Simplistic assumptions of a stimuli-response type then dominate, resulting in poor understanding and underdeveloped theory.

Arguably, institutional, cultural, political and historical factors play a large role in how specific policies, systems and (intended) practices actually influence people (Legge 2005). As we will see, there is often a gap between systems, structures and policy, and the practices and meanings being carried out and developed. Without any considerations of these aspects, reports of input in relationship to results support a technocratic line of thinking, neglecting the human dimensions at work, and viewing HRM as a design outcome of the work of top management and HR specialists. Finding correlations between some of the 'right' HRM practices and performance is thus not necessarily of much help in order to understand what is happening and how organizations are managed and how people think and act. We will come back to this.

Ideology critique

This critical scrutiny of HRM–P claims also overlaps to some extent with ideology critique, although the latter goes beyond scrutinizing this link. Ideology critique is an important part of critical studies, but it is sometimes watered down (or made more nuanced, depending on how you see it) as the term *discourse* is at present more frequently used. Ideology critique circles around the discrepancy between rhetoric and reality, i.e. the use of new and nice-sounding claims that stand in contrast to actual practices, but which have ideological and legitimizing effects for corporations, HRM academics and practitioners. Three overlapping aspects related to this critique can be mentioned.

1. The boosting of (traditional concerns of) personnel management and packaging it as HRM as though indicating that with this label something quite different, and for those concerned, much more impressive has been developed. HRM, it is claimed, involves a concern with organizational performance, the adoption of a unitaristic (rather than a pluralist) perspective, a belief in the alignment of employer and employee interest and the general emphasis of the strategic role of human resources and the pay-off of investments in competence and people. There is a kind of ideological upgrading of personnel administration, not fully or well anchored in organizational practices (Guest & King 2004: 411). In other words HRM, it is suggested, is being 'talked-up'.

2. The making of HRM into something 'strategic'. Sometimes one gets the impression that there is very little 'non-strategic' HRM going on. If there is, it escapes a lot of the attention of researchers, pop-management authors and practitioners producing accounts of what they are doing. There is a general strategy discourse being dispersed and used by ever expanding sets of actors through which they redefine themselves from being administrators and managers to becoming 'strategists'. The strategy discourse often plays a greater role as a source of identification and boosting of status than as a way of understanding what actors do and accomplish (Knights & Morgan 1991). Researchers in HRM – as in many other fields – like to locate themselves in this camp, as do practitioners. As personnel work – like most other forms of management and administration – is mainly on the technical, operative and bureaucratic level, the strategy discourse easily becomes an ideologically imprinted version of what goes on, sometimes conflating contemporary reality with a projected future (Berglund 2002).

3. The perhaps most obvious aspect of HRM as ideology is the heavy use of positive-sounding representations of how organizations view and treat personnel. Competence, development, trust, alignment of interests, communication, investment in people, etc. are terms frequently used. 'People are our most important asset' is a popular expression, but critics are quick to point out that this is only half the picture. Rationalizations and exploitation of this important asset are important and most organizations show a complicated mix of long-term investments in corporate culture, competence, trust and community as well as differentiation beteen groups of employees, cost-cutting, quarterly capitalism, outsourcing, etc. (Watson 1994).

A lot of critical analysis focuses on the gap between rhetoric and reality, especially as indicated by the third aspect above. Organizational practices seldom live up to the ideals of progressive HRM ideals (Legge 1995; Palmer & Hardy 2000). As Guest and King (2004: 412) have observed:

> It seems that when organizations are making money they are too busy to implement best practice HRM and feel that in any case they are doing well enough without it; and when they lack money, they can't afford to implement it.

HRM then can be seen as being stronger on rhetoric, ideology and the legitimation of the personnel function and contemporary forms of people management than on influencing and explaining corporate practice typically falling short of the promises.

Foucauldian ideas on HRM (The HRM–S formula)

According to Foucault (1976, 1980), the most significant form of power in the present context is disciplinary power. This power, which originated at the beginning of the eighteenth century in prisons and clinics in the name of behavioural reform, aided by the emerging human sciences, revolved around systems of surveillance and normalizing judgements. Through systems of observation and careful prescriptions as to what is appropriate (normal, therapeutic), the regulation of conduct was and is accomplished. As Clegg (1989: 156) points out, Foucault focuses on discourses which increasingly limit, define and normalize the motives and meanings which are 'available in specific sites for making sensible and accountable that which people should do, can do and thus do'. Originating in institutionalized contexts, the systems of observation and classification and the normalizing judgements associated with these are taken over by our own reflexive gaze, as we evaluate ourselves and make ourselves objects of discipline according to these prescribed patterns of meanings and standards of conduct.

The form of the subject and its way of relating to itself and its world is constituted through discourse. Such 'things' as motivation and strategy are not merely phenomena existing 'out there', but are things created discursively and materially in the shape of various practices. Any attempts to chart the nature of human motivation or to generate ideas resembling 'natural laws' on the subject of, for example, strategy, leadership, job satisfaction or motivation are thus doomed to failure (see Knights 1992; Townley 1994). Power is thus exercised by binding the subject to a particular identity or form. It is not any autonomous or genuine identity that is meant; rather, Foucault rejects an essentialist view of man (in which the subject is viewed as a fixed and pre-existing object for knowledge and management). All we can study are the discourses and practices which shape the individual and through which he or she emerges as an object of knowledge and influence. 'The individual is the effect of power' (Foucault 1980: 98). The constituted identity limits but also enables some action. The individual's self-perception is controlled and regulated through the effects of power.

Critical HRM scholars have drawn heavily upon Foucauldian thinking, for example, Deetz (2003), Grey (1994) and Townley (1993, 1994). Foucauldian ideas mean that labelling, classification and ranking plus confessions and the providing of templates for being are emphasized (e.g. Foucault 1976, 1980). HRM practices are studies in terms of how they make individuals objects of knowledge and, through this, shape and form them in particular ways, in appraisals and through career ladders. HRM becomes a set of disciplinary technologies that classify, measure, order and fix individuals. People become subordinated to and bear the imprints of these technologies.

This work has a strong critical edge, but tends to be restricted to studies of theories, ideas and recipes in textbooks, and policies and plans in corporations. Not much work in the form of in-depth field studies based specifically on a Foucauldian perspective has been conducted. Exceptions to some extent include Covaleski et al. (1998) who address mentoring and MBO as integrating individual and corporate goals respectively, 'realizing corporate clones when people avow organizational imperatives as their own' (p. 300) and Grey (1994) who investigates career orientation as a self-project.

With a few exceptions, there is thus a neglect of human action, interpretation and power and politics at the local level. Thus, just as it is reasonable to ask if there is any close link between academic texts on HRM and what is actually happening at workplaces, so too, critical work is itself vulnerable to a similar critique. Some would-be critics also fail to unpack the black box. This reinforces a dubious assumption that HRM ideas as expressed in the literature have a strong influence in organizations and over employees. One could talk about a HRM–S tradition (where HRM technologies are supposed to shape subjectivity). But it is unclear if, and if so how, the actual shaping of subjects actually takes place. It might be much weaker and uncertain than indicated by the HRM–S advocates (Newton 1998). The local intentions, usages, practices, interpretations and subjectivity-effects call for close up studies, preferably of an ethnographic type. Some of the HRM–S work also black-box the operations of HRM, assuming that its impact can be read from textbooks and corporate policies.

Critique of critiques

All these critiques offer valuable insights on HRM and certainly contribute to a much more balanced and nuanced view of the subject matter. However, there are problems with a fairly one-sided focus and a mainly 'negative' research agenda. For some critics, there is an exaggerated interest in the rhetoric vs. reality theme in critical HRM studies. This approach reproduces a dominant scheme, it is argued: when critical work challenges existing orthodox studies, 'critical scholars often find themselves locked into a de facto reply genre, narrative analysis shows that the first story to be told tends to be the most persuasive, with the counter story mainly serving to reproduce it' (Harley & Hardy 2004: 393). Critical scholarship reacts to the agenda, but does not set it. Critics claim that it is 'a very sterile way to "contribute" because, even as a criticism, one remains within and reproduces the existing frame' (Steyaert & Janssens 1999: 186). This echoes general critiques of critical research as parasitic and not very helpful. One aspect here, reinforced by the sometimes rather obscure language of much critical work, is that it is too far removed from its key targets within the management camp as well as within mainstream academia. Of course, the very purpose of critical work is not to accommodate the agenda of practitioners or mainstream academics viewing themselves as delivering technically oriented knowledge to management ('servants of power'), but critical work can also offer something contributing to the self-questioning or the revision of mainstream agendas and preoccupations. And here it is motivated with knowledge and ideas that go beyond fault-finding and focusing on what is wrong with dominant ideas, models, claims and perspectives.

Part of this problem is the shortage of critical studies genuinely interested in what goes on in terms of HRM. Critical studies do not need to be empirical and the ideological and other critiques find targets worthy of their criticism, but there are still important themes around HRM as a social practice that have not, with a few exceptions, been investigated in much depth. The entire critical project appears as one-sided, narrow and reactive. It shares with the mainstream work a tendency to black-box HRM. Less reactive and less negative work is also important to support the critique reviewed above and we now move over to such work.

To be clear, my point is not that the reviewed critique in itself is problematic. On the contrary, I think it is most relevant and important. But critical studies need also to include 'positive' work, in the sense of rich and ambitious studies of what is happening, and perhaps also some ideas on how to work with HRM issues in a more productive way, where the employees benefit more. Arguably, critical work as a collective project needs to contribute a combination of critical scrutiny of dominant ideas and representations of HRM ideologies and claims, with practice *and* work curious about what is happening in organizations and with individuals when HRM is put into work. Based on such projects, some input for the critical self-reflection of firms, professionals and mainstream academics should be offered.

Critical studies on the actual use of HRM

Empirical studies of *specific HRM practices* often show the difficulties in making good ideas on paper function well in practice. (Of course, similar observations are made within a range of other subject areas as well – HRM is not unique in this respect.) As one would perhaps expect, there is a lot of variation in the application of HRM policies, leading to strong deviations from the suggested normative order. In-depth research has revealed widespread doubt about the rationality of key HRM practices such as assessment and promotion (Barlow 1989; Jackall 1988; Longenecker et al. 1987; Townley 1999), emphasizing uncertainties and politics.

Coalitions and personal interests generally play a role in assessments, promotions and task assignments. Meritocracy does, for example, tend to be subordinated to senior people wanting reliable co-workers. Judgement is always uncertain, criteria are bent and used in idiosyncratic ways. Senior people want to have discretion and be able to make decisions based on their personal interests and preferences, e.g. on who to work with, without being constrained by aggregates of previous assessments – something that weakens the impact of HRM policies and systems (Barlow 1989; Longenecker et al. 1987). There are frequently conflicts between personnel departments trying to impose these policies and managers wanting to use their discretion, and the former party is frequently the weaker one.

Issues around competence development are also sometimes not well taken care of, as short-term objectives and pressure for results and efficiency take priority. Although the competence of the employees is conventionally viewed as a key resource for professional service firms, management often pays little attention to it in practice (Fosstenløkken 2007).

Practice-near studies typically show the difficulties of organizations fulfilling technocratic fantasies when it comes to people issues. It confirms the common experience of in-depth case studies that 'organizational life seldom lives up to the facade of order it presents' (Batteau 2001: 728).

An important shortcoming of this otherwise valuable research is that it tends to embrace a rather narrow research agenda. Most HRM advocates would argue that it is the overall HRM system that is of importance. Even if one or two of the elements (e.g. socialization, training, appraisals, formal promotion processes, feedback or career planning) fail to work as planned, this may not matter so much if several of the other ingredients work according to plan.

The need for in-depth studies of sets of HRM practices

We have an interesting discrepancy between the reviewed studies pointing at great deviations in practice from what the strategic HRM literature would claim to be guarantees of performance, and great faith in the literature showing that HRM policies and practices deliver the goods. HRM researchers feel that they 'now can say with increasing confidence that HRM works' (Guest 1999: 188) and they can mobilize empirical studies indicating that ambitious use of HRM practices has positive effect on performances (Huselid 1995; MacDuffie 1995, etc.). We earlier referred to reservations about this (e.g. Legge 2001), but leaving our doubts aside, let us ask if HRM, perhaps, sometimes works (at least to a degree), how does it do the trick? Mainstream HRM research views this to be a matter of the competent realization of plans and intentions, leading to a system characterized by instrumentality, validity and consistency (Bowen & Ostroff 2004). It is believed that the success of a HRM system is closely related to the validity of the practices and the consistency of HRM messages. Bowen and Ostroff (2004), for example, emphasize the need to establish 'an *unambiguous* perceived cause–effect relationship in reference to the HRM system's desired content-focused behaviours and associated employee consequences' (p. 210, italics in original). As seen above, research on specific HRM practices indicates there is seldom such an unambiguous perceived cause–effect relationship. However, there is a shortage of studies on what is actually happening more broadly in sets of HRM practices in organizations and what are the experiences and views of those concerned.

Many studies point at only limited aspects and, as Bowen and Ostroff (2004) note, 'little attention has been given to the social constructions that employees make of their interactions with HRM' (p. 206), arguably a key aspect. As Watson (2004) remarks, much of the HRM research neglects the concept that HR, like organizational arrangements and practices in general, are outcomes of human interpretations, conflicts, confusions, guesses and rationalizations (p. 453). A considerable part of the critical research also shares this tendency. Black-boxing is only partially avoided through glimpses of a small part of what is inside the box.

In empirically studying HRM, a range of options, from studying broad and general HRM policies (set of practices) to focusing on specific practices in detail, are possible. A problem is that the former tends to treat HRM as an aggregate and exhibits little knowledge of the specific sets of practices, leading to superficial research in which the HRM package is reified and black-boxed. In the worst case, which is not uncommon, case managers are asked to tick off boxes as to whether they 'have' team organization, invest in competence, and so on, and these are then seen as indicators of the strategic use of HRM. Of course, the result may reflect local beliefs about progressiveness or inclinations to promote the firm as much as any 'objective reality' out there. Often people in organizations see things quite differently, e.g. senior and junior people may have quite different perceptions of possibilities for competence development (Fosstenløkken 2007). A focused study on a specific practice means that only a limited part of the HRM side of an organization is highlighted. Studies of, for example, training or appraisal do give a partial view of HRM, but do not reveal that much of the richness of employment management as a whole. Studies of work organizations, e.g. teams, give important and sometimes rich knowledge of a key dimension of work, but are arguably slightly outside HRM, if this is not defined as involving all kinds of people management (which easily makes HRM equal to management in general).[1] There is a dilemma between the Big Black-Boxed extreme – very popular among HRM researchers – and the one-practice-focused extreme.

HRM, organizational culture and identity (HRM/C)

There is a strong need to go beyond the hard/soft and other distinctions, critique of textbook and other popular formulations of HRM and the HRM–P claiming and testing and take the human and social aspects of HRM much more seriously. There are also good reasons not to focus just on specific aspects of HRM – career structures, appraisals or mentoring – but to look more broadly at the interface between employees and HRM practices. This would mean (i) taking the nature of human beings not as object-like dependent-variables, but as active, interpreting and subjective actors, and (ii) taking the political, ambiguous and often non-rational nature of organizations and managers seriously.

Arguably, neither those managing, nor those managed by, HRM policies and plans act and react according to the blueprints of HRM gurus and advocates. A 'pro-human' move can, for example, be carried out through connecting HRM to how various actors experience, interpret and relate to a set of various policies, systems and practices. Organizational culture and identity theory are useful in throwing light on these issues in organizations in that they capture human and social aspects. Organizational culture is then defined as the shared meanings and symbolism common within a particular setting, which guide understanding and organize experience (Alvesson 2002; Smircich 1983).

Although HRM is typically seen as a functional tool, this perspective indicates that HRM may be more powerfully understood as a device that provides shared meanings about the corporate universe, thus being instrumental in sustaining the normative order. Others view HRM as an expression of culture, most typically as an expression of technocracy and managerialist fantasies of control (c.f. Keenoy 1997; Townley 1993).

In these senses, HRM practices may be understood as key providers and manifestations of culture and cultural material in organizations. HRM and organizational culture are frequently viewed as closely related. Jackson and Schuler (1995), for example, view 'organizational culture as inextricably bound to HRM and therefore not meaningful if separated from it' (p. 238), but they do not express any theoretical view on culture or use it as an interpretive device. Culture is often reduced to a variable affecting HRM or as a managerial tool for accomplishing the wanted workforce. In this chapter culture means the use of an interpretive perspective.

'Culture' indicates a way of thinking that particularly highlights symbolic phenomena. Culture is viewed as 'a framework of meaning, a system of reference that can generate both shared understandings and the working misunderstandings that enable social life to go on. These frameworks of meaning are cultivated, negotiated, and reproduced within behavioural enactments' (Batteau 2001: 726). Thus, we can study HRM from a cultural perspective (c.f. Alvesson 2002; Geertz 1973; Kunda 1992; Martin 2002; Smircich 1983). Culture and HRM are thus not external, but HRM systems and practices are fused with cultural meanings. Compared to the 'external' perspectives of HRM–P or HRM–S (where HRM is viewed respectively as a discursive practice producing performance or subjectivity), one could perhaps capture a cultural view on HRM as HRM/C.

A key dimension here is identity, at individual (Alvesson & Willmott 2002; Collinson 2003) and organizational levels (Albert & Whetten 1985; Dutton et al. 1994; Hatch & Schulz 2002). HRM practices can be viewed as vehicles (in the sense of media for meaning) for the construction of meanings and 'stories' about the individuals – who they are – and the organization – its distinctiveness and coherence. Identity indicates constructions of what is specific and distinct. As will be developed below, this self-view affects employees' identifications with the firm and their sense of who and how they are. A density of HRM structures and practices signal to external and internal audiences that this firm knows what it is doing and that the personnel who are promoted are thoroughly bona fide. HRM is thus about 'the creation of the organization's view of itself' (Keenoy & Anthony 1992: 238), i.e. organizational identity. HRM is not viewed as an objective-functional system but as a meaning-creating device, which organizational members use to develop and reproduce understandings about who they are and what their firm stands for (Alvesson & Kärreman 2007). HRM–P studies often tell us very little.

Culturally speaking, HRM phenomena are understood in terms of the symbolism and meanings that they communicate and/or group members ascribe to (or interpret from) arrangements and practices. From this point of view, promotion practices are significant not because they promote the better candidate, but because they tell us what it meant to be the better candidate in a specific organizational setting. They articulate and propagate shared understandings of the meaning of promotion and candidature in this context. Similarly, cultural resources – rituals, myths, stories, language use – are important building blocks in organizational members' identity work. This HRM/C perspective breaks with the technocratic view of most HRM and has little tolerance with HRM–P (or HRM–S) lines of thinking, favoring an in-depth exploration of what goes on inside the black box.

Unpacking HRM: A case study

Alvesson and Kärreman (2007) studied a large, successful management consultancy firm (Excellence) with very ambitious HRM systems and procedures, characterized by experiences of frequent deviations from policies in feedback, ranking, promotion and assignment planning.

The HRM system of excellence is designed in a way that closely matches the normative ideal typically voiced by proponents of strategic HRM. Recruitment practices, career structure, appraisal systems and development and training are all designed in an elaborate fashion and allocated considerable time and money. The firm invests heavily in the training and development of individual employees: courses, competence development groups, mentors, workshops, invited speakers and publications available for those interested. Promotion receives a lot of attention, and the meritocratic nature of the firm is emphasized. People receive much support for their development and they are promoted based purely on qualifications and competence, it is claimed – by junior as well as senior staff. This is a successful firm with a very ambitious HRM system that works very well, according to those involved. This seems to support the HRM–P view.

However, there are many experiences of deviations from the espoused ideals and ambitions of the HRM system, e.g. people perceive their feedback as being non-ambitious, vague and mainly positive, they note grade inflation and see examples of promotion that makes little sense. But strikingly, organization members do *not* share the world-weary view of the HRM systems emerging from their own experiences of how it in practice functions (or does not function). Actually, all of the informants tend to think that the HRM system delivers. There is a widespread belief that the corporate system for selection, ranking, developing and promotion is reliable and that the resulting hierarchy expresses valid differences in technical and managerial competence. The elaborated formal differentiation system is assumed to register and mirror the actual competence of the employees. As a consequence, the deviations mentioned were reported as surprising and puzzling events.

The study confirms other research that the realization of ambitious HRM designs faces formidable problems. Interestingly, despite these difficulties, people still use HRM systems, practices and ideologies for the construction of positively loaded meanings about organizational identity and the identities of the employees. The observation that 'failed' practices are accompanied by 'successful' symbolism offers an alternative to functionalism (and partly also to Foucauldian studies). Understanding of ambitious HRM from a cultural-theoretical perspective emphasizes its role in aligning individual and organizational identity.

This study shows that (i) the actual practices of HRM can easily fall far behind and contradict ambitious HRM objectives, ideologies, systems and procedures; (ii) HRM may feed into organizational and individual identity projects; and (iii) the 'success' of HRM – the inclination of people to take this seriously and ascribe positive meaning to it – is contingent upon the presence of stories and myths communicating beliefs about the quality and reliability of HRM arrangements and practices, that facilitate the willing suspension of disbelief. All this indicates the need to rethink conventional ideas about HRM – and to some extent also the critiques of HRM.

Perhaps strategic HRM (often) works, at least to some extent, but how? Mainstream HRM research views this to be a matter of the competent realization of plans and intentions, leading to a system characterized by instrumentality, validity and consistency (Bowen & Ostroff 2004). Alvesson and Karreman (2007) suggest that other mechanisms may be even more important. It also demonstrates the usefulness of observing actual HRM practices and listening closely (but not uncritically) to the experiences and voices of those involved, rather than treating them as a black-box phenomenon that reliably converts particular input to predictable outcomes. Doing the latter means that one is just guessing what is actually happening and why. The study would indicate that the impressive machinery of HRM cannot in itself accomplish that much as regards rationality, but in combination with a specific belief system it may produce and uphold faith and encourage a strong motivation to succeed and subordinate oneself to a seemingly rational and superior system.

The study suggests a reconceptualization of HRM *from* a system of structures and practices leading to effective people-processing through techniques *to* a set of meanings and symbols which organizational members draw upon to produce a particular view of the organization as well as themselves. This view means a certain selectivity and closure in how people make sense of their experiences. Rather than functioning as a rational set of practices for developing and using people at work, HRM, at least sometimes, appears as exercising influence through a myth, where it reduces critical reflections and shapes and possibly even freezes people's subjectivities. Like a true Calvinist, guided by the belief that one's inner capacity and performance are reflected in the divine hints of one's value offered by HRM apparatus, the individual works very hard and with few doubts about the logic behind the hints.

Conclusion

The amount of critical work on HRM is not overwhelming (Keegan & Boselie 2006). There is, however, a number of critical texts investigating the assumptions in mainstream HRM, problematic claims about the link between HRM and performance, ideology critique pointing at discrepancy between rhetoric and reality, as well as Foucauldian work on the forming of subjectivity. From a critical perspective, HRM, that is, large parts of it, appears to be one-sidedly promoting an ideological view of employement relations and practices in which there is a close alignment between performance and employee (humanistic) interests. It also expresses a technocratic and managerialist worldview in which the strategy and design of HRM in itself accomplish high performance. The human aspects of HRM are marginalized: interests, politics, interpretations, relations, experiences and actions of people. Critical work on HRM is sometimes not strong in seriously considering, even less empirically investigating these themes. This work tends to concentrate on problematic features in mainstream HRM and then function as a reply to these. It shares with a lot of the mainstream work a tendency to black-box HRM – to study it from a distance and look at effects (or the lack thereof). Various strands of critical HRM argue for the lack of a strong HRM–performance link or a strong effect of HRM on subjectivity. The total picture becomes somewhat confusing – is HRM impotent or too potent? Of course, it can lead to no visible performance effects and operate efficiently on the forming of subjects. Or it can have strong performance effects but not really influence individuals more than locating them based on their abilities and improving these in a technical and intellectual sense. But these two effects could also (and perhaps more likely) combine to either produce powerful effects on results and people or else be unproductive and mainly provide a legitimizing structure (Meyer & Rowan 1977) and have limited impact on individuals. A confrontation of and negotiation between the positions of HRM–P and HRM–S seem motivated.

Critical work needs also to embrace a more 'positive' research agenda, less tied to HRM literature. Studying HRM in terms of social practices and the meanings associated with these offers a richer picture of what goes on as well as an unpacking of HRM. The latter often suggests that there is a discrepancy between a formal system (allocated resources), and actual organizational practices, but also the meanings and experiences involved may suggest another discrepancy and add to the complexity. Shortcomings of HRM in working as planned are common. In-depth studies show how HRM may influence the construction processes, the identities and meanings in organizations, involving power effects such as self-discipline and HRM mediated views of self. Constructions of HRM – despite its shortages in delivering according to plan and promise – may freeze and legitimate a specific organizational order as meritocratic. The possible consequences of HRM for performance may be more in the region of extensive HRM rituals and a local mythology of the salience of HRM practices (and talk promoting these) legitimizing hierarchy and differentiation, creating 'surplus' compliance and increasing career motivation – a possible key aspect obscured by technocratic notions of HRM and studies black-boxing the phenomena.

Note

1   Legge (2005) views work organization studies under High-Performance Work as the critical alternative to 'strategic HRM', but I am limiting my overview to fairly distinct HRM issues, and thus not including studies of labour process and organization of work.

References

Albert S. & Whetten, D. 1985. Organizational identity. *Research in Organizational Behavior*, 7: 263–295.

Alvesson, M. 2002. *Understanding Organizational Culture*. London: Sage.

Alvesson, M. 2004. *Knowledge Work and Knowledge-Intensive Firms*. Oxford: Oxford University Press.

Alvesson, M. 2008. The future of critical management studies. In D. Barry & H. Hansen (eds), *Handbook of New Perspectives on Organizations*. London: Sage.

Alvesson, M. & Deetz, S. 2000. *Doing Critical Management Research*. London: Sage.

Alvesson, M. & Kärreman, D. 2007. Unraveling HRM. Identity, ceremony and control in a management consultancy firm. *Organization Science*, 18 (4): 711–723.

Alvesson, M. & Willmott, H. 1996. *Making Sense of Management: A Critical Introduction*. London: Sage.

Alvesson, M. & Willmott, H. 2002. Producing the appropriate individual. Identity regulation as organizational control. *Journal of Management Studies*, 39 (5): 619–644.

Alvesson, M. & Willmott, H. (eds) 2003. *Studying Management Critically*. London: Sage.

Barlow, G. 1989. Deficiencies and the perpetuation of power: latent functions in management appraisals. *Journal of Management Studies*, 26 (5): 499–517.

Batteau, A. 2001. Negations and ambiguities in the cultures of organizations. *American Anthropologist*, 102 (4): 726–740.

Berglund, J. 2002. *De otillräckliga*. Stockholm: EFL.

Bowen, D. & Ostroff, C. 2004. Understanding HRM–firm performance linkages: the role of the "strength" of the HRM system. *Academy of Management Review*, 29 (2): 203–221.

Boxall, P. & Steeneveld, M. 1999. Human resource strategy and competitive advantage: a longitudinal study of engineering consultants. *Journal of Management Studies*, 36 (4): 443–463.

Clegg, S. 1989. *Frameworks of Power*. London: Sage.

Collinson, D. 2003. Identities and insecurities. *Organization*, 10 (3): 527–547

Covaleski, M. et al. 1998. The calculated and the avowed: techniques of discipline and struggles over identity in Big Six public accounting firms. *Administrative Science Quarterly*, 43: 293–327.

Deetz, S. 2003. Disciplinary power, conflict suppression and human resource management. In M. Alvesson & H. Willmott (eds), *Studying Management Critically*. London: Sage.

Dutton, J., Dukerich, J. & Harquail, C. 1994. Organizational images and member identification. *Administrative Science Quarterly*, 39: 239–263.

Fosstenløkken, S. M. 2007. *Enhancing Intangible Recourses in Professional Service Firms. A Comparative Study of How Competence Development Takes Place in Four Firms*. PhD diss. Oslo: BI.

Foucault, M. 1976. *The History of Sexuality. Vol. 1*. New York: Pantheon.

Foucault, M. 1980. *Power/Knowledge. Selected Interviews and Other Writings 1972–1977*. New York: Pantheon.

Fournier, V. & Grey, C. 2000. At the critical moment: conditions and prospects for critical management studies. *Human Relations*, 53(1): 7–32.

Geertz, C. 1973. *Interpretations of Culture*. New York: Basic Books.

Grey, C. 1994. Career as a project of the self and labour process discipline. *Sociology*, 28: 479–497.

Grey, C. & Willmott, H. (eds) 2005. *Critical Management Studies*. Oxford: Oxford University Press.

Guest, D. 1999. Human resource management and performance: a review and research agenda. In R. Schuler & S. Jackson (eds), *Strategic Human Resource Management*. Oxford: Blackwell.

Guest, D. & King, Z. 2004. Power, innovation and problem-solving. The personnel manager's three steps to heaven? *Journal of Management Studies*, 41: 401–424.

Harley, B. & Hardy, C. 2004. Firing blanks? An analysis of discursive struggles in HRM. *Journal of Management Studies*, 41: 377–400.

Hatch, M. J. & Schultz, M. 2002. The dynamics of organizational identity. *Human Relations*, 55: 989–1018.

Hesketh, A. & Fleetwood, S. 2006. Beyond measuring the human resource management–organizational performance link: applying critical realist meta-theory. *Organization*, 13: 677–699.

Huselid, M.A. 1995. The impact of human resource management practices on turnover, productivity, and corporate financial performance. *Academy of Management Journal*, 38: 635–672.

Iles, P. & Salaman, G. 1995. Recruitment, assessment and selection. In J. Storey (ed), *Human Resource Management – A Critical Text*. London: Thomson.

Jackall, R. 1988. *Moral Mazes. The World of Corporate Managers*. New York: Oxford University Press.

Jackson, S. & Schuler, R. 1995. Understanding human resource management in the context of organizations and their environment. *Annual Review of Psychology*, 46: 237–264.

Keegan, A. & Boselie, P. 2006. The lack of impact of dissensus inspired analysis on developments in the field of human resource management. *Journal of Management Studies*, 43 (7): 1491–1511.

Keenoy, T. 1997. Review article: HRMism and the languages of re-presentation. *Journal of Management Studies*. 34(5): 825–841.

Keenoy, T. 1999. HRM as hologram: a polemic. *Journal of Management Studies*, 36: 1–23.

Keenoy, T. & Anthony, P. 1992. HRM: metaphor, meaning and morality. In P. Blyton & P. Turnbull (eds), *Reassessing Human Resource Management*. London: Sage.

Knights, D. 1992. Changing spaces: the disruptive impact of a new epistemological location for the study of management, *Academy of Management Review*, 17: 514–536.

Knights, D. & Morgan, G. 1991. Corporate strategy, organizations, and subjectivity: a critique. *Organization Studies*, 12: 251–273.

Kunda, G. 1992. *Engineering Culture. Control and Commitment in a High-Tech Corporation*. Philadelphia: Temple University Press.

Legge, K. 1995. *Human Resource Management. Rhetorics and Reality*. London: Macmillan.

Legge, K. 2001. Silver bullet or spent round? Assessing the meaning of the 'high commitment management'/performance relationship. In J. Storey (ed.), *Human Resource Management*. London: Thomson.

Legge, K. 2005. Human resource management. In S. Ackroyd et al. (eds), *Oxford Handbook of Work and Organization Studies*. Oxford: Oxford University Press.

Lengnick-Hall, C. & Lengnick-Hall, M. 1988. Strategic human resource management: a review of the literature and a proposed typology. *Academy of Management Review* 13 (3): 454–470.

Longenecker, C., Gioia, D. & Sims, H. 1987. Behind the mask: the politics of employee appraisal. *Academy of Management Executive*, 1 (3): 183–193.

MacDuffie, J. P. 1995. Human resource bundles and manufacturing performance: organizational logic and flexible production systems in the world auto industry. *Industrial and Labor Relations Review*, 48 (2): 197–221.

Marchington, M. & Grugulis, I. 2000. 'Best practice' human resource management: perfect opportunity or dangerous illusion? *International Journal of Human Resource Management*, 11: 905–925.

Martin, J. 1992. *The Culture of Organizations*. New York: Oxford University Press.

Martin, J. 2002. *Organizational Culture*. Thousand Oaks, CA: Sage.

Meyer, J. & Rowan, B. 1977. Institutionalized organizations: formal structure as myth and ceremony. *American Journal of Sociology*, 83: 340–363.

Newell, S., Robertson, M., Scarborough, H. & Swan, J. 2002. *Managing Knowledge Work*. London: Palgrave.

Newton, T. 1998. Theorizing subjectivity in organizations. The failure of Foucauldian studies? *Organization Studies*, 19: 415–447.

Palmer, I. & Hardy, C. 2000. *Thinking about Management*. London: Sage.

Pfeffer, J. 1994. *Competitive Advantage through People*. Boston: Harvard Business Press.

Purcell, J. 1999. Best practice and best fit: chimera or cul-de-sac? *Human Resource Management Journal*, 9 (3): 26–41.

Schneider, S. 1999. Human and inhuman resource management: sense and nonsense. *Organization*, 6 (2): 277–284.

Smircich, L. 1983. Concepts of culture and organizational analysis. *Administrative Science Quarterly*, 28 (3): 339–358.

Steffy, B. & Grimes, A. 1992. Personnel/organizational psychology – a critique of the discipline. In M. Alvesson & H. Willmott (eds), *Critical Management Studies*. London: Sage.

Steyaert, C. & Janssens, M. 1999. Human and inhuman resource management: saving the subjects of HRM. *Organization*, 6: 181–198.

Storey, J. 2001. Human resource management. In J. Storey (ed.), *Human Resource Management*. London: Thomson.

Storey, J. & Quintas, P. 2001. 'Knowledge management and HRM. In J. Storey (ed.), *Human Resource Management*. London: Thomson.

Thompson, P., Warhurst, C. & Callaghan, G. 2001. Ignorant theory and knowledgeable workers: interrogating the connections between knowledge skills and services. *Journal of Management Studies*, 38 (7): 923–942.

Tichy, N., Fombrun, C. & Devanna, M. 1982. Strategic human resource management. *Sloan Management Review*, 23 (2): 47–61.

Townley, B. 1993. Foucault, power/knowledge and its relevance for human resource management. *Academy of Management Review*, 18 (3): 518–545.

Townley, B. 1994. *Reframing Human Resource Management*. London: Sage.

Townley, B. 1999. Practical reason and performance appraisal. *Journal of Management Studies*, 36 (3): 287–306.

Tyson, S. 1995. *Human Resource Strategy*. London: Pitman.

Watson, T. 1994. *In Search of Management*. London: Routledge.

Watson, T. 2004. HRM and critical social science analysis. *Journal of Management Studies*, 41: 447–467.

Part 3

The external environment of SHRM

The chapters in Part 3 deal with various aspects of the environment – most notably, the legal context, the changing architecture of work organizations and the labour market environment. Acting strategically in relation to HR usually means coping within a dynamic environment and in so far as possible anticipating some of the changes. A number of players at different levels in the 'system' shape and impact the nature of this environment. The most obvious set of environmental changes concerns globalization and the shift of economic activity and power to Asian economies such as China and India. These economies are no longer simply the low-cost producers receiving inward investment from Western corporations 'outsourcing' and 'offshoring' their routine manufacturing and service activities. On the contrary, there are signs that these economies are taking a lead in aspects of quality and innovation and that they are now in a position to acquire Western companies – some of long standing.

Apart from international trade in goods and services there is also a significant shift in the volume of labour migrating between countries and continents. In the face of such heightened competition in both labour and product markets, governments are having to rethink the fundamental principles which guide their regulative activity. Many Western governments, while at times tempted by protectionist tendencies, are seeking a mix of policies which allow some basic standards (such as a minimum wage) while also seeking to ensure flexible labour markets which encourage rather than stifle entrepreneurship. There is often a third leg to this policy architecture and that is to equip people for change by offering incentives and provision for capability development.

That is the kind of context which governs the formulation of new legal regulation. In general, legal regulation in many countries is still increasing its reach. In consequence, as Mark Roehling, Richard Posthuma and Stacy Hickox note, there are relatively few aspects of HRM which are not now covered by laws, regulation and risk of litigation. Their chapter provides a useful framework analysis of types of law (this includes an analysis of 'hard' and 'soft' forms of regulation), the various sources of law, and the implications of the changing forms of legal regulation for HR strategists. The variety of responses to law in the employment field – such as 'technical compliance' as opposed to 'legitimacy seeking behaviour' – is subject to scrutiny. The chapter concludes with a research agenda and some practical implications.

In the next chapter, John Storey examines the emerging variety of forms within which work and enterprise now takes place. The idea of a 'workplace' or 'employing organization' is now much more complicated and variegated than was the case a few decades ago. Work and economic activity is coordinated in a plethora of ways. Even where a direct employment contract persists, the understanding may be very different from that pertaining when some notion of a lifetime's employment with one company or organization was at least some kind of notional norm, albeit one breached in practice. Varieties of partnerships, networking and contracting mean that the HR department may not be dealing with conventional employees. Added to that, the employment deal and sets of underlying assumptions may depart from past conventions. Collective contracts with trade unions are fewer in number and cover only a minority of workers; individualized contracts are increasingly important. The implications for HR strategy deriving from these changes to the structuring of work and enterprise are far-reaching; at the same time, HR strategy is, in many instances, one of the drivers of these changes.

Some of these themes are picked up and explored further in David Coats's chapter on the changing labor market and the future of work. Coats focuses in particular on the nature of work and its relationships with structural changes in national economies. This analysis embraces the various forms of capitalism, including, for example, the employment implications of liberal market economies compared with social welfare state models. Of special interest, for example, is the Danish 'flexicurity' concept which combines a labor market characterized by a strong welfare state, moderately strict employment protection legislation, trade unions and active labor market programs. As he notes, the OECD have judged this approach to be compatible with non-inflationary growth and good employment performance. The kinds of legal regimes which are discussed by Roehling et al. tend to derive from these sorts of political considerations.

A key lesson to be drawn from the Coats's chapter is that national policies do matter a great deal and that there seem to be few policy decisions which simply stem directly from forces such as globalization. Nonetheless, as he points out, there have been significant structural changes – most especially in the profile of industries. Of special note is the immense turbulence in the advanced economies at this time – with the U.S.A., for example, creating and destroying 500,000 jobs every week. As national policies do matter, the message is that getting employment policies right is of crucial importance. Strategic human resource management works within the resulting framework of choices but it can also help to shape the nature of these policies. To this extent SHRM is thus even more important than might otherwise be thought possible.

5

Foundations for understanding the legal environment of HRM in a global context

*Mark V. Roehling, Richard A. Posthuma
and Stacy Hickox*

Introduction

At a general level, the role of the legal environment as an important context for human resource management (HRM) is well recognized by both practitioners and researchers. In addition to an awareness of laws directly regulating day-to-day HRM activities, HRM managers providing input into strategic decisions must have an understanding of the broader legal environment associated with their area of professional expertise (Bagley, 2008; Florkowski, 2006). An awareness of how the legal environment may influence the phenomena they study is also important to researchers investigating a wide range of HRM topics (e.g., HRM decision-making, diffusion of practices, the HR practices–organizational effectiveness link, crosscultural differences). However, for both practitioners and researchers, the challenge of understanding and effectively taking into account the legal environment of HRM is both considerable and growing. Across countries, the legal regulation of the workplace has increased significantly in recent decades. As a result, in many countries, almost all aspects of HRM are now potentially affected by workplace laws, regulations, and/or the risk of litigation. Employers with operations that cross national boundaries face a legal environment with additional layers of complexity. Which country's or countries' laws apply? Must highly publicized international labor standards be complied with? To what extent can "private law" be used to shape employers' and employees' legal obligations?

Purpose of the chapter

The layers of complexity (especially in a global context), the sheer volume of legal regulatory material, and the evolving nature of law preclude any attempt to provide comprehensive coverage of the legal environment of HRM in a single chapter. Instead, this chapter provides readers with a foundation for understanding the legal environment of HRM, giving special attention to the increasingly important global aspects of that environment. The chapter is also intended to promote research that will contribute to the understanding of the legal environment of HRM. The chapter is organized into four sections. It begins by identifying and discussing concepts and issues that are critical to understanding how law operates in theory and practice. An appreciation of these concepts and issues will promote the strategic or "organizationally sensible" consideration of HRM's legal environment (Roehling & Wright, 2006). The second section overviews sources of labor and employment law at the global, regional, and national levels, and then highlights selected HRM-related legal issues with particular relevance to international employers. The third section reviews theory and selected research addressing the impact of the legal environment on HRM strategy and practices, and suggests future research directions. The final section discusses practical issues and makes a number of recommendations for the effective management of the legal environment of HRM.

Critical concepts and issues

"Law," "hard law," "soft law"

Law, broadly defined, encompasses a set of binding customs, practices, or rules. Within that broad definition, there are several distinctions with potential importance to the understanding of the legal environment of HRM. The first distinction relates to whether the law is enforceable by some authority external to the organization. "Hard laws" are legally enforceable, and include laws associated with government (e.g., constitutions, statutes, administrative regulations, judicial decisions; Florkowski, 2006). Hard laws provide "the rules of the game" within which firms compete to create and capture values (Bagley, 2008). In contrast, the term "soft law" refers to instruments that provide non-binding standards for behavior and practice, such as charters, social declarations, codes of conduct, and model acts (Florkowski, 2006). Organizations may agree to be legally bound by soft laws. However, without such an agreement, soft laws merely provide guidance, and may be the basis for interest groups to pressure organizations to treat their workers in accordance with soft law standards.

In addition to labor and employment laws that originate with external authorities and are imposed on organizations, organizations can also create their own "private law" that may affect the responsibilities and rights of employers and workers (Bagley, 2008; Blanpain et al., 2007). Private law may be created, for example, by entering into individual employment contracts or voluntarily adopting corporate codes that make a commitment to international rights and standards. In summary, HRM professionals need to be concerned about two sets of legal obligations: those imposed by external sources of hard law, and those voluntarily assumed by their organization. In addition, in some situations, it will also be necessary to consider soft laws (e.g., where failure to comply with standards established by soft laws may result in negative customer, investor, or public reactions).

International labor and employment law

The terms "labor law" and "employment law" are given different meanings in different countries (Roehling, 2004). In American legal parlance, the term "labor law" typically refers to the legal regulation of collective bargaining and labor relations, and the term "employment law" refers to work-related legal regulations regarding individual employees (e.g., laws prohibiting discrimination, individual work contracts, the regulation of wage and hours). However, in Europe and many other countries the term "labor law" is used more expansively, to cover both of the above-described types of legal regulation. In this chapter, we use the American parlance for the labor and employment law, or the term "workplace law" to encompass both.

"International labor and employment law" is not captured by a single, easily identified, unified body of law. Rather, it has been described as a "confusing" and "unwieldy" patchwork of international treaties and conventions, International Labor Organization standards, national laws (which may include religious laws in some countries), contracts, and voluntary codes of conduct (Hagerman, 2006, p. 860).

Legal requirements versus law-related risk

At a general level, HRM decisions in global contexts involve two related, but distinct, legal concerns: (1) To what extent does the law mandate that a specific policy or practice be followed, a specific behavior demonstrated, or a specific choice made? (2) To what extent is there a threat of litigation or other negative stakeholder reaction based on a perceived failure to comply with hard or soft laws? The first concern is about legal requirements, the second about law-related risk. The distinction between these two legal concerns is critical to understanding and managing the legal environment (Roehling & Wright, 2006).

The term *legal requirements* refers to those policies, practices, or specific behaviors that are either mandated or proscribed by the various sources of hard law described above (Roehling & Wright, 2006). Within a given legal jurisdiction, the extent to which the law requires (or prohibits) a specific course of action will vary depending on the specific employment decision. At one extreme are decisions regarding employment issues that are governed by *clear and specific* legal requirements. Here, the course of action to be followed is clearly prescribed by law, and there is really no decision to be made because the "decision" is dictated by the clear and specific legal requirements. Examples of legal requirements include: the U.S. Occupational Safety and Health Act, which requires compliance with a variety of specific safety-related practices; the Mexican Federal Labor Law's requirement that seniority be used to lay off employees; Japanese law specifying that employees in certain categories receive minimum additional compensation for overtime; and the Netherlands' requirement that to terminate an employment contract by giving notice, a "dismissal permit" must first be obtained from the appropriate state authority. These are, of course, just a few of the many possible examples of legal requirements relating to HRM.

At the other extreme are decisions that clearly do *not* involve legal requirements. These employment-related decisions still may involve litigation or other law-related risks. Examples include decisions on whether to adopt a corporate code of conduct, use a specific kind of selection test not expressly prohibited by law (e.g., an unstructured interview format, cognitive ability tests in the U.S.), provide employees greater job security than mandated by law, hold a "company party" or other social event on the company's premises, or conduct an audit of the company's HRM policies and practices.

Between those employment decisions that are governed by clear and specific legal requirements, and those decisions where the law clearly does not require a specific course of action, there are situations where the applicable legal requirements are ambiguous or uncertain (i.e., the precise nature of the legal requirements cannot be determined with a reasonable degree of certainty). This uncertainty may occur when newly passed legislation first goes into effect, and/or where legal standards for complying with the law are still evolving. For example, while it is clear that the U.S. Family Medical Leave Act (FMLA) imposes legal requirements on covered employers, there is still considerable uncertainty as to the precise nature of those requirements in many situations.

The term *law-related risk* refers to the threat that a perceived failure to comply with hard or soft laws will lead to litigation or other negative stakeholder reactions (e.g., customer boycotts). This risk is a function of both the likelihood of the threat being realized and the magnitude of the threat. While employment-related litigation is perhaps most commonly associated with the

U.S., there is evidence that employees are becoming increasingly militant in the assertion of their rights in many other countries, and there has been a dramatic growth in employment-practices lawsuits around the world (Florkowski, 2006). In addition, the threat of negative reactions by customers or investors to perceived violations of hard or soft employment laws is clearly an international phenomena, and it appears that multinational enterprises (MNEs) are particularly vulnerable to such reactions. The aforegoing considerations suggest that while many employment decisions do not involve legal requirements (i.e., the contemplated action is not strictly mandated or proscribed by law), in an increasing number of countries most employment decisions will involve some level of law-related risk.

HRM professionals' awareness and understanding of the distinction between legal requirements versus law-related risk is critical. If it is determined that an employment decision involves clear legal requirements, then it is appropriate for HRM professionals to defer to a lawyer's judgment as to the specific compliance that is required. However, if the employment decision merely involves law-related risk, and not legal requirements, then a strategic or "organizationally sensible" approach to HRM requires that relevant non-legal considerations be identified, taken into account, and weighed against the law-related risk. Examples of non-legal considerations that may be relevant include whether the decision is consistent with the organization's expressed values, and its likely impact in promoting critical attitudes and behaviors, attracting and retaining talent, or promoting workforce diversity. The failure of an HRM professional to distinguish between decisions involving legal requirements and those only involving an increase in law-related risk may result in employment decisions that are unnecessarily dictated by lawyers, and legalistic advice will limit the HRM professional's ability to use his or her HRM expertise to make valuable contributions to the organization.

Sources of labor and employment law and selected legal issues

Figure 5.1 summarizes the primary sources of labor and employment law, including both law imposed on organizations by external authorities and "private law." As indicated in Figure 5.1, sources of law may exert their influence at various levels: global, regional, national, or organizational (e.g. a binding code of conduct agreed to by the employer). In this section, we review key sources of labor and employment law, and then identify and briefly discuss legal issues with particular relevance to employers with global operations.

Global organizations and the evolution of transnational employment regulation

The International Labor Organization (ILO)

It has been suggested that any discussion of international law relating to employment and labor should start with the ILO (Bilder, 2006). This UN-affiliated agency formulates international labor standards (ILS), monitors compliance with standards by its member states, provides technical assistance to member states, and attempts to enforce the commitments of approximately 175 member states. The ILO issues labor standards in two forms, conventions and recommendations. *Conventions* are treaty-like agreements that must be formally ratified by member states before taking effect. Once ratified by a member state without reservations, an ILO convention is considered a treaty containing binding international obligations. In contrast, *recommendations* are intended to provide guidance, and do not constrain the actions of ILO member states. The ILO core labor standards are viewed as fundamental rights of all workers. They include:

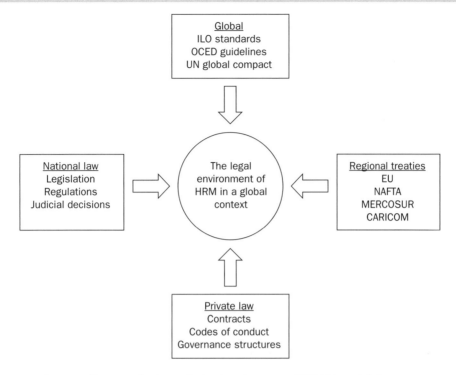

Figure 5.1 Sources of law contributing to the legal environment of HRM in a global context

- freedom of association and the effective recognition of the right to collective bargaining;
- freedom from discrimination in employment (equal opportunity);
- the effective abolition of forced or compulsory behavior;
- the effective abolition of child labor.

There are two main ways that the ILO enforces international labor standards: through the review of reports that members have a recurring obligation to file, and through the initiation of complaints enforced by the ILO. In some countries, once an ILO convention is ratified, it becomes part of the national law, and as a result, enforceable at the national level.

The United Nations Global Compact

The UN has historically played a relatively minor, indirect role in employment law and labor standards. However, in 2000 it began taking a more active role by adopting the Global Compact, a statement of universal principles in the area of human rights, labor standards, and the environment. Its principles relating to labor include normative statements that businesses should comply with the fundamental rights of all workers reflected in the ILO core standards, as set forth above. The Global Compact is a voluntary initiative without an enforcement mechanism, seeking instead to promote its principles through public accountability and the enlightened attitudes of organizations.

Organization of Economic Cooperation and Development (OECD)

The OECD has evolved from an organization of European countries intended to promote reconstruction in Europe following World War II, and now includes 30 countries from five continents, including the U.S., Canada, Mexico, South Korea, Japan, and Australia. With the purpose of promoting foreign investment that benefits both firms and the societies in which they conduct their operations, the OECD has adopted guidelines for responsible business conduct for MNEs in or from member countries. Revised in 2000, the *OECD Guidelines for Multinational Enterprises* advocate numerous policies bearing on "Employment and Industrial Relations," including the following:

- respect the rights of employees to be represented by trade unions;
- provide employees with sufficient information to convey an accurate picture of firm performance;
- avoid discrimination with respect to employment or obligation on the basis of race, color, gender, religion, political opinion, national extraction, or social origin unless doing so furthers established policies to promote EEO or can be justified as job related;
- eliminate child labor and forced labor;
- provide reasonable notice of collective lay-offs and dismissals.

The OECD guidelines are also voluntary. However, member states operate a network of national contact points that field complaints about MNE conduct in violation of the guidelines. Also, countries seeking new membership in the OECD must show that their regulatory practices (e.g., employment laws and related enforcement mechanisms) are consistent with the OECD values and legal instruments as a condition of admission.

Regional trade treaties

There are a number of regional trading blocs that involve treaty or other obligations relating to employment and labor standards. These regional trade treaties vary significantly in the amount of authority given to the central or coordinating institution over member state policy making, and the extent to which an attempt is made to integrate the member states' substantive laws. In this section, we provide an overview of several of the better known regional trading blocs with treaties that have labor and employment law implications.

The European Union (E.U.)

The trading bloc with the most fully developed regulation of the employment and labor standards of member states is the E.U. The E.U. began as a free trade agreement among six Western European states, and has expanded to include 25 countries from throughout Europe. Similar to the federal system in the U.S., where federal laws enjoy supremacy over conflicting state laws, E.U. "community law" is viewed as supreme over conflicting domestic law (e.g., an individual country's law). E.U. law is promulgated in several types of instruments: directives, regulations, opinions, and recommendations. *Directives* require that member states implement the E.U. community policy into their domestic law, but allow the respective national legislative bodies to determine the exact form that the law will take. The E.U. has passed numerous employment directives, including those addressing:

- the protection of employees' right to unpaid wages and other claims in the case of employer insolvency;

- the obligations of employers to inform and consult with workers;
- individual employment contracts;
- working time;
- equal opportunity (e.g., equal treatment regardless of sex, race, ethnic origin, religion, disability, age, sexual orientation);
- parental leave;
- privacy (e.g., personal data protection);
- the operation and supervision of pensions.

Because implementation of E.U. directives is left in the hands of member states, there may be a significant time lag between the E.U.'s adoption of a directive and its adoption by all E.U. member states. In addition, there is the possibility that in implementing a directive, individual member states may pass domestic legislation that, mistakenly or intentionally, falls short of what the E.U. community law contemplated. *Regulations* are a second form of E.U. community law that must be received directly into domestic laws in their exact form.

The last two forms of community law have much less potential relevance to HRM professionals. *Decisions* are case-specific factual determinations that primarily impact the rights of the parties to the dispute at hand, and *recommendations* are nonbinding opinions that member states are free to adopt, or not adopt. Given the potential relevance of E.U. community law to many labor and employment practices, international HRM managers in organizations that have employees working within the E.U., as expatriates or otherwise, should have an awareness and understanding of that body of law that exceeds the coverage of this chapter.

North American Free Trade Agreement

The aim of NAFTA was to promote trade and economic ties between the U.S., Canada, and Mexico. Before gaining ratification in the U.S., the initial agreement created in 1992 was supplemented by an agreement on labor issues in 1993. This supplemental agreement, the North American Agreement on Labor Cooperation (NAALC), committed the member countries to respect and consistently enforce their own labor laws. The NAALC sets forth guiding labor principles that member countries are committed to promote, subject to each country's domestic labor laws. Those principles reflect internationally recognized labor rights (e.g., the elimination of discrimination, the right to organize and bargain collectively, protection of children).

The NAALC also requires that the U.S., Canada, and Mexico ensure that persons with legally recognized rights under domestic law have access to some mechanism for enforcing the respective country's labor laws (e.g., an administrative, quasi-judicial, judicial, or labor tribunal). In addition, the NAALC established a new forum for transnational justice, the Commission for Labor Cooperation, and requires each signing country to maintain a National Administrative Office which receives complaints from any interested party. However, for a penalty to be imposed under the NAALC, a party must follow detailed and time-consuming processes that strive for mutually satisfactory, compromise resolutions (Chew & Posthuma, 2002). In summary, the main focus of the NAALC is on the consistent enforcement of domestic labor and employment laws.

Other regional trade blocs

While the E.U. and NAFTA receive the most attention, global HRM leaders need to be aware that there are numerous other regional trade blocs that may influence the labor and employment standards applying to member states. Examples of important trade blocs receiving less attention include:

- Caribbean Community (CARICOM; 20 member states from the Caribbean region);
- Dominican Republic–Central American Trade Free Area (DR-CAFTA; Dominican Republic, Costa Rica, El Salvador, Guatemala, Honduras, Nicaragua);
- Southern Common Market (MERCOSUR; Argentina, Brazil, Paraguay, Uruguay);
- Southern African Development Community (SADC; 10 southern African member states);
- ASEAN Free Trade Zone (AFTA; the 10 countries that comprise the Association of Southeast Asian Nations).

The extent to which these and other trading blocs influence members' labor and employment practices varies significantly, depending on the amount of authority the regional institution has over member state policy, and the level of substantive integration the member states seek to achieve. For example, AFTA does little to regulate labor and employment matters, reflecting a strong policy of national sovereignty on these matters. In contrast, CARICOM has promulgated a "Declaration of Labor and Industrial Relations Principles," and is seeking to integrate the substantive labor and employment law of member states.

National law and law-related institutions

Workplace law remains primarily a domestic or national matter (Blanpain et al., 2007). Thus, in addition to any applicable global or regional standards that may apply to employment activities, companies operating in the global economy must be prepared to contend with the employment laws in every country in which they operate. This section offers several general observations regarding national labor and employment regulatory schemes, and provides a number of country-specific examples to illustrate the different approaches to employment regulation.

First, workplace rights and obligations in a given country can flow from various sources, including legislation, administrative rule making, court or tribunal decisions, custom, and in some countries, religious texts (e.g., Egypt). The relative importance of a specific source will depend on the type of legal system within which it is embedded. For example, in common law systems, which have their genesis in the legal history of England, the decisions of a judge in a given case may create a legal precedent that has dramatic consequences beyond the case at hand. In contrast, in civil law systems, legislation is the paramount source of law, and judges generally have no authority to create new law.

Second, all countries regulate employment matters to some extent, and most countries have laws regulating at least the following areas:

1. Individual contracts of employment.
2. Protection from dismissal/redundancy.
3. Working conditions and working hours.
4. Wages, benefits, and social security.
5. The right of workers to engage in collective action and the status of unions.

Other areas commonly regulated by national legal systems that may have HRM implications include laws relating to taxation, corporate governance, immigration, and privacy.

Third, in nearly all countries employment practices are subject to multiple layers of employment regulation operating at different levels (e.g., global, regional trade bloc, national, state/province, local). For example, in the United States, private sector employment relationships are regulated by Federal, State, and in some communities, local laws (e.g., a San Francisco city ordinance prohibits discrimination in employment based on body weight). At the various levels, there may be multiple sources of relevant law (e.g., legislation, administrative regulations, judicial or tribunal decisions). For companies with international operations, there may also be United States treaty obligations relating to employment (e.g., NAFTA). In addition, most employers are, at least to some extent, regulated by common law (or judge-made law) principles relating to the employment relationship. Similarly, employment in E.U. countries is governed by the regulations and directives from the Council of Ministers, decisions of the European Court of Justice, the national laws of member states, relevant treaties, and in the case of the United Kingdom, common law principles (to a more limited extent than in the United States). Within some member countries, regional legislative bodies (e.g., the parliament for the Flemish region of Belgium) may enact law regulating employment in their region. Also, since members of the European Union are members of the International Labor Organization (ILO), they are also subject to the extensive labor standards of the ILO.

Fourth, there is significant variation across countries in norms and practices regarding the enforcement of workplace laws. That is, in some countries workplace laws of record are more strictly enforced than in other countries. In particular, pervasive lapses in the enforcement of labor and employment law seem endemic to emerging markets (e.g., China, Vietnam, Guatemala) (Florkowski, 2006). Factors contributing to the lack of enforcement vary across countries, but in general include inadequate structural support (e.g., lack of appropriate trained inspectors and other staff due to insufficient resources), willful neglect or intentional malfeasance (e.g., relaxing enforcement standards to attract or retain MNE operations), or lack of congruence between a formally enacted law and strong cultural norms (e.g., where a country adopts a law prohibiting discrimination based on gender or some other personal characteristic in response to external economic or political pressures even though the law does not reflect widely held cultural norms).

Fifth, the nature of unions, the density of unions (the percent of workers who are union members), and the effects of unionization on employment practices vary significantly from country to country. However, in all instances, when HRM professionals are dealing with union members, they must be aware of the national body of laws relating to collective bargaining and unions, as well as the rights and obligations arising from any collective bargaining agreements covering the union workers in question.

Issues with special relevance to global employers

Application of national laws to foreign-owned enterprises operating within a country

In general, employers must comply with the laws in the countries within which they operate. However, most countries develop choice-of-law principles that determine which nation's law will apply to a dispute in which the parties are from different countries, and there may be some exceptions to that general rule. In particular, a country may have treaty obligations that are incorporated into its national law and, in effect, supersede workplace laws that might otherwise apply to employers operating within the country. For example, in some circumstances U.S. treaties with several countries (e.g., Japan, Italy) give companies from those countries operating in the U.S. the right to discriminate based on citizenship (i.e., hire only their citizens), a policy that might otherwise raise illegal discrimination issues under U.S. law prohibiting discrimination in employment based on national origin.

Extraterritorial applications of national law

Some countries have labor and employment laws that extend their protection to parent-country nationals while they are working abroad. For example, U.S. MNEs must comply with the extraterritorial application of three anti-discrimination laws: The Americans with Disabilities Act, Title VII of the Civil Rights Act of 1991 (prohibiting discrimination based on race, religion, sex, color or national origin), and the Age Discrimination in Employment Act. This means that American citizens working anywhere in the world for a U.S.-owned or -controlled company have the right to sue in a U.S. court for an alleged violation of these three acts. The European Union's Data Protection Directive addressing employee privacy, which provides restrictions on the disclosure or transfer of employee personal data, also has extraterritorial application. That directive provides that relevant practices occurring outside of the E.U. will be treated as though they were performed within the E.U. when compliance determinations are made involving E.U.-based business units.

Nevertheless, the ability of a country to extend the application of its workplace laws beyond its borders has its limitations. International law principles provide that the extraterritorial application of a country's laws to protect its citizens working abroad will not be enforced where the application of the law to foreign operations would cause the employer to violate a law of the foreign country (i.e., the foreign law defense). For example, in *Mahoney v. RFE/RL, Inc* (1995), although the U.S. Age Discrimination in Employment Act (ADEA) provides for its extraterritorial application and would have prohibited the mandatory retirement of employees at age 65, the law was not applied to two U.S. citizens working in Germany for a U.S. non-profit corporation who were forced to retire pursuant to the terms of a collective bargaining agreement requiring employees to retire at age 65. The court ruled that compliance with ADEA would have required the U.S. employer to violate the German collective bargaining agreement, forcing it to violate the law of a foreign country, because in Germany, labor agreements take on the force of law. Therefore, the extraterritorial application of the ADEA was not appropriate.

As the foregoing case suggests, the determination of whether the U.S., E.U., or other countries' employment laws have extraterritorial application in a given situation is a multifaceted question that may involve multiple sources of legal authority, and the resolution of ambiguous factual issues (e.g., Was an assignment abroad "temporary?" Is there a significant conflict in the two countries' laws?). The broader issue for HRM professionals in organizations with employees working in multiple countries is that they need to expressly consider the extent to which their national workplace laws may apply to their employees working abroad. Unless it is possible to clearly conclude otherwise (e.g., based on unambiguous language or opinion of a legal expert), it would be prudent for employers with operations outside of their country to assume that both their parent country's employment laws and the employment laws of the host country will apply to their employees working abroad, and to the extent possible, endeavor to meet the requirements of both.

Individual employment contracts and termination

Union members have some form of protection from the termination of their employment as the result of a collective labor agreement and applicable labor laws. However, according to the employment laws of most countries, even employees not covered by a collective labor agreement are still protected to some extent by an individual contract of employment that defines important terms and conditions of employment and restricts the employer's right to terminate employment unilaterally. Key restrictions relate to notice requirements, the extent to which the law generally requires good or just cause for the dismissal of an employee, and payments to compensate the terminated employee.

The employer obligation to provide employees with advance notice of dismissal varies from a required notice to essentially all employees (e.g., Belgium, Germany, Japan) to no generally required notice (e.g., the United States). The notice requirements of a number of countries fall between these two extremes. For example, Canada has a minimum statutory notice requirement, but no notice is required if termination is for just cause. Also, the mandatory notice requirements of some countries only apply after some minimum length of service has been met (e.g., an agreed upon trial period in France; a period specified by statute in the United Kingdom). In summary, the vast majority of countries require some kind of notice before dismissing an employee, with the required notice period often varying by the length of service of the employee or the specific grounds for dismissal.

The extent to which different countries' regulatory schemes generally require good or just cause for the dismissal of an employee (i.e., provide substantive legal protection against arbitrary dismissals) may also be placed on a continuum. At one end are countries that require that employers establish good cause to effectively terminate employment. If the employer cannot meet that burden, the employee is typically reinstated and compensated (e.g., Canada). At the other end of the continuum, in the United States, absent a contrary agreement, private sector employment is generally presumed to be "at-will" (i.e., there is no need for the employer to establish good cause for the dismissal). A number of countries fall between these extremes by rejecting the presumption that employment is at-will, but allowing employee dismissals even without proof of just cause so long as the dismissed employee is compensated.

In summary, the regulatory schemes of almost all industrialized countries reflect the general belief that employees have some legitimate interest in the continuation of their employment relationships, and therefore, employees should receive some protection from arbitrary dismissals (i.e., compensation and/or reinstatement). The practical effect is that in most countries, an employer's right to terminate or lay off employees is significantly constrained. The discussion in this section has focused on the individual employment contract *as provided for by public law*. The voluntary use of employment contracts as a form of "private law" that may assist MNEs in managing the legal environment of HRM will be addressed in a later section.

Works councils

These provide workers with mechanisms for participation in decision making relevant to their employer operations that is in addition to the representation that may be provided by a union. Works councils play an important role in labor relations in many countries, particularly in Europe, where both E.U. directives and national laws of individual countries provide for them. Works councils are made up of elective representatives of an employer's workforce, with the number of members typically varying by the type and size of the employer. Works councils have the right to receive information and consultation relative to many decisions an employer makes (e.g., mergers, acquisitions, lay-offs, employee dismissal, training). However, the extent to which works councils are empowered to approve (or disapprove) employment-related decisions varies across countries. For example, depending on the issue, work councils in Germany may have a right to codetermination with the employer (e.g, scheduling daily working hours, temporary reduction of work), and on some issues the works council has the right of approval and veto (e.g., hiring, deployment of employees). In contrast, the work councils in France are limited to receiving information, providing consultation, and offering recommendations. It is essential that HRM managers supporting operations in the E.U. and other countries where the law provides for works councils to understand the various ways in which the representation they provide may affect employment practices.

The impact of the legal environment of HR on strategy and HR practices

Despite the widely recognized role of the legal environment as an important context for HRM, and numerous practitioner-oriented articles reporting on legal issues related to HRM, there is relatively little research investigating the impact of legal considerations on HRM decision making and outcomes. The research that does exist is spread over several literatures, most notably those of organizational theory, sociology, economics, and HRM. The following provides an introductory overview of several primary theories that have been applied to examine the impact of legal consideration on HRM, and briefly discusses selected research findings.

Institutional theories

Much, if not most, research investigating the impact of the legal environment on HRM has adopted an institutional theory perspective. According to this perspective, rather than reflecting rational choices, a firm's choice of HR practices reflects the firm's attempt to attain legitimacy in its broader external environment (Kelly & Dobbin, 1999). In the face of uncertain legal requirements, it is argued, the effort to attain legitimacy typically includes monitoring the behavior of their peer organizations (e.g., industry competitors), and mimicking the practices that are observed.

Studies using institutional theory perspectives to examine the effect of employment regulation within a single country emphasize that organizational responses to employment laws tend to result in symbolic compliance (versus substantive compliance) and homogeneity of HRM practices across organizations. For example, a study assessing the effect of a Spanish law mandating that Temporary Help Agencies (THAs) allocate resources to provide their workers training above a certain level suggests that THAs' responses were largely symbolic (technical compliance) rather than substantive. Consequently, implementation of the law did not achieve its aim of increasing the productivity of THA workers (Munoz-Bullon, 2004).

In contrast to studies investigating law-related institutional influences on HRM practices within a single country, studies investigating the effect of institutional forces on the HRM practices of MNEs also considered the potential for institutional forces to produce heterogeneity in HRM practices across MNE affiliates operating in different countries. It is argued that while there is pressure within MNEs to adopt consistent HRM practices throughout its operations, there is counteracting pressure for affiliates located in different countries to comply with local laws and regulations. Therefore, the HRM practices of local affiliates may be compelled to resemble local practices through "coercive isomorphism" (DiMaggio & Powell, 1983).

The potential counteracting institutional forces that MNE affiliates may experience is examined in Ferner, Almond, and Colling's (2005) study of the processes by which diversity policies are "internationalized" by U.S. MNEs. Focusing on a large U.S. MNE and its U.K. affiliates, their findings show a pattern of uneasy affiliate accommodation to transferred diversity policies. The "isomorphic pull" exerted by the U.S. corporate headquarters was not sufficient to produce full compliance with their U.S. law-based diversity agenda in the U.K. affiliates. That is, while diversity policies were implemented by affiliates, it was done with resistance, and without full acceptance of the form and spirit of the U.S. headquarters' agenda. The researchers found that the lack of compliance was due in a part to the fact that differences in relevant laws in the U.S. and U.K. made it harder for U.S. headquarters to assert its diversity agenda, and easier for affiliate managers in the U.K. to mobilize their resistance to their headquarters' initiative.

Economic theories

Classical economic theories view the legal regulation of the workplace as one of many forces that may affect the course of action that offers the greatest financial return. Such regulation is viewed as creating impediments to market efficiency, and organizations are viewed as rational actors with good information who seek the most efficient response with respect to legal constraints. It is assumed that the determination of the most efficient response is based on *objective* assessments of the risk and likely returns associated with the various potential courses of action.

The economic perspective has been applied to hypothesize that competitive labor markets would drive out firms that engage in employment discrimination because discrimination is an inefficient labor practice that would create a competitive disadvantage for discriminating firms (Becker, 1971), and to argue that laws aimed at preventing employment discrimination may actually lead some employers to hire fewer protected workers because of the higher expected litigation-related costs of such workers (Harcourt, Lam, & Harcourt, 2005). The economic perspective has also led to the argument that economic pressures emanating from global competition will lead to ever-increasing workplace deregulation and the erosion of worker protections throughout the world, referred to as "a race to the bottom" (Befort, 2002, p. 2; Blanpain et al., 2007)

Strategic Human Resource Management (SHRM) models

SHRM models address the connection between human resource functions and the achievement of important organizational goals. Models of the SHRM process and outcomes typically give the legal environment brief mention, treating it as an exogenous constraint on SHRM processes. For example, noting that the legal environment surrounding affiliates in other countries can constrain a MNE's ability to transfer HRM practices abroad, Taylor, Beechler, and Napier's (1996) model of strategic international HRM proposes that the greater the "legal distance" between the host country of the affiliate and the home country of the MNE, the lower the degree of similarity between the MNE parent company's HRM system and the affiliate's HRM system.

It has also been argued that the legal environment not only constrains HRM in some ways, but also provides organizations opportunities to gain a competitive advantage. For example, effectively contracting with employees to protect trade secrets and restrict their ability to go to work for competing firms, to the extent permissible, arguably assists companies in preserving intellectual capital and preventing their investments in human capital from directly benefiting their competitors (e.g., Bagley, 2008; Muir, 2003).

As the preceding suggests, while it is widely acknowledged that the legal environment plays a role in the strategic HRM process, relatively little attention has been given to explicating the nature and extent of that role. A notable exception is an article by Florkowski and Nath (1993) identifying the following dimensions of legal issues that may impact an MNE's strategic use of human resources:

1. Heterogeneity: The degree of similarity in the legal systems that must be accommodated. To what extent are employer obligations and rights similar across the locations in which the MNE and its affiliates are located?

2. Complexity: The level of knowledge needed to ensure compliance with the prevailing set of employment laws. It includes the diversity of the issues addressed by the regulatory system as well as the extensiveness of the substantive and procedural requirements within each area.
3. Relevance: The extent to which enforcement efforts will be directed against the MNE.
4. Stability: The likelihood that significant, employment-related changes (substantive or procedural) will occur in the governing legal systems, varying from unstable to highly stable environments.
5. Predictability: The extent to which the MNE can accurately forecast material changes in the applicable employment laws.

Florkowski and Nath (1993) articulate a series of propositions regarding how MNEs would adapt their HRM structure, programs, and practices in response to different legal environments reflecting the different dimensions. For example, a legal environment with high levels of regulatory heterogeneity, complexity, and relevance is expected to impede an MNE's ability to respond quickly to institute corrective measures when, for example, there is a negative reaction among locals to their current operations. Although they provide interesting directions for future research, based on our review, those propositions await empirical testing.

Future research directions

The importance of understanding the legal environment of HRM is widely accepted, and given the relatively underdeveloped nature of the literature, there are many opportunities for researchers to contribute to that understanding. Here we identify and briefly discuss some of those opportunities.

There is still a significant need for descriptive research documenting the levels and trends of many variables of interest. For example, to what extent is there significant variation in the degree to which governments attempt to regulate labor and employment practices, and are there significant trends in that regulation? Is *variation* in regulation increasing (decreasing in some areas of the world and increasing in others), or is there truly a global "race to the bottom" that is resulting in lower standards and lower variation in workplace regulations around the world? Are there identifiable patterns in organizational practices addressing workplace law-related concerns, including both legal compliance efforts and litigation management strategies, and if so, at what level(s) are they occurring: across trading blocs, countries, industries, units within MNEs? Research addressing these basic questions will help researchers to more systematically identify the critical variables influencing organizational responses to the law, and provide policy makers with empirical evidence regarding the practical effects that their lawmaking efforts are having (or not having) on organizational practices.

It is clear that perceptions of the law and law-related risk play key roles in mediating the impact of workplace laws on organizational behavior. Evidence from the U.S. suggests that inaccurate perceptions of the workplace laws may be widespread, and that perceptions of law-related risk may be greatly inflated (see Roehling & Wright, 2006). However, many questions remain either unanswered or in need of further investigation. To what extent are law-related risks perceived as significant concerns by key organizational actors (e.g., managers, lawyers, and HRM professionals) in the various countries of the world? Do differences in the perceptions of the law, or the role of regulatory enforcement agencies, influence how organizations adapt to legal constraints? To what extent do perceptions of customary or ethical practices (e.g., bribery) influence adaptations to legal environments in different countries?

Although the question of the extent to which MNEs should seek to apply uniform policies and practices across their affiliates versus allowing local adaption to local circumstances involves more than legal considerations, there appears to be increasing recognition of the need for MNEs to develop policies and practices that harmonize national differences in substantive law across the countries in which their affiliates are located (e.g., Blanpain et al., 2007). To what extent are MNEs attempting to harmonize policies and practices? What are the most significant challenges? What legal requirements are difficult to reconcile? How do cultural differences or cultural distance influence harmonization? Findings from research addressing these and related issues should be used to inform interdisciplinary efforts (lawyers, HRM researchers and practitioners) to identify HRM policies and practices that "travel well" (i.e., meet legal requirements and are culturally acceptable across countries).

The issue of separating out the effects of cultural norms from the effects of legislation and other formal statements of law is one that warrants closer attention. While a country's culture may affect the laws it adopts, and the laws it adopts, over time, may influence its cultural values, there are many other factors that may lead to the adoption of a specific law (e.g., external political or economic pressure). Therefore, researchers should avoid using a country's formal laws as a surrogate measure of its cultural norms. Also, when attempting to investigate the unique effect of a national law, national culture should be separately assessed and taken into account to the extent possible (e.g., controlled for), and vice versa.

Conceptual models that reflect the cognitive judgment and behavioral decision-making perspectives in their attempts to explain how the law impacts HRM decisions and outcomes suggest the value of empirical research drawing on those literatures. Roehling and Wright's (2006) legal-centric decision-making model seeks to explain how various actors in the HRM process (e.g., HRM professionals, lawyers, employees), and micro-level processes (e.g., perceptions, motivations), may interact to cause HRM decision making to be unnecessarily legalistic, and produce results that are counter-productive. Also, Fuller, Edelman, and Matusik's (2000) legal readings model addressed the intraorganizational structure of law and how it impacts employee reactions and behaviors, which in turn influence substantive outcomes (e.g., grievances, female representation in the workplace). While both models are based on logical extensions of existing theory and available empirical evidence, they remain highly propositional, a situation that should be addressed by future research.

Although a growing body of research from diverse literatures (e.g., sociology, law, economics, psychology, HRM, organizational theory) provides evidence bearing on the impact of the legal environment on HRM decisions and outcomes, the literature is highly fragmented, and firm conclusions are not manifest. For example, studies can be cited to support the claim that increased legal regulation of HRM tends to have a significant negative impact on employer–employee relations and HRM practices (e.g., Gooderham, Nordhaug, and Ringdal's 1999 study of employers from six European countries found that employers in legal environments with more comprehensive regulation of the workplace were less willing to communicate with employees about the company's strategy and goals; Dobbin, Sutton, Meyer, and Scott's 1993 longitudinal study of the impact of increased legal regulation on the personnel practices of U.S. companies suggested that organizations were declining to use valid selection tools due to perceived legal risks that were not accurate). However, other research indicates that the impact of legal consideration on HRM is relatively insignificant (e.g., Rosenzweig and Nohria's (1994) study of the HRM practices of U.S. affiliates of foreign-based nationals indicated that the affiliates' consistent adoption of local practices was better understood as normative, and not due to coercive effects such as local regulation; Waters and Johanson's (2001) survey results indicated that the vast majority of the HRM professionals surveyed did not view the U.S. Americans with Disabilities Act as having had a significant impact on their organization).

A comprehensive review that integrates relevant findings from the various literatures would be a valuable contribution. The findings from such a review would help researchers address another important need: the development of conceptual models that provide frameworks for organizing the wide ranges of factors (e.g., formal statements of law, perceived litigation risk, cultural norms, industry, organizational cultures, professional biases), operating at various levels (national, organizational, group, individual), that existing theory and research suggests interact to influence the impact of the legal environment on HRM decision making and outcomes.

Practical implications: managing the legal environment of HRM

It is increasingly important that HRM executives involved in global operations, or in organizations *contemplating* global operations, have a global perspective of labor and employment law if they want to be able to provide valuable strategic input to their employers (Berkowitz & Müller-Bonanni, 2006; Florkowski, 2006). Such a perspective should include an awareness of the basic legislative and regulatory frameworks that may be involved when operations cross national borders, the potential relevance of so-called "soft laws," and the common legal issues associated with developing and maintaining a global workforce. It should also include an appreciation of the increased layers of complexity and uncertainty when dealing with the legal environment of HRM in a global context, and the corresponding increased need for a more proactive, less legalistic, approach to managing the legal environment. In developing such an approach, consideration should be given to the following policies and practices.

HR audits

HR audits involve examining policies, procedures, documentations, systems, and practices with respect to an organization's HR functions. This examination may be relatively narrow in scope, focusing on the compliance of HR policies and practices with applicable laws (also referred to as "legal compliance audits"). All HR audits address legal compliance issues. However, some HR audits are much broader in scope, also examining the extent to which HR policies and practices are aligned with the organization's strategic plans and values, and the extent to which they are effectively implemented to bring about desired behaviors and outcomes (sometimes referred to as "strategic HR audits"). While the challenge of conducting an HR audit in a global organization is considerable, their potential value is also considerable. HR audits should go beyond technical legal compliance issues, to examine the effectiveness of policies and practices that may also have a less direct impact on law-related risk. For example, a selection process may meet all legal requirements, but if it is ineffective in assessing the applicant's job performance ability or "fit" within the broader organizational cultures, the result will be avoidable involuntary terminations. These, in turn, increase the risk of employment litigation. Finally, a critical issue in any HR audit is "Who should participate?" While it is important to have a senior HRM executive and corporate counsel involved in the process, the audit itself should be conducted by external, truly independent professionals with relevant expertise. In the case of an HR audit of an MNE, these outside professionals should have expertise in international labor and employment law and/or international HRM.

Use of employment contracts

Written employment agreements are an increasingly attractive option for specifying relevant terms and conditions in international employment settings. From a legal perspective, written documentation provides evidence that is given great weight by the courts, and is often viewed as dispositive on the issue of which country's laws apply (Sabiru-Perez, 2000). International treaties and the law in most countries generally permit the parties considerable autonomy in designating the law that will apply to their employment contract, so long as a substantial relationship exists between the country chosen and the parties or their transactions (Posthuma, Roehling, & Campion, 2006). From a behavioral science perspective, written contracts help create clear expectations that guide performance for both supervisor and employee, and help avoid ambiguities that may lead to conflict (e.g., length of stay in assignment abroad, reporting relationships, reimbursable expenses).

HRM professionals also need to be aware of the limitations on MNEs' freedom to contract with employees. Contractual provisions that are highly recommended and legally enforceable in one country may not be enforceable in another. For example, noncompete agreements (or "covenants not to compete") have been recommended as a tactic for gaining a competitive advantage by preventing former employees from using human capital they developed on the job to aid a competitor. However, some countries do not permit noncompete agreements (e.g., Mexico, Chile). Among countries that allow such agreement, there may be significant restriction on the length of time they are enforceable, or compensation due the employee for his or her agreement.

Global corporate codes of conduct

Private global corporate codes set forth general standards for a company's business operations, including practices relating to the management of its workforce. They typically include prohibitions on child labor, forced labor, and discrimination in employments. Other common code provisions address employee safety and health issues, freedom of association, the right to organize and bargain collectively, workplace privacy, gifts and bribes, conflicts of interest, other ethical behavior of employees and officers, and protection of the environment. Most corporate codes of conduct are voluntarily adopted, and unless an organization agrees to be legally bound by its terms, the code remains soft law. However, this may change in the not too distant future. Based on litigation trends, government enforcement of corporate codes, *even when the organization did not agree to be legally bound*, may not be far off (Hagerman, 2006).

Several factors have contributed to the growth of global corporate codes, including the absence of an enforceable, internationally agreed-upon, labor and employment law regime, increased emphasis on corporate governance and standards of behavior in the corporate workplace, pressure from non-governmental interest groups, the desire to be seen as socially responsible, and the belief that corporate codes promote desired behaviors by establishing clear expectations. Although most empirical research to date has focused on the content of corporate codes, available evidence suggests that corporate codes can have a significant impact in promoting desired behaviors (e.g., Helin & Sandström, 2007).

Employment practices liability (EPL) insurance

EPL insurance provides protection against claims by employees, former employees, or potential employees that arise from an employer's employment practices (e.g., illegal discrimination, wrongful termination, sexual harassment, breach of contract). Insurance underwriters in North

America, Europe, and some Asian markets offer EPL in a variety of forms. However, EPL policies typically reimburse employers for expenses associated with defending a lawsuit, and paying judgments or settlements. The cost of EPL insurance depends on various risk factors such as the nature of the employer's business, number of employees, and its history of employee lawsuits. In general, EPL is viewed as an expensive risk management strategy. Nonetheless, it may provide net positive benefits in allowing organizations to manage the uncertainty of litigation risk, especially in the early stages of an organization's entry into global operations when an employer may be dealing with the complexity of multiple, and sometimes conflicting, layers of legal regulations for the first time.

Alternative dispute resolution

The benefits of arbitration and other alternative dispute resolution (ADR) practices (reduced cost, speedier resolution of disputes, avoidance of unfamiliar and/or potentially hostile legal forums) make it particularly attractive in international employment settings (Westfield, 2002). However, national laws may have provisions that affect the legality of ADR practices, or the specific form they must adhere to, and therefore must be consulted in crafting an ADR policy. For example, while mandatory arbitration of employee disputes may be viewed by some employers as having potential advantages over a voluntary policy, mandatory arbitration may be prohibited in some countries.

References

Bagley, C. E. (2008). Winning legally: The value of legal astuteness. *The Academy of Management Review*, 33(2), 378–390.

Becker, G. S. (1971). *The Economics of discrimination*, 2nd edition. Chicago: University of Chicago Press.

Befort, S. F. (2002). Labor and employment law at the new millennium: A historical overview and critical assessment. *Boston College Law Review*, 43, 351–460.

Berkowitz, P. M. & Müller-Bonanni, T. (2006). *International labor and employment law*. Chicago: American Bar Association.

Bilder, R. B. (2006). The emergence of transnational labor law. *The American Journal of International Law*, 100, 725–733.

Blanpain, R., Bisom-Rapp, S., Corbett, W. R., Josephs, H. K., & Zimmer, M. J. (2007). *The global workplace: International and comparative employment law*. New York: Cambridge University Press.

Briscoe, D. R. & Schuler, R. S. (2004). *International human resource management*, 2nd edition. New York: Routledge.

Chew, D. & Posthuma, R. A. (2002). International employment dispute resolution under NAFTA's side agreement on labor. *Labor Law Journal*, 53, 38–45.

DiMaggio, P. J. & Powell, W. W. (1983). The iron cage revisited: Institutional isomorphism and collective rationality in organizational fields. *American Sociological Review*, 48, 147–160.

Dobbin, F., Sutton, J. R., Meyer, J. W., & Scott, W. R. (1993). Equal opportunity law and the construction of internal labor markets. *American Journal of Sociology*, 99(2), 396–427.

Ferner, A., Almond, P., & Colling, T. (2005). Institutional theory and the cross-national transfer of employment policy: The case of 'workforce diversity' in US multinationals. *Journal of International Business Studies*, 36(3), 304–329.

Florkowski, G. W. (2006). *Managing global legal systems*. New York: Routledge.

Florkowski, G. W. & Nath, R. (1993). MNCl responses to the legal environment of international human resources management. *International Journal of Human Resource Management*, 4, 305–324.

Fuller, S. Riggs, Edelman, L. B., & Matusik, S. F. (2000). Legal readings: Employee interpretation and mobilization of law. *The Academy of Management Review*, 25(1), 200–216.

Gooderham, P. N., Nordhaug, O., & Ringdal, K. (1999). Institutional and rational determinants of organizational practices: Human resource management in European firms. *Administrative Science Quarterly*, 44(3), 507–531.

Hagerman, J. L. (2006). Navigating the waters of international employment law: Dispute avoidance tactics for United States-based multinational corporations. *Valparaiso University Law Review*, 41, 859–891.

Harcourt, M., Lam, H., & Harcourt, S. (2005). Discriminatory practices in hiring: Institutional and rational economic perspectives. *The International Journal of Human Resource Management*, 16(11), 2113.

Helin, S. & Sandström, J. (2007). An inquiry into the study of corporate codes of ethics. *Journal of Business Ethics*, 75(3), 253–272.

Kelly, E. & Dobbin, F. (1999). Civil rights law at work: Sex discrimination and the rise of maternity leave policies. *The American Journal of Sociology*, 105(2), 455–492.

Mahoney v. RFE/RL, Inc., 310 U.S. App. D.C. 307 (D.C. Cir. 1995), cert. denied, 516 U.S. 866 (1995).

Muir, D. M. (2003). *A Manager's Guide to Employment Law: How To Protect Your Company and Yourself*. San Francisco: Jossey-Bass.

Munoz-Bullin, F. (2004). Training provision and regulation: An analysis of the temporary help industry. *International Journal of Manpower*, 25, 656–672.

Posthuma, R., Roehling, M. V., & Campion, M. (2006). Applying U.S. employment discrimination laws to international employers: Simplifying a complex legal structure. *Personnel Psychology*, 59(3), 705–740.

Roehling, M. V. (2004). Legal theory: Contemporary contract law perspectives and insights for employment relationship theory. In Coyle-Shapiro, J. A-M., Shore, L. M., Taylor, M. S., & Tetrick, L. E. (eds), *The employment relationship: Examining psychological and contextual perspectives*, pp. 65–92. Oxford, UK: Oxford University Press.

Roehling, M. V. & Wright, P. W. (2006). Organizationally sensible versus legal-centric approaches to employment decisions. *Human Resource Management Journal*, 45, 605–627.

Rosenzweig, P. M. and Nohria, N. (1994). Influences on human resource management practices in multinational corporations. *Journal of International Business Studies*, 25(2), 229–251.

Sabiru-Perez, M. (2000). Changes of the law applicable to an international contract of employment. *International Labour Review*, 139, 335–358.

Taylor, S., Beechler, S., & Napier, N. (1996). Toward an integrative model of strategic international human resource management. *Academy of Management Review*, 21(4), 959–985.

Waters, K. W., & Johanson, J. C. (2001). Awareness and perceived impact of the Americans with Disabilities Act among human resources professionals in three Minnesota cities. *Journal of Disability and Policy Studies*, 12(1), 47–56.

Westfield, E. (2002). Governance, and multinational enterprise responsibility: Corporate codes of conduct in the 21st century. *Virginia Journal of International Law*, 42, 1075–1108.

6

New organizational structures and forms

John Storey

Introduction

The purpose of this chapter is to explore the links between organizational forms and human resource management. In recent years, many organizations have been seeking greater flexibility and agility, and as a result, they are relying more on market and market-like forms of coordination. The ways in which work contributions are brought together and are coordinated have thus become much looser and more variegated. Even the term 'organization' begins to seem too restrictive a concept to capture the variety of forms which the multiplicity of modes of coordinated work now takes. Externally, networks, supply chain management, various forms of contracting and outsourcing all tend to loosen the construct of a singular employing organization. Internally, we see a growing reliance on market-oriented projects, network structures, and process management approaches. Increasingly, cooperation runs alongside competition both within and between organizations. This admix of the principles of hierarchy, market and trust (Adler 2001: 2670) leads not only to some interesting and novel forms but also throws up some novel human resource management challenges which have, to date, remained largely unexplored.

Shifts in organizational forms carry many important HR implications. These include, for example, implications for career opportunities, for job design and job satisfaction, for learning and development opportunities, work content and skill levels. Moreover, in some senses these new forms themselves constitute alternative people-management approaches, such as when organizational boundaries are redrawn based on an assessment of which skills are considered 'core'. The causal link between organizational structures and human resource management strategies thus run in both directions. The purpose of the chapter is not to try to locate the prime mover here. Rather, the aim is to explore the mutual ramifications and the patterns of fit and misfit between these aspects of organizing.

To a large extent, the aspirations and principles underlying many recent structural changes seem to reflect those which also underpin the ideas of HRM. There are even the same 'hard' and 'soft' logics at play. From an organizational restructuring point of view the 'hard' aspects are to be found in cases of downsizing and outsourcing. The 'soft' side of the rationale is to be found in cases of empowerment, learning and teamworking. The main thesis of this chapter is that the hard and soft approaches proceed apace: that capitalism marches on two legs – market discipline and mutual commitment – and that these two legs sometimes work together and sometimes undermine each other.

The analysis of these issues in this chapter is organized as follows. We begin with a brief review of the interplay between the organizing principles of bureaucracy and market; we then present a figure which maps the variety of forms which have emerged or are emergent; each of these is examined in turn in order to tease out the implications for human resource management.

From bureaucracy to market

The large organizations which grew after the end of the Second World War typically took a form described by Edwards (1979) as 'bureaucratic control'. The key attributes of bureaucracy in the descriptive, social science sense (as distinct from perjorative, colloquial sense) were a clear division of work with stipulated boundaries of responsibility; officials given authority to carry out their assigned functions; referral by role occupants to formal rules and procedures which ensure predictability and routinization of decisions; a well-defined hierarchy of authority; appointment to posts arranged not through patronage or bribery but on the basis of technical competence.

This bureaucratic form was based on internal labour markets and winning employee commitment through the prospect of long-term career advancement, job security, welfare packages and seniority pay systems. The elaborate job ladders were underpinned by company-provided training and development. Where they existed, trade unions also supported these internal labour markets. Such arrangements formed the matrix within which emerged the principles of modern human resource management. The material elements were in place to encourage a psychological contract based on commitment; extensive investment in training and development made sense; the system ought to have encouraged careful recruitment and selection, systematic appraisal and elaborate performance management systems. To this extent the fit between this organizational model and human resource management was rather promising.

But there were limitations. The model in its totality gave rise to impersonality – this was one of its intended characteristics. Impersonality had the advantage of overcoming nepotism, favouritism and arbitrary decision making; the principles seemed well suited to the administrative needs of the new democratic states and the emerging large industrial enterprises. On the other hand, however, the emphasis on control prompted rigidity of behaviour and defensive routines. The division of task and responsibility elevated departmental goals above whole system goals – that is, led to sub-optimizing behaviour. Rules and procedures often became ends in themselves. These 'unanticipated consequences' and 'dysfunctions' of bureaucracy gave rise to a voluminous literature that helped buttress bureaucracy's bad press (Gouldner 1954; March and Simon 1958; Merton 1957; Selznick 1966).

If bureaucracy's internal structure was too rigid, its external structure – the form it gave to inter-organizational relationships – seemed no more reliable. In their relations with peer organizations, big bureaucratic 'core' firms appeared to be all too comfortable in their oligopolistic 'easy life'. On the other hand, the big core firms held their smaller suppliers at arms' length, forcing them into brutal price competition with each other, and keeping them in a subordinate, 'peripheral' sector.

In sum, the bureaucratic form tended to degenerate. Complacency and the link with customers became tenuous; as competitive conditions changed, these systems found it hard to adapt; bureaucracy was used to command and control; initiative was stifled; supplier relations became markedly antagonistic. As a result, much of the innovation in organizational form over the past few decades has been a response to the perceived limitations of bureaucracy and to the very real limitations of its degenerate forms.

The uncertain place of bureaucracy in an 'age of enterprise' has attracted considerable academic scrutiny (see, for example, the Special Issue of *Organization* in January 2004). Some reform initiatives suggest a desire to restore the integrity of the bureaucratic form. In many of these 'restorative' cases, the goal has been to strip away unnecessarily complex structures and to streamline key processes; General Electric's famous 'Work-out' process reflects this faith in the power of streamlined bureaucracy. The then CEO, Jack Welch, said the purpose was to abolish bureaucracy; but a more sober assessment is that GE was simply streamlining it – and with great benefits to the organization's efficiency and profitability. This effort to restore bureaucracy has often been accompanied by greater attention to the fabric of informal relations needed to allow it to function effectively. New forms of 'soft bureaucracy' can be detected (Courpasson 2000; Reed 1999).

Other reform initiatives, often in combination with these restorative ones, sought to partially or wholly replace the process-based controls characteristic of bureaucracy with market-like output-based control. This has led many organizations to decentralize – to reduce subunit size, and devolve responsibility. Starting in the 1950s, many large corporations moved to a division-alized form, based on strategic business units. In recent decades, this move has continued, with many organizations breaking up large divisions into a number of smaller ones that are more rigorously market-focused. Down in the business units, this reorientation towards the market prompts trends towards project and process management approaches.

In their external structure too, we see a proliferation of reforms aimed at creating simultaneously greater market discipline and mutual commitment. On the one hand, firms are outsourcing non-core activities and encouraging more rigorous supply chain management. On the other hand, organizations are increasingly forming alliances and joint ventures, partner-ships and networks. Information and communication technologies carry the capacity to bridge – in some sense, abolish – organizational boundaries and allow work to be done in new ways on a distributed basis. A related reform has been the shift from hierarchy to network or modular forms in order to increase flexibility (Schilling and Steensma 2001). The past identity of an organization, resting as it did on a physical place and associated perhaps with distinct products, is becoming less important and even less valid.

In this buzzing landscape of changing organizational forms, ideas and practices have been powerfully shaped by an ideological shift which urged the primacy of the market. There was a parallel attempt internally to promote the idea of 'enterprise'. This logic led to extensive deregulation and the consequent pressure on large organizations which had previously enjoyed oligopolistic conditions. It also manifested itself in the pressure to shift from internal transactions and process controls in favour of actual or near-market controls.

Faced with rapidly changing environments and encouraged by this market ideology, many employers engaged in radical downsizing and in the process also retreated from long-term commitments to employees which the internal labour market model allowed and facilitated. Littler (2004) has analysed patterns of downsizing across the world. In the United States it is estimated that over one million middle managers lost their jobs as organizations flattened organizational structures.

However, this push towards the market has provoked a backlash, and not only among its victims. A growing chorus of consultants and managers argue that even if market forms support flexibility, they do not create the collaborative commitment needed for innovation. As a result of these moves towards a market logic, Hamel and Prahalad noted,

In many companies, one cannot speak meaningfully of a 'corporate strategy' because the corporate strategy is little more than the aggregation of the independent strategies of standalone business units. Where the corporate role has been largely devolved, corporate officers have no particular responsibilities other than investor relations, acquisitions and disposals, and resource allocation across independent business units.

(Hamel and Prahalad 1994: 288)

In adopting a 'hard' market model, the synergies and the potential advantages of the big company are lost: the potential to use core competencies across units is undermined, and the creative combinations that generate innovative products become less likely.

Figure 6.1 locates the diverse initiatives on a conceptual map. While some authors see a simple spectrum between markets and hierarchies, we follow Adler (2001) and others in arguing that both market and bureaucratic organizing principles can be more or less salient in structuring real institutions, and that some institutional forms reflect powerful influences of both. Our argument is that recent decades have seen a 'swelling' of the middle zone between the top left (pure market relations) and the bottom right (pure bureaucracy), and the emergence of forms that combine strong influences of both market and hierarchy.

The human resource dimensions of these intra- and inter-organizational changes in organizational form have been under-explored. In the following sections, we sketch the nature of each of the forms shown in Figure 6.1, and then identify its human resource management dimensions. In the final section of the chapter, we address the implications for the *strategic*

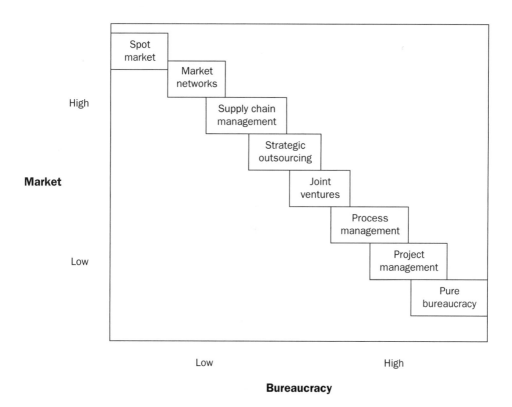

Figure 6.1 Mapping the forms of work coordination

93

potential in HRM presented by these structural developments. The journey through the chapter reflects the climb from the bottom right of the figure to the top left. Having considered aspects of bureaucracy above, we begin the review at the next stage with project management.

Project management

Project management has been perfected over centuries by civil engineers as a way of mobilizing people and skill sets towards a market goal. However, over recent decades, project management has penetrated an increasingly broad spectrum of industries and firms. As the business environment becomes more turbulent, and as customer demands become more idiosyncratic, many businesses find they need to respond with less standardized, more customized solutions. Even where customer needs are relatively standardized, competitive pressure pushes firms to find ways to optimize the resolution of the competing considerations of the contributing functions (marketing, engineering, manufacturing, etc.)

Project management implies significant changes to the traditional bureaucratic form. New roles are needed. Project leaders assume more authority and influence. The resulting 'matrix' forms of organization have become almost ubiquitous in a growing number of industries. Structural forums for reconciling the competing demands of concurrent project emerge. In their most radical form, these project-based organizations do away with functions altogether, and the organization adopts a 'network' form discussed below.

The logic of project management has also been scaled up to a more aggregated level with the 'front-back' structure. Here multi-divisional firms redefine the charter of their units so that a first set serves distinct customer or market segments, and a second set serves as internal resources for this first set. Galbraith describes the way Nokia and other big corporations have reconfigured themselves in this manner (Galbraith 2002: 2677).

Human resource management considerations

Project management requires new skills. Individual contributors need to learn some of the skills used by other project participants, leading to the idea of 'T-shaped' skill sets. Rotational assignments become more valuable in this environment. Team members also need new interpersonal, teamworking skills, since more of their work now requires face-to-face discussion of how best to resolve the competing functional requirements. Project managers need both 'managerial' skills of coordination, budgeting, and planning, and 'leadership' skills that equip them to lead heterogeneous teams towards goals that are often ambiguous. Functional managers also learn to operate in a more complex political landscape, where their power is counter-balanced by that of project leaders.

Evaluation and rewards shift in a project-oriented organization. Organizations find that they need to reward teams not just individuals. Galbraith (2002) identifies some further implications for the front-back model. Most importantly, where the traditional multi-divisional firm typically rewards people based on the performance of their own division, now rewards need to recognize their contributions to the performance of the organization as a whole.

Evaluations and rewards are typically set not only by the functional manager or the project leader, but by the two jointly. Moreover, these people often find they need input on employees' performance from other team members and other people outside the team that the focal team member may have worked with. As a result, a growing number of project-oriented organizations are using '360 degree' evaluation methods.

The inherent capability of ICT to allow 'virtual teams' to operate across the globe raises new questions for HR. Typically, these include whether to encourage face-to-face interaction or not, if so how much, and to what extent they should be empowered. A study by Kirkman and Rosen (2004) of 35 virtual sales and service teams revealed that team empowerment was positively associated with both process improvement and customer satisfaction. The degree of face-to-face interaction however played a mediating rather than a direct role in that its effects depended upon the amount of empowerment. Other studies too have found that social cohesion and network range affect the efficacy of knowledge transfer within a network (Reagons and McEvily 2003). People management choices are thus closely associated with organizational choices.

Process management

While project management represents a temporary structure laid over the bureaucratic functional structure, the market can influence the internal organization of the firm even more strongly with the introduction of process management. The starting point of process management is the discovery that operational improvements and innovations are often located across, rather than within, existing activities. In its more modest forms, workers are encouraged to collaborate in occasional 'process improvement projects' to seek out improvements in the way their work is divided up and coordinated. In its more radical forms – as 'business process reengineering' – the power of new technologies is marshalled to automate activities, allowing whole families of activities to be combined and correspondingly reducing labour costs and administrative, coordination costs (Storey 2002). It can apply to services such as healthcare just as much as manufacturing (McNulty and Ferlie 2002). The objectives are drastic cost reductions, and major improvements in quality, flexibility and service levels.

Proponents of process management claim that it has far-reaching implications for organizational structures and human resource management. Thus, according to the founders of the business process reengineering (BPR) movement, 'everything that has been learned in the twentieth century about enterprises applies only to task-oriented organizations, everything must be rethought' (Hammer and Champy 1992). In this statement the originators of the business process reengineering concept make clear their radical intent. The central idea of reengineering was that companies should re-orient themselves around their core processes – the start-to-finish sequence of activities which create customer value – no longer arranging themselves according to the vertical authority structure of bureaucracy but horizontally, towards their market targets. The key elements of this more radical BPR programme are:

- a 'fresh start', 'blank sheet' review;
- a process rather than functional view of the whole organization;
- cross-functional solutions;
- step change;
- the exploitation of information technology;
- attention to work activities on and off the shop floor;
- adoption of a customer's view of the organization/producing value for customers;
- processes must have owners.

Hammer (1996) in *Beyond Reengineering* explains how the 'process-centred organization' differs from traditional functional structures. In a process organization, workers engaged in operating a machine will see their role is not just running the machine but contributing to the 'order fulfilment process'. Hence, if production-flow backs-up, these operatives will be expected first to investigate and then seek to resolve the problem. Such behaviour will simply be part of the new job. According to BPR proponents, the term 'worker' should be replaced by the term 'process performer'.

Further new roles are required beyond the 'process performer'. There is a need for 'process leaders', 'process owners' and 'process managers' whose jobs are to engage in process design and redesign, coaching, and advocacy. This last means it is the process owner's job to obtain the necessary financial and other resources to meet the process needs; and to occupy a seat on the 'process council' (which is a forum of process owners and heads of remaining support services to discuss the business as a whole). Such a body is seen as necessary to avoid functional silos being replaced by 'process tunnels' or process protectorates.

This kind of process focus implies jobs that are considerably enlarged: jobs which require understanding, insight, autonomy, responsibility and decision making. Supervision is not supposed to be required. Hammer (1996) talks bluntly about 'the end of the organization chart'. There are no departments or departmental managers and very little hierarchy. This, in retrospect, seems like hype, since the creation of a whole hierarchy of process performers/leaders/owners/managers/councils signals that the old bureaucracy is being updated to reflect the new pattern of interdependencies. Moreover, the old functions persist, although they are now an overlay on the process-oriented structure, as 'centres of excellence'. These are to be thought of as in-house versions of professional associations. They are supposed to enable skill formation and continual development, and are intended to provide channels of communication which enable the sharing of knowledge and expertise.

The origins of BPR are traced to the late 1980s when a few companies such as Ford, Taco Bell and Texas Instruments began programmes of business improvements which differed in kind from the usual run-of-the-mill variety. They engaged in radical changes and redesigned their processes. The take-up of reengineering worldwide has been very extensive. In Britain, for example, it has been reported that 70 per cent of large organizations have embarked on what their own managers say was a BPR programme. In America, Ingersoll Rand, Shell, Levi Strauss, Ford, GTE, Chrysler 'are all concentrating on their processes' (Hammer 1996: 8). In 2005 one could still find major organizations seeking to adopt a process-based review of their organization and operation.

Initially, this process approach was adopted in a highly coercive, top-down manner: it was an effort to streamline bureaucracy without the participation of the people doing the bureaucracy's work. BPR programmes thereby often dramatically undermined whatever trust may have existed. Subsequently, Hammer himself argued for a version of process redesign closer to the vision propounded by the humanistic wing of lean production and proponents of 'continuous process improvement' – where workers themselves learn the art and science of process (re-)design and work together with managers and engineers to improve processes.

Human resource management considerations

The implications of process redesign for HR according to Hammer are far-reaching:

> For a world of process-centred organizations everything must be rethought: the kinds of work that people do, the jobs they hold, the skills they need, the ways in which their performance is measured and rewarded, the careers they follow, the roles managers play, the principles of strategy that enterprises follow.

> (1996: xiii)

HR needs to help in the changing of mindsets and behaviours which are required under such a radically different organizational form. One crucial such change is the job enlargement discussed above. Evaluation and rewards need to change too, to reflect these broader responsibilities. New process measurements are important in order to track performance and plan improvements.

Shifting from a traditional mode of operating to a process-based one is no easy task. Employees fear that a process reengineering initiative means job losses and extensive change. They are usually correct on both counts. Even years after the introduction of such a change employees may harbour resentment and blame the consultancy firm that was used. The implications for future commitment-winning measures can be problematical. More recent BPR programs therefore often take a more participative approach and attempt to allay job-loss concerns by assuring employees that process innovation will not lead to firings although perhaps to attrition.

In the more radical form of BPR, process management has often brought to the fore in a rather stark way some of the fundamental contradictions of the capitalist enterprise and in the process, challenged the hegemony of the unitary view of the firm. In a telling section, Hammer criticizes those corporate heads who so readily nowadays mouth the mantra of the primacy of 'shareholder value'. This is not what business enterprises are about, he maintains: they should instead serve to create 'customer value'. The tension here is between the alienating effects of subordinating the enterprise to the pursuit of exchange-value and the motivating effects of orienting the organization to the creation of use-value. BPR programs often appeared as brutal, job-destroying exercises aimed only at enhanced profit.

Joint ventures and alliances

Partnering for the acquisition or development of capabilities which the organization does not currently have is an increasingly common strategy. In the UK, for example, BT alone has more than 70 joint ventures and overseas distribution arrangements. Some pharmaceutical companies form as many as 20 to 30 new alliances per annum. The iPod was not successful until Apple developed the alliances necessary to manage and sell digitized music using iTunes.

Companies often use partnerships in order to innovate. Those which succeed in this have to handle a multiplicity of variables. According to the results of a worldwide study on collaborative innovation by MacCormack such firms

> figure out how collaboration can improve the top line as well as the bottom line, and they organize themselves to work effectively with partners. What isn't widely appreciated is how much time and effort these companies put into getting better at collaborating.
>
> (MacCormack and Forbath 2008)

Through joint ventures, organizations are able to achieve a number of objectives. Large companies using their marketing expertise and systems can bring new products developed by smaller companies to market rather faster than a small company acting alone. For example, this is common in the area of genetic research enterprises. Additionally, large companies may seek a joint venture in order to gain a foothold in new product areas and to acquire new expertise rapidly. This has been the case with large agrochemical companies which have allied with small and medium sized biotechnology companies. A third reason for joint ventures is to enable the partners to reduce their cost base by pooling resources. Companies have often cut their staffing levels and reduced their distribution costs. A fourth factor is that certain developing countries such as India and China may disallow inward investment which is not tied to some form of joint venture with a domestic concern. Salomon Brothers, the American investment bank, and Dresdner Bank of Germany have both entered into joint ventures with Chinese financial companies as a result. Likewise, Royal Dutch/Shell invested in a power generation plant in India in a joint venture with Essar Group, an Indian industrial company.

Despite these attractions and the frequency of occurrence, failure is high and one of the most frequently cited causes of such failures has been that the organizational and HRM issues were not adequately addressed.

Human resource management considerations

The human resource management aspects have usually been neglected by companies embarking on new alliances and joint ventures. There are, however, a few exceptions. Merck, for example, in the USA, has a high reputation for the way it uses the HR role in managing joint ventures. Numerous joint ventures, both national and international in character, have been entered into by Merck and in each case the HR staff have been involved from the outset. Staffing solutions are devised, procedures and policies drawn up. Communication and education are given an especially high priority in order to ensure that the partners not only understand each other but can learn from each other. The overall HRM challenge involves blending corporate cultures, compensation schemes, and overcoming staffing problems. According to the results of the study by MacCormack and Forbath (2008), the successful firms

> alter their recruitment, training, evaluation, and reward systems to focus on 'soft' skills such as communication so that managers can better learn to motivate and coordinate team members who are outside the firm and, sometimes, in vastly different cultures. Many of these companies also help to train partners – for example, by inviting them to internal development programs so that future teams learn together what it takes to collaborate.

Strategic outsourcing

'Outsourcing' refers to the situation when a company subcontracts to another supplier work that it was previously performing in-house. In recent times it has been one of the more popular ways to cut costs and to re-focus on core competencies. One graphic sign of the trend was that by the mid-1990s the labour agency Manpower Inc. had displaced General Motors as the largest employer in the United States. While some sporadic signs of in-sourcing can be found, the general trend has been towards continued outsourcing. For example, in the US, the growth of off-shore IT outsourcing in the two-year period 2003–5 was estimated at 55 per cent (www.intergroup.com).

The reasons for the growth of outsourcing are many. In a complex, fast-moving market it is a speedy way to gain access to specialist services. Alternatively, it can be a means to reduce costs by sourcing from low-cost producers many of whom are likely to be non-unionized. In this regard, advances in information and communication technologies have played a part in that companies headquartered in high-wage cosmopolitan areas can outsource routine billing and so on to remote stations almost anywhere in the world.

Problems of scrap can be drastically reduced or even eliminated as defective components can simply be rejected. Outsourcing also enables flexibility in that supply can be more readily turned on or off – at least in theory. In some instances it is merely a device to respond to pressures of 'headcount control' – i.e. a means, on paper at least, to show that the critical measure of direct employee numbers is being kept under control. But, according to the more cutting-edge theories of 'winning' companies, the outsourcing phenomenon is, above all, a manifestation of enterprises clearing out peripheral, distracting activities, in order to focus on core functions and core competencies.

In practice, there are many different types of outsourcing activity and usage. Some of the instances are piecemeal and opportunistic with little strategic character. Office cleaning is an example in most circumstances. The commissioning client has low vulnerability in relation to this kind of service and likewise the contribution to competitive advantage is not likely to be high. Here arm's length market contracting is the norm.

But for other services the outsourcing decision might permit strategic advantage. Nike thus considers it a strategic advantage to outsource all of its manufacturing; similarly Apple Computers outsources 70 per cent of its components, while GM has outsourced its car body-painting activities. In these cases, outsourcing often necessitates much closer ties between supplier and customer: here arm's length market relations are replaced by a complex mix of market and bureaucratic mechanisms.

Human resource management considerations

In addition to the commonly outsourced services such as catering, security, IT services and the like, various HR functions can themselves be outsourced. To date, the most popular candidates have been training, retirement planning, outplacement services, relocation, counselling, and various forms of consultancy. American Express, for example, has outsourced its retirement plan and benefits system. In February 2005, BT signed a renewed contract with Accenture for the provision of HR transactional work including recruitment, payroll, employee benefits, health and safety and some HR advisory services. This new long-term (ten-year) deal covers 87,000 BT employees in the UK and 180,000 pensioners plus another 10,000 BT employees in 37 countries. BT's Group HR Director said that the agreement would enable BT's own remaining in-house HR staff to concentrate on the strategic aspects of the HR role (see also (Adler 2003: 2285).

A variant on outsourcing is an arrangement whereby companies enter into cooperative arrangements to invest in and share common services – such as a local training facility. In a more formal way this was exemplified by the Shared Service Centre established for the BBC by a joint venture company formed by Coopers & Lybrand and EDS, the US systems group. A ten-year contract was signed under which staff would eventually work for the joint venture company – but on BBC premises. The shared service centre allowed the finance function the opportunity to offer career development to two quite different groups of staff. High-quality finance staff were 'not going to spend a lifetime pushing debits and credits. We want to build skills in the value-added areas', claimed the Finance Director. In time, other companies could use the SSC as it effectively became an outsourcing centre. At the beginning at least, it was located inside the BBC. Shared service arrangements have also been launched by General Electric, Seagram, Bristol Myers Squib and Whirlpool. Essentially an SSC does all those tasks that do not need to be kept close to the heart of a business. Placing an order with a supplier is a decision that must be taken at the centre – but the payment of the bill and recording of the transaction can be done at the SSC. Meanwhile, the staff working on processing transactions found themselves in a larger, single organization with greater career opportunities. There was also a need to put management structures in place to ensure the main customer/contractor was able to keep a measure of strategic control.

There are many consequences for human resource management deriving from outsourcing. Organizational hierarchies are somewhat simplified, since there are fewer functions to be coordinated. On the other hand, relationship management and the negotiation of contracts with the providers become critical. There are issues of confidentiality, risk sharing, continual improvement and so on. Even where there are clear opt-out clauses for non-compliance, the management of the actual occurrences may prove difficult.

A critical strategic human resource management issue is the potential loss of expertise in certain areas which may be difficult to recover. There is a danger of a serious 'hollowing-out' of the organization. The modern tenets of organizational learning, corporate culture and shared visions may all be put in some jeopardy if this occurs. Likewise, the sources of innovation needed in order to keep pace with rapidly changing markets may be put in jeopardy if a company is heavily reliant on strictly delineated services from a host of outside suppliers. Arranging the wherewithal to forestall this problem is an important HR challenge under conditions of extensive outsourcing.

The HR function could potentially assume a key role when outsourcing occurs. In fact our data suggest that HR departments already usually play some role in outsourcing cases in the advanced economies, at least in the larger corporations. So, while the search and selection team ideally involves a top executive, the respective department manager and a legal expert, human resources often play a critical role as facilitators and coordinators of the entire process. Indeed, it ought to be a natural role for human resource professionals to play.

Part of the human resource management function is to attract and retain people who have the appropriate skill sets required under the new conditions. A series of decisions to buy rather than to make, taken individually, may make economic sense, but collectively they may undermine the ability of a firm to compete.

While not all contracted staff are in the vulnerable, low-pay category, there has been some widening of inequalities as the remaining few permanent staff enjoy higher earnings, fringe benefits and better access to skill acquisition. This presents a further challenge to the maintenance of an organization which is low on formal control structures but is supposed to score high on shared values.

Supply chain management

Traditionally, supplier relations were managed by a specialized purchasing function. Personnel here identified potential suppliers and made contracts with those who could produce to the organizational specifications at the lowest price. Over recent decades, a growing number of firms have seen potential competitive advantage in developing a more strategic approach to the management of this function. The process management logic can extend beyond the organizational boundaries to encompass the entire 'supply chain' – not only direct suppliers, but these suppliers' suppliers further 'upstream'. Supply chain management has been stimulated by the globalization of supply options, which creates opportunities for cheaper suppliers, but also greater risk of disruption. These concerns are exacerbated (in some industries) by activists who want corporations to take responsibility for the labour and environmental practices of their suppliers.

In some cases, supply chain management consists of enforcing a strict market discipline on suppliers, demanding sizeable price reductions with every successive contract on pain of losing the contract to competing suppliers. In other cases however, customer firms work to establish a denser fabric of relations with their suppliers. This typically takes the form of what Stinchcombe (1986) calls 'hierarchical contracts', where the purchase agreement stipulates not only the standard enforcement clauses but an extensive specification of how the two firms will coordinate their activities – effectively introducing important elements of bureaucracy into interfirm market relations, especially where continual cost reductions, quality improvement, and timeliness are critical. This kind of supply chain management is also often characterized by higher levels of trust and collaboration – especially where innovation is expected.

Human resource management considerations

Supply chain management means that middle managers and first-level supervisors often find themselves dealing directly with external suppliers. This is a role that previously was reserved for top executives and for specialized staff in the purchasing department. Middle-managers now need to learn the art of 'influence without authority', which is a skill managers have typically been expected to acquire only at more senior levels. HR is pressured to respond with new criteria for selection, promotion, training, and rewards.

Organizational members need to adjust their mindsets so that the well-being of the whole value chain is kept in mind and enhanced. For example, GE Appliances collaborated with key suppliers. Together they can plan for and respond more quickly to changes in the production schedules. Production, inventory, sales, specification and scheduling data can be coordinated. A monthly data package is shared with 25 main suppliers. An organization may be considered well linked into its value chain if it scores high on a set of measures of joint development in marketing plans, product development planning, production and inventory planning, distribution planning and information systems planning. For the management of resources and capabilities the indicators would be shared resources, as opposed to separate resources, in the areas of technical expertise, financial expertise, management skills, information systems, and training and development.

Networks and virtual organizations

Network forms have attracted immense attention in recent years, as signalled by the Special Issue devoted to the theme in both the *Academy of Management Journal* (December 2004) and the *Academy of Management Executive* (November 2003). An organization such as Benetton is characterized by its organized network of market relations based on complex forms of contracting. It operates a retail system based entirely on franchising. On the other hand, its sourcing for garments is based on a putting-out system which has a long history. Nowadays, information and communication technology allows the total complex system to operate with rapid feedback system enabling it to operate with the absolute minimum of stock. In this system it is the wider network rather than the organization which is the interesting unit of analysis – indeed arguably Benetton, as such, is not an 'organization' at all in the conventional sense (Clegg 1990). Organizations such as Coca Cola and Visa, despite their strong worldwide presence, are likewise not traditional organizations. It is very hard to pin down the 'ownership' of these forms, as some of them have no fixed assets. Some commentators maintain that they really are 'virtual organizations'.

A network organization has been defined as an economic entity that operates through a cluster of compact business units, driven by the market, with few levels of decision making and a willingness to outsource whatever can be better done elsewhere (Snow 1992). It can be expected that new management functions will be needed – for example, brokers, architects, lead-operators, and caretakers.

However, we can also find network forms of organization within the ownership boundary of the firm, such as have been documented in several large consulting firms. Here teams are continually formed and reformed, regardless of administrative or geographic location, as a function of the clients' needs. Functional or divisional structures recede into the background, as mere support for this constantly evolving pattern of interactions. There can be wide variation in the strength of network ties from weak to strong over time depending upon founding conditions and network processes (Elfring & Hulsink 2007).

This free-flow across internal or external organizational boundaries can reach a stage when the organization per se becomes indefinable and unrecognizable – what Davidow and Malone (1992) have described as the 'virtual organization'. They ask:

> What will the virtual corporation look like? There is no single answer. To the outside observer it will appear almost edgeless, with permeable and continuously changing interfaces between company, supplier and customers. From inside the firm the view will be no less amorphous, with traditional offices, departments and operating divisions constantly reforming according to need. Job responsibilities will constantly shift, as will lines of authority – even the very definition of employee will change as some customers and suppliers begin to spend more time in the company than will some of the firm's own workers.
>
> (Davidow and Malone, 1992: 5–6)

Human resource management considerations

The management or coordination of network organizations demands attention to HR issues. The underlying logic of network organizations as presented by their advocates and practitioners is that 'know-how' and resource capability are now critical factors and these are increasingly difficult to locate within the boundaries of a single organization. Know-how and capability are increasingly distributed across a network of different businesses and contractors. But if this is so, the human resource management challenges, to identify, retain, develop and appropriate such scarce resources, are immense.

Part of the know-how resides in the identification of the parties and the capability to bring them together. In the 'boundaryless organization' there are huge uncertainties about who, if anyone, is managing these processes. External boundaries are barriers between firms and the outside world including customers and suppliers but also government agencies, special interest groups and the community at large. In traditional organizations there are clear demarcation lines separating 'insiders' from 'outsiders'. Role expectations were relatively clear. Management dealt with the former group and had mechanisms and techniques to help them do this. But these traditional methods are of doubtful validity in the network situation.

Under the network arrangement, there are contracts of a more commercial nature. Equally, there are connecting lines based on repeat business, trust and reputation. Mindsets and attitudes have to change considerably. Traditional methods of negotiation, competition, win-lose, information withholding, power plays and the like may cause difficulties.

Increasingly, boundary maintenance behaviour is seen as having dysfunctional consequences. When the boundaries are dissolved or drastically reduced, customers and suppliers may be treated as joint partners. Employees, as such, may be hard to identify. A range of parties may be expected to help the firm solve problems and to innovate. Effective network organizations need to make permeable the external boundaries that divide them from their customers and suppliers. The key concept here is that of the value chain. This is the set of linkages which create services and products of value to the end user. In the traditional view each company is supposed to maximize its own success with disregard for that of others. The overriding idea is that of competition. Under the new value chain concept the idea is to loosen external boundaries so as to create win-win relationships across the whole value chain.

Under the network concept cooperative relations between organizations are given high priority. As the cost of innovation increases, as complexity increases and everything changes so much faster, many companies have come to the conclusion that they simply cannot work alone (Storey and Salaman 2005). Business partners, customers and suppliers are urged to work together to co-produce value. This entails reconfiguring roles and relationships. The use of cooperative arrangements of a network kind has long been well developed in Japan. The *keitsu* consists of cross-locking companies often straddling very different sectors. They have shares in each other's equity but there is no governing holding company.

The successful network companies cooperate in both strategic and operational business planning. Network organizations require managers and staff to change their assumptions and behaviours. Instead of developing plans and strategies independently, planning needs to be coordinated and even shared with other participants in the network. Information therefore must not be hoarded and protected but shared to allow joint problem solving. Moreover, measurement and auditing systems need to be coordinated.

How, and why, does a company become a core organization in a network's value chain? The main identifying feature of a core organization is that it 'manages the network' – a role that is not, however, legally recognized. The actual process of managing such a network is a difficult one and it requires skills for which, as yet, little or no formal training is usually offered. Boyle (1993) examines the role of the core as a user organization, as the provider and/or user of goods and services, and as the link organization. He sees the possibility of the role of the core organization changing over time, as exemplified by Esso's shift away from being a petrol station franchiser to becoming a link organization by moving into forecourt convenience stores.

According to proponents of networks, the human resource management implications include the involvement of as many employees as possible so that they become familiar with customer and supplier needs. This can be done through inviting customers and suppliers to meetings where outlines of plans, goals and problems can be explained, by sending employees on customer and supplier field trips to encounter the detailed operations of day-to-day work, and by collecting and collating customer and supplier information. An additional stage can involve experiments with collaboration through, for example, organizing cross-value-chain task forces, and sharing technical services. A more ambitious step involves companies integrating their information systems and reconfiguring roles and responsibilities in the light of the collaboration achieved across the networks.

An overview of the implications for strategic human resource management

The host of structural developments reviewed in this chapter could be seen as offering a major opportunity for human resource management to raise its strategic profile. This case rests partly on the observation that the many failures in initiatives of this kind have been traced to shortcomings in human resource management and therefore this presents a strategic opportunity. It also rests in part on the point that many of the challenges thrown up by such initiatives put a premium on strategic thinking about human resource issues.

There is, however, an altogether different case that can be made: this suggests that these structural developments are highly inimical to a strategic approach to human resource management and that they rather express and impel the short-term financial denominator management approach in place of the sustained, numerator approaches extolled, for example, by Hamel and Prahalad.

There are a number of factors limiting the strategic potential. Outsourcing and other moves to market-based contractual arrangements are likely to reduce the investment by the organization in long-term skill formation activities. This is likely to apply as much to management development as it is to employee development and training more generally. There are still uncertainties about the possible loss of intellectual capital when extensive outsourcing occurs. An organization which contracts for services may, even though it initially gains a cheaper and perhaps more specialized service in the short term, lose the capability to undertake an activity close to its core.

These potential drawbacks are of course not an argument for simply retaining large internal labour markets. What seems to be required is a new type of strategic management within the context of the new form of 'boundaryless' or extended 'organization'. But managing these looser boundaries requires new skills (Lynn 2005) and the full nature of these new skills has not as yet been fully realized.

Classic bureaucracies harbour a *dual potential*. They can emphasize the rigid rules, multiply hierarchical levels and impede horizontal communication along with a command-and-control approach to worker management. Or, they may emphasize the psychological contract of security for long-term commitment and loyalty along with an infrastructure of training and development and corporate identity. In so far as the classic form has not been entirely abandoned, these dualities remain.

But, as we have seen in this chapter, there have also been very many and very significant departures from this classic form. The alternatives have been numerous. Descriptions and prescriptions of these have proliferated. And, to a large extent, the alternatives are still unfolding. No one has a firm fix on the emergent form. Various key attributes have been championed: prominent front runners have been the process–oriented company, the network, joint ventures and strategic alliances, the boundaryless organization and the virtual organization. We have argued in this chapter that there are some significant overlaps in these conceptualizations. For example, Ashkenas et al.'s (1995) concept of 'boundarylessness' both within and between enterprises shares many features with Davidow and Malone's (1992) 'virtual organization'. Likewise, Nonaka's (1995) description and proselytizing of the features of 'the knowledge-creating company' has a great deal in common with Senge (1992) on 'the learning organization', Quinn (1992) on 'the intelligent enterprise', and even Hamel and Prahalad (1994) on the vital strategic importance of building core competencies. Further discussion of the variety of meanings hidden in similar language can also be found in Palmer et al. (2007).

Thus, similarities and overlaps abound. Each management consultant and would-be guru is seeking to crystallize a complex set of developments into a central idea which can be made appealing, be packaged and sold. The variations around certain underlying themes should not therefore be too surprising. This is not to say, however, that the whole set can simply be dismissed as manipulated 'fads'. The numerous accounts of the nature of 'the new organization' are capturing, albeit in a selective and partial way, critical features of important trends in organizational formation and re-formation.

References

Adler, P. (2001). "Markets, hierarchy and trust: The knowledge economy and the future of capitalism." *Organization Science* 12(2): 215–234.

Adler, P.S. (2003). "Making the HR outsourcing decision." *Sloan Management Review* 45(1): 53–60.

Ashkenas, R., Ulrich, D., Jick, T. and Kerr, S. (1995). *The Boundaryless Organization*. San Francisco: Jossey-Bass.

Boyle, E. (1993). "Managing organizational networks." *Management Decision* 31(7): 22–31.

Clegg, S. (1990). *Modern Organizations: Organization Studies in a Postmodern World.* London: Sage.

Courpasson, D. (2000). "Managerial strategies of domination: Power in soft bureaucracies." *Organization Studies* 21(1): 141–162.

Davidow, W. H. and Malone, M. S. (1992). *The Virtual Corporation: Structuring and Revitalizing the Corporation for the 21st Century.* New York: Harper Business.

Edwards, R. (1979). *Contested Terrain: The Transformation of the Workplace in the Twentieth Century.* London: Heinemann.

Elfring, T. and Hulsink, W. (2007). "Networking by entrepreneurs: Patterns of tie-formation in emerging organizations." *Organization Studies* 28(12): 1849–1872.

Galbraith, J.R. (2002). "Organizing to deliver solutions." *Organizational Dynamics* 31(2): 194–207.

Gouldner, A. (1954). *Patterns of Industrial Bureaucracy.* New York: The Free Press.

Hamel, G. and Prahalad, C. K. (1994). *Competing for the Future.* Boston: Harvard Business School Press.

Hammer, M. (1996). *Beyond Reengineering.* London: HarperCollins.

Hammer, M. and Champy, J. (1992). *Reengineering the Corporation.* London: HarperCollins.

Kirkman, B. L. and Rosen, B. (2004). "The impact of team empowerment on virtual team performance: The moderating role of face to face interaction." *Academy of Management Journal* 47(2): 175–192.

Littler, C. R. and Innes, P. (2004). "The paradox of managerial downsizing." *Organisation Studies* 25(7): 1159–1184.

Lynn, M. L. (2005). "Organizational buffering: Managing boundaries and cores." *Organization Studies* 26(1): 37–61.

MacCormack, A. and Forbath, T. (2008). "Learning the Fine Art of Global Collaboration." *Harvard Business Review* 86(1): 10–11.

March, J. G. and Simon, H. A. (1958). *Organizations.* New York: Wiley.

McNulty, T. and Ferlie, E. (2002). *Re-engineering Healthcare: The Complexities of Organizational Transformation.* Oxford: Oxford University Press.

Merton, R. (1957). *Social Theory and Social Structure.* Chicago: The Free Press.

Nonaka, I. and Takeuchi, H. (1995). *The Knowledge-creating Company: How Japanese Companies Create the Dynamics of Innovation.* Oxford: Oxford University Press.

Palmer, I., Benveniste, J., and Dunford, R. (2007). "New organizational forms: Towards a generative dialogue." *Organization Studies* 28(12): 1829–1847.

Quinn, J. B. (1992). *Intelligent Enterprise.* New York: Free Press.

Reagons, R. and McEvily, A. (2003). "Network structure and knowledge transfer: The effects of cohesion and range." *Administrative Science Quarterly* 48: 240–267.

Reed, M. (1999). "From the iron cage to the gaze? The dynamics of organizational control in late modernity," in Morgan, G. and Engwall, L. (eds) *Regulation in Organizations.* London: Routledge.

Schilling, M. and Steensma, H. K. (2001). "The use of modular organizational forms: an industry level analysis." *Academy of Management Journal* 44: 1149–1168.

Selznick, P. (1966). *TVA and the Grass Roots.* Berkeley: University of California Press.

Senge, P. (1992). *The Fifth Disciplne: The Art and Practice of the Learning Organization.* London: Century Business.

Stinchcombe, A. (1986). "Contracts as hierarchical documents", in Stinchcombe, A. and Heimer, C. (eds) *Organizational Theory and Project Management.* Oslo: Norwegian University Press.

Storey, J. (2002). "What are the general manager issues in supply chain management?" *Journal of General Management* 27(4): 65–79.

Storey, J. and Salaman, G. (2005). *Managers of Innovation: Insights into Making Innovation Happen.* Oxford: Blackwell.

7

Changing labour markets and the future of work

David Coats

Introduction

The purpose of this chapter is not to describe the world as it might look to an HR practitioner in twenty years' time but to map the terrain of "what we know" and make a modest assessment of the challenges that we face. It explores the changes that have taken place in the labour market, identifies the forces influencing these developments, looks at the shifting structure of organisations and at the reshaping of work – with some discussion of the question of job quality. Inevitably, the account given here reflects the author's experience in the UK, but evidence is drawn from other countries too.

Futurist speculation is the curse of any discussion about the changing world of work. In the early 1990s popular commentators predicted with great confidence that the permanent full-time job was a thing of the past, that we would all have to get used to a world of persistent employment insecurity, that increases in contingent work were inevitable and that employees would need to become footloose, opportunistic and flexible (Handy 1994). It was never explained how this vision of the future could be squared with the high-volume protestations that "our employees are our greatest asset", or with the other "inevitability" that comparative advantage, productivity and performance would increasingly depend on the skills, knowledge and talents of motivated, committed employees.

Other analysts speculated that we were about to witness "the end of work", as information technology unleashed a wave of job destruction across the developed world (Rifkin 1996). It was asserted that this could explain the inexorable rise in US unemployment from the 1960s (average 4.8%) to the late 1980s (average 7.3%). One might attribute this line of thought to an almost pathological technophobia, but it is much better understood as an effort to construct an alarmist argument on rather shaky economic foundations.

Those with slightly longer memories might recall that a similar prospectus was offered in the UK in the late 1970s (Jenkins and Sherman 1979, 1981), with the suggestion that technology would lead to an "excess" of leisure time rather than unemployment. Both hypotheses have proved wanting when tested against events. "The end of work" cannot explain the return of something close to full employment in the liberal market (and Nordic) economies and the rapid pace of technological development has not led to a significant reduction in working hours

(Coats 2006). The selective use of evidence has proved to be no more reliable than gazing directly into a crystal ball.

For our purposes the lesson is clear. We should all tread a little warily before we start making overconfident predictions about the likely direction of change; although that does not mean that we must abandon all efforts to assess the likely challenges. Perhaps there is more to be gained by eschewing futurism in favour of an accurate description of the world today, reflecting the scale and pace of change since the 1980s. Once we can see how much (or how little) is different we might be rather better positioned to make a judgment about the course of developments over the next twenty years. But even this more modest approach raises some difficulties. Apparently "new" "trends" tend to be exaggerated and then projected forward – hence the suggestion that we are witnessing the exponential growth of short-term and temporary contracts.

So even though the past can never be a guide to the future, it should be possible, exercising a judicious degree of caution, to detect trends in the present that were also observable in the recent past. Some constructive thinking about the likely shape of the future is unavoidable if government and employers want to be well positioned to anticipate change. Of course, we should recognise that sometimes predicted events will fail to materialise, that the unexpected will happen and that governments, employers and other stakeholders will continue to be surprised by Rumsfeldian "unknown unknowns".

Perhaps the most important part of the story is that national policies still matter – the level of unemployment, the extent of income inequality, the impact of minimum wages, the perception of workplace justice and even the general health and life expectancy of workers all remain within the purview of domestic policy influence (Layard 2005, Marmot 2004). This is a rather positive story, offering a direct response to that of "global pessimism", which tells us that there are unstoppable economic forces sweeping across the world and that we must all adapt to these new realities or suffer the consequences.

Structural changes and the labour market

A useful place to start our discussion is the basic structure of the labour market. How much change have we really witnessed over the last two decades? Certainly so far as the UK is concerned some of the changes have been profound – a big fall in employment in manufacturing, a continued feminisation of the workforce, rising skill levels and a burgeoning of employment in business services, particularly knowledge-intensive services. Yet an observer from the mid-1980s would also find much that is familiar (see Figure 7.1). Most jobs are permanent and full-time. Part-time work has grown slightly over the last two decades, but most of the growth took place in earlier periods. Temporary and contingent employment as a share of total employment has remained stable for much of the last twenty years. In short, on these dimensions, today looks much like yesterday.

A swift glance at the data reinforces the judgment that the guru-driven narratives of the early 1990s have proved to be rather unreliable guides. There is no significant evidence to endorse the view that we will all be flexible, self-employed portfolio workers in the future; most second job holders are low-paid and work part-time. Nor has Rifkin's "end of work" prediction been vindicated. The UK has a high employment rate (74.6% in 2006), relatively low unemployment and a lower rate of labour market inactivity (people who say they would like to work if they could find a job, but have abandoned active job search) than was the case in 1971 (Brinkley et al. 2007). A dispassionate observer might conclude that this is a rather remarkable achievement, given the high rates of unemployment that were experienced in the 1980s and 1990s.

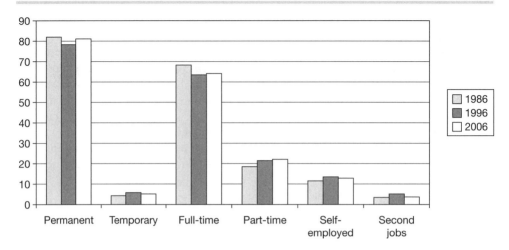

Figure 7.1 Employment change in the UK labour market 1996–2006 (% share of total employment)

Source: Labor Force Survey, Social Trends No 30.

Of course, it is important to understand that these experiences are not universal. Indeed, the labour markets of the OECD countries display a wide range of diverse characteristics – experiences have been as different as one could imagine. For example, France and Germany have experienced high unemployment at the same time as the UK and the USA have seen unemployment fall and long-term unemployment virtually disappear. The Nordic countries have retained the essence of their social model – strong welfare states, limited income inequality, high unemployment benefits, strong trade unions and widespread coverage of collective bargaining – at a time when welfare states elsewhere have been under pressure, trade unions have seen membership decline and income inequality has grown (especially in the "liberal market economies" of the Anglo-Saxon world).

The extent of contingent employment reflects this diversity too. Around a third of jobs in Spain are classified as temporary but, despite the rhetoric of "labour market flexibility", the Anglo-Saxon economies have the lowest levels of temporary work (EU Labour Force Survey, 2006). Indeed, we might conclude that there seems to be an inverse relationship between the level of labour market regulation and the extent of contingent work – although we might observe too that the flexibility of liberal market economies means that regular work at the bottom of the labour market looks much like contingent work elsewhere.

In the early part of the 1990s, many reputable commentators were suggesting that there was only "one right way" to achieve low unemployment and stable non-inflationary growth. For want of a better phrase we might describe this as the "orthodox" or "neo-liberal" view that there was simply no alternative to weak welfare states, low taxation, and a low level of labour market regulation, weak trade unions, low unemployment benefits and coercive welfare to work regimes for the unemployed. The OECD offered the following definitive advice to developed countries in their 1994 Jobs Strategy: follow our prescription or suffer the consequences. Now, thirteen years on, the position looks a little more complex. Indeed, in their recent review of the Jobs Strategy the OECD have abandoned the "one right way" thesis and have accepted that there is something positive to be said for the Nordic model too, particularly the Danish notion of "flexicurity".

This is a particularly important development because it suggests that a labour market characterised by a strong welfare state, moderately strict employment protection legislation, strong trade unions, high unemployment benefits (albeit with strong job search conditions attached) and active labour market programmes (rather than passive support for the unemployed) are, according to the OECD, all compatible with non-inflationary growth and good employment performance (OECD 2004, 2005). Indeed, the developing discussion about social policy in the EU draws inspiration from these findings and may offer a useful framework for a revival of the social dimension of the EU.

It might be an overstatement to say that the OECD have performed an abrupt U-turn, but there can be no doubt that their position has changed. Even the strongest enthusiast for the neo-liberal model must concede the point.

There are two self-evident conclusions to be drawn from this very rapid review. First, national policies really do matter. Second, there are no *irresistible* forces constraining national policy choices. Countries can choose to have more or less income inequality, they can choose to offer a high or low level of workplace justice and they can choose more or less coercive regimes for the unemployed – sometimes a carrot can be more effective than a stick (Coats 2006). In other words, the impact of global trends is highly differentiated across countries.

Returning to our earlier theme, it would be wrong to give the impression that *nothing* has changed in the labour markets of developed countries. Perhaps a better characterisation is that we have seen both continuity *and* change. Certainly the most significant development, in the UK at least, is not in the structure of the labour market but in the "rise and fall of industries". It is this phenomenon which explains why the labour market of 2007 looks very different from the labour market of 1977. At that time slightly more than one in four workers were employed in manufacturing, whereas today the figure is close to one in ten; employment in services has grown apace, rising from 69% of total employment in 1986 to 75% in 1996 and 81% in 2006.

Looking to the future, the big story is the growing importance of employment in high-value *knowledge-intensive* services. The phenomenon can be observed across Europe, with the biggest increases in employment to be found in knowledge services, as widely defined, including business services, financial services, communications, education and health. Indeed, recent research suggests that the UK has a significant advantage in these sectors, which are contributing an increasing share of the country's international trade and in which the UK has a large trade surplus, valued at around 3.4% of GDP (Brinkley 2007).

Moreover, the best projections of occupational change in the UK suggest that by 2014 more than 45% of all employees will be in the top three occupational groups (managers, professionals and associate professionals), which might be contrasted with the position in 1984, when the same groups accounted for around 30% of employees (see Figure 7.2). To some extent the changing occupational structure is a consequence of the rise and fall of industries too, with fewer manual workers in manufacturing and more white-collar employees elsewhere.

This change in the structure of the economy can be observed across the developed world, with technology as the principal driver – the number of units produced by UK's car industry is at roughly the same level as in the 1970s although the workforce is much smaller; and the same might be said of the UK's steel industry, which has levels of output similar to the 1970s (albeit in more specialised products) but with a much smaller workforce. A simple way of describing the process is to say that we are moving from an economy where a worker could make a decent living by using their physical capabilities, to an economy where a premium is placed on intellectual or cognitive qualities. The most striking phenomenon described by Figure 7.2 is the dramatic fall in employment in elementary occupations – there will be relatively few jobs that require brawn alone; workers will need to live by their wits. It is this phenomenon which explains why policy makers place so much emphasis on the importance of the "knowledge economy" and devote relentless attention to skills policy.

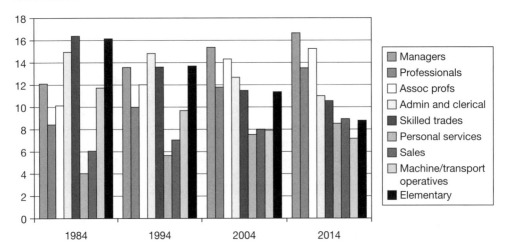

Figure 7.2 Occupational change in the UK 1984–2014 (% of all in employment)

Source: SSDA (2006).

Of course the experience has not been painless and some communities have been severely disadvantaged as a result. But the important point to note is that the phenomenon is ubiquitous. Indeed, one might even say that it reflects no more than the process of "creative destruction" that has always been the fundamental dynamic of capitalism (Schumpeter 1943). For policy makers the most important question is to find instruments that can manage the adverse consequences equitably without losing the self-evident benefits of competitive markets. How this outcome can be achieved is the issue to which we now turn.

Explaining the changing world of work

Some commentators have suggested that all these "trends" are best explained by "globalisation", but that term is so loaded with both positive and negative associations that it is of limited analytical use. While some NGOs call for "global resistance", market fundamentalists argue that "resistance is useless". Both fall into the trap of believing that "globalisation" can account for almost anything good or bad in the global economy and both believe that nation states are powerless. As we shall see, the truth is slightly more complex than either side will allow.

Three preliminary points may help to clarify our discussion. First, structural change has been a constant in economic history – often with devastating consequences for the workers affected. Handloom weavers were legitimately worried that steam-powered looms and the factory system were threats to a well-established way of life. Their response (machine breaking) may have looked rational in the short term, but there can be little doubt that industrialisation laid the foundations on which our modern democratic welfare states have been built. The process may have been messy, unpleasant and a cause of social conflict, but few would contest the argument that in the long run the sacrifices of previous generations made today's prosperity possible.

Second, disruptive change was taking place before anybody coined the term "globalisation"; indeed, it has been suggested that the world was just as globalised in 1900 as it is today (Hirst and Thompson 1996, Wolf 2004). Capital was free to move across borders, real-time financial information could be transmitted across continents, tariff barriers were relatively low (market

110

liberalisation had been an instrument of British policy since the repeal of the Corn Laws), there was a regime of fixed exchange rates and a single global currency (gold) and huge movements of populations across national borders. In that sense the world in which we live today contains many features that were observable a century ago and, taking account of some likely perplexity about modern technology, a time traveller from 1900 with an analytical cast of mind would not find the structure of today's global economy either particularly novel or astonishing.[1]

Third, managing restructuring has always posed a problem for policy makers and other stakeholders. Public agencies can either anticipate change or adopt a "wait-and-see" approach, dealing with negative consequences after they have materialised. Employers can either anticipate the likely impact on their business of emerging technologies, new competitors and new markets or find themselves the victims of economic transformation. Trade unions can either recognise change as a constant and equip their members for a very different world of work or play a rather negative role by campaigning to "save all the existing jobs".

Referring explicitly to globalisation, the development economist and philosopher Amartya Sen makes the case for public policy to observe the following principles:

> The appropriate response has to include concerted efforts to make the form of globalisation less destructive of employment and traditional livelihood, and to achieve gradual transition. For smoothing the process of transition there have to be opportunities for retraining and acquiring new skills . . . in addition to providing social safety nets for those whose interests are harmed – at least in the short run – by globalising changes.
>
> (Sen 1999)

This is both an intelligent and humane response, but other commentators have suggested that there *is* something new and historically unprecedented about our situation that requires a more radical reaction. The argument can be expressed in two words – India and China. It is said that both countries are so huge, with a growing human capital stock (millions of scientists and engineers) that the West will struggle to compete. It is argued further that skills upgrading may have been an appropriate answer when competition was intensifying between *developed* countries, but it is an inadequate response to the integration of China and India into the world trading system.

Alan Blinder, an eminent US economist and former adviser to President Bill Clinton, has suggested that millions of American service jobs will be potentially "offshoreable" in the near future (Blinder 2007). Low labour costs and the availability of technology will make it much cheaper and therefore more profitable to locate in the emerging markets of the new global superpowers. And these jobs will not necessarily be low-skill jobs. Blinder is quite explicit: the middle classes are about to experience a degree of insecurity fuelled by international competition that hitherto has been confined to relatively low-skill groups. And the process could lead to some reduction in living standards: "In addition to job losses, it is quite likely that, by stripping away their previous immunity to foreign competition, offshoring will depress the real wages of many service workers who do not lose their jobs" (Blinder 2007, p. 9).

Richard Freeman, an equally renowned labour economist, has talked of the "great doubling" of the global workforce following the collapse of the Soviet Union and the ready availability of labour in India, China and Russia (Freeman 2005). Joseph Stiglitz, another former Clinton adviser and former chief economist at the World Bank, has been equally explicit: the wages of low-skilled workers in developed countries are *already* being adversely affected by globalisation (Stiglitz 2006). Thomas Friedman, the *New York Times* columnist, has told us that "the world is flat" and all developed countries are now in direct competition with lower cost and highly skilled workers elsewhere in the world (Friedman 2005).

And Lord Digby Jones, former director general of the CBI (the UK's principal employers' organisation) and now a trade minister in Gordon Brown's government, has suggested that China and India will "eat our lunch" unless the UK becomes a lean, mean knowledge economy with a relentless focus on the reduction of costs, low levels of business taxation, weak trade unions and a small welfare state. Those of a nervous disposition will already be terrified by these predictions, but even the most imperturbable citizen might be rather discomfited by forecasts that amount to little more than "be afraid, be very afraid".

The risk with this kind of rhetoric is that some people might be persuaded to embrace a protectionist response. Anxiety about change leads people to demand that government act to "save all the jobs", increase tariff barriers and insulate national economies from international competition. It is something of a paradox that Alan Blinder, who is now perhaps quite wrongly associated with the "be afraid" camp, is also an enthusiastic free trader and an advocate of liberalisation on the grounds that trade openness leads to higher global prosperity. Unfortunately, by talking about a "new industrial revolution" and "great dislocation" he adds fuel to the protectionist fire, even as he concludes that in the long run global prosperity will be higher.

How might we answer these influential voices? What possible arguments might we use? To begin with, we could quite reasonably observe that the process of economic development has never, in the past, led to the immiseration of the already affluent. In other words, a rising tide can lift all boats. The emergence of Germany as an industrial power did not make the UK poorer; the same might be said of the United States or the countries of Southern Europe that have become much more prosperous since joining the EU, or the newly industrialised Asian countries that joined the world trading system in the 1990s.

Enabling India and China to grow their economies and join the world trading system is a route to higher overall global prosperity and higher incomes in both those countries. Developing countries may benefit from an element of "infant industry" protection at the early stage of development (as was the case for now prosperous Western economies in the early phase of industrialisation) but the objective must be eventually to achieve full integration into the world trading system (Chang 2002). Competition between *developed countries* leads to the more effective exploitation of comparative advantage and a more efficient allocation of capital. Allowing China and India to continue on this path would be the greatest anti-poverty programme the world has seen.

There is also a serious question whether Richard Freeman's "great doubling" is a real phenomenon anyway. For example, much of the labour force in India and China remains rural rather than urban, even though rapid urbanisation is taking place. India suffers from widespread illiteracy and China may be reaching the limits of its current growth model (Hutton 2006). Skilled workers in the West have little to fear from the theoretical possibility that agricultural workers in Asia are now part of the global labour force.

We might also ask whether the prediction of widespread offshoring is consistent with recent experience. Applying a crude version of Alan Blinder's argument leads to the inevitable conclusion that the economies of developed countries in the future will be wholly constituted by non-tradable services, simply because nobody believes that it makes any economic sense to travel to Bangalore for a cheaper haircut or a manicure. Yet contrary to all the arguments advanced above, some developed countries with high labour costs are continuing to perform well in industries that are exposed to intense international competition. Germany may have relatively high unemployment, but it remains the world's largest exporter and has doubled its exports to China over the past five years. The Nordic countries have high labour costs and high taxes but have continued to experience moderately strong non-inflationary growth and low unemployment. Common sense suggests that there are only weak reasons to be "afraid" of the emerging economic strength of India and China.

Empirical data support this conclusion. The USA creates and destroys around 500,000 jobs every week. As Will Hutton has pointed out, in any one year around one-fifth of the nation's jobs have been eliminated and another one-fifth have been created (Hutton 2006). By way of comparison, even the most hawkish commentators have only attributed around 100,000 jobs per year in lost job opportunities to trade with China in the period 1989–2005, which equates to about 2.24 million in total. This could be said to be a relatively small number in the context of the US economy overall during this same period (Palley 2005).

So far as offshoring is concerned (where jobs are directly transferred from the developed to the developing world), on one measure the numbers are smaller still in both the UK and the USA. According to the Bureau of Labour Statistics only 16,000 workers in the USA were affected by offshoring in 2005 (1.7% of mass layoffs) and the European Restructuring Monitor identified 19,000 jobs offshored from the UK in the same period (Hutton 2006, Palley 2005). However, we should note that these figures are contested and that other commentators have suggested that up to 406,000 US jobs were offshored in 2004 (Bronfenbrenner and Luce 2004). However, while almost half a million jobs sounds like a big number, it is still relatively modest in the context of the whole US economy.

It should be obvious that not all these figures can be right. So is the fear of globalisation more myth than reality? There can be no doubt that the level of anxiety is rising and that reputable commentators are worried, particularly in the USA. But it would be wrong to view this discussion only through an American lens. Experiences elsewhere offer a more positive outlook; the debate about offshoring in the UK and in Northern Europe seems to be following a slightly different trajectory.

One possibility of course is that the USA is being affected by an openness to trade which other countries have experienced for some considerable time. According to the OECD, the Nordic countries are *more* open to trade than the USA, have opened their markets with more enthusiasm over the last decade *and* still have employment rates that are amongst the highest in the developed world (OECD 2007). Perhaps the real cause of the problem is that the USA remains one of the *least open* economies in the OECD, despite all the rhetoric of liberalisation. In other words, while the UK and some other European economies have got used to dealing with the "creative destruction" that comes with openness, the USA is still learning how to manage these processes; a conclusion that returns us directly to Amartya Sen's injunction about how "globalisation" should be handled.

Indeed, despite the rather crude interpretation of some of his recent public statements, Alan Blinder would not necessarily disagree. The important conclusion is to recognise that there can be losers as well as winners from these economic processes (although open trade benefits global prosperity in the long run). Governments must act to compensate the losers – or more accurately, equip them with the wherewithal to succeed in a knowledge economy. His most recent work offers a policy prospectus that would look familiar to policy makers in the Nordic countries: higher unemployment benefits and a stronger welfare state, high-quality active labour market programmes and investment in education and skills (particularly communication and problem-solving skills).

In other words, the critical challenge for policy makers is to manage difficult economic transitions with sensitivity. A degree of labour market flexibility may help and there are already models in operation in Scandinavia that offer real promise for the rest of the developed world. Indeed, from a more parochial perspective, much of the policy mix in the UK is already consistent with Blinder's proposals and the emerging discussion about "flexicurity" at EU level offers real promise for the future (European Commission 2007). There is no reason therefore why "globalisation" should necessarily have either an adverse impact on employment or lead to increasing income inequality (OECD 2007).

This latter consideration is particularly important because there is a widespread view that increases in income inequality are in large measure attributable to "globalisation". It is undeniable of course that income inequality grew in many countries over the course of the 1980s and has continued to accelerate in the USA since that time (Esping-Anderson 2005). The position in the UK is a little more complex, with the trend towards greater inequality halting in the early part of this decade and some evidence of a small reduction in the period 2001–05 (Jones 2006).

A particular concern has arisen around the incomes of the group best classified as the super-rich, the top 0.1% of the income distribution or, in Robert Frank's words, the inhabitants of Richistan (Frank 2007). Yet even here experiences across the developed world are not uniform. Certainly, those in the top 0.1% of the income distribution have got significantly richer in the UK, the USA and Canada over the last thirty years. But the same cannot be said for the same group in either France or Japan, which leads the OECD to conclude that: "differences in national policies and institutions also play an important role in determining the income share going to the top 0.1% and how it is affected by economic integration" (OECD 2007, p.117).

How might we describe these national variations? Self-evidently, there will be differences in tax systems, in the remuneration strategies of large corporations, in the extent of social norms of "acceptability" that place limits on executive pay, in the structure of capital markets, in the ease of merger and acquisition and in corporate governance arrangements. And the fact that these differences exist at all shows us that nations continue to have real social, economic and political choices available to them.

Andrew Glyn makes a similar point in noting that the extent of the growth in inequality has varied significantly between countries operating at a similar level of economic development and with similar exposure to international trade (Glyn 2000). And the OECD's analysis confirms that the USA and Japan, with similar degrees of trade openness, have had very different experiences of income inequality. Whatever is happening here, it cannot be attributed exclusively to globalisation.

We would therefore be wrong to conclude that the continued growth of India and China will lead to the impoverishment of the West or that rising income inequality is an inevitable consequence of these developments. Our experience shows us that the developed world can remain affluent if productivity continues to grow and wages rise broadly in line with productivity. Certainly, there is an irresistible case for investing in training and skills, but that has more to do with being able to respond to the changing nature of consumer demand in developed countries combined with the impact of technology than it does with supposed trade effects. Indeed, having suggested that globalisation is to blame for falling wages, Joseph Stiglitz contradicts himself and concedes our point by accepting that technology is the proximate cause of the deteriorating position of the unskilled (Stiglitz 2006, p. 273).

This is a useful step forward, but there may be other factors that are equally important in the US context. For example, the USA has witnessed rapid inward migration from Central and South America and, at the same time, has seen trade union influence decline and the federal minimum wage fall from what was, in international terms, an already low level. The basic laws of economics suggest that when the supply of a commodity increases significantly the price can be expected to fall if demand rises somewhat more slowly. This is a reasonably accurate description of the US labour market over the last decade and it helps to explain why the incomes of workers below the median have been under pressure. Experience in the UK offers a lively counter-example. Inward migration has been relatively high, but the National Minimum

Wage has continued to rise rapidly over the 2001–06 period. Low-paid workers have done well and there is no evidence of downward pressure on average earnings as a result of migration, trade or any other external factor (Coats 2007). Our previous conclusion still holds: national policies matter.

If we really want to understand how labour markets are changing then we would be better advised to look at the domestic institutional factors that reflect national policy choices and cultural preferences. Capital markets are of great importance, particularly because they shape the market for corporate control; and regulatory requirements can affect the extent of mergers and acquisitions, the role of private equity and the extent to which transactions are highly leveraged. A debt-laden company controlled by a private equity house may be highly sensitive to interest rate changes and may, as a result, have a relentless focus on reducing labour costs. As Martin Wolf has pointed out, the financial architecture of the so-called "new capitalism" is a much more important influence on the nature of work than the supposed effect of international trade (Wolf 2007).

Changing organisations

Alongside all these changes attributed to trade and technology are changes that have taken place in the nature of corporate organisation and the design of jobs. Richard Sennett has suggested that there has been a significant shift in the strategies adopted by multi-national companies in highly competitive international markets (Sennett 1998, 2006). These are the organisations that have downsized and delayered, moved from networks to hierarchies, instituted new forms of corporate organisation and now look more like an archipelago than a conventional "command-and-control" pyramid.

Virtual teams, flat hierarchies and porous departmental boundaries are all fundamental features of what Sennett also calls the "new capitalism". Whether these are widespread developments remains an open question, and Sennett is very careful to restrict his account to multi-nationals operating in global markets. Nonetheless, the story that he tells has some resonance in popular consciousness and, even though his work is almost entirely qualitative, the argument is supported by quantitative research which finds some evidence of similar phenomena (Gallie et al. 2004, White and Hill 2004).

Even if we accept the critique that Sennett is talking about a narrow rather than a widespread experience, we are still left with a profound question about the implications for organisations engaged in permanent structural change:

> How can we decide what is of lasting value in ourselves in a society which is impatient, which focuses on the immediate moment? How can mutual loyalties and commitments be sustained in institutions that are constantly breaking apart or continually being redesigned?
> (Sennett 1998, p. 10)

Sennett argues further that there is something to be said for hierarchy in a traditional "command-and-control" model, principally because employees know where they stand and they know who to blame when things go wrong. We might say that a traditional "Fordist" organisation is characterised by predictability and stability – things may change but they will not change fast, partly because of the complexity of the products being produced and the relative inflexibility of traditional mass production systems. Second, tasks are clearly delineated, workers know what they have to do and have the opportunity to build strong relationships with colleagues over time. Third, in the past, workers in a mass production environment would

115

probably have been trade union members with access to effective voice institutions. Simply put, in a Fordist organisation workers are secure about their own position, they know who to go to if they have a problem, they know they can make themselves heard and they know that they will be dealt with fairly.

Whatever one makes of this argument, companies must be adopting new strategies for a reason; it cannot be the case, for example, that some persuasive management consultants have convinced firms to behave quite irrationally and adopt practices that are ineffective. An obvious answer is that new organisational forms enable companies to be nimbler in reacting to consumer demand in an economy where the tastes of an affluent population are becoming increasingly differentiated.

HR and high-performance working

Much of the management rhetoric suggests that these developments are an unqualified good for both employers and employees; "flexibility" is definitionally benign because it offers workers more autonomy and guarantees higher productivity for employers. A more determined application of "high-performance" management practices will lead us to the sunlit uplands where "work is more fun than fun". Continuous change is a fact of life and workers must learn to embrace uncertainty with enthusiasm; anything less is a retreat from an increasingly complex world and little more than wishful thinking.

This characterisation may seem a little extreme, but a swift glance at the smorgasbord of HR conferences shows that organisations are always in search of a magic bullet. Better employee engagement, higher effort levels and increased commitment are all supposed to follow the application of "enlightened" HR practices in redesigned and re-engineered organisations. Individual employee involvement is said to be a necessary condition for engagement. Relating pay more closely to individual effort is said to generate higher individual productivity. Yet what is perhaps most striking is the relatively weak evidence supporting the supposed superiority of new organisational models, new forms of work organisation and the bundle of "high-performance" HR practices. Put crudely, management gurus may claim to know "what works" and even "what works best" in our "globalised" world, but their models rarely reach the exacting standards of social science and as we have seen are sometimes founded on rather weak evidence.

An array of studies purport to demonstrate that people management has a direct and beneficial impact on productivity. However, as Toby Wall and Stephen Wood have pointed out, most of the efforts to prove causal relationships have so far produced little more than persuasive associations (Wall and Wood 2005). Much of the research is cross-sectional rather than longitudinal and the performance measures are often not robust enough to withstand rigorous stress testing. Moreover, there may be some "contamination" between measures of HRM and measures of performance, making it difficult to disentangle the direction of causation. Wall and Wood conclude that the evidence is "encouraging but ambiguous", even though there are "strong theoretical grounds for believing an HRM system centred on enhancing employee involvement should be beneficial for organisational performance" (Wall and Wood 2005, p. 454). In other words, we probably know less than we think about the importance (or otherwise) of HR as a strategic function that is supposed to ensure the alignment of individual aspiration with organisational mission and the delivery of strong organisational performance.

One can also find more critical commentaries, suggesting that applying the full bundle of "high-performance" practices can be self-defeating (Godard 2004). It is said that "high-performance" practices lead to an increase in labour costs and employers respond to these rising costs through an intensification of work. As a result employees lose faith in the practices, withhold discretionary effort and any further effort to apply the practices is abandoned because employers have become convinced that the business benefits are small or non-existent. This may be a rather harsh assessment, but it might explain why practices that are widely believed to improve performance have been applied so sparingly – or, in the words of the most comprehensive account of these developments, why the "diffusion of so-called 'high involvement management' practices has been rather muted in recent years" (Kersley et al. 2006, p. 107).

A consequence of the critical line of thinking promoted by Wood and Wall is that HR practitioners should begin to question some of their most cherished assumptions. Is it true, for example, that relating pay to individual performance is such an unqualified good that we can reasonably anticipate a world where every organisation has a system of individual performance pay? On one view the answer might be taken to be a slightly qualified "yes". After all, there is ample evidence to show that the adoption of performance pay proceeds apace – especially in the UK's public sector. But the evidence supporting PRP is at best ambiguous and at worst suggests that employers would be well advised to abandon the individualisation of reward at the earliest possible opportunity.

Perhaps the biggest surprise here is that individual performance pay continues to be so popular when the weight of the evidence suggests that there are serious difficulties associated with the practice. One leading commentator has suggested that "much of the conventional wisdom about pay today is misleading, incorrect and sometimes both" (Pfeffer 1998, p. 110). It is said that individual performance pay has been shown to undermine teamwork, encourage employees to focus on the short term and lead people to "link compensation to political skills and ingratiating personalities rather than to performance". Sometimes half-truths and total nonsense can get in the way of the hard facts that are needed for effective evidence-based management (Pfeffer and Sutton 2006).

We might take the view that this amounts to little more than a plea for better data, but practitioners may be a little too impatient to wait for a robust longitudinal study and have to make immediate decisions using the best research available. What might we say to them about new organisational forms, new forms of work organisation and new HR practices? How might these phenomena shape developments over our twenty-year time horizon?

Perhaps we should start with research findings that are at least moderately persuasive. So far as the pay question is concerned, this would suggest that organisations would be well advised to consider collective forms or remuneration (team-based pay) and abandon the focus on individualisation and intrusive performance management – of which more later.

Similarly and despite the critical assessment that we have already explored, there is evidence to show that "high-performance" practices can have a beneficial impact on performance when they are allied to effective arrangements for both direct and indirect employee participation (OECD 1999, Sisson et al. 1997). Other studies have reached similar conclusions, suggesting that "high-trust" relationships with trade unions when combined with "high-performance practices" deliver better results than either no employee involvement or individual employee involvement alone (Black and Lynch 2000). There is also evidence to show that, in the UK at least, high-performance practices are more widespread in unionised workplaces (Cully et al. 1999, Kersley 2006). Furthermore, another study shows that the level of openness is lower in those enterprises that only used direct forms of voice (individual employee involvement) and that multiple channels for consulting the workforce (trade unions, consultative committees, works councils and individual involvement methods) have proved to be mutually reinforcing (Wood and Fenton O'Creevy 2005).

All of this may seem a little distant from Sennett's new capitalism, but a moment's reflection will show that there is a link to the problems that he has identified. The real criticism of the

117

"archipelago" model of the organisation is that it leaves employees feeling rootless, disconnected and the victims of events, with little or no control over their circumstances. The studies looking at the application of "high-performance practices" suggest that these practices can be made to work most effectively where organisations have a high level of social capital. Most importantly, perhaps, the strength of interpersonal relationships is sustained by the effectiveness of both direct employee involvement and collective consultation. For example, teamworking demands more effective interactions between members of the team. Joint problem solving can only be successful if individuals know that they can trust each other and trust their managers. Looking to the future, we might say that organisations with a proven capability to create and sustain high-trust relationships are also most likely to demonstrate resilience in the face of an increasingly competitive business environment.

Robert Putnam has offered us the very helpful observation that:

> A society characterised by generalised reciprocity is more efficient than a distrustful society, for the same reason that money is more efficient than barter. If we don't have to balance every exchange instantly, we can get a lot more accomplished. Trustworthiness lubricates social life.
>
> (Putnam 2000, p. 21)

Life at work is simply a variety of social life and what applies to society at large applies in microcosm to the workplace. There may be no escaping the "new capitalism", whether we use Martin Wolf's definition of a new financial architecture or Richard Sennett's definition of new organisational forms, but we now have some compelling research findings that are at least suggestive of an agenda that can enable employers to reconcile efficiency and productivity with workers' demands for justice in the workplace.

Job quality in a changing labour market

Of course, a sceptic may say that this is all far too positive, and that the sad reality is that the new capitalism has been associated with work intensification, declining job satisfaction and the more widespread use of intrusive performance management systems. The story is widespread, popular and comes from the same stable as the argument that "globalisation" is a threat to both decent wages and high-quality jobs. The evidence offers a somewhat more ambiguous picture which, in its essentials, suggests that we should be optimistic rather than pessimistic about the future.

For the avoidance of doubt, it has to be made clear that a wholly positive account is open to the accusation of Panglossian optimism. There is substantial evidence to suggest that the quality of work has deteriorated in the recent past. In a paper for the UK's Economic and Social Research Council, Robert Taylor identified declining satisfaction with work throughout the 1990s, particularly dissatisfaction with pay and working time (Taylor 2002). The UK's Workplace Employment Relations Survey confirmed this finding and also suggested that employees had less influence over key workplace decisions than they would like (Kersley 2006). We know from the epidemiological research that autonomy and control over the process of work can have a significant impact on health and life expectancy (Marmot 2004). But recent studies have shown a decline in autonomy and task discretion in British workplaces, with barely two in five workers reporting that they can choose or change the order of tasks, choose or change the method of work, choose the speed or rate of work, influence their choice of working partners or take breaks when they wish (DTI 2007, Gallie 2004). Using a composite measure of job content suggests that the UK has something of a problem, being ranked with countries that languished under Soviet-style command economies for forty years (Romania, Bulgaria, and Lithuania) rather than the Nordic social democracies (DTI 2007).[2]

Yet, once again, we might observe that these experiences are not universal and wide variation can be observed across the EU's twenty-seven member states. For example, workers in the Nordic countries and the Netherlands all report a high level of autonomy at work, workers agree that their jobs often involve learning new things and they report a high level of "functional flexibility" (autonomous teamworking and job rotation). In general the process of work in all these countries is more intense than in the UK. The critical question here is the extent to which workers have control over what they do. Working at high intensity need not necessarily have an adverse impact on employees as long as they possess appropriate skills and are offered a high level of task discretion. As Michael Marmot has pointed out, contrary to the widespread perception, the security guard on the front desk is a more likely victim of coronary heart disease than the "highly stressed" senior manager on the executive floor (Marmot 2004). Richard Layard has offered a slightly more polemical account:

> Perhaps the most important issue is the extent to which you have control over what you do. There is a creative spark in each of us, and if it finds no outlet then we feel half-dead. This can be literally true; among British civil servants of any given grade, those who do the most routine work experience the most rapid clogging of the arteries.
>
> (Layard 2005, p. 68)

Skills development is obviously part of the answer to the job-quality conundrum, but the quality of management matters too. Those studies that identified the phenomenon of work intensification in the 1990s also suggested that rising skill levels had not been matched by a consequent change in employer policies and practices (Green 2003). Simply put, skills were not being fully utilised by employers, leaving workers frustrated and dissatisfied. Employers' skills requirements may have been rising (see our earlier discussion) but workers' levels of formal qualification were rising faster, leaving an increasing proportion of employees overqualified for the jobs that they did.

Of course, this might be a temporary or transitional effect that will disappear as the labour market assumes a new shape, but employers would be wise to pay close attention to the phenomenon, simply because it could have a damaging impact on recruitment, retention and business performance.

Throughout the 1990s, authoritative surveys consistently showed that people believed they were working harder (Green 2003) – work intensification was a well-documented phenomenon. However, the process has either slowed or been halted in the current decade (Brown et al. 2006, Green 2003). In part this can be attributed to an increasing employee familiarity with information and communications technologies (ICT). For example, PCs, laptops and email had become ubiquitous by the end of the 1990s, but initially at least employees were uncertain how to handle these technologies. Devices that were supposed to be productivity enhancing came to be seen as instruments that demanded more effort from workers – handling a raging torrent of emails, for example – and allowed employers to monitor performance more closely (counting keystrokes as a measure of productivity is a particularly egregious example). As time passed employees, however, learned how to manage the new technologies at lower levels of effort, with the consequence that the work intensification phenomenon was brought to a halt. Of course, it might be that we are about to witness another wave of technology-induced work intensification (the Blackberry syndrome) but so far the evidence for such an effect is either patchy or anecdotal.

Once again, the best conclusion is that national policies can have a decisive effect on the relationship between organisational change and job quality – otherwise it would be impossible to explain the differences between the UK, the Nordic countries and the Netherlands. Workplace institutions seem to be particularly important. In each of the "high-performing" countries workers have some opportunity to influence the course of events, both as individuals and through representative institutions like works councils or trade unions. Employee voice and the quality of management are therefore critical factors in ensuring that an appropriate trade-off is achieved between business efficiency and workplace justice.

Some final reflections

We have seen that the world of work remains the proverbial curate's egg – good in parts – and that while the basic structure of the labour market today has some similarities with twenty years ago the big story is about the transformation of the occupational structure and the rise and fall of industries. Although this chapter has sought to avoid the pitfalls of predicting the future it is reasonable to assume that some of the trends we have witnessed in the recent past are likely to continue.

First, we might anticipate that competition will intensify, partly as a result of technological change and rising prosperity but also because of conscious public policy decisions like the completion of the EU single market and the liberalisation of the global trading regime.

Second, demographic trends (which have not been discussed in detail in this chapter) will continue to play an important role in reshaping the labour market, employer strategies and government policies. For example, falling fertility rates and the changing dependency ratio will lead to somewhat later retirement and longer working lives, with both employers and government needing to change policy as a result. Moreover, demographic change will also require employers and governments to make it easier for women in particular to reconcile work and their caring responsibilities. Unless action is taken on this front then skills shortages are likely to emerge and a huge amount of productive potential (women's skills) will be wasted. And finally on this point, if the economy is to continue to grow at its trend rate (around 2.5% per annum) then government will need to have a positive attitude to managed migration to ensure that employers have access to an adequate supply of skilled labour.[3]

Third, there will be some disruption to established patterns of employment. As we have seen, it would be wrong to attribute this phenomenon exclusively to "globalisation", largely because "creative destruction" is an unavoidable consequence of capitalism. There is some disagreement about the scale and pace of change but rather more agreement about the appropriate policy response that is designed to *anticipate* change – investment in skills, an enabling welfare state ("a hand up, not a hand-out"), high unemployment benefits, active job-search obligations, moderate employment protection legislation and a fairly high level of labour market flexibility. To use the European jargon, a "flexicurity" model will enable developed countries to manage the consequences of structural change with a degree of sensitivity and humanity.

Fourth, we have seen that organisations are changing too in response to changing technologies and changing markets. These developments have not necessarily been an unqualified good for workers and it is not entirely clear either that all the "new" organisational models have had a positive effect on business performance. Yet while some uncertainty remains, we can still be confident in saying that good management matters for high performance (Bloom et al. 2007) and that effective workplace institutions that lubricate workplace relationships and create or sustain trust are important ingredients in the overall mix.

This brief review of international experience demonstrates that national policies matter. We are not at the mercy of impersonal or unmanageable forces that have been unleashed by neo-liberalism. There is still ample room for social, economic and political choice. And the same might be said of business models too. Capitalism is protean, multi-faceted and diverse – with open market economies being entirely compatible with very different institutional patterns and wide variations in the extent of income inequality. There is no "one right way" to economic success and no inevitable convergence on a single business model. These are essential facts to bear in mind if we are to face the future with confidence and rise to the challenge posed by the rapid restructuring of developed economies.

Notes

1 Although they might, like most of us, struggle to understand the bewildering array of financial instruments traded in derivatives markets.
2 The composite measure of job content includes whether the job involves monotonous tasks, learning new things, resolving unforeseen problems on your own and handling complex tasks (DTI 2007).
3 The USA does not have quite the same problem as most countries of the EU. Fertility rates are somewhat higher and we have already observed that there has been a large influx of migrant labour over the last two decades.

References

Black, S. E. and Lynch, L. (2000), *What's Driving the New Economy: The Benefits of Workplace Innovation*, National Bureau of Economic Research Working Paper 7479.

Blinder, A. (2007), *Offshoring: Big Deal or Business as Usual?* CEPS Working Paper No 149, June.

Bloom, N. et al. (2007), *Management Practice and Productivity: Why They Matter*, Centre for Economic Performance LSE and McKinsey.

Brinkley, I. (2007), *Trading in Knowledge and Ideas*, The Work Foundation, London.

Brinkley, I., Coats, D. and Overell, S. (2007), *Seven out of Ten: Labour under Labour 1997–2007*, Work Foundation, London.

Bronfenbrenner, K. and Luce, S. (2004), *The Changing Nature of Corporate Global Restructuring*, report prepared for the US-China Economic and Security Review Commission.

Brown, A. et al. (2006), *Changing Job Quality in Britain 1998–2004*, Employment Relations Research Series No 70, Department of Trade and Industry, London.

Chang, H.-J. (2002), *Kicking Away the Ladder*, Anthem Press, London.

Coats, D. (2006), *Who's Afraid of Labour Market Flexibility?*, The Work Foundation, London.

—— (2007), *The National Minimum Wage: Retrospect and Prospect*, The Work Foundation, London

Cully, M. et al. (1999), *Britain at Work*, Routledge, London.

DTI (2007), *Job Quality in Europe and the UK*, Employment Relations Research Series No 71, Department of Trade and Industry, London.

Esping-Anderson, G. (2005), Inequalities of Incomes and Opportunities, in Giddens, A. and Diamond, P. (eds), *The New Egalitarianism*, Polity Press, Cambridge, UK.

European Commission (2007), *Towards Common Principles of Flexicurity: More and Better Jobs Through Flexibility and Security*, Communication from the Commission to the Council, the European Parliament, the Economic and Social Committee and the Committee of the Regions, June.

Frank, R. (2007), *Richistan*, Piatkus Books, London.

Freeman, R. B. (2005), What Really Ails Europe and America: The Doubling of the Global Workforce, *The Globalist*, 3 June.

Friedman, T. (2005), *The World is Flat*, Allen Lane, New York.

Gallie, D. et al. (2004), Changing Patterns of Task Discretion in Britain, *Work Employment and Society*, 18: 243–66.

Glyn, A. (2000), Unemployment and Inequality, in Jenkinson, T. (ed.), *Macroeconomics*, OUP, Oxford, UK.

Godard, J. (2004), A critical assessment of the high performance paradigm, *British Journal of Industrial Relations*, 42(2): 349–78.

Green, F. (2003), The Demands of Work, in Dickens, R. (ed.), *The Labour Market Under New Labour*, Palgrave, Basingstoke.

Handy, C. (1994), *The Empty Raincoat*, Hutchinson, London.

Hirst, P. and Thompson, G. (1996), *Globalization in Question*, Polity Press, Cambridge, UK.

Hutton, W. (2006), *The Writing on the Wall*, Little Brown, New York.

Jenkins, C. and Sherman, B. (1979), *Collapse of Work*, Eyre Methuen, London.

—— (1981), *Leisure Shock*, Methuen, London.

Jones, F. (2006), *The Effects of Taxes and Benefits on Household Incomes, 2004/05*, Office of National Statistics.

Kersley, B. et al. (2006), *Inside the Workplace*, Routledge, Abingdon, UK.

Layard, R. (2005), *Happiness: Lessons From a New Science*, Allen Lane, New York.

Marmot, M. (2004), *Status Syndrome*, Bloomsbury, London.

OECD (1999), *OECD Employment Outlook*, OECD.

—— (2004), *OECD Employment Outlook*, OECD.

—— (2005), *OECD Employment Outlook*, OECD.

—— (2007), *OECD Employment Outlook*, OECD.

Palley, T. (2005), Trade Employment and Outsourcing: Some Observations on US–China Economic Relations, in Auer et al. (eds), *Offshoring and the Internationalisation of Employment*, ILO.

Pfeffer, J. (1998), Six Dangerous Myths About Pay, *Harvard Business Review*, May–June: 109–19.

Pfeffer, J. and Sutton, R. (2006), *Hard Facts, Dangerous Half-truths and Total Nonsense*, Harvard Business School Press, Cambridge, MA.

Putnam, R. (2000), *Bowling Alone*, Touchstone, New York.

Rifkin, J. (1996), *The End of Work*, Warner Books, Clayton, Australia.

Schumpeter, J. (1943), *Capitalism Socialism and Democracy*, Unwin edition 1987.

Sen, A. (1999), *Development as Freedom*, Random House, New York.

Sennett, R. (1998), *The Corrosion of Character: Personal Consequences of Work in the New Capitalism*, WW Norton and Co., London.

—— (2006), *The Culture of the New Capitalism*, Yale University Press, New Haven, CT.

Sisson, K. *et al.* (1997), *New Forms of Work Organisation: Can Europe Realise its Potential?*, European Foundation for the Improvement of Living and Working Conditions.

Stiglitz, J. (2006), *Making Globalisation Work*, Allen Lane, New York.

Taylor, R. (2002), *Britain's World of Work: Myths and Realities*, Economic and Social Research Council.

Wall, T. and Wood, S. (2005), The Romance of Human Resource Management and Business Performance, and the Case for Big Science, *Human Relations*, 58(4): 429–62.

White, M. and Hill, S. (2004), *Managing to Change*, Palgrave, Basingstoke.

Wood, S. and Fenton-O'Creevy, M. (2005), Direct Involvement, Representation and Employee Voice in UK Multinationals in Europe, *European Journal of Industrial Relations*, 11(1): 27–50.

Wolf, M. (2004), *Why Globalisation Works*, Yale University Press, New Haven, CT.

—— (2007), Unfettered Finance is Fast Reshaping the Global Economy, *Financial Times*, 18 June.

Part 4

The strategic role of HR

This part of the volume starts to look directly at the strategic role of HR. It tackles the big themes of knowledge, the practice of strategic HR and the management of change.

'Strategic HRM' and the 'knowledge-based theory of the firm' have been two of the most prominent ideas in recent analyses of management discourse. While there are many actual and potential links between these two they have, in the main, remained as separate fields of theory and practice. The first chapter in this part examines the interplay between knowledge and strategic HR. In particular, John Storey seeks to examine the nature of the underlying knowledge upon which practitioners of strategic HR draw. This is an unusual way to address the question of the management of knowledge.

It is generally agreed that the advanced economies have entered an era when human capital and the knowledge which underpins it has become especially critical. It is arguably the key vital resource which can help explain the differences between firm success and failure. This realization has led to a huge focus on intellectual capital and the place of knowledge. The 'management of knowledge' has become a virtual industry. However, Storey's chapter cautions against excessive zeal. It seeks to rebalance the assessment. Knowledge is not always positive and advantageous. The knowledge which managers and others bring to their work may also carry negative consequences. It can blind them to alternative ways of thinking and channel their modes of analysis and their solutions down all too familiar channels. HR strategy should be developed with a cognizance of these potential problems. Hence, this chapter shows how HR strategy can be formulated and delivered using four complementary pathways. Each of these pathways brings into play and leverages different types of knowledge. By balancing out these different types and sources of knowledge, managers will have a greater chance of reaching more mature and considered conclusions.

In Chapter 9, Anthony Rucci makes a robust case for a significant shift in thinking by HR practitioners. The objective, he argues, should not be to make HR more strategic but rather for HR specialists to focus on making organizations more effective. The way this can be done, he suggests, is to focus on the core purpose of HR which should be to 'build organizational capabilities that help achieve sustained value creation, by focusing the commitment of people's energy, effort and ideas on a common vision'. This means working on four key themes: *value creation*; *focus and vision*; *commitment*; and *ideas*. HR specialists should aim to be not business

123

partners but business people. They should aim to help get people focused on the vision and core purpose, and promote commitment so that people feel responsible for the whole operation and seek to contribute creatively to it.

In order to act strategically in the way recommended by Tony Rucci there would be a need for HR to engage more widely and more fully in managing organizational change. This in itself is likely to be a challenge. As David Buchanan shows in Chapter 10, the HR function is often under-represented in shaping and influencing the change process in most organizations. It 'punches below its weight' in this regard. In order to be more effective players in the strategic change game, human resource practitioners need to be able to compete more effectively with change agents in other management functions. This in turn means that human resource professionals must be able and willing to use more sophisticated political skills. In this final chapter of this part of the book, Buchanan makes a systematic analysis of the components of the practice of political skills. These include an array of tactics, including image building, alliance formation, networking, compromise, issue selling and so on.

Without the effective deployment of these skills the HR function is in danger of remaining on the periphery of strategic organizational change. Human resource professionals need to work with the political dimensions of change agency and to play a more sophisticated game. While the term 'manipulation' is often used in a negative sense, suggesting devious, disreputable behaviour, many commentators argue that managers who are not prepared to use such methods are likely to find that their good ideas do not attract attention, and are not pursued, while competing initiatives find support and resources. The human resource professional, as is the case for any other change agent, is unlikely to succeed without the political skills required to sell, initiate, drive, and deliver strategic organizational change. Even that combination may not be enough. The acquisition of political skill merely gives the function a ticket to the game. Also significant is the manner and context in which such skills are deployed, and the nature and efficacy of the tactics used by the other players.

8

The knowledge underpinning HR strategy

John Storey

Introduction

'Strategic HRM' and the 'knowledge-based theory of the firm' have been two of the most prominent ideas and debates in recent management discourse. While there are many actual and potential links between these two domains they have, in the main, remained as separate fields of theory and practice. The purpose of this chapter is to explore the links between them.

This exploration is worthwhile because while a great deal of attention has been paid to *types* of HR strategies (such as commitment or control oriented), to the *processes* of strategy construction (such as incremental or ab initio), to the various frameworks and indeed to the capacity of HR directors through their position on the Board to shape strategy, much less attention has been paid to a number of underlying, more fundamental questions. These underlying questions concern the rationales, principles, orientations and knowledge out of which strategic choices may derive.

Approaches to the practice of human resource management can be many and varied. Organizations may proceed with a highly pragmatic and ad hoc set of practices and policies or they may seek to act in a more strategic way. The proportion of firms and other employing organizations acting in one or other of these ways is an empirical question amenable to answer through survey or other research work. This is not the question we seek to answer here. Rather, there is a rather more important prior question: this concerns the *kinds of knowledge* upon which managers draw when formulating HR strategy. In other words our purpose here is to 'get behind' the more familiar discussions in order to explore the bedrock out of which HR strategy emerges. The lengthy discussions about best practice versus best fit, necessary and useful as they are, tend to suggest a strongly analytical basis to management action. And yet we know that in reality managerial practice is also impelled by other forces including beliefs, assumptions, emotions and a string of non-rational impulses. Even when using the services of external consultants, top management teams tend to select those consultancies which are within the existing comfort zone and which from the outset seem to 'make sense' – i.e. that operate within an existing frame of sense-making and understanding.

A great deal of research in knowledge management has emphasised both the tacit as well as the explicit dimension of knowledge (Nonaka 1994; Nonaka and Takeuchi 1995; Polanyi 1966).

While the explicit dimension is codified the tacit dimension includes hunches and intuitions. It is rooted in experience and context. Thus, managerial knowledge and action involves the way managers establish patterns, identify what are the key issues and features and create connections between identified elements. Practice typically involves situated knowing; thus strategic choice in HR is likely to be influenced by a range of personal, institutional, social and political factors.

Illustration

TD is an HR Director of a major financial institution in London. She is a graduate in her mid-forties, and is professionally qualified in HR. She has progressed through the ranks in this firm over the past 15 years and has patiently developed what she regards as an integrated approach to HR policy. Selection and development procedures are very systematic. There is a strong emphasis on employee engagement; employee attitude surveys are conducted four times a year and the resulting data are used in a serious and applied manner in order to help steer course corrections in each department. Morale scores according to these surveys are high and staff are also committed to the organization to a level which exceeds the industry norm. During TD's time with the firm it has grown year on year and it is judged as a very successful organization. A key theme of TD's approach was to develop a narrative based on the nurturing and management of the best 'talent'.

DS is a new Managing Director with this firm. He is in his early fifties and has been with this firm just 12 months having previously enjoyed a successful career in a range of companies. In December, he calls TD to a meeting to discuss the HR implications of the new business strategy which includes substantial outsourcing of routine work to a country in the Far East. Also present at the meeting is the Finance Director and the Operations Director. DS explains the outline plan and asks TD to work on a more detailed set of proposals ready for a Board Meeting in late March. TD is initially surprised by the request and is shocked by the implications for the London-based staff. She spends the next month reviewing the possibilities and the implications for the HR strategy as a whole. In mid-February, TD seeks a meeting with the Managing Director but is redirected to the Director of Finance. By the end of that month, a draft paper is circulated by the MD which outlines the new strategy and indicates the number of posts to be reallocated. TD finds herself alone in expressing significant reservations about the plan in a meeting in early March where the Managing Director, the Finance Director, the Operations Director and newly appointed Director of Strategy are all present. TD decides to write a paper with full supporting data showing the rationale for the current HR strategy. This is circulated to all executive directors and is discussed at a pre-Board executive directors' meeting on 20 March. At this meeting the competing conceptions of HR strategy are debated. Very different understandings about people management are revealed. The debate occurs at a more fundamental level than has ever before been attempted. Participants state what they know about the labour market, the competitive edge of the firm, and the elements of the strategy which matter most. At the end of the meeting these competing understandings and the varying 'knowing' about the fundamentals of the business and the place of HR strategy within it, remain unresolved. TD leaves HQ that evening bewildered and resentful. The next morning she tenders her resignation.

This episode reveals some of the key linkages between knowledge and HR strategy. The HR director in this case had spent considerable time making explicit the nature of the HR strategy and the logic and values which underpinned it. She had indeed become the main exponent of the values statement which was supposedly central to the organization's purpose. The quarterly and annual reports provided ample data to underpin the strategy. It appeared plain to the HR Director – and to many others – that the strategy was firmly accepted and well understood. There had been no clear challenge to it before. Yet, from the moment of that fateful meeting with the Managing Director in December, the solid ground of 'knowing' seemed to become far less stable than had ever been imagined.

Strategic HR and the link with knowledge

This case and many others like it raise fundamental questions about the basis of knowledge within HR. Researchers have drawn upon a range of perspectives to help explain the bases of such knowledge. Psychologists emphasize the processes of human cognition while institutional theorists suggest that strategic choices in HR will be influenced by social readings as to which solutions are deemed acceptable and legitimate (DiMaggio and Powell 1983; Greenwood and Hinings 1996).

Strategic choices in the HR domain include decisions about what competences to recruit and develop, decisions about outsourcing and insourcing (Lepak and Snell 1999), organizational design, the shaping of appropriate organizational values and culture, and so on. Each of these depends upon judgement – which in turn is based on perception, and pre-existing frames of reference and knowledge. As Mintzberg observes:

> Strategy formation is judgemental designing, intuitive visioning, and emergent learning; it is about transformation as well as perpetuation; it must involve individual cognition as well as social interaction, cooperative as well as conflictive; it has to include analysing before and programming after as well as negotiating during. . . .
>
> (Mintzberg and Lampel 1999: 27)

In a recent study, I asked corporate directors (including but not exclusively HR directors) in a number of countries how they went about devising their HR strategies. There were, in essence, three broad categories of response. The first type referred to the use of various formal analytical models and approaches – for example, environmental analyses, SWOT and so on. The second type indicated less reliance on formal models and more reliance on an 'evidence-based' approach which suggested that they were driven by systematic data concerning 'what works'. This empiricist approach included, for example, drawing on employee attitude survey data and linking this with performance data of various sub-units and then discerning which approaches elicited which outcomes. Thus, the resulting pattern of responses was perceived as data driven rather than theory driven. The third type of response came from senior managers who seemed to be acting in accord with certain underlying beliefs, intuitions and tacit knowledge.

These three categories of response to how HR strategy was devised can each be regarded as different forms of knowledge. They are shown in Figure 8.1.

These three types of knowledge used by these HR directors merit further exploration.

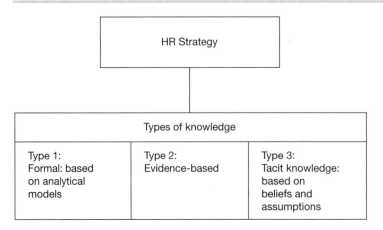

Figure 8.1 Types of knowledge underpinning HR strategy

Type 1: Formal knowledge: based on analytical models

Many HR directors remain uncertain about how to respond to the expectation that they should be able to produce and deliver a HR strategy for their organization. Often, in consequence, they produce a document based on an agglomeration of the current set of policies, practices and initiatives. Alternatively or additionally, they may undertake some environmental scanning and commence their strategic review with some statistical profiles of demographic trends and similar economic, social and legal reviews. The existing suite of policies may then be appended to that analysis as, with some suitable statement of caveats, it is not normally too difficult to justify the continuance of current policy if it is stated in a sufficiently vague and aspirational manner – as these documents often tend to be.

There are also cases where HR directors draw upon the kind of formal analytical frameworks and approaches as sold by leading management consultancies.

The HR directors in the survey mentioned a wide range of external consultants which they had used. But for illustrative purposes it may be helpful to take one example of a cited company. One of the largest global HR consultancies is Mercer. It offers a perspective which locates HR investments alongside potential investment options in outsourcing and offshoring. As their corporate marketing states:

> Organizations around the world, of all sizes, are recognizing the payback and competitive advantage of developing the right human capital and related outsourcing and investment strategies. Helping clients get this right is Mercer's passion. Our core strengths in consulting, outsourcing and investments, from advice to solutions, put Mercer in a unique position to help.
>
> (http://www.mercer.com)

Their claimed unique and innovative approach is based on "*proprietary tools* to objectively support our recommendations for shareholder-sensitive outcomes" and the use of "business economics and strategy to determine implications for human capital strategies and organizational alignment".

Type 2: Evidence-based knowledge informing HR strategy

The second type of response differed substantially from the first. Instead of references to a framework or theory-led approach, directors in this category talked about the ways in which they relied primarily upon data and evidence in order to devise their policies and interventions.

It could reasonably be argued that this category of response from directors, albeit emphasizing data, is not entirely theory-free. For example, one of its classic contemporary manifestations is the approach to people management which relies heavily on a series of regular attitude surveys and performance monitoring exercises. Lloyds/TSB bank in the UK currently surveys some of its units four times a year and the HR function uses the resulting massive dataset to guide line managers in their responses.

In some cases this approach could be said to derive from an underlying theory of the importance of 'employee engagement' at the outset. None the less, in other regards, many practitioners of this approach do seem heavily wedded to a data-led response to devising HR policies and practices. These empiricists profess to proceed largely on the basis of 'what works'.

An example of this approach has been the notion of the employee-service-profit chain as described most famously in the work of Heskett, Sasser and Schlesinger (1997). They write:

> we sought to understand why some service organizations succeed year-in and year-out. In addition to collecting lore and listening to countless stories emanating from outstanding service organizations, we did a risky and audacious thing. We started to collect data. Our work has grown a data base comprising inputs from several dozen well-known service organizations operating in a number of different competitive environments. In addition to seeking facts, we developed measurements and began looking for relationships in our data that could shed light on ways of achieving service excellence and organizational success.

Rucci et al. (1998) describe how the American retail chain Sears used the employee-service-profit chain approach to turn around a loss-making situation. The focus was on detailed information about employee attitudes and behaviours and the way this affected customer service and the customer experience. The resulting econometric model included an elaborate set of 'total performance indicators'. The key to the approach is measurement. The measures of employee and customer satisfaction are described as "an ongoing process of data collection, analysis, modelling and experimentation" (Rucci et al. 1998: 84).

As noted, the employee-customer-profit chain approach started with an empirical approach but it has matured into a more conventional theory-driven mode. In part, the origin can be traced to a tacit-knowledge-based approach. It is to a consideration of this form of HR knowledge that we can now turn.

Type 3: Tacit knowledge, beliefs and assumptions

Tacit knowledge, as revealed in the knowledge management literature, is hugely important. In most of that literature it is treated and regarded as inherently positive and valuable; the only problem is supposedly how to convert it into explicit knowledge so that it can be shared and made more easily accessible.

However, from a strategic HR perspective we need to note its potential negative aspects. Underlying sets of assumptions, beliefs and propositions become embedded through application and success. This sort of knowledge also tends to accrue a presumed basis in morality. Regimes of truth can have negative or limiting consequences, not only in their own right (knowledge can be erroneous, incomplete or flawed), but also because what is known can limit what is learned, what is held to be 'right' both practically and morally can limit the identification, discussion or assessment of new strategic options or new organizational designs. The knowledge held collectively by the top team can impact on the team's ability to discuss and agree new directions and structures. This phenomenon is illustrated in the international finance case discussed above.

Managers' shared knowledge of the external world (markets, competition and industrial structure) is influenced by entrenched shared organizationally generated and disseminated schemas (Calori et al. 1992; Weick 1979). These pieces of research support the conclusion that managers learn to see and know the world in terms of simplified and established frameworks. These serve to minimize data-processing time and are necessary. But these routines may also become counter-productive under new circumstances (Lant 2002; Stubbart and Ramaprasad 1988). And as Van de Ven (1986: 596) observes, "the older, larger, and more successful organizations become, the more likely they are to have a large repertoire of structures and systems which discourage innovation while encouraging tinkering".

Michael Porter has long argued that cost/price strategies are inherently limited not only because of global competition but because competitive advantage based on operational effectiveness is inherently short term, because it can be replicated and thus negated by competitive convergence. Porter recognizes that strategies based on improving operational efficiencies are not only limited and ultimately insufficient, they are also counter-productive – "a series of races down identical paths that no one can win" (Porter and Ketels 2003: 13). The way out of the war of attrition of competition based on increased (but non-sustainable) operational effectiveness is to compete on a completely different basis – strategic differentiation. Firms, he argues, can only compete successfully and sustainably when they compete not on being like competitors but by being *different* – "deliberately choosing a different set of activities to deliver a unique mix of value" (Porter and Ketels 2003: 13).

Why is this insight – about the limits and the self destructive nature of competing on the basis of operational efficiency and the performance advantages of competing on the basis of the identification and achievement of a distinct market position supported by a distinct and different set of organizational activities – not more prevalent? Why can he see these benefits but business leaders – to whom these issues of the bases of organizational performance matter a great deal more than they do to Michael Porter – apparently not see them? Why do business leaders continue to behave in a way that is damaging to their businesses by failing to recognise the need for offering value to customers through differentiation strategies? Indeed why do they seem to have trouble in recognising the need to rethink what they are doing and develop new ways of competing or the need to escape from historic but now declining success recipes? His answer – and our answer – lies in the nature and impact of the knowledge that exists at senior levels of organizations and which underpins how – or when or if – executives think and make decisions on strategic issues and choices.

Porter notes that writers on organizations (like government spokespersons and consultants) tend to stress the threats to organizational strategies that arise outside the organization from competitors and technological change. This is also true of the authorities whose views on the implications of the global knowledge economy were discussed earlier. But as this chapter has argued, the real threat is *internal* – in the various beliefs, assumptions and convictions held by senior managers which limit how they think about strategy and how they frame and define and assess strategic options. Porter notes that senior managers are prone to "misguided views of competition", are "confused about the necessity of making choices", "and un-nerved by forecasts of hyper-competition", and that what is required is a "clear intellectual framework to guide strategy" (2002: 28–9).

But how do we explain these weaknesses and vulnerabilities? Why is a 'clear intellectual framework to guide strategy' so often missing or incomplete? Why are the threats and opportunities of the knowledge economy ignored by so many business leaders? The answer proposed by this chapter is that executives' ability to develop new strategies and new organizational forms is not because of executive ignorance but because of particular types of executive knowledge. Executives' understanding and definition of the world facing their organization and of the options available to the organization are shaped by the cognitive and normative tools they use – shared and strongly held generalizations, judgement and rules. Furthermore, the significance of these cognitive tools is that they often remain implicit. They remain therefore unchallenged. Executive work therefore focuses on *using* the shared knowledge but not on discussing and assessing it and its merits. In Argyris and Schon's (1978) terms, executives operate at model 1 level – competently using the available rules and assumptions, correcting things when they are going wrong – but are less likely to work at model 2 – surfacing examining and challenging the assumptions underlying their decisions. Sometimes this is because these assumptions are tacit and taken-for-granted, other times because the status of these assumptions, hallowed by time and use, make it, according to shared corporate values, awkward or difficult to challenge them.

Reflections on the three types of knowledge

Having described the three types of knowledge underpinning HR strategy, it is now necessary to discuss the theoretical and the practical implications.

Theoretical implications

What senior managers know can impact negatively – as well as positively – on the performance of the firm. Knowledge affects orientations as well as ability to direct and modify the organization. Aspects of existing organizational knowledge can create situations where there develops "a satisfaction with the status quo, and a general lack of incentive to abandon a certain present (which is profitable) for an uncertain future" (Markides 2002: 246). There are different levels to the sourcing of knowledge – from societal to individual. The role of fads and fashions has been discussed and analysed elsewhere (Abrahamson 1991). Above the organizational level there are societal and indeed even near-global trends in fads and fashions which impel certain ideas and kinds of knowledge into privileged status. The HRM narrative itself could be seen as carried by just such a tide in the 1980s and beyond. New interpretations of the nature of competition and new definitions of the place of people in adding value and in competing became known. The trends which develop, for example, towards downsizing during certain periods, to outsourcing and offshoring at other periods and to talent management, etc. are evident.

Current knowledge suggests that fundamental changes are occurring in the global economy. One consequence is that low-cost strategies are or will be increasingly untenable for firms in the advanced economies for they will be unable to compete on cost. Therefore organizational success or even survival is – or soon will be – dependent on a move away from cost-centred strategies and business models towards strategies based on value-adding differentiation (quality, delivery, innovation) supported by knowledge-based organizational forms and skilled employees. Knowledge thus becomes critical to, and synonymous with, successful performance. The current emphasis on knowledge represents a fundamental step change in the development of the modern business and the emergence of the knowledge economy not only represents a major shift in the nature of consumer demand but also a change in the basis on which businesses compete – and succeed or fail.

In the knowledge economy, firms must be capable of moving through a series of stages, each of which is essential to success, as they move from environmental analysis to strategy and finally to organizational capability. They must be able to recognize the shift in the nature and basis of competition and in consumer expectations; must be capable of developing strategies and business models whereby they can compete in the new competitive landscape; and finally they must translate these strategies into very new forms of organization with new structural forms, new ways of relating to suppliers and customers and new and enhanced capacities to attract, retain and develop employees with new and greater quantities of knowledge and expertise. In a 'knowledge-intensive environment' it is argued that firms must understand and enhance their knowledge assets and capabilities and deploy them in the development and achievement of strategies which understand and comply with the new bases of competition – using organizational knowledge to develop products, processes or delivery channels which meet and exceed customers' (ever-changing) expectations.

Theoretically, the function of the executive is to make decisions about key issues of strategy and organizational capability. In particular, it has been argued that the ability of executives to be reflexive about and be capable of moving beyond existing competences and established knowledge is critical. Many analysts within the knowledge management and strategy literatures have argued this point. Its expression by Teece et al. (2002: 183) is typical:

> The global competitive battles . . . have demonstrated the need for an expanded paradigm to understand how competitive advantage is achieved. . . . Winners in the global market-place have been firms that can demonstrate timely responsiveness and rapid and flexible product innovation, coupled with the management capability to effectively co-ordinate and redeploy internal and external competences . . . we emphasise the key role of strategic management in appropriately adapting, integrating, and reconfiguring internal and external organizational skills, resources, and functional competences to match the requirements of a changing environment.

However, there is substantial evidence that many organizations have not in fact formulated HR strategies. Even large organizations with substantial HR departments often struggle to produce a full-blown HR strategy and struggle equally to explain what their strategy is. HR departments seem able to operate quite happily without formal strategies. This leaning towards the *ad hoc* has triggered much discussion among HR academics. It has also provided ample opportunity for management consultancy firms to step in with ready-made, more systematic approaches.

Executive judgements on key organizational issues are based on their knowledge of, and beliefs about, what strategies are available, which are appropriate for the organization, which strategies are best for different environmental conditions, or are best suited to different strategies. This knowledge, as we have seen above, is often tacit rather than explicit. As Nonaka and Takeuchi (1995: 310) observe, it often consists of "schemata, mental models, beliefs and perceptions so ingrained that we take them for granted. The cognitive dimension of tacit knowledge reflects our image of reality (what is) and our vision for the future (what ought to be)."

None the less, whether found in tacit or explicit form, the nature and quality of the assumptions and knowledge which underpin and inform strategic thinking are critical to the quality of organizational strategy and capability. Business strategies are developed in response to managers' perceptions of the business environment and the business, as seen through lenses which are coloured by their beliefs and political interests (Fahey and Narayanan 1989). Senior managers' knowledge, and understanding of, and response to, identified external or internal pressures is a consequence of what managers know and how they think. As noted already, what managers know and think can become deeply embedded in ways which can obstruct change. Managers tend to become committed to established routines. As Valentin (2002: 41) observes:

> Some businesses fail not because resources or systems needed to cope effectively with the real external environment cannot be acquired or implemented economically and expeditiously but because various behavioural factors impair strategic problem-sensing or effective strategy development and implementation.

In other words, past successes and ideological rigidities can foster dysfunctional inertia and mindsets.

Knowledge touchstones may be found at various levels – national, industry sector, organizational and functional. For example, Spender (1989) explored 'industry recipes'. He found that managers "turn to a body judgement which is shared by those socialised into the industry" (1989: 214). At the organizational level, Bettis and Prahalad (Bettis and Prahalad 1995; Prahaland and Bettis 1986) emphasize the pervasive influence of 'dominant logic' within certain organizations. This is the term they use to describe the way managers in an organization often collectively conceptualize the business and the basis on which they make critical resource allocation decisions. Similarly, Ransom et al. point to the important role in organizational strategic decision making of underlying 'interpretative schemes' which underpin and are embodied in organizational strategies and systems (Ransom et al. 1980). These and various other analysts point to the way logics and 'tools of rationality' orient behaviour towards the external world and influence how it is classified, defined and understood. The implication is that such knowledge does not simply reflect that same external world but has some independent existence.

Drawing upon such knowledge, top-level managers are often expected to make strategic decisions in the face of scant information and considerable uncertainty. They make judgements which in effect involve making 'sense' of the world and from this make further judgements about how best to achieve organizational purposes. By implication, knowledge (ways of understanding) can be detrimental to achieving optimal organizational performance.

Practical implications

Having an awareness of the different modes of knowledge which HR directors use is one thing but what practical implications can flow from such an awareness? Work with organizations in both the public and private sectors leads me to suggest that, from a practical point of view, it is possible and indeed usually beneficial for HR directors to craft their strategy in multiple ways and not to rely too heavily on just one approach or indeed one mode of knowledge. While it is usually easier to form some consensus through the use of one approach – whether that be a values-based approach, scenario planning, SWOT analysis or a data-led approach – reliance on just one of these tends to make the resulting strategic HR approach more vulnerable. In order to help avoid the kind of isolation and exposure to changing logics which was illustrated in the international finance case vignette at the start of this chapter, managers would be well advised to broaden their knowledge base.

Top management teams which are aware of the above tendencies have the option to open up their horizons of strategic thinking by using multiple methods. Instead of relying entirely on familiar routines they can challenge, compare, and in effect triangulate their approaches by working through a series of alternative approaches.

I suggest that this can be done through the use of *simultaneous pathways*. Each can be used to check and qualify or support the other. Four pathways to knowledge building for the purposes of constructing a HR are suggested. These are shown in Figure 8.2.

An organization's formal approach to HR strategy can usually be constituted by an amalgam of these four approaches. The first pathway, 'good practices', means the inclusion of policies and practices which at the very least accord with current law and codes of practice and which preferably exceed these. This approach can normally be justified on the grounds that social legitimacy is ensured in this way and further that the organization may avoid the unnecessary expense of high labour turnover or resentment deriving from standards which are out of line with the prevailing norms. Through this pathway the organization may reap the benefits of reputation value and provide the basis for smooth as possible routines.

The 'best-fit pathway' may, at the extreme, compete with the first and it has to be accepted that conflicts can occur between these two. However, I have found that, in most circumstances, the two are reconcilable – the good practices approach can be used as the foundation, and then each organization needs to explore which special factors (of skill levels, time demands, travel requirements, market conditions and so on) require which adjustments to be made so that alignment with organization mission can be achieved.

The third pathway, response to trends, is again normally a useful one to follow. This is the one which helps to ensure that due note is taken of changes which may threaten business as usual.

The fourth pathway, the resource-based approach, means taking advantage of the insights from the resource-based view of the firm perspective. While pathways 2 and 3 tend to emphasize responsiveness to external changes it is also normally wise to approach the crafting of strategy by paying regard to internal factors – most especially internal capabilities. Of course there will often be some tension between these two perspectives – the internal and the external – but revealing the nature and depth of that tension is indeed one of the purposes of these multiple analyses.

The self-conscious use of such a variety of approaches can help management teams escape at least to some degree the tyranny of their interpretive frames. Systematic work of this kind is a practical expression of the 'reflective practitioner' (Schon 1983) in action. This multiple-component approach can also help to limit and challenge embedded ways of thinking of either

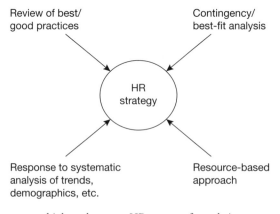

Figure 8.2 Complementary multiple pathways to HR strategy formulation

dominant individuals or whole teams. The discipline helps surmount the tramlines of learned responses noted by Schneider (1997) whereby teams repeat patterns of behaviour learned over time in the context of a given industry and so on.

When are teams willing or inclined to work in this pluralistic mode? The answer to this question is that this is rare: it tends to occur only when the pre-existing model has gone awry. But by that time it may be too late. The ideal time to be cognizant of the unreliability of much 'existing knowledge' and the often flawed yet deeply embedded inclination towards existing schemas and formulations is when the business is stable and performing. At that point the formula may already have reached its zenith and be about to be a hindrance. Likewise, this is also the time to seek to deploy the raft of multiple approaches to strategy formulation described above. This is advisable for top teams as a whole in order to monitor the ongoing relevance of their strategic models and strategic thinking. But, it is also advisable for HR directors in order to monitor the degree of commitment to the espoused strategy. TD's failure to do this in her financial instruction left her isolated and exposed, with fateful consequences.

Conclusions

As noted at the outset to this chapter, strategic HRM and the knowledge-based theory of the firm have been two of the most prominent ideas and debates in recent years. There are many interconnecting links between the two. This can be seen most clearly in relation to the resource-based view of the firm. Human capital is one of the key vital resources which can help explain the differences between firm success and failure. For a decade or so now the importance of knowledge – and indeed of ever-changing knowledge – has been a central theme and message. As large industrial behemoths struggled and collapsed when faced with new, smaller, but more vibrant competitors, so the idea of knowledge as the crucial explanatory factor grew in prominence. But, as we have seen in this chapter, the enthusiasm for knowledge at times was pursued with uncritical zeal. This chapter has sought to rebalance the assessment. Knowledge is not always positive and advantageous. The knowledge which managers bring to their work may also carry negative consequences. It can blind them to alternative ways of thinking and channel their modes of analysis and their solutions down all too familiar channels. Within the HR field, we have shown that HR strategy can be developed with a cognizance of these potential problems. Hence, the focus of this chapter has been to show the ways in which HR strategy can be formulated and delivered using multiple pathways. Each of these pathways brings into play and leverages different types of knowledge. By balancing out these different types and sources of knowledge managers will have a greater chance of reaching more mature and considered conclusions.

Acknowledgement

I am pleased to acknowledge the invaluable contribution of my colleague Graeme Salaman to much of the thinking underpinning this chapter.

References

Abrahamson, E. (1991). "Managerial fads and fashions: the diffusion and rejection of innovations." *Academy of Management Review* 16(3): 586–612.

Argyris, C. and Schon, D. (1978). *Organisational learning: A theory of action perspective*. Reading, MA: Addison Wesley.

Bettis, R. A. and Prahalad, C. K. (1995). "The dominant logic: retrospective and extension." *Strategic Management Journal* 16: 5–14.

Calori, R., Johnson, G. and Sarnin, A. (1992). "French and British top managers' understanding of the structures and dynamics of their industries: a cognitive analysis." *British Journal of Management* 3(2): 61–78.

DiMaggio, P. W. and Powell, W. (1983). "The iron cage revisited: institutional isomorphism and collective rationality in organizational fields." *American Sociological Review* 48: 147–160.

Fahey, I., and Narayanan, V.K. (1989). "Linking changes in revealed causal maps and environmental change: an empirical study." *Journal Of Management Studies* 26(4): 361–378.

Greenwood, R. and Hinings, C. R. (1996). "Understanding radical organizational change: bringing together the old and the new institutionalism." *Academy of Management Review* 21(4): 1022–1054.

Heskett, J. L., Sasser, E. and Schlesinger, L. A. (1997). *The Service Profit Chain*. New York: Free Press.

Lepak, D. P. and Snell, S. A. (1999). "The human resource architecture: toward a theory of human capital allocation and development." *Academy of Management Review* 24: 31–48.

Lepak, D. P. and Snell, S.A. (2002). "Examining the human resource architecture: the relationships among human capital, employment, and human resource configurations." *Journal of Management* 28: 517–543.

Markides, C. (2002). "Strategic innovation in established companies." In M. Mazzucato (ed.), *Strategy for Business*. London: Sage.

Mintzberg, H. and Lampel, J. (1999). "Reflecting on the strategy process." *Sloan Management Review*, spring: 21–30.

Nonaka, I. (1994). "A dynamic theory of organizational knowledge creation." *Organization Science* 5(1): 14–36.

Nonaka, I. and Takeuchi, H. (1995). *The Knowledge-creating Company: How Japanese Companies Create the Dynamics of Innovation*. Oxford: Oxford University Press.

Polanyi, M. (1966). *The Tacit Dimension*. New York: Doubleday.

Porter, M. and Ketels, C. (2003). *UK Competitiveness: Moving to the Next Stage*. London: DTI/ESRC.

Prahalad, C. K. and Bettis, R. A. (1986). "The dominant logic: a new linkage between diversity and performance." *Strategic Management Journal* 7: 485–501.

Ranson, S., Hinings, C. R. and Greenwood, R. (1980). "The structuring of organizational structures." *Administrative Science Quarterly* 25: 1–7.

Rucci, A. J., Kirn, S. P. and Quinn, R. T. (1998). "The employee-customer-profit chain at Sears." *Harvard Business Review*, January–February: 82–97.

Schneider, S. C. (1997). "Interpretations in organizations: sensemaking and strategy." *European Journal of Work and Organizational Psychology* 6(1): 93–102.

Schon, D. A. (1983). *The Reflective Practitioners: How Professionals Think in Action*. London: Basic Books.

Spender, J. C. (1989). *Industry Recipes: The Nature and Source of Managerial Judgements*. Cambridge, MA: Blackwell.

Teece, D. J., Pisano, G. and Shuen, A. (2002). "Dynamics capabilities and strategic management." In M. Mazzucato (ed.), *Strategy in Business*. London: Sage.

Valentin, E. K. (2002). "Anatomy of a fatal business strategy." In J. G. Salaman (ed.), *Decision Making for Business*. London: Sage.

Van de Ven, A. (1986). "Central problems in the management of innovation." *Management Science* 32: 591–607.

Weick, K. (1979). "Cognitive processes in organizations." In B. M. Staw (ed.), *Research in Organizational Behavior* (pp. 41–74). Greenwich: JAI Press.

9

The pursuit of HR's core purpose

The practical doing of strategic HRM

Anthony J. Rucci

HR management is about managing people. 'Strategic' HR management is about making people and organizations successful. It should be noted that these are two very different things.

The focus of this chapter will not be on making HR more strategic, but rather on making organizations more effective. I would suggest that no matter how inelegant or unsophisticated the strategic framework of the HR strategy in an organization may look or sound, any HR professional or function that helps align human and intellectual capital behind the successful achievement of an organization's goals is, by definition, 'strategic'. Over the past twenty years or so, the HR profession has been littered with conferences on 'becoming a strategic partner'. So much so, that in the search for the holy grail of a good HR strategy, the profession may actually have lost its focus on *why we exist*.

So, for the duration of this chapter, let me ask you to suspend disbelief. Let us forget about making the HR profession strategic. In doing so, we may find that our definition of 'strategic HR' has been misplaced and misguided for some time. The entire premise of this treatment is that it's *not* about making HR strategic, it's about making organizations strategically successful.

HR's core purpose

In 1996, Collins and Porras published a now classic article in the *Harvard Business Review* entitled "Building your company's vision". In particular, Collins and Porras describe an organization's 'core ideology', a combination of two factors which those authors take great pains to define operationally. They encourage organizations to be very deliberate about *discovering* these two factors. The two factors of core ideology are: core values and core purpose. It may surprise you to learn that we are going to skip over the core values discussion here in search of the strategic role of HR. We will do this not because core values are not vitally important, but because core purpose is so fundamentally related to strategy.

Collins and Porras describe core purpose as an organization's "reason for being". It goes beyond strategy, beyond goals and beyond business objectives. It gets to the deeper meaning for an organization's existence. A core purpose "reflects people's idealistic motivations for doing the company's work" (p. 68). Does Disney 'operate theme parks', or do they exist to make people happy? Does Fannie Mae 'grant mortgage loans', or do they democratize home ownership? The difference in those two examples illustrates the important affective and inspirational value of a core purpose.

So, what if we were presumptuous enough to attempt to articulate a core purpose statement for the entire HR profession around the world? And not just for HR in for-profit companies, but any variety of organizations . . . universities, philanthropies, governments, publicly traded companies, religions, military agencies, sports franchises and charities? What might that core purpose statement look like? *Why does HR exist?* Based on practicing, studying and observing for over thirty years, my admittedly subjective attempt at a statement of core purpose for the HR profession would look something like this: "To build organizational capabilities that help achieve sustained *value creation*, by *focusing* the *commitment* of people's energy, effort and *ideas* on a common *vision*."

There are four key themes evident in the italicized words in the above core purpose statement for HR. Each of the four themes – 1. *value creation*, 2. *focus and vision*, 3. *commitment* and 4. *ideas* – has profound implications for the practice of HR as a profession, and in judging when HR is strategic, and when it's not. These themes will create the architecture for the discussion and practical considerations treated here. We will come back at the very end of this discussion to focus on HR itself.

Value creation

This is *not* a financial reference. Any organization exists to create value, whether it be a for-profit, charitable, educational, military or religious organization. In fact, organizations *must* create value, for someone – customers, shareholders, employees, members, society – or they will cease to exist, period. Religions can create value spiritually for their members by enabling them to find meaning and order in their lives, and spiritual peace of mind. If a religious entity doesn't do that, it will cease to exist. Military and police organizations create value by protecting the domestic security of their citizens. If they fail to do that they will cease to exist. And for-profit companies create value by producing goods and services that consumers will purchase on financial terms that generate acceptable returns on invested capital for the owners of the firm. If a for-profit company fails to do that, it will cease to exist, because investors will not continue to channel capital into that entity.

Historically, the very term 'value creation' has been used to describe economic benefit generated, but in the proposed core purpose statement for the HR profession it is not meant to connote only economic value creation. In fact, we will come back to this topic later and argue that successful organizations define value creation much more broadly than economics in order to achieve sustained high performance.

Focus and vision

Focus is all about alignment behind the Vision. Value creation cannot be achieved without human energy, effort and ideas being channeled toward the achievement of a desired outcome. When human creativity and effort are focused on the accomplishment of a common, desirable goal the outcome can be powerful.

The key elements here are: (1) alignment of an organization's intellectual and human capital behind a goal; and (2) a 'clear line of sight' for every employee – from the CEO to the fork-lift operator – as to how each of their jobs contributes to the achievement of the value creation goal. In order for human beings to contribute their energy, effort and ideas to a goal *they must know what the goal is.* This seems like a stunningly simple statement, but it is disheartening how many organizations fail to explain their strategies and goals to their employees, volunteers, soldiers, ministers. In fact, many organizations tend to keep their goals and strategies a secret, for fear of giving away competitive information. It is possible to convey strategic focus without disclosing proprietary information.

Commitment

This is a pivotal concept in our statement of core purpose for the HR profession. It speaks to active *commitment* by people to the purpose and goals of the organization, rather than passive acceptance of what they are told to do. But be careful what you wish for. When you unleash people's energy and ideas and ask them to channel those toward a goal, they can become inspired but non-compliant if they see a better way.

The greatest gift you can be given by a member of your organization is a conversation that starts out with them saying something like this, "You know, I was thinking last night at home about our issue and . . .". In that simple statement you know you enjoy the commitment of that individual. They've given you the two most valuable things they have to contribute to your organization . . . their time and their ideas.

Ideas

We could easily have isolated energy and effort here as well, but the true value creator in any organization today is ideas . . . new, different and energizing ideas. How does an organization foster, encourage, acknowledge and reward ideas? Large organizations by their very size tend to suppress human innovation and creativity. As organizations get older, larger and more complex there's an unseen 'regression to the norm' effect. Unwittingly or not, organizations seek and reward uniformity and conventional behavior and thinking. How can a company's people practices provide a needed counter-balance to this inexorable regression to the norm?

We know that highly successful organizations are those that conceptualize how to *differentiate* themselves from competitors, not just replicate best practices (Porter, 1996). Ironically, much of HR's heritage in the latter half of the twentieth century was designed to create order in organizations as they became bigger and more diffused. In today's complex world of value creation, dependency on uniformity is not only non-strategic, it can actually be a value destroyer.

Those four key themes from our core purpose statement for HR – value creation, focus and vision, commitment and ideas – will frame our discussion of the strategic role of HR in organizations at both a conceptual and practical level. Let's broadly define the strategic implications for HR for each of those four right now, and then through the remainder of this chapter we will consider the practical implications of each one.

Table 9.1 HR's core purpose and strategic implications

Core purpose: To build organizational capabilities that help to achieve sustained value creation, by focusing the commitment of people's energy, effort and ideas on a common vision.
Strategic implications: 1. Define value creation broadly to include intangible factors. 2. Get people focused on the vision and their role in driving achievement of that vision. 3. Promote employee commitment by involving people in the strategy. 4. Generate ideas and innovation by selecting leaders who encourage open, enlightened debate.

Strategic implication #1: Define value creation broadly

HR must help organizations 'mature' into a broader definition of value creation than merely the historic, myopic, economic-viability definition. In other words, HR must help organizations build models that reflect the value generated by intangibles.

Strategic implication #2: Focus people on the organization's vision

Help your organization to frame its purpose, goals and strategies in ways that capture the imagination of people, and which can be readily communicated and understood by people throughout the organization.

Strategic implication #3: Promote commitment

Work on gaining the discretionary energy, effort and ideas of people in your organization by focusing on people management practices that foster commitment.

Strategic implication #4: Select leaders who generate ideas from people

Support and promote leaders, managers and supervisors who are not threatened by ideas that may end up being better than their own.

Strategic implication #1: Define value creation broadly

Traditionally, value creation was a concept viewed as pretty much the exclusive domain of economists and finance professionals: "Does an organization in the for-profit domain generate returns on invested capital greater than their average weighted cost of cumulative capital employed?" If so, then intrinsic economic value has been generated. Historically, in line with this economic definition of value creation, an organization's market value moved in direct ratio to its book value. In fact, going back to the mid-1960s through the late 1980s, the best predictor of an organization's market value was its book value.

Book value, in laymen's terms, is what the 'hard assets' of the firm would be worth if you threw a gigantic, global garage sale. Put all the plants, warehouses, equipment, raw inventories and real estate out at the curb – how much could you get for the hard assets? From the 1960s until 1990, the ratio of market value to book value was roughly 1:1 for the typical publicly traded company. Between 1990 and 1995 that increased to approximately 4:1. In the late 1990s the ratio climbed even spuriously higher in the 'irrationally exuberant' dot-com period. Post the 2000 market decline, the market-to-book ratio of companies recovered to about 3:1 in 2003, and in mid-2008 that ratio once again stands at about 4:1. What does that 4:1 ratio tell us? It means that only 20–25% of the market value of companies today can be explained by their hard assets. Conversely, it means that over 75% of the market value of companies can be attributed to 'soft' assets. Or to use the more common term, 'intangible' assets.

What are intangible assets? It could be a long list, but ultimately intangible value drivers boil down to two broad categories: customer equity as represented in brand reputation and customer service excellence, and intellectual and human capital. Much of the thought leadership on intangible asset valuation referenced here is based on the work of economist Baruch Lev (2001), who has been tracking company market values and performance indicators for nearly forty years, first at Berkeley and later at New York University. Lev and other insightful economists have challenged the 'tangible assets' model of value generation in favor of a more balanced model that also considers the value-added contribution of intangible assets. In fact, Lev has argued that intangible assets can be economically valued, in what he calls the 'Value Chain Scoreboard', and he has provided algorithms for estimating the actual economic value of a company's intangible assets.

So why is Lev's work so relevant here? It illustrates what other non-economists have been researching and hinting at for a number of years. Authors such as Heskett, Sasser and Schlesinger's (1997) work on the 'service-profit chain'; Rucci, Kirn and Quinn's (1998) work on the 'employee-customer-profit chain'; and Ulrich, Zenger and Smallwood's (1999) work on results-based leadership clearly show that 'soft' (read *intangible*) factors like customer service, customer loyalty, leadership effectiveness and employee commitment are significant leading indicators of economic value creation. In fact, some of these authors have developed mathematical algorithms that quantify what a 5% improvement in employee or customer satisfaction will translate into in increased revenues at a later point in time. More recently, Ulrich and Smallwood (2003) have extended the concept of intangibles to organizational capability and leadership effectiveness.

The strategic implication for HR professionals for this work on intangibles is that it is possible to build a model for your organization that quantifies the economic value of intangibles. Measure what matters. Instead of wasting your time and energy on secondary or intermediary factors related to human capital, build models that show how customer satisfaction and employee commitment directly drive economic value growth like revenue, earnings and cash flow. Such models have been built and demonstrated at Sears Roebuck and Co., Cardinal Health and the Ohio State University Medical Center, and many other organizations are working toward such models, including Starbucks, Home Depot and others. Kaplan and Norton's fine work on the Balanced Scorecard (1996) was an important early conceptual model that considered employee, customer and operational factors as leading indicators of value creation. More recently, David Norton and the Balanced Scorecard Collaborative have been working with a number of global organizations on quantifying intangible value creators and building predictive models (Kaplan and Norton 2004a, b).

In order to do this, however, HR executives and professionals need to understand the competitive strategy of their organizations, understand how their organizations create value, be economically literate and then figure out how people management practices map directly back onto value creation. In short, strive to be a business *person*, not just a business *partner*. You can no longer expect your organization's leadership to accept the platitude that 'people are our most important assets' as an article of faith. You need to demonstrate that fact in economically viable terms. It is possible to do this. Broaden your organization's definition and frame of reference regarding value creation to include intangible value creation for customers and employees as leading indicators of economic value growth.

Strategic implication #2: Get people focused on the organization's vision

Before beginning to read this section, ask yourself three questions:

1. Does my organization currently have a simple statement of vision – *a clear, elevating goal*?
2. Has this clear, simple statement been widely communicated at all levels of the organization?
3. Do people's individual performance objectives reflect how they will personally support the vision? In short, does the vision translate to individual employee behavior?

If you answered no to any one of the above questions, you now have a golden opportunity to help accelerate value creation in your organization.

Vision and strategy are important. And it's important to get it right. People like Porter (1996) and Hamel and Prahalad (1994) have done a very effective job over the past fifteen or twenty years of impressing on organizations how critical good strategy is to their success at value creation. Organizations have taken it to heart and have improved their discipline in the area of strategy, often introducing comprehensive planning efforts throughout their organizations. This has presumably led to better strategies within organizations. But increasingly, leaders are discovering that the most elegant and well-thought-out strategies will under-deliver on the promise unless that strategy, (a) can be stated simply to any level of employee in their organization, and (b) people's efforts are aligned behind the successful achievement of the strategic goals. In fact, in a 2007 survey by the Conference Board of CEOs from global companies with over $5 billion in sales, 'consistent execution of strategy' was the number one area of greatest concern for those CEOs, with 42% agreeing with that issue. That concern ranked ahead of 'sustained top line growth' (39%), and 'profit growth' (33%)!

More recently, Bossidy, Charan and Burck (2002) and Kaplan and Norton (2004a, 2006) have begun to address the issue of strategy *execution*, rather than strategy *formulation*, as the 'missing ingredient' to translating good strategy into value creation outcomes. Through the application of the Balanced Scorecard methodology, Kaplan and Norton (2006) have focused organizational attention on how to operationalize a strategy to achieve performance results. What is particularly encouraging about Kaplan and Norton's work is that they are increasingly focused on the 'intangible' dimensions of strategy execution like human capital and customer equity. In fact, much of Kaplan and Norton's work (2004b) has outlined three intangible areas of necessity in order to drive strategy to value creation: human capital, information capital and organization capital.

In short, the opportunity to identify a simple statement of strategy, communicate it effectively and then align human capital behind the strategy is a big value creation opportunity for organizations today, and for HR. So, as an HR professional how can you make a strategic intervention into your company's value creation efforts? If your answer to any or all of the opening three questions was 'no', try the following (Warning: this section has nothing to do with HR, per se, and may even get you looked at a little askance the first time you talk to your CEO, CFO or head of corporate development about it):

- Offer to lead an effort to capture your organization's vision and articulate it in a clear, simple phrase.
- Once armed with that simple statement of strategy, communicate it broadly to every individual in your organization in a personal way.
- Once they understand the simple statement of strategy, require people at all levels to translate the strategy into what it means in their job – in practical terms – in their day-to-day behaviors.

People cannot support the strategy unless they know it and understand it. A blinding flash of the obvious, perhaps, but many organizations don't take the time to articulate the strategy in simple terms and then communicate it to their employees. So, how can you accomplish the three steps outlined above?

Get three or four of your senior managers together in a room for about ninety minutes and ask them each to describe the current vision of your organization. They'll have a difficult time doing this. They'll ask questions about whether you mean vision, mission, goal or strategy, because they think those four things are different. That will be a stall tactic, because they're just feeling awkward about not being able to accomplish the simple task you requested. Don't let them off the hook. Keep pressing. If you want to help them, ask them to tell you what they'd say to their brother-in-law across the Thanksgiving dinner table the next time he asks, "Hey, what does your organization actually do?". If you can get your senior managers to answer that simple question in twenty-five words or less . . . no, fifteen words or less, you are well on your way to adding real strategic value.

Next, get someone who's got the creative 'right brain' thing going to give you a hand in making whatever your senior managers came up with even simpler. The goal here is to be as brief and concise as possible, and not to have this sound like something a Harvard B-School MBA team dreamed up. It has to be a simple, credible statement that can be communicated to anyone, at any level and have them nod their head. Pressure test that simple statement with your senior managers one more time. Now begin to communicate this simple statement throughout your company. Whatever your intuition tells you is the right amount of communication, triple that amount and you'll start to reach the level of communication needed. Use a variety of ways to communicate it: town hall meetings, group presentations, videos, websites, newsletters. Do *not* rely exclusively on wall plaques and laminated wallet cards. Those can be used, but they are not sufficient. Leadership needs to take this message out to people face-to-face in order to be effective.

Once people know what the simple strategy is, ask them to consider how their job can directly support the achievement of that vision. Ask them to write it down. In fact, ask people at all levels to develop individual performance objectives in support of the vision as part of the performance management system of the organization, and get their manager to agree to those objectives.

There it is. In those three steps you have taken a major step toward focusing and aligning your organization behind the strategic vision. Don't over-complicate this process. Sacrifice some precision and wordsmithing in favor of engaging as many people as possible in knowing the direction in which you want them to head.

Strategic implication #3: promote commitment

The premise for this third piece of HR being strategically relevant is based on a simple idea (see Figure 9.1). *Employee commitment* is a leading indicator of customer outcomes and value creation. In Figure 9.1, you see an employee-customer-profit value creation chain. Ultimately, we want to generate sustained value creation, however we define that (e.g. financially, socially, spiritually, militarily). This is the outcome we exist to create. The model in Figure 9.1 suggests that two critical, intangible factors can be a leading indicator of value creation: customer satisfaction and employee commitment. In fact, a number of practitioners and researchers across a wide spectrum of organizations have demonstrated this empirically (Buckingham and Coffman, 1999; Heskett et al., 1997; Rucci et al., 1998).

If employee commitment is such a powerful value creator, what is it and what factors contribute to strengthening it? Rucci, Ulrich and Gavino (1998) have defined 'employee commitment' as "*gaining discretionary energy, effort and ideas from people*". Commitment is not

Employee commitment	+	Customer satisfaction	=	Value creation
(leading indicator)		(leading indicator)		

Figure 9.1 A simple idea about intangible value creation

'satisfaction', and is not 'loyalty', two terms that have been used historically as an explanation for the emotional attachment an employee feels toward an organization. The evidence to date is pretty clear. You can have satisfied employees; you can have loyal employees, but those factors are not leading indicators of customer satisfaction and other value creation outcomes. Commitment speaks to a much more active *involvement* by people in the achievement of strategic goals. Employees' answers to satisfaction questions like "I like my pay", "I like my benefits" are important to know, but those types of traditional employee survey questions do not measure commitment. How do you know if you enjoy 'commitment' that leads to better customer and value creation? Ask your employees how strongly they agree with the following kinds of statements:

> *My work gives me a sense of accomplishment.*
> *I am proud to say I work here.*
> *I have a good understanding of our business strategy.*
> *We are making changes necessary to compete effectively.*
> *We make customers a top priority.*
> *We are investing in innovative products and services for our customers.*
> *I see a direct connection between my job and the goals of the organization.*
> *I feel good about the future of the organization.*
> *We are driven to achieve high standards of performance.*
> *People take personal accountability for their actions here.*
> *I have a good understanding of our core values.*
> *I like the kind of work I do.*
> *Dignity of the individual is never compromised here.*

Questions like these are not an index of how 'happy' or satisfied employees are. They are an indicator of how much an employee understands the strategy of the organization, how confident they feel in helping to drive strategic outcomes, and finally how they feel they are treated as individuals by their leaders. In fact, LaFasto and Larson (2002) talk about a virtuous cycle that summarizes the two themes here of *focus and vision* and *commitment*. Their simple algorithm is:

> *Clarity* → *Confidence* → *Commitment*

Employees who are *clear* about the goals of the organization will have a greater degree of *confidence* in their ability to contribute effectively to that goal, and will therefore be more *committed* to the goal, and to the organization. Driving employee commitment is a major determinant of successful strategic execution, and we've already discussed that execution of strategy is a critical value creator.

So, what organizational factors and practices lead to greater employee commitment? The list is pretty concise, pretty clear and pretty simple. People remain committed to three things in organizations:

- an inspiring vision that they relate to;
- teams they value being part of;
- leaders they choose to follow.

As an HR professional, if you want to make a meaningful strategic contribution to your organization's success, focus on efforts in these three areas. We've already discussed how important it is to help the organization frame and communicate its vision in an earlier section, and we will leave team effectiveness for a later day. But now, let's focus on the final strategic implication theme: ideas, and the crucial role of leaders who drive employee commitment and ideas.

Strategic implication #4: select and promote leaders who generate ideas from people

Earlier we suggested that it is ideas which drive value creation in organizations today. Market valuations and market multiple premiums go to organizations that take hard assets and add incremental value in the form of innovation, design and customer awareness (Hamel 2000). The earlier discussion of Lev's (2001) work on market-to-book-value ratios clearly illustrates that this intangible idea 'premium' is very real. Once again, the value creation potential of 'intangible' factors is increasingly recognized.

It is leaders who either promote idea generation from people, or suppress it. So, if your goal is to gain the discretionary energy, effort and *ideas* from people, then as an HR professional you should focus your efforts on helping the organization select leaders who will accelerate the idea generation capacity of your culture. First, have processes in place that facilitate the identification, selection and development of leaders. This includes things like: have a clear set of leadership competencies your organization looks for, have a leadership planning process in place, be serious about development efforts for future leaders, take selection of supervisors and managers very seriously, and use things like 360-degree survey information on leaders. We could review about fifty years of research literature here (see, for example, Bennis, 1989; Collins, 2004; Goleman, 1998; Rucci, 2001; Zaleznik, 1977) on what makes a good leader, but very simply, as an HR professional if you want to help your organization select leaders who drive idea generation, then help it to select leaders who do the following four things:

- create a vision and involve and inspire others;
- achieve results and hold people accountable;
- reinforce values and hold people accountable;
- treat people with dignity and build their confidence.

These four leadership capabilities are fairly self-descriptive, except perhaps for the theme of 'accountability' in both numbers two and three. Successful organizations and successful leaders are not about making people happy or creating a nice place to work. They are about achieving value creation, doing it the right way and holding people accountable for both 'what' they achieve, but also 'how' they achieve it. And really effective leaders do not tolerate employees who are not contributing and performing; they are equally intolerant of employees who are behaving in ways that are not consistent with the core values of the organization.

Leaders who demonstrate the above four capabilities are more likely to gain the discretionary ideas from those they lead. And ideas drive value creation. Put processes in place in an organization which cause it to focus on selecting these kinds of leaders.

Adding strategic value in HR

This chapter has attempted to focus on ways to make HR a meaningful contributor to an organization's success at sustained value creation. By focusing on HR's core purpose, more than an HR strategy, the profession can actually become strategically integrated. Ironically, the less we focus on being 'strategic in HR', and the more we focus on helping organizations create value the more relevant we become. In fact, I look to the day when we don't have to discuss the strategic role of HR. The debate only serves to beg the question and detracts from HR's core purpose: to help organizations achieve sustained value creation, by focusing the commitment of people's energy, effort and ideas on a common vision. And the way to realize that core purpose, as suggested here, is for HR professionals to focus not on strategy in HR, but rather on value creation in four ways, as discussed and summarized in Table 9.1.

What does this mean for HR?

So what conditions need to exist within an HR organization that will enable it to make the contribution required in each of the four areas above? There are any number of things that could be considered to answer that question, including: Does HR have a plan for itself? Has HR translated the strategic goals of the organization into its people implications? Does HR have the resources needed to carry out the mission? But I would like to conclude this chapter on the strategic relevance of HR by focusing on the one question that I believe will ensure that the HR profession is making a meaningful contribution to value creation in organizations: Do we have the right people in HR in our organizations?

What do the very best HR professionals look like?

They have personal credibility

The most successful HR professionals are also those who enjoy a personal reputation for trust and credibility. That doesn't merely mean that they are nice people. It means that they honour commitments they make. They follow through on promises. They personally achieve results and have high performance standards. They hold themselves accountable for their performance, and don't make excuses when they or the function fail to perform. They maintain confidences and they operate confidently based on a clear sense of purpose, both about the profession and themselves and what they stand for.

They are business people

Notice this didn't say 'they have business acumen', or 'they are a business partner'. Rather, the very best HR professionals are those who not only understand business, but actually enjoy it. This is the biggest liability among the profession and its professionals today (see Hammonds, 2005). We should expect HR professionals and executives to be no less a business person and leader than we expect from a CFO, a general manager or a CEO. In order to accomplish that, HR professionals must understand their organization's business. They must not just be able to understand financial numbers, but know the business of the organization. They should be able to answer three simple questions: Who is the customer? Who is the competition? Who are we? This should reflect a realistic assessment of their own organization. An HR professional should be able to conduct a credible twenty-minute business discussion about their organization with a customer, a supplier, an investment manager, an investment analyst, a community leader.

They are change agents

More than ever, organizations need an internal catalyst for change in order to remain competitive. HR professionals are in a unique position to be drivers of change, rather than merely be asked to help manage change. But that requires some real assertiveness and personal risk taking. It means being willing to put yourself on an operating leaders' calendar and discussing issues of concern well beyond HR issues, raising issues that you see anywhere in the organization and having credible recommendations about how to address those issues. In order to be taken seriously in your efforts to command the attention of non-HR leaders in your organization, you can see why personal credibility and business understanding discussed above are so critical. You will not be able to create change, or even be taken seriously, if you cannot exhibit those two capabilities.

They have excellent professional skills

It should go without saying that in order to be effective in a professional HR role you need to have excellent professional skills. Understand the professional areas of importance: employee relations, labour law, compensation, benefits, development, organization development, information technology and systems, etc. However, the critical concept here may be a bit surprising to you. Have good professional skills and knowledge, just don't strive to be known for that. Keep your professional knowledge and skills low-key, particularly among non-HR leaders in your organization. They assume you know what you're doing professionally, and want to be assured that you are focusing on their business and strategic issues, not any parochial professional issues.

They are employee advocates

Despite all of the prior rhetoric in this chapter, this is the final (seemingly inconsistent?) requirement for effective HR professionals. Beyond helping organizations create value, beyond being strategic, beyond being business relevant, have real courage of conviction about your 'ultimate' role as an advocate for employees. Nothing about the importance of business relevance or the strategic relevance of what HR does in any way excuses or absolves an HR professional from the professional obligation of protecting the dignity of people in organizations. If we believe that the commitment of people's energy, effort and ideas are what create value in organizations, then this final requirement is not only consistent with that core purpose, but is the foundation of that purpose. The very best HR professionals and executives, the very best business people and the very best leaders will put their own personal interests at risk to protect the dignity of the people they lead. It is the foundation of value creation in organizations where 'intangibles' drive sustained strategic success.

References

Bennis, W. and Bennis, W.G. (1989) *On Becoming a Leader*. Perseus Publishing, New York.
Bossidy, L., Charan, R. and Burck, C. (2002) *Execution: the discipline of getting things done*. Crown Business, New York.
Buckingham, M. and Coffman, C. (1999) *First, Break all the Rules*. Simon & Schuster, New York.
Collins, J. (2004) Level V leadership. *Harvard Business Review*, 79(1): 66–76.
Collins, J. and Porras, J. (1996) Building your company's vision. *Harvard Business Review*, 74(5): 65–77.

Goleman, D. (1998) What makes a leader. *Harvard Business Review*, 76(6): 92–102.

Hamel, G. (2000) *Leading the Revolution: How to thrive in turbulent times by making innovation a way of life.* Harvard Business School Press, Boston.

Hamel, G. and Prahalad, C. (1994) *Competing for the Future.* Harvard Business School Press, Boston.

Hammonds, K. (2005) Why we hate HR. *Fast Company*, 97: 42–47.

Heskett, J., Sasser, W. and Schlesinger, L. (1997) *The Service Profit Chain.* The Free Press, New York.

Kaplan, R. and Norton, D. (1996) *The Balanced Scorecard: translating strategy into action.* Harvard Business School Press, Boston.

Kaplan, R. and Norton, D. (2004a) Measuring the strategic readiness of intangible assets. *Harvard Business Review*, 82(2): 52–63.

Kaplan, R. and Norton, D. (2004b) *Strategy Maps: converting intangible assets into tangible outcomes.* Harvard Business School Publishing, Boston.

Kaplan, R. and Norton, D. (2006) *Alignment: using the balanced scorecard to create corporate synergies.* Harvard Business School Publishing, Boston.

LaFasto, F. and Larson, C. (2002) *When Teams Work Best.* Sage Publications, London.

Lev, B. (2001) *Intangibles: management, measurement and reporting.* Brookings Institution, Washington DC.

Losey, M., Ulrich, D. and Meisinger, S. (2005) *The Future of Human Resource Management: 64 thought leaders explore the critical issues of today and tomorrow.* John Wiley & Sons, New York.

Porter, M. (1996) What is Strategy? *Harvard Business Review*, 74(6): 61–78.

Rucci, A. (2001) What the best business leaders do best. In R. Silzer (Ed.), *The 21st century executive.* Jossey-Bass, San Francisco.

Rucci, A., Kirn, S. and Quinn, R. (1998) The employee-customer-profit chain at Sears. *Harvard Business Review*, 76(1): 82–97.

Rucci, A., Ulrich, D. and Gavino, M. (1998) Unpublished work. *The VOICE Model of Leadership.*

Ulrich, D. and Smallwood, N. (2003) *Why the Bottom Line Isn't!: How to build value through people and organization.* John Wiley & Sons, New York.

Ulrich, D., Zenger, J. and Smallwood, N. (1999) *Results Based Leadership.* Harvard Business School Press, Boston.

Zaleznik, A. (1977) Managers and leaders: Are they different? *Harvard Business Review*, May–June: 67–73.

10

Managing strategic change

David A. Buchanan

Objectives and context

This chapter has three objectives. First, we will examine potential roles for the human resource management function in relation to strategic organizational change. Second, key aspects of the nature and processes of organizational change are outlined. Third, following that analysis, the implications for practice are considered. With compelling evidence for the impact of human resource policy on organizational performance, the function is positioned to contribute in significant ways to corporate strategy. However, this chapter argues that, curiously, the function is often under-represented in the change process, and 'punches below its weight' in this regard. Consequently, in order to be more effective players in the strategic change game, human resource practitioners need to be able to compete more effectively with change agents in other management functions. This in turn means that human resource professionals must be able and willing to use more sophisticated political skills.

Given the pattern of change that most organizations now experience, the role of the human resource function should be pivotal, but this contribution is rarely recognized in the change management and organization development literature. Tracking the top 50 companies in Britain through the 1990s, Whittington and Mayer (2002) observe that, by the beginning of the twenty-first century, large businesses were implementing major reorganizations every three years, on average. In addition, most businesses were also regularly conducting many minor reorganizations. This pattern of repeat change, they argue, is driven by three factors:

1. intensified competition and stockmarket turbulence in the private sector, and consumerism and government pressures in the public sector;
2. the pace of technological innovation;
3. increasing knowledge-intensity, placing a premium on good organization design to reduce barriers to information flows.

This study also observed that change outcomes are often poor, in terms of financial returns and damaged morale. One of the main reasons for these results lies with the focus on technical and structural issues (such as expensive new accounting and information technology systems) in major change programmes, and the relative lack of attention to cultural and behavioural factors. And as Caldwell (2001) observes, major strategic investments will rarely be deferred on human resource management grounds, although such issues will almost always arise. Whittington and Mayer (2002) thus argue that, as 'the soft stuff' becomes more important, so does the role of the human resource management function, which is central to the success of repeat change through the knock-on effects this has on organization culture, leadership styles, and senior management succession, along with staff recruitment, retention, careers, rewards, training, and skills. One of the main conclusions from this study is that repeat change puts a premium on the skills of *adaptive reorganization*, constantly redesigning in response to trends and opportunities. Managing change is no longer a one-off task with clear start and end points, but an ongoing, and critical, responsibility. A more important conclusion, perhaps, is that the ability to redesign the organization frequently contributes more significantly to competitive advantage than one particular structure.

The necessary organizational capabilities for repeat reorganization include clear formal structures and reporting relationships, standardized performance metrics, consistent organization-wide compensation policies, propensity to organize in small performance-oriented units, and culture of change (Whittington and Mayer, 2002, p. 26). They conclude that the attributes of those leading repeat organizational change should include:

- action- and results-oriented;
- able to play many roles, from visionary to organizer to lobbyist;
- self-critical and restless in seeking improvements;
- involvement in collegial interactions across boundaries;
- politically sensitive but not politically motivated.

Despite these findings, the human resource management function had a leading role in organizational change in only one in five of the organizations involved in this research. In exploring how the function's influence and contribution can be strengthened in this respect, we will consider in this chapter the significance of political skill in particular, accepting the need for sensitivity in this domain. However, it will be necessary to challenge as unhelpful the advice that the human resource manager should not be politically motivated.

Typologies of typologies

With respect to the role, or roles, of the personnel or human resource management function, a major concern over the past two decades has been the development of appropriate typologies. Definitions of the concept of strategic human resource management, contrasted with that of the traditional personnel function, consistently emphasize the function's role in organizational change. Storey (1992) characterizes the strategic, interventionist orientation of human resource 'changemakers', in sharp contrast to the personnel function's stereotypical roles as 'regulators', 'advisors', and 'handmaidens'. Revisiting his earlier typology of personnel roles, including 'clerk of works', 'contracts manager', and 'architect', Tyson (1995) argues that the pace of change creates opportunities for the human resource management function to contribute to major change initiatives. Ulrich (1998) argues that the function needs a 'new agenda' with four components, noting that competency in change management in particular is vital to the career success of the human resource professional. These four components are:

1. strategic partners, working with line managers in strategy execution;
2. administrative experts, offering expertise to reduce costs and improve quality;

3. employee champions, representing staff concerns and working to increase employees' contribution to performance;
4. agents of continuous transformation, developing capacity for change.

Schuler, Jackson and Storey (2001, p. 127) similarly argue that human resources has four roles, as 'strategic partner', 'innovator', 'collaborator', and 'change facilitator'. But is the function's change role itself open to further clarification? Considering in particular Storey's changemakers and Ulrich's change agents, Caldwell (2001) sought to establish in more detail the nature of the various roles that human resource professionals play in organizational change. From his survey of 98 British companies, followed by 12 interviews, the typology in Figure 10.1 was developed, based on the distinction between transformative and incremental change, and between providing a vision in contrast to providing expertise. Almost 70 per cent of respondents, in personnel and human resource jobs, identified change agency as one of their roles, and the model identifies four types of change agent:

- **champions**: senior executives who lead major human resource initiatives and policy changes;
- **adapters**: middle managers who build support for change, translating visions into action;
- **consultants**: specialists and external consultants who implement discrete projects;
- **synergists**: senior managers and external consultants who co-ordinate and integrate multiple large-scale change initiatives.

Caldwell (2001) supports the view that current trends allow the human resource management function to move beyond the traditional personnel role and to make decisive contributions to organizational effectiveness by leading significant changes to employment policies and practices.

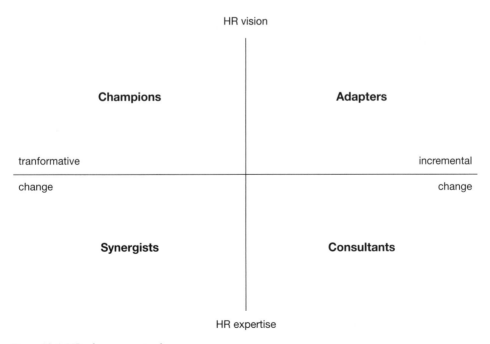

Figure 10.1 HR change agent roles

However, Caldwell also argues that any neat typology, including his own, cannot adequately capture the overlaps, ambiguities, confusions, conflicts, and tensions of the human resources role, and of these various contributions in practice. Some of his human resource interviewees, for instance, felt that the role of 'change champion' was an unrealistic one for their profession, as this involved the risks that accompany the sponsorship of strategic change, in contrast with the safer ground of providing advice. However, that view was not shared by all of his respondents. The function, he concludes, will always have multiple roles and role combinations, shifting over time with circumstances. These typologies perhaps reflect an unrealizable set of ideal stereo-types, but they also characterize the aspirations of many members of the function with regard to a strategic change champion role.

With the exception of Caldwell (2001), most commentators advocating a change-orientated role for the human resource management function have not then asked, 'What kind of change agent?'. The generic literature of change agency, or change leadership as this is now often styled, is itself dominated by role types and typologies. Schön (1963) highlights the importance of the 'change champion'. Stjernberg and Philips (1993) refer to 'souls of fire', from the Swedish 'eldsjälar' meaning 'driven by burning enthusiasm'. Change, of course, is rarely implemented by one person: Hutton (1994) talks of a 'cast of characters'. Ottaway (1983) thus identifies ten roles in three categories, of change generators, implementers, and adopters. Beatty and Gordon (1991) distinguish patriarchs who originate ideas, from evangelists who implement them. Buchanan and Storey (1997) identify the eight change-related roles summarized in Table 10.1. Accompanying these typologies, typically, is discussion of the skills, knowledge, and other attributes required in those roles.

In the second half of the 1990s, the iconic agent of strategic change was the transformational leader (Bass and Avolio, 1994; Burns, 1978). However, the charismatic, visionary, heroic transformational leader has recently attracted widespread criticism. Denis et al. (2001) describe instead the role of 'leadership constellations' in driving major change. Various commentators have been critical of transformational figures, describing them as 'a dangerous curse' (Khurana, 2002), and emphasizing the role of middle managers who implement 'quiet change' by 'stealth', working 'below the radar' (Badaracco, 2002; Huy, 2001; Meyerson, 2001). The human resource management role is absent from these perspectives, although the consequences of repeat organizational transformation can include stress, initiative fatigue, and burnout, which potentially damage individual and organizational effectiveness. These observations led Abrahamson (2000) to advocate 'painless change' that is more sensitively timed and paced to allow individuals and social systems to make appropriate adjustments.

The generic literature of change agency is too broad to summarize here, but two observations are particularly significant. First, the analysis of change agent (or change leader) roles and competencies does not appear to have informed analysis of the change-related role, or roles, of the human resource management function. Second, the potentially controversial political

Table 10.1 Change agency roles

initiator	the ideas person, the heatseeker, the project or process 'champion'
sponsor	the main beneficiary, the focal person, the project or process 'guardian'
agent or driver	promotes, implements, delivers – often the process or 'project manager'
subversive	strives to divert, block, interfere, resist, disrupt
passenger	is carried along by the change
spectator	watches while others change
victim	suffers from changes introduced by others
paramedic	helps others through the traumas of change

skills of change agency, in influencing, persuading, negotiating, and manipulating others into accepting, if not welcoming, change proposals, do not appear to have been recognized as significant to the change-oriented strategic human resource management function. The relevance of political skills will be examined after we have considered current thinking with regard to the nature of organizational change processes.

Recipes and processes

The literature of organizational change is large and fragmented, and is difficult to summarize for several reasons (Iles and Sutherland, 2001). First, it contains work from different theoretical and practical perspectives; there are several *literatures*. Second, while valuable contributions have been made over the past five or six decades, recent work has not necessarily reduced the relevance, interest, or value of earlier work. Third, the evidence draws from a range of organizational settings, using a range of methodologies with varying degrees of rigour, and it is difficult to reach sound generalizable conclusions. In addition, there are major problems in establishing clear cause and effect relationships across complex, iterative change processes that unfold over extended periods of time. This causality problem is exacerbated by two other sets of issues. First, even straightforward changes are often multidimensional, both in their nature and outcomes, and causality is always difficult to establish in such settings. Second, organizational change usually implicates numerous stakeholders, who may have quite different views of the nature of the problem, appropriate solutions, and desirable outcomes; this generates the problem of whose criteria to use.

Two strikingly different perspectives on organizational change are currently influential. One is described by Collins (1998) as offering 'n-step guides' to change implementation which, as this label suggests, provides a plethora of numbered checklists. One of the most widely cited of these guides is that developed by Kotter (1995), whose 'recipe' has eight ingredients: establish a sense of urgency, form a powerful guiding coalition, create a vision, communicate the vision, empower others to act on the vision, plan for and create short-term wins, consolidate improvements and produce still more change, and finally institutionalize new approaches. In Britain, the professional body for human resource management, the Chartered Institute for Personnel and Development (2006), has developed a similar change recipe, identifying 'the seven Cs of change': choosing a team, crafting the vision, connecting organization-wide change, consulting stakeholders, communicating, coping with the stress of change, and capturing the learning. Gustafson *et al.* (2003) develop a recipe for predicting the success of organizational change, identifying 18 ingredients under six headings: the solution, the adoption decision, external links, structural support, organizational and people readiness, and change agency. These recipes all claim, broadly, that if their respective ingredients are present, then change is more likely to be successful. None of these guidelines makes explicit mention of the role of the human resource management function.

A second influential perspective concerns the processual-contextual theories of change developed by, for example, Pettigrew (1985), Van de Ven and Poole (1995), and Dawson (2003). Critical of the neat and tidy 'rational linear' assumptions on which n-step guides are based, this approach argues that the outcomes of change are influenced instead by the interaction between change nature or substance, the organizational context (inner and outer), and the implementation process. Change here is seen as messy, iterative, and highly politicized, as different individuals and groups jostle and manoeuvre to establish the legitimacy of their own proposals, and weaken the credibility of others. This untidiness renders inappropriate any universal solution or 'best practice' recipe for implementing change. In addition, a theory that tries to link independent variables (changes) to dependent variables (outcomes) is inappropriate. Instead of variance theory, process theory sees change as an event sequence unfolding over time, as a narrative with many authors (Buchanan and Dawson, 2007), where the human resource function is one of a number of stakeholder groups seeking to influence the nature, direction, pace, and outcomes of change.

One implication of this brief overview is that, if human resource managers are to play a more proactive role in strategic organizational change, the nature of this task is not immediately apparent. Will this involve the routine implementation of a series of preplanned steps? Will this instead involve a more contingent and iterative process in which political skill matters as much as conventional change management technique? It is almost certainly the case that, the more significant the changes in terms of their impact on the organization, its working practices, and its employees, the more politicized the change process is likely to be (Buchanan and Badham, 2008; Frost and Egri, 1991). Any manager, and not just human resource managers, lacking political skills when engaging this kind of process is likely to struggle.

A further implication is that, if there is no one best approach to change, it is difficult to specify one perspective with regard to change agency (or leadership), which in turn is contingent and fluid. And where the outcomes are open to the competing assessments of different stakeholders, this creates opportunities for results to be represented as successful, on carefully selected criteria, even where results have been less than impressive in other respects. While it is important to be able to establish the legitimacy of one's proposals for change, it is equally significant to be able to present the consequences in a positive manner, especially where negative outcomes attract accusations of error or failure, and can damage the reputation of those responsible for advocating those initiatives in the first place.

Something to sell

The function's contribution to strategic change has been reinforced by welcome evidence that links human resource policies and practices demonstrably to organizational performance. Put crudely, treat your staff properly, and your profits will rise. Proof of returns on investment in human resource initiatives is clearly important to the adoption of those initiatives, and those returns also have implications for the status and influence of human resource practitioners. At the core of this argument lies the concept of *high performance work practices*. In order to measure their use, Huselid (1995) identifies 13 such practices, in two categories, concerning skills and structures, and motivation, respectively:

Employee skills and organizational structures
1. information-sharing programmes;
2. job analysis;
3. internal appointments for promoted posts;
4. workforce attitude surveys;
5. quality of work life programmes, quality circles and participative teams;
6. company incentive and profit-sharing plans;
7. training hours per employee;
8. formal grievance procedures and complaint resolution systems;
9. employment testing for new recruits;

Employee motivation
10. performance appraisals to determine financial reward;

11. formal performance appraisals;
12. promotion based on merit or performance rating, not seniority;
13. the number of qualified applicants for the five most often recruited posts.

Huselid (1995) surveyed around 3,500 organizations to measure the use of high performance work practices in American organizations, predicting that these would reduce labour turnover, and increase productivity and profitability. His main findings were that:

- organizations using high performance work practices had higher levels of productivity and financial performance;
- organizations using high performance practices in the employee skills and organization structure category had lower employee turnover;
- a significant proportion of the impact of high performance practices on financial performance was due to lower labour turnover, or higher productivity, or both;
- high performance practices contributed US$18,500 per employee in shareholder value, and almost $4,000 per employee in additional profits (1995 prices).

Investment in human resource policies can thus bring demonstrable financial returns in the form of reduced employee turnover, improved productivity, and profitability. These findings support the argument that high performance work practices improve financial performance regardless of the organization's strategy. Huselid's findings were among the first to present a major challenge to those who would dismiss human resource management (in its new or traditional personnel management guise) as commercially irrelevant.

Pfeffer (1998) similarly argues that human resource practices can raise an organization's stock market value by US$20,000 to $40,000 per employee. He claims that 'profits through people' are produced by seven people management policies:

1. emphasis on job security;
2. recruiting the right people in the first place;
3. decentralization and self-managed teamworking;
4. high wages linked to organizational performance;
5. high investment in employee training;
6. reducing status differentials;
7. sharing information across the organization.

In Britain, research by the Sheffield Group (Patterson *et al.*, 1997) has also revealed a measurable impact of human resource management on productivity and profitability. This work involved a ten-year study of over 100 manufacturing companies, using 'human resource management variables' similar to Huselid's (1995) high performance practices. This study also assessed the contributions to organizational performance of other management strategies and tactics, finding that none had the same positive impact on business performance as human resource management. The findings showed that two clusters of high performance practices were significantly related to productivity and profitability. These clusters are similar to the main factors in Huselid's perspective:

1. skills development: the acquisition and development of employee skills, through selection, induction, training and the use of performance appraisal systems;
2. job design: the design of jobs, including skill flexibility, job responsibility, variety, and the use of teams.

155

The main findings from this study were that:

- high overall job satisfaction and organizational commitment are positively linked to high company profitability;
- an organization culture that demonstrates concern for employee skill development and well-being is linked to high productivity and profitability;
- skills development and job design practices such as teamworking are positively linked to increased productivity and profitability;
- human resource management practice is a good predictor of performance: quality emphasis, corporate strategy, technological sophistication and investment in research and development contribute only weakly to productivity and profitability.

Comparative research by this team showed that British manufacturing companies place less emphasis on empowering and capturing the ideas of employees, and on adopting high performance practices than Australia, Japan, and Switzerland. Problems of poor comparative productivity and innovation may thus lie with work organization and management processes.

One of the most intriguing findings in this line of research is that human resource practices reduce hospital mortality rates. West *et al.* (2002) surveyed 61 hospitals in England and carried out ten case studies, asking chief executives and human resource directors about human resource practices covering all clinical, administrative, support and managerial staff. Data were then collected on the numbers of deaths following emergency and non-emergency surgery, admission for hip fractures and heart attacks, and readmission. Care was taken to account for variations in mortality due to region, local population, hospital size, and doctor–patient ratios. Analysis showed that mortality rates were significantly lower in hospitals with human resource practices related to appraisal (with extensive and sophisticated systems), training (with well-developed policies and budgets), and teamwork (with high staff numbers working in teams, and trained to do so). These relationships were even stronger where the human resources director was a full voting member of the hospital management board.

Surely it is the skills and knowledge of nurses, doctors, and surgeons which affect patient care and survival, and medical staff were suspicious of these research findings. How can human resource practices applied to staff who are not involved in patient diagnosis and treatment affect mortality rates? West and Johnson (2002, p. 35) reply:

> Our answer is simple, though it may seem strange to those who deal with individuals rather than organizations. If you have HR practices that focus on effort and skill; develop people's skills; encourage co-operation, collaboration, innovation and synergy in teams for most, if not all, employees, the whole system functions and performs better. If the receptionists, porters, ancillary staff, secretaries, nurses, managers and, yes, the doctors are working effectively, the system as a whole will function effectively.

A hospital is a community which depends on the interaction of all its members. Although clearly important, the skills and performance of doctors is not the only factor which affects the quality of patient care. The impact of human resource practices, therefore, is *systemic*. It is unlikely that this conclusion is limited to healthcare organizations.

From those research findings, the human resource manager seeking to influence organization strategy not only has a clear agenda concerning the kinds of changes that are likely to contribute significantly to performance (with appropriate adaptation to local circumstances), but can also point to proof demonstrating that these methods work. Scepticism concerning 'the soft stuff' can now be confronted with hard evidence. The empirical research supporting the positive, quantifiable impact of human resource policies and high performance practices is difficult for other senior managers to ignore. In short, the function has something valuable to sell. Why, then, do so few human resource functions play leading 'change champion' roles in their organizations (Guest and King, 2004), why are most organizations struggling with the concept of the human resource function as 'strategic partner' (Arkin, 2007), and why do most organizations employ so few of those high performance practices? The answers seem to lie with the observation that good ideas and compelling evidence, on their own, are rarely sufficient to promote a new idea, a new product, or a change initiative.

Making things happen, getting things done

Organizational change is a politicized process because it typically generates conflict, over the definition of problems, and over the nature and timing of the solutions that are required to address them. Conflict is often regarded in negative terms, as an undesirable condition that must be resolved, if not avoided. Organization politics are typically seen as a damaging waste of time, as 'dirty tricks', as behaviours to be shunned. However, not all new ideas are good ideas, and conflict can be desirable, in order to stimulate appropriate debate and to sharpen the quality of decisions. Mangham (1979, p. 16) observes that reasonable people often disagree, with regard both to ends and means, and can thus be expected 'to fight for what they are convinced is right and, perhaps more significantly, against that which they are convinced is wrong'. Butcher and Clarke (1999) thus describe politics as 'battles over just causes'. Hardy (1996) argues that political forces generate the energy for organizational change. To shut down political behaviour is to turn off this source of energy.

Change agents who are not able and willing to engage with the politics of the organization are thus likely to fail in their enterprise. Pfeffer (1992, p. 30) argues that, 'unless we are willing to come to terms with organizational power and influence, and admit that the skills of getting things done are as important as the skills of figuring out what to do, our organizations will fall further and further behind'. This means abandoning the notion, popular in the field of organization development, that change agents are 'neutral facilitators' using appropriate techniques to encourage information-sharing, joint problem-solving and collaborative action planning among the organization's willing members. Zanko et al. (2008) explain the absence of attention to the evident human resource management issues in the implementation of an innovative approach to product development in a military electronics manufacturing company with reference to power and political structures in the organization, and to the political positions and tactics of the various key management players.

At any given time in an organization, there are likely to be in circulation several innovative ideas, proposals, projects, or initiatives, competing for management attention and resources. This is especially the case in the current context of repeat organizational redesign. The process through which ideas attract support is based in part on a reasoned business case. But good ideas do not sell themselves. As ideas compete, the selection process is a political one, and the human resource manager, like any other manager wishing to facilitate or drive change, has to play the politics game. The manager who is politically aware, but who is not politically motivated, as Whittington and Mayer (2002) advise, will thus find it difficult to engage effectively with the organization's change agenda.

Organization politics is also usually defined in terms of getting one's own way despite resistance. It is important to note that 'one's own way' can often involve organizational as well as individual benefits, and potentially both at the same time. While political behaviour is typically equated with self-interest, there is no reason why personal and corporate gain cannot both be pursued through the same actions. Indeed, maintaining or enhancing one's interests, to no corporate gain, may be appropriate and desirable in order to protect personal credibility for use on future occasions. The successful implementation of clusters of high performance work practices, for instance, may thus improve corporate profitability while simultaneously enhancing the reputation, and continuing influence, of the human resource manager responsible for the design of this initiative. It is significant, however, that Ferris *et al.* (2000, p. 30) define political skill as:

> an interpersonal style construct that combines social astuteness with the ability to relate well, and otherwise demonstrate situationally appropriate behaviour in a disarmingly charming and engaging manner that inspires confidence, trust, sincerity, and genuineness.

Skilled organization politicians may thus have to disguise their self-serving intentions to avoid being labelled as 'political', even where their proposals will deliver corporate gain. Traditionally, the human resource function has not only lacked organizational power, but has also been suspected of being unwilling to engage with organization politics (Legge, 1978, 2005; Watson, 1977). Lack of influence may be explained in part by structural conditions, but also by the willingness of the function's members to engage with their organization's political system, for a blend of personal and professional reasons.

Organization politics is a particularly rich and creative aspect of management activity. In an attempt to capture this variety, Buchanan and Badham (2008) identify the ten categories of tactics summarized in Table 10.2. Those category labels stand for a variety of tactics wider than the indicative examples. There is a range of image-building or impression management methods beyond dress and appearance (Singh *et al.*, 2002). Managers create and use different kinds of networks in different ways (Ibarra and Hunter, 2007). In advocating and driving strategic organizational change, two of these sets of tactics are particularly significant to the human resource management function: positioning, and issue-selling.

Table 10.2 Political tactics

image building	we all know people who didn't get the job because they didn't look the part – appearance is a credibility issue
information games	withholding information to make others look foolish, bending the truth, white lies, massaging information, timed release
scapegoating	this is the fault of another department, external factors, my predecessor, a particular individual
alliances	doing secret deals with influential others to form a critical mass, a cabal, to win support for and to progress your proposals
networking	lunches, coffees, dinners, sporting events, to get your initiatives onto senior management agendas, to improve visibility
compromise	all right, you win this time, I won't put up a fight and embarrass you in public – if you will back me next time
rule games	I'm sorry, but you have used the wrong form, at the wrong time, with the wrong arguments; we can't set inconsistent precedents
issue-selling	packaging, presenting, and promoting plans and ideas in ways that make them more appealing to target audiences
positioning	switching and choosing roles where one is successful and visible; avoiding failing projects; position in the building, in the room
dirty tricks	keeping dirt files for blackmail, spying on others, discrediting and undermining, spreading false rumours, corridor whispers

Positioning

Earlier in this chapter, Table 10.1 summarized eight typical roles that actors play in relation to organizational change: initiators, sponsors, drivers, subversives, passengers, spectators, victims, and paramedics. One individual may play several roles with regard to one particular change initiative, while simultaneously holding different positions in relation to other concurrent projects. That role typology is a useful analytical tool, as different skills and behaviours are required in different roles (even though they may be held by the same person). So, for example, the role of the initiator is to stimulate enthusiasm for change in others; that is quite different, in terms of behaviours and timescales, from the role of delivering change.

That role typology is also a political tool, with interesting practical consequences, in prompting the obvious question, 'which position, or positions, do you want to play?' Assuming that one has a choice, the pattern of positions that one adopts has significant implications, not merely for current workload, but also for skills development, personal reputation, career prospects, and the ability to continue to influence the organization in ways that one believes to be desirable. Thus, the human resource manager (indeed any manager) who consistently plays the roles of passenger and paramedic in relation to the organization's major changes is unlikely to develop an influential voice with regard to shaping future initiatives, and will develop few skills in change management. In contrast, the initiators, sponsors, and drivers of successful strategic initiatives are more likely to grow their reputational capital, develop their expertise (actual and perceived), and maintain their credibility and voice in the organization. Change roles may sometimes be vacant ('we need a sponsor for this initiative') and can be occupied opportunistically, when appropriate. But as indicated earlier, initiating or sponsoring major change programmes can entail risk, and if it is likely that an initiative will stumble, or fail, with consequent reputational damage, it may be more appropriate to revert to a spectator or passenger role, while avoiding becoming a victim.

The pattern of roles that the human resource manager decides to play at any one time is highly contingent on organizational circumstances and personal aspirations. Nevertheless, to be an effective strategic change agent, careful and considered positioning with regard to current and future initiatives is a vital element of political skill, which commentary on the evolving change roles of the function appears to have neglected.

Issue-selling

If the human resource management function has something to sell, this is not going to happen just because there is good supporting evidence. Good marketing is also necessary. The role of evidence in the diffusion of innovation, and in organizational change, is problematic. Products and ideas are rarely accepted just because they have research evidence to back them. For example, the American diplomat, Henry Kissinger, once said that,

> Before I served as a consultant to Kennedy, I had believed, like most academics, that the process of decision-making was largely intellectual and all one had to do was walk into the President's office and convince him of the correctness of one's view. This perspective I soon realized is as dangerously immature as it is widely held.
>
> (Pfeffer, 1992, p. 31)

To initiate and successfully deliver strategic changes, human resource managers thus need to be aware of the concept and techniques of issue-selling.

How do change proposals get off the ground? Problems have to be recognized as such, and be interpreted as significant, before they attract attention and get onto the senior management agenda. The factors influencing problem interpretation include the attributions of those involved, organization design and culture, the availability of resources, external pressures, and the promise of irresistible opportunities. A problem gets little or no attention when those in positions of influence do not recognize the issue as important, or where the causes of the problem are attributed to other factors, which may be beyond their control. Issues can be sidelined when the solution is perceived to benefit only some other (competing) group or function, or where key decision-makers have already decided that resources need to be deployed to higher priority tasks, or believe that the opportunities in this case are minimal. Change proposals which are perceived to benefit only employees, which will drain resources from other strategic issues, and which promise only vague or uncertain financial returns, are thus less likely to find senior management backing.

How, then, should the available evidence be presented and communicated? How can human resource managers ensure that what they regard as priorities for improvement are also regarded by the organization as a whole as priorities? For those who wish to initiate major change, therefore, a key political task is to ensure that their proposals figure prominently on a management agenda which is likely to be crowded with other competing initiatives. March and Olsen (1983, p. 292) refer to this as the 'organization of attention'. Dutton *et al.* (2001) refer to this as marketing ideas, as orchestrating impressions, and as 'issue-selling', observing that an organization is 'a market-place for ideas', each competing for decision and resources. Ideas do not appear on the management agenda because they are 'obvious' or even where they are supported by evidence. Ideas rise to prominence by the efforts of their advocates to market or to sell those issues to colleagues. This helps to explain why some lousy ideas are often implemented, and why some great ideas stay on the shelf. While some issue-selling methods are public and visible, others occur backstage, and while those may be less easy to identify, they involve methods that are just as common and easy to use.

Dutton describes three categories of techniques for manipulating senior management perceptions, agendas, decisions, and actions. *Packaging moves* concern ways in which ideas can be 'wrapped' to make them more appealing, more urgent, more acceptable, and include presentation tactics and bundling tactics. *Involvement moves* concern ways in which relationships and structures can be exploited to build support for ideas. *Process moves* concern preparation, timing, and degree of formality in issue-selling.

Packaging moves

Presenting

- using the logic of the business plan, 'running the numbers', using lots of figures and charts, conveying a logical and coherent structure, emphasizing bottom-line impacts;
- continuous proposal-making, raising issues many times over a period, prepare the target to better 'hear' a full proposal;
- making changes appear incremental, by 'chunking' ideas into components to make them more palatable to potential targets.

Bundling

- tying issues to profitability, market share, organizational image;
- tying issues to the concerns of key constituents.

Involvement moves

- targets of involvement; knowing who to involve and when;
- involving senior management in supporting ideas;
- clearing the idea with your immediate superior;
- involving colleagues and other departments in supporting ideas;
- involving outsiders, like consultants, to gain credibility;
- customizing issue-selling to stakeholders;
- using formal committees and task forces to legitimize issues;
- creating a task force with a diverse membership.

Process moves

Formality

- deciding appropriate degree of formality in issue-selling.

Preparation

- collecting background information on context before selling, preparing people to support an idea when the time comes;
- understanding social relationships, organizational networks, and strategic goals and priorities.

Timing

- being persistent through a lengthy issue-selling process;
- sensing when to hold back and when to move forward, based on level of support;
- involving relevant others at an early stage.

Sonenshein (2006) develops a similar approach to 'issue-crafting', which involves the manipulation of public language to make issues appear to be more legitimate, urgent, and trustworthy for the audience. Issues are crafted through embellishing (emphasizing particular features), subtracting (playing down parts of the argument) and through consistency (we all share the same values and goals). These tactics can rely either on a normative perspective (fairness, obligation, values, do the right thing) or on an economic perspective (objective, rational, commercial, business-oriented). In Sonenshein's study, the most common issue-crafting tactics involved economic embellishing and normative subtracting, in other words emphasizing commercial gain and paying less attention to values. It is tempting to observe that human resource management initiatives may often do the opposite, emphasizing welfare, health and safety, skills development, while advocating the values of a 'good employer'. These are not complex techniques that require extensive skills training, but routine everyday behaviours that require awareness and informed judgement for their effective use.

If you don't play, you can't win

In conclusion, despite the human resource implications of adaptive reorganization, and the accumulation of evidence concerning the impact of human resource policies, the function rarely appears to be at the forefront of strategic organizational change. This chapter has argued that one explanation for this lack of involvement concerns the need for human resource professionals to work with the political dimensions of change agency, to play a more sophisticated game. While the term 'manipulation' is often used in a negative sense, suggesting devious, disreputable behaviour, many commentators argue that managers who are not prepared to use such methods are likely to find that their good ideas do not attract attention, and are not pursued, while competing initiatives find support and resources.

It is not enough to categorize the function as strategic partner or change champion, in the hope that a fresh label will generate new actions. Commentary on the role of human resource management in strategic change has focused on role typologies, idealized models of implementation, and unrealistic assumptions concerning the power of evidence to persuade. The failure of change initiatives is variously attributed to lack of coherence across multifaceted agendas, to lack of project management skills, to inadequate training in new technologies, to poor communication, to resistance to the content and process of change, and to ineffective leadership. These explanations overlook the politics of change, and do not address the need to act politically to progress proposals. The failure of change to deliver is rarely attributed in public to lack of political skill (but see Buchanan and Badham, 2008).

For Whittington and Molloy (2005), the competencies relevant to the human resource manager as change champion include the ability to make a strategic business case, to align change initiatives with overall corporate functioning, and to use sound project management techniques. This chapter has sought to demonstrate that, while those skills and capabilities may be necessary, they are not sufficient. The human resource professional, like any other change agent, is unlikely to succeed without the political skills required to sell, initiate, drive, and deliver strategic organizational change. Equipped with that combination of conventional and political expertise, is the function's problem solved? No. The acquisition of political skill merely gives the function a ticket to the game. Also significant is the manner and context in which such skills are deployed, and the nature and efficacy of the tactics used by the other players. But as Frankel (2004, p. 19) observes, 'if you don't play, you can't win'.

References

Abrahamson, E. (2000) 'Change without pain', *Harvard Business Review*, 78(4): 75–79.

Arkin, A. (2007) 'Street smart', *People Management*, 5 April: 24–28.

Badaracco, J.L. (2002) *Leading Quietly: An Unorthodox Guide to Doing the Right Thing*. Boston, MA: Harvard Business School Press.

Bass, B.M. and Avolio, B.J. (1994) *Improving Organizational Effectiveness through Transformational Leadership*. Thousand Oaks, CA: Sage Publications.

Beatty, C.A. and Gordon, J.R.M. (1991) 'Preaching the gospel: the evangelists of new technology', *California Management Review*, 33(3): 73–94.

Buchanan, D.A. and Badham, R. (2008) *Power, Politics, and Organizational Change: Winning the Turf Game*. London: Sage Publications (second edn).

Buchanan, D. and Dawson, P. (2007) 'Discourse and audience: organizational change as multi-story process', *Journal of Management Studies*, 44(5): 669–686.

Buchanan, D. and Storey, J. (1997) 'Role taking and role switching in organizational change: the four pluralities', in Ian McLoughlin and Martin Harris (eds), *Innovation, Organizational Change and Technology* (pp. 127–145). London: Thomson International.

Burns, J.M. (1978) *Leadership*. New York: Harper & Row.

Butcher, D. and Clarke, M. (1999) 'Organizational politics: the missing discipline of management?' *Industrial and Commercial Training*, 31(1): 9–12.

Caldwell, R. (2001) 'Champions, adapters, consultants and synergists: the new change agents in HRM', *Human Resource Management Journal*, 11(3): 39–52.

Chartered Institute for Personnel and Development (2006) *Approaches to Change: Key Issues and Challenges*. London: Chartered Institute for Personnel and Development.

Collins, D. (1998) *Organizational Change: Sociological Perspectives*. London: Routledge.

Dawson, P. (2003) *Reshaping Change: A Processual Approach*. London: Routledge.

Denis, J.-L., Lamothe, L. and Langley, A. (2001) 'The dynamics of collective leadership and strategic change in pluralistic organizations', *Academy of Management Journal*, 44(4): 809–837.

Dutton, J.E., Ashford, S.J., O'Neill, R.M. and Lawrence, K.A. (2001) 'Moves that matter: issue selling and organizational change', *Academy of Management Journal*, 44(4): 716–736.

Ferris, G.R., Perrewé, P.L., Anthony, W.P. and Gilmore, D.C. (2000) 'Political skill at work', *Organizational Dynamics*, 28(4): 25–37.

Frankel, L.P. (2004) *Nice Girls Don't Get The Corner Office: Unconscious Mistakes Women Make That Sabotage Their Careers*. New York: Warner Business Books.

Frost, P.J. and Egri, C.P. (1991) 'The political process of innovation', in L.L. Cummings and B.M. Staw (eds), *Research in Organizational Behaviour, Volume 13* (pp. 229–295). Greenwich, CT: JAI Press.

Guest, D. and King, Z. (2004) 'Power, innovation and problem-solving: the personnel managers' three steps to heaven?', *Journal of Management Studies*, 41(3): 401–423.

Gustafson, D.H., Sainfort, F., Eichler, M., Adams, L., Bisognano, M. and Steudel, H. (2003) 'Developing and testing a model to predict outcomes of organizational change', *Health Services Research*, 38(2): 751–776.

Hardy, C. (1996) 'Understanding power: bringing about strategic change', *British Journal of Management*, 7(special conference issue): 3–16.

Huselid, M.A. (1995) 'The impact of human resource management practices on turnover, productivity, and corporate financial performance', *Academy of Management Journal*, 38(3): 635–672.

Hutton, D.W. (1994) *The Change Agent's Handbook: A Survival Guide for Quality Improvement Champions*. Milwaukee, WI: ASQC Quality Press.

Huy, Q.N. (2001) 'In praise of middle managers', *Harvard Business Review*, 79(8): 72–79.

Ibarra, H. and Hunter, M. (2007) 'How leaders create and use networks', *Harvard Business Review*, 85(1): 40–47.

Iles, V. and Sutherland, K. (2001) *Organizational Change: A Review for Health Care Managers, Professionals and Researchers*. London: National Co-ordinating Centre for NHS Service Delivery and Organization Research and Development.

Khurana, R. (2002) 'The curse of the superstar CEO', *Harvard Business Review*, 80(9): 60–66.

Kotter, J.P. (1995) 'Leading change: why transformation efforts fail', *Harvard Business Review*, 73(2): 59–67.

Legge, K. (1978) *Power, Innovation, and Problem Solving in Personnel Management*. London: McGraw-Hill.

Legge, K. (2005) *Human Resource Management: Rhetorics and Realities (Anniversary Edition)*. Basingstoke: Macmillan Business.

Mangham, I. (1979) *The Politics of Organizational Change*. Westport, CT: Greenwood Press.

March, J.G. and Olsen, J.P. (1983) 'Organizing political life: what administrative reorganization tells us about government', *American Political Science Review*, 77(2): 281–296.

Meyerson, D.E. (2001) 'Radical change, the quiet way', *Harvard Business Review*, 79(9): 92–100.

Ottaway, R.N. (1983) 'The change agent: a taxonomy in relation to the change process', *Human Relations*, 36(4): 361–392.

Patterson, M.G., West, M.A., Lawthom, R. and Nickell, S. (1997) *Impact of People Management Practices on Business Performance*. London: Institute of Personnel and Development.

Pettigrew, A.M. (1985) *The Awakening Giant: Continuity and Change in ICI.* Oxford: Basil Blackwell.

Pfeffer, J. (1992) *Managing With Power: Politics and Influence in Organization.* Boston, MA: Harvard Business School Press.

Pfeffer, J. (1998) *The Human Equation: Building Profits by Putting People First.* Boston, MA: Harvard Business School Press.

Schön, D.A. (1963) 'Champions for radical new inventions', *Harvard Business Review*, 41(2): 77–86.

Schuler, R.S., Jackson, S.E. and Storey, J. (2001) 'HRM and its link with strategic management', in John Storey (ed.), *Human Resource Management: A Critical Text* (pp. 114–130). London: Thomson Learning (second edn).

Singh, V., Kumra, S. and Vinnicombe, S. (2002) 'Gender and impression management: playing the promotion game', *Journal of Business Ethics*, 37(1): 77–89.

Sonenshein, S. (2006) 'Crafting social issues at work', *Academy of Management Journal*, 49(6): 1158–1172.

Stjernberg, T. and Philips, A. (1993) 'Organizational innovations in a long-term perspective: legitimacy and souls-of-fire as critical factors of change and viability', *Human Relations*, 46(10): 1193–1221.

Storey, J. (1992) *Developments in the Management of Human Resources: An Analytical Review.* Oxford: Blackwell Business.

Tyson, S. (1995) *Human Resource Strategy: Towards a General Theory of HRM.* London: Pitman Publishing.

Ulrich, D. (1998) 'A new mandate for human resources', *Harvard Business Review*, 76(1): 124–134.

Van de Ven, A.H. and Poole, M.S. (1995) 'Explaining development and change in organizations', *Academy of Management Review*, 20(3): 510–540.

Watson, T.J. (1977) *The Personnel Managers.* London: Routledge & Kegan Paul.

West, M. and Johnson, R. (2002) 'A matter of life and death', *People Management*, 8(4): 30–36.

West, M.A., Borrill, C., Dawson, J., Scully, J., Carter, M., Anelay, S., Patterson, M. and Waring, J. (2002) 'The link between the management of employees and patient mortality in acute hospitals', *International Journal of Human Resource Management*, 13: 1299–1310.

Whittington, R. and Mayer, M. (2002) *Organizing for Success in the Twenty-First Century: A Starting Point for Change.* London: Chartered Institute of Personnel and Development.

Whittington, R. and Molloy, E. (2005) *HR's Role in Organizing: Shaping Change.* London: Chartered Institute for Personnel and Development.

Zanko, M., Badham, R., Couchman, P. and Schubert, M. (2008) 'Innovation and HRM: issues, absences and politics', *International Journal of Human Resource Management*, 19(4): 562–581.

Part 5

The HR function

HR professionals often spend so much time coaching, facilitating, and designing systems for others that their own function languishes. Like the proverbial cobbler's children who have no shoes, the minister's rowdy children, or the teacher's uneducated child, HR professionals often preach more than they practice. This section is about HR for HR. Rather than just having responsibility to do HR work for business leaders who are trying to clarify and deliver strategy, HR professionals need to turn their knowledge inward, building a strong and vibrant HR function.

Lacking a viable HR function, HR professionals advise but do not do, and are subject to legitimate criticism that if they cannot live what they advocate, they have little credibility advocating it. Sometimes what we do speaks more loudly than what we say and we need to lead by example more than by rhetoric. In this part, we examine two areas where HR can apply HR principles: (1) HR professionals and competencies, and (2) HR strategy and structure.

Competency models have been in place now for fifty years. Consultants and HR professionals distinguish high and lower performers and identity the critical incidents and behaviors that distinguish the two groups. Competency models can then be used to hire, train, and pay employees. Competencies have become an accepted standard for helping leaders balance between results and behavior. But, defining HR competencies has not occurred as clearly. The chapter by Brockbank and Ulrich reports Round 4 of their twenty-year HR competency study. This study comprises a large global data set of HR professionals and identifies five domains of HR competence that these HR professionals must master. This longitudinal and sizeable data set defines for HR professionals and line managers what knowledge, skills, and abilities they need to possess to accomplish their work. In this chapter, we learn that associates or users of HR services find HR professionals more competent when they are able to: (1) make a strategic contribution, (2) know the business, (3) have personal credibility, (4) deliver HR practices, and (5) know and use HR technology. The chapter reports the relative impact of these five competence domains on the performance of the HR professionals. This information can be very useful as a standard for hiring, training, and paying HR professionals.

The chapter by Ulrich, Younger, and Brockbank suggests how the HR function should operate in the future. Their basic premise is that the HR function should operate like a business within a business, and like any business it requires a strategy and structure to be effective. The strategy of an HR function are the outcomes of the HR practices often called capabilities (see Part 7 of this book). The structure of the HR function of the future is the focus of this chapter. In this chapter, they show that the HR organization should be aligned with the business organization. Single businesses would have functional HR organizations. Holding companies would have separate HR organizations. Allied diversified organizations would have shared service HR organizations. Since the majority of organizations are allied/diversified, they lay out five roles and responsibilities for this new organization. This work especially develops the operational executor role which many large companies are headed towards.

When HR can do HR for HR, credibility follows. These chapters suggest what types of investments can be made in HR to build both the function and the people who work in it.

11

HR competencies that
make a difference[1]

Wayne Brockbank and Dave Ulrich

The competency approach has emerged from being a specialized and narrow application to being a leading logic for diagnosing, framing and improving virtually every aspect of human resource management. This chapter addresses the question: "What are the competencies that are required of HR professionals if they are to add substantial value to key stakeholders?"

The competency approach to HR management

The competency approach to human resource management has its origins in military staffing decisions during World War II. Over the ensuing years, the theory and application of competencies has become a central paradigm in HR practices (McClelland 1976; Boyatzis 1982a; McClelland & Boyatzis 1982; McLagan & Suhadolnik 1989; Spencer & Spencer 1993; Schoonover 1998). In 1982, Boyatzis (1982b, p. 221) defined a competency to be "a characteristic of a person that results in consistently effective performance in a job". These characteristics may be conceptualized to include values, knowledge, abilities and skills that are required for job performance.

Over the years the competency approach has been specifically applied to the following purposes:

1. to specify human characteristics that are required for job performance (McClelland 1973);
2. to communicate and train people to improve performance (McClelland 1973);
3. to monitor and measure performance (McClelland 1976);
4. to predict superior human performance (Spencer & Spencer 1993);
5. to match individuals with jobs (Kolb 1984);
6. to implement business strategy and create competitive advantage (Intagliata, Ulrich & Smallwood 2000);
7. to integrate and harmonize potentially fragmented management and HR practices (Intagliata, Ulrich & Smallwood 2000);
8. to develop high value adding HR departments (Ulrich 1987; Nadler & Nadler 1989; Schuler 1990; Morris 1996; Ulrich 1997; Losey 1999).

While it is difficult to trace the first application of the competency approach to the HR function, early studies include the work of the Ontario Society for Training and Development in 1976 (Kenny 1982) and an American Society of Training and Development sponsored study in 1967 (Lippitt & Nadler 1967; McCullough & McLagan 1983). These were followed by extensive studies of HR competencies by Patricia McLagan for the American Society for Training and Development in 1983 and 1987 (McLagan & Bedrick 1983). These important studies detailed the competencies for specialists in human resource development and documented the variety of possible roles for the human resource profession as a whole (see McLagan and Suhadolnik 1989).

In the late 1980s, Dave Ulrich and Wayne Brockbank from the Ross School of Business at the University of Michigan and The RBL Group initiated the longest and largest ongoing study of the competencies of HR professionals. This study has been conducted in four major waves over sixteen years.[2] The foundational work of this study began with the work of Dave Ulrich who surveyed 600 HR professionals (Ulrich 1987). From this data set, three categories of HR professional competencies were identified: knowledge of business, HR delivery and change management.

In 1988, Ulrich was joined by other colleagues at the University of Michigan including Wayne Brockbank, Dale Lake and Arthur Yeung. The 1988 Human Resource Competency Study was designed to include more elaborate questions and a larger number of participants. This survey was designed on the basis of 360° logic in which individual HR professional participants evaluated themselves and were, in turn, evaluated by HR and non-HR associates (who were familiar with the participant's functioning as an HR professional). Of the approximately 10,000 respondents from 91 firms in the survey, almost 9,000 were associates. Thus, their work avoided many of the problems inherent in self-evaluation. The study included HR professionals from every HR position and from virtually every industry. It also accounted for the strategic as well as the operational aspects of HR (Ulrich et al. 1989). The result of the study was a benchmark of effective HR competencies using rigorous quantitative statistical methods to analyze a large-scale survey population.

In the 1992 round of the Human Resource Competency Study, the survey questions were almost exactly the same as their first survey in 1989. Repeating the same survey enabled the HR field to track important trends as they occurred. This second round found the following:

- the importance of knowledge of finance and external market dynamics had increased;
- change management was becoming a more critical category of HR value contribution;
- interpersonal skills and communications emerged as important contributors to personal success;
- high-performing firms were spending increasingly more time and effort on strategic HR issues whereas the low-performing firms were focused relatively more heavily on operational-level HR issues.

The 1992 iteration verified that the three main types of HR competencies were management of change competencies, delivery of HR practices, and knowledge of the business (Ulrich et al. 1995).

In 1997, the third iteration of the Human Resource Competency Study (Brockbank et al. 2001) sought a larger cross-section of medium and smaller companies at the expense of fewer overall participants. In this round 3,000 respondents from 142 companies were involved. Utilizing findings from extensive pre-survey focus groups, this round examined the influence of two additional categories of HR competencies: personal credibility and culture management. The results identified the following trends:

■ Many of those activities that HR professionals did best mattered least and some activities that HR professionals did not do so well had substantial influence on business performance. For example, HR professionals in the low-performing firms and the high-performing firms had similarly high levels of knowledge about HR practices. HR professionals in the high-performing firms distinguished themselves in their knowledge of external business realities. This contrasted with the relatively low knowledge of external market dynamics in the field as a whole, and especially among HR professionals in low-performing firms. This round established the importance of the personal credibility of HR professionals in working with their internal clients. They had to have good interpersonal skills, had to achieve their promised results, and had to contribute to business decisions.

■ This round continued to confirm that HR matters most under conditions of change. In companies whose business environments were relatively stable, HR as a whole had little differentiating influence on business performance.

This current chapter relies on the 2002 data set and the fourth round of the Human Resource Competency Data. In this chapter we also introduce the preliminary findings of the 2007 data set.

Characteristics of the 2002 data set

Questions that have been included in our competency research have been identified through interviews with hundreds of HR professionals and line managers and through extensive reviews of the academic literature. We have asked questions about every mainstream HR competency.

In order to relate the competencies of HR professionals to business performance, we also asked about business performance: "Compared to *the major competitor* in 'your business' in the last three years, how has 'your business' performed financially[3]?" This question has clear limitations; however, it does embody three issues. It focuses on financial performance; it has a built-in time perspective; and it represents performance relative to the competition.

Our competency research applies a 360° methodology. Each HR participant evaluates herself or himself on a "participant survey". Each participant selects a set of three to seven associates who are familiar with the participant's functioning as an HR professional. Associates could be either from HR or not from HR. This chapter relies solely on the US non-HR associates[4] as data sources (N = 646). The following additional aspects of the data are noteworthy.

■ Primary role of associate raters: The non-HR associates are dominated, in order, by general management, marketing and sales, finance, and manufacturing.

■ Company size: The data set is relatively balanced in terms of size including small, medium and large sized companies.

■ Industry of participation: The data set cuts across virtually all industry sectors.

Competencies for HR professionals

To identify the basic categories we applied exploratory factor analysis. This objective sorting of the data generated the competency model in Figure 11.1.

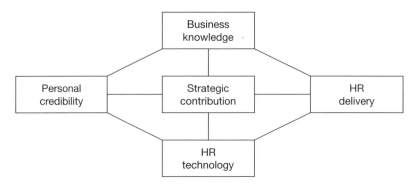

Figure 11.1 Competency model for the HR value proposition

This initial analysis identifies the competencies of HR professionals and establishes that these competencies may be divided into five categories or factors:

- strategic contributions (HR has influence on large-scale strategic contributions such as culture management, fast change, strategy decision making and market-driven connectivity);
- personal credibility (HR has personal credibility if they get results, have good interpersonal skills, and are effective communicators.);
- HR delivery (HR professionals deliver the foundational HR infrastructure of staffing, training and development, organization design, and performance management);
- business knowledge (HR professionals have knowledge of the integrated business value change, the business value proposition, and labor law);
- HR technology (HR professionals know how to apply technology to HR processes).

Having identified these factors, we then went on to address a second research objective: "What are the competencies of HR professionals in high-performing firms that are different from the competencies of HR professionals in low-performing firms?" In other words, we set out to identify those competencies that have the greatest influence on firm performance.

Table 11.1 provides information about two categories of performance.

Column 1 in Table 11.1 responds to the question, "How effective is HR at each competency category?" It shows that HR professionals are best at personal credibility (4.13). They achieve

Table 11.1 HR effectiveness in each competency category and the influence of each competency category on business performance

Competency category	HR effectiveness (1 = low; 5 = high) (Column 1)	Linear regressions of business performance on competency categories (Column 2)	Significance (Column 3)
Strategic contribution	3.65	.16	.000
Personal credibility	4.13	.11	.002
HR delivery	3.69	.06	.027
Business knowledge	3.44	.06	.029
HR technology	3.02	.04	.075

basic results; they have good interpersonal skills; they are effective communicators. There is a large drop-off in effectiveness for the next competency category – HR delivery. HR professionals do a moderately effective job at designing and delivering the foundational HR practices. Coming in at a very close third is HR's strategic contribution. This is followed by business knowledge and HR technology. These numbers reveal how well HR professionals undertake each competency category but they do not tell us which of these categories has the greatest influence on business performance.

Column 2 in Table 11.1 shows that the greatest influence of HR professionals on business performance is through the competencies of strategic contribution. HR professionals who are actively involved in culture management, fast change, strategic decision making, and market-driven connectivity have substantive influence on business performance.[5] The HR professionals in high-performing firms exhibit these competencies to a much greater degree than do the HR professionals in low-performing firms. The next category, personal credibility, accounts for significantly less business performance than strategic contribution. HR delivery and business knowledge account for approximately less than half of the business performance variance when compared to personal credibility. At a statistically insignificant R^2 of .04, the HR technology category has the least influence on business performance.

Thus what HR professionals do best (personal credibility) has moderate influence on business performance. And what HR professionals do only moderately well has greatest influence on business performance – when it is done well. These findings do not discount the importance of personal credibility, HR delivery and business knowledge. Rather, they suggest that to have the knowledge and legitimacy to be involved in strategic issues, HR professionals must first exhibit these more basic competencies. However, if HR professionals limit their professional aspirations and activities to personal credibility, HR delivery and business knowledge, they substantially limit their total influence that they might have on business performance.

With this awareness, we examine each of these five competency categories in more detail.

Strategic contribution

Our competency model emphasizes that the largest influence of HR on business performance is accounted for by strategic contribution. Through additional analyses, we identify four sub-factors that comprise the strategic contribution category.[6] In order of importance, these factors include culture management, fast change, strategic decision making, and market-driven connectivity.

Culture management

In high-performing firms HR professionals exhibit the competencies of culture management. Culture management consists of a number of steps that fit into an integrated framework. HR professionals in the high-performing firms make sure that they define the culture to be consistent with the balanced requirements of external customers, the business strategy, and employees. They ensure that the company's HR practices are designed and delivered to create and reinforce the desired culture by translating the desired culture into specific employee and executive behaviors.

Fast change

In high-performing firms, HR professionals make change happen successfully and thoroughly. They are centrally involved in planning and implementing change processes. But most critical is that they ensure that change happens quickly. They focus on getting decisions made quickly. They effectively involve key leaders in fast change. They ensure that the human, financial and informational resources required for effective change are aligned with the desired changes. They monitor progress of key change initiatives, capture important learnings and apply these learnings to improve future change efforts. They not only set the broad framework for effective change management but also have the facilitation skills to move change initiatives forward in a "hands-on" manner.

Strategic decision making

In high-performing firms, HR professionals play two roles in the making of key decisions. First, they know the business in enough detail that they are able to proactively set the direction of change. They walk into the strategy room with an opinion about the future of the business. They are willing to take strong stands. They not only facilitate change but they also set the direction of change. And, most interesting, they bring intellectual rigor to business decision making; that is, when HR walks into the room in the high-performing firms, the average of the "business IQ points" in the room goes up – not down. Second, they also play a reactive role relative to the business decision making. They ask insightful questions; they encourage others to be strategic; they forecast obstacles to achieving the strategy. In so doing they must have the interpersonal skills as well as the intellectual capacity to play an effective "devil's advocate".

Market-driven connectivity

The first three competency factors are reasonably well known in the HR literature. This last factor, market-driven connectivity, is new to the literature. To our knowledge, prior to the 2002 iteration of the HR Competency Study, the combination of specific competencies that make up this factor had not been empirically identified as an area for HR involvement. In this iteration of the Competency Study, it was not only identified as an issue but it was also identified as a distinguishing factor between the HR professionals in high-performing firms and those in low-performing firms. In high-performing firms, HR professionals play an important role in amplifying important signals (customer information) from the external environment and ensuring that these signals are fully disseminated throughout the company so that people may act in harmony with each other in responding to market place demands. Furthermore, they reduce the presence of less important information that frequently blocks attention to more critical information. By so doing HR professionals help to successfully "navigate" the organization through changing customer and shareholder requirements. We call the process of leveraging dynamic market information to create a unified and responsive organization "market-driven conductivity".

Personal credibility

Personal credibility has the second greatest influence on business performance. Our data indicate that there are a significant number of HR professionals who have personal credibility but who do not go to the next step of translating personal credibility into strategic contribution. However, to be allowed to make strategic contributions, HR professionals must first have credibility with the line managers with whom they work. Without credibility they will not be invited to strategy forums nor will they be able to generate commitment to the strategic agendas that they might bring to "the table". Personal credibility consists of three sub-factors: achieving results, effective relationships and communication skills.

Achieving results

The most important aspect of personal credibility is achieving a track record of results. HR professionals must have a reputation of meeting their commitments, of doing what they say and saying what they will do. The results they achieve should be error free. One important category in which results should occur is in the areas of asking important questions that help to frame complex ideas in useful ways. All of this must be done with personal integrity. It is noteworthy that in the Human Resource Competency Study, the integrity variables factored together with the "achieving results" variables. Therefore, in the minds of line executives, HR professionals must achieve results but they must do so in a way that meets the highest standards of integrity.

Effective relationships

Given that HR professionals focus on the human side of business, the expectation that HR professionals are able to foster and maintain effective interpersonal skills is reasonable. These skills enable them to work well with colleagues, with individual line executives and with the management team as a whole. They must be able to diagnose and improve, if necessary, intra-personal as well as interpersonal problems. They must be able to create an atmosphere of trust in their relationships. Trust comes about by being consistent relative to an agreed-upon set of behavioral and achievement standards. With trust comes the capacity to "have chemistry" with key constituents. In our work with effective HR executives we have noticed that "having good chemistry" occurs when core values are shared, when there are some elements of common interests that go beyond work boundaries, when HR executives are helpful and empathetic in addressing non-direct work-related concerns and when the HR executive can decompress tense interpersonal issues.

Communication skills

HR professionals must have effective written and verbal communication skills. Over the past twenty years, the average span of control has more than doubled. This requires that HR professionals must be able to communicate effectively to large numbers of people in shorter time periods. In a world where the speed of information has increased approximately 16,000,000% in the past twenty-four years or so, the mandate to communicate clearly is obvious. Multiple messages compete for airtime in the limited mental space of virtually all organizations. To have personal credibility HR professionals must be able to accurately select and clearly communicate the most critical messages for organizational success. They must communicate not only through formal communication lines; they also recognize that virtually all activities in which HR is involved have an important communication component. When HR professionals hire, promote and fire certain people, when they design and implement measurement and reward systems, and when they offer specific training programs, they are sending powerful messages about what is important to the organization and to its success.

HR delivery

HR professionals deliver both traditional and operational HR activities to their businesses. The HR delivery category entails the HR activities that are traditionally associated with the HR function. They are the tools of the trade. These include staffing, training and development, organization design,[7] performance management, legal compliance and HR measurement.

This category of HR involvement is akin to one of the dominant HR frameworks of the 1970s and 1980s: "Right person, right people, right place, doing right things."

HR Delivery has a small though statistically significant influence on business performance. The conclusion is that increasingly the HR delivery tools do not highly differentiate the HR professionals in the high-performing firms from those in the low-performing firms. However, there is a fascinating and important conclusion that can be drawn when HR delivery is applied in the context of HR's strategic contribution. Recall that elements of the HR delivery tools are included in both culture management (i.e. alignment of HR with the desired culture) and fast change (i.e. alignment of people, information, measurement and incentives with fast change). Thus, when applied in the context of powerful cultural or change agendas, the foundational HR tools strongly contribute to business performance. When these foundational HR tools are applied without powerful business direction, their differentiating impact is weak. This does not suggest that these practices do not need to be done well. Rather, it suggests that the well-designed and delivered HR basics are the "price of entry" into the strategy game.

Staffing

HR professionals should have the ability to develop comprehensive staffing processes. They must competently design and deliver each phase of the staffing process; they must be able to hire, promote, transfer and fire people as individual and discrete steps. They must also be able to carry out these tasks as part of an overall staffing agenda. They must integrate the full breadth of staffing practices into a comprehensive system that supports the overall HR strategy as described above.

In a world of change, the required individual competencies and organizational capabilities need to be continually defined and created. Your company will need to keep some competencies and capabilities through aggressive programs that retain the key talent. Your company may need to develop other key competencies. Still other competencies and capabilities may no longer be needed because of the changing nature of the competitive environment. These need to be reduced through divestitures or through outplacement. Thus, staffing practices play a central role in continually updating the capabilities that are required by a company. Of the HR basics, staffing practices have greatest influence on financial performance.

Development

Effective development defines and integrates two key sets of activities: training and organization development. This is noticeable since it sometimes occurs that HR activities become dominated by psychologists with a decided bent toward individual development. On other occasions, developmental activities may be dominated by organizational development specialists who focus on organizational interventions. As a result of this distinction, some companies have experienced a fragmentation between the training specialists and the OD specialists. Occasionally the segmentation deteriorates into dysfunctional one-upmanship – each trying to outdo the other in importance, impact, and image. In the high-performing firms, these two sets of activities are integrated into a cooperative whole and are conceptually and practically linked into a single and comprehensive agenda. Training programs may consist of four major sets of activities:

- basic skills (reading, writing, arithmetic), technical skills (activity-based costing, inventory management), or leadership skills (strategy, organizing, coaching);
- training programs that promote overall cultural and strategic agendas;

  ▦ training that is linked to career development for individual participants;
  ▦ training that engages employees in high value-added and challenging work assignments.

Organization development is also a key component of an overall developmental agenda. In the HR field, there are probably as many different definitions of OD as there are companies that employ OD specialists. At a minimum, OD generally refers to change interventions at the organization and team levels. In the Human Resource Competency Study, we identified two key OD activities:

  ▦ developmental intervention programs that facilitate change;
  ▦ large-scale communication initiatives that help people to know where the organization is headed and how it will get there.

Structure

HR professionals assist in the design of effective organizations. The Human Resource Competency Study differentiates two aspects of organization design: organization structure and process design. To play a substantial role in restructuring activities, HR professionals must apply four key principles of organizational structure.

  ▦ First, the primary purpose of structure is to place those people together structurally who need to interact most to create the greatest wealth. This principle applies whether corporate wealth is created by developing a close relationship with customers (market-based structure), by creating and producing products (product-based structure), by being highly efficient (functionally based structure), by leveraging synergies (matrix structure) or by responding to regionally segmented markets (geographically based structure).
  ▦ Second, organizational structures bring people together to solve one problem but in so doing structures inevitably separate people who must still have working relationships. HR professionals can help design mechanisms that foster coordination among separated functions or products groups such as meetings, task forces and committees, common goals, measures and rewards, lateral and diagonal transfers, and work process integration.
  ▦ Third, we live in a world that mandates greater speed, flexibility, efficiency, empowerment, productivity and innovation. In this world, hierarchical delayering and staff reductions continue as an ongoing way of life in many organizations. When these occur, HR must establish control mechanisms which replace the traditional managerial hierarchy. Such control mechanisms include the following:
    ▦ training programs that enhance technical, team and personal competencies, financial and process knowledge, and skills in conflict resolution;
    ▦ team-based goal setting, measurement, feedback and incentives;
    ▦ intensive communications about company direction and strategy, cultural and technical requirements, and financial and operational matters;
    ▦ delegation of authority to make decisions and take action with minimal supervisory oversight (because there are fewer supervisors).
  ▦ Fourth, HR professionals should not only be experts in the structuring of organizations but should also be expert in the process of organizational restructuring. They should work with organization design teams to ensure that political considerations are minimized and that business logic receives predominant consideration. They should be the integrity shepherds and primary proponents of the pre-specified strategic objectives of

the restructuring. They should make sure that the right people are selected to be on the design team, that design team members have the correct instructions and that they have the opportunity to receive information and instructions from key stakeholders. Finally, HR professionals should ensure that measures are in place to evaluate the effectiveness of the new structure within pre-specified time frames.

The second aspect of organization design is process design. Redesigning organizations around processes is becoming a more prevalent trend. Two considerations are central in process redesign:

- First, process-based organization design generally presumes that the processes begin with a target customer or group of target customers in mind. With the target customer as the focal definer of the process, information and activities flow backward from the customer into the organization through sales and marketing, delivery, service, logistics, manufacturing (or the equivalent in a service-based company), product or service design, R&D, and market research. The key issue in this flow is the maintenance of consistency of customer focus.
- Second, processes must be concurrent and integrated. Concurrency requires that organizational processes be designed so that heretofore sequential steps are planned and executed simultaneously. Integration occurs, as processes are designed to move away from individual assembly line-based processes to more team-based workflow. As these are done, time, quality and costs are mutually improved.

HR measurement

As part of the basic HR delivery, HR professionals must be able to measure how much their activities add value. They must have a concept of the full HR value proposition. They must be able to provide measures for each component of the HR value proposition and verify the statistical relationship among the levels of the HR value proposition (Ulrich & Brockbank 2005).

As the mandate for greater productivity continues to impress itself on most corporations, HR departments are expected to provide quantitative indicators of value added. Two categories of HR measurement may be distinguished: efficiency measures and effectiveness measures.

- The HR measurement literature has traditionally been dominated by measures of efficiency. These measures tend to focus on how well HR does specific HR activities (e.g. costs per hire, time to fill a job, training hours per year per employee).
- In recent years substantial progress has been made in measuring the contributions of HR to business success. The premise of these recent trends is that measuring HR is easy; the difficult aspect of HR measurement is not the measurement but rather knowing what to measure. Before measurements can be taken, the dominant and focal contributions of HR to the firm must first be determined. Once these are decided then the measurement process may proceed rather easily by statistically connecting marketplace results, strategy implementation results, organizational capability results, and HR practice implementation results.

Legal compliance

To be effective in working with the human side of business, HR professionals must know the legal issues that influence and safeguard people at work:

- the rights of people to work free from discrimination based on gender, race, religion, sexual orientation, ethnicity, age or disability;
- legal protection of an environment that is free from physical threat or forms of psychological harassment;
- legal rights of people at work relative to testing, evaluation, discipline, compensation, and privacy;
- legal issues that have direct influence on labor relations;
- legal issues that have ethical overtones including honesty in financial and other kinds of reporting.

Performance management

HR professionals should have the ability to design and deliver performance management systems. Of the four sub-factors that constitute HR delivery, the performance management factor is the weakest predictor of business financial performance. There are probably several reasons for this result:

- other factors influence pay besides performance, such as seniority, guaranteed base pay, hierarchical level, and functional category;
- companies frequently pay large compensation packages as part of pre-employment agreements rather than solely on the basis of performance;
- many companies link compensation to performance when business is good and cash flow is strong; fewer companies substantially reduce total compensation when business is bad and cash flow is weak.

To be a driver of business performance, performance management systems must consist of two basic elements: measurements and rewards.[8] Effective measurement systems have four important features:

- high-performing teams and individuals from low-performing teams and individuals can be differentiated;
- measurements should be simple but complete; they should measure both results and behaviors including ethical integrity;
- measurements should come from several sources so as to be credible in the mind of the person being evaluated and to capture the full richness of multiple perspectives;
- measurements should be comparable to key benchmarks such as previous year-to-date performance, other individuals doing the same tasks, and preset targets or goals.

Effective reward systems also have seven important characteristics:

- effective reward systems acknowledge that certain components of the reward system are required to get people to go to work for you (e.g. benefits and some form of base compensation);
- rewards motivate when they are of value to the receiver and not to the giver;
- rewards are most motivating when they are visible to both the receiver and to those whose opinions are valued by the receiver;
- rewards that are given close to the achievement of the desired results or to the expression of the desired behaviors are more effective at reinforcing those desired results and behaviors;

- rewards are more effective if they are performance contingent and can therefore be taken away if performance is not sustained;
- non-financial rewards can be important sources of motivation; these include office size, titles, and public acknowledgement;
- of the non-financial rewards, one that is often overlooked and yet has great motivating influence is the option to do challenging and high value-added work that may be outside of the formal job description.

Business knowledge

Business knowledge likewise accounts for a small though statistically significant portion of HR's influence on business performance. It is not that business knowledge is unimportant but it is the case that HR professionals in low-performing firms tend to know as much about business as those in high-performing firms. Knowledge by itself is not a differentiator of performance. What does differentiate performance is not what you know but rather what you do with that knowledge. Specifically, what matters is how effectively you apply that knowledge to making strategic contributions to the business.

Knowledge of the value chain

HR professionals need to have knowledge of the full breadth of activities that comprise the value chain. The value chain consists of several elements which together link the market demand with internal supply. The value chain factor starts with knowledge of external customers, suppliers and competitors. The dynamics and requirements of the competitive environment are then translated into internal financial and production requirements. Finally, the supplied products and services are then distributed to the marketplace through alternative channels. By applying this knowledge a major contribution of HR is to make the value chain whole greater than the sum of the parts.

Knowledge of the firm's value proposition

The Human Resource Competency Study identifies three key categories of wealth creation that determine the context within which other value-creating activities occur and about which HR professionals should be knowledgeable.

- First, companies create wealth by developing a portfolio of businesses that maximize leverage and returns while concurrently mitigating risks. Company leaders (including HR leaders) determine which businesses they will buy, which they will keep, and which they will close or divest. This must be done with the focused consideration of the risk tolerance of the investment community. They must also determine which activities will be conducted through which internal channels (within business units, within corporate headquarters, and within shared services) or which should be outsourced.
- Second, in harmony with determining which businesses they will emphasize, companies must also determine which markets they will pursue and through which marketing activities they will approach their selected markets.
- Third, they must know the basic processes through which products and services will be provided and the quality standards to which these processes will be held accountable.

Labor knowledge

As might be anticipated, HR professionals need to have knowledge of labor issues. Labor issues may be divided into four categories:

- general infrastructure, personnel, and logic of unions;
- how to avoid disputes by knowing the issues that are of greatest importance to the work force, maintaining accurate mechanisms to track employee satisfaction relative to these key issues, ensuring that the company is proactive in meeting the key needs of employees, and maintaining ongoing two-way communications with the workforce;
- key legal and ethical issues of collective bargaining;
- how to effectively work within the provisions of the labor contract, acting within the spirit as well as within the letter of the law.

HR technology

In the last decade, there has been a substantial increase in the application of electronic technology to HR administrative services. HR departments are regularly inventing new applications to accomplish a multitude of HR goals. These goals focus on helping HR to be more efficient as well as more effective. Nonetheless, the Human Resource Competency Study has found that HR technology has a statistically insignificant influence on business performance. There are at least two reasons for this finding:

- First, approximately 10% of business IT projects is delivered on time and on budget. HR specific projects are probably consistent with this general statistic.
- Second, even if the projected cost savings are realized, it is likely that these cost savings are a relatively small percent of the firm's total cost structure.

The above logic does not, of course, lead to the conclusion that companies should not invest in HR technology. Rather, it does suggest that the likelihood of HR information systems directly and significantly impacting bottom-line financial performance is rather low. In fact, one might argue that the direct influence of HR technology on financial performance will never be very high. Rather, the influence of HR technology on financial performance will occur because it will free up the time, focus and energy of HR professionals so that they can make important strategic contributions (as discussed above).

Conclusions and what's next

This chapter indicates the competencies of HR professionals that relate to business performance. It, therefore, suggests the specific competencies that HR professionals should identify and master to fully contribute. These findings have important implications for the selection, development, and performance management processes for those in HR. If and when we know what is expected for an HR professional to contribute to business success, then HR leaders can use that information for investing in their HR professionals.

This study reported data from the 2002 data set. At this time, we are culling the data from the 2007 data set with about 10,000 total respondents. Our initial findings on the 2007 data set suggest that most of the key findings of this 2002 data set continue to be valid, with the 2007 data showing an ever-increasing importance of what we now call "credible activist" (in this chapter, personal credibility). It is not enought for HR professionals to be credible, they must also have a point of view on how to influence the business.

We anticipate further refinements as the HR profession continues to move forward.

Notes

1 We express our appreciation to Dave Yakonich and Jon Woodard for their contributions to this chapter.

2 During four iterations of the Human Resource Competency Study, we have had the opportunity to work with a number of outstanding colleagues. In 1987 and 1992, Arthur Yeung and Dale Lake contributed heavily to the project. In 1997, Connie James played a central role. In 2002, David Yakonich capably managed the increasing complexity of the project.

3 We consciously selected the concept of business for reasons that were consistent with the intent of the research project. The term "business" is used to describe the organizational units in which the HR participants generally provide services. Businesses are "identifiable units that are commonly understood within the firm". Thus, "business" could refer to corporate offices, group (Household Products group), division (Software Division), plant (Ann Arbor Manufacturing), function (Financial Services, or geography (Asia-Pacific Region). We avoided the term "business unit" due to the fact that "business unit" has different meaning in different firms. For example, in some companies Asia Pacific Region may be the "business" which an HR professional may serve but the Asia Pacific Region may not be a "business unit" in the vernacular of a specific firm.

   We also consciously decided to focus on the participant's business rather than on the corporation as a whole. The rationale for this decision is based on the assumption that the HR practices and competencies that may be important for one business may be less relevant for another business even if they are part of the same corporation. However, companies were not willing to provide "business"-level performance measures such as ROI, margins, sales, profitability or revenue growth. Thus we were left with a perceived measure of financial performance.

   To confirm the reliability of this indicator, the research team undertook a two-phase process:
   1. Data from multiple business units from the same corporation were aggregated to the corporate level.
   2. These aggregated data were then correlated with the publicly available ROA figures for the past three years (1999, 2000. 2001).

   The resultant correlation is .5645. Given that virtually none of the companies for which ROA figures were available had 100% of their respective "businesses" involved in the study, this result supports the convergent validity assumption between the perceived and objective performance measures.

4 The entire 2002 data set consisted of 7082 respondents. In this chapter, we used only US and non-HR associates. The logic for the utilization of this sub-sample is as follows. In this analysis we are examining the influence of HR on business performance. Through the four rounds of the Human Resource Competency Study, we have found that non-HR associates view the work of HR professionals differently in important ways from how HR professionals view themselves. Non-HR professionals tend to be more critical and more business focused in their judgments of HR professionals. We chose to use the US portion of the sample because of the relatively more competitive business conditions that exist in the US when compared to many other parts of the world. For example, in controlled or developing economies, business performance may be primarily dependent on government influence rather than on the inherent competitiveness of the company.

5 The authors recognize that the data set is based on cross-sectional data from which it is difficult to attribute causality. What we know from the cross-sectional results is that the HR professionals in high-performing firms exhibit these competencies more than do those in the low-performing firms. Additional analysis will be conducted to further test the causal nature of our conclusions.

6 The additional analysis consists of second-level exploratory factors analysis of the items that comprise the strategic contribution category.

7   The "organization design" factor is the most complex of the entire study. Several variables factored together which make sense but only a very high level of conceptual abstraction. While they make conceptual sense as a single factor, from a practical standpoint it makes less sense to address them at the same time. Therefore, we divide this factor into three categories:
   ▓   organization design;
   ▓   HR measurement;
   ▓   legal compliance.
8   The criteria for effective measurements and rewards are based on the work of Steve Kerr whose substantial influence on the HR field we gratefully acknowledge.

References

Boyatzis, R., 1982a. *The Competent Manager*. New York: John Wiley & Sons.

Boyatzis, R., 1982b. Competence at work. In A. Stewart, ed. *Motivation and Society*. San Francisco: Jossey-Bass, pp. 221–243.

Brockbank, W., Sioli, A. & Ulrich, D., 2001. So . . . We are at the table! Now what? Available at http://webuser.bus.edu/Programs/hrcs/res_NowWhat.htm [accessed July 23, 2002].

Intagliata, J., Ulrich, D. & Smallwood, N., 2000. Leveraging leadership competencies to produce leadership brand. *Human Resource Planning*, Dec., 12–22.

Kenny, J., 1982. Competency analysis for trainers: a model for professionalization. *Training and Development Journal*, 36 (5), 142–148.

Kolb, D., 1984. *Experiential Learning*. New Jersey: Prentice-Hall, Inc.

Lippitt, G. & Nadler, L., 1967. Emerging roles of the training director. *Training and Development Journal*, 21 (8), 2–10.

Losey, M., 1999. Mastering the competencies of HR management. *Human Resource Management*, 38 (2), 99–102.

McClelland, D., 1973. Testing for competence rather than intelligence. *American Psychologist*, 28 (1), 1–14.

McClelland, D., 1976. *A Guide to Job Competency Assessment*. Boston: McBer.

McClelland, D. & Boyatzis, R., 1982. Leadership motive pattern and long-term success in management. *Journal of Applied Psychology*, 67 (6), 737–743.

McCullough, M. & McLagan, P., 1983. Keeping the competency study alive. *Training and Development Journal*, 37 (6), 24–28.

McLagan, P. & Bedrick, D., 1983. Models for excellence: The results of the ASTD training and development study. *Training and Development Journal*, 37 (6), 10–20.

McLagan, P. & Suhadolnik, D., 1989. *Models for HRD Practice: The Research Report*. Alexandria: American Society for Training and Development.

Morris, D., 1996. Using competency development tools as a strategy for change in the human resources function. *Human Resource Management*, 35 (1), 35–51.

Nadler, L. & Nadler, Z., 1989. *Developing Human Resources*. San Francisco: Jossey-Bass.

Schoonover, S., 1998. *Human Resource Competencies for the Year 2000: The wake up call!* Alexandria: Society for Human Resource Management.

Schuler, R., 1990. Repositioning the human resource function: Transformation or demise? *Academy of Management Executive*, 4 (3), 49–59.

Spencer, L. & Spencer, S., 1993. *Competence at Work*. New York: John Wiley.

Ulrich, D., 1987. Organizational capability as a competitive advantage: Human resource professionals as strategic partners. *Human Resource Planning*, 10 (4), 169–184.

Ulrich, D., 1997. *Human Resource Champions*. Boston: Harvard Business School Press.

Ulrich, D. & Brockbank, W., 2005. *The HR Value Proposition*. Boston: Harvard Business School Press.

Ulrich, D., Brockbank, W. & Yeung, A., 1989. Beyond belief: A benchmark for human resources. *Human Resource Management*, 28 (3), 311–355.

Ulrich, D., Brockbank, W., Yeung, A. & Lake, D., 1995. Human resource competencies: An empirical assessment. *Human Resource Management*, 34 (4), 473–495.

12

The next evolution of the HR organization

Dave Ulrich, Jon Younger
and Wayne Brockbank

HR departments are increasingly seen and managed as a business within a business. Like any business, the HR department must have a vision (or strategy) that defines where it is headed, a set of goals (objectives, outcomes, or deliverables) that focus the priorities for its work and investments, and an organization structure to allow HR to deliver on its vision and goals. We have discussed elsewhere the emerging vision of an HR department, which is, simply stated, to create value (Ulrich and Brockbank, 2005). Value is created when stakeholders receive desired outcomes because the HR department designs and delivers the HR practices that stakeholders require. When HR does its work well, value is created for each HR stakeholder (Ulrich et al., 1999):

- employees have the right set of competencies and are committed to the organization and its goals;
- line managers have increased confidence that business strategies will be executed;
- external customers buy more products or services resulting in greater loyalty and customer share;
- investor confidence leads to increases in market value through recognition of the company's growth prospects as measured by intangible shareholder value (Ulrich and Smallwood, 2003);
- communities in which organizations participate have more confidence in the organization's ability to deliver on sustainability and other social responsibility agendas.

The goals or outcomes of the HR department have also been well documented. HR has traditionally been measured by the quantity or cost of its activities, e.g., how many people were hired in a given time period, the percentage of employees who received 40 hours of training, or the financial cost of staffing and training. An evolution has occurred where the goals and measures of HR have progressively shifted from quantity of activities to quality of outcomes. Instead of focusing on the relatively easy to measure activities of staffing, training, or other functional operations, HR departments are better assessed by the outcomes they create in support of the organization's objectives. These outcomes may generally be defined as the capabilities an organization requires for its strategy to succeed on a sustained basis (Ulrich and Smallwood, 2004).

For example, organizations may require competitive superiority in speed to market (a consumer products firm bringing new products to market), collaboration (a firm growing through mergers and acquisitions), culture change (a firm trying to shift its firm brand to be more connected with new customer expectations), efficiency (a firm competing on price), service (a firm working to deepen relationships with key customers), innovation (a firm competing based on the creation of new products and services), accountability (a firm dedicated to meeting deadlines), or leadership brand (a firm focused on building confidence in the quality of its leaders and leadership as a competitive tool). These, and other, capabilities represent what the organization is known for and this identity may be enhanced because the HR practices are aligned with the desired capability. The organization's efforts in recruitment, development, communication, compensation, and work design may now be integrated around the capabilities they are trying to deliver. Tracking and measuring an organization's capabilities shifts the focus of HR from activities to outcomes. This focus also makes sure that HR activities inside the firm deliver value to customers, investors, and communities outside the firm. Capabilities become the deliverables of HR that show up in employee value propositions, investor intangibles, and firm brand.

While the vision of *value* and the outcomes of *capabilities* continue to be refined, these concepts set the foundation that permits an HR department to act as a business within the business (Reilly and Williams, 2006; Reilly et al., 2007). The business of HR now has a vision and outcomes that matter. What's next is to figure out how the HR department can and should be organized to deliver on this vision and reach these outcomes (Christensen, 2005). This chapter offers observations and proposes alternatives for how to organize an HR department so that the vision of value and the outcomes of capabilities occur. We suggest two basic premises which define how to organize HR departments, then propose five roles and responsibilities for the new HR organization in progressive firms. We conclude with implications for the management of the transition to implement this next evolution in HR organization.

Premise 1 of the HR organization: structure HR to reflect the business organization

As a business within a business, the HR organization should be structured in a way that reflects the structure of the business. Business organizations align with the strategies of the business they support, and HR should follow suit.[1] Companies typically organize along a grid of centralization–decentralization, which leads to three basic ways in which a company operates (see Figure 12.1): holding company, functional organization, or diversified/allied organization (Lawler and Galbraith, 1995). The HR department should mimic the structure of its business operations.

Functional organization

When the company is comprised of a single business it competes by gaining leverage and focus. The role of HR in the single business is to support that business focus in its people practices. Generally, start-ups and small companies have little or no HR staff. Until a company has 50 to 75 employees, it hardly needs a full-time HR professional; a line manager can usually handle required basic HR activities. As the business grows, so does the HR workload, with the business eventually hiring someone to oversee HR, set basic policies and practices for hiring, training, and paying employees and perhaps also running the office and administrative side of the business. This HR generalist will normally be part of the management team and be consulted on organization needs and changes.

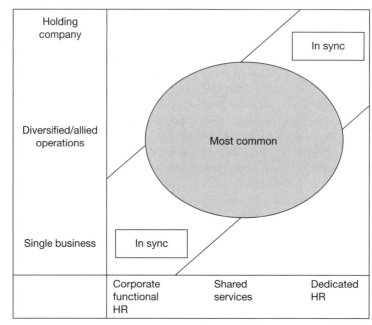

Figure 12.1 Alignment of business organization and HR organization

As companies grow, HR departments and staffs grow as well. But as long as the organization remains primarily a single line of business, HR expertise most logically resides at corporate, establishing company-wide policies, with HR generalists in the plants or divisions responsible for the implementation of these policies. They do so because there is no meaningful differentiation between the business and the corporation.

Herman Miller, for example, was founded in 1923 as a home furniture manufacturer and branched out into office furniture and ergonomics, becoming the world's second-largest company in the field.[2] It now employs over 6,000 people worldwide who work in functional departments. Their HR department has corporate specialists in recruitment, development, and compensation who design policies and practices that apply throughout the company. While thought leadership for HR policies comes from corporate specialists, the responsibility for employee engagement rests with line managers, and local HR generalists tailor corporate policies to plant conditions and participate in employee-related decisions.

Herman Miller is by no means the largest company to use this format. McDonald's has over 13,000 outlets in the U.S. alone, and employs over half a million people. Most of its employees receive similar treatment because they are in relatively similar operations. The standardization and integration of services ensures efficiency, low cost, and consistency across the company, while the corporate HR specialists work to create policies that will work across the McDonald's enterprise and help deliver the company's overall strategic agenda.

In a single-business organization, a strong HR functional organization usually makes most sense. This means identifying staff specialists who can design HR practices that match the needs of the business and deliver them to all corners of the company. Employees who move from site to site want to find familiar terms and conditions of work. Managers want to know what is expected of them regardless of where they work. HR professionals in local plants or operations need a solid line to their HR hierarchy while supporting local business leaders.

HR departments in single business companies are susceptible to the following common mistakes:

- *Hyperflexibility.* Many HR professionals want their work to be flexible (coming up with unique HR systems and practices for their unit), not standardized, even though flexibility can do more harm than good when the basic business is similar across the organization. Flexibility in HR should match diversity of business operations. For example, National City Corporation – similar to many banks – has over 200 different incentive compensation schemes, even though the operations of the company are similar across businesses and geography. When a company has similar strategies, products, and operations, HR practices should likewise be similar.
- *Separating corporate and operating unit HR.* As single businesses expand, the increasing workforce seems to generate a need for operating unit HR specialists. Both corporate and operating units add HR staff, creating a financial and administrative burden and leading to unnecessary proliferation and redundancy of HR practices.
- *Isolation.* Corporate staff specialists who distance themselves from business realities respond slowly to business changes. Barricaded in corporate offices, they are at risk of designing HR practices for the past and not for the future.
- *Disintegration.* Functional HR specialists often settle into silos that separate them from one another. When recommendations come from separate specialties, it may become difficult to weave the resulting practices into a unified whole. Too many companies hire based on one set of criteria, train based on a different set, and evaluate performance on yet a third. Then, their leaders wonder why employees lack a common set of goals and objectives.

The HR functional organization suits a single business strategy. It should not be abandoned in favor of the more popular shared service organization unless the structure and strategy of the business mandate the choice. We see only about 10% of large organizations following this functional organization alignment.

Holding company

When the company is composed of multiple, unrelated businesses that are managed independently, it is best described as a *holding company*. While pure holding companies are rare (probably about 10% of overall businesses) although we see some resurgence of holding company structure associated with the rise of large and well-capitalized private equity and investment firms such as Carlyle, Berkshire Hathaway and Blackstone. For example, Berkshire Hathaway owns or controls Dairy Queen, NetJets, GEICO Insurance and Fruit of the Loom. Blackstone has owned such varied companies as Celanese, Houghton Mifflin, Southern Cross/NHP, SunGard Systems, TRW Automotive, and Vanguard Health Systems.

In a holding company, there is often little or no HR at a corporate level, and little impetus to put it in. Each business is expected to create and manage its own autonomous HR practices based on the specific needs of the business. Therefore, HR is embedded within the businesses. GEICO has an HR department, as does Dairy Queen and NetJets, but Berkshire Hathaway has no corporate HR. Realistically, so long as the corporation is managed as a group of independent businesses, tied together only by a common treasury function (how investment funding is raised), and perhaps investor relations (if the company is publicly traded), the requirements for HR, and the benefits of interaction among subsidiary HR groups, are minimal. Even in those cases where there is a corporate HR function, it is likely to be small and focused primarily on executive talent recruiting and managing executive compensation.

While each independent organization may work well, the corporate value is by definition no more (and often less) than the sum of the independent parts. If organizing HR for a holding company, the requirement is to embed dedicated HR departments within the business units, and ensure they are well led. Here are the common mistakes to avoid:

- *Corporate interference.* A true holding company should have limited corporate involvement in the HR work done at the business unit level. Corporate should set general directions and philosophy, but HR policies, practices, and priorities belong to the business units.
- *Lack of sharing.* Diverse business units find it easy to slide from autonomy into isolation. In the absence of a business imperative for coordination, HR leaders and professionals need to make extra efforts to stay in touch with one another, sharing lessons through learning communities, technology, or other forums. Without a corporate HR function to host and sponsor such meetings, HR departments within independent businesses need to make extra efforts to avoid the "out of sight, out of mind" trap.
- *Repatenting the wheel.* Even when business unit HR departments are in touch with one another, they often prefer to develop programs on their own. In the holding company context, the "not invented here" syndrome is especially alive and well, and many professionals are reluctant to utilize programs they didn't create. Business HR units in holding companies should consider some form of regular communication that facilitates coordination in areas when unique business solutions are not needed.
- *Linearity.* We are strong advocates of HR focusing on the needs of the business. A danger for HR professionals in holding companies is that they may become overly focused on the short-term needs of the business and overlook longer term business implications of HR's involvement. HR must not only focus on those issues that are central to market share growth and short-term profitability; they must also ensure that the business is in compliance with regulatory mandates such as affirmative action, disability issues, Sarbanes Oxley, and labor law.

While relatively few true holding companies exist, the closer a firm comes to that model, the more its HR work needs to be located in dedicated business unit operations.

Diversified/allied businesses

The choice between functional and dedicated HR is often put as an either/or question: HR exists either at corporate or business unit levels, and is either centralized or decentralized, efficient or effective, standardized or flexible. Business units have similar HR practices or dissimilar ones, the flow is top down or bottom up, and so forth. In the kind of reorganization that only looks like progress, companies often shift from one extreme to the other, not realizing that the key requirement is not form per se but, rather organizing to reflect the requirements of the business organization.

Most large companies are neither pure single businesses, nor are they true holding companies. They lie somewhere in between, either in related or unrelated spectra of diversification. They create operating or business units to compete in different markets, yet try to find synergy among them. The best of these organizations align their portfolio of businesses around a core set of strategic capabilities that are leveraged across operations. GE is an exemplar of the diversified/allied model. For these business organizations, a relatively new way to organize HR resources has emerged called Shared Services (Bergeron, 2003; Ulrich, 1995). From a distance, shared services looks a lot like centralization, but it is not. Table 12.1 marks some of the ways functional HR, shared services, and dedicated HR differ from one another.

Shared services became popular among most staff groups, not just HR, beginning in the late 1990s as a response to general cost pressures. Staff leaders couldn't simply choose the cheapest and most efficient approach – centralize and standardize all processes – because centralized staff work cannot keep up with the differentiated needs of each unit within a diversified/allied business. For example, the different businesses within IBM gain leverage from a common approach to talent and performance management, but require different HR solutions in areas such as compensation where competitive pressures are distinct and different across sectors. Hence, in a number of areas, business consulting – a major and growing commercial focus of IBM – has very different needs than the hardware and software divisions of the company, or IBM's IT services business, or its R&D operations. In a world where corporate growth and industry consolidation leads to the increased presence of diversified/allied organization structures, shared services has become a useful means by which organizations balance the efficiencies of centralization with the flexibility required for competing in different markets and/or geographies.

Table 12.1 Functional HR, shared services, and dedicated HR

Dimension	Functional	Shared Services	Dedicated
Business organization	Single business	Related or unrelated diversification	Holding company
Design of HR policies	Performed by corporate functional specialists	Alternatives created by specialists in centers of expertise	Designed and delivered by functional specialists within a business
Implementation of HR practices	Governed by corporate specialists	Governed by local HR professionals who select options from center of expertise menu	Governed by local HR specialists embedded in the business
Accountability	Corporate HR	Split between operations and HR	Local business leader
Services orientation	Standardized services across the corporation	Tailored to business needs with consistency through learning and sharing	Unique services for each business
Flexibility	Mandates use of internal resources	Has flexibility as governed by the centers of expertise	Each business creates what is required
Chargebacks	Business units pay an allocation of HR costs	Business units pay for use of service	Business units fund their own HR costs
Location	Strong corporate presence with HR generalists on site	Wherever makes sense	Small corporate HR office, with HR staff at local level
Skills requirements for HR	Technically expert in design and delivery	Design expertise, but also consulting and support	Business expertise and technical specialty in business
Wealth creation criteria	Corporate shareholder value	HR value creation for line managers, employees, customers, and investors	Business unit profitability

Premise 2 of the HR organization: split HR into transaction and transformation activities and deliver on five roles and responsibilities

HR work is increasingly being split into two fundamental types of work: (1) administrative, transactional, and standardized work; and (2) strategic, transformational, and non-routine work (Lawler et al., 2006; Ulrich and Brockbank, 2005). This split parallels a similar split in other disciplines. The management of money within the firm has over time been divided into accounting (more transaction oriented and routinized) and finance (more transformational and non-routine); the management of customers has been divided into sales (more transactional) and marketing (more transformational); the management of information has been divided into data centers (more transactional) and information systems and management analytics (more transformational).

HR's history and legacy is primarily transactional, focused on administering the terms and conditions of work and the related duties of hiring, paying, basic skill training, and enforcing the policies that manage employee performance and conduct. Even as HR has shifted to do more strategic work – for example – helping to define and align individual competencies and organization capabilities with the business, these administrative tasks must be done and done well (Reilly et al., 2007; Tamkin et al., 2006).

HR's evolution in recent years has been to focus on the strategic or transformational work of helping the firm deliver on its strategy, be more competitive, and create value through translating external customer expectations into internal employee actions. By transformation, we mean the activities that leverage the performance of the enterprise: how HR enables the strategic performance of the company by acquiring the right people with the right skills and/or facilitating the organization capabilities required for the strategy to be successfully executed. Both the transactional and transformational, administrative and strategic work of HR must be done well for HR to meet its vision of delivering value and the essential outcome of building capabilities.

The HR organization creates value and delivers capabilities when it both reflects the structure of the business and effectively manages both the work of administrative transactions and strategic transformation. This leads to questions about how to specifically organize an HR department to fulfill these needs. An overview of the HR organization that facilitates the achievement of these two fundamental ends is shown in Figure 12.2. As the figure points out, the evolving HR organization has five distinct, specific, and at times overlapping, roles and responsibilities. Below, each of these five roles and responsibilities within the new HR structure are discussed.

HR role and responsibility 1: Service centers

Service centers emerged in the late 1990s as HR leaders (and other functional organizations such as purchasing) realized that many administrative tasks are more efficiently done in a centralized, standardized way (Reilly, 2000; Ulrich, 1995). The maturation of information technology has also contributed to the growth of service centers and the ability to locate them in lower cost geographies (e.g., India, Eastern Europe). There's no real limit to centralization. As one HR executive said, "If we move the HR work 400 yards, we might as well move it 3,000 miles." It works because employees are increasingly willing to find answers to routine, standard questions through a service center and because technology enables these centers to access employees and meet basic transactional needs as well or better than other ways.

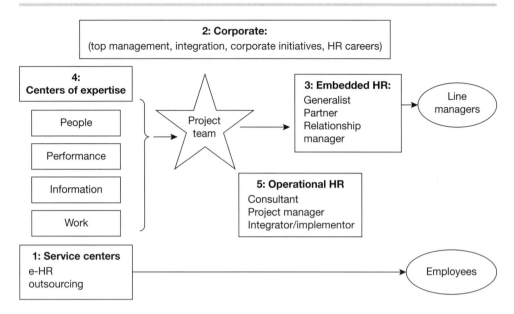

Figure 12.2 Overview of the HR organization

Service centers enjoy economies of scale, enabling employee needs and concerns to be resolved by fewer dedicated HR resources. In addition, service centers require a standardization of HR processes, thus reducing redundancy and duplication. For example, a global oil services firm had more than ten separate ways to register for training; its new service center created a single, standard, procedure that increased efficiency and reduced costs. Service centers can also be accessible 24 hours a day, seven days a week, from inside or outside the company, because of technology, which enhances the service level to employees and retirees.

Service centers offer new ways to do traditional HR work like employee assistance programs, relocation administration, benefits claims processing, pension plan enrollment and administration, applicant tracking, payroll, and learning administration. Employee-related transactional processes need to be performed, and performed well; performed badly they have the potential to damage employee morale and destroy HR's reputation (as one HR executive pointed out, "If we drop the ball on paying people, we will have a very difficult time recovering"). But, it is work that we think of as "table stakes", a requirement to be in the game, but certainly not a basis of winning. HR organizations are increasingly addressing their transactional needs primarily through technology-enabled employee self-service and through outsourcing. We review the trends and challenges of each in turn.

Service centers through technology-enabled employee self-service

Properly designed technology enables employees to manage much of their own HR administrative work. They can access information on HR policy and usage, such as vacation days allotted and taken, retirement provisions such as 401(K) status, job or career opportunities and qualifications needed, and their own skill levels (via self-assessment surveys). They can also take care of many routine transactions whenever they wish, because automated systems don't keep office hours.[3]

We estimate that 60% of employee HR questions or transactions (e.g., 401K investment choices) can be answered online by employees themselves. If employees feel uncomfortable with the online service, or if the issue is unusual, they can contact a service center and talk with someone. Customer service representatives at service centers can usually deal with about 85% of the remaining queries. The remaining 15% are allocated to a case manager who responds. Some estimates of the cost savings of these tiered solutions are as high as 50% of HR transaction costs (McRae, 2003).

Relying on technology to perform HR transactions offers a number of benefits. First, it requires that the HR practices involved are standardized, which avoids duplication, reduces costs, and ensures consistency. Since employees can access HR transactions at their convenience, their perception of service quality also increases. In addition, accuracy improves because employees update and modify their own records. As a result, managers have access to personnel information (such as training and salary history) and are often able to make better decisions.

For example, Boeing has integrated its employee services through a personalized Web-based portal and phone center. Through this portal, called TotalAccess, Boeing employees have a secure and convenient system for accessing HR. They can find information to make decisions, instructions for performing transactions, and access to Web-based services to complete those transactions.

As technology-based solutions to routine HR administration increase, a few trends are worth considering – and some emerging pitfalls are well worth avoiding (Lawler et al., 2003).

- *Building from scratch or excessive customization.* Companies often regard themselves as unique, but it is best to avoid the temptation to design and implement a unique HR data portal and service, or to significantly customize one. Many effective products are on the market, and adapting one of them is much simpler and less expensive than building something new or massively customizing a purchased system.
- *Believing that channel is content.* Occasionally IT specialists become more enamored with the design and implementation of their technology than with the business success that they should be trying to create. This was a fundamental cause in the dot.com boom and bust of the late 1990s. They fail to remember that information technology is a channel for providing and disseminating information but is ultimately the content of information that drives business performance. They need to maintain their business focus and not just their technology focus.
- *Forgetting the importance of the employee relationship.* For many HR transactions the employee goal is to finish as quickly and painlessly as possible. Nonetheless, HR is not like retail banking, where customers happily manage transactions by ATM and don't want a real relationship with the bank. It is more like investment banking, where relationships still offer the best long-term approach to customer share. Relationship HR, designed to build loyalty between individual employees and the firm, likewise offers the best long-term approach to employee care.
- *Data without insight.* One clear benefit of self-service is the ability to collect data on trends and needs. For example, knowing there are differences between younger and older employees in the use of e-learning can be helpful in planning and employee communication. But, data does not improve decision making unless it is used. If ware-housed in files and never fully deployed, it might as well not exist. Good decisions start with good questions that require managerial insight and foresight, and then data collected through technology-based self-service can be used to assess alternatives and test hypotheses.
- *Intrusiveness.* Concerns over privacy continue to be a major challenge. The more data accumulates, the more the firm knows about the employee, and the harder it is to keep

the data secure. And useful and convenient as 24/7 access to employee data can be, it blurs the boundaries between work and social life. While each employee needs to find ways to manage this balance, technology may become increasingly intrusive and remove the balance that gives employees purpose and passion.

Even with these concerns and challenges, technology will increasingly be used to facilitate employee transactions. As the technology becomes more user-friendly and accessible, it will help employees to manage their personal careers and leaders to use employee data and resources to produce value for the company.

Service centers through outsourcing

As we pointed out earlier, organizations are taking two distinct approaches to dealing with routine transactional HR tasks. The above section describes how organizations in-source HR transactions through technology-enabled self-service. Other firms are outsourcing them.

Outsourcing draws on the premise that knowledge is an asset that may be accessed without ownership. HR expertise can be shared across boundaries by means of alliances, where two or more firms get together to create a common service, or by outright purchase from vendors who specialize in offering it (Cook, 1999; Scott-Jackson et al., 2005).

Vendors take advantage of economies of both knowledge and scale. Economy of knowledge allows them to keep up with the latest research on HR issues and with the latest technology, so as to offer transaction support that accesses the most recent ideas and is delivered in the most efficient way. Economies of scale make it possible to invest in facilities and technologies beyond what is realistic for a single company. Firms like Hewitt, Accenture, and Towers Perrin are therefore able to offer bundles of HR services with the goal of moving client companies away from the traditional idea of outsourcing to multiple vendors – one for staffing, another for training, another for compensation, and so on, all taking somewhat different approaches to their work.

Increasingly, companies who are utilizing HR outsourcing seek integrated solutions rather than isolated practices. For example, in hiring, HR systems can identify the skills required for certain jobs and then use these skills in sourcing and screening talent. However, when considered as an integrated solution, the skill requirements can be applied to training, compensation, and job assignments as well, not just hiring. Integrated solutions require vendors with expertise in multiple areas, not single HR practice areas. BP, Prudential, Bank of America, and others have pioneered the outsourcing of HR transactions (Lawler et al., 2003). Though outsourcing on this scale is too new for results to be definitive, these firms have encountered several potential benefits of outsourcing:

- *Cost savings.* Savings have been in the 20–25% range – a substantial amount for large companies, which spend an average of $1600 per employee per year on administration. Firms with 10,000 employees, for example, could estimate saving $3,200,000 per year (20% of $1600 × 10,000).
- *Standardization.* Outsourcing requires consistent HR transactions. Many large firms have grown through mergers and acquisitions, accumulating diverse HR systems. Simply contracting out this work forces a level of consistency that might have taken years to accomplish internally.
- *Increased speed and quality of service.* As we mentioned above, outsourcing vendors generally rely on technology, and have the economies of scale to stay up to date with

new developments that continuously improve their service to client companies. Employees often perceive service as actually improving with effective outsourcing.

- *HR focus.* Outsourcing enables HR professionals to focus on more strategic work. The act of outsourcing increases the likelihood that HR professionals will become strategic in thought and action.

These benefits do need to be analyzed over a longer time to assure the value of outsourcing. Nonetheless, early indicators suggest that outsourcing offers positive returns. Outsourcing has its risks and pitfalls, as well:

- *Picking the wrong vendor.* As with any new business, not everyone who offers the service is really able to deliver excellent work, keep up with the volume, and ensure continuity. However, it seems likely that increasing competition will winnow vendors to those who can meet these criteria.

- *Unbalanced contracts.* The contract between the outsourcing provider and the organization may be skewed toward one party or the other, and contractual terms may make dispute resolution difficult. It is essential to specify current and desired service levels in mutually agreeable terms, outline a procedure for dispute resolution that both parties find fair and equitable, and include incentives for performance for the vendor and cooperation for the company.

- *Lack of change management.* The changeover from internal to external vendors is often difficult, time consuming, prone to early errors and therefore upsetting to employees, line managers, and HR professionals. While some confusion is inevitable, change processes that plan for alternative scenarios, engage employees and other affected parties in the process, and learn from self-correcting systems are important in increasing the probability of successful change.

- *Sprawling efficiency.* Outsourcing firms who want to expand their revenues sometimes do so by convincing a line manager who has an antiquated view of HR that the outsourcing firm should take over all of the HR functions and design and implement them against the primary criterion of transactional efficiency instead of business sensitivity. Such thinking moves HR back a generation in which we saw ourselves as a cost to be reduced instead of partners who drive the business. Internal HR professionals should be on guard for this tendency among some HR outsourcing firms.

- *HR role conflict.* Outsourcing changes HR's role in the company. Employees who used to know who to see and how to get things done now have to rewire their expectations and work norms. HR professionals who developed an identity and reputation based on effectively serving the transactional needs of employees and managers now need to reorient themselves to different issues.

- *Loss of control.* The firm surrenders control of outsourced transactions – but the need for the transactions will not go away. If outsourcing vendors have business problems, they will dramatically affect the firm's ability to relate to its employees.

Despite these risks, we believe large firms will continue to outsource bundles of HR transactions to increasingly viable vendors. Smaller firms will probably outsource discrete HR practices. Both types of outsourcing reflect the kind of collaborative work across boundaries that will characterize the organizations of the future.

HR role and responsibility 2: Corporate HR

HR professionals who perform Corporate HR roles address six important areas of need within the emerging HR organization. These are as follows:

- they create a consistent firm wide culture face and identity;
- they shape the programs that implement the CEO's agenda;
- they ensure that all HR work done within the corporation is aligned to business goals;
- they arbitrate disputes between Centers of Expertise and Embedded HR;
- they take primary responsibility for nurturing corporate-level employees;
- they ensure HR professional development.

The first contribution made by Corporate HR professionals is the creation of a consistent cultural face and identity for the corporation. No matter how diversified the business strategy, a variety of important external stakeholders form broad relationships with the entire firm. Shareholders tend to care mainly about overall performance, and large customers tend to engage with many different divisions. Likewise, the image of the entire firm is often what attracts potential employees to specific divisions. Corporate HR professionals build the firm's culture and reputation by focusing on values and principles. Hewlett-Packard, for example, has diversified dramatically, but the guidance of the HP Way continues. A similar thing could be said for Johnson & Johnson and its credo, or Takeda Pharmaceutical Company and its philosophy of Takeda-ism. Line managers own the principles, but corporate HR architects are the ones who institutionalize them. It takes more than publishing a set of values; they have to be a guiding factor, used and reinforced in all interactions with shareholders, suppliers, customers, and employees.

Second, Corporate HR professionals shape the programs that implement the CEO's agenda. Most CEOs have a corporate strategic agenda – for example, globalization, product innovation, customer service, or social responsibility. Corporate HR professionals are expected to convert this agenda into a plan for investment and action, and build organizational readiness to deliver this agenda through a three-step process:

1. Determine what capabilities are required to deliver the strategy.
2. Choose HR practices from the flows of people, performance management, information, and work that would best deliver those capabilities.
3. Build an action plan for designing and delivering those HR practices throughout the organization.

This action plan does *not* involve Corporate HR in doing all the work, or even in refining all the details. Instead, it will call on centers of expertise to create menus of specific choices, embedded HR professionals to appropriately tailor solutions to each business, and line managers to accomplish strategic goals through the HR service. However, Corporate HR plays the role of quarterback in ensuring that the work is done well, and coordinated effectively, to achieve the goals.

Third, Corporate HR has responsibility to make sure that all HR work done within the corporation is aligned to business goals. This means that Corporate HR should not mandate business unit initiatives since they probably do not understand the business unit realities as well as the embedded HR professionals. But they should mandate a clear and definitive linkage between business strategy and HR within the business units. One metaphor we have found helpful is to describe Corporate HR as playing the role of "devil's advocate" for strategic HR, challenging the need for both sameness and difference in HR practices across operations and specific businesses. In addition, Corporate HR should ensure that business unit HR is involved in setting measurable objectives. They should also be actively involved in facilitating the measurement process in order to eliminate the conflict of interest problems that would occur in business unit HR doing its own measurements.

Fourth, Corporate HR professionals arbitrate disputes between centers of expertise and embedded HR (HR professionals within the businesses or operations). The former naturally lean toward consistency; the latter equally naturally prefer flexibility and choice. Corporate HR won't have a magic answer or uniform formula for deciding when to standardize practices and when to vary them, but it can focus on value creation for multiple stakeholders and shift HR practices to create that value in each specific instance. We call this managing the push (centers of expertise) and pull (embedded HR) which requires conversation and at times arbitration.

Fifth, Corporate HR professionals take primary responsibility for nurturing corporate-level employees – a role both like and unlike that elsewhere in the firm. Like all employees, corporate employees should learn to perform their transaction HR work through service centers or technology. However, some corporate employees are unique in that their relationship with the firm is visible and symbolic. Public reports of executive compensation, for example, require extra care to ensure the right messages are communicated. Senior HR professionals also frequently play significant coaching roles for senior executives, offering advice ranging from personal leadership style to dealing with key employee transitions and succession issues to observations and assistance in evolving the corporate culture.

Finally, Corporate HR is responsible for HR professional development. Too often HR professionals are the cobbler's barefoot children – designing learning experiences for others, for example, while going without a similar investment in their own development.. HR corporate staff should work at helping HR professionals to grow as professionals, unlearn their old roles and learn new ones. This may require hiring a new breed of HR professionals, moving established HR professionals to different roles, and investment in HR development and training.

HR role and responsibility 3: Embedded HR

In shared service organizations, some HR professionals work in organization units defined by geography, product line, or functions such as R&D or engineering. These HR professionals whom we call "Embedded HR" go by many titles: Relationship Managers, HR Business Partners, or HR Generalists. Whatever their specific title, they work directly with line managers and with the leadership team of an organizational unit to clarify strategy, perform organization audits, manage talent and organization, deliver supportive HR strategies, and lead their HR function (Brown et al., 2004). Embedded HR professionals play a number of important roles that include the following:

- they engage in business strategy discussion;
- they represent employee interests and implications of change;
- they define requirements to reach business goals, and identify where problems may exist;
- they select and implement the HR practices that are most appropriate to the delivery of the business strategy;
- they measure and track performance to see whether the HR investments made by the business deliver the intended value.

In the first of these roles, Embedded HR professionals engage in business strategy discussions, offering insights and helping identify where their organization can invest resources to win in new business ventures. They should help to frame the process of business strategy development, should be proactive in providing insights into business issues and should facilitate effective strategy development discussions within the management team.

In the course of assisting in strategic decision-making, HR professionals also represent employee interests and highlight implications for employees that follow from the changes or developments that are inevitable as a result of strategy decisions and changes, for example, how much of the workforce needs to be retrained, reorganized, or resized. HR professionals help to develop a clear strategic message that can be communicated to employees and translated into action. In the process, they watch out for the tendency to groupthink, encouraging everyone to participate and clearly valuing dissent while seeking consensus (CIPD, 2005).

Once strategies are set, and even while being set, the third role played by Embedded HR professionals is auditing the organization to define what is required to reach the goals, and where problems may exist. Sometimes this is an informal process whereby HR professionals reflect on and raise concerns about strategy delivery. Other audits may involve a formal 360-degree review to determine what capabilities are required and available given the strategy (Ulrich and Smallwood, 2004). These audits will help to identify whether the corporate culture on the inside is consistent with the culture that is required to make customers happy on the outside. In doing these organization audits, embedded HR professionals partner with line managers and collect data that lead to focused action.

Based on organization audit information, Embedded HR professionals select and implement the HR practices that are most appropriate to the delivery of the business strategy. In doing so, they are expected to bring their unique knowledge of the business and its people in the selection of practices that add value, integrating them to deliver capabilities and sequencing them to ensure implementation. Embedded HR professionals pull guidance and support from the centers of expertise, and adapt the guidance and support of the centers of expertise to the requirements of the business. This process of accessing resources rather than owning them means that embedded HR professionals must be adept at influencing and working collaboratively with colleagues, because centers of expertise have agendas which are corporate in nature. They must be effective at managing temporary teams, and often multiple teams.

Finally, embedded HR professionals measure and track performance to see whether the HR investments made by the business deliver their intended value. In essence, embedded HR professionals diagnose what needs to be done, broker resources to get these things done, and monitor progress to make sure things have gotten done.

HR role and responsibility 4: Centers of expertise

The fourth HR role is the Center of Expertise. Centers of Expertise operate as specialized consulting firms inside the organization. Depending on the size of the enterprise, they may be corporate-wide or regional (Europe) or country-based (Germany). They often act like businesses with multiple clients (business units) using their services. In some cases a fee for use or a "chargeback" formula plus an overhead charge for basic services may fund them. The financing of Centers of Expertise is sometimes set to recover costs and in other cases is comparable to market pricing. Typically, businesses – through their embedded HR units – are directed to go to the Center before contracting for independent work from external vendors. If, in working with the Center experts, the decision is made to go to outside vendors, the new knowledge provided by these vendors is then added to the menu for use throughout the enterprise. Centers are demand pull operations – if businesses do not value their services, they will not continue.

Royal Dutch/Shell, for example, uses Centers of Expertise that operate on two dimensions: setting strategic direction for each specialty and designing the conceptual architecture and processes for its implementation. Design experts master the latest trends in a particular area, such as rewards or leadership development. They know best practices and create strategies and objectives that would work at Shell. Then experts in process design and delivery consult with embedded HR professionals, contract for delivery of programs to businesses, and lead implementation teams to apply HR expertise to business problems. These roles enable Shell's Centers to respond to requests in a timely and cost-effective way. To accommodate Shell's global reach, HR service centers are established regionally so that they can respond quickly and with sensitivity to local customs.

Center of Expertise HR professionals play a number of important roles:

- they create service menus aligned with the capabilities driving business strategy;
- they diagnose needs and recommend services most appropriate to the situation;
- they collaborate with Embedded HR professionals in selecting and implementing the right services;
- they create new menu offerings if the current offering is insufficient;
- they manage the menu;
- they shepherd the learning community within the organization.

As internal design and process consultants, HR professionals in Centers of Expertise are responsible for creating menus of what can be done that are aligned with the capabilities driving strategy. The menus are finite. Embedded HR professionals are expected to choose from these menus, which legitimates the HR practices in use company-wide. Process experts consult with Embedded HR to help pick the options that best solve specific business problems.

This also points out the second role of the Center of Expertise HR professional, which is to work with Embedded HR professional colleagues in selecting the right practice or intervention for the situation. For example, say an Embedded HR generalist realizes the need for a first-line supervisory training program in his or her organization. The Center of Expertise should already have a menu of choices, perhaps including an in-house workshop, relationships with externally provided workshops (through consultants or a local university), a video program, a self-paced computer learning exercise, a 360-degree feedback exercise, and other development experiences. (If one doesn't exist, the design experts will assemble a menu based on their knowledge of the field and the company.) A process expert takes this menu to the Embedded HR professional and helps them diagnose the need and select the services most appropriate for the business and situation, offering advice on how to implement the selected choices.

The Embedded HR professional is responsible for making the selection and for implementing the right development experiences for improving first-line supervision. However, as a third important role, the Center is expected to collaborate in making the selection and to provide support for implementation.

If the Embedded HR and Center expert agrees that existing menu items are not sufficient, the design experts are invited to create new solutions that will then be added to the menu for the entire enterprise. Hence, the fourth role is the creation of new offerings when the current slate is insufficient or inadequate for the need. For example, in many cases the need for additional menu offerings will be prompted by a company acquisition or decision to diversify and invest in new businesses. For example, we mentioned earlier the growth of IBM into global consulting services. As the organization shifted from products to services, new HR offerings were established to respond to the need.

This points out the next role of the Center of Expertise, which is to manage the size and breadth of the process or service menu. In general, the size of the menus will depend on the degree of business diversification. In related diversification, the menus will be smaller, ensuring that different businesses use similar management practices; in unrelated diversification, the menus will be larger, allowing more flexibility. But, in all cases, there is an important need for the Center of Expertise to manage the boundaries of what is helpful, acceptable, and permitted. As a very simple example, a large regional bank conducted an audit of its training practices and discovered that no less than 12 distinct and different coaching programs were used in various parts of the organization. That number was reduced by the Center of Expertise from 12 to one, with both a cost benefit to the organization (better contracting) and the creation of a common language and skill base in coaching.

Finally, Centers of Expertise also shepherd the learning community within the enterprise. They initiate learning when design experts generate new ideas for the menu; then process experts generalize learning by sharing experiences across units. For example, they share the experiences of supervisory training from one unit to another so that each business does not have to recreate its own training programs. The process experts may transfer the learning or they may have the requesting organization unit communicate directly with those who have previously done the work.

Centers of expertise provide a number of very important benefits to the HR organization, and are found broadly. However, they also create a number of risks that need to be managed by the HR leadership team:

- *One size fits all.* Center experts tend to fall into routines and push programs that are familiar to them; left to themselves, they may fail to adapt their programs to the needs of each business. It takes careful attention to ensure that menus continue to evolve.
- *Out of touch with reality.* If Center experts isolate themselves from day-to-day business problems, their menus are apt to offer solutions that are academically rigorous but irrelevant. Design experts must bridge future ideas to current problems. They need to turn theory and best practice into effective action. The Centers need to bring more than a fixed menu. They need expertise, knowledge base and foresight to address specific issues (i.e. loss of talent in flywheel developing markets such as China and India, for instance). Their work and contribution has to be differentiated enough from the "normal" solution so that the "We have already done this? What else can you bring?" syndrome does not emerge.[4]
- *Canned solutions.* It is much easier to have a solution in search of a problem than to design a solution for a problem. Like independent consultants, Center experts are often tempted to craft single solutions that they sell to multiple businesses. This is particularly true when Centers service global operations. Tailoring solutions to diverse global markets requires agility and thoughtfulness.
- *Not invented here.* Embedded HR professionals who worry more about personal credibility than impact are reluctant to use the best practices proposed by Center experts. If either Center experts or Embedded HR professionals declare themselves more important to the business, the entire process falters.
- *Unquestioned authority.* When business units are required to use the Center, the experts there find it easy to assume the units are happy to do so. They need to monitor their customer service scores as measured by Embedded HR professionals, and pay attention to the response.

- *Excess demand.* Given that Centers serve multiple businesses, demand can easily exceed capacity, leaving neglected businesses to flounder on their own or reinvent the wheel on the sly.
- *Seduction of power.* In some HR functions, Centers of Expertise have had a tendency to become a law unto themselves. That is, instead of framing their role as consultants whose role it is to help business unit HR drive business unit agendas, they arrive in the business units with corporate authority and drive their functional agendas instead of those of the business units.

While none of these risks are insurmountable, they indicate that centers will inevitably evolve as they refine their approach to delivering HR resources.

HR role and responsibility 5: Operational executors

A large number of HR departments have attempted to operationalize the above model with shared services (service centers and Centers of Expertise) and Embedded HR. But, many of these departments are finding that some work continues to fall through the cracks (Reilly and Williams, 2006). In research on the HR organization, Peter Reilly under the auspices of CIPD surveyed 800 senior HR professionals about their experience with their HR organization. Among their findings were:

> The survey results bear out that introducing shared services has produced boundary problems (identified by 55% of respondents), gaps in service provision (42%) and communication difficulties (37%). Communication with the rest of the function was a key problem with centres of expertise (34%) and the difficulty of separating out transactional work (45%) was even more of an issue. Similarly, "getting drawn into the 'wrong' activities" was the number one problem with business partners.
>
> (Reilly et al., 2007)

While the Embedded HR professionals are asked and expected to be strategic and do organization diagnosis, they often find themselves overwhelmed by operational HR work that conflicts with their main purpose and renders them unable to make time to be strategic. They report that they spend a growing time doing individual casework (e.g., handling disciplinary issues), performing operational tasks (e.g., setting up and attending recruiting interviews), doing analysis and reporting (e.g., managing compensation reviews), delivering initiatives (e.g., creating development experiences), implementing business initiatives (e.g., doing the analysis and execution for a new organization structure), or implementing Center of Expertise initiatives.[5] For example, Laurene Bentel, the VP of HR at Takeda Pharmaceuticals North America points out, "The operational demands on our HR generalists make it extremely hard for them to remain focused on their strategic agenda."[6]

Service centers typically do not perform these operational tasks since they require personal attention; Centers of Expertise do not do them since they usually require deep and unique knowledge of the business, and strong internal business relationships; line managers do not do them since they lack the technical expertise. Hence, Embedded HR professionals feel drawn into this operational work by the volume of it, even when they have the skills and self-confidence to be more strategic and are encouraged to focus on their transformational role.

A second driver is the velocity of program change emanating from Corporate HR. Particularly in times of corporate change and transformation, Embedded HR professionals are expected to keep up with a wide number of corporate initiatives: from new measures and measurement to required corporate training and communication programs, to new modifications to the performance management and development system. As a result, many Embedded HR people are encouraged to do strategy by their line management, but are required to do implementation by Corporate HR. One senior embedded HR executive, for example, described it this way: "We are asked to be business partners and strategists, but we end up acting as 'pairs of hands' for Corporate HR."

It is also the case that often these Embedded HR professionals come from an implementation background and lack the self-confidence and skills to comfortably play a more strategic role. For these individuals, the urgency (and comfort) of the operational present outweighs the importance (and developmental interest) of the more strategic future. And, too often HR professionals in Centers of Expertise offer insight and menus of choice, but they do not facilitate or partner in the operational implementation of these ideas. Service centers deal with administrative challenges, but they do not deal with implementation of new administrative systems and practices at the business level.

What has been suffering in some HR restructurings is the capacity to deliver and implement the ideas from the Center while maintaining focus on the business and its customers. While this work ideally occurs through an integrated team (see Figure 12.2), someone needs to be charged with this team and how it works. We are finding that companies are responding to these missing implementation requirements in different ways:

- One company established the role of junior Business Partners assigned to the HR Generalists or Business Partners. These individuals would be required to turn the strategic ideas into operational practice within the business.
- Another company created a team of "HR Operational Consultants" who were assigned to a business to help turn the strategy into action. They were focused on project work with an emphasis on implementing specific projects within the business. The Consulting Pool had HR professionals who were gifted at making HR initiatives happen, and secondarily served as a preparatory and testing ground for individuals who are slated as potential incumbents for senior Embedded HR professional roles.
- Another company uses a Case Advisor who comes from the service center to follow through on employee requests.

Kellogg offers an interesting example. As Kellogg transforms into a truly global foods company, there is a greater need for common practice in how people are developed, for succession management, and for the development of leadership competencies. Thus, the Centers of Excellence deliver a steady flow of innovative HR practices, with the expectation that embedded HR groups within business units will implement them. But, embedded groups are already extremely busy managing the strategic and day-to-day requirements of their business units. Tensions have inevitably arisen. At a recent offsite with the HR leadership team, Kellogg began to think through how it might establish an Operations HR unit that will provide support to both the Centers of Expertise and to Embedded HR units.

National City, a large regional bank headquartered in Cleveland Ohio, faces a similar challenge and has been a pioneer in the development of Operational HR. Their solution has been to create a fifth leg, which they call the HR Consulting Pool. The Consulting Pool operates as a team of high-performing mid-level HR professionals and are managed as a cohesive unit. The unit reports to the head of Regional (i.e., Embedded) HR. They are deployed to assist joint Center and Embedded HR teams to implement solutions to important HR projects, for example, to develop and implement a strategy to reduce attrition in call centers run by the Consumer bank. Historically, Center and Embedded HR professionals would have worked together to scope the need, but would not have had the resources to actually implement. Inevitably, the problem – while well defined – would not be effectively addressed and would often be "delegated" to line management, the worst possible outcome. The Operational HR Pool solves this problem, and has been responsible for a number of important deliverables.

Each of these companies, and others, are experimenting with how to solve a common problem: how to make sure that HR implements state-of-the-art strategies that are tailored to the needs of the business. We call this an Operational Executor role. These HR professionals will be required to meld what the business requires for success (driven by the embedded HR professionals) with innovative and state-of-the-art HR practices (driven by the Centers of Expertise) into an operational plan that can be executed in a timely way.

There are some identifiable challenges for organizations that are thinking of creating an Operational HR capability that need to be addressed for it to be successful. Our discussions with HR leaders suggest the following factors are particularly important:[7]

- *Selecting the right individuals.* Operational HR roles require a particular set of competencies. They are best for people who are execution and implementation oriented, rather than focused on strategic relationships (Embedded HR), or new knowledge creation (Centers of Expertise). However they can also be excellent developmental opportunities for both Embedded and Center professionals. We think that over time, HR organizations will find that Operational HR is a mix of long timers (people who like to do this work) and rotational resources.

- *Developing the skills needed to be successful.* Project and implementation management skills are crucial for Operational HR professionals, but also team skills. They must quickly understand what is expected, bring together the Embedded, Business and Center HR professionals in clarifying goals, roles, specific actions and measures, and make the changes happen. Some diagnostic skills are also important. Operational HR resources should not be seen as simply "pairs of hands" to implement but rather, involved early in the development of solutions.

- *Managing priorities and workloads.* Choosing what projects are appropriate for Operational HR is an important process task. HR doesn't have infinite resources, and it could be easy for HR to use its precious Operational HR resources on lower priority work that other HR professionals do not want to do. This would be a mistake, and would both trivialize the Operational HR work and Operational HR resources. If so, these resources will leave.

- *Maintaining business focus.* In all considerations, Operational HR must maintain an unrelenting focus on a business logic that is consistent with the logic of the corporate business portfolio. Regardless of whether the corporation is a single business unit, diversified or a holding company, HR should maintain its focus on making the corporate business logic successful.

- *Getting the structure right.* Organizations are trying out different structures for operational HR. Sometimes they are a distinct unit (National City), other times they are distributed in Embedded HR as junior professionals (Nestle, Takeda Pharmaceutical Company) or in Centers of Expertise (Royal Bank of Scotland). Smart organizations have found ways to connect these resources to one another, and provide common training and team-building experiences.

■ *Measuring contribution.* Because operational HR is project- and implementation-oriented, how performance is measured should also be project- and implementation-based.

This operational executor role will continue to become more clear as these HR professionals make sure that HR investments turn into capabilities that deliver on the vision and goals of HR.

Conclusions and steps for implementation

For HR to be a successful business within the business it must have a clear strategy that delivers value. It must also have outcomes that focus on the organization's technical and organizational capability requirements. We additionally propose that it must have an organization that appropriately reflects the business model and organization. In most cases, that HR organization will require responsibilities in five areas.

As HR leaders gain commitment to a value proposition for HR contribution, they often realize the need to reshape their organization to deliver value to their multiple stakeholders. While each HR reorganization is likely to contain unique dynamics, the following steps generally occur over a three- to five-year period:

1. *Diagnose the business strategy and organization.* HR leaders need to make sure they understand the model of the business they support (holding company, allied/diversified, or single business). Also, HR leaders must understand how the business organization matches with its vision and strategy.
2. *Align HR and business organization structures.* Make sure you align your HR organization with your business organization. Do not fall prey to modern HR practices just because others are doing them.
3. *Differentiate transaction and transformation work.* Realize that both transaction and transformation work are important, but are different types of work. Make sure you appreciate that these two types of work need to be managed differently. With transaction work, the goal is efficiency through standardization, automation, and consolidation. In contrast, transformation work has greater performance impact, is likely to be non-routine, needs to be focused on stakeholder requirements, and should have the flexibility to meet and exceed all stakeholders' expectations.
4. *Create a project team.* Set up a project team including key stakeholders – line managers, HR professionals from corporate, business unit, and specialist staffs – plus external consultants if needed, and charge it with creating the business case for HR transformation. Once that is done, the team needs to lay out the full road map for transformation, define roles and responsibilities in the new organization, implement the project, and measure success.
5. *Build transaction efficiencies.* The options for transaction processing include service centers and call centers, technology that enables employees to do their own HR work, and outsourcing targeted or integrated HR actions to a third party.
6. *Develop transformational effectiveness.* Clearly define the roles and responsibilities for Corporate, Centers of Expertise, Embedded HR, and Operational HR. Make sure that those who staff those roles have the competencies and commitment to do so.
7. *Maintain balance.* Work to maintain the optimal balance between corporate, functional, and business units' demands. Drive business growth through strategic HR while

201

efficiently delivering HR services. Encourage the development of HR knowledge and skill while meeting the mandate for business acumen on the part of HR professionals.

8. *Monitor progress.* Measures of success should include HR costs, which can be tracked from HR staff ratios and HR budgets. But measures of success should also include organization capabilities which are the outcomes of HR and track how HR delivers on its vision of adding value.

When these steps are followed, the HR department not only has strategies and goals that deliver value, but an organization structure that reflects the business that it supports. As a result, the HR business within the business is positioned to deliver value.

Notes

1 We recognize that there are generally two types of "business strategy": (1) Corporate strategy focuses more on the portfolio or mix of businesses, and (2) business unit strategy focuses on how a particular business unit anticipates and services customers to make money. Each view of strategy leads to business organization choices which then lead to HR organization choices.

2 This description of Herman Miller comes from "About Us" on its website: http://www.herman miller.com. Access date: May 25, 2007.

3 Many consulting firms have built their business on HR shared services, designing and delivering an array of HR technologies. For example, see Mercer Human Resource Consulting (http://www.mercerhr.com/service/details.jhtml?idContent=1000310) and Deloitte (http://www.deloitte.com/dtt/section_node/0,2332,sid%253D26557,00.html).

4 We appreciate Dennis Shuler's insights on the global role of centers.

5 We are grateful to Peter Reilly for his observations on the operational executor role and responsibility. Our conversations with him have informed our thinking a great deal.

6 Personal communication, October, 2007.

7 The corporate members of the RBL Institute for Strategic HR who contributed to the March, 2007 discussion of the Operational Executor are gratefully acknowledged.

References

Bergeron, B. 2003. *Essentials of Shared Services.* Hoboken: John Wiley & Sons.

Brown, D., Caldwell, R., White, K., Atkinson, H., Tansley, T., Goodge, P. and Emmott, M. 2004. *Business Partnering, A New Direction for HR.* London: CIPD.

Christensen, R. 2005. *Roadmap to Strategic HR: Turning a Great Idea into a Business Reality.* New York: AMACOM/American Management Association.

CIPD Impact Report. 2005. *Why HR Must Seek to Become a Business Partner.* London: CIPD.

Cook, M.F. 1999. *Outsourcing Human Resources Functions.* New York: AMACOM.

Deloitte Consulting. 2006. *Global HR Transformation.* Available online: http://www.deloitte.com/dtt/cda/doc/content/UK_C_GlobalHRTransformation.pdf. Access date: July 3, 2008.

Lawler, E.E. and Galbraith, J. 1995. *Organizing for the Future: New Approaches to Managing Complex Organizations.* San Francisco: Jossey-Bass.

Lawler, E.E., Boudreau, J.W. and Mohrman, S.A. 2006. *Achieving Strategic Excellence: An Assessment of Human Resource Organizations.* Palo Alto: Stanford Press

Lawler, E., Ulrich, D., Fitz-enz, J. and Madden, J. 2003. *Human Resources Business Process Outsourcing. Transforming How HR Gets Its Work Done.* San Francisco: Wiley.

McRae, K. 2003. "HR shared services – a growing trend," *Human Resources,* December 3. Available online: http://www.humanresourcesmagazine.com.au/articles/8c/0c01a08c.asp. Access date: June 11, 2004.

Reilly, P. 2000. *HR Shared Services and the Realignment of HR*. IES Report 368. Brighton: Institute for Employment Studies.

Reilly, P. and Williams, T. 2006. *Strategic HR: Building the Capability to Deliver*. Aldershot, UK: Gower Publishing.

Reilly, P., Tamkin, P. and Broughton, A. 2007. *The Changing HR Function: A Research into Practice Report*. London: Chartered Institute of Personnel and Development.

Scott-Jackson, W., Newham, T. and Gurney, M. 2005. *HR Outsourcing: The Key Decisions*. Executive briefing. London: Chartered Institute of Personnel and Development.

Tamkin, P. Reilly, P. and Strebler, M. 2006. *The Changing HR Function: The Key Questions*. London: Chartered Institute of Personnel and Development. Available at: http://www.cipd.co.uk/change agendas.

Ulrich, D. 1995. "Shared services: from vogue to value," *Human Resource Planning* 18.3: 12–22.

Ulrich, D. and Brockbank, W. 2005. *HR Value Proposition*. Boston: Harvard Business Press.

Ulrich, D. and Smallwood, N. 2003. *Why the Bottom Line Isn't*. New York: Wiley.

Ulrich, D. and Smallwood, N. 2004. "Capitalizing your capabilities," *Harvard Business Review* June: 119–27.

Ulrich, D., Zenger, J. and Smallwood, W. 1999. *Results Based Leadership*. Boston: Harvard Business Press.

Part 6

Areas of practice

In a back-to-school night with parents and students, one of our children was asked, "What does your father do for a living?" After a little thought, her answer was "He goes to lots of meetings; he must be a meeting-attendor for the company where he works." In some ways, she had it right, those of us who study and work in HR attend a lot of meetings. These meetings are with employees, other professional groups, peers, leaders, and even those outside the company for the *process* of what we do at work. But, we also need to know the *content* . . . what do we do in those meetings?

Many have tried to create a typology of HR practices.[1] At times HR practices have been defined as processes since they have discernible flows of activity.[2] At other times these HR practices have been called the activities of HR.[3] And, at other times, the practices are described as policies which define how the organization will treat its employees. Regardless of the label, HR practices represent the content of what HR professionals do in all those meetings.

HR practices have evolved over time. Early HR work emerged in the 1930s when industrial and labor relations practices were conceived to enable management to have a unified voice to deal with unions. These early practices focused on terms and conditions of work and established formal policies to govern employee work. In subsequent decades, HR practices have emerged to deal with how organizations manage the flow of people, performance, information, and work within an organization.

The chapters in this section offer insights into how HR practices will need to continue to evolve to adapt to changing work conditions. Many of the basic practices remain the same: getting the right people in the right job at the right time with the right incentives to do the right work. But, the details of these practices have and will continue to advance.

The most basic and primary task of any view of HR is to recruit and select who will work in the company. If an organization is staffed with people who have the right skills and the dedication to use those skills in the right way, issues of training, compensation, and career management are moot. But, if the wrong people are hired, leaders may never be able to overcome these errors. Collins and Kehoe offer a useful insight in making sure that recruiting and selection approaches match the organization. One size does not fit all. If an organization is in a relatively low change, low uncertainty state, then more mechanistic staffing models may be used. If an organization is in a state of flux, uncertainty and change, then staffing models will need to be more focused on the commitment and professionalism of their employees. Linking internal staffing approaches to organizational settings ensures an alignment between the organization context and employee response.

Once people are hired, employees have to be paid. Compensation serves many purposes. It signals to employees what they should focus on; it motivates employees to allocate discretionary energy on the right work; and it helps employees decide if they should stay with a company or move to another (called sorting). Compensation has become both an art which requires judgment and a science which operates according to a predictable set of rules. Gerhart offers an outstanding overview of the compensation issues in today's organization. This overview synthesizes theory and research on how much to pay and how to pay. He also shows that compensation choices should be tightly aligned to the organization context in which they occur. His chapter offers compelling evidence that compensation (especially pay for performance) is an incentive that drives productivity, particularly among high performers, but he also cautions us about the risks of these programs. When compensation programs align with the organization context and when these programs are well executed and communicated, they are much more likely to succeed.

Performance management deals with goal setting, monitoring performance, and setting standards. London and Mone introduce a five-step performance management cycle (set goals, seek and digest feedback, participate in development and change behavior, perceive and evaluation, and determine expectations) that can be adapted to multiple settings. This chapter provides the conceptual underpinnings of this cycle and offers specific guidelines for practitioners who adapt the cycle to their unique work setting. They also suggest specific challenges to bridging theory and practice in the future. They offer a compelling case where the performance management process helped employees translate organization direction into daily action.

Once employees have been recruited, paid, and focused on performance, the reality hits that they also need to change. There is a half life of knowledge and as organizations must adapt to changing customer and investor expectations, employees must also adapt. This employee adaptation comes from training and development. Investments in training and development help employees continue to learn and grow so that they can meet future business requirements. Noe and Tews offer a thorough overview of the strategic training and development theory and research and suggest opportunities for future study and research. They lay out a process for training that begins with an understanding of business strategy, then turns those business requirements into strategic training and development initiatives and activities that can be measured to demonstrate value. For training to have full impact, it needs to begin with strategy and be tracked in a rigorous way.

Each of the above chapters on selection/recruitment, compensation, performance management, and training and development suggest similar directions. First, these HR practices should be aligned with strategy. There is no one best practice, but the practice should match the direction of the organization which deploys the practice. Second, the HR practices need to be a constant source of creativity and innovation. Just doing something because it is popular does not make it right. Finally, theory, research, and practice need to come together. Theory offers a rational approach and a means of replication; research builds confidence in future results; and practice makes the investments relevant to business and individual results.

Gratton and Erickson expand the areas on which HR practices should focus. The HR systems of staffing, compensation, performance management, and training need to be supplemented with serious attention to teams. They convincingly show that in modern organizations the ability to work in collaborative teams is not only inevitable, but a source of real competitive advantage. Their chapter lays out clearly why teams matter, challenges to creating successful teams, and specific actions to ensure team success. They offer a number of cases where organizations have applied these ideas and built teams that help their organization perform better.

Storey, Ulrich, Welbourne, and Wright's chapter on employee engagement reminds us that one of the critical outcomes of all the investments in HR practices is to ensure that the employees of today and tomorrow are fully engaged.

Notes

1   A few samples of HR practice lists: Gary Dessler, *Human Resource Management*, 9th edn. (New York: Prentice Hall, 2002); Anne Bogardus, *PHR/SPHR: Professional in Human Resources Certification Study Guide* (New York: Sybex, 2003); Mark Effron, Robert Gandossy, and Marshall Goldsmith (eds.), *Human Resources in the 21st Century* (New York: Wiley, 2003).
2   See a flow logic in Dave Ulrich and Wayne Brockbank, *HR Value Proposition*. Cambridge, MA: Harvard Business Press, 2005.
3   See the difference of activity (HR practice) vs. deliverables (HR outcomes) in Dave Ulrich, *Human Resource Champions*. Cambridge, MA: Harvard Business Press, 1997.

13

Recruitment and selection

*Christopher J. Collins
and Rebecca R. Kehoe*

Throughout the end of the twentieth century and into the start of the twenty-first, scholars and practitioners have argued that firms are in a war for talent, and that the firms that are best able to attract and retain employees will be in a position to outperform their rivals (e.g., Michaels et al., 2001; Woodruffe, 1999). In a global economy, companies are seeking new growth opportunities and hiring new staff at a pace to help them achieve this growth. At the same time, labor markets are beginning to shrink as the baby boom generation employees begin to retire and are replaced by a reduced supply of younger workers (Dohm, 2000). In the midst of these significant environmental changes, the staffing function, including recruitment and selection, has emerged as arguably the most critical human resource function for organizational survival and success.

Firms across a wide range of sectors and especially those in knowledge-based industries (financial services, high technology, pharmaceuticals) are finding themselves engaged in fierce and continuing battles with their competitors for the recruitment of the best and brightest new hires. Further, because of the increasing importance of employees in driving competitive advantages (Collins & Smith, 2006), mistakes in selection have potentially catastrophic consequences for organizational success and survival. Across all industries, individual employees must possess the requisite mix of skills, aptitudes, motivations, and so on, that will enable their firms to compete effectively and create competitive advantage in their given market space and to help their organization adapt to future unknown challenges. For many companies, recruiting and selection have become essential tools in ensuring that they have the human resources necessary to achieve their current strategic direction and to continue innovating and growing in the future.

Despite the theoretical importance of recruitment and selection to organizational competitive advantage and performance, there are a number of issues that limit the prescriptive advice that recruitment research provides practitioners regarding these components of staffing. First, the vast majority of the published research on recruitment and selection has been conducted at the individual level of analysis. Indeed, the paucity of empirical research that has examined the effects of recruitment and selection practices at the firm level of analysis is surprising given that researchers have argued that research that examines independent and dependent variables at the firm level is likely to provide better prescriptive advice regarding the choices of recruitment and selection systems (e.g., Rynes & Barber, 1990; Taylor & Collins, 2000).

Second, these studies have drawn on theories that explain individual reactions or outcomes, leaving little understanding of how or if these staffing practices may affect firm-level performance or how the effects of these practices may vary across firms or types of employees. What empirical work that does exist tends to be atheoretical or has lumped recruitment or selection with other human resource functions as part of a larger system of human resource practices. There is no or at best little theory for researchers to draw on to make specific predictions regarding the impact on performance of choices in recruitment and selection practices within an overarching staffing system. Thus, the field needs a theoretical model to serve as a framework for firm-level strategic research on recruitment and selection.

In this chapter, we look to address the second issue by developing a theoretical model of the link between different staffing systems and firm-level performance. We first look to existing theory on organizational design and structure to better understand the role of recruitment and selection. Specifically, we argue that organizations are structured into unique subunits of employees based on the equivocality of available information in their jobs and the resulting need for organizational rationality or openness. Drawing on existing empirical work on strategic human resource management, we argue that unique systems of recruitment and selection practices are necessary to provide the level of employee knowledge, skills, and abilities to match the level of information equivocality faced by the employees in these roles. In particular, we put forth arguments that recruitment and selection systems that match with the mechanistic organizational structure are the best fit for subunits of employees facing low information uncertainty; whereas recruitment and selection systems that match with the organic organizational structure are the best fit for subunits of employees facing high informational uncertainty.

Based on contingency theory, we argue that there are likely to be multiple recruitment and selection systems that fit with either the mechanistic or organic structural principles. Further, the alternative recruitment and selection systems may be based on competing management philosophies that lead to greater or lower levels of role specialization and required skills and abilities. Specifically, as shown in Figure 13.1 below, we identify two recruitment and selection systems that fit with the mechanistic structure: an autocratic system of recruitment and selection practices that is a fit for subunits requiring lower skill specialization, and a bureaucratic system

Figure 13.1 Alternative staffing system models

of recruitment and selection practices that is a better fit for subunits requiring higher levels of skill specialization. We also identify two recruitment and selection systems that fit with the organic organizational structure: a commitment system that is a better fit for subunits with lower levels of skill specialization and a professional system that is a better fit for subunits with higher levels of skill specialization. Finally, we draw conclusions and identify areas for future empirical research in the area of strategic recruitment and staffing.

Organizational structure and information processing

In the strategic human resource management literature, a growing number of researchers have noted that organizations are made up of different groups of employees; and organizations are likely to achieve optimal levels of performance by matching employment systems to the unique set of characteristics associated with the responsibilities tied to these roles (Collins & Smith, 2006; Lepak & Snell, 1999). Further, work by Baron and colleagues (Baron & Hannan, 2002; Baron et al., 2001) suggests that there are a multitude of philosophies regarding how to best manage employees that result in a potentially wide array of HR systems even within a single industry and within individual firms.

While not directly focused on recruitment and selection systems, this body of literature suggests that there may be a wide array of alternative recruitment and selection systems that companies can use to attract and select employees with the right knowledge, skills, and abilities (KSAs) required to drive maximum firm performance. Research on contingency theory (e.g., Lawrence & Lorsch, 1967; Thompson, 1967) would also suggest that there is not a single best recruitment and selection system and not all of the potential systems will be ideal for every type of employee. Thus, our first priority is to identify different groups of employees and to clearly articulate the differences in KSAs between these positions. Our second priority is to identify the best recruitment and selection systems that will ensure that the employees in these unique subunits have the requisite skills, abilities, and aptitudes required to deal with the level of information uncertainty that they face. To accomplish this task, we draw on organizational theory research to identify two broad groups of employees and identify the KSAs tied to each.

Management scholars have long been arguing and writing about the purpose of organizations and the resulting implications for organizational design and structure. Indeed, there has been an extensive line of research in the field of organizational theory that has looked to identify the different organizational designs and structures that will be most effective under alternative conditions. Etzioni (1964), for example, noted that organizations are often in a perpetual struggle in regard to organizational structure and are continually trying to balance choices between the formal and informal, the rational and non-rational, and controlling and freeing up employees to make decisions. These constant tensions and struggles are the result of work-related uncertainties created by the combination of pressures and changes from the external environment (Lawrence & Lorsch, 1967) and the complexity of organizational technology and coordination inter-dependencies in the internal environment (Galbraith, 1973; Hage & Aiken, 1969). Therefore, the critical task of the organization is to create the ideal organizational structure to collect and process information.

Taking these ideas a step further, Thompson (1967) noted that organizations face differing types of pressures across the different elements of the external environment with which they interact. Further, he argued that organizations should seek to isolate parts of the organization from external pressures to achieve optimal efficiency, while simultaneously structuring other parts of the organization as boundary spanners to deal with the uncertainty of the external environment. In particular, the organization can be optimally structured by separating those subunits of the organization that face less change and uncertainty in the external environmental pressures from those subunits that face higher degrees of external environmental turbulence and uncertainty (March & Simon, 1958; Thompson, 1967).

Organizations must also deal with differences in complexities across groups of employees in terms of task complexities and task interdependencies in completing work. For example, there are differences in task complexity and task interdependencies across groups of employees depending on the work being completed, resulting in differences in information-processing needs across units within the organization (Galbraith, 1973; March & Simon, 1958). Therefore, organizations may be best viewed as a collection of employee groups or subunits, each with specialized organizational design needs given the complexity of the information-processing needs created by the uncertainty and complexity of the external and internal issues faced by the particular unit. Below, we examine separately the organizational structure and resulting employee KSAs for those subunits facing low uncertainty and information-processing needs and those subunits facing high uncertainty and information-processing needs.

Structure and positions with low information uncertainty

While organizations are open systems that face uncertainty in their external environment, there are some subunits within the organization that may be isolated to achieve a greater degree of rationality when there is a high level of stability on the part of the external environment with which they interact (Thompson, 1967). There are several reasons that would lead organizations to seek greater rationality in some subunits. For example, some subunits have a lower need for information-collection and processing capability because they face a consistent pattern of information in the external environment. In addition, other subunits in the organization face low uncertainty and information-processing demands because this subunit is using particular existing technology or process that matches well with the external environment and can be exploited for a particular period of time (Galbraith, 1973; Hage & Aiken, 1969). Thus, while the overarching goal of organizations is information processing, organizations should look to ensure repeatability for as long as the environment stays stable in those subunits where information processing has been completed and shown positive results (Weick, 1969).

In each case where subunits are pursuing the exploitation of an existing technology or process or where the subunit clearly understands and has accurately responded to a stable set of external environment conditions, the job roles in these subunits require reliable replication for the efficient production of existing products and services (Thompson, 1967). Indeed, the main concern for these subunits should be a focus on organizational structure that increases the consistency of execution of routines, and repetitive processes which ensure the consistent execution of the existing processes and technology that is being exploited. In particular, these subunits of the organization are looking for an organizational form that increases consistency, as mistakes are costly, and deviation from standards is undesirable.

The subunits in this category are clearly looking to exploit the stability in their external environment and this necessitates that employees fully understand and adhere to the defined requirements of their work roles (Galbraith, 1973). There are a number of key KSAs associated with the roles in these types of subunits. First, efficiency and reliability are key capabilities that will drive employees' performance if they are to consistently perform tasks without mistakes. Similarly, employees would be expected to be willing to meet standards and have a strong ability to carry out pre-determined routines with a high level of attention to detail. Because of the low variability in external conditions, the company would also gain increased efficiency and consistency by keeping decision making at higher levels, increasing the importance of the ability to take and follow directions.

A mechanistic organizational structure is likely to be the best organizational structure for subunits that face low uncertainty and in which the organization is trying to exploit an existing technology or process. In fact, there is empirical evidence that the mechanistic structure is conducive to a strategy in which an organizational subunit is looking to exploit an existing technology or process (Hage, 1980). Specifically, the mechanistic structure involves high centralization, high formality, and the use of vertical communication (Burns & Stalker, 1994; Hage, 1965, 1980). High levels of centralization allow a few individuals at the top of an organization to set precise rules and standards. Vertical communication is then used to alert employees at lower organizational levels of the uniform rules and standards to be followed. A high degree of formalization ensures that employees in a particular position are extremely familiar with the expectations and standards for their role, allowing work roles to be routinized in a way that ensures maximum efficiency and reliable quality (Hage, 1965, 1980). Based on these findings we argue that recruitment and selection systems that match the prescriptions of the mechanistic model will be the best fit to organizations and subunits that face relatively stable environments or that are looking to exploit an existing technology or process.

Based on the above, we propose that organizational subunits with low information uncertainty will achieve the highest level of performance when instituting recruitment and selection practices that match with the mechanistic organizational structure.

Recruitment and selection systems matching with mechanistic structure

As we noted, a mechanistic structure is likely the best fitting organizational structure to support a strategy of exploitation. However, the mechanistic structure is really an archetype and prescription of required elements of an organizational structure rather than an implemented system or set of HR practices. Based on the arguments of contingency theory, it is likely that multiple systems of HR practices exist that match the attributes of the mechanistic structure. Contingency theory holds that there is likely not a single best practice or system that would achieve optimal outcomes across all conditions; instead the best results are achieved by matching the particular system or systems of practices to the environmental or competitive conditions faced by the firm (Lawrence & Lorsch, 1967). Applying this proposition more specifically to recruitment and selection, it is likely that firms can implement different systems of recruitment and selection practices, each of which match with the key attributes of the mechanistic structure. Further, the best results will be obtained by matching the system of recruitment and selection practices to both the internal and external conditions faced by the subunit of employees. For example, research by Baron et al. (2001) suggests that there are at least two unique systems of HR practices – autocratic and bureaucratic – that are mechanistic in nature. Below, we outline these two systems of HR practices and develop specific outlines of the recruitment and selection requirements that would be associated with each.

The autocratic recruitment and selection model

The autocratic model of recruitment and selection, identified by Baron et al. (2001), is one system of management that fits with the definitions of a mechanistic structure as it reflects

213

a strict centralized managerial philosophy. The autocratic system follows specific philosophical guidelines around entry into the organization, management control, and employee attachment (Baron & Hannan, 2002; Baron et al., 2001). The autocratic model specifies employee selection on the basis of specific task abilities which enables the subunit of the organization to fill job roles with employees who are already qualified in a relevant area. Also matching with a mechanistic structure, subunits following an autocratic management style seek to achieve control of employees through direct managerial supervision of tasks. Further, this style of control would lead to jobs that are narrowly defined in scope and responsibilities; therefore, employees filling these roles are likely to be of lower skill and easily replaceable. Finally, employee attachment in the autocratic model is created through monetary rewards linked to individual performance in a given work role. While we would expect that the individual monetary rewards would motivate employees to achieve specific, measured objectives, we do not expect particularly high levels of employee tenure under the autocratic model. Based on these defining philosophical attributes, as shown in Table 13.1 below, we next identify specific recruitment and selection practices that fit with this HR management system.

Recruitment under the autocratic management philosophy

In terms of the scope of the recruitment effort, organizations and sub-units under this model will focus on recruitment and employment brand building efforts only in the local labor market because they are looking to fill low skilled jobs managed with tight control. Further, the main source of employee affiliation is pay, suggesting that employment brand building efforts should be based on establishing the relative strengths of the pay versus labor market competitors. Because companies following the autocratic model are likely to experience higher turnover

Table 13.1 Components of alternative recruitment and staffing models

Models	Recruitment and selection practices
Autocratic	Local recruitment – low-skilled labor sources Continuous recruitment in expectation of high turnover Employment brand based on individual pay Select for skills to perform immediately in job Select for willingness and ability to follow direction
Bureaucratic	Targeted recruitment at labor sources with specialized skills Employment brand based on development opportunities Recruitment and selection are centralized Selection based on skills to perform immediately in job Selection for ability to follow rules and procedures
Commitment	Targeted recruitment at labor sources that match company culture Employment brand based on development opportunities and long-term employment Selection based on fit to company culture and values Selection carried out by peers in position Selection based on adaptiveness and ability to grow with company
Professional	Targeted recruitment at labor sources with specialized skills Employment brand based on challenging work National search and employment brand-building efforts Selection based on certification of specialized skills Selection based on ability to collaborate and work across teams Components of alternative recruitment and staffing models

than those following other management philosophies, there will likely be pressure on the company to continually source applicants to fill openings. Therefore, recruitment is more focused on building a continual stream of applicants than on attracting applicants with specific skill sets or attributes. In other words, recruitment should be focused on attracting a continuous stream of applicants who are able to immediately fill open vacancies, rather than conducting extensive searches for applicants with specific skill sets.

Selection under the autocratic management philosophy

As noted above, companies and subunits that follow an autocratic management philosophy rely on a high degree of constant, direct oversight, resulting in jobs that require limited or easily found skills and abilities. Further, this philosophy would suggest that employees that are hired will be seen as relatively interchangeable and expendable, so the organization is also unlikely to expend resources on employee development. Based on these premises, organizations or subunits under this philosophy will exert little resources on selection activities, because mistakes in selection will be quickly terminated from the role and have limited ability to impact performance because of continual direct oversight. For those that do invest some effort on selection, the selection practices should be focused on two aspects. First, because there will be no investment in employee development and the relatively low skills required, selection practices would be used to test for any specific limited skills or attributes required for the job. Second, because of the style of management, companies should also look to select based on ability and willingness to follow direct supervision. Finally, to maintain tight control, any selection activities will be conducted by the senior managers of the company or subunit.

Based on the above, we propose that organizational subunits with low information uncertainty and low task and role specialization will achieve the highest level of performance when instituting an autocratic recruitment and selection model.

The bureaucratic recruitment and selection model

As with the autocratic model, the bureaucratic model of recruitment and selection is also consistent with the ideals of the mechanistic structure and would create the workforce characteristics that would be supportive of the requirements of a subunit that is exploiting an existing technology or process and/or competing in a stable environment. As defined by Baron et al. (2001), the bureaucratic management philosophy also follows specific guidelines regarding entry into the organization, employee coordination and control, and employee attachment. Organizations following this management philosophy typically have centralized control regarding entry of new employees into the organization and entry decisions emphasize narrow expertise and skills required for a particular role. This type of strict control of entry into the organization clearly fits with the control and formalization of the mechanistic structure.

Employee coordination and control in the bureaucratic model is handled through formal policies and procedures that are strictly adhered to through managerial supervision. The regulation of employees and tasks by management can help to ensure that employees are not straying from organizational routines at the cost of efficiency. Opportunities for development, promotion within functional or departmental roles, and challenging work are the bases for attachment in the bureaucratic model. Promotions within a particular task domain provide rewards for individual performance in a given job. Consequently, we would expect employees working under a bureaucratic model to report greater job involvement and fewer intentions to turnover than employees working under the autocratic management philosophy. The

215

components of the bureaucratic approach help to ensure that employees in any given role are experts with regard to their particular job and are, therefore, more likely able to efficiently and consistently carry out their tasks. Based on these defining philosophical attributes, we identify specific recruitment and selection practices that fit with the bureaucratic management philosophy.

Recruitment under the bureaucratic management philosophy

Subunits of employees under the bureaucratic model are likely to develop and invest in more advanced recruitment efforts than are their autocratic counterparts. First, in terms of scope, bureaucratic recruiting efforts should span a broader geographical region yet simultaneously be targeted at a specific pool of labor in order to attract applicants with expertise in the specific areas needed for open positions. The philosophy guiding the bureaucratic model calls for less direct supervision of tasks than in the autocratic model and emphasizes the availability of internal development opportunities for employees. While the organization provides training over the long run, new employees should already possess sufficient skills to enter and succeed in their job roles at the time of hire. For these reasons, the attraction of employees with more advanced and specialized skill sets is especially important.

Because of the nature of how this model of management seeks to create employee attachment, companies following the bureaucratic model should look to build an employment brand with a focus on opportunities for challenging work and long-term internal development and promotion. Additionally, bureaucratic organizations and subunits may incorporate an emphasis on order and structure into branding efforts to attract applicants particularly drawn to more organized, controlled work environments. Overall, recruitment should take the form of targeted messages emphasizing challenge and development, directed at a skilled labor pool qualified for the company's current job openings.

Selection under the bureaucratic management philosophy

Selection decisions, like all other significant decisions, are centralized under the bureaucratic model. Hiring procedures are standardized and rule-based and favor candidates whose skill sets best match the requirements of open positions. As noted, bureaucratic units aim to immediately place new hires into their positions with minimal initial training. For this reason and because job tasks are likely to require more complex knowledge and understanding than are job tasks performed by employees in autocratic organizations, the bureaucratic unit is likely to weight the levels and appropriateness of applicants' skill sets heavily. Additionally, because this model relies on employee adherence to organization or subunit standards and managerial oversight is not as close or direct as in the autocratic model, the bureaucratic organization or subunit should consider applicants' ability to follow rules and procedures in selection decisions.

Based on the above, we propose that organizational subunits with low information uncertainty and higher task and role specialization will achieve the highest level of performance when instituting a bureaucratic recruitment and selection model.

Rapidly changing environment and high information-processing uncertainty

Where there is a high degree of uncertainty, organizations need to follow communication-behavior cycles in which participants exchange information and develop interpretations of the new or changing information to which they are exposed (Weick, 1969). These outcomes require flexibility, creativity, and appropriate mechanisms to handle uncertainty (Hage & Aiken, 1969). Organizations facing this type of external environment must be flexible enough to adapt to the changing demands of their competitive environments in order to meet the unstable and emerging needs of consumers typically through pursuing continuous innovation (Hage, 1965, 1980; Zammuto & O'Connor, 1992). Further, the ability to deliver continuous innovation requires creativity in solutions to environmental demands, which is driven through the exchange and creation of knowledge and investigation of uncharted intellectual territory – tasks typically considered as very high in uncertainty (Hage, 1980).

Employees in a subunit that is more adaptable and innovative must be able to effectively mobilize skills, ideas, and knowledge across departments (Hage, 1965, 1980). Communication and collaboration are effective tools for achieving these objectives of increasing creative efforts by allowing for the incorporation of ideas from diverse perspectives and can enhance information-processing capacities by employing multiple skill sets in problem-solving tasks (Collins & Smith, 2006). The cross-fertilization of ideas across an organization is often most effectively achieved by having employees take active roles in projects in multiple departments. For this boundary-spanning to be most productive, more adaptable organizational subunits must also employ workers with diverse areas of expertise (Hage, 1965).

In addition to free and open collaboration across departments, subunits of employees are also more adaptable and innovative when employees embrace risk-taking attitudes. Without confidence in taking risks, employees are less likely to produce profitable ideas and solutions to problems (Collins & Smith, 2006). In sum, the workforce characteristics most advantageous to a boundary-spanning subunit are open and active cross-departmental communication networks, the possession of unique and diverse skill sets by many employees, and a risk-taking culture that facilitates creative experimentation.

An organic organizational structure appears to be the most effective structure for eliciting the workforce characteristics required by boundary-spanning activities and the need to adapt to rapidly changing environments. For example, empirical research has demonstrated that organizations competing on innovation have fared better with organic-like structures (Damanpour, 1991; Hage, 1965). Organic structures are characterized by low centralization, low formalization, high specialization, and the regular use of horizontal communication throughout the firm (Hage, 1965, 1980; Zammuto & O'Connor, 1992). The characteristics of the organic structure also lead to employees constantly crossing job and departmental boundaries in their everyday work roles and facilitate horizontal communication between employees across the same level of an organization which increases the degree to which information and advice is shared (Hage, 1980; Zammuto & O'Connor, 1992).

The characteristics of the organic structure complement each other and support the level of adaptation and innovation required by subunits facing environments with high levels of uncertainty and change. Specifically, the decentralization of power allows for more department-level decision making, enabling employees at non-managerial levels to contribute more directly to decisions regarding the products and processes on which they have the most expertise and in meeting the changing demands of the respective competitive environments. The use of horizontal communication combined with high levels of employee specialization fosters a creative environment where employees with diverse skill sets can combine and create knowledge freely. The low level of formalization also contributes to the flexible movement of employees and employee knowledge across departmental boundaries and promotes an organization-wide environment of collaboration. In sum, the organic structure facilitates the flexibility, adaptiveness, skill mobilization, and creative problem solving required by an innovation strategy.

Based on the above, we propose that organizational subunits with high information uncertainty will achieve the highest level of performance when instituting recruitment and selection practices that match the organic organizational structure.

Recruitment and selection systems matching organic structure

As we noted, the organic organizational structure is likely the best fitting organizational structure to support subunits facing a high degree of information uncertainty or pursuing a strategy of innovation. As with the mechanistic structure, the organic structure is really an archetype and prescription of required elements of an organizational structure rather than an implemented system or set of HR practices. Further, based on contingency theory, it is likely that there are multiple systems of HR practices that match the attributes of the organic structure, each of which may be a better fit for a particular subunit given other important subunit characteristics. For example, research by Baron and colleagues (Baron & Hannan, 2002; Baron et al., 2001) suggests that there are at least two unique management philosophies – commitment and professional – that are organic in nature. Below, we outline these two management philosophies and develop specific outlines of the recruitment and selection requirements that would be associated with each.

The commitment recruitment and selection model

The commitment model, as identified by Baron and colleagues (Baron et al., 2001), is one management approach that is consistent with the characteristics of an organic structure. As with the other models of management, the commitment model follows a specific set of guidelines regarding organizational entry, employee coordination and control, and employee attachment. In particular, the commitment model aims to facilitate a family-like environment and emphasizes an employer–employee relationship in which long-term commitment to and tenure with the organization are emphasized. Companies following a commitment model of management are looking to attract and select new employees to the organization who fit with the organization's culture. Further, these firms complement attraction and selection based on company-fit by implementing socialization events and regularly held social activities to promote strong, family-like employee relationships throughout the organization.

Firms following the commitment model also look to achieve employee coordination and control through the use of peer feedback and performance management. As an outcome of peer group control, subunits of employees under the commitment model of management will have a work environment that facilitates horizontal communication and decentralization of authority. As noted above, we expect these processes to lead to higher levels of collaboration among employees. Further, collaboration in the commitment model will be based on trust among employees and mutual commitment to the goals of the organization. Finally, the basis for attachment in the commitment model is based on employees' love of their job and work environment and sense of ownership and belonging to the organization as a whole. This form of attachment is driven and facilitated by creating a family-like environment through participation, close-knit and similar cultural fit between employees, and incentive pay that creates an ownership stake in the firm. Because of their close attachment to the firm, we would expect a lower likelihood of employee turnover in the commitment model compared to levels found under other management models.

Recruitment under the commitment management philosophy

The recruiting efforts used by organizations and subunits following the commitment model will aim to attract employees who will fit well with the organization's existing culture and who are likely to remain with the organization for an extended period of time. Subunits following the commitment model will best be served by implementing recruiting initiatives that primarily focus on openings in entry-level positions and are targeted at labor sources that closely match the organizational culture. Because of the nature of employee attachment and organizational entry in the commitment model, companies should look to build an employment brand that focuses on the specific unique aspects of their company culture and the long-term development opportunities available in the organization. This form of employer brand-building effort will help to attract applicants who are the right cultural fit to the organization and help to provide a realistic preview that may lead others who are not a fit to self-select out of the recruitment process.

Selection under the commitment management philosophy

As previously indicated, while other employment models emphasize the importance of employees' knowledge and skills, the primary selection criterion in the commitment model is applicants' fit with organizational culture and values. Because the commitment model places a great emphasis on family-like relationships and trust among employees in the organization, it is important for new employees to naturally fit with existing employees to some extent upon hiring. To help ensure this fit, selection decisions are often made by peer employees, the likely colleagues of potential hires.

An additional consideration in selection in the commitment model is an applicant's ability to adapt and grow with the organization. Job tasks are likely to be modified with the changing demands of the environment. Therefore, applicants who appear able and willing to adapt to the changing needs of the organization are likely to be greatly valued. Finally, the commitment model's emphasis on employee development and extended tenure play an additional role in selection considerations. Organizations following this model are likely to select employees who seem committed to and likely to succeed in a long-term career with the firm. Only through the hiring of this type of employee is an organization able to promote the trust-filled, family-like relationships on which its culture and success are based.

Based on the above, we propose that organizational subunits with high information uncertainty and lower role and task complexity will achieve the highest levels of performance when instituting a commitment recruitment and selection model.

The professional recruitment and selection model

The professional model (originally called the engineering model by Baron and colleagues) also appears to be reflective of the organic structure and supportive of the employee outcomes desirable under an innovation strategy. Based on the work of Baron et al. (2001), the professional model specifies selection based on specific task abilities, peer-group control, and employment attachment through challenging work. The professional model is characterized by loose definitions of job roles, employee relationships based on expertise and task interdependence, and high levels of employee flexibility and discretion. The professional model's specification of selection on the basis of specific task abilities promotes the high levels of specialization that are characteristic of the organic structure and fruitful for the cross-fertilization of diverse ideas which drives the innovation approach. This basis for selection is also likely to result in an employee base with high levels of industry experience, as employees who have spent the most time in the industry are most likely to have developed the advanced skill sets sought by organizations using this approach. Additionally, selection for task abilities is likely to result in greater productive task conflict among employees, as diverse functional and educational backgrounds lend themselves to different strengths and perspectives in problem-solving contexts.

The use of peer-group control requires and facilitates the horizontal communication and decentralization of power implicit in an organic structure. Horizontal communication is likely to create increased opportunities for collaboration, and involvement in peer control mechanisms is likely to instill greater interest among employees in other employees' work. The attachment mechanism of the professional model, challenging work, is consistent with the multitude of novel tasks in the innovation strategy. Additionally, it reflects the strong task focus that is prevalent in an professional model approach. Taken together, the various dimensions of the professional model select and connect employees primarily for the work they perform. Hence, it is likely that employees working in the context of this model are likely to report greater job involvement than employees working under other models of management.

Recruitment under the professional management philosophy

The recruitment efforts of organizations following the professional model are likely to be widespread in scope and well funded. Because organizational success under this model depends on the diversity and quality of employees' skill sets, organizations following this model should invest heavily in recruitment efforts directed at labor sources with advanced, specialized skills. National brand-building efforts are likely to be used in an attempt to attract the most skilled applicants from a wide variety of specialties. Companies should also focus the message of their employment branding along the dimension of the challenging work offered by the organization in order to better attract top talent to the firm.

Selection under the professional management philosophy

Selection under the professional model is based on applicants' specialized knowledge and skill sets. While recruiting efforts are aimed at attracting specialized talent to apply, selection decisions consider which applicants' skill sets best complement and uniquely contribute to the skill base of existing employees in the firm. Therefore, organizations following the professional model are likely to invest substantially in the certification of applicants' skills. Additionally, organizations under this model may consider applicants' abilities to collaborate with colleagues, as collaboration is essential to the cross-fertilization of ideas and knowledge required for these organizations' success.

In contrast to organizations following the commitment model, organizations following the professional model do not invest substantially in skill-specific employee development and do not expect particularly long tenure by employees. Therefore, organizations under the professional model are more focused on selecting for skill sets immediately required for the completion of current business goals and that match with current market needs. Instead, these firms are likely to tolerate and even encourage turnover among employees whose skill sets are no longer required because of changes in the external environment. In fact, turnover of this variety helps to ensure that the organization is able to fill open jobs with new talent that has skills and knowledge that match with the company's dynamic market conditions. Finally, firms following the professional model should also look to select employees based on their ability to collaborate and work across teams as this is an essential component to the knowledge sharing required to adapt and innovate.

Based on the above, we propose that organizational subunits with high information uncertainty and higher levels of role and task complexity will achieve the highest levels of performance when instituting a professional *recruitment and selection model*.

Conclusions

The goal of this chapter was to provide a new, macro-level model of strategic staffing to close the gap in our knowledge regarding how practices within recruitment and selection systems can work to provide companies with a competitive advantage. In particular, we were looking to identify multiple systems of recruitment and selection systems that would be the right fit for attracting and selecting employees with the right KSAs that fit the strategy or business context faced by particular organizations. To meet this challenge, we felt that it was first necessary to identify groups of employees where there are potentially meaningful differences necessitating different recruitment and selection systems. We drew on research in the area of organizational theory (e.g., Thompson, 1967; Weick, 1969) to make the argument that companies should create distinct subunits of employees based on the extent of information equivocality in their jobs.

Further, we noted that some subunits of employees will experience relatively low information uncertainty either because of stability in the external business environment or because the company is looking to exploit an existing technology or process on a continuing basis. In contrast, other subunits of employees face high information uncertainty because of the dynamism in the external environment and the resulting need for continued innovation and change internally. Drawing on emerging research in the area of strategic human resource management, we went on to argue that unique systems of recruitment and selection practices are necessary to create a workforce with the requisite level of knowledge, skills, abilities, and motivation to match the differing levels of information equivocality faced by the subunits of employees. We went on to argue that recruitment and selection systems that match the mechanistic organizational structure are the best fit for subunits of employees facing low information uncertainty; whereas recruitment and selection systems that match the organic organizational structure are the best fit for subunits of employees facing high informational uncertainty.

Finally, based on contingency theory, we noted that there are multiple systems of recruitment and selection systems that may match the employee workforce requirements created by information equivocality depending on the extent to which tasks within the subunit differ in terms of complexity. We went on to present four models of management – two that match a mechanistic structure and two that match an organic structure – as a basis for identifying specific systems of recruitment and selection practices. First, we presented the autocratic model of recruitment and selection and argued that this is the best fit for subunits that face low information equivocality and lower role complexity. Second, we presented the bureaucratic model of recruitment and selection and argued that this model is the best fit for subunits facing low information equivocality and higher levels of role and task complexity. Third, we presented the commitment model of recruitment and selection and put forth the argument that this model is the best fit for subunits facing high levels of information equivocality and lower levels of role and task complexity. Finally, we presented the professional model of recruitment and selection and argued that the professional model is the best fit for subunits that face high levels of both information equivocality and role complexity.

While we feel that this chapter helps to provide an important stride forward in terms of macro-level theory for staffing, there are a number of important areas for future research in this field. First, there is a great need for empirical research on the effects of recruitment and selection at the macro-level of analysis. In particular, we feel that it is critical to test the ideas put forward in this chapter in order to empirically test our contingency argument that particular systems of recruitment and selection will be more efficacious given the nature of the information equivocality and role and task complexity faced by a particular subunit of employees. However, there is such a lack of empirical research at the macro-level of analysis that any empirical work examining the effects of recruitment and selection on key organizational outcomes would be welcome. Second, there is a great need for continuing theoretical development of our understanding of how systems of recruitment and selection practices affect firm performance and firm-level employee outcomes (e.g., human capital, employee engagement). For example, we would encourage researchers to identify additional systems of recruitment and selection practices. Further, more research and thinking is needed to identify employee profiles and outcomes that may be a match to other organizational conditions and then identify the matching systems of recruitment and selection practices.

We believe that we have presented an interesting set of propositions to encourage readers to think about and theorize the effects of recruitment and selection at a more strategic, macro-level of analysis. However, we strongly encourage readers to view our chapter as a start in moving the field of strategic staffing forward and to take this as a challenge to continuing pushing forward our knowledge of how different systems of recruitment and selection practices affect firm performance through the workforce attributes of different subunits of employees.

References

Baron, J. N. & Hannan, M. T. 2002. Organizational blueprints for success in high-tech startups: Lessons from the Stanford project on emerging companies. *California Management Review*, 44(3), 8–36.

Baron, J. N., Hannan, M. T., & Burton, M. D. 2001. Labor pains: Change in organizational models and employee turnover in young, high-tech firms. *The American Journal of Sociology*, 106, 960–1012.

Burns, T. & Stalker, G. M. 1994. *The Management of Innovation*. Oxford: Oxford University Press.

Collins, C. J. & Smith, K. G. 2006. Knowledge exchange and combination: The role of human resource practices in the performance of high-technology firms. *The Academy of Management Journal*, 49, 544–560.

Damanpour, F. 1991. Organizational innovation: A meta-analysis of effects of determinants and moderators. *Academy of Management Journal*, 34, 555–590.

Dohm, A. 2000. Gauging the labor force effects of retiring baby boomers. *Monthly Labor Report*, 123(7), 17–25.

Etzioni, A. 1964. *Modern Organizations*. Englewood Cliffs, NJ: Prentice-Hall.

Galbraith, J. 1973. *Designing Complex Organizations*. Reading, MA: Addison-Wesley.

Hage, J. 1965. An axiomatic theory of organizations. *Administrative Science Quarterly*, 10, 289–320.

Hage, J. 1980. *Theories of Organizations: Form, Process, and Transformation*. New York: Wiley.

Hage, J. & Aiken, M. 1969. Routine technology, social structure, and organizational goals. *Administrative Science Quarterly*, 14, 366–377.

Lawrence, P. R. & Lorsch, J. W. 1967. *Organization and Environment: Managing Differentiation and Integration*. Cambridge, MA: Harvard Graduate School of Business Administration.

Lepak, D. P. & Snell, S. A. 1999. The human resource architecture: Toward a theory of human capital allocation and development. *Academy of Management Review*, 24, 31–48.

March, J. G. & Simon, H. A. 1958. *Organizations*. New York: The Free Press.

Michaels, E., Handfield-Jones, H., & Axelrod, B. 2001. *The War for Talent*. Boston, MA: Harvard Business School Press.

Rynes, S. L. & Barber, A. E. 1990. Applicant attraction strategies: An organizational perspective. *Academy of Management Review*, 15, 286–310.

Taylor, M. S. & Collins, C. J. 2000. Organizational recruitment: Enhancing the intersection of theory and practice. In C. L. Cooper & E. A. Locke (Eds), *Industrial and Organizational Psychology: Linking Theory and Practice* (pp. 304–334). Oxford: Blackwell.

Thompson, J. D. 1967. *Organizations in Action*. New York: McGraw-Hill.

Weick, K. 1969. *The Social Psychology of Organizations*. Reading, MA: Addison-Wesley.

Woodruffe, C. 1999. *Winning the Talent War*. New York: Wiley.

Zammuto, R., & O'Connor, E. 1992. Gaining advanced manufacturing technologies benefits: The role of organizational design and culture. *Academy of Management Review*, 17, 701–728.

14

Compensation

Barry Gerhart

To be successful over time, organizations must be effective in formulating and executing their product market strategies. Although strategy is often framed as a macro topic, what happens at the organization level depends on the nature of decisions that are made by individuals at every level in the organization, as well as the success with which these decisions are executed. Although many factors influence the effectiveness of strategy formulation and execution, one key factor, and the focus of this chapter, is how people in the organization are compensated. Whether the goal is to have executives formulate and execute a strategy that benefits shareholders, or the goal is that of a first-level manager seeking to have his or her work group make a successful contribution to strategy execution and success, it is likely that the design of compensation for these groups (executives, managers, and employees) will play an important role in effectiveness. Thus, effective compensation design can play a major role in strategy formulation, execution and effectiveness.

Definition

Compensation, or remuneration, can be defined to include "all forms of financial returns and tangible services and benefits employees receive as part of an employment relationship" (Milkovich & Newman, 2008, p. 9). "Total rewards" include monetary compensation and nonmonetary rewards. This distinction and the related different general forms of compensation are shown in Figure 14.1 below.

Compensation can alternatively be defined and studied in terms of its key decision/design areas, which include (Gerhart & Milkovich, 1992; Milkovich & Newman, 2008): how pay varies across (and sometimes within) organizations according to its level (how much?); form (what share is paid in cash versus benefits?); structure (how is pay linked to job content, individual competencies, and progression and does pay vary across business units?); basis or mix (what is the share of base pay relative to variable pay/performance-based pay and what criteria determine payouts?); and administration (who makes, communicates, and administers pay decisions?).[1]

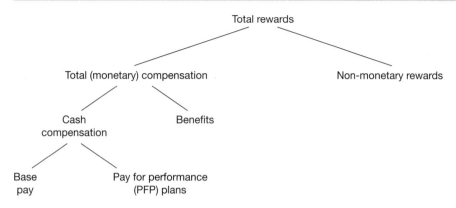

Figure 14.1 Dimensions of total rewards and total compensation

Alternatively, compensation can be organized around two broader dimensions: *how much* (total compensation level) to pay and *how* (e.g., cash or benefits, structure, degree of PFP) to pay (Gerhart & Milkovich, 1992; Gerhart & Rynes, 2003). Some evidence suggests that organizations may have more discretion regarding the how compared to the how much decision (Gerhart & Milkovich, 1990). Labor market competition pressures (the need to offer a competitive compensation package to attract and retain employees) and product market competition pressures (the need to control labor costs to keep product costs competitive) may set lower and upper bounds respectively on pay level for particular skills and occupations. In contrast, decisions regarding how payments are made (e.g., the mix of base versus variable pay) and the criteria used in awarding such payments (e.g., individual, group, organization effectiveness) can vary widely across (and within) organizations without necessarily generating significantly different labor costs. Or, if labor costs are higher, it is hoped that these higher costs are a natural consequence of higher productivity, quality, and/or other measures of effectiveness that are a result of a well-designed compensation strategy.

In addition to specifying the content of compensation decisions and thinking about where there is the most discretion in design choices, the compensation literature also seeks to understand their causes (e.g., organization strategy) and consequences (e.g., organization effectiveness). Additionally, the compensation literature has sought to understand whether the consequences (for effectiveness) of compensation decisions depend on alignment or fit with contextual factors (e.g., organization strategy, which is studied as both a causal and moderator variable).

Finally, it should be acknowledged that compensation could be defined to include nonmonetary rewards as well. There is no doubt about the fact that both monetary and nonmonetary rewards are important in the workplace. However, monetary rewards are unique in at least a few ways (Gerhart & Rynes, 2003; Lawler, 1971; Rottenberg, 1956). First, compensation is one of the most visible aspects of a job to both current employees and job seekers. Second, unlike some other job characteristics (e.g., job responsibility, working in teams), most people prefer more money to less. Third, money can be instrumental for meeting a wide array of needs, including, where preferences differ, economic consumption, self-esteem, status, and feedback regarding achievement. Given the central importance of monetary compensation, as well as limits on what can be covered in a single chapter, the main focus here is on pay or monetary rewards.

Chapter plan

I organize this chapter around the "how much to pay" and "how to pay" decisions identified above.[2] I focus primarily on the "how to pay" decision, especially pay-for-performance (PFP) plans. Most of my attention is devoted to the potential consequences of PFP decisions (both good and bad) and how these consequences may depend on contextual factors (i.e., alignment) and on design choices. First, however, it is necessary to address the fundamental issue of money's role as a motivator.

Does pay motivate?

Campbell and Pritchard (1976) observe that motivation can be defined in terms of its intensity, direction, and persistence. (Together with ability and situational constraints/opportunities, motivation contributes to observed behavior.) Thus, to fully evaluate the impact of pay on motivation, one must look not only at (enduring) effort level, but also the degree to which effort is directed toward desired objectives.

The role of pay, specifically PFP, and its effect on the level and direction of motivation in the workplace has long been a source of debate.[3] In some psychology-based treatments, the view is that "money is the crucial incentive" (Locke et al., 1980, p. 379). In a similar vein, Lawler (1971) stated that "the one issue that should be considered by all organization theories is the relationship between pay and performance" (p. 273). Lawler presented a model showing that pay is important because it is instrumental for meeting so many needs, both tangible (e.g., Maslow's (1943) frequently mentioned "lower order" needs such as food and shelter) and less tangible (or "higher order" needs such as security, status, esteem, and feedback about achievement). The importance of compensation in economics-based theories is taken as a given, as a reading of agency, efficiency wage, and tournament theories reveals.

In contrast, especially in recent years, there has been a tendency to ignore compensation in treatments of motivation and performance management in the psychology-based literature. Rynes et al. (2005, p. 574) observe that "at least three historical theories of motivation have dampened psychological interest" in pay: Maslow's (1943) need hierarchy theory, Herzberg et al.'s (1957) motivator-hygiene theory, and Deci and Ryan's (1985) cognitive evaluation theory. The scholarly literature has, for the most part, come to the conclusion that many of the core propositions of the Maslow and Herzberg models have not been empirically supported, including the peripheral role given to pay in motivation. Likewise, while the empirical support for cognitive evaluation theory, specifically the idea that PFP undermines intrinsic motivation (in nonwork settings) is still being debated, Gerhart and Rynes (2003) argue that such an effect is unlikely in work settings and find no empirical evidence in such settings. Rynes et al. (2005) observe that these ideas nevertheless seem to have continued influence in both the academic and practitioner worlds.[4]

Finally, a third view does not question the motivational impact of pay as an incentive. To the contrary, the concern is that it sometimes motivates "too well" resulting in unintended consequences (e.g., lack of teamwork, lack of quality, gaming the system) caused by people (mis)directing their effort in a way that earns the incentive payout, but which is ultimately not beneficial to the organization. Thus, the concern is not with effort level, but with its direction. These potential problems have received a good deal of attention across disciplines and in both the academic and practice literatures (e.g., Gerhart, 2001; Kohn, 1993; Lawler, 1971; Pfeffer, 1998; Whyte, 1955).[5]

Each of the above perspectives on compensation has some validity and relevance in at least some situations. As I show below, the evidence clearly indicates that PFP can be a powerful motivator of effective behaviors. Just as important, I also discuss the evidence (often anecdotal, but compelling) of the risks associated with PFP and some of the things that can go wrong. In any event, the question of whether to use compensation as an incentive may be largely irrelevant, given that organizations around the world already, as a rule, use compensation to motivate *something*, whether it be high performance, promotion, seniority, or avoidance of discharge or other discipline.

Effects of pay: incentive, sorting, and other intervening mechanisms

There are many theoretical processes, both in psychology and in other social sciences that have been used to explain the impact of pay in organizations, including reinforcement, expectancy, equity, utility, agency, efficiency wage, and tournament theories. (For a summary and review, see Gerhart & Rynes, 2003.) To greatly simplify, these theories indicate that pay operates on motivation and performance in two general ways (Gerhart & Milkovich, 1992; Gerhart & Rynes, 2003; Lazear, 1986).

First, there is the potential for an *incentive effect*, which we define as the impact of PFP on current employees' motivational state. The incentive effect is how pay influences individual and aggregate motivation, holding the attributes of the workforce constant. The incentive effect has been the focus of the great majority of theory and research in compensation, especially in management and applied psychology (in earlier years when monetary incentives received more attention).

Second, there is the potential for a *sorting effect*, which we define as the impact of pay on performance via its impact on the attributes of the workforce. Different types of pay systems may cause different types of people to apply to and stay with an organization (self-select) and these different people may have different levels of ability or trait-like motivation, or different levels of attributes (e.g., team skills) that enhance effectiveness more in some organizations than in others. Organizations may also differentially select and retain employees, depending on the nature of their pay level and/or PFP strategies. The self-selection aspect of sorting and its application to the effects of pay is based primarily on work in economics (e.g., Lazear, 1986), but the idea is consistent with Schneider's (1987) attraction-selection-attrition (ASA) idea in the applied psychology literature.

The sorting and incentive idea provides one broad conceptual framework for thinking about intervening processes in studying the effects of compensation. Another is the ability-motivation-opportunity to contribute (AMO) framework (Appelbaum et al., 2000; Boxall & Purcell, 2003; Gerhart, 2007). Compensation seems most likely to influence workforce ability and motivation, less likely to come into play in the 'O' component, which has more to do with job design and participation in decisions. (As noted later, however, the 'O' component and the AMO dimensions in general are quite relevant in addressing horizontal alignment in HR and compensation.)

Gerhart and Milkovich (1992) called for compensation research to include intervening variables (and) at "multiple levels" of analysis in studying compensation and performance, because "if a link is found . . . possible mediating mechanisms can be examined to help establish why the link exists and whether (or which) causal interpretation is warranted" (p. 533). Beyond the general mediating mechanisms discussed above, more detailed intervening variables might include employee attitudes, individual performance and/or competencies, and employee turnover (broken out by performance levels). Other relevant mediators, depending on the particular goals of the unit or organization would be citizenship behavior, teamwork, climate for innovation, motivation, and engagement.

Effects of pay level

Higher pay levels result in higher labor costs per worker, which, by itself, makes a firm less price competitive in its product market. In addition, the costs of a high pay-level policy tend to be easier to measure and more certain than its benefits. Thus, as may be the case with human resource policies generally, it is possible that costs tend to be given more weight than benefits in deciding on a pay-level policy. While competitive pressures drive firms to minimize costs and maximize benefits, the cost side means that firms must control labor costs by controlling total compensation per employee and/or by controlling employee headcount. In a global world, cost control includes an ongoing search for the lowest cost location for production, all else being equal (e.g., proximity to customers and suppliers, worker skill levels) which is to varying degrees, depending on the product, technology, and work organization, a partial function of labor costs. As Table 14.1 makes clear, labor costs differ significantly across the world.

Efficiency wage and other economics-based theories argue that some firms, for a variety of reasons (e.g., their technology depends more heavily on having higher quality workers or monitoring performance is more difficult) do indeed have efficiency reasons to pay higher wages.[6] Higher pay levels, either for the organization as a whole or for critical jobs, may be well suited to particular strategies, such as higher value-added customer segments (e.g., Batt, 2001; Hunter, 2000). Similarly, evidence suggests that organizations making greater use of so-called high-performance work practices (teams, quality circles, total quality management, job rotation) and computer-based technology and having higher skilled workers also pay higher wages (Osterman, 2006).

The observable benefits of higher wages may include (Gerhart & Rynes, 2003): higher pay satisfaction (Currall et al., 2005; Williams et al., 2006; for a review, see Heneman & Judge, 2000), improved attraction and retention of employees (for a review, see Barber & Bretz, 2000), and higher quality, effort, and/or performance (e.g., Klaas & McClendon, 1996; Yellen, 1984).

Table 14.1 Average hourly labor costs for manufacturing production workers, by country 2005 (in equivalent US dollars)

United States	$24
Canada	24
Germany	33
France	25
United Kingdom	26
Spain	18
Czech Republic	6
Japan	22
Mexico	3
Hong Kong[a]	6
Korea	14
Sri Lanka[b]	0.52
China[c]	0.57

Note: Wage rates rounded to nearest dollar except when rate is less than one dollar.

Sources: U.S. Bureau of Labor Statistics, www.bls.gov
[a] Special Administrative Region of China; [b]2004; [c] 2002

I conclude the discussion of pay level at this point because it is only at an organization's peril that it follows a high pay-level policy without also linking high pay to high performance, whether it be the performance of the individual, team, unit, organization, or some combination. While it is possible to decouple pay level and performance in the short run, especially where there are forces that dampen market-based competition, by contrast, where market forces dominate, this decoupling is expected to work against organization survival and success in the longer run. In addition, as noted earlier, it may be that organizations have more discretion in terms of how they pay than in terms of how much they pay. Thus, the how to pay or PFP issue is perhaps the more strategic of the two decisions (Gerhart & Milkovich, 1990) and it is an issue that is (or should be) made in tandem with the how much to pay decision (Gerhart & Rynes, 2003).

Effects of pay for performance (PFP)

I begin by recognizing that PFP can take on many forms. When it is claimed that PFP did or did not work in a particular context, it is important to know the particular types of pay-for-performance programs being discussed, as different programs may be more or less suitable for different situations. Further, it is important to examine the impact of PFP plans on both incentive and sorting effects, as both are important and may operate differently.

Types of PFP programs include profit sharing, stock plans, gain sharing, individual incentives, sales commissions, and merit pay (Milkovich & Newman, 2008). As Figure 14.2 shows, these programs can be classified on two dimensions: level of measurement of performance (e.g., individual, plant, organization) and type of performance measure (results-oriented or behavior-oriented).

This distinction has also been drawn by Gerhart and Rynes (2003) and Milkovich and Wigdor (1991). It is important to note that, in practice, many employees are covered by what might be called hybrid pay programs. In other words, rather than working under either merit pay alone or under profit sharing alone, in many cases, employees will be covered by both types of plans and perhaps others as well.

Type of performance measure	Level of performance measure			
	Individual	Facility/plant	Organization	Multiple levels
Behavior-based	Merit pay		Merit pay for executives	Hybrid
Results-based	Individual incentives sales commission	Gain sharing	Profit-sharing stock plans	Hybrid
Results-based and behavior-based	Hybrid	Hybrid	Hybrid	Hybrid

Figure 14.2 Pay-for-performance (PFP) programs, by level and type of performance measure

229

Some of the many companies in the United States that are well known for their use of PFP include Lincoln Electric, Nucor Steel, Whole Foods, Hewlett-Packard, Southwest Airlines, and General Electric, to name just a few. Each uses a different form of PFP, with varying degrees of relative emphasis on individual, group/unit, and/or organization-level performance. Outside the United States, in countries with less of a tradition of PFP, there appears to be a movement in some cases (e.g. Japan, Korea) toward greater emphasis on PFP at all organization levels. In these and many other countries, there has been a clear movement toward greater use of PFP for selected employee groups (e.g., executives; Towers Perrin, 2006).

Incentive effects

In a meta-analysis of potential productivity-enhancing interventions in actual work settings, Locke, Feren, McCaleb, Shaw, and Denny (1980) found that the introduction of individual pay incentives increased productivity by an average of 30%. This meta-analysis is particularly compelling, since the authors only included studies that were conducted in real organizations (as opposed to laboratories), used either control groups or before-and-after designs, and measured performance via "hard" criteria (e.g. physical output) rather than supervisory ratings. Based on these multi-study findings, Locke et al. concluded that "money is the crucial incentive . . . no other incentive or motivational technique comes even close to money with respect to its instrumental value" (1980, p. 379).

Subsequent research also supports the powerful incentive effects of pay. Another meta-analysis by Guzzo, Jette, and Katzell (1985) also examined the average effects of both monetary incentives and work redesign on productivity (physical output). They found that financial incentives had a large mean effect on productivity (d = 2.12).[7] More recent meta-analyses (Jenkins et al., 1998; Judiesch, 1994; Stajkovic & Luthans, 1997) likewise provide strong support for a significant positive relationship between financial rewards and performance. Thus, there is compelling evidence that PFP, on average, is associated with substantially higher productivity in these settings.

In studies of executives, PFP plan design seems to influence a wide range of strategic decisions (Gerhart, 2000), including staffing patterns (Gerhart et al., 1996); diversification (Hitt et al., 1996; Phan & Hill, 1995); research and development investment (Galbraith & Merrill, 1991; Hill & Snell, 1989); capital investment (Larcker, 1983); and reaction to takeover attempts (Buchholtz & Ribbens, 1994; Kosnik, 1992; Mallette & Fowler, 1992). Likewise, over time, organizational strategy is more likely to change when (executive) pay strategy changes (Carpenter, 2000). Thus, there is consistent evidence that pay strategy does influence managerial goal choice.

Sorting effects

After reading the studies reviewed above, the reader would be well aware of the incentive mechanism, but quite possibly unaware of the sorting mechanism as a possible explanation for the observed effects. To the extent that the above studies track the same individuals before and after the intervention, they do indeed estimate incentive effects. However, to the degree that the individuals making up the workforce changed in response to a PFP intervention, then at least some of the improvement in performance might be due to a sorting effect. Lazear (2000), for example, reported a 44% increase in productivity when a glass installation company switched from salaries to individual incentives. Of this increase, roughly 50% was due to existing workers increasing their productivity, while the other 50% was attributable to less productive workers quitting and being replaced by more productive workers over time.

Cadsby, Song, and Tapon (2007) likewise found that both incentive and sorting effects explained the positive impact of PFP on productivity. Their study, set in the laboratory, was designed so that subjects went through multiple rounds. In some rounds, subjects were assigned to a PFP plan, while in other rounds they were assigned to work under a fixed salary plan. In yet other rounds, they were asked to choose either the fixed salary or the PFP plan to work under (i.e., they were asked to self-select). Cadsby et al. found that by the last rounds in their experiment, the PFP condition generated 38% higher performance than the fixed salary condition and that the sorting effect (less risk-averse and more productive subjects being more likely to select the PFP condition) was actually about twice as large as the incentive effect in explaining this 38% difference. In explaining why they found a sorting effect that was larger than that found by Lazear (which was also substantial), Cadsby et al. observe that in the Lazear study, few employees chose to leave the organization, presumably because there was no down-side risk to the PFP plan implemented there. Thus, most of the sorting effect in the Lazear study was probably attributable to new hires being more productive than current employees on average, without much of the sorting effect being due to lower performing employees leaving the organization.

Evidence suggests that PFP is more attractive to higher performers than to lower performers. For example, Trank and her colleagues (2002) found that the highest achieving college students place considerably more importance on being paid for performance than do their lesser achieving counterparts. Likewise, persons with higher need for achievement (Bretz et al., 1989; Turban & Keon, 1993), and lower risk aversion (Cable & Judge, 1994; Cadsby et al., 2007) also prefer jobs where pay is linked more closely to performance. Since these are all characteristics that some or most employers desire, such individual differences are important for employers to keep in mind.

Other research shows that high performers are most likely to quit and seek other employment if their performance is not sufficiently recognized with financial rewards (Salamin & Hom, 2005; Trevor et al., 1997). Conversely, low performers are more likely to stay with an employer when pay–performance relationships are weaker (Harrison et al., 1996).

Finally, to the degree that sorting effects are important, they may make it appear as though the relationship between pay and performance is weaker than it really is (Gerhart & Rynes, 2003). For example, to the degree that organizations are selective and valid in their decisions regarding who to hire and who to retain, the remaining group of employees will be unrepresentative in that their average performance level should be high as selectivity and validity increase (Boudreau & Berger, 1985). So, even if there is little observed variance in performance and/or pay within this group (i.e., there is range restriction), this selected group of employees may have above-market pay and above-market performance. Thus, in this example, there is no (observed) relationship between pay and performance within the firm, but there would be a significant relationship between pay and performance between firms. Similarly, on the employee side of the decision, it may be that high performers self-select such that they are more likely to join and remain with organizations that have PFP. In summary, even when there is little observed variance in performance ratings and/or pay within an organization, it may nevertheless be the case that PFP, via sorting effects, has resulted in major differences in performance between organizations (Gerhart & Trevor, 2008).

Concerns, cautions, and challenges

The discussion of the motivational impact of PFP might convey an impression that any organization can readily benefit from PFP and that there is little risk in such a strategy. That, however, is not the case, for reasons noted earlier. First, some critics say pay has no important impact because it is a secondary motivator. In other words, it does not energize and sustain motivation and behavior. While the value that employees attach to pay certainly does vary, we believe that in workplaces where PFP does not appear to motivate, it is often because there is not a sufficiently strong pay–performance link.

Consider the case of two employees, each earning US$50,000 per year. Suppose that the first receives an "excellent" performance rating and a 5% merit increase, while the second receives a "very good" rating and a 4% increase. On an annual basis, the differential is only 1%, or $500. On a weekly basis, the differential is $500/52 = $9.62. With a marginal tax rate of say 40%, the after-tax weekly differential is $5.77. Is this performance payoff sufficient to motivate Employee A to maintain the same level of high performance or to motivate Employee B to aspire to higher performance? Many people would say "no." Furthermore, given the imprecision of performance ratings, there is no assurance that better performance by Employee B would actually result in a higher rating and the modestly higher take-home pay.

Thus, even where (e.g., in the United States) most private sector organizations tend to claim that they have PFP policies (or researchers claim that they are studying PFP policies), there is, in fact, sometimes little meaningful empirical relationship between pay and performance (Gerhart & Milkovich, 1992; Gerhart & Rynes, 2003; Trevor et al., 1997). Not surprisingly then, when employees are asked about how much PFP there is in their own organizations, they tend to say "not very much." For example, in a survey of employees in 335 companies conducted by the HayGroup (2002), employees were asked whether they agreed with the statement, "If my performance improves, I will receive better compensation." Only 35% agreed, whereas 27% neither agreed nor disagreed, and 38% disagreed with this statement.

PFP, if weakly implemented, is not expected by anyone to have much impact. Thus, like any policy, its success depends on the success (including the strength) with which it is implemented. It is also worth noting that PFP is often narrowly defined as annual merit increases. If defined more broadly to include the cumulative effects over time of such increases and importantly, the effect of merit ratings on pay over time via their influence on promotion, the pay–performance relationship begins to look bigger. It is possible that doing a better job of communicating these facts would contribute to stronger performance–pay relationships among employees.

While the above concern focuses on the problem of PFP being too weak to motivate, a very different concern is that PFP motivates "too well" in other cases. Here, the danger is that a PFP program can act as a blunt instrument that may result in unintended and harmful consequences. Several supporting examples can be cited. One is the range of executive pay scandals in the United States, which have involved gaming of the system (e.g. manipulating profits, backdating stock options) as a means to maximize stock option and other incentive plan payouts for themselves. Other examples (see Gerhart (2001) for further details) have to do with "churning" practices in the insurance industry, miscoding health conditions at hospitals to get higher reimbursement from the government, and even auto repair shops finding (non-existent) mechanical problems with automobiles so they could sell more repairs, thus increasing sales and bonus payments, which depend on sales growth.

These and other examples make clear that people do respond to incentives, so great care must be taken in designing such incentives. This issue must, in our opinion, be accorded significant weight and be given serious consideration by any organization implementing or revising a PFP program. There are many potential pitfalls in the use of PFP. One general problem is that there are multiple objectives in organizations and a PFP system cannot maximize them all simultaneously. Thus, a balancing act is required. A system that too aggressively rewards one objective may compromise other objectives. People tend to do what is rewarded and objectives not rewarded tend to be ignored (Lawler, 1971; Milgrom & Roberts, 1992).

How long a PFP plan remains in place is sometimes used as a measure of its success. While a short-term gain in performance from a pay plan that does not last long should not be dismissed, a plan that generates longer term performance gains is preferred and changing plans too often can result in a counterproductive "flavor-of-the-month" perception among employees (Beer & Cannon, 2004). So, survival is a useful indicator.

In addition, evidence on survival is important in terms of drawing statistical conclusions for at least two reasons (Gerhart et al., 1996). First, plans that survive for shorter periods are more likely to be excluded from studies of pay plan effectiveness. To the degree that PFP plans have significant "failure" rates and this results in failed plans not being studied, it would result in a sample of plans that are more effective on average than the full population of plans. Second, while it is useful to know how effective different PFP plans are, on average, just like an investor looking at different types of investments, an organization should be interested in information not just on the average "return," but also information on the variance or risk of the PFP plan.

Beer and Cannon (2004) provide an analysis of 13 PFP "experiments" conducted at Hewlett-Packard in the mid-1990s. In 12 of the 13 cases, the program did not survive. They concluded that "Despite the undisputed instrumentality of PFP to motivate, little attention has been given to whether the benefits outweigh the costs or the 'fit' of these programs with high-commitment cultures like Hewlett-Packard was at the time" (p. 3). In the Hewlett-Packard case, the PFP initiatives had "unintended consequences" and managers eventually decided that performance could be more effectively improved "through alternative managerial tools such as good supervision, clear goals, coaching, training, and so forth" (p. 13). Beer and Cannon note that "This decision [did] not imply that managers believed that pay did not motivate or that it could not be used effectively in other settings" (p. 13). Rather, managers decided that at Hewlett-Packard, there were better alternatives.

Gerhart and colleagues have made similar observations on the risk in implementing PFP programs: "One must consider whether the potential for impressive gains in performance" from such plans is "likely to outweigh the potential problems, which can be serious" (Gerhart, 2001, p. 222) and that such plans are best thought of as representing "a high risk, high reward strategy" (Gerhart et al., 1996, p. 222).

While the risks of PFP programs must be acknowledged and understood, it is also necessary to use some caution here so that one does not get too carried away with the risk issue. Several points are in order. First, Ledford (2004) observed that we need to be clear regarding what specific types of PFP programs we are addressing. For example, the programs that Hewlett-Packard experimented with appear to be mostly team-based programs. Although these did not survive, as both Beer and Cannon and Ledford observe, Hewlett-Packard has for many years used other PFP programs such as broad-based stock options and profit sharing. These PFP programs have survived. So, it is not possible to make any broad statement about PFP programs overall. Second, the evaluation of PFP program success can depend on the timeframe. Beer and Cannon state that "Hewlett-Packard's performance since Carly Fiorina [its former chief executive] introduced pay-for-performance at the executive level has been less than stellar" (p. 16). That statement may have been accurate then, but looking back from the later vantage point of 2007, Hewlett-Packard's performance over the preceding several years was very strong relative to the market and its peers. Does that mean the introduction of more PFP for executives has actually been a success?

Third, it should be understood that in cases where PFP programs generate sorting effects (see earlier discussion), the risk element of PFP programs may be diminished in some respects.

For example, problems causes by a lack of fit with the current culture or employee preferences should be more avoidable in a start-up situation to the extent that an organization can exercise considerable control from day one over who it hires and how well they fit its PFP system.

Fourth, as Cannon and Beer (2004) and others (e.g., Gerhart & Rynes, 2003) have pointed out, risk, defined in terms of lack of fit, disruption, dissatisfaction, and so forth, is not necessarily a bad thing. Indeed, it may be a goal of the plan to reshape the workforce by replacing those that are less effective under a new PFP plan with those that would be more successful (Sturman et al., 2003).

Finally, whenever the risk of implementing a new PFP plan is discussed, it is also necessary to discuss the risk of not implementing such a plan as well (Gerhart et al., 1996). What are the costs and benefits of acting versus not acting? What is the cost of a program not surviving? Is it large enough that it should play an important role in the implementation decision? What happens if the status quo continues while competitors are making changes that, while not necessarily warmly received in the short run, do result in more long-run competitiveness, and thus returns to shareholders and continued employment and earnings for employees?

Factors in PFP success: alignment and performance measurement issues

Given the preceding discussion's emphasis on the need for caution in designing and implementing PFP plans, a couple of natural questions might be "What contextual factors affect whether a PFP plan is successful?" and "How should performance be measured for a PFP plan to succeed?" The former question has to do with alignment/fit and the latter question has to do with pros and cons of different performance measures.

Alignment

Terms such as alignment, synergy, fit, and complementarity describe the idea that the effects of two or more factors are nonadditive and dependent on contextual factors.[8] An example given by Gerhart and Rynes (2003) is where a gain-sharing program alone results in an average performance increase of 10%, while a suggestion system alone results in an average performance increase of 10%. However, when used in combination, their total effect is not additive (i.e., 20%), but is rather nonadditive (e.g., 30%). So, the effect of the gain-sharing program is contingent on a contextual factor, in this case, another aspect of HR (Gerhart & Rynes, 2003).

There are two general classes of contingency factors: person and situation. Our earlier discussion of sorting effects highlighted some of the relevant person factors (e.g., risk aversion, need for achievement, academic performance, performance) that predict preference for PFP. In addition, other person characteristics may predict preferences for particular types of PFP. For example, Cable and Judge (1994) found that individual-based PFP was preferred, on average, by those with high self-efficacy, but as might be expected, less preferred, on average, by those scoring high on collectivism.

There are three key aspects of pay strategy alignment or fit that focus on the situation or environmental context (Gerhart, 2000; Gerhart & Rynes, 2003): horizontal alignment (between pay strategy and other dimensions of HR management, as in the gain-sharing example above), vertical alignment with organizational strategy (i.e., pay strategy with corporate and business strategy), and internal alignment between different dimensions of pay strategy (e.g. pay level and pay basis). Only a brief review is provided here. (For more detail, see Gerhart, 2000; Gerhart & Rynes, 2003; Gomez-Mejia & Balkin, 1992; Milkovich, 1988.)

The primary focus of the pay strategy literature has been on vertical alignment. It has been shown that aspects of corporate strategy such as the process, degree and type of diversification (Gomez-Mejia, 1992; Kerr, 1985; Pitts, 1976) and the firm's life cycle (e.g., growth, maintenance; Ellig, 1981) are associated with different compensation strategies (Gomez-Mejia & Balkin, 1992; Kroumova & Sesis, 2006; Yanadori & Marler, 2006). Evidence also suggests performance differences based on fit such that growth firms perform better with an incentive-based strategy (Balkin & Gomez-Mejia, 1987) and that the effectiveness of an incentive-based strategy depends to a degree on the level of diversification (Gomez-Mejia, 1992). Alignment of pay strategy with business strategy (e.g., Miles & Snow, 1978; Porter, 1985) may also have performance consequences (e.g., Rajagopolan, 1996). Another stream of work on nonexecutives at the business unit level focuses on the alignment between pay strategy and manufacturing strategy (Shaw et al., 2002; Snell & Dean, 1994). Finally, other work shows, consistent with agency theory, that companies having more financial risk tend to have less risk sharing in their compensation for managers and executives (Aggarwal & Samwick, 1999; Bloom & Milkovich, 1998; Garen, 1994). Thus, both the risk aversion of the individual and risk properties of the situation are relevant (Wiseman et al., 2000).

In contrast to the work on vertical alignment, horizontal alignment of pay strategy with other employment practices has been studied mostly using nonexecutive employees and mostly in the context of work on so-called high-performance work systems and HR systems. The effect of an HR system on effectiveness is thought to operate via the intervening variables of ability, motivation, and opportunity, or AMO (Appelbaum et al., 2000; Batt, 2002; Boxall & Purcell, 2003; Gerhart, 2007). One problem with studying horizontal fit, however, is that the hypothesized role of pay and/or PFP, as well as the way these constructs are operationalized, tends to differ across studies, making it difficult to draw robust conclusions about what other HR strategy elements work best with particular pay and PFP approaches (Becker & Gerhart, 1996; Gerhart & Rynes, 2003).

Nevertheless, certain potential areas of fit and mis-fit can be identified (Gerhart & Rynes, 2003; Rynes et al., 2005). For instance, with respect to the 'O' component, it seems likely that group-based incentive plans (e.g., gain sharing, profit sharing) will be more effective in smaller groups (Kaufman, 1992; Kruse, 1993) than in larger groups or organizations. In addition, in situations where work is more interdependent, it may be that some shift in emphasis from individual performance to group performance will be more effective (e.g., Shaw et al., 2002). Nevertheless, it must be kept in mind that even where tasks are interdependent, if there are individual differences in ability and/or performance that are important, then placing too little weight on individual performance in compensation can lead to undesired sorting effects, such that high performers may not join or remain with the group or organization.

To use a sports example, by not paying high competitive rates for high individual performance in basketball, football/soccer, American football, or hockey, a team may find itself left with a set of individuals with less talent, on average, than on other teams. The lack of dispersion in pay may generate some form of harmony and cooperation, but can a team low on talent and high on harmony be competitive? And, if not, how long will the harmony last? If it does last, is it harmony in the form of resignation to the lack of competitiveness?

The third area of fit, internal alignment, has been the least studied. The work of Gomez-Mejia and Balkin (1992) has sought to identify overarching compensation strategies, but more work is needed to document which aspects of pay tend to cluster together in organizations and whether certain clusters are more effective and/or what contingency factors are most important. In any event, the modest evidence that exists concerning the degree of actual alignment between pay and other HR strategy dimensions suggests that there is less alignment than one might wish (Wright et al., 2001).

Although it could be included as a part of vertical alignment, another type of alignment that is important is that between pay strategy and country. Countries differ on a multitude of dimensions that can affect management practice (Dowling et al., 2008), including the regulatory environment (e.g., requirements for worker participation in firm governance), institutional environment (e.g., strength of labor unions, accepted HR practices in areas like compensation), and cultural values (e.g., Hofstede's (1980) dimensions of individualism/collectivism, long-term orientation, masculinity–femininity, power distance, and uncertainty avoidance). As such, a good deal of attention has been devoted to the constraints that organizations face when it comes to choosing which HR and pay strategies (a) can be implemented, and (b) if able to be implemented, which will be effective. Thus, organizations must decide how best to balance standardization and localization in designing HR and pay practices.

While practices that are effective in one country are not necessarily going to be effective or even feasible in another country due, for example, to legal or strong institutionalized traditions, I would like to caution against giving too much weight to contingency factors generally, including country. For example, in the case of the five cultural values dimensions made famous by Hofstede (1980, 2001), evidence shows that country actually explains only a small percentage of variance in individual employee cultural values (Gerhart & Fang, 2005). There is good reason to believe that organizations have considerable room to be different from the country norm in many countries in at least some key areas of HR and pay strategy (Gerhart, 2007). Also, country norms as they relate to HR and pay strategy can and do change. As mentioned earlier, one example is executive compensation. Countries like Germany, South Korea, and Japan changed from essentially no use of long-term incentives (e.g., stock options, stock grants) for top executives in 1998 to substantial use by 2005 (Towers Perrin, 2006). Another example mentioned earlier is the significant change in South Korea (Choi, 2004) and in Japan (Jung & Cheon, 2006; Morris et al., 2006; Robinson & Shimizu, 2006) away from seniority-based pay toward PFP. A third example is the dramatic decline in private sector unionism in the United States, which stands at 7.4% of the workforce in 2006. A fourth example is the decentralization (e.g., from industry to firm or plant level) of collective bargaining in many parts of the world (Katz et al., 2004).

Some of these examples are changes that occurred over the long run. So, a fair question is, how relevant are these examples of changing national conditions in the somewhat shorter run that organizations and managers must survive to make it to the longer run? My point is only that it is important to recognize not only institutional pressures toward conformity in a country, but also that at least in some respects, depending on the country, the timeframe, and the particular policy, there can be room to be unique and the strategy literature tells us that being the same as everyone else is unlikely to generate anything more than competitive parity, whereas being different, while perhaps being more risky, has the potential to generate sustained competitive advantage (e.g., the resource-based view of the firm; Barney, 1991). Some evidence indicates that there is indeed substantial variability in employment practices within countries (Katz & Darbishire, 2002).

Turning to methodology, a challenge in studying contextual or contingent effects is that if only firms and units that achieve some minimal level of alignment survive (Hannan & Freeman, 1977), alignment may be so important that it is almost impossible for the researcher to observe substantial departures from alignment (Gerhart et al., 1996; Gerhart & Rynes, 2003). In this case, restricted range in alignment would reduce the statistical power available to observe a relationship between alignment and performance. This may help explain why the idea of fit, while often thought to be critical, has not received as much support as might be expected in HR research broadly and in the area of compensation specifically (Gerhart et al., 1996; Gerhart, 2007; Wright & Sherman, 1999).

A final observation, on the conceptual side, as alluded to earlier, is that pay strategy work needs to think about how the resource-based view (RBV) of the firm may be relevant to pay strategy. The RBV emphasizes how firms "look inside" for resources that are rare and difficult to imitate and that can be leveraged to build sustained competitive advantage. Industry characteristics and business strategy are still important under the RBV because they place some limits on managerial discretion. However, within these limits, firms are viewed as having considerable discretion in how they compete. Some work has been done addressing how the RBV is relevant to HR strategy broadly (Barney & Wright, 1998; Becker & Gerhart, 1996; Colbert, 2004), but beyond Gerhart et al. (1996), there has not been much application to pay strategy.

Performance measurement issues

A limitation of the meta-analytic evidence reviewed earlier on the effects of PFP is that in most of the studies included, physical output measures of performance (e.g., number of index cards sorted, number of trees planted) were available, (related to this) tasks were simple, and individual contributions were usually separable (Gerhart & Rynes, 2003). In contrast, in many jobs, some or all of these three characteristics do not apply. The widespread use of merit pay and its subjective performance measures is, to an extent, a result of this fact (Milkovich & Wigdor, 1991).

In deciding on which performance measures to use in PFP programs, there are at least two key choices. First, how much emphasis can or should be placed on results-oriented performance measures (e.g., number of units produced) relative to behavior-based ones (e.g., supervisory evaluations of effort or quality)? Second, how much emphasis should be placed on individual contributions relative to collective contributions (an issue discussed briefly above)? Although we discuss each choice separately, in practice, many organizations use multiple performance measures to balance multiple (and sometimes conflicting) objectives.

Behavior-based (subjective) and results-based (objective) measures

Behavior-oriented measures (such as traditional PE ratings) offer a number of potential advantages relative to results-based measures (Gerhart, 2000). First, they can be used for any type of job. Second, they permit the rater to factor in variables that are not under the employee's control, but that nevertheless influence performance. Third, they permit a focus on whether results are achieved using acceptable means and behaviors. Fourth, they generally carry less risk of measurement deficiency, or the possibility that employees will focus only on explicitly measured tasks or results at the expense of broader pro-social behaviors, organizational citizenship behaviors, or contextual performance (see e.g., Arvey & Murphy, 1998; Wright et al., 1993).

On the other hand, the subjectivity of behavior-oriented measures can limit their ability to differentiate employees (Milkovich & Wigdor, 1991). In addition, meta-analytic evidence finds a mean inter-rater reliability of only .52 for performance ratings (Visweswaran, Ones & Schmidt, 1996), making it difficult for organizations to justify differentiating employees based on such error-laden performance measures, especially if a single rater, often the immediate supervisor, is the source. (A 360-degree appraisal, with its multiple sources/raters, may be helpful in this regard.)

Even if subjectivity in PE could be sufficiently controlled and performance reliably and credibly differentiated, managers may be reluctant to do so because of concerns about adverse consequences for workgroup cohesion, pro-social behaviors, and management–employee relations (Heneman & Judge, 2000; Longenecker et al., 1987). Perhaps for these reasons, as we saw earlier, evidence indicates that most employees do not believe that better performance results in higher compensation (HayGroup, 2002).

At first blush, objective measures of performance, such as productivity, sales volume, shareholder return, and profitability, would seem to provide the solution to the above problems. However, relevant objective measures are not available for most jobs, especially at the individual level. Moreover, agency theory emphasizes that results-based plans (e.g., individual incentives, gain sharing, profit sharing) increase risk bearing among employees (Gibbons, 1998). Because most employees derive the bulk of their income from employment, they cannot diversify their employment-related earnings risk, making them more risk averse than, say, investors. This then is the classic trade-off between designing plans that maximize incentives while keeping the negative effects of risk under control.

Risk aversion is less of a problem where objective measures are seen as credible and performance on such measures is high, providing significant payouts to employees. However, poor performance on such measures (and thus decreasing or disappearing payouts), especially if attributed to factors employees see as beyond their own control (e.g., poor decisions by top executives), often results in negative employee reactions (Gerhart & Milkovich, 1992). Often, there will be pressure to revise (e.g., the experience at GM's Saturn division, Gerhart, 2001) or abandon the plan (e.g., Petty et al., 1992).

Finally, even though objective measures are possibly more reliable, they may also be more deficient. Lawler (1971) warned that "it is quite difficult to establish criteria that are both measurable quantitatively and inclusive of all the important job behaviors," and "if an employee is not evaluated in terms of an activity, he will not be motivated to perform it" (p. 171).

Individual versus group (or collective) performance

Criticisms have been leveled at organizations for focusing too much on individual performance and rewards. For example, Pfeffer (1998b) critiqued individual merit and incentive plans as being ineffective, inciting grievances, and reducing product quality. Similarly, Deming (1986) argued that management's "excessive" focus on individual performance often obscures apparent differences in individual performance that "arise almost entirely from the system that (people) work in, rather than the people themselves" (p. 110). Deming and Pfeffer also argue that focusing on individual performance discourages teamwork: "Everyone propels himself forward, or tries to, for his own good . . . The organization is the loser" (Deming, 1986, p. 110).

While the potential pitfalls of individually based PFP are important, the literature is quite clear that group-based plans also have their own drawbacks. One is that most employees (at least in the U.S.) prefer that their pay be based on individual rather than group performance (Cable & Judge, 1994; LeBlanc & Mulvey, 1998). Another is that this preference is strongest among the most productive and achievement-oriented employees (e.g., Bretz et al., 1989; Lazear, 1986; Trank et al., 2002; Trevor et al., 1997). These facts suggest, as noted earlier, that group-based pay can have unfavorable sorting effects, causing the highest performers to choose alternative opportunities where individual results will be rewarded more heavily.

Yet another drawback has to do with the potential for weakened incentive effects under group plans among those that do join and stay with the organization: "Unless the number of individuals in a group is quite small, or unless there is coercion or some other special device to make individuals act in their common interest, rational self-interested individuals will not act to achieve their common or group interests" (Olson, 1965, pp. 1–2).

This last phenomenon has been widely studied (Kidwell & Bennett, 1993) and goes by many names (e.g., the common-resource problem, public-goods problem, free-rider problem, or social loafing problem). The general idea is that when people share the obligation to provide a resource (e.g., effort), it will be undersupplied because the residual returns (e.g., profit-sharing payouts) to the effort are often shared relatively equally, rather than distributed in proportion to contributions. Evidence suggests that the free-rider problem is sufficiently important (see Gerhart & Rynes (2003) for a summary of evidence) that researchers have devoted considerable attention to how free-rider effects might be mitigated.

One potential solution is to give differentiated rewards to group members based on their individual contributions (an approach used for many years by Lincoln Electric). As mentioned earlier, differentiating rewards based on performance can yield benefits via both incentive and sorting effects (Bishop, 1984). In the same vein, differentiating pay on the basis of individual performance, even within group systems, may reduce the tendency of high-performing employees to leave organizations that switch to group-based pay systems (e.g., Weiss, 1987).

In summary, there are important trade-offs involved in choosing how to measure performance. Performance measures must have a meaningful link to what the organization is trying to accomplish, be sufficiently inclusive of key aspects of performance, balance sometimes competing objectives, and be seen as fair and credible by employees. As noted earlier, organizations often attempt to achieve these goals by using multiple measures of performance, aggregate and individual, results and behavior-oriented (e.g., as in a Balanced Scorecard), and adjusting incentive intensity, to an important extent, on the degree to which valid and credible performance measurement is believed to be achievable.

Conclusion

Compensation involves decisions in multiple areas. My focus in this chapter has been on PFP and, to a lesser extent, pay level. I have highlighted the potential for well-designed PFP plans to make a substantial contribution to organization performance through effects on intervening mechanisms such as incentive and sorting. I have also noted the potential for PFP plans to cause serious problems, often as a result of unintended consequences. I suggested that the probability of success of PFP plans might be improved by effective alignment with contextual factors such as organization and human resource strategy, as well as through careful selection and balancing of performance measures. Still, it may be that the stronger the incentive intensity of such plans, the greater their potential positive impact as well as their potential negative impact. Finally, regardless of how well designed the PFP plan is, its probability of success also rests on how well it is executed and communicated.

Notes

1 Benefits represent a substantial share of compensation cost to employers in the United States, for example, given that many (especially larger) companies fund retirement and health care for employees.

2 Another approach is to organize around the level of analysis and/or type of employee being studied. Studies of executives often use the organization as the level of analysis, whereas studies of non-executives use organization, unit, or individual levels. I focus primarily on non-executive compensation. There is a very large literature on executive compensation. (Publicly traded companies are required in the United States by the Securities and Exchange Commission to publicly disclose how and how much they pay their five highest paid officers.) For reviews, see Devers et al., 2007.

3 This section draws freely on Gerhart and Rynes (2003) and Rynes et al. (2005).

4 It is certainly the case that not all people have pay as their primary motivator and also that the motivational impact of pay is contingent to a degree on these individual differences as well as on situational contingencies (e.g., declining marginal utility at higher pay levels, the strength of the link between pay and performance) (Rynes et al., 2004).

5 One of the more formal treatments of incentive problems and challenges is provided by agency theory and its central focus on agency costs, which are seen as arising from goal incongruence and information asymmetry. Milgrom and Roberts (1992) provide a helpful review.

6 A strict traditional neoclassical economics view would find the notion that employers (at least within a particular market) have a choice when it comes to pay level to be misguided, because the forces of supply and demand yield, in the long run, a single going/market wage that all employers must pay to avoid too high costs in the product market on the one hand and the inability to attract and retain a sufficient quantity and quality of workers in the labor market on the other. The only way that an employer could pay higher wages than other employers would be if better quality workers were hired. In that case, the ratio of worker quality to cost would be unchanged, meaning both that the apparent difference in pay levels was not real, disappearing upon appropriate adjustment for worker quality and that employers would not necessarily realize any advantage from using a high-wage, high-worker quality strategy. However, evidence of persistent and arguably non-illusory differences in compensation levels (see Gerhart & Rynes (2003) for a review) between companies operating in the same market has resulted in greater attention to why such differences exist and more general acknowledgment, including in economics (Boyer & Smith, 2001), recognition that employers have some discretion in their choice of pay level. In response, efficiency wage theory provides an economics-based rationale for why some firms may benefit from higher (lower) wages.

7 The d statistic is defined as the difference between the dependent variable mean for Group A versus Group B, divided by the pooled standard deviation of Groups A and B. Thus, it gives the difference between Group A and B in terms of standard deviation units.

8 This section draws freely on Gerhart and Rynes (2003).

References

Aggarwal, R.K. & Samwick, A.A. (1999). The other side of the trade-off: The impact of risk on executive compensation. *Journal of Political Economy*, *107*, 65–105.

Appelbaum, E., Bailey, T., Berg, P. & Kalleberg, A. (2000). *Manufacturing Advantage: Why high performance work systems pay off*. Ithaca, NY: Cornell University Press.

Arvey, R.D. & Murphy, K.R. (1998). Performance evaluation in work settings. *Annual Review of Psychology*, *49*, 141–68.

Balkin, D.B. & Gomez-Mejia, L.R. (1987). Toward a contingent theory of compensation strategy. *Strategic Management Journal*, *8*, 169–82.

Barber, A.E. & Bretz, R.D. Jr. (2000). Compensation, attraction and retention. In S.L. Rynes & B. Gerhart (Eds), *Compensation in Organizations* (pp. 32–60). San Francisco, CA: Jossey-Bass.

Barney, J.B. (1991). Firm resources and sustained competitive advantage. *Journal of Management*, *17*, 99–120.

Barney, J.B. & Wright, P.M. (1998). On becoming a strategic partner: The role of human resources in gaining competitive advantage. *Human Resource Management*, *37*, 31–46.

Batt, R. (2001). Explaining intra-occupational wage inequality in telecommunications services: Customer segmentation, human resource practices, and union decline. *Industrial and Labor Relations Review*, *54*(2A), 425–49.

Batt, R. (2002). Managing customer services: Human resource practices, quit rates, and sales growth. *Academy of Management Journal*, *45*, 587–97.

Becker, B. & Gerhart, B. (1996). The impact of human resource management on organizational performance: Progress and prospects. *Academy of Management Journal*, *39*, 779–801.

Beer, M. & Cannon, M.D. (2004). Promise and peril in implementing pay-for-performance. *Human Resource Management*, *43*, 3–20.

Bishop, J. (1984). The recognition and reward of employee performance. *Journal of Labor Economics*, *5*, S36–S56.

Bloom, M. & Milkovich, G.T. (1998). Relationships among risk, incentive pay, and organizational performance. *Academy of Management Journal*, *41*, 283–97.

Boudreau, J.W. & Berger, C.J. (1985). Decision-theoretic utility analysis applied to employee separations and acquisitions. *Journal of Applied Psychology*, *73*, 467–81.

Boxall, P. & Purcell, J. (2003). *Strategy and Human Resource Management*. Basingstoke, UK: Palgrave Macmillan.

Boyer, G.R. & Smith, R.S. (2001). The development of the neoclassical tradition in labor economics. *Industrial and Labor Relations Review*, *54*, 199–223.

Bretz, R.D., Ash, R.A., & Dreher, G.F. (1989). Do people make the place? An examination of the attraction-selection-attrition hypothesis. *Personnel Psychology*, *42*, 561–81.

Buchholtz, A.K. & Ribbens, B.A. (1994). Role of chief executive officers in takeover resistance: Effects of CEO incentives and individual characteristics. *Academy of Management Journal*, *37*, 554–79.

Cable, D.M. & Judge, T.A. (1994). Pay preferences and job search decisions: A person–organization fit perspective. *Personnel Psychology*, *47*, 317–48.

Cadsby, C.B., Song, F., & Tapon, F. (2007). Sorting and incentive effects of pay-for-performance: An experimental investigation. *Academy of Management Journal*, *50*, 387–405.

Campbell, J.P. & Pritchard, R.D. (1976). Motivation theory in industrial and organizational psychology. In M.D. Dunnette (Ed.), *Handbook of Industrial and Organizational Psychology*. Chicago, IL: Rand McNally.

Carpenter, M.A. (2000). The price of change: The role of CEO compensation in strategic variation and deviation from industry strategy norms. *Journal of Management*, *26*, 1179–98.

Choi, J.T. (2004). Transformation of Korean HRM based on Confucian Values. *Seoul Journal of Business*, *10*, 1–26.

Colbert, B.A. (2004). The complex resource-based view. *Strategic Management Journal*, *29*, 341–58.

Currall, S.C., Towler, A.J., Judge, T.A., & Kohn, L. (2005). Pay satisfaction and organizational outcomes. *Personnel Psychology*, *58*, 613–40.

Deci, E.L. & Ryan, R.M. (1985). *Intrinsic Motivation and Self-determination in Human Behavior*. New York: Plenum.

Deming, W.E. (1986). *Out of the Crisis*. Cambridge, MA: MIT, Center for Advanced Engineering Study.

Devers, C.E., Cannella, A.A., Reilly, G.P., & Yoder, M.E. (2007). Executive compensation: A multidisciplinary review of recent developments. *Journal of Management*, *33*, 1016–72.

Dowling, P.J., Festing, M., & Engle, A.D. Sr. (2008). *International Human Resource Management* (5th Edition). London: Thomson Learning.

Ellig, B.R. (1981). Compensation elements: Market phase determines the mix. *Compensation Review* (Third Quarter), 30–8.

Galbraith, C.S. & Merril, G.B. (1991). The effect of compensation program and structure of SBU competitive strategy: A study of technology-intensive firms. *Strategic Management Journal*, *12*, 353–70.

Garen, J.E. (1994). Executive compensation and principal-agent theory. *Journal of Political Economy*, *102*, 1175–1200.

Gerhart, B. (2000). Compensation strategy and organizational performance. In S.L. Rynes & B. Gerhart (Eds), *Compensation in Organizations*. San Francisco: Jossey-Bass.

Gerhart, B. (2001). Balancing results and behaviors in pay for performance plans. In C. Fay (Ed.), *The Executive Handbook of Compensation*. New York: Free Press.

Gerhart, B. (2007). Horizontal and vertical fit in human resource systems. In C. Ostroff & T. Judge (Eds), *Perspectives on Organizational Fit*. SIOP Organizational Frontiers Series. New York: Lawrence Erlbaum Associates, Taylor & Francis Group.

Gerhart, B. & Fang, M. (2005). National culture and human resource management: Assumptions and evidence. *International Journal of Human Resource Management*, *16*, 975–90.

Gerhart, B. & Milkovich, G.T. (1990). Organizational differences in managerial compensation and financial performance. *Academy of Management Journal*, *33*, 663–91.

241

Gerhart, B. & Milkovich, G.T. (1992). Employee compensation: Research and practice. In M.D. Dunnette & L.M. Hough (Eds), *Handbook of Industrial & Organizational Psychology*, 2nd edn (pp. 481–570). Palo Alto, CA: Consulting Psychologists Press, Inc.

Gerhart, B. & Rynes, S.L. (2003). *Compensation: Theory, evidence, and strategic implications*. Thousand Oaks, CA: Sage.

Gerhart, B. & Trevor, C.O. (2008). Merit pay. In A. Varma, P.S. Budhwar, & A. DeNisi (Eds), *Performance Management Systems: A global perspective*. Abingdon, UK: Routledge.

Gerhart, B., Trevor, C., & Graham, M. (1996). New directions in employee compensation research. In G.R. Ferris (Ed.), *Research in Personnel and Human Resources Management*, pp. 143–203.

Gibbons, R. (1998). Incentives in organizations. *Journal of Economic Perspectives, 12*, 115–32.

Gomez-Mejia, L.R. (1992). Structure and process of diversification, compensation strategy, and firm performance. *Strategic Management Journal, 13*, 381–97.

Gomez-Mejia, L.R. & Balkin, D.B. (1992). *Compensation, Organizational Strategy, and Firm Performance*. Cincinnati, OH: Southwestern Publishing.

Guzzo, R.A., Jette, R.D., & Katzell R.A. (1985). The effects of psychologically based intervention programs on worker productivity: A meta-analysis. *Personnel Psychology, 38*, 275–91.

Hannan, M.T. & Freeman, J. (1977). The population ecology of organizations. *American Journal of Sociology, 82*, 929–64.

Harrison, D.A., Virick, M., & William, S. (1996). Working without a net: Time, performance, and turnover under maximally contingent rewards. *Journal of Applied Psychology, 81*, 331–45.

HayGroup. (2002). Managing performance: Achieving outstanding performance through a 'culture of dialogue.' Working Paper.

Heneman, H.G. III & Judge, T.A. (2000). Compensation attitudes. In S.L. Rynes & B. Gerhart (Eds), *Compensation in Organizations*. San Francisco: Jossey-Bass.

Herzberg, F., Mausner, B., Peterson, R.O. & Capwell, D.F. (1957). *Job Attitudes: Review of research and opinion*. Pittsburgh: Psychological Service of Pittsburgh.

Hill, C.W.L. & Snell, S.A. (1989). Effects of ownership structure and control on corporate productivity. *Academy of Management Journal, 32*, 25–46.

Hitt, M.A., Hoskisson, R.E., Johnson, R.A., & Moesel, D.D. (1996). The market for corporate control and firm innovation. *Academy of Management Journal, 39*, 1084–119.

Hofstede, G. (1980). *Culture's Consequences: International differences in work-related values*. Beverly Hills, CA: Sage.

Hofstede, G. (2001). *Culture's Consequences: Comparing values, behaviors, institutions, and organizations across nations*, 2nd edn. Thousand Oaks, CA: Sage.

Hunter, L.W. (2000). What determines job quality in nursing homes? *Industrial & Labor Relations Review, 53*, 463–81.

Jenkins, D.G. Jr., Mitra, A., Gupta, N., & Shaw, J.D. (1998). Are financial incentives related to performance? A meta-analytic review of empirical research. *Journal of Applied Psychology, 83*, 777–87.

Judiesch, M.K. (1994). *The Effects of Incentive Compensation Systems on Productivity, Individual Differences in Output Variability, and Selection Utility*. Unpublished doctoral dissertation. Iowa City, IA: University of Iowa.

Jung, E. & Cheon, B. (2006). Economic crisis and changes in employment relations in Japan and Korea. *Asian Survey, 46*(3), 457–76.

Katz, H.C. and Darbishire, O. (2002). Convergences and divergences in employment systems. In S. Estreicher (Ed.), *Global Competition and the American Employment Landscape as We Enter the 21st Century*. New York: Kluwer.

Katz, H.C., Lee, W., & Lee, J. (2004). *The New Structure of Labor Relations: Tripartism and decentralization*. Ithaca, NY: ILR Press/Cornell University.

Kaufman, R.T. (1992). The effects of Improshare on productivity. *Industrial and Labor Relations Review, 45*, 311–22.

Kerr, J.L. (1985). Diversification strategies and managerial rewards. *Academy of Management Journal, 28*, 155–79.

Kidwell, R.E. & Bennett, N. (1993). Employee propensity to withhold effort: A conceptual model to intersect three avenues of research. *Academy of Management Review, 18*, 429–56.

Klaas, B.S. & McClendon, J.A. (1996). To lead, lag, or match: Estimating the financial impact of pay level policies. *Personnel Psychology, 49*, 121–41.

Kohn, A. (1993). Why incentive plans cannot work. *Harvard Business Review, 71*(5): 54–63.

Kosnik, R.D. (1992). Effects of board demography and directors' incentives on corporate greenmail decisions. *Academy of Management Journal, 33*, 129–50.

Kroumova, M.K. & Sesis, J.C. (2006). Intellectual capital, monitoring, and risk: What predicts the adoption of employee stock options? *Industrial Relations, 45*, 734–52.

Kruse, D.L. (1993). *Profit Sharing: Does it make a difference?* Kalamazoo, MI: Upjohn Institute.

Larcker, D. (1983). The association between performance plan adoption and corporate capital investment. *Journal of Accounting and Economics, 5*, 3–30.

Lawler, E.E. III (1971). *Pay and Organizational Effectiveness.* New York: McGraw-Hill.

Lazear, E.P. (1986). Salaries and piece rates. *Journal of Business, 59*, 405–32.

Lazear, E.P. (2000). Performance pay and productivity. *American Economic Review, 90*, 1346–61.

Le Blanc, P.V. & Mulvey, P.W. (1998). How American workers see the rewards of work. *Compensation & Benefits Review, 30*, 24–8.

Ledford, G.E. (2004). Commentary on "Promise and peril in implementing pay-for-performance". *Human Resource Management, 43*, 39–41.

Locke, E.A., Feren, D.B., McCaleb, V.M., Shaw, K.N., & Denny, A.T. (1980). The relative effectiveness of four methods of motivating employee performance. In K.D. Duncan, M.M. Gruenberg, & D. Wallis (Eds), *Changes in Working Life* (pp. 363–88). New York: Wiley.

Longnecker, C.O., Sims, H.P., & Gioia, D.A. (1987). Behind the mask: The politics of employee appraisal. *Academy of Management Executive, 1*(3), 183–93.

Mallette, P. & Fowler, K.J. (1992). Effects of board composition and stock ownership on the adoption of "poison pills". *Academy of Management Journal, 35*, 1010–35.

Maslow, A.H. (1943). A theory of human motivation. *Psychological Review, 50*, 370–96.

Miles, R.E. & Snow, C.C. (1978). *Organizational Strategy, Structure, and Process.* New York: McGraw-Hill.

Milgrom, P. & Roberts, J. (1992). *Economics, Organization, & Management.* Englewood Cliffs, NJ: Prentice-Hall.

Milkovich, G.T. (1988). A strategic perspective on compensation management. *Research in Personnel and Human Resources Management, 6*, 263–88.

Milkovich, G.T. & Newman, J.M. (2008). *Compensation,* 9th edn. Boston: McGraw-Hill/Irwin.

Milkovich, G. & Wigdor, A. (1991). *Pay for Performance: Evaluating performance appraisal and merit pay.* Washington, DC: National Academy Press.

Morris, J., Hassard, J., & McCann, L. (2006). New organizational forms, human resource management and structural convergence? A study of Japanese organizations. *Organization Studies, 27*, 1485–1511.

Murphy, K.J. (1999). Executive compensation. In O. Ashenfelter & D. Card (Eds), *Handbook of Labor Economics,* Volume 3. Amsterdam: Elsevier.

Olson, M. (1965). *The Logic of Collective Action: Public goods and the theory of groups.* Cambridge, MA: Harvard University Press.

Osterman, P. (2006). The wage effects of high performance work organization in manufacturing. *Industrial & Labor Relations Review, 59*, 187–204.

Petty, M.M., Singleton, B., & Connell, D.W. (1992). An experimental evaluation of an organizational incentive plan in the electric utility industry. *Journal of Applied Psychology, 77*, 427–36.

Pfeffer, J. (1998). Six dangerous myths about pay. *Harvard Business Review, 76*, 108–20.

Phan, P.H. & Hill, C.W. (1995). Organizational restructuring and economic performance in leveraged buyouts: An ex post study. *Academy of Management Journal, 38*, 704–39.

Pitts, R.A. (1976). Diversification strategies and organizational policies of large diversified firms. *Journal of Economics and Business, 8*, 181–8.

Porter, M. (1985). *Competitive Advantage.* New York: Free Press.

Rajagopalan, N. (1996). Strategic orientations, incentive plan adoptions, and firm performance: Evidence from electric utility firms. *Strategic Management Journal, 18,* 761–85.

Robinson, P. & Shimizu, N. (2006). Japanese corporate restructuring: CEO priorities as a window on environmental and organizational change. *Academy of Management Perspectives, 20*(3), 44–75.

Rottenberg, S. (1956). On choice in labor markets. *Industrial & Labor Relations Review, 9,* 183–99.

Rynes, S.L., Gerhart, B., & Minette, K.A. (2004). The importance of pay in employee motivation: Discrepancies between what people do and what they say. *Human Resource Management, 43,* 381–94.

Rynes, S.L., Gerhart, B., & Parks, L. (2005). *Annual Review of Psychology, 56,* 571–600.

Salamin, A. & Hom, P.W. (2005). In search of the elusive U-shaped performance-turnover relationship: Are high performing Swiss bankers more liable to quit? *Journal of Applied Psychology, 90,* 1204–16.

Schneider, B. (1987). The people make the place. *Personnel Psychology, 40,* 437–53.

Shaw, J.D., Gupta, N., & Delery, J.E. (2002). Pay dispersion and workforce performance: Moderating effects of incentives and interdependence. *Strategic Management Journal, 23,* 491–512.

Snell, S.A. & Dean, J.W. Jr. (1994). Strategic compensation for integrated manufacturing: The moderating effects of jobs and organizational inertia. *Academy of Management Journal, 37,* 1109–40.

Stajkovic, A.D. & Luthans, F. (1997). A meta-analysis of the effects of organizational behavior modification on task performance, 1975–1995. *Academy of Management Journal, 40,* 1122–49.

Sturman, M.C., Trevor, C.O., Boudreau, J.W., & Gerhart, B. (2003). Is it worth it to win the talent war? Evaluating the utility of performance-based pay. *Personnel Psychology, 56,* 997–1035.

Towers Perrin. (2006). Worldwide Total Remuneration, 2005–2006.

Trank, C.Q., Rynes, S.L., & Bretz, R.D. Jr. (2002). Attracting applicants in the war for talent: Differences in work preferences among high achievers. *Journal of Business and Psychology, 17,* 331–45.

Trevor, C.O., Gerhart, B., & Boudreau, J.W. (1997). Voluntary turnover and job performance: Curvilinearity and the moderating influences of salary growth and promotions. *Journal of Applied Psychology, 82,* 44–61.

Turban, D.B. & Keon, T.L. (1993). Organizational attractiveness: An interactionist perspective. *Journal of Applied Psychology, 78,* 184–93.

Viswesvaran, C., Ones, D.S., & Schmidt, F.L. (1996). Comparative analysis of the reliability of job performance ratings. *Journal of Applied Psychology, 81,* 557–574.

Weiss, A. (1987). Incentives and worker behavior: Some evidence. In H.R. Nalbantian (Ed.), *Incentives, cooperation, and risk taking.* Lanham, MD: Rowman & Littlefield.

Whyte, W.F. (1955). *Money and Motivation.* New York: Harper & Row.

Williams, M.L., McDaniel, M.A., & Nguyen, N.T. (2006). A meta-analysis of the antecedents and consequences of pay level satisfaction. *Journal of Applied Psychology, 91,* 392–413.

Wiseman, R.M., Gomez-Mejia, L.R., & Fugate, M. (2000). Rethinking compensation risk. In S.L. Rynes & B. Gerhart (Eds), *Compensation in Organizations* (pp. 32–60). San Francisco, CA: Jossey-Bass.

Wright, P.M. & Sherman, W.S. (1999). Failing to find fit in strategic human resource management: Theoretical and empirical problems. In P. Wright, L. Dyer, J. Boudreau, & G. Milkovich (Eds), *Strategic Human Resources Management in the Twenty-first Century.* Supplement to G.R. Ferris (Ed.), *Research in Personnel and Human Resources Management.* Stanford, CT: JAI Press.

Wright, P.M., George, J.M., Farnsworth, S.R., & McMahan, G.C. (1993). Productivity and extra-role behavior: The effects of goals and incentives on spontaneous helping. *Journal of Applied Psychology, 78,* 374–81.

Wright, P.M., McMahan, G., Snell, S., & Gerhart, B. (2001). Comparing line and HR executives' perceptions of HR effectiveness: Services, roles, and contributions. *Human Resource Management, 40,* 111–24.

Yanadori, Y. & Marler, J.H. (2006). Compensation strategy: Does business strategy influence compensation in high-technology firms? *Strategic Management Journal, 27,* 559–70.

Yellen, J.L. (1984). Efficiency wage models of unemployment. *American Economic Review, 74,* 200–5.

15

Strategic performance management

Issues and trends

Manuel London and Edward M. Mone

Performance management refers to the process of goal setting, performance monitoring for feedback and development, and performance appraisal for evaluation as input to compensation and other administrative decisions. As a process, performance management is not a single event or a series of discrete events, but rather an integrated series of interactions. As a system, the components relate to each other in a continuous cycle that is affected by external factors (e.g., demands and opportunities) and internal factors (e.g., self-expectations and monitoring). At the individual level, we speak of an employee's or manager's goals and performance in relation to the strategies of the organization and department. At the group level, we speak of the department's or work team's goals and performance as affected by organizational expectations and the demands from other work groups. Departmental goals affect individual employees' goals and performance, which in turn affect those of the department, other departments, and the entire organization. In this chapter, we present critical issues for practitioners and researchers for today and the future. We also present a case that illustrates the design and implementation of an organization-wide performance management process.

The performance management cycle, depicted in Figure 15.1, evolves as people perceive and evaluate environmental conditions, determine others' and their own expectations, set goals, seek and digest feedback, participate in developmental experiences, change behavior, alter their performance, and benefit from the consequences of goal achievement and/or suffer the consequences of failing to achieve goals. It involves others, such as one's supervisor, peers, and customers, who convey expectations, participate in goal setting and performance monitoring, provide feedback and coaching, and deliver rewards. It is continuous or ongoing in that it occurs over time, and it is repetitive or cyclical, with multiple and overlapping components. Goals are revised as expectations change, competition shifts, feedback is received and interpreted, and training is experienced. Performance management tools and tactics are designed by the human resource department to support each step of the process from guidelines for joint goal setting to rating forms for performance appraisal. The design process includes ensuring that the methods are reliable (meaning, for example, that behaviors are perceived similarly by multiple raters who have similar roles) and valid (meaning, for example, that performance ratings accurately reflect important performance outcomes).

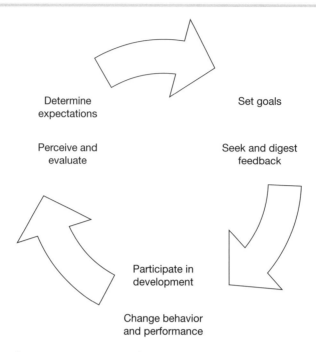

Figure 15.1 The performance management cycle

Table 15.1 lists theories that guide the elements of performance management, describes implications for practice, and provides key references. These theories address key processes in the performance management cycle, such as goal setting, feedback, motivation and self-regulation, social cognition, feelings of fairness about how rewards are distributed, and self-verification and impression management. Theories also deal with processes that support performance management, such as rater accuracy, multi-source ratings, coaching, supervisors' and coaches' implicit views about whether people can be developed, and methods for creating a feedback-oriented, performance-centered work environment. The citations in the table indicate that there is a rich body of knowledge from which to draw in understanding how to formulate and implement effective performance management programs.

Performance management processes apply to groups and organizations as well as to individuals. We usually think of performance management from the standpoint of an individual's performance (e.g., individual employees setting goals jointly with supervisors, supervisors appraising their performance, etc.). However, groups and organizations also engage in goal setting, performance measurement, and feedback giving, seeking, and receiving. Performance management can and should be strategic in that at each level of analysis (individual, group, or organization), it is tied to accomplishing higher level objectives (for example, those of specific functions or the overall organization) and overall organization results. So, for instance, an individual manager's goals need to be aligned with the goals of the department, and the department's goals need to be aligned with the goals of the function and the overall organization. More generally, the nature of an individual's goals and dimensions of performance will depend on the function of the department and the role of the individual. Examples of organization strategies guiding performance expectations, goals, and measurement include: moving from a domestic to global business; becoming number one in the marketplace; increasing return on investment (ROI) by 10%; and building a culture that values integrity, open communication, fair treatment, and differences. We illustrate these relationships in Table 15.2 with an example of an HR department and manager, in this case, a manager of recruiting, whose efforts are in alignment with the organization's goals of reducing costs by 10%. The table indicates how each main component of the performance management process requires action at the organizational, departmental, and individual managerial level. So, for instance, the human resource department can find ways to reduce its costs, including reengineering the company-wide recruitment process. The recruiting manager can set a time line for accomplishing this and track cost data per candidate recruited. The performance appraisal will measure the extent to which the manager completed the reengineering project and is rewarded accordingly.

This chapter focuses primarily on methods for assessing and improving individual performance. Comprehensive performance management programs include support mechanisms and guidelines for use. Comprehensive, strategic performance management programs that incorporate appraisal, feedback, and compensation at multiple levels are Management by Objectives (MBO) (Drucker, 1993; Odiorne, 1968), Balanced Scorecards (Kaplan & Norton, 1996), and Dashboards (Alexander, 2006). These strategic performance management (SPM) programs facilitate setting goals in relation to larger objectives, measuring results, and seeking improvement. These programs usually start from the top of the organization and cascade down, conveying organization-wide goals that should be reflected in department and team goals, which in turn should be reflected in each individual's goals and performance.

SPM programs evolve over time as strategies change and as instruments for measurement and methods for linking the components together are fine-tuned. As a result, SPM affects the culture of the organization, making employees and managers more comfortable with discussing performance issues, providing and receiving feedback, and supporting and engaging in development for performance improvement. SPM programs in one organization or setting may not work in another because of the organization's history of using performance management methods, the management philosophy of the organization's leaders, and the resources and emphasis placed on the investment in performance management tools and processes. Overall, SPM is a developmental process that promotes individual and organizational learning.

Periodically, the strategic performance management system may need to be refreshed to reflect (a) changes in organizational objectives and strategies (e.g., moving from a domestic to a global business), (b) changes in key elements of performance (which may evolve as technology changes), (c) the need to create a performance management culture and awareness of key organizational goals and performance dimensions, (d) take advantage of employees' increasing commitment to performance improvement and comfort with, and sophistication in dealing with, feedback and coaching, and (e) increase the value of the organization's investment in performance measurement, feedback, development, and continued performance improvement.

Issues for practitioners

Based on the authors' experience and the literature (cf. Table 15.1), we have identified five concerns of practitioners who design and support SPM: (1) eliciting the active involvement and buy-in of executives and managers to the design, roll-out, and ongoing use of the program elements, (2) linking the components of the program to the strategy of the organization overall while maintaining relevancy to departments and individuals throughout the organization, (3) keeping the program current so that managers and employees will find it valuable and will be motivated to use it, (4) capturing the learning so that managers and employees become more able to focus on performance issues and creating an environment in which it is acceptable to

Table 15.1 Examples of seminal theories and research guiding performance management policies and programs

Theories	Implications for practice	Key references
Goal setting theory	Help employees set specific, difficult, yet achievable goals which focus attention; easy, "do your best," and assigned goals result in lower performance.	Locke & Latham (1990, 2002)
Feedback intervention theory	Provide feedback that focuses on specific behaviors and goal progress. Avoid giving feedback that focuses on personal characteristics; threatens self-esteem, and lowers performance.	Kluger & DeNisi (1998)
Temporal motivation theory (integration and extension of expectancy, prospect, and need theories)	Recognize time as a motivational factor along with expectancy of goal achievement, loss aversion, values of success, and needs. Enhance motivation by parceling tasks into subgoals that focus behavior, avoid temptation to be distracted, and clarify expectancy and value of achievement. However, avoid subtasks that are so small, immediate, and easy to achieve that they lose their tie to the whole and decrease motivation.	Steel & Cornelius (2006)
Social cognitive theory; control theory	Enhance motivation, increase self-esteem, and attain goals by helping people adopt goal challenges (proactive discrepancy production) and then reduce the discrepancy (i.e., meet their goals). (Note that this contradicts control theory's position that people maintain self-esteem by setting low challenges for themselves.)

Support employees' self-efficacy by reinforcement, training, and encouraging setting realistic, achievable, yet challenging goals. Self-efficacy influences managers' goal achievement both directly and through its effects on their goal setting and analytic thinking. | Bandura & Locke (2003); Wood & Bandura (1989) |
Fairness of process and outcome (equity theory)	Provide clear explanations for performance ratings. Ratings that enhance the employee's self-concept are perceived to be the most fair, indicating the importance of explanations in enhancing perceptions of fairness. Both the perceived fairness of the ratings process and the fairness of the rating are important to understanding an employee's reaction to the appraisal. The process includes (a) the structure, policies, and support of the formal appraisal system, and (b) the appraisal-related interactions that occur throughout the year between supervisors and subordinates.	Giles, Findley, & Field (1997); Greenberg (1991)
Self-verification and impression management	Give employees an opportunity to describe their strengths and weaknesses to others and seek feedback to test how well the people with whom they interact know them. Generally, people want to verify their self-concept by (a) providing others with an accurate view of their capabilities, and (b) seeking feedback from others.	Polzer, Milton, & Swann (2002)
Rater accuracy–self-ratings	Recognize that employees will not immediately agree with an appraisal of their performance. People, in general, and especially lower performers, tend to rate themselves higher than others rate them. Also, they, in general, overestimate the similarity between how they see themselves and the way they think others see them.	Atwater, Rousch, & Fischthal, (1995); Harris & Schaubroeck (1988); Mabe & West (1982)

Rater accuracy – ratings from supervisors, peers, and others	Use easily measured and observable, behaviorally based performance dimensions to increase the accuracy of employees' self-ratings and ratings from supervisors and peers. Train raters in ways to observe key behaviors, request clarifying information, and search for disconfirming evidence. Provide raters with a frame of reference (e.g., standards, norms, expectations, examples) for evaluating the accuracy of ratings. Hold people accountable for their ratings (chance they will have to justify them) so they perceive a cost as being inaccurate.	Klimoski & Donahue, (2001); London (2003); London, Smither, & Adsit (1996); Mone & London (2003)
Multisource (360-degree) feedback surveys, self-other agreement, and setting developmental goals	Use 360-degree feedback surveys (ratings from subordinates, peers, supervisors, customers, and self) to support and direct manager development; avoid its use for making administrative decisions about managers since raters are less likely to be honest if they know that the ratings will be used for this purpose. Recognize that people tend to overrate themselves compared to how others see them.	London (2003); London & Smither (1995); Smither, London, & Reilly (2005)
Supplement feedback with coaching	Use coaching to increase the value of multisource feedback by encouraging managers to set specific goals, ask for ideas for improvement, and improve their performance over time.	Smither, London, Flautt, Vargas, & Kucine (2003)
Supervisors' implicit personality theories and their role as coach and developer	Demonstrate to supervisors that employees' personal attributes can be changed and developed (recognizing that supervisors who believe that employees' key characteristics can't be changed will not be effective coaches). Train managers in coaching techniques to provide guidance, facilitation, and inspiration.	Dweck (1999); Heslin, Vandewalle, & Latham (2006)
Acceptance of feedback and the likelihood of behavior change	Consider the effects of individual characteristics on reactions to performance appraisal. People who are mastery learners (those who are motivated to learn and improve continuously for the sake of their development) are more likely to seek feedback and react positively to it compared to those who are performance oriented (those who demonstrate competence and avoid failure). Self-monitors are more sensitive to feedback and more willing to respond constructively to it; low self-monitors do not modify their behavior to meet the needs of the situation. People are more likely to change their behavior when they accept others' evaluations of their weaknesses.	Stamoulis & Hauenstein (1993); Vandewalle, Brown, Cron, & Slocum (1999)
Creating a feedback-oriented, performance-centered environment	Foster an environment that provides resources for and rewards continuous learning and performance feedback.	London & Mone (1999); London & Smither (2002); Sessa & London (2006)

Table 15.2 Example of strategic performance management relationships – an HR department and recruiting manager

Performance management component	The organization	The HR department	The recruiting manager
Goal setting	Reduce overall costs by 10%.	Reengineer HR processes and systems to reduce costs by 10%.	Reengineer the company-wide recruitment process to reduce costs by 10% and increase process efficiency and effectiveness.
Feedback and development	Review financial reports for each department and the overall organization at monthly intervals. Take appropriate action if interim targets are not being met.	Review department finance and measures of internal customers' satisfaction with HR processes and systems monthly to monitor overall performance. Take appropriate action if performance and satisfaction levels are not being achieved.	Meet time lines for reengineering initiative and monitor overall effort monthly for increased efficiency and satisfaction of internal customers' with the recruiting process. Take appropriate action if time lines are not being met and/or if satisfaction levels are not being achieved.
Appraisal	Measure the extent to which the overall organization met the cost reduction goal of 10%.	Measure extent to which financial and customer satisfaction measures where achieved.	Measure extent to which reengineering was completed on a timely basis, costs were reduced and customer satisfaction with the recruiting process increased.
Connection to compensation and rewards	Improved financial position for the company; allows for an organization-wide, all employee cash bonus if key targets are met.	HR department enjoys eligibility for participation in company-wide and departmental-level bonus awards if targets are met at the company-wide and/or department level.	Recruiting manager eligible to receive various bonus awards based on individual, HR department and organization-wide performance in meeting or exceeding targets.

discuss difficult performance issues, and (5) evaluating the program, assessing its impact on individual, departmental, and organizational performance and regularly fine-tuning the program to improve its effectiveness.

Human resource and/or organizational development professionals are likely to be responsible for the design and implementation of the SPM program. However, these professionals need the active engagement of the employees and managers who will use the program. The elements of the program need to be helpful in doing their jobs. Their active involvement in designing the process is likely to ensure the right aspects of performance are measured and rewarded. If they believe the program is imposed from above and is the work of outside consultants who have little understanding of their organization's goals and their individual roles and functions, then they are not likely to take the process seriously. Their involvement in the program design may be critical because they know the organization and the performance expectations that need to be measured by the program. Off-the-shelf performance rating forms and 360-degree performance surveys that measure generic dimensions of performance are likely to have little specific relevance to the organization and will excite little interest. Customizing performance dimensions and incentive plans to the organization, and having the people who will use the program involved in the customization, is likely to result in a program that will be accepted and valued.

The performance management process should be viewed as developmental and evolutionary. Working on its design, educating managers and employees during its initial roll-out, and supporting the use of the program over time helps educate managers about the meaning of performance management. They can then grow more comfortable dealing with performance issues and incorporate performance discussions into their daily activities. Over time, performance management becomes part of the way the organization does business. A performance-based culture is created. However, this is not a natural process. People usually shy away from giving and seeking feedback because it is potentially threatening to their self-esteem and leads to defensiveness and uncomfortable interpersonal situations (London, 2003). Consider a program that emphasizes an annual performance appraisal followed by a formal performance interview with the supervisor and an accompanying change in salary. This puts the supervisor and subordinate on edge. Both are likely to be defensive, unclear, and unhappy. Next, consider a program that emphasizes feedback for development throughout the year. The supervisor and subordinate can become a team focused on enhancing performance. They can be creative in suggesting performance improvement strategies, trying them out, and jointly evaluating their effects. They are "in this together." The formal annual evaluation is a culmination of these formative processes, and the results are not a surprise and an occasion to feel threatened or be defensive. Indeed, individuals will feel more responsible for monitoring their own performance in conjunction with their supervisors. Their self-evaluations will likely be critical and accompanied by ideas for behavior change. Human resource professionals can help managers and employees be ready to participate in the excitement of ongoing improvement by providing resources that help managers to be better coaches and help both managers and employees to participate in constructive feedback discussions.

Overall, when creating strategic performance management programs, HR professionals can generate higher degrees of commitment to both the program and the process of performance management by inviting managers and employees to contribute to the design, implementation, and evaluation of the program. HR professionals should strongly consider forming a design task force for development and implementation with representatives from different functions and levels of the organization. This will not only help build commitment, it will also help to ensure that key components (e.g., performance dimensions) that are important to the overall

251

organization, as well as those that are unique to specific departments or functions, will be included in the program. After the program has been implemented, HR professionals should consider forming a performance management council to oversee the program's assessment and use. As a result, monitoring the use of the program becomes more than the bureaucratic exercise of being sure forms are completed; rather, it becomes an examination of how people are using the process, what they think about it, and ways they would like it changed to be even more valuable.

Sustaining interest in the process and ensuring compliance are two different things. Compliance can be enforced by requiring that annual appraisal forms be completed before salary increases or other administrative changes, such as promotions, can be implemented. However, completing appraisals because they are required can result in a pro forma exercise with little meaning or effect. Sometimes organizations try to refresh their programs by changing formats, rating methods, and performance dimensions. Training can be used to explain these changes and create more awareness of performance issues and how the process might be used to evaluate and improve performance. However, both employees and managers may become jaded quickly when new performance programs are introduced every year or two.

Performance management programs that are redesigned to reflect changes in organizational strategy can go hand-in-glove with the implementation of the new strategy. For instance, an organization that is implementing a new global strategy may expect employees to acquire and use multicultural competencies and will want to incorporate this expectation in the performance management process, perhaps in setting and evaluating development goals.

Another potential reason for redesigning a performance management program is to build on the skills and competencies both employees and managers have developed in performance management. For example, as managers become adept at giving feedback and supporting development, they may need to rely less on formal processes, such as 360-degree surveys. Instead of a semi-annual 360-degree survey for all managers, for instance, the organization may implement a just-in-time, online process that allows managers to formulate their own surveys when they believe they need feedback to understand how their peers, subordinates, or customers are responding to their decisions and actions. In other words, they learn when to ask "how am I doing," and how to gather information that will help them guide their efforts.

Knowing when to adapt or devise an entirely new performance management program requires constant assessment. Assessment is usually the job of the human resource or organization development professionals in the organization. They need to devise and implement methods for assessment, and they need to convince top executives of the importance of investing in assessment. Perhaps the best way to do this is to conduct a trial program and study to demonstrate its effectiveness. The program might be implemented in one department in one region of the company. A similar department in the same region and the same department in another region might be used for comparison purposes. In general, assessment should be built into the design of the program itself so that it is expected and recognized as an integral part of the program.

There are four types of assessment data: (1) attitude surveys that ask about the perceived value of the performance management program; (2) behavioral data, which may be self-report (part of a survey that asks not only about value but use; for instance, "Did you complete the annual performance appraisal form for all your subordinates?," "How often do you and your manager discuss your job performance?"), or it may be frequency counts of use (e.g., number of managers who completed appraisal forms for their employees); (3) behavior change reflected in changes in performance ratings over time or external measures (e.g., number of times a behavior was carried out, such as a successful sales call); and (4) improvement in bottom-line performance and outcomes associated with the organization's strategic goals (e.g., change in profits, sales, new clients, employees hired, employees retained, etc.) and objectives (methods for accomplishing the goals).

Each of these measurements has potential problems. Ratings may be subject to response biases, such as central tendency (ratings in the middle of the scale) or halo (ratings at the top end of the scale). In either case, the result is that managers are not truly differentiating between dimensions of performance but instead rating one employee or all employees the same on all performance dimensions. So when the data are averaged across employees to consider performance change in a department or the organization as a whole, the results would be confounded by rater error. Behavioral and performance ratings may be a function of many factors other than an honest assessment of performance as defined by the performance management program in place. This is why multiple measures are needed to understand the performance management program from different perspectives and to recognize the diverse factors that influence performance, including faulty measurement. Insights result as data from different sources and indicators converge to tell a consistent story. So, for instance, attitude survey results may indicate that performance dimensions are difficult to understand or too time consuming to complete. This may explain why managers leave items blank, fill out the appraisal forms in a cursory way, or don't meet with employees to discuss performance results.

Program evaluation, alternatively called action or applied research, faces greater challenges than basic research because program evaluation is not designed to eliminate alternative explanations. So the data are likely to be subject to a variety of unavoidable confounds. However, consistent measurement procedures repeated over time that take into account subgroup differences are likely to produce meaningful results. These results can be used to understand how people are using and reacting to the elements of a performance management program, and can also be used to fine-tune the program. When the program undergoes a major transition in response to changes in the organization's strategic goals, or to increase awareness of performance issues, or to reinvigorate motivation to apply performance management techniques, the assessment methods can be changed accordingly. Some measures may stay the same in order to assess change over time. Others may be added to reflect performance relative to the new goals and program objectives. In the case we present at the end of the chapter, the organization development group used the results of the company-wide employee opinion survey to track use and satisfaction with its performance management process, and to design specific training to meet skill gaps in setting strategic goals, giving and receiving feedback, and conducting the performance appraisal conversation.

Issues for researchers

Here we raise five concerns of basic and applied researchers who are interested in understanding how people and groups monitor and change their performance, including: (1) generating theory that informs practice – that is, expressing theories that underlie, and so predict, human and organizational behavior that suggest fruitful directions for methods to improve performance; (2) formulating and carrying out research designs that clearly identify the unique and joint effects of the elements of performance management as a longitudinal, systemic process; (3) developing and applying reliable and valid measures of behaviors and outcomes at the individual, group, and organizational level; (4) finding opportunities to partner with organizations to conduct research; and (5) generating results that inform theory and practice.

Basic research explains the reasons for phenomena and improves our ability to predict and control performance behaviors and interactions that contribute to the performance

improvement of individuals and groups. There is no shortage of theories that inform performance management. Each component has its own set of theoretical frameworks, including those
listed in Table 15.1. So, for example, theories suggest that goals should be specific, challenging
but possible to achieve, and involve the employee in setting them (e.g., Locke & Latham, 2002).
Feedback should be specific, occur soon after the event that occasioned the feedback, and
behaviorally focused (Ilgen et al., 1979; London, 2003).

Performance management theories are continuously being tested, revised, and extended.
In fact specific research shows how the program components work together to develop comprehensive approaches to performance management. Research designs in the laboratory and
the field have examined the joint effects of goal setting and feedback (e.g., see Locke & Latham,
2002), feedback and coaching (Smither et al., 2003, 2005), and leadership schemas and ratings
(Lord & Maher, 1993). As an example, one study in a major global bank collected 360-degree
performance survey data from more than 700 senior managers (Smither et al., 2003). Managers
rated themselves and were rated by their peers, subordinates, and immediate supervisor.
A portion of the sample received the results from an executive coach and then worked with
the coach to establish a development plan for performance improvement. The results showed
that those who worked with a coach had statistically significant higher ratings a year later when
the 360-degree performance survey was repeated compared to the group that did not receive
coaching, but the difference accounted for only 4% of the change in performance. Although
small, even practically, 4% of the bottom line controlled by each of these managers was substantial (in millions of dollars) and well worth the investment in the performance management
process. The research had practical suggestions for the value of external coaching and suggested
to the bank that it could train managers to be coaches to lower level managers and employees,
thereby cascading coaching throughout the organization.

Performance measures need to be reliable and valid for use in basic and applied research.
One difficulty is that changes in performance ratings over time may be due to changes in
perceptions of the instrument, performance standards, or changes in the level of difficulty of
goal achievement. Measures that are external to the performance management system (e.g.,
objective indicators of individual performance, such as sales data) may be needed to validate
improvements in performance ratings.

Although basic research strives to control conditions to isolate effects, this is often difficult
to do, especially in field studies. Laboratory studies (for example, undergraduate students rating
descriptions of managers' performance) are often artificial, and the results do not necessarily
transfer directly to work settings, although these results usually have implications for work that
needs to be tested in the field. On the other hand, isolating individual effects is difficult in
research on comprehensive performance management programs that may be influenced by
multiple factors. Also, comparison groups may be hard to find, the program may not be
randomly assigned to groups but may be used in groups that need it the most, and measures
may be influenced by a variety of factors that are external to the program, such as market or
economic conditions.

Basic and applied research are not necessarily distinct. Program evaluations to examine
reactions of raters and employees to feedback tell us something about how sensitive individuals
are to various elements of a performance management program and suggest the extent to which
goal setting, ratings, and/or feedback are likely to affect behavior.

Basic research is likely to be artificial and not directly transferable to all work settings. Applied
research is likely to use measures of questionable reliability or validity and compare results to
groups that are not equivalent and so produce ambiguous results. Still, as long as we recognize
the limitations of research results and continue to conduct research to build a repository of

knowledge, we are likely to increase our understanding of performance management from a variety of perspectives and under different conditions. So, for instance, we will learn when and how organizational goals inform individual goals, the extent to which performance dimensions need to be customized to specific functions and positions or can be general and apply across departments and functions, and when and why different types of feedback and coaching are useful.

Challenges for future research and practice

Before presenting a case example, we conclude with five challenges for the future.

(1) Business is global, and managers and executives need to interact effectively with people from multiple cultures. This suggests that designing and implementing performance management programs that reflect cultural issues will be a challenge, especially in multinational organizations. Performance expectations and dimensions will need to be communicated clearly especially when multiple languages are involved. Cultural issues may affect raters' willingness to participate and provide meaningful feedback. For example, subordinates rating supervisors may not be viewed in the same way in hierarchical, collectivistic cultures, for instance, in Asia, compared to individualistic cultures in which there is power equalization, for instance, in Scandinavian countries (Hofstede, 2003).

(2) We now have online methods of conveying and gathering information about performance management. As a result, challenges include developing and using online ratings, feedback through emails and other forms of electronic communication, survey generation systems that allow managers to seek feedback themselves when they want it, and comparative data on a host of performance topics that become public information.

(3) Organizations will face the challenge of understanding performance management from the standpoint of new-generation (e.g., X and Y) employees. This may encompass dealing with discontinuities between organizational expectations for performance, standards, and behavior and the thinking of new generation employees regarding career goals, concerns for work–life balance, and modes of communication. Younger generations may not have the same performance standards, career goals, and desires for development compared to older generations. Of course, this is a continuously evolving picture (Huntley, 2006).

(4) Another challenge is linking performance management programs to the many interfaces that employees and managers have, including input from customers, suppliers of outsourced functions, and joint venture partners, to name a few stakeholders in performance management. These are constantly shifting, yet these various constituencies all have a stake in the performance management process. They contribute to an individual's performance and are able to provide a perspective about the individual's performance (Amabile & Kramer, 2007). So performance management systems need to recognize the contributions of others to an individual's performance and also collect information about the individual's performance from people who make these contributions.

(5) Overall, a principal challenge is preparing for, and creating, the workplace of the future. Strategic performance management systems can help create a learning, feedback-oriented culture that incorporates the above shifts in globalization, technology, and workforce attitudes, and attract, develop, and retain talent to maintain high standards and strive for continuous performance improvement.

Case study: GHT Corporation

The following describes the evolution of strategic performance management (SPM) at a global, high-tech company (GHT), a firm with more than 10,000 employees and revenues in billions of dollars.

Background

GHT was a successful company, but it was undergoing a transition. To remain an industry leader, it created a new business model, restructured operating units, and began to shift away from a heroic, founder-driven view of leadership toward becoming a professionally managed organization. GHT had a culture of compliance. Employees, in general, did what they were asked to do, often rallying resources to meet unique business challenges and events. If you were to ask most GHT employees about their next job or career aspirations, the answer, most likely, was "whatever GHT wants me to do." At the same time, GHT did not have a process focus, viewing, for example, performance appraisal as an event rather than being part of an overall performance management process. In fact, the company's human resource (HR) function, as well as its HR processes and systems, were immature. To say the least, HR was not considered a strategic business partner.

Although the company was successful it lacked a clearly articulated vision, mission and overarching goals. As a result, its performance management process was less than effective from a goal-setting perspective. In addition, the form used for the year-end appraisal had a number of faults, including poor scale design, unclear scale definitions, no established set of competencies for evaluating behavior, and a system-generated overall rating that had no consistency to its meaning across different parts of the organization.

The beginning

After the hiring of a successful, senior HR professional several years ago to lead HR, and the subsequent staffing of other senior HR and organization development (OD) professionals in key functions, the OD team was charged with creating a new performance management process while the compensation team was charged with building a total rewards strategy and program. Both teams were expected to and did work together and align efforts.

The current automated performance management process, in its design, was more an outcome of IT system designers than performance management experts. The system design drove what could and could not be done from a performance management perspective. The changes to performance management at GHT, described next, occurred over a four-year period.

Early work

There were a number of factors inhibiting effective performance management at GHT. These are outlined in Table 15.3 below. Also identified in Table 15.3 are those factors, over years two and three in this journey, that helped to make performance management a more successful and effective process at GHT.

In spite of the lack of an explicit corporate mission, vision and overarching goals, work was done to transform the performance management process. The new appraisal process would now include a focus on both behavior and performance, with all employees being assessed against the behaviors supporting the company's values, and behaviors explicitly defined for both

Table 15.3 Strategic performance management at GHT

Initial inhibiting factors	Later factors promoting a strategic performance management process
A non-professional management team	A professional management team
Insular, limited-experienced HR team	International, experienced HR team
Leader-founder driven	Leadership team driven
Sales focus	Business focus
Lack of robust strategic plan, budget-driven focus	Strategic planning process in place, strategic focus
Implicit, not widely shared, strategic direction	Explicit mission, vision and key priorities
No cross-functional planning	Cross-functional planning part of strategic planning process
Poor performance appraisal and process	Appraisal focusing on goal achievement, development and behavior
Lack of HR process integration	Key HR process integration, e.g., compensation and appraisal
No explicit statement about culture and performance	Key priority established as "building a performance-based culture"
Minimal training on performance management process	Regular, updated training available on aspects of performance management process
Appraisal and performance management process not clearly linked to rewards	Clear link between year-end appraisals and rewards
Appraisal ratings influenced by distribution expectations	Overall appraisal ratings based on objective measures of performance

managers and individual contributors. Along with a strong emphasis on performance goals, these two aspects became the focus of the new appraisal, which also included a development action plan.

The new appraisal process was approved by senior management, and within one year, a system was built to automate the new process. The overall performance management process now formally included goal setting, feedback, and mid-year and year-end appraisals.

Compliance culture

Although we stated previously that GHT had a culture of compliance, its managers did not feel a strong need to comply with the requirements of the new performance management process and its related time lines. In fact, managers' prevailing belief backed by experience was that extensions would be granted for all deadlines, as managers and employees always considered themselves "too busy" to meet the official time lines. As a result, setting goals and completing appraisals was typically a "right down to the wire" exercise.

As outlined in Table 15.4, GHT achieved nearly 100% completion of year-end appraisals (though not always within the official timeframe) because overall ratings were required for compensation administration. And to move to the compensation phase, both managers and their employees had to sign the official year-end appraisal. At first, the HR department was reluctant to push for firmer deadlines for completion because of the extraordinary changes going on in the business. However, it was not until the policy was changed to "no extensions will be

Table 15.4 Improvement in "compliance to deadlines" over time

▦ GHT had both a mid-year appraisal process that managers could adopt for their departments ("strongly recommended") and a required year-end appraisal.
▦ Generally, several transmittal letters, reminder emails, etc., needed to be sent to managers and employees to achieve compliance with the policy and timelines.
▦ Initially extensions were typically granted and expected (part of the culture).
▦ Near 100% compliance was attained for year-end appraisal completion as overall ratings were required for compensation administration.
▦ In year one, due to issues in business, only 75% voluntary compliance with mid-year appraisal completion was attained, even after extending the period from the normal two months to four and a half months.
▦ In year two, 90% compliance was reached for mid-year appraisals, with only a one-month extension granted (three months' total). The extension was granted because there was a change in the timing of the appraisal process, moving from a calendar-year-based to a fiscal-year-based process.
▦ In year three, the policy was changed and extensions were no longer granted; this was communicated at the beginning of the process. An 83% completion rate for mid-year appraisals was achieved in two months. However, a 93% rate was achieved if those appraisals completed up to one week past the deadline were included.
▦ Before the year-end appraisal phase in year four, employee opinion survey ratings showed a significant increase in satisfaction (as measured by percent favorable response) with the set of performance management-related questions, although still in the 60%–70% favorable range.
▦ In year four, 92% of year-end appraisals were completed on time.

granted" that practically all managers complied by meeting the official deadlines for both mid-year and year–end appraisals. In fact, for the most recent year–end appraisal period, year four of the journey, more than 92% completed appraisals *on time*, the highest percentage ever at GHT.

Performance management process support

During this period of transition, the OD team provided extensive communication and training on performance management including how to set strategic goals, complete appraisal forms, and conduct a performance appraisal discussion. In addition, the development of an explicit mission and vision, as well key priorities, including "establishing a performance–based culture," went a long way toward creating the framework for team and individual goal setting. Again, Table 15.3 describes those promoting factors, which in the case of GHT, helped to make performance management a more effective and respected process.

Lessons learned

As in most case studies, there are specific lessons learned at GHT that can be applied elsewhere. These lessons are described in Table 15.5 and focus mostly on the need for training managers and employees in the performance management process and regular communication about the process throughout the year. Not included in the table, however, is a very critical lesson learned as a result of GHT's most recent employee opinion survey.

The survey included six questions on performance management. The prior year's results averaged a 60% favorable response – fair but not outstanding. The current results showed a statistically significant increase, but still averaged only 63% favorable, lower than HR had anticipated given all the recent training efforts for, and process improvements to, performance management and positive changes in the business. In fact, a new question was added to the current year's survey, "Is performance management valued at GHT?", to which there was only a 53% favorable response.

Table 15.5 Lessons learned from GHT

- Need to clearly articulate the process for each phase of performance management (goal-setting feedback, development planning, appraisal).
- Need to train managers and employees for how to effectively conduct each phase – tell them what to do and how to do it.
- HR/OD must regularly support the process with:
  - emails;
  - websites with tools, techniques, strategies for performance management;
  - HR partners counseling leaders throughout the performance management process.
- Using systems-based vs. paper-based processes creates an additional set of concerns:
  - the system must be designed to be both user-friendly and the process it supports must be based on sound HR practices;
  - system changes and maintenance impact usage and may be difficult to support, as dedicated IT resources are required;
  - managers and employees, and particularly senior leaders, need to take time to learn the system, regardless of its perceived ease of use.
- As the business changes, performance management process changes have to be made.
- It takes time to change behavior (almost four years).

What happened? Open-ended comments revealed that employees did not see a strong connection between their overall performance ratings and their subsequent merit increases. Many felt the positive feedback they had received throughout the performance year and their overall ratings justified a higher increase. Increases were moderated, however, by a relatively small merit increase budget driven by business conditions, so distinguishing and rewarding strong performance was difficult. As a result, a strong performer might not have received the level of rewards he or she expected. Managers did not adequately explain this situation, adding to the general dissatisfaction with and confusion about the performance–pay relationship. Some employees also expressed the feeling that their ratings were suppressed because of an implied "20–70–10" ratings distribution, where only 20% of employees could achieve a rating of "exceeded expectations." From a corporate perspective, "20–70–10" was a general guideline, not an absolute; it helped to express a "pay-for-performance" philosophy. Although there was an explicit connection at GHT between pay and performance, managers in general did not adequately communicate how they were related, and they did not communicate the purpose of the distribution guidelines and how they were to be used.

Given increasing manager and leadership support for the performance management process, the ongoing training and communication provided by OD, the focus on building a performance-based culture, and recent efforts to further clarify for all employees the linkage between pay and performance, GHT anticipates increased satisfaction with performance management over the next year. Current senior leadership are counting on this fact. They see performance management as critical to achieving business results, maintaining GHT's industry leadership position, and driving the overall success of GHT in the marketplace.

Finally, based on lessons learned, the OD team will also be taking additional steps to:

- better align and integrate performance management with business planning and strategic goal setting to make the connections more transparent;
- drive a paradigm shift regarding performance management from one of "a bureaucratic, compliance-oriented process" to "a process of business value";
- make performance management the way of doing business;
- help managers to understand and be able to customize general ratable behaviors to reflect individual job performance;

help managers (train them) to establish and formulate goals where performance measures may be more qualitative, for example, in staff roles such as finance, marketing, software and administration.

Conclusion

Our case illustrates challenges for practice, theory, and the future that we described earlier in the chapter. Performance management requires executive buy-in, clearly articulated program elements with strong linkages with each other and with organizational goals, and a system to track success and improve the process over time. Performance management components draw on a strong theoretical foundation, and this case demonstrates the value of goal setting, evaluation, feedback, and development as integrated functions. The case recognizes the changing corporate world, utilizing technological advances for program delivery and communications. It also recognizes the dynamic nature of performance management in a business-focused, internationally experienced, growing organization. Senior leaders learn the system along with the new generation of managers entering the business, building a fluid yet focused culture of performance assessment and improvement. Organization culture change through performance management takes time, commitment, and involvement of staff at all levels, with human resource professionals closely aligned with business functions to implement a system that all employees respect and value. This is not an easy process, but it is one that can result in dividends through improved performance and the ability to adapt to future needs.

References

Alexander, J. (2006). *Performance dashboards and analysis for value creation.* New York: Wiley.

Amabile, T. M., & Kramer, S. J. (2007). Inner work life: Understanding the subtext of business performance. *Harvard Business Review, 85*(5), 72–83.

Atwater, L., Roush, P., & Fischthal, A. (1995). The influence of upward feedback on self and follower ratings of leadership. *Personnel Psychology, 48,* 34–60.

Bandura, A., & Locke, E. A. (2003). Negative self-efficacy and goal effects revisited. *Journal of Applied Psychology, 88,* 87–99.

Drucker, P. F. (1993). *Management: Tasks, responsibilities, practices.* New York: Collins.

Dweck, C. S. (1999). *Self-theories: Their role in motivation, personality, and development.* Philadelphia, PA: Psychology Press.

Giles, W. F., Findley, H. M., & Field, H. S. (1997). Procedural fairness in performance appraisal: Beyond the review session. *Journal of Business, 11,* 493–506.

Greenberg, J. (1991). Using explanations to manage impressions of performance appraisal fairness. *Employee Responsibilities and Rights Journal, 4,* 51–60.

Harris, M. M., & Schaubroeck, J. (1988). A meta-analysis of self-manager, self-peer, and peer-manager ratings. *Personnel Psychology, 41,* 43–62.

Heslin, P. A., Vandewalle, D., & Latham, G. P. (2006). Keen to help? Managers' implicit person theories and their subsequent employee coaching. *Personnel Psychology, 59,* 871–902.

Hofstede, G. (2003). *Culture's consequences: Comparing values, behaviors, institutions, and organizations across nations* (2nd edn). Newbury Park, CA: Sage Publications.

Huntley, R. (2006). *The world according to Y: Inside the new adult generation.* Crows Nest, New South Wales, Australia: Allen & Unwin.

Ilgen, D. R., Fisher, C. D., & Taylor, M. S. (1979). Consequences of individual feedback on behavior in organizations. *Journal of Applied Psychology, 64,* 349–371.

Kaplan, R. S., & Norton, D. P. (1996) *The balanced scorecard: Translating strategy into action*. Boston: Harvard Business School Press.

Klimoski, R. J., & Donahue, L. M. (2001). Person perception in organizations: An overview of the field. In M. London (Ed.), *How people evaluate others in organizations* (pp. 5–43). Mahwah, NJ: Erlbaum.

Kluger, A. N., & DeNisi, A. (1998). Feedback interventions: Toward the understanding of a double-edged sword. *Current Directions in Psychological Science, 7*, 67–72.

Locke, E. A., & Latham, G. P. (1990). *A theory of goal-setting and task performance*. Englewood Cliffs, NJ: Prentice-Hall.

Locke, E. A., & Latham, G. P. (2002). Building a practically useful theory of goal setting and task motivation: A 35 year odyssey. *American Psychologist, 57*, 705–717.

London, M. (2003). *Job feedback*. Mahwah, NJ: Erlbaum.

London, M., & Mone, E. M. (1999). Continuous learning. In D. R. Ilgen & E. D. Pulakos (Eds), *The changing nature of work performance: Implications for staffing, personnel actions, and development* (pp. 119–153). San Francisco, CA: Jossey-Bass.

London, M., & Smither, J. W. (1995). Can multi-source feedback change self-awareness and behavior? Theory-based applications and directions for research. *Personnel Psychology, 48*, 803–840.

London, M., & Smither, J. W. (2002). Feedback orientation, feedback culture, and the longitudinal performance management process. *Human Resource Management Review, 12*(1), 81–101.

London, M., Smither, J. W., & Adsit, D. J. (1996). Accountability: The Achilles Heel of multisource feedback. *Group and Organization Management, 22*, 162–184.

Lord, R. G., & Maher, K. J. (1993). *Leadership & information processing: Linking perceptions and performance*. New York: Routledge.

Mabe, P. A., & West, S. G. (1982). Validity of self-evaluation of ability: A review and meta-analysis. *Journal of Applied Psychology, 67*, 280–296.

Mone, E. M., & London, M. (2003). *Fundamentals of performance management*. London: Spiro Press.

Odiorne, G. S. (1968). *Management by objectives: A system of managerial leadership*. New York: Pitman Publishing Corporation.

Polzer, J. T., Milton, L. P., & Swann, W. B., Jr. (2002). Capitalizing on diversity: Interpersonal congruence in small work groups. *Administrative Science Quarterly, 47*, 296–324.

Sessa, V. I., & London, M. (2006). *Continuous learning in organizations*. Mahwah, NJ: Erlbaum.

Smither, J. W., London, M., & Reilly, R. R. (2005). Does performance improve following multisource feedback? A theoretical model, meta-analysis, and review of empirical findings. *Personnel Psychology, 58*(1), 33–66.

Smither, J. W., London, M., & Richmond, K. R. (2005). The relationship between leaders' personality and their reactions to and use of multisource feedback: A longitudinal study. *Group & Organization Management, 30*, 181–210.

Smither, J. W., London, M., Flautt, R., Vargas, Y., & Kucine, I. (2003). Can working with an executive coach improve multisource feedback ratings over time? A quasi-experimental field study. *Personnel Psychology, 56*, 23–44.

Stamoulis, D. T., & Hauenstein, N. M. A. (1993). Rater training and rating accuracy: Training for dimensional accuracy versus training for rate differentiation. *Journal of Applied Psychology, 78*, 994–1003.

Steel, P., & Cornelius, J. K. (2006). Integrating theories of motivation. *Academy of Management Review, 31*, 889–913.

Vandewalle, B., Brown, S. P., Cron, W. L., & Slocum, J. W. Jr (1999). The influence of goal orientation and self-regulation tactics on sales performance: A longitudinal field test. *Journal of Applied Psychology, 84*, 249–59.

Wood, R., & Bandura, A. (1989). Social cognitive theory of organizational management. *The Academy of Management Review, 14*, 361–384.

16

Strategic training and development

Raymond A. Noe and Michael J. Tews

Recently, there has been a greater emphasis on strategic training and development initiatives to enhance human capital and help organizations adapt to compete effectively in the marketplace (Kozlowski & Salas, 1997; Martocchio & Baldwin, 1997; Tannenbaum, 2002). Based on the resource-based view of the firm (Barney, 1991), human resources can be resources which are rare, valuable, difficult to imitate, and non-substitutable, and thus provide a means for organizations to achieve a competitive advantage. Employees' knowledge and skill sets help organizations develop valuable technologies and services which other companies cannot easily duplicate or imitate. Strategic training and development is particularly relevant in helping organizations achieve a competitive advantage by developing competencies not readily available in the labor market, developing firm-specific skill sets, and promoting innovation and creating new knowledge.

Given the interest in strategic training and developing and its potential in helping organizations achieve their goals, the aim of this chapter is to further explore this human resource management (HRM) domain. The chapter begins by providing a conceptualization of strategic training and development. Next, we identify key issues, review relevant research, and present opportunities for future research attention in the areas of needs assessment, organization of the training function, knowledge management, transfer enhancement systems, and evaluation. An important point of emphasis in the chapter is that there have been more theoretical discussions than empirical research on strategic training and development. Thus, in order to further advance the strategic training and development domain, concerted research effort is necessary. We should note that this chapter does not provide a comprehensive review of training and development research at the micro-level. Comprehensive reviews are provided by Kraiger (2003), McCauley & Heslett (2001), and Salas, Cannon-Bowers, Rhodenizer, & Bowers (1999).

What is strategic training and development?

Strategic training and development focuses on the design and implementation of training systems to successfully impact organizational performance. Tannenbaum (2002) provides one of the most comprehensive models of the strategic training and development process, which is

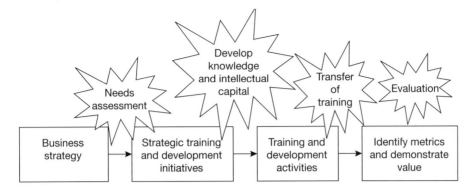

Figure 16.1 The strategic training and development process

presented in Figure 16.1. First, the strategic process begins with identifying the business strategy. Second, strategic learning imperatives (strategic training and development goals) to support the strategy are identified. Although Tannenbaum (2002) acknowledges that strategic learning imperatives should be unique for each organization based on its unique goals and challenges, he does provide eight common learning imperatives shown in Table 16.1. Third, the strategic learning imperatives are then translated into specific training and development activities, which could include formal and informal learning opportunities utilizing a variety of traditional and newer methodologies. The final step in the strategic training and development process involves evaluating whether training helped contribute to the goals of the organization utilizing appropriate metrics.

To what extent can a strategic perspective on training and development be differentiated from the traditional, micro-perspective which focuses on needs assessment, transfer of training, training methods, and evaluation? As Figure 16.1 suggests, strategic training and development cannot be differentiated. All training interventions should be carefully planned, designed, and evaluated in support of organizational goals and objectives. Several authors suggest that most organizational training and development initiatives that have occurred in the last decade have been strategic because they have emphasized knowledge management, continuous learning, and development programs to help organizations increase their ability to detect change, adapt, and anticipate trends (Kraiger & Ford, 2006; Sessa & London, 2006).

Although strategic training and development cannot (and should not) be completely divorced from the traditional perspective and vice versa, we contend that strategic training and development can and should be conceptualized at a broader level. With respect to needs assessment, the emphasis is on aligning training systems with an organization's business strategy and operating constraints. Further, the emphasis for training design is on the development of systems of interventions to support knowledge and skill acquisition and transfer, rather than on

Table 16.1 Tannenbaum's (2002) strategic learning imperatives

1. Diversify the learning portfolio.
2. Expand the view of whom we train.
3. Accelerate the pace of employee learning.
4. Prepare employees to deal better with customers.
5. Make sure employees believe they have opportunities to learn and grow.
6. Capture and share knowledge more effectively.
7. Ensure that training and learning supports the strategic direction.
8. Diagnose and modify the work environment to support transfer and learning.

the design and implementation of discrete training activities or methods. Finally, evaluation is focused on demonstrating an organizational impact of training investments. These perspectives have been advocated in the traditional training and development domain, yet have not been the focus of substantial research attention.

Needs assessment: linking business strategy to training and development initiatives

The goal of needs assessment from a strategic perspective is to link training initiatives with the overall goals of the organization. Needs assessment is critical because it helps evaluate whether training is a viable option for the organization based on its resources and strategy, determines the type of training that should be provided, and identifies the outcomes or metrics for subsequent evaluation.

There are many anecdotal examples and case studies of how strategic training and development has been integrated with business strategy. For example, IBM, which reinvented itself in 2002, adopted a new business strategy to transform itself from a high-tech industrial age company to an information and knowledge-driven company to better serve its clients' needs (Davenport, 2005). Implementing this strategy required a massive cultural shift. IBM needed to transform its workforce; its employees needed to become more dedicated to clients and more adaptable and innovative. Training was deemed to be critical in helping the company achieve its strategic objectives, and this function was reoriented toward "learning through work," where training was conducted on location and was linked explicitly to client needs. For example, learning teams designed training opportunities into the work itself, a concept known as "work-embedded learning." Employees worked via computers to connect with experts, participate in specialized online communications, and completed online learning modules. The amount of time spent on learning and training grew 32% from 2003 to 2004 through the expansion of work-embedded learning, and the company was to commit more than $700 million to learning initiatives deemed to be critical for achieving its business strategy.

Noe (2008) suggests that different business strategies call for different human capital requirements and thus place different demands on the training function. A *concentration* strategy focuses on increasing market share, reducing costs, or creating and maintaining a market niche for products and services. In this context, companies need to emphasize skill currency and the development of their existing workforce. An *internal growth* strategy focuses on new market and product development innovation and joint ventures. The training and development emphasis should be placed on keeping employees up-to-date with new products and services. An *external growth* strategy emphasizes acquiring vendors and suppliers or acquiring businesses that allow the company to expand into new markets. Companies adopting such a strategy need to help employees adapt to the change and learn about organizational culture. Further, training under both internal and external growth strategies should focus on preparing employees for new leadership and other roles that may emerge as a result of growth. Finally, a *disinvestment* strategy emphasizes liquidation and divestiture of business, where the training and development should emphasize helping employees find new jobs and cross-training those employees who find themselves with greater responsibilities.

Lepak and Snell (1999, 2002) contend that the strategic value and uniqueness of occupational groups are key considerations in the design of HR systems. These researchers have focused on the adoption of different employment modes with occupational groups which vary in strategic value and uniqueness. The employment modes and their training foci include:

(1) *commitment* (providing employees with long-term internal development opportunities); (2) *productivity* (training employees quickly in core skills; offering limited development opportunities); (3) *collaboration* (training employees in teamwork and relationships; providing incentives to transfer and share information); and, (4) *compliance* (training employees in compliance issues focused on policies, procedures, and systems). In turn, the specific occupational groups were: (1) knowledge employees (strategically valuable and unique); (2) job-based employees (strategically valuable but not unique); (3) alliance/partnership employees (unique but not strategically valuable); and (4) contract employees (neither strategically valuable nor unique). Lepak and Snell (2002) found different patterns of adoption of the employment modes across the employee groups. The prevalence of the commitment configuration was slightly higher for knowledge employees. The productivity configuration was used for job-based and knowledge employees, while the collaborative configuration was used equally for alliance/partnership and knowledge employees, as well as job-based employees. These findings suggest that strategic value and uniqueness should be considered in designing an overall strategic training and development architecture.

A variety of needs assessment models have been proposed to explicitly link training and development interventions to specific contexts. Leigh, Watkins, Plat, and Kaufmann (2000) reviewed a variety of needs assessment models that have been developed over the past forty years. They differentiate the models based on the outcomes addressed (societal, organizational, and individual or small group), efforts and activities, and resources. Debate persists as to which models are best, as the different frameworks vary in scope, timeframe, and content addressed. However, models that link training and development needs to what organizations use, do, produce, and deliver are best suited for strategic training and development purposes.

Several models included in Leigh et al. (2000) may be particularly relevant from a strategic perspective. For example, Nelson, Whitener, and Philcox's (1995) model, which draws on Ostroff and Ford's (1989) content-level application matrix, focuses on processes and inputs at the organizational, small-group, and individual levels. In addition, Witkin and Altschuld's (1995) framework addresses process improvement and the achievement of organizational goals for individuals and small groups. Moreover, Kaufman's (1972, 1992, 1998) organizational elements model addresses linkages between societal, organizational, small group, and individual results and organizational resources and activities. The strength of these frameworks from a strategic perspective is the multi-level systems perspective.

Competency modeling may be a valuable means to link training and development systems to organizational objectives (Shippmann et al., 2000). Competencies refer to areas of personal capability that enable employees to perform their jobs by achieving specific outcomes or accomplishing tasks (Lucia & Lepsinger, 1999), and a corresponding model identifies competencies required for a job along with the requisite knowledge, skills, behaviors, and personality characteristics for each competency. In a dynamic business environment, competency modeling may have more advantages than traditional needs assessment approaches. Frequently, needs assessment has focused on aligning training content with narrowly defined knowledge and skill sets appropriative for specific work roles. Such a traditional focus may be appropriate where jobs are narrowly defined and static, but less so where jobs are broader and evolving. Research has demonstrated that broad competency models were more likely than results from traditional job analysis to link to company goals and that competencies are more generalizable across occupational groups, levels or jobs, and organizations (Shippmann et al., 2000). Further, competency models can serve as a foundation for integrating systems of HRM practices thereby creating *horizontal fit*, a key tenet in strategic human resource management (SHRM) (Huselid, 1995). Organizations have utilized competency models for integrating several HRM practices, such as formal performance appraisal, succession planning, ongoing coaching and performance feedback, and formal training and development interventions (e.g., Sallie-Dosunmu, 2006).

Research suggests that competency ratings may not necessarily be accurate, however. Competency statements represent combinations of tasks and performance requirement, which may not always be applicable to the job, and thus overall ratings may be inflated. Morgeson, Delaney-Klinger, Mayfield, Ferrara, and Campion (2004) found inflation in individuals' ratings of competencies. Distortion in raters' evaluations may increase as competency statements become more abstract and less verifiable. Further, a series of studies has found that inexperienced raters have difficulty distinguishing among competencies and their ratings have poor inter-rater reliability and discriminant validity (Lievens, Sanchez, & DeCorte, 2004; Lievens & Sanchez, 2007). Frame of reference training (i.e., providing raters with the appropriate schema for rating competencies) may be useful for increasing the quality of competency ratings, and its effects are enhanced by having prior experience in competency modeling (Lievens & Sanchez, 2007).

A final issue to be addressed with respect to needs assessment content is the assessment of training support in the broader organizational context. Tannenbaum (2002) argues that needs assessment should focus on whether appropriate support is present in the work environment to support transfer of training (i.e., the application of trained skills). If transfer of training does not occur, training will not have an organizational impact. Research has demonstrated that transfer can be facilitated through rewards, incentives, and social support (Rouiller & Goldstein, 1993; Tracey et al., 1995). Prior to implementing a formal training intervention, practitioners should assess whether the necessary training support mechanisms are present. Where they are not, remedies should be instituted. A detailed discussion on the transfer enhancement supports is presented later in the chapter.

It should be emphasized that research on needs assessment has been limited. There is much more research on the effectiveness of training interventions and design features, activities which have (or should have) resulted from a carefully designed assessment of organizational needs. However, nearly twenty years ago, Ostroff and Ford (1989) provided many recommendations for research on organizational-level needs assessment that have been largely ignored, but which may still serve to advance the field. For example, they suggested that research focus on the effectiveness of strategies for scanning and acquisition that training personnel use to identify organizational and environmental changes. In addition to Ostroff and Ford's suggestions, it may be worthwhile to examine factors external and internal to the organization that may influence individual decisions to invest in strategic training initiatives. Such factors could include labor market conditions, the availability of new instructional design methods, and levels of trust between senior management and the training and development personnel.

Organization of the training function: deploying training resources to create value

An important strategic issue is whether an organization should assume responsibility for training or outsource this responsibility to outside vendors. A survey conducted by the Society for Human Resource Management (SHRM) found that 57% of the HR and training professionals outsourced all or portions of their training and development programs (Johnson, 2004). Training experts predict that within ten years, half of all trainers will work for outsourcing providers. Companies may elect to outsource their training for a variety of reasons, such as cost savings, time savings to focus on business strategy, expertise in compliance training mandated by legislation, lack of internal expertise, and the desire to access best practices. Some of the reasons companies do not outsource include the inability of external companies to meet the needs of their clients, uncomfortable with less organizational control over training design and delivery, and beliefs that outsourcing reduces employees' and managers' perceptions of the value of training among organizational members.

Outsourcing firms offer a variety of training services to organizations. For example, Convergys, an outsourcing company, offers a range of services focused on the planning and development of training content, delivery with up-to-date technologies, administration, and evaluation (Harris, 2004). Convergys helped SonicWALL, an Internet security company, transition from instructor-led workshops to e-learning by providing Web-based training for employees as well as customers.

Although outsourcing is increasing, most companies only outsource smaller projects and not the complete training and development function. Texas Instruments (TI) is a company that utilizes a hybrid approach. TI contracts with General Physics, a training outsourcing provider, to offer open-enrollment courses for professional technical training (Cornell, 2005). However, TI remains in charge of its customized professional development offerings—programs believed to add strategic value to the company. Due to a desire to reduce costs, frequent technology changes, and the cyclical nature of the semiconductor business, the technical skills programs were deemed to be the most viable candidates for outsourcing. To enhance control over its outsourced training, TI was careful to include language in its contact with General Physics that allowed TI to raise and lower the amount of training it was buying on an as-needed basis.

The limited research on outsourcing provides some guidance on how to ensure that outsourced training interventions are successful. Gainey and Klaas (2003) found that company–supplier trust (e.g., loyalty between managers from each company and concern for each other's interests) and contract specificity (e.g., clear specification of responsibilities in the contract) enhanced a company's satisfaction with outsourced training responsibilities. Additional research is needed on the factors used in the decision to outsource training, the relative importance of these factors, and on the conditions under which outsourcing training is successful.

Another strategic issue is how to structure the training and development function to ensure that training and development initiatives and activities contribute to the company's business strategy. Carliner (2004) discusses the different models used for organizing and using training and development resources. These include the consulting firm (a group from outside the organization that advises on training and development issues and implements solutions), internal profit center (internal group that offers training and development services and makes a profit), internal cost center (internal group that offers training and development services at cost), leveraged expertise (small internal group of trainers), development shop (external group that builds courses on a contract basis), and course marketers (builds courses).

Noe (2008) suggests that the business–embedded model (BE) is becoming popular. The BE model provides the opportunity to gain the benefits of centralized training, while ensuring programs meet business needs. A BE training function not only views trainees as customers, but also managers who make decisions to send employees to training and allocate money for training. Cingular Wireless is a company that has adopted a BE model (Oakes, 2005). The company's training function comprises two areas: *core services* and *functional design and delivery*. The core services function from headquarters provides training coordination, content management, resource and budget management, and links to other HR functions. Core services eliminates redundant training processes and content. The functional design and delivery function, in turn, is accountable for the execution of Cingular's learning strategies. It develops and delivers specific content in the field for sales, customer service, and billing personnel.

The corporate university model centralizes training to ensure that best training practices are disseminated across the company. Also, the corporate university model enables organizations to control costs by developing consistent training practices and policies. Both large and small organizations in a variety of industries (e.g., McDonald's, Target, Milliken, and Capital One) have started their own universities to train new employees and update the skills and knowledge of current employees (Fenn, 1999). For example, Caterpillar University consists of six colleges: leadership, marketing and distribution, technology, business and business processes, Six Sigma, and product support. Caterpillar's CEO, vice presidents, and the two group presidents provide guidance, approve budgets, and identify the university's priorities. One priority was to support new business growth through the development of leaders who are willing to collaborate with others, have a global mind set, and understand the financial aspects of the business. The College of Marketing and Distribution focuses on providing a comprehensive curriculum for sales professionals and sales marketing managers. It includes product knowledge, sales skills, and management skills. All learning goals are tied to business goals. Caterpillar University staff members help the business units deal with their learning needs. Lead learning managers in each unit have a dual reporting relationship with the university and the unit's human resource manager. The learning managers work with the business unit managers to set up learning plans. There is some anecdotal evidence that corporate universities have a positive impact on the business by improving product and service quality, reducing operating costs, and increasing revenues (Training, 2005, Corporate University Exchange website at www.corpu.com). Research needs to examine the prevalence of the different models of organizing the training function, their appropriateness for different business strategies and organizational contexts, as well as their effectiveness.

In addition to becoming more aligned with the needs of the business, training functions that have a distinctive competency in a certain area of expertise are becoming profit centers by selling training services to other companies. For example, Walt Disney Company sells training on customer service and organizational creativity at the Disney Institute in Florida. The Institute gives employees from other companies the opportunity to understand how Disney developed its business strengths, including leadership development, service, customer loyalty, and team building. Randstad sells training courses to its customers and sends selected employees to customer service call centers (Sussman, 2005). While the company makes revenue selling the training, the greater benefit is realized from building a relationship with the client. Within a one-year period, Randstad was able to show that US$45 million of business was influenced by providing access to the training to clients who chose the company (or stayed with them).

Knowledge management systems: promoting knowledge exchange and creation

Knowledge and the sharing and creation of knowledge are increasingly believed to be key sources of competitive advantage. But what exactly is knowledge? Knowledge is information that is relevant, actionable, and at least partially based on experience (Leonard & Sensiper, 1998). Nonaka and Takeuchi (1995) classify knowledge into two categories: tacit knowledge and explicit knowledge (see also Polanyi, 1969). Tacit knowledge refers to personal knowledge based on individual experience which is subconsciously understood; whereas explicit knowledge refers to more easily codified knowledge. Explicit knowledge can be communicated to others through manuals, formulae, and specifications with relative ease; whereas tacit knowledge is more difficult to convey, requiring personal discussions and demonstrations. Both types of knowledge are important in organizations, but ultimately the goal is for individuals to apply tacit knowledge to enhance performance.

Given the strategic importance of knowledge, scholars have focused on understanding knowledge management, i.e., the development of systems for recognizing, generating, documenting, distributing, and transferring knowledge (Davenport & Prusak, 1998; Rossett, 1999). Knowledge management involves developing an infrastructure for collecting and maintaining data, information, experiences, and lessons, as well as a social system to enhance knowledge exchange. The former involves information technology or hardware development; while the latter involves training and development activities, the physical arrangement of the work environment, and effective processes for work teams.

In practice, companies facilitate knowledge sharing using a variety of resources including information systems (networks and software) that allow employees to store information and share it with others; electronic catalogues that identify each employee's expertise; informational maps that identify where different types of knowledge are available in the company; online libraries of resources such as journals, manuals, training and development opportunities; and work areas that facilitate employees' exchange of ideas (Tobin, 1998).

Because most knowledge management systems emphasize the use of technology, they often fail to recognize the social system as a key ingredient for effectiveness. For example, the results of a study of 431 U.S. and European business organizations found that most firms' priorities were directed toward developing knowledge management technology (e.g., creating an intranet, knowledge repositories, and decision-support tools) and not toward creating a social system to support knowledge development and sharing (Bassi et al., 2000; Ruggles, 1998). The largest barriers to knowledge sharing were cultural barriers, lack of top management support, lack of a shared understanding of the business strategy, and lack of an appropriate organizational structure. The emphasis on information technology at the cost of creating social conditions to facilitate knowledge exchange parallels the historic emphasis in training placed on learning methods rather than the social conditions to improve transfer of training. This emphasis is unfortunate because the management development, socialization, and knowledge management literatures all emphasize that most explicit and tacit knowledge sharing occurs informally through job experiences and relationships with peers, customers, managers, and mentors (e.g., Brown & Duguid, 1991; McCauley et al., 1994; Morrison & Brantner, 1992).

Nahapiet and Ghoshal (1998) emphasize the importance of social networks in enhancing intellectual capital. Social capital, the sum of the actual and potential resources available that are derived from the relationships possessed by an individual or social unit, is the key means through which individuals and organizations enhance knowledge and skills, or intellectual capital. Intellectual capital is created through combination and exchange. Combination refers to the connection of elements previously unconnected or by developing novel ways of combining elements previously associated. Exchange refers to social interaction between parties though teamwork, collaboration, and sharing. Nahapiet and Ghoshal suggest four conditions for combination and exchange:

1. Parties must have the opportunities to make the combination or exchange, due to aspects of their work environment or technology.
2. Parties must anticipate that interaction, exchange, and involvement will create value.
3. Parties must feel that interaction, exchange, and involvement will be valuable for them personally.
4. Parties must have the capability to engage in combination or exchange, due to the existence of relevant prior knowledge.

Nahapiet and Ghoshal's model for the creation of intellectual capital proposes that structural, cognitive, and relational dimensions of social capital influence the combination and exchange of intellectual capital, which then directly affects intellectual capital creation. The structural dimension refers to the relationships or network ties among employees. The relational dimension refers to the degree to which the relationships are characterized by trust and reciprocity norms. The cognitive dimension refers to shared paradigms that relate to common understanding and shared action. For example, the "network ties" structural dimensions refers to: (a) access people have for combining and exchanging knowledge and anticipating the value of such an exchange; (b) ability of personal contacts to provide information sooner than it becomes available to people without such contacts; and (c) processes providing information on available opportunities to people. Network ties may influence the access to parties for combining and exchanging intellectual capital and the value of doing so.

In turn, the cognitive dimension in Nahapiet and Ghoshal's model suggests that the availability of shared narratives, myths, and stories enables the creation and transfer of new interpretations of events between persons. Shared language and communication codes are important because they are the means through which people discuss and exchange information, ask questions, and conduct business.

Finally, the relational dimension of the model suggests that trust, norms, obligations, expectations, and identification are dimensions of social capital that influence combination and exchange by affecting the access to other parties and the motivation of those parties. Trust, or willingness to be vulnerable to another party, is needed for persons to be open to the exchange of information. Similarly, norms of openness and teamwork, cooperation, and experimentation facilitate the exchange and value of information (DeLong & Fahey, 2000).

Kang, Morris, and Snell (2007) emphasize that a firm's ability to explore and exploit knowledge through social relationships is the fundamental means through which human resources contribute to a company's competitive advantage. They suggest that social networks between core employees and internal partners (cooperative archetype) and between core employees and external partners (entrepreneurial archetype) are most important. Kang et al. suggest that a number of training and development interventions can facilitate effective knowledge exchange between parties. Traditional training interventions can be used to build knowledge among core employees and internal partners. Orientation and socialization programs can be used to help employees and internal partners understand unique values, history, and firm culture and share tacit knowledge. Mentoring and on-the-job training can be used to build social relationships between employees and internal partners and facilitate shared representations and meaning. Team building can help expand and integrate the mental models of internal/external partners and core employees. Finally, cross-training, job rotation, and knowledge management systems can be used to help employees develop the breadth and depth of expertise to interact effectively with external partners and to explore new ideas with them. Empirical research is necessary to substantiate these propositions to determine the role that training and development activities have in building social relationships and promoting subsequent knowledge acquisition.

Brown and Van Buren (2007) suggest that while research on the relationship between training and intellectual capital has been conducted, research on the influence of training on the structural, relational, and cognitive dimensions of social capital is needed. They provide thirteen propositions about the relationship between training and social capital. Examples of these propositions include: (1) a greater percentage of employees in training will create a denser social network; (2) training which emphasizes a shared organizational identity will lead to greater levels of institutional trust among employees; and (3) training focused exclusively on organizational mission, values, and beliefs will lead to more employees with shared common vision.

We should note that a variety of individual factors may directly impact intellectual capital or moderate the interplay between intellectual capital and social capital. Training research suggests that there are many individual characteristics (e.g., attitudes, personality variables) that affect motivation to learn and learning (Colquitt et al., 2000). These types of individual characteristics, which are not aspects of social capital, may directly affect knowledge sharing. For example, individuals who lack self-confidence or are low in self-efficacy may be less likely to participate in sharing due to concerns over their capability. There may also be a relationship between participation in knowledge sharing and organizational commitment or collectivism. Individuals with high organizational commitment, or individuals who believe that the interests and well-being of the collective take precedent over personal interest, may participate more frequently in knowledge sharing because of a stronger sense of personal value.

Both action learning and communities of practice facilitate the creation of intellectual capital through social interactions. It is important to note that little empirical research has evaluated the effectiveness of action learning and communities of practice, although case studies suggest they are effective (e.g., Marquardt, 2004).

Action learning involves assigning teams a real business issue to resolve, having them collectively work on the issue and commit to an action plan, and holding them accountable for executing their plan (Dotlich & Noel, 1998). The teams typically consist of employees from different functional areas. Issues assigned to the teams vary, but typically relate to cultural change, raising revenue, or reducing costs. In order to more fully understand issues and devise the most effective solutions, teams typically conduct research, such as through meetings with customers and clients. Action learning provides a medium for knowledge sharing because employees are required to work together, share their perspectives and expertise, and seek out information to report back to their teams. Intellectual capital is generated because teams may devise innovative solutions to achieve their goals.

Communities of learning and practice, where groups of employees who work together learn from each other and develop a common understanding of how to get work accomplished, provide a context for dealing with workplace problems in real time. These communities often exchange information typically addressed in a traditional classroom environment, but this information is contextualized through the social interactions among members (Beer, 2000). Internet or intranet-based discussion boards, listservs, or other forms of computer-mediated communication represent examples of these communities. Human capital can be enhanced because knowledge can be tapped relatively quickly, and employees can share information and experiences in a way that benefits others who might otherwise not communicate. One unique benefit of communities of learning and practice is that they are often built around practice- or person-based networks, not geography or organizational function, which allows for a broader distribution of knowledge (Sena & Shani, 1999).

We need to know more about the organizational conditions and the individual differences that influence individuals' participation in communities of practice. A number of theoretical and conceptual reviews are available to guide studies on knowledge sharing (e.g., Alavi & Leidner, 2001; Ipe, 2003). Ipe (2003) proposes that motivational factors related to power, reciprocity and rewards for sharing, relationships with the knowledge recipients, the value of knowledge, the type of knowledge, and opportunities to share influence knowledge-sharing behavior. Wasko and Faraj (2005) found that individuals contribute knowledge when they (a) believe it enhances their reputation, (b) have experiences to share, and (c) have a high degree of centrality in the electronic network (i.e., exchange messages with many different people). A drawback to communities of practice is that participation is often voluntary and therefore, some individuals may not share their knowledge (Williams & Cothrel, 2000). Employees may

271

not share knowledge for several reasons including perceptions that others may not consider their knowledge as valuable, loss of expert power, and beliefs that knowledge sharing takes too much time away from their work (Starbuck, 1992). If participating in communities of practice is viewed as an extra-role behavior, the literature on organizational citizenship behavior may serve as a useful theoretical basis for studies on the development of intellectual capital and knowledge exchange in communities of learning and practice.

Transfer supports: facilitating the application of knowledge and skills

For training and development interventions to have organizational impact, knowledge and skill sets must be successfully applied, or *transferred*, on the job. However, discrete learning activities alone may be insufficient to support transfer (Baldwin & Ford, 1988). Individuals' knowledge and skills may not always be fully developed during training, a necessary but insufficient condition for transfer. Further, individuals may not always be motivated to transfer training content on the job, and knowledge and skill decay may occur over time. Researchers have argued that attention should be paid to factors beyond the formal learning experience to enhance transfer (Baldwin & Ford, 1988; Baldwin & Magjuka, 1991; Kozlowski & Salas, 1997; Yelon & Ford, 1999). Training effectiveness is grounded in the proper design and delivery of the formal learning experience, yet training should not be an isolated classroom activity if benefits are to be fully realized. A large amount of research has focused on three general factors beyond the design of the formal learning experience to promote transfer: individual differences, organizational climate and culture, and specific transfer enhancement interventions.

A variety of individual difference variables have been examined in previous research and shown to influence employee participation in development activities, knowledge and skill acquisition, and subsequent transfer. These variables have included personality characteristics (conscientiousness, goal orientation, and anxiety), trainability factors (cognitive ability), and attitudes (organizational commitment, job involvement, career exploration, and perceived value of training) (Colquitt et al., 2000; Ford et al., 1992; Noe & Wilk, 1993; Quinones et al., 1995). There are two strategic implications of these findings for training and development. First, organizations should hire for key individual differences which are stable, such as personality characteristics and cognitive ability. Second, organizations should strive to manage more malleable employee attitudes through specific interventions and by creating a favorable climate and culture toward training and development (as discussed below).

At the organizational level, transfer research has focused on climate and culture. Climate for transfer refers to trainees' perceptions about work environment characteristics that facilitate or hinder the use of what was learned in training. Different transfer climates do exist in organizations and climate does affect learning and transfer of training. Rouiller and Goldstein (1993) developed a measure of organizational transfer climate that included situational cues and consequences. These situational cues included goal cues (cues reminding trainees to use trained skills), social cues (behavior and influence cues exhibited by supervisors, peers, and subordinates), and task and structural cues (cues relating to the design and the nature of the job itself). Consequences included positive and negative feedback and rewards. In a study focused on the development of supervisory skills of managers from multiple units of a restaurant chain, they found that trainees from locations with more positive transfer climates demonstrated more trained behaviors and performed more effectively on the job. Tracey et al. (1995) investigated the impact of transfer climate and what they called a continuous learning culture on the transfer behavior of individuals who attended training focused on entry-level supervisory skills. A continuous learning culture is one in which members share perceptions and expectations that learning is important on a daily basis. Both transfer climate and continuous learning (aggregated to the group level) predicted transfer behavior.

Both Rouiller and Goldstein (1993) and Tracey et al. (1995) provide support for the relationships between social capital and intellectual capital proposed in Nahapiet and Ghoshal's (1998) model. Culture and climate contain many of the social capital dimensions illustrated in the authors' model, from network ties to shared language, to norms and obligations. Nonetheless, further research is warranted to examine the relationship between an organization's continuous learning culture or climate and other types of intellectual capital.

Holton and colleagues (Holton et al., 1997, 2000, 2003) have focused on the development of a "learning transfer systems inventory" (LTSI) that includes a comprehensive set of personal, training, and organizational factors to enhance transfer. The LTSI comprises sixteen factors which can be grouped into four dimensions: (1) ability (lack of opportunity to use learning; lack of personal capacity to try out learning); (2) motivation (belief that expended effort will change performance; belief that changed performance will lead to valuable outcomes); (3) work environment factors (feedback and performance coaching about learning use; amount of support for learning use; the extent to which supervisors oppose using new knowledge); and (4) secondary influences affecting motivation (self-efficacy and learner readiness). Given the comprehensiveness of the LTSI, this instrument may be particularly well suited for organizational diagnostic purposes.

Because climate and related factors are linked to training effectiveness, research is needed on what actions top-level and mid-level managers can take to create positive climates in their organizations. Future research should examine the impact of specific interventions such as policies (e.g., tuition reimbursement, mandatory hours of training), and reward systems on employees' perceptions of organizational support for training, knowledge and skill acquisition and transfer.

Previous research on specific interventions to support transfer has focused on two general types of post-training supplements. One is goal-setting supplements that aim to promote transfer by focusing trainees on the implementation of training content (Reber & Wallin, 1984; Richman-Hirsch, 2001; Wexley & Baldwin, 1986; Wexley & Nemeroff, 1975). The rationale for utilizing such supplements is that competing demands and interests inhibit transfer, and thus mechanisms are necessary to direct skill application. Goal-setting supplements have addressed the importance of transfer, characteristics of effective goals, and specific implementation priorities. Some goal-setting supplements have been implemented within the classroom (e.g., Richman-Hirsch, 2001), while others have involved meetings with trainers or supervisors after training has been complemented (e.g., Reber & Wallin, 1984; Wexley & Baldwin, 1986; Wexley & Nemeroff, 1975). On the whole, goal-setting supplements have been found to have a favorable impact on transfer beyond the effects of classroom training only.

Self-management training is a second commonly researched supplement to promote transfer. This training is related to goal setting with a focus on the implementation of training content. However, self-management training specifically aims to equip individuals with skills to overcome obstacles to transfer (Marx, 1982; Richman-Hirsch, 2001; Wexley & Baldwin, 1986). Proponents of self-management training assume that trainees will encounter obstacles on the job, such as time pressure or lack of social support, and then relapse into previous patterns of behavior. This training is implemented within the classroom, and it typically focuses on identifying obstacles to transfer, establishing performance maintenance goals, identifying strategies to overcome obstacles, monitoring progress toward goal attainment, and self-administering rewards and punishments. Support for this post-training supplement has been mixed. While some research has demonstrated a post-training impact for self-management training in comparison to classroom training only (e.g., Noe et al., 1990; Tziner et al., 1991); other studies have not (e.g., Burke, 1997; Gaudine & Saks, 2004; Richman-Hirsh, 2001; Wexley & Baldwin, 1986).

The growing body of research on transfer indicates that a variety of different support interventions may have utility in ensuring that skills are successfully applied on the job. However, Yelon and Ford (1999) have argued that one size does not fit all and that research is necessary to develop and validate interventions tailored to specific skill sets and work contexts. Yelon and Ford contend that two key factors be considered in designing transfer enhancement systems. The first of these is task adaptability, the degree of flexibility and variability required for successful performance. This dimension ranges from closed to open tasks. Performing a closed task involves responding to predictable situations with standardized responses. In contrast, performing an open task involves responding to variable stimuli with variable responses. There is one best way to perform closed tasks; whereas performance on open tasks is contingent upon numerous situational variables. The second dimension is the degree of supervision under which training content is applied on the job. Under heavily supervised conditions, supervisors can closely monitor employee performance on trained skills, and can thus provide positive and negative feedback and appropriate rewards. Further, under such conditions, employees may be more apt to engage in appropriate behaviors with the knowledge of close observation. Under autonomous working conditions, however, employees have more discretion whether to engage in trained behaviors and must be more responsible for ensuring that behaviors are appropriately executed.

Yelon and Ford suggest a variety of design elements, individual differences, and work environment factors that vary along the two key dimensions. For example, for training closed tasks, the authors suggest training standardized procedures and attitudes toward compliance, utilizing identical elements, providing standardized checklists, and offering rewards for compliance to standards on the job. Developing meta-cognitive competence and strategic knowledge (knowing when and why to pursue a course of action), teaching general principles, and selecting those with a mastery goal orientation are all suggested for training open tasks. Regarding performing under supervised working conditions, the authors recommend training favorable attitudes toward supervision, training supervisors in training content, and rewarding supervisors for monitoring employee performance on the job. Finally, examples for training skills performed under autonomous working conditions include developing trainee commitment toward performing training content, assessing trainees' transfer intentions, conducting obstacle assessments, developing meta-cognitive competence, and selecting those with a mastery goal orientation. Yelon and Ford's model provides a valuable framework for understanding the conditions under which different individual differences, environmental support factors, and design elements may be relevant in enhancing the effectiveness of training interventions. The authors presented a number of provocative propositions, which are worthy of future research attention. Such research will continue to enhance the theoretical basis for training design.

The majority of research on transfer has been conducted in single organizational contexts. To gain a better perspective on the extent to which transfer of training differs across organizations, Saks and Belcourt (2006) surveyed members of a professional training and development society in Canada. The respondents reported that 62% of employees apply what they learned in training immediately after attending a training program, but that number dropped to 44% after six months and 34% after one year. Unfortunately from a strategic training and development perspective, organizations rarely utilized interventions to support transfer in their training designs. However, organizations that did incorporate transfer enhancements before training (e.g., trainee input and involvement, training attendance policies, and supervisor involvement), during training (e.g., identical elements), and after training (e.g., supervisor and organizational support) reported higher levels of transfer. Given the variability of organizations in instituting transfer enhancements, research is necessary to determine the factors which facilitate or inhibit their adoption.

Evaluation: establishing metrics and demonstrating the strategic value of training and development

The central aim of strategic training and development initiatives is to support business strategy and enhance organizational performance. Thus, systematic evaluation efforts linking training and development to meaningful business outcomes are critical. Kozlowski and Salas (1997) refer to the link between training and development and higher level organizational outcomes as *vertical* transfer, which they distinguish from *horizontal* transfer, the application of knowledge and skills across different settings and contexts. Evaluating the extent to which training and development systems impact organizational outcomes serves to demonstrate their value and illuminates whether modifications to existing systems are necessary to further enhance organizational performance.

Researchers suggest that a collaborative approach between training professionals and business partners is needed to develop an appropriate strategy for demonstrating training–organizational performance linkages (Kraiger et al., 2004; Nickols, 2005; Russ-Eft & Preskill, 2005). Kraiger et al. (2004) suggest that collaborative planning for training impact involves developing a theory of impact (identify relationships between training, training outcomes, and business metrics), reframing the point of evaluation from proof to evidence, isolating the effects of training, and establishing accountability for training in trainees, supervisors, and other key players in the organization. Moreover, Tannenbaum and Woods (1992) present fifteen evaluation designs which vary based on the importance of evaluation, the research design employed, and the training outcomes collected. Tannenbaum and Woods argue that the choice of design be based on a variety of factors, such as the importance of the training for key organizational outcomes related to the business strategy, the expertise available to conduct and analyze a complex study, cost of evaluation, time constraints, and the scale of the training effort.

One key issue in strategic training development and evaluation is identifying appropriate measures of human/intellectual capital for use as independent variables, mediators, moderators, or dependent variables. The American Society for Training and Development (ASTD), in partnership with several companies, identified a set of core intellectual capital measures (see Van Buren, 1999), which may be useful for such purposes. As shown in Table 16.2, these include human capital, innovation capital, process capital, and customer capital. Human capital includes the knowledge, skills, and competencies of employees. Innovation capital is the capability of an organization to develop new products and services. Process capital includes the organization's processes, systems, and tools, particularly as they relate to information technology. Finally, customer capital is the value of the organization's relationship with its customers. In addition, McBassi and Company, a consulting company that helps organizations measure "return on people," utilizes five dimensions for assessing human capital (Bassi & McMurrer, 2004). These five indicators include: (1) leadership and managerial practices (e.g., communications, performance feedback); (2) workforce optimization (e.g., processes for getting work done, good hiring choices); (3) learning capacity (e.g., company's ability to learn, innovate, and improve); (4) knowledge accessibility (e.g., ability to make knowledge and ideas available to employees); and (5) talent engagement (e.g., job design, how employees' time is used).

Table 16.2 Intellectual capital indicators and sample measures

Human capital	Retention of key personnel
	Ability to attract talented people
	▪ information technology literacy
	▪ training expenditures as a percent of payroll
	▪ employee commitment
	▪ employee satisfaction
	▪ replacement costs of key employees
	▪ portfolio of employee skills according to core competencies
	▪ number and quality of external knowledge links
	▪ number of "lessons learned" workshops
Innovation capital	Research and development ependitures
	▪ percentage of workforce involved in innovation
	▪ products introduced in the last three years
Process capital	Processes documented and mapped
	▪ use of documented processes
Customer capital	Customer satisfaction
	Customer retention
	▪ product and service quality
	▪ average length of customer relationship
	▪ repeat orders
	▪ response time to customer queries

Based on Van Buren, M. (1999). A yardstick for knowledge management. *Training & Development, 53*, 71–8; and Sveiby, K. (1997). *The new organizational wealth: Managing and measuring knowledge based assets.* San Francisco, CA: Berrett-Koehler Publishers, Inc.

Researchers and practitioners interested in showing the relationship between training and development interventions and organizational-level outcomes such as revenue or customer satisfaction need to ensure that the level of analysis is considered (e.g., individual training programs versus aggregate training programs), the direct and indirect effects of the intervention on the outcomes is considered, and an appropriate design is used to isolate the effects of training on organizational outcomes (see Kraiger, 2002; Kraiger et al., 2004; Russ–Eft & Preskill, 2005).

In addition to quantitatively assessing the strategic impact of training interventions, other tools can be used to demonstrate that training delivers bottom-line results. The demonstration of *success cases* is one such approach. Success cases refer to concrete examples of how learning leads to worthwhile results for the company and that managers find credible (Brinkerhoff, 2005). Success cases do not attempt to isolate the influence of training but to provide evidence that it was useful. For example, Federated Department Stores wanted to determine the impact for its Leadership Choice program designed to increase sales and profit performance in Federated stores by helping leaders enhance personal effectiveness, develop a customer-focused plan to improve business performance, and recognize the impact of decisions on business result (Wick & Pollock, 2004). Because the managers in the program had a wide range of responsibilities in Federated's different divisions, it was necessary to show that the program produced results for managers with different responsibilities. As a result, it was decided to illustrate the value of the program to management with concrete examples. Keeping in mind Tannenbaum and Woods' (1992) considerations in choosing an evaluation design, it is important to emphasize that story telling was an important part of Federated's culture.

From a research perspective, most evaluation efforts on the strategic impact of training and development activities draw from the SHRM literature which has focused on establishing the relationship between the overall HR system and firm performance (see Becker & Huselid (2006) for the most recent comprehensive review). Research has addressed whether different combinations of HR practices influence firm effectiveness, if the effects are additive or if the effect of any one practice is dependent on other HR practices, and whether the effects of any specific HR practice or HR system depend on contextual factors such as business strategy (Gerhart, 2007). Training and development has been studied in this research as part of a larger HR system or policies (e.g., work design, staffing, performance management, compensation, and employee participation).

A number of studies have examined the role of strategic HR systems (and training practices) in influencing organizational performance. In one of the first published studies in this area, Huselid (1995) found that high-performance work practices were significantly related to turnover, productivity, and financial performance. Delery and Doty (1996), however, found no significant interaction between training or internal career opportunities and business strategy in impacting firm performance in the banking industry. Training and internal career opportunities were unrelated to firm performance. Welbourne and Andrews (1996) found that human resource value which included training (measured by whether training investments were highlighted in a company's prospectus) predicted initial investor reactions and long-term survival of initial public offering companies. Schroeder, Bates, and Junttila (2002) found that competitive advantage in manufacturing was related to use of "internal learning" (e.g., training of multifunctional employees and incorporating employee suggestions into process improvements and product developments) and "external learning" (e.g., establishing problem-solving routines with customers and suppliers). Hayton (2003) found that HR practices that promoted employee discretionary behavior, knowledge sharing, and discretionary learning were positively related to entrepreneurial performance in small and medium firms. Firms in high technology benefited more from use of both "strategic" and "discretionary" HR practices than firms in non-high-technology industries. Discretionary HR practices included investment in socialization and orientation activity, as well as employee participation and empowerment, and incentives.

Overall, based on Combs, Liu, Hall, and Ketchen's (2006) meta-analysis, we can confidently conclude that high-performance work practices are related to organizational performance. Combs et al. (2006) estimated an effect size of .20, providing evidence that the use of high-performance work practices can significantly enhance return on investment and reduce turnover. An examination of individual high-performance work practices indicated that training had a significant relationship with firm performance (effect size = .12). Further, the effect size for the high-performance work practices–performance relationship was almost twice as large for manufacturers as for service organizations. Such practices may be more relevant for manufacturing firms due to the high levels of knowledge and skill required for interacting with complex machinery, control quality, and adapting to constant change.

A number of additional research opportunities are worth pursuing. One avenue for future research is examining the strategic impact of training and development systems with more refined measures. Typically in SHRM research, study participants, typically HR managers or executives, are asked to respond to a few general questions about training practices (see Table 16.3). This approach is appropriate for examining how global HR configurations, practices, or systems relate to different types of employees, strategies, or firm performance. However, the training and development measures which have been utilized do not assess specific information about needs assessment, training methods, evaluation, transfer of training, or training department resources and organization. Further, few if any questions in the SHRM research to date relate to development activities such as mentoring programs, tuition reimbursement, assessment

Table 16.3 Examples of training and development measures used in SHRM research

---

Delery & Doty (1996)

Training
- extensive training programs are provided for individuals in this job
- employees in this job will normally go through training programs every few years
- there are formal training programs to teach new hires the skills they need to perform their jobs
- formal training programs are offered to employees in order to increase their promotability in this organization

Internal career opportunities
- individuals in this job have clear career paths within the organization
- individuals in this job have very little future with the organization
- employees' career aspirations within the company are known by their immediate supervisors
- employees in this job who desire promotion have more than one potential position they could be promoted to

Huselid (1995)

What is the average number of hours of training received by a typical employee over the last twelve months?

Lepak & Snell (2002)

Our training activities for these employees:
- are comprehensive
- are continuous
- emphasize improving current job performance
- emphasize on the job experiences
- focus on compliance with rules, regulations, and procedures
- focus on team building and interpersonal relations
- require extensive investments of time and money
- seek to increase short-term productivity
- strive to develop firm-specific skills/knowledge

Takeuchi, Lepak, Wang, & Takeuchi (2007)
- training is continuous
- training programs are comprehensive
- training programs strive to develop firm-specific skills and knowledge
- the training programs emphasize on-the-job experiences

Wright, Gardner, Moynihan, & Allen (2005)

On average, how many hours of formal training do employees in this job receive each year?

Lepak, Taylor, Tekleab, Marrone, & Cohen (2007)
- training comprehensiveness
- formalization
- use of outside instruction
- use of on-the-job experiences
- focus on increasing current job performance
- increasing short-term productivity

(360-degree feedback), or formal courses such as MBA or certificate programs. While SHRM research suggests that training as part of the bundle of HR practices is related to firm performance, more specific study of training and development systems is needed outside of the context of broader HR system or high-performance work systems.

Development of valid and reliable measures of training and development practices is needed. Researchers need to develop questions that ask appropriate organizational representatives (e.g., trainers and training executives) about strategic training initiatives. Tannenbaum (2002) suggests that leaders in organizations who take a strategic view of training periodically perform an overall strategic assessment of their organizations identifying capability requirements and how training and development is being utilized to meet them. Tannenbaum provides specific questions that would be a useful starting point for developing questions to assess the degree to which an organization has specific learning imperatives and the extent to which they are linked to training and development activities. In addition, seven capabilities identified by Accenture Learning can be utilized to characterize organizations engaged in strategic training and development (Hughes & Beatty, 2005). These capabilities include alignment of learning goals with business goals, measurement of the overall business impact of the learning function, movement of learning outside of the company to include customers, vendors, and suppliers, focus on developing competencies for the most critical jobs, integration of learning with other HR functions, and training delivery including classroom instruction as well as e-learning and design and delivery of leadership development courses. Finally, perceptual survey measures of strategic training and development should be supplemented with more objective measures such as coding the emphasis given to training and development activities in corporate annual reports or using data of actual hours and expenditures spent on training and development.

A second area for future research is to examine more fully the causal direction between strategic training systems and organizational performance outcomes. While it is tempting to conclude that training and other HR practices cause firm performance, the causal direction of the HR–firm performance relationship is still unknown. Wright, Gardner, Moynihan, and Allen (2005) found that HR practices are strongly related to both past and future performance, suggesting that causal inferences about HR practices should be made with caution until studies that gather HR and firm performance data at multiple points in time are conducted.

A third recommendation for research is examining training and development interventions with respect to strategic employees. SHRM scholars have suggested that because HR's strategic impact is contingent on its contribution to the effectiveness of strategic business processes, the value of this impact can be most realized by focusing on strategic jobs or the strategic core of the workforce related to critical business processes (Becker & Huselid, 2006; Cable, 2007; Delery & Doty, 2001; Huselid et al., 2005). A number of questions should be addressed. What makes these jobs strategic, particularly from a knowledge perspective? Do these jobs involve more tacit than explicit knowledge? What training methods are most effective in helping employees in these jobs acquire the tacit knowledge they need? How do training and development practices vary across these jobs? What combination of training and development practices is necessary for these jobs? Answering these questions would be a useful complement to the work of Lepak and Snell (1999, 2002) and Lepak, Taylor, Tekleab, Marrone, and Cohen (2007) who investigated the alignment of HR practices with different occupational groups differing in strategic value and uniqueness.

Fourth, future research should also examine the linkages among training and development interventions, business strategy, and organizational performance, as there have been few studies in this area. One notable example is the work of Raghuram and Arvey (1994). Using Miles and Snow's (1978) generic strategy types (defenders, prospectors, and analyzers), these researchers examined whether the practices of buying versus building skills varied according to business strategy and whether different functional skills were associated with different business strategies. Using data collected from 176 business units across industries, they found that most of the relationships between strategy and training practices were low. The strongest relationship they found was between the prospector strategy and buying new skills. Businesses emphasizing new products or services tended to buy or rely on staffing or selecting employees with the new skills needed rather than building them internally through training. Research is necessary to extend this work by examining additional strategic training practices as well as their influence with additional models of business strategy. Further, research is warranted to identify how factors such as industry capital intensity, growth and differentiation, and other industry, strategic and market factors influence training and development systems and relationships with firm performance (Datta et al., 2005).

A final recommendation for further research is examining the mechanisms by which training and development systems impact organizational performance and how such vertical transfer can be enhanced. Kozlowski and colleagues (1997, 2000) present a multilevel model of training effectiveness which draws on systems theory and emergent processes and discuss how individual outcomes influence higher level outcomes. These issues have not received concrete attention in training and development research and thus merit attention. Kozlowski et al. (2000) pose a number of research questions related to vertical transfer and needs assessment, design and delivery, and evaluation that can serve as a basis for such efforts.

Conclusion

Strategic training and development is important for knowledge creation and sharing and the development of intellectual capital which are the means through which organizations gain and maintain a competitive advantage. Although models of strategic training and development exist in the literature and are advocated for practitioner use, our review suggests that additional research is necessary to validate these models and prescriptions for practice. Research is especially necessary in order to examine how the organization of the training function influences training practices and how these in turn contribute to the business strategy. It is necessary also to investigate the link between specific training practices and organizational-level outcomes of various kinds.. Such work will enhance the strategic training and development knowledge base and ultimately provide a basis for improving organizational effectiveness.

References

Alavi, M., & Leidner, D. (2001). Review: Knowledge management and knowledge management systems: Conceptual foundations and research issues. *MIS Quarterly*, *25*, 107–36.

Baldwin, T., & Ford, J.K. (1988). Transfer of training: A review and directions for future research. *Personnel Psychology*, *41*, 63–105.

Baldwin, T., & Magjuka, R. (1991). Organizational training and signals of performance: Linking pretraining perceptions to intentions to transfer. *Human Resource Development Quarterly*, *2*, 25–36.

Barney, J. (1991). Firm resources and sustained competitive advantage. *Journal of Management*, *17*, 99–120.

Bassi, L., & McMurrer, D. (2004). *What to do when people are your most important asset*. Golden, CO: McBassi & Company.

Bassi, L., Lev, B., Low, J., McMurrer, D., & Siesfeld, G. (2000). Measuring corporate investments in human capital. In M. Blair & T. Kochan (Eds), *The new relationship: Human capital in the American corporation* (pp. 334–82). Washington, DC: Brookings Institute.

Becker, B., & Huselid, M. (2006). Strategic human resources management: Where do we go from here? *Journal of Management*, *32*, 898–925.

Beer, V. (2000). *The web learning fieldbook: Using the worldwide web to build workplace learning environments*. San Francisco, CA: Jossey-Bass.

Brinkerhoff, R. (2005). The success case method: A strategic evaluation approach to increasing the value and effect of training. *Advances in Developing Human Resources*, *7*, 86–101.

Brown, J., & Duguid, P. (1991). Organizational learning and communities of practice: Toward a unified view of working, learning, and innovation. *Organization Science*, *2*, 40–57.

Brown, K., & Van Buren, M. (2007). Applying a social capital perspective to the evaluation of distance training. In S. Fiore & E. Salas (Eds), *Toward a science of distributed learning* (pp. 41–64). Washington, DC: American Psychological Association.

Cable, D. (2007). *Change to strange*. Upper Saddle River, NJ: Wharton School Publishing.

Carliner, S. (2004). Business models for training and performance departments. *Human Resource Development Review*, *3*, 275–93.

Colquitt, J., LePine, J., & Noe, R. (2000). Toward an integrative theory of training motivation: A meta-analytic path analysis of twenty years of research. *Journal of Applied Psychology*, *85*, 678–707.

Combs, J., Liu, Y., Hall, A., & Ketchen, D. (2006). How much do high-performance work practices matter? A meta-analysis of their effects on organizational performance. *Personnel Psychology*, *59*, 501–28.

Cornell, C. (2005). Changing the supply chain. *Human Resource Executive*, *19* (4), 32–5.

Datta, D., Guthrie, J., & Wright, P. (2005). Human resource management and labor productivity: Does industry matter? *Academy of Management Journal*, *48*, 135–45.

Davenport, R. (2005). A new shade of big blue. *T+D*, *59*, 35–40.

Davenport, T., & Prusak, L. (1998). *Working knowledge*. Boston, MA: Harvard University Press.

Delery, J., & Doty, D. (1996). Modes of theorizing in strategic human resource management: Tests of universalistic, contingency, and configurational performance predictions. *Academy of Management Journal*, *39*, 802–35.

DeLong, D., & Fahey, W. (2000). Diagnosing cultural barriers to knowledge management. *Academy of Management Executive*, *14*, 113–27.

Dotlich, D., & Noel, J. (1998) *Action learning: How the world's top companies are re-creating their leaders and themselves*. San Francisco, CA: Jossey-Bass.

Fenn, D. (1999). Corporate universities for small companies. *Inc.*, *21*, 95–6.

Ford, J.K., Quinones, M., Sego, D., & Sorra, J. (1992). Factors affecting the opportunity to perform trained skills on the job. *Personnel Psychology*, *45*, 511–27.

Gainey, T. & Klaas, B. (2003). The outsourcing of training and development: Factors affecting client satisfaction. *Journal of Management*, *29*, 207–29.

Gaudine, A., & Saks, A. (2004). A longitudinal quasi-experiment on the effects of posttraining transfer interventions. *Human Resource Development Quarterly*, *15*, 57–76.

Gerhart, B. (2007). Horizontal and vertical fit in human resource systems. In C. Ostroff & T. Judge (Eds), *Perspectives on organizational fit* (pp. 317–50). New York: Lawrence Erlbaum Associates, Taylor & Francis Group.

Harris, P. (2004). Outsourced training begins to find its niche. *T+D*, *58*, 36–42.

Hayton, J. (2003). Strategic human capital management in SMEs: An empirical study of entrepreneurial performance. *Human Resource Management*, *42*, 375–91.

Holton, E., Bates, R., & Ruona, W. (2000). Development of a generalized learning transfer system inventory. *Human Resource Development Quarterly*, *11*, 333–60.

Holton, E., Chen, J., & Naquin, S. (2003). An examination of learning transfer system characteristics across organizational settings. *Human Resource Development Quarterly*, *14*, 459–82.

Holton, E., Bates, R., Seyler, D., & Carvalho, M. (1997). Toward a construct validation of a transfer climate instrument. *Human Resource Development Quarterly*, *8*, 95–113.

Hughes, R., & Beatty, K. (2005). Five steps to leading strategically. *T+D*, *59*, 46–8.

Huselid, M. (1995). The impact of human resource management practices on turnover, productivity, and corporate financial performance. *Academy of Management Journal*, *38*, 635–72.

Huselid, M., Becker, B., & Beatty, R. (2005). *The workforce scorecard: Managing human capital to execute strategy*. Boston, MA: Harvard Business School Press.

Ipe, M. (2003). Knowledge sharing in organizations: A conceptual framework. *Human Resource Development Review*, *2*, 337–59.

Johnson, G. (2004). To outsource or not to outsource . . . That is the question. *Training*, *41*, 26–9.

Kang, S., Morris, S., & Snell, S. (2007). Relational archetypes, organizational learning, and value creation: Extending the human resource architecture. *Academy of Management Review, 32*, 236–56.

Kaufman, R. (1972). *Educational system planning.* Englewood Cliffs, NJ: Prentice-Hall.

Kaufman, R. (1992). *Strategic planning plus: An organizational guide.* Thousand Oaks, CA: Sage.

Kaufman, R. (1998). *Strategic thinking: A guide to identifying and solving problems.* Arlington, VA: American Society for Training & Development; Washington, DC: International Society for Performance Improvement.

Kozlowski, S., & Salas, E. (1997). A multilevel organizational systems approach for the implementation and transfer of training. In J.K. Ford, S. Kozlowski, K. Kraiger, E. Salas, & M. Teachout (Eds), *Improving training effectiveness in work organizations* (pp. 247–87). Hillsdale, NJ: Erlbaum.

Kozlowski, S., Brown, K., Weissbein, M., Cannon-Bowers, J., & Salas, E. (2000). A multilevel approach to training effectiveness: Enhancing horizontal and vertical transfer. In K. Klein and S. Kozlowski (Eds), *Multilevel theory, research, and methods in organizations* (pp. 157–210). San Francisco, CA: Jossey-Bass.

Kraiger, K. (2002). Decision-based evaluation. In K. Kraiger (Ed.), *Creating, implementing, and managing effective training and development* (pp. 331–75). San Francisco, CA: Jossey-Bass.

Kraiger, K. (2003). Perspectives on training and development. In W. Borman, D. Ilgen, & R. Klimoski (Eds), *Handbook of psychology* (vol. 12, pp. 171–92). Hoboken, NJ: Wiley.

Kraiger, K., & Ford, J.K. (2006). The expanding role of workplace training: Themes and trends influencing training research and practice. In L. Koopes (Ed.), *Historical perspectives in industrial psychology* (pp. 281–309). New Jersey: Erlbaum and Associates.

Kraiger, K., McLinden, D., & Casper, W. (2004). Collaborative planning for training impact. *Human Resource Management, 43*, 337–51.

Leigh, D., Watkins, R., Plat, W., & Kaufmann, R. (2000). Alternate models of needs assessment: Selecting the right one for your organization. *Human Resource Development Quarterly, 11*, 87–93.

Leonard, D., & Sensiper, S. (1998). The role of tacit knowledge in group innovation. *California Management Review, 40*, 112–32.

Lepak, D., & Snell, S. (1999). The human resource architecture: Toward a theory of human capital allocation and development. *Academy of Management Review, 24*, 31–48.

Lepak, D., & Snell, S. (2002). Examining the human resource architecture: The relationships among human capital, employment, and human resource configurations. *Journal of Management, 28*, 517–43.

Lepak, D., Taylor, M., Tekleab, A., Marrone, J., & Cohen, D. (2007). An examination of the use of high-investment human resource systems for core and support employees. *Human Resource Management, 46*, 223–46.

Lievens, F., & Sanchez, J. (2007). Can training improve the quality of inferences made by raters in competency modeling? A quasi-experiment. *Journal of Applied Psychology, 92*, 812–19.

Lievens, F., Sanchez, J., & DeCorte, W. (2004). Easing the inferential leap in competency modeling: The effects of task-related information and subject matter expertise. *Personnel Psychology, 57*, 881–904.

Lucia, A., & Lepsinger, R. (1999). *The art and science of competency models: Pinpointing critical success factors in organizations.* San Francisco, CA: Jossey-Bass/Pfeiffer.

Marquardt, M. (2004). Harnessing the power of action learning, *TD*, June, 26–32.

Martocchio, J., & Baldwin, T. (1997). The evolution of strategic organizational training. In R. G. Ferris (Ed.), *Research in personnel and human resource management* (vol. 15, pp. 1–46). Greenwich, CT: JAI Press.

Marx, R. (1982). Relapse prevention for managerial training: A model for maintenance of behavioral change. *Academy of Management Review, 7*, 433–41.

McCauley, C., & Heslett, S. (2001). Individual development in the workplace. In N. Anderson, D. Ones, H. Sinangil, & C. Viswesvaran (Eds), *Handbook of industrial, work, and organizational psychology* (vol. 1, pp. 313–35). London: Sage Publications.

McCauley, C., Ruderman, M., Ohlott, P., & Morrow, J. (1994). Assessing the development components of managerial jobs. *Journal of Applied Psychology, 79*, 544–60.

Miles, R., & Snow, C. (1978). *Organizational strategy, structure, and process.* New York: McGraw-Hill.

Morgeson, F., Delaney-Klinger, K., Mayfield, M., Ferrara, P., & Campion, M. (2004). Self-presentation processes in job analysis: A field experiment investigating inflation in abilities, tasks, and competencies. *Journal of Applied Psychology, 89*, 674–86.

Morrison, R., & Brantner, T. (1992). What enhances or inhibits learning a new job? A basic career issue. *Journal of Applied Psychology, 77*, 926–40.

Nahapiet, J., & Ghoshal, S. (1998). Social capital, intellectual capital, and the organizational advantage. *Academy of Management Review, 23*, 242–66.

Nelson, R., Whitener, E., & Philcox, H. (1995). The assessment of end-user training needs. *Communications of the Association for Computing Machinery, 38*, 27–39.

Nickols, F. (2005). Why a stakeholder approach to evaluating training. *Advances in Developing Human Resources, 7*, 121–34.

Noe, R. (2008). *Employee training and development*. New York: McGraw-Hill/Irwin.

Noe, R., Sears, J., & Fullenkamp, A. (1990). Relapse training: Does it influence trainees' post-training behavior and cognitive strategies? *Journal of Business and Psychology, 4*, 317–28.

Noe, R.A., & Wilk, S. (1993). Investigation of the factors that influence employees' participation in development activities. *Journal of Applied Psychology, 78*, 291–302.

Nonaka, I., & Takeuchi, H. (1995). *The knowledge-creating company: How Japanese companies create the dynamics of innovation*. New York: Oxford University Press.

Oakes, K. (2005). Grand central training: Part 2. *T+D, 59*, 22–5.

Ostroff, C., & Ford, J.K. (1989). Assessing training needs: Critical levels of analysis. In I. Goldstein (Ed.), *Training and development in organizations* (pp. 25–62). San Francisco, CA: Jossey-Bass.

Polanyi, M. (1969). *Knowing and being*. Chicago, IL: University of Chicago Press.

Quinones, M., Ford, J.K., Sego, D., & Smith, E. (1995). The effects of individual and transfer environment characteristics on the opportunity to perform trained tasks. *Training Research Journal, 1*, 29–48.

Raghuram, S., & Arvey, R. (1994). Business strategy links with staffing and training practices. *Human Resource Planning, 17*, 55–73.

Reber, R., & Wallin, J. (1984). The effects of training, goal-setting, and knowledge of results on safe behavior: A component analysis. *Academy of Management Journal, 27*, 544–60.

Richman-Hirsh, W. (2001). Posttraining interventions to enhance transfer: The moderating effects of work environments. *Human Resource Development Quarterly, 12*, 105–20.

Rossett, A. (1999). Knowledge management meets analysis. *Training & Development, 53*, 62–8.

Rouiller, J., & Goldstein, I. (1993). The relationship between organizational transfer climate and positive transfer of training. *Human Resource Development Quarterly, 4*, 377–90.

Ruggles, R. (1998). The state of the notion: Knowledge management in practice. *California Management Review, 40*, 80–9.

Russ-Eft, D., & Preskill, H. (2005). In search of the holy grail: Return on investment evaluation in human resource development. *Advances in Human Resource Development, 7*, 71–85.

Saks, A., & Belcourt, M. (2006). An investigation of training activities and transfer of training in organizations. *Human Resource Management, 45*, 629–48.

Salas, E., Cannon-Bowers, J., Rhodenizer, L., & Bowers, C. (1999). Training in organizations: Myths, misconceptions, and mistaken assumptions. In G. Ferris (Ed.), *Research in personnel and human resource management* (vol. 17, pp. 123–61). Greenwich, CT: JAI Press.

Sallie-Dosunmu, M. (2006). Born to grow. *TD*, May, 33–7.

Schroeder, R., Bates, K., & Junttila, M. (2002). A resource-based view of manufacturing strategy and the relationship to manufacturing performance. *Strategic Management Journal, 23*, 105–17.

Sena, J., & Shani, A. (1999). Intellectual capital and knowledge creation: Towards an alternative framework. In J. Liebowitz (Ed.), *Knowledge management handbook* (pp. 8.1–8.16). Boca Raton, FL: CRC Press.

Sessa, V., & London, M. (2006). *Continuous learning in organizations*. Mahwah, NJ: Lawrence Erlbaum.

Shippmann, J., Ash, R., Battista, M., Carr, L., Eyde, L., Hesketh, B., Kehoe, J., Pearlman, K., Prien, E., & Sanchez, J. (2000). The practice of competency modeling. *Personnel Psychology, 53*, 703–40.

Starbuck, W. (1992). Learning by knowledge-intensive firms. *Journal of Management Studies, 29*, 713–40.

Takeuchi, R., Lepak, D., Wang, H., & Takeuchi, K. (2007). An empirical examination of the mechanisms mediating between high-performance work systems and the performance of Japanese organizations. *Journal of Applied Psychology, 92*, 1069–83.

Tannenbaum, S. (2002). A strategic view of organizational training and learning. In K. Kraiger (Ed.), *Creating, implementing, and managing effective training and development* (pp. 10–52). San Francisco, CA: Jossey-Bass.

Tannenbaum, S., & Woods, S. (1992). Determining a strategy for evaluating training: Operating within organizational constraints. *Human Resource Planning, 15*, 63–81.

Tobin, D. R. (1998). *The knowledge-enabled organization*. New York: AMACOM.

Tracey, J., Tannenbaum, S., & Kavanagh, M. (1995). Applying trained skills on the job: The importance of the work environment. *Journal of Applied Psychology, 80*, 239–52.

Training (2005). Corporate University Exchange website at www.corpu.com.

Tziner, A., Haccoun, R., & Kadish, A. (1991). Personal and situational characteristics influencing the effectiveness of transfer of training improvement strategies. *Journal of Occupational Psychology, 64*, 167–77.

Van Buren, M. (1999). A yardstick for knowledge management. *Training & Development, 53*, 71–8.

Wasko, M., & Faraj, S. (2005). Why should I share? Examining social capital and knowledge contribution in electronic networks of practice. *MIS Quarterly, 29*, 35–57.

Welbourne, T., & Andrews, A. (1996). Predicting the performance of initial public offerings: Should human resource management be in the equation? *Academy of Management Journal, 39*, 891–919.

Wexley, K., & Baldwin, T. (1986). Post-training strategies for facilitating positive transfer: An empirical exploration. *Academy of Management Journal, 29*, 508–20.

Wexley, K., & Nemeroff, W. (1975). Effectiveness of positive reinforcement and goal-setting as methods of management development. *Journal of Applied Psychology, 60*, 446–50.

Wick, C., & Pollock, R. (2004). Making results visible. *T+D, 58*, 46–50.

Williams, R., & Cothrel, J. (2000). Four smart ways to run online communities. *Sloan Management Review, 41*, 81–91.

Witkin, B., & Altschuld, J. (1995). *Planning and conducting needs assessments: A practical guide*. Thousand Oaks, CA: Sage.

Wright, P., Gardner, T., Moynihan, L., & Allen, M. (2005). The relationship between HR practices and firm performance: Examining causal order. *Personnel Psychology, 58*, 409–46.

Yelon, S.L., & Ford, J.K. (1999). Pursuing a multidimensional view of transfer. *Performance Improvement Quarterly, 12*, 58–78.

17

Collaborative teams

Lynda Gratton and Tamara J. Erickson

All over the world one of the powerhouses of organizational productivity and innovation is teams of people working collaboratively on complex tasks.[1] Over the last decade the study of these collaborative teams has been at the centre of our research.[2] In this chapter we show why collaboration is so crucial by describing some of the tasks faced by the teams we have studied, and the extent of the challenges these teams are confronted with as they execute these tasks.

It is clear that collaboration across and within complex teams is both crucial to business success – and yet at the same time, very difficult. In this chapter we focus on these difficulties by identifying the actions based on 'good practice' that can be taken to ensure that – however difficult the task and complex the team – it is possible for complex teams to be both productive and innovative. When considering these aspects of 'good practice', we distinguish between good practice based on actions which many companies can take, and those actions – which we term 'signature processes' – that are difficult to replicate, being unique to a company and the result of a specific context, culture and executive attitudes.

To get a flavour of what work contemporary teams are currently engaged with, consider these five examples taken from our recent study of 55 teams from 15 multinational companies. Each of these examples highlights the extent and frequency with which corporations are faced with challenges that can only be met by teams prepared to collaborate with each other.

- For example, when the executives of the Royal Bank of Scotland are planning an acquisition, they do so by creating large task forces of specialists whom they rapidly bring together from across the businesses across the company. These task forces are required to work on the acquisition strategy of the corporation; during this period they are working under intense time pressure.
- This pressure is also apparent in the consultancy practice PwC. The practice services the needs of its many multinational clients by creating chains of consultants often spread across multiple locations. These networks of consultants are required to both work closely with each other, and with client organizations. As we discovered when we studied these teams, an extra complexity to these teams is that many of the members are highly educated and come from different specializations.

■ The sheer size of teams was very apparent as we studied the BBC. This corporation regularly pulls together teams of specialists to cover events such as the World Cup or the Olympics. In order to meet the needs of the scale of the task, these teams are large, and made up of a wide variety of specialists, many of whom have not met prior to the project. Like the RBS acquisition task forces, these teams work under the highly charged pressures of a 'no-retakes' environment – everything must be captured successfully the first time.

■ This scale is clear in the teams we studied at Nokia. Here the collaborative agenda is further complicated by the extent to which Nokia teams are collaborating with teams from the company's many partnerships and joint ventures.

■ The virtual nature of many of the teams we observed was very apparent in the news agency Reuters. Here executives frequently create teams to look at emerging world events. When this happens, almost all the members of the team are working virtually from different places. Yet, despite this virtual working, when delivering major news stories, perspectives have to be shared and synthesized, and meaning derived through rapid collaboration.

These five team stories are a snapshot of the many teams we have studied over the last five years. Each is unique in its scope and membership. However, beyond this uniqueness it is possible to see that there are emerging trends in the context in which these teams operate that make collaboration ever more crucial to organizational success.

Why collaboration is increasingly crucial

These teams represent a growing organizational phenomenon – that the value held within a company is vested in both skilled and competent individuals – and in the networks and relationships that bind these individuals together. We believe that this shift from individual to collective value will continue and even increase as a result of a number of intersecting trends.

The rise of strategies of partnership

The first trend is the fundamental changes around what constitutes good business strategy and wise strategic positioning. Over the last decade it is becoming increasingly clear that executives and their businesses are not in fact competing for a piece of finite cake. Instead they are interested in making a bigger cake. In the jargon of business strategy, the emphasis is less on 'value appropriation' and more on 'value creation' often in the context of co-creation.[3] Markets can be created – but to do so often requires erstwhile competitors, customers and clients working together in partnerships. This was first apparent in the pharmaceutical industry that had for decades created and marketed its products through alliances and joint ventures that allowed companies to pull together the breadth of talent and experience required to bring blockbuster drugs to the market. Working with partners has required this sector to hone their partnership skills and build their collaborative capabilities. These patterns of collaborative working are now apparent in the telecom sectors and IT. As we saw with Nokia, it is becoming increasingly untenable for these companies to 'go it alone'. The alliances and partnerships they are rapidly developing require their managers to develop the capacity to work collaboratively with a range of stakeholders including suppliers and consumers.[4]

The emergence of the knowledge economy

The second trend is the rapid move into the knowledge economy and the focus on innovation of products or services. Research into the history of innovation shows clearly that in the majority of cases, innovations arise as the result of the collective experience and conversations of groups of people.[5] It is in this combination of ideas and insights that innovation is borne. Yet, and here is the real issue, people do not willingly work with each other and share knowledge unless they respect and trust each other. Simply put, innovation is unlikely to occur without some degree of a collaborative culture.

The working styles of GenY

These first two trends are about the business environment. The third trend that influences the extent to which collaboration is crucial and possible is the subtle but profound generational changes that are emerging. To understand these subtle changes let's step back for a moment and think about the basic attitudes and values of many of today's CEOs and senior executives, many of whom are 'baby boomers'. These postwar 'baby boomers' entered a world of competition and individual endeavour. Typically they had to battle to get a university education, to get a job and to make it in a career. Competition was the name of the game and they honed their competitive skills and practices as they rose through the corporate hierarchy.

These generational cohorts are now in their late forties and fifties. They may still have their hands on the corporate steering wheel – but coming up after them are two generations with very different attitudes. Coming up behind them are Gen Xs and Gen Ys. Both of these generation cohorts are more collaborative – and GenY (now up to age 27) is particularly adept at collaborating with others. This is a community-based generation who place enormous value on working with their peers and shy away from the individual competitive nature that marked many 'baby boomers'. So, as the power of the 'baby boomers' and their competitive style begins to wane, so we might expect a more finely tuned collaborative style to occur – championed by GenYs – for whom collaboration is a basic attitude and competency, and for whom collaborative technology is second nature.[6]

Advances in collaborative technology

The final trend is technological. In the five examples described earlier, for many of these teams the collaboration they are involved in relies on advanced technology to support their interactions.[7] For example, the virtual teams at Nokia and Reuters rely on asynchronous communication technology such as voice mail, e-mail, text messaging, and blogs to keep co-ordinated on the tasks they are engaged with. Technology has made possible what demography has made plausible – a wired-up generation for whom communities is central.

Thinking back to our opening team examples, it is clear that these complex collaborative teams are created with the expectation that the extent and breadth of experience within the team enables the team to address the complex task at hand. The design assumption is that this combination of skills and insights creates greater insight and opportunity for innovation than might be possible with a small group, or with individuals working alone.

For these complex teams to deliver to this promise they need to be able to rapidly and openly share knowledge with each other and with those outside the task team; to be prepared to volunteer to help each other to balance their workload; to be flexible about switching responsibilities; to be prepared to help each other complete jobs and deadlines, and to actively share their sources and information.

Collaborative challenges and risks

And here is the challenge. For whilst business strategies, generational values, and technological advances are allowing the emergence of teams to work on difficult and challenging tasks – the very nature of these teams makes productivity and innovation a low probability event. There are real challenges and risks involved with these complex teams.

The extent of this challenge was brought home to us in our study of 55 of these complex collaborative teams. When we looked at their productivity and innovative capacity we found that some of these teams failed to deliver on expectations. We discovered that there are five characteristics associated with complex teams that – though necessary in the fundamental performance of the task – paradoxically often work against the team achieving the desired levels of cooperation and innovation. These five characteristics, without carefully designed counter-balancing approaches, have within them the possibility of dysfunctionality and rapid degrading of performance. Let us take a look at each of these five characteristics and then explore the counterbalancing approaches.

Challenge #1: Teams are becoming ever larger

As we saw in the opening examples, the reality of today's complex tasks is that they often involve large numbers of people working collaboratively to solve. So whilst a decade ago the commonly accepted view of teams was that true teams rarely had more than 20 members, our research shows that many of today's teams are significantly larger. In fact in both Nokia and PwC we saw teams with over 100 members. These large teams are often formed to ensure that a wide stakeholder group is consulted and involved, diverse sets of activities are coordinated, and multiple skills are leveraged. However, our research shows that as the size of the team increases from a baseline of about 20 members, so the level of natural cooperation between members of the team decreases.

The risk: As teams become larger, so the proportion of strangers increases and the relationships that hold the network together are put under greater strain. The risk is that the team fractures into subgroups that fail to share knowledge across the boundaries.[8]

Challenge #2: Teams are often more virtual

Many of the teams presented at the beginning of this chapter involve people working at a distance from each other. Again, the logic is that the tasks they are engaged with require the insights and knowledge from people in many different locations. Virtual working can range from simply working in offices in the same city, to working in offices strung across the world. While 40% of the teams in our sample were co-located in one physical location, the remainder were spread in multiple locations.

Our research shows that the extent of a collaborative culture declines as teams become more virtual. Simply put – it is easier to be collaborative with someone down the corridor, than someone on the other side of the world. Decades of social science research have revealed the power of proximity.[9] Long-term friendships are often forged with people who had adjacent rooms in college, and proximity is a powerful indicator of who married whom. When people spend time together, particularly in informal settings, they begin to understand and like each other and they develop a number of social norms that serve to lubricate their interactions and to develop trust. Without the power of proximity, virtual teams are continuously in danger of breaking up through misunderstanding and lack of trust.

The risk: As teams become more virtual, so the number of strangers increases, and with diversity, so too decreases the extent of a shared mindset. The risk is that team members fail to trust each other sufficiently to work productively together.

Challenge #3: Teams are increasingly made up of strangers

Large and virtual teams have to work particularly hard to cooperate because the chances are many of the members were strangers when the teams were created. This meeting of strangers is exacerbated by the often rapid assembly of teams of people many of whom have rarely, if ever, met each other. The diverse insights and views from people who have not worked closely together in the past can create sparks of insight and innovation. However, our research shows that the higher the proportion of strangers in the team and the greater diversity, the less likely the team is to share knowledge with each other. With lack of proximity also comes inevitably an increase in the proportion of strangers in the team.

This can be a real disadvantage. Typically in a team where some members are already acquainted with each other, these 'heritage relationships' serve as points of triangulation whereby the networks between two people rapidly evolve to triangles where a third person is introduced. These triangles of relationships are crucial to the development of wider networks across the company. However, without these heritage relationships to fuel this process, virtual teams are in danger of remaining a collection of strangers without the networks and relationships to enable them to relate to each other.

The risk: Cooperation is easier between people who know each other – and more challenging between people who are strangers. The risk is that these strangers fail to trust each other, fail to share knowledge and instead develop conflicts with each other.

Challenge #4: Teams span the world

Complex teams frequently work across time zones. We found that co-located teams abound with shorthand ways of keeping in touch and coordinating their activity; 'let's meet for coffee', 'see you at five' are all simple coordination practices. But what does 'coffee time' mean when one person is in Delhi, another is in New York, and a third in London?

And finally, since complex teams often include members of different nationalities, they face all the potential challenges of cultural misunderstanding. Our research abounded with examples of cross-cultural misunderstanding. In fact even the research team itself, consisting of German, Lithuanian, British and American scholars, ran temporarily aground when one of the American team wrote that they 'quite liked' the first draft of one of the reports. High praise in the USA, but a sign of disapproval in the UK. It took over a week of conversation to clear up what on the face of it is a simple word difference.

Challenge #5: Team members are often highly educated specialists

The potential value created in complex collaborative teams often arises from the combination and synthesis of specialist knowledge and a variety of skills that together create new products and insights.[10] Again, our research shows that whilst these teams of highly educated specialists can indeed bring value, the higher the proportion of highly educated specialists, the more likely the team is to disintegrate into non-productive conflict.[11]

The risk: Highly educated specialists have developed their own heuristics and ways of seeing and describing their world. So when confronted by other specialists, it can be difficult

289

to build a shared understanding. The risk is that each specialist group creates boundaries around each other which become barriers. These barriers stop any innovation based on synthesis occurring.[12]

To summarize, the competitive environment is increasingly pushing executives towards creating teams of people that are large, virtual, diverse and highly educated. However, our research shows that while these very characteristics can be essential to driving the innovation of these teams and their ultimate ability to perform complex tasks well, paradoxically, they are also likely to sub-optimize the effectiveness of these very same teams unless carefully managed. There are real risks to creating these teams. However, it is possible to carefully develop counter-balancing approaches that enable the promises of complex teams to be delivered. Let us take a look at what these counterbalancing approaches may be.

Investing in counterbalancing the risks

The challenge and the risks are clear. So how can executives build the organization's capacity to perform complex collaborative tasks – to ensure that they maximize the effectiveness and innovation of these teams – whilst minimizing the disadvantages posed by their structure and composition? What might be these counterbalancing approaches?

To answer this question we looked carefully at the 55 teams in our research sample and considered those where the most challenging characteristics (large, virtual, diverse, specialists) had nonetheless resulted in performance and innovation.

Our interest was in looking at those factors that executives could potentially lever to ensure that the teams they had created to address complex collaborative tasks resulted in performance and innovation. We examined a wide range of possible factors affecting team performance, including:

- *The general culture of the company*: We designed a wide range of survey questions to measure the extent to which the team had a cooperative culture and their attitudes to knowledge sharing.
- *Human resource practices and processes*: We studied the way staffing took place and the process by which people were promoted. We measured the extent and type of training and the way in which the reward systems were configured, and we examined the extent to which mentoring and coaching took place,
- *The socialization and network-building practices*: We measured how often people within the team participated in informal socialization, and the type of socialization that was most common. We also asked a wide range of questions about the extent to which team members participated in and were active in informal communities of practice.
- *The design of the task*: We asked team members and team leaders about the actual task itself. Our interest here was in how they perceived the purpose of the task, how complex it was, the extent to which the task required members of the team to be interdependent, and the extent to which the task required members of the team to engage in boundary-spanning activities with those outside of the team.
- *The leadership of the team*: We studied the perceptions team members had of their leader's style, and how the leaders described their own style. In particular we were interested in the extent to which the leader practised relationship-orientated and task-orientated competences, and the extent to which they set cooperative or competitive goals.
- *The behaviour of the senior executive*: We asked team members and the team leaders to comment on their perceptions of the senior executives of the business unit of which

the team was a part. In particular we were interested in whether senior executive behaviour and the way the senior team worked together were described by team members as cooperative or competitive.

In total we considered more than 100 factors. Using a range of statistical analyses, we were able to discover which of the 100 factors actually impacted on the performance and perceived innovation of the team.

In our study of complex teams that were productive and innovative we identified the following conditions that counterbalanced the risk of complexity. These factors are crucial in the design and operation of high-performing complex teams:

- *Leadership role modelling*: Employees are unlikely to behave collaboratively and to value collaboration if they see senior executives competing with each other. Later we will see how leaders at Standard Chartered Bank demonstrate over and over again that they operate a team – a practice that sends a strong cue to the rest of the company about team behaviour.
- There are a number of *people practices* that appear to support a culture of collaboration, in particular, selecting for collaborative attitudes and induction are particularly important. Later we see how the induction process at Nokia encourages people to build wide collaborative relationships. Another key people practice concerns career development practices, such as those at BP, that encourage people to build broad and cooperative networks.
- Collaboration is more likely to take place when people also collaborate in more *informal ways* – for example, through shared social activities, communities of practice or social enterprise activities.
- Leaders who are able to be both *task and relationship orientated* are particularly adept at counterbalancing the risks of complexity. In fact, the two styles, rather than being mutually exclusive, are both found in successful team leaders.

There are also a number of choices that can be made about the design and membership of teams that can reduce the risks.

- *Co-location*: There are many advantages of co-locating teams for whom cooperation is crucial. For the complex teams at Royal Bank of Scotland, co-location in the Edinburgh headquarters significantly increases their capacity to work cooperatively together.
- *Building on heritage relationships*: One of the ways that the risks of complexity can be reduced is by ensuring that within the network there are heritage relationships that can fuel and support the rapid development of relationships – something that Nokia has been particularly skilled at.

These enablers together create a culture where the probability of collaboration is increased. However, for collaboration to be productive, there needs to be a focus on the competencies of people and the task itself:

- The *general skills* of appreciating others' diversity, managing conflict and commitments are crucial to productive collaboration.
- The *task itself* is important. Tasks that encourage collaboration are complex, ambiguous and meaningful and require people to collaborate if the goal is to be achieved. As we shall see at Nokia and BP, tasks that are strong in purpose are crucial to creating a focus for the potential energy within a complex team.

291

Shaping 'signature' collaborative practices

In the high-performing complex teams we studied, we discovered that the executive team had made a significant investment in creating counterbalances that ensured the formation and maintenance of high-quality relationships throughout the business. They used a combination of these counterbalances to ensure that they reduced the risks of complex teams.

We discovered that whilst each company had made this significant investment, the manner in which they did so was unique to each. The best had a practice that was unique to them – and in a sense represented what we call a 'signature' that was both memorable and difficult for others to replicate.[13] Yet whilst each had their own signature, what they all had in common was the depth and quality of these investments. Let us see how RBS, BP, Standard Chartered Bank and Nokia have reduced the risk of complex teams by creating a 'signature' collaborative process using one or more of the counterbalances described earlier.

1. Reducing risks through co-location

In 2005 the CEO of RBS, Fred Goodwin, made a £350 million investment in moving the many separate businesses of RBS from offices across Scotland into a new headquarters outside of Edinburgh.

Built around an indoor atrium (important in the chilly climate of Scotland), over 3,000 people daily rub shoulders with each other. Many of the offices are open plan and look over the central atrium. The main floor is an arcade of shops, serving virtually any and all employee needs – essentially a private 'main street' running through the building. Multiple coffee shops, mobile phone vendors, restaurants, drycleaners, and numerous other retail shops ensure that most employees stay on the campus throughout the day – and out of their offices mingling with colleagues for at least a portion of it. So that even if people are not meeting, they can see each other go about their daily business.

This configuration is not simply an architect's dream. When CEO Fred Goodwin made the investments to move all the disparate parts of RBS into a single site, the impact on productive collaboration was one of his driving concerns. He reinforced this by commissioning an adjoining 70-bedroom Business School where staff from across the world could meet and learn. The result of this productive collaboration is that knowledge flows easily across the members of the community, and strangers meet as they share a cup of coffee or take their clothes in to be drycleaned. Proximity, daily contact, and the rapid assimilation of strangers – all elements we know drive collaboration. So whilst the teams at RBS are very large, the potential negative of this has been reduced by ensuring that they work together either in the headquarters, or through the programs in the Business School.

The RBS teams we studied, all of which were based primarily in the Gogarburn facility, had some of the highest levels of cooperation among any of the teams we studied. This cooperative working was unquestionably facilitated by the personal relationships that have formed over many years among the employees. For these teams, the physical headquarters is a significant and powerful investment in reinforcing the development of social relationships.

2. Reducing risks by investing in career development to build cooperative relationships

Like RBS, the senior team and the corporate staff of BP are located in a single open plan office in London's Finsbury Square. BP's then-CEO, John Browne, made a call on this significant investment. However, the collaborative challenge that BP faces is that, with employees located all over the world, only a relatively small proportion can be located in Finsbury Square.

In order to create networks of relationship at BP, another sort of signature investment was required. In this case it was the investment that the senior team made in supporting career development planning that encourages people to move across functions, businesses and countries.[14]

BP's corporate evolution is through a conglomerate of numerous smaller oil companies – BP, Amoco, Castro, Arco and others. Between 1998 and 2002, BP assimilated a large number of formerly independent firms. Through the M&A phase, the leadership development committee of BP invested in deliberately and methodically migrating employees from the various acquired companies throughout the corporation, both from business to business and internationally. Whilst the easier call would have been to leave the executives in their own companies, they chose instead to support them through training and coaching to take on new roles outside their immediate area of competency and knowledge. As a consequence of this heritage of investing in building networks of social relationships, today, any senior team is likely to be made up of people from a variety of heritages. This significant migration of people, with movement typically every two to three years, has created a highly collaborative culture. Changing roles frequently – it would not be uncommon for a senior leader to have been in four different businesses and three different geographic locations over the past decade – necessitates becoming very good at talking to strangers and rapidly forming cooperative relationships with a diverse group of people.

The clear implication of our research is that executives must create an environment that provides the opportunity for people to develop trusting personal relationships – whether through physical proximity or processes that ensure broad exposure and frequent personal interaction. Our research shows that this can take different forms – from investing in physical location, as RBS has done, to investing in the formal processes at BP. Executives in both companies know that networks of relationships are crucial, and have been prepared to make a significant investment in these high-quality networks.

3. Reducing risks through executive 'job sharing' as a role model of senior collaboration

Standard Chartered Bank also has strong executive role models of cooperation, emanating, many believe, from the firm's global trading heritage. Chartered Bank received its remit from Queen Victoria in 1853, with the goal of supporting the emerging trade routes to the East. The bank's traditional business was in cotton from Mumbai (Bombay), indigo and tea from Calcutta, rice from Burma, sugar from Java, tobacco from Sumatra, hemp from Manila and silk from Yokohama. The Standard Bank was founded in the Cape Province of South Africa in 1862 and was prominent in financing the development of the diamond fields of Kimberley and later the gold mines in Johannesburg. Today, the bank has 57 operating groups in 57 countries, with no home market. Although the bank is officially headquartered in London, the bank's current footprint is predominantly Asia, Africa and the Middle East. Diversity lies at the heart of the bank's values.

Standard Chartered occupies a unique niche in the banking world. As a major participant in consumer and retail banking, the organization is positioned between the large global-scale players Citibank and HSBC and a host of rapidly growing local players. The bank competes by leveraging its historic pioneering spirit into agility and speed. Today's organization is highly matrixed, with strong functional and geographic roles, and an informal culture that favours direct peer-to-peer decision-making.

Given this history, the culture of collaboration pervades and is reinforced by the behaviours of the senior team. One of the most unique aspects of this behaviour is that the collaborative role modelling extends to the acceptance that members of the General Management Committee will frequently substitute for each other. It's accepted that the executives all know and understand the entire business, and can fill in for each other easily on almost any task – comfortable that they will behave in a way that is acceptable to the person they are substituting for.

Whilst the behaviour of the executive team is crucial to supporting the development of a culture of collaboration – the challenge for any executive is to create situations when their behaviour can be observed. At SCB the executive team travel extensively; the norm is to travel even for relatively brief face-to-face meetings. This creates many opportunities for people across the company to see the executive team in action. Internal communication is frequent and open and, maybe most telling, every site around the world is filled with photos of groups of executives – country and functional leaders working together.

At SCB, the stories about the collaborative behaviour of the top team, the photos of them working together across the world, and their capacity to substitute for each other all create a cohesive vision of a senior team able to work effectively on complex collaborative tasks.

The role model set by senior executives reinforces the importance of developing collaborative relationships across the company. For example, there is recognition in the bank that there is no obvious formal way to get most specific tasks done. The optimum approach is seldom reflected in formal charts. Rather, employees quickly learn that the way to succeed is to go through the informal network. It's essential to have fast access to 'who's who'. The culture favours those with high responsibility (people who would never say 'we have to look at this' but then fail to follow up) and high relational skills.

Our study results clearly show that executive teams with dysfunctional, aggressive and competitive behaviour send out strong messages about what is acceptable. The legitimization of non-collaboration that comes from this significantly decreases the probability that teams in the company will collaborate effectively on complex tasks.

The implication is that senior executives must be coached to understand the impact their behaviour has. Collaboration starts from the top – so, a broad range of symbolic collaborative acts (such as the senior team group photos) and collaborative stories are needed to reinforce a culture of collaboration.

4. Reducing risks through mentoring

At Nokia establishing possible coaching and mentoring relationships begins as soon as someone takes a new job. When a new employee comes aboard, managers typically work with the newcomer on a simple exercise. The manager sits down with the new member and lists all the people in the organization, no matter in which location, which it would be useful for the newcomer to meet. The manager raises what topics the newcomer should discuss with each and why establishing a relationship with each person is likely to be of future importance. The newcomer will then set up meetings, including making arrangements to incorporate visits into other travel as appropriate. The manager will systematically follow up, asking: 'Have you met this person, what did you get out of it, what did you learn, and what do you think?'

This is not a formal practice, but rather more a habit that has just evolved within Nokia, probably from a time when Nokia was a smaller and simpler organization and self-organizing was common. People frequently approached new challenges by asking, 'Who can help with this?' You would be invited to join in. If you accepted the invitation, you would become part of a new set of relationships. As a result, establishing your network, understanding who does what, who can be of importance for you, and how you can be important to them is in the Nokia DNA. As people told us: 'It's just something you do. You share your network. And you encourage the newcomer to develop his or hers.'

5. *Reducing risks by building on heritage relationships*

Complex teams are much more likely to be productive and innovative if they contain a relatively small proportion of people who are motivated to build the networks between the members. Without this motivation the team is destined to remain a group of strangers. Typically the motivation to introduce people to each other comes from two sources. In some cases the networks within the team were rapidly expanded because there were some 'heritage relationships' that had existed prior to the formation of the team. In many cases these people with heritage relationships introduced their old acquaintances to new acquaintances and by doing so rapidly expanded who knows whom.

The other source of motivation to build networks is the presence within the virtual team of what I call 'boundary spanners'. These are people who as a result of their personality and skills, or their past experience of working in multiple functions and businesses, are particularly well placed to introduce people to each other. These 'boundary spanners' are a crucial source of glue in complex teams – particularly those that are working virtually. For example, in one of the most successful virtual teams we studied, a skilful boundary spanner had regular brunches in which she made a point of introducing the people she had worked with across her varied career – to the current members of the virtual team. By doing so she created much deeper knowledge of who knows what and had kickstarted the development of trust.

Some companies place a significant emphasis on encouraging boundary spanners. At Nokia, for example, there is a significant focus on supporting activities that enable people to gain cross-functional and cross-boundary work experience. A huge range of routines, practices and processes support and encourage employees to expand their networks. Some of these establish external links, for example, to over 100 university faculties; others are internal routines, like formally introducing new hires to at least ten people from within and across the teams; to practices such as every six months bringing volunteers together from across the company to work on crucial business questions. The executive team at Nokia also encourages boundary spanners by placing a premium on executives who have taken the risk to move outside their initial skill and function. For example, a recent head of manufacturing for the company had been in a factory only a couple of times prior to taking the post. Importantly though, the senior team at Nokia reduce these potential risks by systematically creating strong mentoring relationships between new hires and old hands.

6. *Reducing risks by creating purposeful tasks*

One of the most common reasons why complex teams working in a virtual environment fail is because they don't have anything interesting to do with each other. They simply fade away, with fewer and fewer team members dialing into the weekly conference calls, and fewer and fewer ideas being posted on the shared site. It is not that the team doesn't like each other, it is simply that it has become more like a 'country club' than a dynamic collection of inspired people.

We found that when teams really buzz it is because they are ignited by a question or a task that is so compelling and exciting that people from across the company are drawn towards it. This was clear, for example, at BP when over a decade ago CEO John Browne asked the whole community how BP could become what he termed 'a force for good'. This igniting question – at a time when oil companies were not seen as 'forces for good' – sparked a whole host of virtual teams to gather around the question. For example, one team of young people, the self-styled 'Ignite team', looked at the whole sustainability agenda. It was their energy and focus that resulted in BP's early commitment to the sustainability agenda.

The exciting question is an important element of successful team working. However, to be sustainable, the task of the team must also have meaning for each individual team member. Virtual team working often takes place unsupervised and with minimum leadership; without personal meaning virtual team working can simply disintegrate under the sheer weight of disinterest.

Conclusions: developing a collaborative signature

Across the world executives are putting together complex teams in order to perform tasks that require insight and innovation. Inevitably these complex teams have risks associated with them since they are large, often virtual, may contain many strangers, and have sub-groups of specialists. However, as we have seen, there are ways to reduce these risks. We have found that executives often reduce these risks by focusing on one or more practices and processes that they believe to be important and resonate with their values. The development of these 'collaborative signatures' can be a crucial part of reducing risk. When executives are developing these signatures we have found that there are four choices executives can take that will make a significant impact on the probability of complex collaborative tasks being successfully completed.

1. They can decide the extent to which they themselves are prepared and able to become a 'cooperative architect' through their collaborative behaviours and the collaborative practices – such as mentoring and coaching – they personally support.
2. They can make a choice to focus on, resource and champion one or more of a range of possible HR practices available to them, such as induction and career development.
3. They can develop a point of view on how team leaders are selected and developed and how they perform as team leaders.
4. They can make choices around the structuring of the task and the manner in which it is resourced.

By thoughtfully considering each of these choices, executives have the possibility of reducing the potential risks of complex teams. Understanding the potential levers or cooperation while creating signature processes can be the basis for building high-performance complex teams.

The research

The work is based on a major research initiative conducted jointly by The Concours Institute and the Cooperative Research Project of London Business School, based on funding received from the Advanced Institute for Management Research and 15 global corporate sponsors. The initiative was created as a way to explore the reality of cooperative working in contemporary organizations. The objectives were to identify pragmatic approaches to support successful collaborative working, while modelling how the norms of cooperation develop.

The results described in this summary are based on data collected through an extensive, academically valid survey, administered to individuals in 55 work teams in 15 European and American global corporations. Selected work teams had tasks related to the development of new products, process reengineering, or other tasks that require the identification of new solutions to business problems. These companies included four telecommunication companies, eight companies from the financial services or consulting sectors, two media or advertising companies, and one oil company. The size of the teams ranged from four to 183 people, with an average of 43 team members.

We administered surveys to 2,420 team members; a total of 1,543 responded, giving a response rate of 64%. Separate surveys were administered to group members, to group leaders, to the group's evaluating executive(s), and to the group's associated HR leader. Through this comprehensive approach, we have developed an extraordinary body of data on this complex subject.

Notes

1 The way in which teams collaborate with each other is increasingly seen as central to their effectiveness. An overview of this argument is provided by Alper, S., Tjosvold, D., and Law, K.S. (1998). 'Interdependence and Controversy in Group Decision Making: Antecedents to Effective Self-Managing Teams.' *Organizational Behavior and Human Decision Processes*, 74: 33–52.

2 This research at the London Business School was made possible by a Fellowship from the Advanced Institute of Management – a part of the UK's Economic and Social Science Research Council. The research was carried out by a team that included Dr Janine Nahapiet, Dr Anne-Katrina Neyer, Dr Modestas Gelbudas and Andreas Voigt. The team also had an important partnership with the Concours Institute, directed by Tamara Erickson.

3 The creation of innovation through the combination of elements is central to our understanding of innovation. For an overview of this, see, for example: Nahapiet, J., and Ghoshal, S. (1998) 'Social Capital, Intellectual Capital, and the Organizational Advantage.' *Academy of Management Review*, 23: 242–66. For an overview of the changing nature of strategic intent, see, for example, Mintzberg, H. (1994). *The Rise and Fall of Strategic Planning*. New York: Prentice Hall. Knowledge sharing has been argued to be central to the innovative capacity of a company. A number of important insights have been made about this – see, for example, Nonaka, I., and Takeuchi, H. (1995). *The Knowledge-creating Company*. New York: Oxford University Press.

4 The impact of the horizontal structures was described by Galbraith, J. (1973). *Designing Complex Organizations*. Reading, MA: Addison-Wesley. A more detailed description of such horizontal mechanisms has been provided by Bartlett, C.A., and Ghoshal, S. (1988). *Managing Across Borders: The Transnational Solution*. Boston: The Harvard Business School Press.

5 That high-quality relationships are a conduit for business to be done is the starting assumption of Adler, P., and Kwon, S.W. (2002). 'Social Capital: Prospects for a New Concept.' *Academy of Management Review*, 27: 17–40, and is described in depth in Cross, R., and Parker, P. (2004). *The Hidden Power of Social Networks: Understanding How Work Really Gets Done in Organisations*. Boston: Harvard Business School Press.

6 Tamara Erickson has shown clearly the impact of the generational cohorts on the world of work. See, for example, *Workforce Crisis: How to Beat the Coming Shortage of Skills and Talent*. Boston: Harvard Business School Press, 2006, or catch her blog at Harvard Business Review Press.

7 This impact of the web on cooperation and team work can be easily inferred from the analysis of Daft, R.L., and Lengel, R.H. (1986). 'Organizational Information Requirements, Media Richness, and Structural Design.' *Management Science*, 32: 554–71.

8 We have described the challenges of team fractures in Gratton, L., and Voigt, A. (2007). 'Bridging Faultlines in Diverse Teams.' *Sloan Management Review*, 48: 4.

9 The research on proximity began at MIT in the 1970s with a particular focus on proximity and technology. See Allen, T.J. (1977). *Managing the Flow of Technology: Technology Transfer and the Dissemination of Technology Information within the R&D Organisation.* Cambridge, MA: MIT Press.

10 With regard to the differences between people, a distinction has been drawn between surface level and deep level. Surface-level attributes (age, gender, nationality) have been explored in more detail by Jackson, S.E., May, K.E., and Whitney, K. (1995). 'Understanding the Dynamics of Diversity in Decision Making Teams.' In Guzzo, R. A., and Salas, E. (Eds), *Team Effectiveness and Decision Making in Organizations*: 204–261. San Francisco: Jossey-Bass. For a more academic treatment of the theory, see Harrison, D.A., Price, K.H., and Bell, M.P. (1998). 'Beyond Relational Demography: Time and the Effects of Surface- and Deep-level Diversity on Work Group Cohesion.' *Academy of Management Journal*, 41: 96–107.

11 The study of in-groups and out-groups has been a central theme of group analysis. For an overview of some of the key concepts, see, for example, Tajfel, H., and Turner, J. C. (1986). 'The Social Identity Theory of Inter-group Behavior.' In Worchel, S., and Austin, L.W. (Eds), *Psychology of Intergroup Relations*. Chicago: Nelson-Hall.

12 The challenge of team faultlines is currently being studied by a number of scholars, For an academic description of faultline theory, see Lau, D.C., and Murnighan, K.M. (1998). 'Demographic Diversity and Faultlines: The Compositional Dynamics of Organizational Groups.' *Academy of Management Review*, 23: 325–40.

13 For a further description of the role of signature processes see Gratton, L., and Ghoshal, S. 'Beyond Best Practice.' *Sloan Management Review*; and for more examples of signature processes see Gratton, L., and Erickson, E. (2007). 'What It Is to Work Here.' *Harvard Business Review*, March.

14 For an early description of the power of careers see Edstrom, R.G., and Galbraith, J.R. (1977). 'Transfer of Managers as a Coordination and Control Strategy in Multinational Organizations.' *Administrative Science Quarterly*, 222. A further description of this is provided by Hansen, T., and von Oetinger, B. (2001). 'Introducing T-shaped Managers: Knowledge Management's Next Generation.' *Harvard Business Review*, March.

18

Employee engagement

John Storey, Dave Ulrich,
Theresa M. Welbourne and Patrick M. Wright

The aspiration to involve, engage and win commitment from employees has long been high on the agenda of a select portion of enlightened management. However, there has been a notable resurgence of interest in employee engagement in recent times and it seems that the phenomenon has evolved and been redrawn. Distinctive posts are now advertised which call, for example, for 'Directors of Employee Engagement' rather than, or sometimes in addition to, Director of HR. Recent conferences linking employer branding to employee engagement also indicate the nature of the trend, and the professional associations for HR professionals in the USA and the UK have both paid close attention to the issue (Chartered Institute of Personnel and Development 2006, 2007; SHRM 2008). The Australian Human Resource Institute has engagement as a key component of its 'Model of Excellence' which incorporates the latest research results from the HR Competency Model developed by Dave Ulrich and Wayne Brockbank of the University of Michigan. The practices and the remit are being reimagined and reinvented. The intensity of interest has been such that the Editor of T&D has moved to ask: 'What's the Big Deal About Employee Engagement?' (Ketter 2008). The purpose of this chapter is to explore the meanings and manifestations of employee engagement in its revitalized mode. We will answer four questions about employee engagement:

1. What does employee engagement mean?
2. What are the outcomes?
3. What are the methods?
4. What are the future theoretical and practical challenges?

Answering these four questions will help academics and consultants synthesize and advance engagement work and assist managers and HR professionals to make wiser choices about employee engagement activities and investments.

The meaning of employee engagement

We want to begin by seeking to clarify the meaning of employee engagement. Because it has grown so quickly in popularity, many consultants, companies, and researchers have developed their own definitions of engagement, resulting in confusion of meanings and of approaches. We begin with some commercial definitions and then move on to consider some academic definitions.

The Caterpillar Company defines it as: 'The extent of employees' commitment, work effort, and desire to stay in an organization.' Dell Inc declares that, 'To compete today, companies need to win over the minds (rational commitment) and the hearts (emotional commitment) of employees in ways that lead to extraordinary effort.' The Corporate Leadership Council defines it as 'The extent to which employees commit to something or someone in their organization, how hard they work and how long they stay as a result of that commitment.' The Gallup Organization simply states that it 'is the involvement with, and enthusiasm for, work' (Vance 2006a, b). The Gallup Organization (2006) has elaborated their understanding by referring to 'engaged employees' as those who 'work with a passion and feel a profound connection to their company and drive innovation and move the organization forward'. In the UK, the CIPD (2007) refers to it as 'passion for work' and the willingness to go the extra mile.

Academic researchers have defined employee engagement as 'the harnessing of organization members' selves to their work roles; in engagement, people employ and express themselves physically, cognitively, and emotionally during role performances' (Kahn 1990). Others have noted the centrality of 'vigor' in the idea of engagement – that is, feelings of strength and emotional energy in the workplace (Shirom 2003). Shaw (2005) defined engagement as 'translating employee potential into employee performance and business success'. This means changing the way employees perform 'by utilizing the tools in the armoury of internal communication professionals'.

International Survey Research (ISR) defines employee engagement as 'a process by which an organization increases commitment and continuation of its employees to the achievement of superior results'. The ISR separates commitment into three parts: cognitive commitment, affective commitment and behavioral commitment. In other words, the three dimensions are: think, feel and act.

The challenge with most of these definitions is that they define the construct in terms of its outcomes more than the construct itself. The definitions also suggest an overlap between engagement and commitment and yet the argument has been posited that engagement exists 'as a distinct and unique construct that consists of cognitive, emotional, and behavioral components that are associated with role performance' (Saks 2006: 602). When applied to organizational settings, however, the concept tends to exhibit considerable overlap with constructs such as affective organizational commitment and organizational citizenship behavior (OCB). There are overlaps too with ideas about (i) role expansion, (ii) the taking of initiative and (iii) the voluntary giving of discretionary – and even extraordinary – effort. Thus, employee engagement is hard to distinguish conceptually from this range of constructs relating to cognitive and emotional commitment. It is also important to ask 'engagement in or to what?' – the answer could be the immediate task, the social life of the group, the department or the organization as a whole. Each of these behaviours is of course rather different from the others.

For the purposes of this chapter 'employee engagement' is understood to mean the affective commitment which employees make in practice. Affective commitment implies discretionary energy and working hard on the job versus 'satisfaction' which focuses on 'liking' a job. There are cognitive, emotional and physical dimensions to engagement. We can demonstrate the distinction of satisfaction versus commitment with a simple illustration. When conducting a company workshop, we often ask participants the satisfaction question: 'Do you like your job (boss, pay, or other job features)'? To get at commitment means asking a different set of questions such as: 'To what extent do you go beyond your job description to do your best for the organization?' Someone can like or be satisfied with their job, but not work very hard at doing it well. Conversely, someone may work hard but not like the work they do. Thus, we define engagement as: *a set of positive attitudes and behaviours enabling high job performance of a kind which is in tune with the organization's mission.* To bring this about usually requires a mix of human resource practices built around involvement, perceived appropriate rewards, a set of learning and development opportunities and good leadership at multiple levels.

Contemporary approaches to employee engagement in practice almost invariably involve some systematic attempt to measure the phenomenon and to act upon the results over a series of iterations. We have undertaken a wide-ranging assessment of such surveys. The questions used in engagement surveys indicate the nature of the construct. Some typical core questions are shown below (these are normally accompanied by a Likert scale of responses):

- I am proud to work for this company
- I put my heart into the job
- I would recommend this company to a friend
- Our company is energizing and exciting
- I enjoy the challenges in my work
- I like to stay until the work is done.

This affective commitment should, and as we will show under the appropriate conditions does, impact employee behaviour in ways that can result in positive organizational outcomes. There are of course conditional factors such as team leader behaviour, job design and energy. We will focus later in the chapter on the 'energy' variable as we have conducted extensive research in this area both with managers' energy and that of employees.

The outcomes from employee engagement

When employees experience engagement or commitment, a number of positive outcomes occur. Some of the outcomes of engagement link to other employee affective responses to work. For example, the UK Workplace Relations Survey found that more engaged employees had higher employee participation in company programs, retention, receptiveness to change, and loyalty. In addition, employee engagement has also been found to be related to less:

- role conflict and stress;
- cynicism about the organization and its goals;

and more:

- sense of control over one's work environment;
- confidence in the future of the organization;
- sense of self-confidence in the ability to make change happen in the organization;
- willingness to learn and experiment;
- willing to stay with the company (lower turnover or higher retention);

- motivation;
- creative ideas and solutions; continuous improvement;
- team working;
- organization identity.

Most people can reflect on a personal experience when they felt more engaged with the organization and when conversely they felt less engaged or even disengaged. These feelings of engagement are associated with a greater willingness to work hard, feeling connected to both the work and cohorts doing the work, there is a sharper focus on achieving the goals of the organization, and a feeling of being part of the 'flow' of the organization. Researchers have confirmed and generalized these personal experiences. For example, work by Saks (2006: 613) revealed that engagement levels are predicted by perceived support granted to employees by the organization and that measures of engagement themselves predict levels of job satisfaction, commitment measures, intentions to quit, and positive behaviours within the organization.

In addition to these personal outcomes, when an organization has more engaged employees, the organization performs better. The relationship between employee engagement and performance seems to have been found in much of the empirical research that has tried to relate it to business unit or firm outcomes. For instance, the following quotes illustrate these empirical findings:

> Companies in which 60 percent (or more) of the workforce is engaged have average five-year total returns to shareholders (TSR) of more than 20 percent. That compares to companies where only 40 to 60 percent of the employees are engaged, which have an average TSR of about six percent.
>
> (Baumruk et al. 2006: 24)

> Highly engaged employees achieve 12 percent more of their goals than employees with low engagement. Twelve percent of an employee salary of $35,000 equates to $4,200. When considering the impact on an organization with 10,000 employees, the value of engagement can yield a major impact of $42 million.

A meta-analysis by Harter et al. (2002) of data collected by the Gallup Organization produced similar findings. This revealed the strong effects employee engagement can have on levels of customer satisfaction and loyalty. A weaker, but practically significant, effect was also found between measures of engagement and satisfaction and business-level outcomes. In another meta-analytic study, Riketta (2002) found a correlation between measures of attitudinal organizational commitment – defined as 'the relative strength of an individual's identification with and involvement in a particular organization' (Mowday et al. 1979: 226) – and job performance. Interestingly, the strength of this correlation was found to be moderated by the type of data collected and was stronger when self-ratings were used as compared to objective and/or supervisor-rated measures. Additionally, Luthans et al. (2002) examined the role of managers with regard to employees' levels of engagement and determined that levels of manager self-efficacy partially mediated the relationship.

Thus, research conducted by both academic and consulting firms seems to suggest that engagement (or commitment) is related to outcomes that are considered important by managers of organizations at both individual and organization levels.

Ways of achieving employee engagement

Many consulting firms, such as Accenture, Concours, Gallup, Hewitt, Mercer, Towers Perrin, Watson Wyatt and others, have created engagement surveys. We have assessed each of these products and we have identified seven common factors, briefly defined and then developed below.

- *Vision*: The work unit has a clear sense of the future that engages hearts and minds and creates pride among employees.
- *Opportunity*: The work on offer provides a chance to grow both personally and professionally, through participation in the work unit's activities.
- *Incentive*: The compensation package is fair and equitable, including base salary, bonus, and other financial incentives.
- *Impact*: The work itself makes a difference or creates meaning, particularly as it connects the employee with a customer who uses the employee's work.
- *Community*: The social environment includes being part of a team when appropriate, and working with co-workers who care.
- *Communication*: The flow of information is two-way, so employees are in the know about what is going on.
- *Experimentation*: The work hour, dress, and other policies are flexible and designed to adapt to the needs of both the firm and the employee.

We call these inducements VOI2C2E. This framework stems from the work of Anthony Rucci and it has been elaborated in Ulrich and Brockbank (2005). Each of the elements represents a set of choices which leaders can make to increase employee engagement. An individual may differ on his/her interest in each of these seven factors (e.g., some may be more interested in community than in communication). Over a career span, employees may also vary on the relative weighting of each of these elements (e.g., early in a career, incentives or financial rewards may be more important than later in a career). These seven elements can be woven into an employee value proposition, representing what employees get in return for their dedication to the firm. They are shown diagrammatically in Figure 18.1.

In the following commentary on the figure we discuss the meaning of each term and we also in each case focus especially on the implications for leaders of teams, departments and organizations.

Vision

Defining a future direction for an organization unit goes by many names: strategy, goals, objectives, aspirations, themes, values, milestones, mission, intent, and purpose. While there are nuances of differences among these concepts, they all focus on a future direction and investments to make tomorrow's direction real today.

When employees understand, accept, and align their actions to the direction of the organization, they are more likely to be engaged. There are a number of specific dimensions of the vision that lead to employees being more engaged:

- *Clarity*. Visions should combine analytics which lay out statistical projections of the future and stories which capture the impact of the future investments on employees and customers. In consulting, we often ask members of a management team to write in

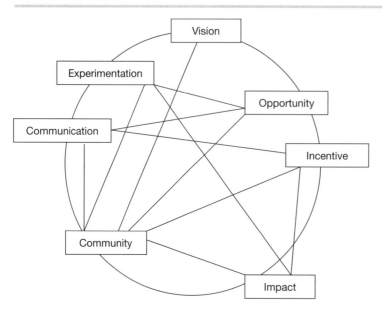

Figure 18.1 The VOICE framework

20 words or less 'What are we trying to accomplish?' We can quickly discern the extent to which there is a shared vision among the managers of the management team. Visions engage employees when they offer them a sense of purpose that has meaning to each of them.

- *Line of sight.* Visions in the abstract remain at the hoped-for-but-not-likely level. When visions translate to employee actions, they become real. Employees who can see how their day-to-day behaviour links to longer term organization visions become more engaged. This is consistent with expectancy theory which advocates the alignment between an employee's effort and performance and performance and outcomes. When this line of sight exists, employees feel engaged because they believe that their work will have impact.

- *Future focused.* Visions focus on what can be, not what has been. By creating the future, visions engage employees in working together to deliver a desired result.

- *Emotive and cognitive.* Visions create energy by generating passion among employees about what can be. Energy often comes from emotions that may exist within a company or from the leaders of the company. Cognitive visions ensure that the passions are grounded in reality.

When leaders build purpose-driven organizations, employees are more engaged. Employees in these organizations act like volunteers because they believe in the cause or purpose of the organization. At times, a crisis may create a temporary purpose-driven organization. In utility firms, when a storm creates power outages, utility employees find a clear and unifying purpose to their work. Employees think much less about distracting politics or policies and focus on restoring power. These employees are engaged. The greater challenge for leaders is to ensure a continuity of engagement with the benefit of an external crisis.

Implications for leaders

Leaders who create visions that lead to employee engagement should identify and connect with leading customers, anticipate technology and industry trends, determine how to leverage their core competencies to move into new markets, and find ways to involve employees in defining and shaping their strategy. Nokia leaders knew that the cellular phone devices strategy which had been so successful had to morph to being an internet company where content on the devices defined their future. They held broad-based employee 'café' meetings where employees throughout the company could learn about the future and engage in discussing the strategy. As the Nokia internet strategy emerges, employees who participated in it will be more engaged with it.

Opportunity

Opportunity means that employees are given the chance to learn and grow through their participation in the work's activities. Opportunities to participate may come from direct participation involving individual employees, indirect or representative participation through the intermediary of employee representative bodies, such as works councils or trade unions, and financial participation. Each of these forms is discussed in more detail below. Through all of these forums, employees participate in decision making and work impact.

■ Direct participation can be seen as taking two main forms: *consultative participation* where management encourages employees to make their views known on work-related matters, but retains the right to take action or not; and *delegative participation* where management gives employees increased discretion and responsibility to organize and do their jobs without reference back.

Both *consultative* and *delegative participation* can involve individual employees or groups of employees. The two forms of consultative participation can be further subdivided. Individual consultation can be 'face-to-face' or 'arm's-length'; group consultation can involve temporary or permanent groups.

■ Indirect or representative participation includes co-determination or rights of works councils in some EU member countries, notably Germany. The decision forums make social policy decisions jointly with management. Joint consultation may also exist, where management seeks the views of the union and takes them into account in making its decision. The most obvious example of a 'dual system' is to be found in Germany where it is enshrined in the legal framework. Joint regulation is largely the responsibility of the employers' organizations and trade unions and takes place outside the workplace at the level of the industry or the Land. Inside the workplace, the task of representing the interests of employees is taken over by the statutory works councils, which have limited rights of joint regulation but extensive powers of joint consultation as well as information, which means a much wider range of issues is discussed between management and employee representatives.

As these forums for participation increase, employees are given more opportunities to join in how the organization defines and delivers work. When employees participate, they feel more engaged. Research on commitment among self-employed workers shows that their engagement scores are higher because they participate in and have control over decisions.

Opportunity also means that employees have prospects of learning and growing at work. This growth may come from formal training and development experiences, but it may also come from work assignments. Learning also comes when a culture exists that encourages risk taking and reflection. Employees are more engaged when they have opportunities to learn.

Implications for leaders

Leaders lead by doing, but also by getting others to do. Leaders recognize that their ultimate responsibility is to help others nurture and growth their talents. The participation and learning opportunities for employees should be a constant leadership action item. As decisions are made, leaders can ask questions such as: Who should be involved in this decision? Who are the next generation of talented employees and how do we give them learning opportunities? What is our workforce plan and how do we make sure we have employees prepared for what is coming? As leaders open their decision processes to more employees, these employees will be more engaged.

Impact

Hackman and Oldham's (1974) work on motivation showed that when employees could see the outcome of their work, they were more likely to be committed to it. Impact means that employees feel that their hard work will lead to desired results. In this present volume, the chapter by Bowen and Pugh (Chapter 30) shows the impact of employees seeing that their work will affect customer response to the firm. When employees realize that their attitude and behaviors will show up in customer attitude and behaviours, these employees are more engaged as they know that what they do makes a difference.

Leaders can help employees see the impact of their work by helping them understand how their work fits into the overall process of customer service. Every employee has a customer, either inside or outside the organization. When an employee can see the ways in which his or her work delivers value to customers, the employee is more likely to be emotionally engaged in delivering the work.

Some of the nature of this impact can be found in the empowerment literature especially in relation to those circumstances where employees are empowered to make decisions that affect customers. But good empowerment is not just about decentralizing decision making and sharing authority; it also means making sure that employees have the information required to make good decisions and the competencies to use that information to serve customers.

Implications for leaders

Leaders often have information about the connection of activities inside a company to users of the activities. Leaders can see the beginning of the processes to the end. As they open these processes to employees, employees become equally engaged with the impact that they have. This means getting more employees touching and thinking like customers. A large retail chain asked all of its 200,000 sales associates to interview ten people in a thirty-day period and ask questions like: Why do (or don't) you shop at our company? How would you rate your last experience in our store? What could we do to improve? What do you tell your friends about our company? At first, the leaders were excited about building a data base with all this data, but then they realized that the real impact was having employees throughout the company connecting with customers so that they could better experience the impact of their work.

Rewards and incentive

Few like to admit publicly that they are motivated by something so crass as money but, as the chapter in this volume by Barry Gerhart suggests (Chapter 14), financial incentives can shape employee behaviour. There are two main forms of financial participation: profit sharing and share ownership. Both have a long history in the UK. The John Lewis Partnership, for example, which embraces Waitrose, the multiple food retailer, as well as the general household stores, has long been a strong advocate of profit sharing and the organization in recent years has outperformed the industry sector.

Although a regular feature in the remuneration of many managers, however, profit sharing and share ownership among employees in general has not been extensively practised. In the UK, for example, the number of workplaces with an employee share ownership scheme for non-managerial employees amounts to no more than 15 per cent, while profit-sharing schemes cover about 30 per cent of workplaces. Typically, too, the amounts of money involved in profit sharing or the number of holdings in share ownership are relatively small.

Employee engagement increases when employees receive financial benefits from their engagement. Remuneration sends communication signals about what matters, serves as a scorecard for performance, and also meets the needs of some employees. Profit sharing and share ownership can be very useful in sensitizing employees to the state of the business. It is a moot point, however, whether they do a great deal for involvement and participation on a day-to-day basis. Arguably, they need to be raised to the levels available to senior managers to have a serious impact in this respect.

Implications for leaders

Creating an incentive system that drives the right behaviour starts by being very clear about the behaviour that reflects the strategy. Behaviours or standards that put strategic directions into actions that employees understand may come when leaders share directions with employees and then ask employees what they should do more or less of to make the direction actionable. The responses to these questions become the basis for employee standards. Then, as employees reach these standards, they receive positive financial or non-financial consequences. If employees miss these standards, this has negative consequences. Leaders need to continually audit their incentive systems to make sure that they are measuring the right things, having clear standards, connecting rewards to standards, and providing employees with feedback on how they are doing.

Community

Community affects employee engagement in two ways. First, a community represents cohorts of teams with whom the employee works. Peer pressure and social networks encourage employees to commit to their job. Gallup's finding of having a friend at work as a source of engagement implies a reciprocal relationship between the employee and his/her peers. Because of personal relationships, employees have goodwill towards their peers and will try to not let them down, and to make sure that they are not the weak link on the team. Richard Hackman's (2002) research on high-performing teams shows that when employees feel like they are part of a social network, or community, they allocate more effort to supporting the goals of the team.

Community is often rooted in leadership. Clearly, leadership matters. When an employee works for a respected and admired leader, the leader is able to engage the employee to work hard by personal relationship or influence. Leaders who engage employees, listen, reinforce positive behaviour, help employees meet their personal goals, care for employees, and deliver results, are generally surrounded by employees who reciprocate by being more engaged. Obviously visible and immediate leaders have more impact than distant leaders who are higher in the hierarchy. However, we are finding that with internet blogs and other corporate transparency, employees in the bowels of the organization relate to the leaders at the top of the organization. When senior executives communicate an environment of openness and caring, employees throughout the organization feel more engaged.

Implications for leaders

Leaders who build community model what they want others to do. Employees hear what leaders say, but they watch closely what leaders do. Leaders who build the right community start with customer expectations by answering the question: What do we want to be known for by our best customers in the future? The answers to this question then should be translated into leadership behaviours that leaders should model. If customers want a firm to be innovative, leaders need to take risks, ask questions, spend time on new products, and be open to change. In addition, leaders set the tone for the community they serve. This team work shows up in how the team makes decisions, processes information, manages relationships, and learns from good and bad experiences. Leaders who build community have employees who are more engaged.

Communication

Employees are more engaged when they know what is going on and why. Communication systems that inform employees help employees feel more a part of the organization. Communications can, of course, be two-way. Thus there can be channels of communicating *with* employees and channels for 'listening' *to* employees Sometimes the terms 'top-down' and 'bottom-up' are used. For the purposes of analysis and exposition, however, it makes sense to use the term communications or information disclosure to describe the former and consultation the latter. The importance of communications hardly needs emphasizing. Lack of understanding is a major source of inefficiency and lack of motivation. More worrying from a management perspective is that, in the absence of clear information, the infamous 'grapevine' takes over.

Leaders who build top-down, bottom-up, side-to-side, and inside-out communication plans ensure that employees understand what is expected and why it is expected. Employees are more engaged when they are more informed. Some employees like to be at the centre of the information network and become transmitters of information to others. Engaging these employees happens when they become spokespeople for the organization.

Implications for leaders

Leaders who communicate well have clear messages that they share redundantly. They share at both the cognitive and emotive levels. They are open to feedback and are constantly trying to improve. They use multiple tools to share information, from one-on-one meetings, to town hall meetings, to blogs, to videos, to e-mails depending on the purpose of their communication. They think carefully about the audience for their messages and tailor common messages to different audiences.

Entrepreneurship or flexibility

Finally, we know that employees, particularly the next-generation employees, enjoy flexibility. The playlist generation of employees has been raised on choices through computer technology.

In the work setting, flexibility about terms and conditions of work may help engage employees. Flexibility might include work hours, benefits, work location, work attire, office space, and other policies that give employees more choice over their work setting.

Flexibility gives employees choice. When an employee makes a choice about his or her work setting, they are more engaged because they have a feeling of ownership.

Implications for leaders

Leaders who encourage flexibility focus on the outcomes of an activity more than the activity. They are open to innovative and creative ways to accomplish the outcomes. They invite employees to find new ways to deliver on important goals. They are willing to experiment and learn by trying new things, and then learning from those experiments. They treat each employee as an individual, with clear performance expectations, but with flexibility on how to reach business goals.

Three future challenges

Our research and consultancy work in the domain of employee engagement suggests a need for more concentrated effort along three dimensions. These are challenges mainly for leaders and managers though by implication there are also research challenges involved here.

Challenge 1: Leadership energy

We find that despite the exhortations, in practice many managers are often resistant to employee engagement programs. This can be for two underlying reasons – first, some inherent uncertainty about the implications for the leader role and second, due to the perceived additional work required by the leader. It can be argued from afar that engagement would in fact lighten the leader's role, but the perception is real and is a barrier to be overcome. We have found that those leaders who feel overburdened tend to judge that an 'engagement' programme will be an added cost to them personally. Our research also suggests that unless these interpretations are faced at the outset, it is difficult to embed and sustain a major engagement initiative in any organization.

The awareness-raising elements of an employee engagement initiative such as training, surveys, posters, action planning and the like are in fact the easy bits. Then comes the problem of implementation proper. This may be simple in an environment where leaders have the time for the additional work required for engagement initiatives; however, our work shows that many leaders are overworked and may even be burned out. They have little energy to embed the initiative in any meaningful sense. One of us in particular (Welbourne) has focused on this problem. Data have been collected from 4,000 leaders every two months since 2003 to track their energy at work[1] and gather comments about what is affecting energy. Using this data we can show that over the past few years, the measure of overall leadership energy has in fact been declining among this sample. These leaders are reporting their energy levels are at a rate that is lower than where they are most productive. These leaders say they have no time to get the most critical elements of their core work jobs done, and this is the key factor they report as negatively affecting their personal energy levels at work. Given that engagement implies activity 'above and beyond' (a common expression used for engagement), the problem is that these leaders are working at suboptimal energy levels and cannot even engage themselves properly because they are too busy just trying to cope with their personal workloads; still less do they feel that they have time or inclination to engage others.

The leadership study described above was inspired by two separate research initiatives. The first was a longitudinal study covering over a thousand firms which examined the predictors of earnings growth, stock price growth and firm survival. The second was the case study work within organizations that grew from the firm-level research. The key finding in the firm-level work was that organizations with higher, long-term performance had high energy cultures. The work involved surveying individual employee energy levels over time – in some cases at weekly intervals. The case study data found that, using the individual employee measure of energy established for the project, energy measures predicted levels of labour turnover, absenteeism, productivity, safety outcomes, patient satisfaction in hospitals, and customer satisfaction.

The case study also discovered that leader energy predicted employee energy. And so it is especially disconcerting to find in the ongoing leader study (that began in 2003) that leader energy is not optimal. If leader energy is falling and/or suboptimal, the overall outcome is negative for bottom-line productivity and firm performance because leader energy predicts employee energy, and high energy cultures predict organizational outcomes (stock price growth, survival). Therefore, exploring and dealing with the root causes of suboptimal leader energy is important for understanding long-term firm performance and the potential for employee engagement initiatives to work in any organization.

In order to provide some context for the above leader energy findings and the link of falling leader energy to employee engagement, we now briefly describe how it was measured for the studies mentioned. 'Energy' is a construct that is different from the constructs explored through traditional questions used in most employee surveys and it has been shown to be predictive in some unique ways. First, the ideal energy level varies from individual to individual and from occupation to occupation. The measurement process uses a 0 to 10 scale, where 0 = no energy, 8 = high energy, and 10 = too much energy.[2] Thus, energy is an optimization versus a maximization scale. A point can be reached where people are exerting so much energy they cannot find time to replenish themselves fast enough. An employee can have too much stimulus at work, and this can result in burnout. However, the definition of 'too much' differs from person to person, and it is important when measuring energy to ask more than one question. The measurement process used in the above-mentioned studies produces a variety of scores: energy overall, most productive energy level, and the gap between where one is most productive and where one is today.

When energy is measured, a few unique things are done: employees are asked to rate their energy frequently (bimonthly or even weekly); they rate where they are most productive using the same energy question; the 'most productive' rate is used to establish control zones, which are zones where the employee is most productive (similar to target heart zones when exercising); and variance over time in energy is measured and tracked.

Challenge 2: Role-based performance to define engagement

Leaders cannot get their core jobs done when they are overworked and near burnout. What does that mean for engagement? In order to delve into this question in more detail and add a theoretical perspective to the topic of engagement, we introduce the role-based performance model.

Five different categories of work behaviour can be defined via the roles that employers set up at work and reward within organizations. Short descriptions of each and an overall model follow:

1. Core job holder role (what is in the job description);
2. Entrepreneur or innovator role (improving process, coming up with new ideas, participating in others' innovations);
3. Team member role (participating in teams, working with others in different jobs);
4. Career role (learning, engaging in activities to improve your skills and knowledge);
5. Organizational member role (citizenship role or doing things that are good for the company).[3]

(Welbourne et al. 1998)

When the role-based approach to work is combined with a resource-based view of the firm, a link between role-based behaviour and firm performance can be derived. The resource-based view of the firm states that firms 'win' when they create long-term competitive advantage from resources that are valuable, rare, inimitable, and for which substitutes do not exist (Barney 1991, 1995). Researchers in human resource management strategy applied this work, suggesting that employees are a key strategic asset that meets the requirements of providing competitive advantage.

However, it is what people are doing at work specifically (or what roles they are engaged in) that drives results. If the role-based model of performance is applied, long-term competitive advantage does not come with people simply doing their core jobs. If employees are only doing core jobs (for which job descriptions are easily available), the competition can hire people, train them to do those same jobs, and do this in a location where wages and other costs are much lower.

But, if employees engage in behaviours above and beyond the core job, then true competitive advantage from people materializes. When employees have firm-specific knowledge and use that information to develop new ideas, to improve the organization, to assist new team members, and to continue to escalate their careers, then the synergy that comes from all of these above and beyond behaviours starts to drive long-term competitive advantage, which then affects firm performance.

If one starts with firm performance in mind and works backwards, then it becomes clear why employee engagement is so popular today. It makes sense that 'emotional commitment', 'above and beyond' behaviours, or 'discretionary' efforts (all terms found in the work on employee engagement) are desirable. A clear understanding of what these words mean is essential for anyone who expects to improve engagement and improve performance through their employees' efforts. Also, the link between extra role (entrepreneur, team, career, and organizational member) and core-job role performance needs to be clearly understood because if employees cannot find enough time to do the core job role, then the odds on engaging in any non-core roles are very low.

Going back to the leadership findings, leaders are saying they are de-energized because they do not have enough time to get their core jobs done. In such an environment, how can these leaders be expected to work on an employee engagement initiative? By adding yet one more piece of work to overburdened leaders, organizations run the risk of further de-energizing them.

Thus, the lesson learned from all of this discussion of energy and research is that engagement programmes need to start at the top. Start with leader energy and leader role-based performance. Leaders themselves need to have time to go 'above and beyond' so that they exemplify what employee engagement can be by being engaged leaders. Only when leaders have the time they need will they be able to help the managers and employees who report to them reach their own optimal energy levels, balance their work in core and non-core job roles and engage in the behaviours that will drive the organization's strategy.

Challenge 3: Engaging low energy employees

As noted above, seeking to engage low energy leaders can be a problem; in a supplementary stream of research we also found that engaging non-manager employees can decrease employee performance. At the Society for Industrial and Organizational Psychology conference in 2007, several consulting firms presented tales of employee engagement noting that there is 'something more' going on with the data. In other words, there was a non-specific but consistent reference to engagement not being enough, at least when discussed in terms of raising engagement survey scores. Additional research linking engagement to energy in non-leader populations helps translate what is now becoming a concern or 'feeling' about employee engagement work (Welbourne 2007). The findings of a series of in-depth case studies with organizations in multiple organizations indicates that raising employee engagement survey scores for low energy employees has a negative effect on their performance. Figure 18.2 shows an example of what the resulting interaction effect looks like.

Although these same results were found in multiple within-organization case studies done with surveys developed by our team, with traditional, engagement-like survey questions, perhaps the more interesting study is with an organization that has been doing its own engagement survey, using its own questions, for the last five years. In addition to running their traditional employee engagement survey, the organization collected monthly energy data for a subpopulation of about 1,200 employees. At the end of the project, an analysis was done using data collected for the change in the firm's own employee engagement scores, average employee energy (over 12 months), change in the employees' performance appraisal scores and a series of control variables (location, job level, salary, gender, ethnicity). The analysis predicts change in employee performance appraisal scores as a function of both the change in their employee engagement scores and average energy. As can be seen from Figure 18.2, increasing employee engagement scores of high energy employees had a positive impact on their performance over the year. However, increasing employee engagement scores for employees with low energy scores backfired – it lowered their performance.

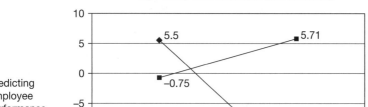

Energy and traditional engagement surveys (results from linkage study with employee performance)

Figure 18.2 Interactive effect of energy and engagement on individual employee performance

It should be noted that this organization may or may not be increasing 'real' employee engagement in this situation; we are improving employee engagement survey scores. According to Macey and Schneider (2008: 11–12) who did a very extensive literature review of the academic work surrounding employee engagement:

> The measures of "engagement" we have seen in the world of practice are highly similar to measures used for assessments of job satisfaction (or climate or culture), albeit with a new label. While there may be room for satisfaction within the engagement construct, engagement connotes activation while satisfaction connotes satiation . . . [these surveys] do not directly tap engagement.

There are two potential reasons for the negative outcome. The first may be the same cause uncovered in the leader studies. The employees with low energy scores may have been reporting low levels of energy due to burnout and not getting their core work done. Trying to engage these low energy employees could have led to more distractions from the core job and resulted in lower performance appraisal scores because, in reality, most performance appraisals focus on core job (vs. non-core job roles). There is, however, a second possibility that has been borne out in some of our interview data with non-manager employees.

This second possibility only makes sense if we consider that much of what is studied in the engagement survey are really factors related to satisfaction or 'satiation'. Low energy employees are given better communications, more attention, made to feel more valued, cared about and nurtured, while all the time, employers may be simply enhancing the comfort level of the already 'low energy' employees.

If this were the case, then clearly there could be problems associated with including employee engagement survey scores as part of a balanced score card. There could be conditions under which the employer is doing more harm than good.

Taken together, we think that two key processes need to be added to employee engagement initiatives. First, start with the leaders. Second, improve energy before trying to increase employee engagement.

What these cautionary tales are telling us

Too often in HR there is a search for the 'holy grail', the thing that will improve performance overnight. There is a worry that employee engagement has the potential to become yet one more HR fad because after millions of dollars being spent on this intervention, there is still a lack of a clear, actionable, definition. In addition to being a field with many fads, HR also often generalizes more than is warranted or needed. Not everyone needs to be retained, trained, motivated, or indeed engaged at the same time. The faster we move to clear understanding of interventions and when they work and do not work, the better.

We believe that employee engagement should be treated as any other HR intervention. It should be a strategic programme, derived from an organizational need to change behaviour in order to achieve a strategic outcome. This means the starting point is not engagement. We should not be implementing 'engagement' because it is now in vogue.

The most important question anyone contemplating spending time and money on employee engagement should be asking is: 'Engaged in what?' Only when this question is asked first will employee engagement be a useful part of an organization's strategy.

Conclusions

Employee engagement is attracting a great deal of interest from employers across numerous sectors. In some respects it is a very old aspiration – the desire by employers to find ways to increase employee motivation and to win more commitment to the job and the organization. In some ways it is 'new' in that the context within which engagement is being sought is different. One aspect of this difference is the greater penalty to be paid if workers are less engaged than the employees of competitors, given the state of international competition and the raising of the bar on efficiency standards. A second aspect is that the whole nature of the meaning of work and the ground rules for employment relations have shifted and there is an open space concerning the character of the relationship to work and to organization which employers sense can be filled with more sophisticated approaches.

But there is reason to worry about the lack of rigor that has, to date, often characterized much work in employee engagement. If we continue to refer to 'engagement' without understanding the potential negative consequences, the core requirements of success, and the processes through which it must be implemented, and if we cannot agree even to a clear definition of what people are supposed to be engaged in doing differently at work (the engaged 'in what' question), then engagement may just be one more 'HR thing' that is only here for a short time. On a positive note, there is now a wider array of measurement techniques with which to assess trends in engagement and an associated array of approaches to effect some change. Thus, aspiration can more feasibly be translated into action.

Notes

1 Energy is defined as the degree to which they are energized or motivated at work. The construct has been validated (predicts turnover, productivity, customer service scores, and more) by numerous studies done since 1993. References to this work are available at www.eepulse.com.
2 The energy metric used in these studies is trademarked and copyright protected; use of the measure requires the written permission of Dr. T.M. Welbourne.
3 Validation research for this approach is available in: Welbourne, T.M., Johnson, D., & Erez, A. (1998). 'The role-based performance scale: Validity analysis of a theory-based measure of performance', *Academy of Management Journal*, 41(5): 540–55.

References

Barney, J. (1991). 'Firm resources and sustained competitive advantage', *Journal of Management*, 17: 99–120.

Barney, J. (1995). 'Looking inside for competitive advantage', *Academy of Management Executive*, 9(4): 49–61.

Baumruk, R., Gorman, Jr., B., & Gorman, R.E. (2006). 'Why managers are crucial to increasing engagement: Identifying steps managers can take to engage their workforce', *Strategic HR Review*, 5(2): 24–7.

Chartered Institute of Personnel and Development (2006). *Working Life: Employee Attitudes and Engagement*, London: CIPD.

Chartered Institute of Personnel and Development (2007). *How Engaged are British Employees?* London: CIPD.

Gallup (2006). 'Engaged employees inspire company innovation', *Gallup Management Journal*, http://gmj.gallup.com/content/default.aspx?ci=24880&pg=1.

Hackman, J.R. (2002). *Leading Teams: Setting the Stage for Great Performances*, Boston, MA: Harvard Business School Books.

Hackman, J.R. & Oldham, G.R. (1974). 'Motivation through the design of work', *Organizational Behaviour and Human Performance*, 16(2): 250–79.

Harter, J.K., Schmidt, F.L., & Hayes, T.L. (2002). 'Business-unit-level relationship between employee satisfaction, employee engagement, and business outcomes: a meta-analysis', *Journal of Applied Psychology*, 87(2): 268–79.

Kahn, W.A. (1990). 'Psychological conditions of personal engagement and disengagement at work', *Academy of Management Journal*, 33(4): 692–724.

Ketter, P. (2008). 'What's the big deal about employee engagement?', *American Society for Training & Development*, January: 45–49.

Luthans, F., Peterson, S.J., & Farmer, R.T. (2002). 'Employee engagement and manager self-efficacy', *Journal of Management Development*, 21(5): 376–87.

Macey, W.H. & Schneider, B. (2008). 'The meaning of employee engagement', *International and Organizational Psychology: Perspectives in Science and Practice*.

Mowday, R.T., Steers, R.M., & Porter, L.W. (1979). 'The measurement of organizational commitment', *Journal of Vocational Behavior*, 14: 224–47. In M. Riketta (2002). 'Attitudinal organizational commitment and job performance: a meta-analysis', *Journal of Organizational Behavior*, 23: 257–66.

Riketta, M. (2002). 'Attitudinal organizational commitment and job performance: A meta-analysis', *Journal of Organizational Behavior*, 23: 257–66.

Saks, A. M. (2006). 'Antecedents and consequences of employee engagement', *Journal of Managerial Psychology*, 21(7): 600–19.

Shaw, K. (2005). *Employee Engagement: How to Build a High-performance Workforce*, Chicago, IL: Melcrum Publishing Limited.

SHRM (2008) White Paper: Employee Engagement and Organizational Performance: How do you know your employees are engaged? www.shrm.org/hrresources/whitepapers_published/CMS_012127.asp.

Shirom, A. (2003). 'Job-related burnout: A review', in J.C. Quick & L.E. Tetrick (Eds.), *Handbook of Occupational Health Psychology* (pp. 245–65). Washington, DC: American Psychological Association.

Ulrich, D. & Brockbank, W. (2005) *HR Value Proposition*. Cambridge, MA: Harvard Business Press.

Vance, R. (2006a). *Employee Engagement and Commitment*. Alexandria, VA: SHRM.

Vance, R.J. (2006b). 'Employee engagement and commitment: A guide to understanding, measuring and increasing engagement in your organization', *Society for Human Resource Management*, 1–45.

Welbourne, T.M. (2007). 'Employee engagement: Beyond the fad and into the executive suite', *Leader to Leader*, spring: 45–51.

Welbourne, T.M., Johnson, D. & Erez, A. (1998). 'The role-based performance scale: Validity analysis of a theory-based measure of performance', *Academy of Management Journal*, 41(5): 540–55.

Part 7

The capability-building perspective

In one of our first graduate courses on organizational behavior, the professor emphasized the concept, "organizations don't think people do." He showed his bias that organizations are social constructions and that to really understand organizations meant understanding the people who comprise the organization. Over the last few decades, we have learned that he was half right. People who make up an organization make decisions to create and/or change the organization. People matter. But organizations often create identities and essentially lives of their own. These organizational lives shape how people behave as much as the people shape the organization.

In the field of HR today, there seems to be an emphasis on the people dimension. We hear about human capital, talent, and individual differences. These person-centric approaches highlight the importance of the individual in understanding how organizations work. And, we believe they are half right. The other half is a focus on organizations, the culture, processes, and patterns that influence how people behave within the organization. An employee who chooses to work at Nordstrom with an organizational bias to service may behave very differently than if the same employee chose to work at Wal-Mart with an organizational focus on efficiency.

Managing the balance of individual abilities and organization capabilities is a future challenge for the HR profession. When individuals are very talented, but do not work well together, they essentially form an all-star team who may not outperform the well-functioning team. On the other hand, even if team work is superb, a lack of talent may keep the well-functioning team from succeeding.

When we begin to think about organizations, we need to move beyond definitions of structure and roles and think about organizations as capabilities. The organization capability logic was initially noted by Igor Ansoff in his classic book on strategy.[1] He acknowledged that organizations have identities or routines that need to be aligned with strategy. In *Organization Capability* Ulrich and Lake worked to define what organization capability means and how to integrate HR practices to support key capabilities.[2] In further work, efforts have been made to identify capabilities that an organization might possess, then how to do organization diagnosis to discover and align critical capabilities.[3]

In this section the organization capability argument is enhanced by tying it to existing organization theory. Wright and Snell do a superb job showing that the resource view of the firm (an organization exists to acquire or bundle critical resources) offers a conceptual underpinning for a capability argument. They show that with this more rigorous theoretical approach, strategic human resource management may be more linked to existing organization theories. They also posit that with a capability-laced logic, more robust explanations of how HR can help make strategy happen and deliver firm performance may be forthcoming.

The chapter by Bhattacharya and Wright offers a unique look into how organizations operate. In the first article, Wright and Snell use a resource theory to discuss capabilities an organization may need to succeed. In the second paper, we learn about organization hiring practices (and capabilities) through an options theory lens. The options theory suggests that investments in capabilities hedge the future risks of an organization. So, an organization treats talent as an option, finding ways to secure future streams of talent through current temporary arrangements. Like stock or other financial options, talent options secure a future resource with today's payment. In talent terms, today's payment is around a temporary work arrangement where employees are engaged part time in the firm with an option to go full time. The options approach may enable organizations to increase flexibility for securing future talent and hedge talent risks. When organizations can project possible future capabilities, instead of securing talent to deliver those capabilities, they might take options on future talent.

Dave Hatch's chapter focuses on leadership development and talent management more generally. He notes how HR is increasingly playing a key role in building organizational capacity by attracting, assessing, selecting, and developing new forms of talent. As he observes, "What was once a quiet, out of the way function is suddenly thrust forward in one of the most important roles in almost any organization." In the first part of his chapter he analyzes the increasing emphasis on leadership in organizations and he explores how positive development of leadership can occur. He reveals how much of this development has to be experiential, though he also contends that a balance of classroom and experience-based development can be most effective. He develops the analysis by demonstrating how leadership development can be tailored to different contexts and challenges and he builds on this in order to develop a model of progressive leveraging of developmental experiences. In the second part of the chapter he widens the analysis to include 'talent management' more generally. He unfolds a systematic review of the core components of talent management and goes on to present a framework for delivering an integrated talent management process.

The sum of these chapters is to redefine and refine our view of organizations. Rather than think of organization in terms of its structure with roles, rules, and routines, we see organizations as a set of capabilities. These capabilities become critical to turning strategies into realities. Leaders and HR professionals who have become comfortable doing leadership 360-degree audits may not also learn to do organization capabilities audits. Once the critical capabilities required to deliver a strategy are identified, these capabilities may become the deliverables or outcomes of HR work. For example, HR has traditionally measured success by activity (e.g., how many people received 40 hours of training, how many were hired, how many received pay for performance). A capability, or HR deliverable, focus shifts from the activity to the outcome of the activity. What happens because of the staffing, training, or payment practices? The result should be a capability that helps the organization succeed. Further, these capabilities may be seen as intangibles that investors value. We know that a publicly traded firm's market value is increasingly made up of intangible assets, but defining those intangible assets is difficult. The work in this section helps to define capabilities which may become those intangible assets that investors value.[4]

Clearly, more work can and should be done in this area. We can learn more about which capabilities have the most impact on which strategies, about which theoretical frameworks (resource dependence, transaction cost, options) help explain how capabilities operate, and about how capabilities can be tied to investor and customer expectations.

Notes

1 Igor Ansoff. *Corporate Strategy*. New York: McGraw–Hill, 1965.
2 Dave Ulrich and Dale Lake. *Organization Capability: Competing from the Inside Out*. New York: Wiley, 1990.
3 Dave Ulrich and Norm Smallwood. Capitalizing your capabilities. *Harvard Business Review*, July 2004.
4 Dave Ulrich and Norm Smallwood. *Why The Bottom Line Isn't*. Cambridge, MA: Harvard Business Press, 2003.

19

Leadership development and talent management

David D. Hatch

Talent, especially leadership talent appears to be in short supply. Given the growing demand in emerging markets the need is likely to intensify. In fact, there is a large and growing gap between supply and demand (Dychtwald et al. 2006).

The globalization of business has redistributed the supply and demand for all kinds of talent. New technologies, changing consumer expectations, and market-driven organizations reshuffle how businesses make money and how organizations get things done every day, resulting in a continual evolution of skills and capability requirements across the world, and Human Resources is right in the middle of everything. HR has increasingly played a pivotal role in building organizational capacity by attracting, assessing, selecting, and developing the talent required by organizations. What was once a quiet, out of the way function has suddenly been thrust into one of the most important roles in almost any organization. Stakeholders of all types look to HR to acquire the necessary resources, tools, systems, programs and so on to ensure that the organization's current and foreseeable needs for leadership and quality talent are being met.

The challenge of leadership

There are of course, many kinds of leaders. There are the highly visible and famous leaders like politicians who inspire the people of their nation to do great things, or military commanders who take their troops into battle and save their country. Leaders come from the other end of the popularity continuum as well, such as a soft-spoken nun who captures the respect and admiration of the world as she helps the poor and downtrodden, or a frail little man who fasts to give birth to a new nation.

All leaders need followers, most importantly, followers with the skills and abilities to do what is needed, get results, and bring to life the vision of their leaders. To accomplish great objectives or realize grand visions requires talented people who can be mobilized, innovate and get things done. Despite all of the technology, innovation, and progress in the world, success or failure still depends on the talent of people in organizations and the leadership to guide and direct them.

Technology has shrunk the world to the point of instantaneous communication across the globe. Transportation has put the world at our doorstep. Organizations and markets are integrated to the point where the ripples of almost any decision or event are felt everywhere. Leaders are not only expected to understand these effects, but anticipate them, predict their consequences, and control them in a way that leads to a competitive advantage. Leaders are required to deal with issues, solve problems, make decisions, and chart the new course for their organizations on a truly global scale, and those that are not global typically face markets and environments experiencing a steady pace of change.

As a result, leaders are needed who are experienced in a much wider range of disciplines than in the past. And by leaders, we do not just mean Chief Executives, or general managers of businesses. Everyone who is called upon to lead whether they are a project manager, department head, sales, marketing, manufacturing, service, finance, the list goes on and on, are all required to know so much more than leaders of just a decade ago. They need to understand the cultural, social, political, regulatory, and economic factors that influence the businesses or environments they work in. They need to be confident in taking risks, open to new ways of doing things, and have a keen understanding of how to bring together diverse types of people to compete in an increasingly complex and integrated world.

Evolution of leadership

The pace of change, complexity, and integration in the world is changing the nature of required leadership. Our understanding of what leadership is has evolved over the last seventy years as well as our view on how it should be developed. Early theories of leadership (Stogdill 1974) focused on traits and characteristics of leaders (Yukl 2002). This perspective tended to suggest that leaders were born not made. Most of the effort to get good leadership focused not on developing it, but finding it. Psychological tests and selection tools focused largely on identifying key traits that leaders were thought to be born with. Leadership development as we think of it today was not mainstream.

Over time, more rigorous studies of leadership were undertaken. Science got involved, and field and laboratory studies were launched to determine what leaders did, how they did it, what made some more successful than others, and what could be done to improve measurement and selection techniques. It was soon discovered that leadership was much more than genetically endowed characteristics and traits.

Leadership behaviors tied to specific skills were identified, and new ways to measure what leaders did were pioneered. Soon the models of leadership shifted from traits to skills, and behaviors. Most importantly, much of what successful leaders were doing could be learned – and the era of leadership development was born. Leadership emerged from the "either you have it or you don't" realm of traits and aptitudes to the more exciting and robust world of knowledge, skills, and abilities, often referred to as "KSAs" or competencies.

Leadership research efforts began to focus on what was observed to be influencers of successful leadership outcomes. For example, psychologist Kurt Lewin observed that some leaders were more participative in their decision making and communications with subordinates and less autocratic or directive, leading to his participative leadership model (Lewin et al. 1939). In the early 1950s the Ohio State Leadership Studies found that two consistent style characteristics of leaders could be observed. Their findings defined two sets of leadership behaviors differentiated by the degree leaders focused on the task, and the degree they focused on people

These studies sparked even more research to understand the nature of the relationships that leaders have with their people, and began to define those relationships in greater detail. Early on, one of the most commonly used typologies of leadership style examined a leader's decision-making style, and involvement of followers as primary determinants of success, ranging from autocratic to participative (Likert 1961).

With mounting evidence that leadership was more than a result of a person's genetic endowment, leadership development began to emerge as a key resource for human resource professionals focused on getting the best talent for their organizations. As research on leadership increased, so did the quality and value of their findings, and efforts in organizations to train and develop their current and future leaders.

Leadership development has always been directly tied to the theories and models of leadership that were popular at the time. For example, popular models for developing leadership in the early stages were Blake and Mouton's Managerial Grid (1964), and Hersey and Blanchard's Situational Leadership model (1977). Both models (as well as many others) focused on matching various leadership styles or behaviors, or their "fit" with the type of situation or environmental factors the leader was faced with, and the maturity or readiness of those who were being led.

One of the most important evolutions in leadership development in the last twenty years has been to differentiate management from leadership. Although they overlap considerably, management is generally defined by a set of competencies that focus on achieving tasks and accomplishing objectives within a defined set of parameters and within a fairly structured process. Planning, budgeting, organizing, controlling and so on are central elements of what a manager is expected to do. They represent the core building blocks of the supervision of people, and the management of resources within an organization. Although almost all leaders are expected to manage, they are expected to do more.

Not only has leadership been differentiated from management, leadership researchers began to differentiate two types of leadership: transactional and transformational. Transactional leaders focus on efficiently achieving the organization's goals and objectives, gathering and managing the resources necessary for the task at hand, and getting things done. In contrast, transformational leadership focuses on transformation or change, not simply getting things done, but also deciding which things need to be done, and changing or innovating how things should be done to fit the requirements of the ever-changing world, as discussed earlier.

In less turbulent times, leaders did more managing than leading; they were often simply someone in charge, someone who managed the organization's resources and was accountable for getting things done. Today's leaders have a much more challenging course to navigate. Business leaders must not only know how to plan, organize and control, but also set stretch goals, create winning strategic plans, acquire and sell businesses, and meet or beat Wall Street's estimates for their quarterly earnings. Leaders of government or non-commercial organizations face no less of a challenge to do more with less, meet the rigorous and increasingly intrusive requirements of oversight entities, and deal with demanding and knowledgeable consumers.

Almost without exception, modern leadership models focus on the leaders' ability to lead their organization safely and competitively through the forces of change in the environments or markets they are in. Although there are many leadership models, all are change oriented and most focus on three types of skills or abilities that a leader must have: envision the future path or direction of the organization, align people and resources around that vision, and motivate and inspire the people and manage the resources to achieve it (Kotter 1990).

Today's leadership opportunity

The building blocks of management such as planning, organizing, and controlling tend to focus on the task or work that is to be performed. These have been supplemented with a greater focus on people. New innovations in management continue to evolve to meet the needs of increasingly integrated and global organizations; for example, management of virtual teams, large spans of control, empowerment and self-managed teams.

As we travel further down the continuum, the requirements and opportunities for today's leaders are even more significant. Despite innovations in management practices, more is being demanded from today's leaders. Recent changes in the definition of what leaders must do and a wider array of resources and organizational levers at their disposal continues to create a broad, ever-changing playing field. Hamel (2007) has called for even newer models of leadership, declaring that given today's dynamic, global world, management theories and practices haven't evolved enough and are no longer the stuff that great leaders are made of. Ulrich and Smallwood (2007) have argued for companies to develop a Leadership Brand that not only embodies the unique challenges facing their leaders, but also results in real economic value to shareholders.

Gary Hamel and other researchers have observed that innovation in leadership and organization is likely to become a significant source of competitive advantage in the business world (Bryan and Joyce 2007; Hamel 2007). What was once thought of as a genetic trait is now emerging as a powerful force that may determine the way businesses compete, and who wins in a competitive global economy.

A leadership development model

The good news about leadership development is that as we have discovered and learned more about what leaders do and how they do it; we have also been learning how to develop it. As indicated earlier, in most organizations, corporations, bureaucracies, and non-profit entities, Human Resources has the stewardship over identifying, hiring and developing future leaders. It is HR's responsibility to carefully select those with the greatest potential and make sure they receive every opportunity to grow and develop to their fullest capacity. When the supply of leadership seems insufficient for the organization's needs, whether due to growth, demographic shifts, market inflections or strategic changes, it is HR's responsibility to attract, hire, and develop talent to meet those needs.

Perhaps the most parsimonious and effective model for development has been Morgan McCall's General Model for Executive Development (McCall 1998). The model has three simple elements: Talent, Experience, and what he calls "The right stuff."

Talent

In the classical sense, talent refers to those innate gifts that one might possess that predisposes one to exceptional performance, such as unusual eye–hand coordination, quick reflexes,

Figure 19.1 The right stuff

creativity, or charisma. In addition to innate gifts, talent would also include things that are developed to the point where they are a central part of the person. For example, tenacity, discipline, hard work, and the passion to excel and develop talents can become significant assets from a developmental perspective. In fact, McCall indicates that perhaps the most valuable trait or skill a person could possess is the ability to learn.

Starting with the right kind of talent increases the chance that given the right experiences, the individual will grow and develop to be successful in their role in the organization. Talent refers to the basic raw ingredients such as courage, intelligence, integrity, risk taking, drive to make a difference, etc. Generally, these are traits that are by definition difficult or at least costly and time consuming to develop. In a practical sense, talent can even be construed to include things like education, or training that requires a significant amount of time to accumulate or demonstrate a level of expertise.

Experience

Experiences are what shape and mold talent. Most of what we learn is by doing it, watching others do it, having those who have done it coach and mentor us, or by making our own mistakes and learning from them. The best development solutions integrate learning from experience wherever possible. Our intuition and research agree, experience truly is the best teacher (Lindsey et al. 1987). Some experiences are, of course, better teachers than others, or at least teach us more valuable things. The best developmental experiences are rarely if ever easy, instead they are often full of adversity, stretch, and introspection. McCall et al. (1988) established a framework for thinking about the different developmental value of experiences by studying the experiences leaders had and determining what lessons they learned. Additional studies have added to the list of experiences and lessons, including what makes an experience developmental, and how individuals can best take advantage of their learning opportunities or assignments (Eichinger and Lombardo 1990; Lombardo and Eichinger 1989).

The right stuff

In McCall's model, The right stuff doesn't have a single definition, especially in today's turbulent world. There is no single profile of what a successful leader does; accordingly, there is no single definition of what the right stuff is for a great leader. Leadership requirements in changing environments emerge, shift and redefine themselves as the landscape and terrain evolves and changes.

Despite statements to the contrary, successful leaders in one setting or company will not always be successful in another. Great leaders vary significantly in their skills and talents, and a perfect profile for the successful leader doesn't exist. Leaders are successful because of their own personal and unique combinations of talent that match the requirements of the leadership role they are in. Harold Geneen, former Chairman and CEO of ITT, was in many ways the opposite of D. Wayne Calloway, former Chairman and CEO of PepsiCo. Both were exceptionally talented leaders who led their businesses and achieved phenomenal success in very different ways, and in dramatically different environments. What the right stuff for leadership development is then dependent on what the leader is called upon to do, and what type of environment they are required to do it in.

With this brief introduction to McCall's General Model for Executive Development, we can now turn to how it is used.

Determining what leaders must do

The value of the statement of The right stuff is driven by its utility to identify raw talent and learning experiences to develop future leaders. Although it is the third element in McCall's model, leadership development architects often "begin with the end in mind." They start by defining what the leadership environment is, and kinds of leadership challenges they will likely face to ensure the organization's success.

Typical analytical questions are:

- What leadership capabilities do today's most successful leaders have?
- Why do some of today's leaders fail?
- What kinds of leadership challenges face our organization in the future?
- What will the business environment be like in the future?
- What new skills must leaders possess to become high performers as we move into the future?
- What kinds of experiences should they have to be successful in the future?
- How will leadership requirements be affected by our business strategy?
- Where have our leaders come from in the past, and where are they likely to come from in the future?
- How many leaders are needed, and when, where?

Answering these and other questions requires a significant amount of insight and analysis, but they are key to building a leadership development system that is firmly grounded and focused on the "right stuff." To be valuable, the answers to these questions must be as concrete and specific as possible, avoiding broad generalizations that fail to differentiate between average and great leadership. They require a deep understanding of current and future business requirements in order to match up with the KSAs required to win in the marketplace. For example, the following should be taken into account:

- current and future market conditions;
- anticipated business challenges from competition;
- new product requirements;
- regulatory changes;
- demographic shifts and workforce trends.

The answer to many of these questions typically varies by business unit, geography, function, market, product, organizational structure, business model or several other variables that can significantly impact what a leader must do. Organizations vary greatly in their approach to these questions. Some leadership development professionals launch sophisticated studies of what successful leaders do and perform exhaustive analyses of the environments, cultures, and market dynamics and so on. Some interview top management and conduct focus groups to create a list of leadership skills, knowledge, and abilities, to define as clearly and specifically as possible what will be required of successful leaders. Others simply sit down and write out what they think leaders must do using lists and statements of leadership requirements defined by other organizations, which they refine and customize to meet their organization's situation.

The most important requirement of any statement of leadership requirements is that they be concrete enough for assessment, selection, and development of leadership talent. For

Table 19.1 Contrast between changing global business and a mature domestic business environment

Changing global business	Mature domestic business
Understand changing customer priorities and workflow	Increase quality of service to new customers
Understand competitor strategies	Reduce operating costs to meet competitive challenges
Re-segment customers	Exploit cross-business synergies
Develop a new business model for an emerging market	Reduce healthcare and pension costs
Develop a new pricing model	Outsource call center operations

example, a typical list of strategic leadership requirements will look different for businesses in two different environments. (See Table 19.1 for an example.) The results of these studies are often distilled down to a succinct set of leadership competencies that attempt to define what is required of a leader in clear and behaviorally anchored terms.

Although leadership competencies are, as McCall puts it, the result of the development process, they have become a succinct description of what leaders need to know, be, and do. Competencies have evolved to include a wide range of elements including traits, knowledge, motives, attitudes, values, knowledge, or skills (Spencer and Spencer 1993). However, when each element is concretely defined and illustrated, they have proven to be an effective resource to define, communicate, and assess what a leader must do.

The right number of competencies used to define leadership requirements has to balance the specificity and accuracy of a long and detailed list, with the utility and user friendliness of a small set. Often the balance seems to be in favor of a focused core of eight to ten competencies defined in ways that are meaningful to managers and leaders within the organization, yet simple enough for them to use them to identify, assess, and develop talent within the organization. Keeping the number down to a manageable number sometimes works against the need to be as specific and concrete as many would prefer, but enhances the chances that they will be accepted and used within the organization.

The flexibility to add one or two additional competencies can help bridge the need for additional competencies to meet diverse leadership needs of different cultures or geographies; these should always work to achieve a balance between usability and accuracy to keep their value as a development tool high. Effective leadership competencies are often used in a wide range of HR systems, including selection, assessment, 360-degree feedback, development planning, career planning, performance management, internal communications, and coaching.

The challenge facing leadership development architects today is similar to that facing behavioral science. To add value, analysis must be specific and comprehensive enough to capture all the key variables that define and contribute to leadership success. However, too much specificity and too much detail overwhelms the user, especially line management, who then revert back to their old paradigms and models, casting analysis aside in favor of intuition and gut feel.

As a result of all of the study and analysis, a clear leadership profile or definition of the "right stuff" emerges. This profile drives the design of leadership development systems, processes, and tools to concentrate effort on those areas for most important leadership development.

Talent

With a clear definition of what a leader must do, the immediate challenge is to identify individuals with the raw talent needed to be developed into the leader of the future. It takes time and money to develop leadership talent, and talent that doesn't have the potential to learn or develop what is required for the future, in the time available to develop it, is a poor investment. Without the proper ingredients to begin with, or ingredients that will develop with the time and resources available, the result will fall short of what is needed.

McCall's research into what kind of talent organizations should be looking for has focused on elements that distinguish between high potential and solid performers. He has identified 11 characteristics of high potential global executives:

- seeks opportunities to learn;
- acts with integrity;
- adapts to cultural differences;
- is committed to making a difference;
- seeks broad business knowledge;
- brings out the best in people;
- insightful, sees things from a new angle;
- has the courage to take risks;
- seeks and uses feedback;
- learns from mistakes;
- open to criticism.

(Spreitzer et al. 1997)

A closer look at the list reveals that over half of the characteristics deal with the desire and ability to learn. Being gifted, or good at something, is not sufficient. People with high potential have to develop their gifts by continuing to learn, improve, and develop them into towering strengths.

Although dominant, the ability to learn isn't everything. Those with potential were found to have five other important qualities: integrity, commitment to making a difference, respect for people, insightfulness, and the courage to take risks. Without integrity even high performers are ultimately left out in the cold. Commitment to make a difference demonstrates the drive and passion often cited as a leader, and differentiates their performance. Sometimes their drive helps draw attention to their potential. Respect for people suggests "soft skills" for dealing with people to do their best. Insightfulness increases the likelihood of innovation and creativity, a powerful combination in changing environments. And finally, courage to take risks means that their ideas will either be proven good, or give them opportunities to learn from their failures, to readjust and try again.

Experience

The third element of McCall's model is perhaps where the greatest (and most under-utilized) power of McCall's development model lies. Research indicates that people learn more from experience than any other method (McCall et al. 1988). Accordingly, many of the things leaders and highly talented people must learn cannot be taught, but must be experienced. Self-confidence, perspective, and deep technical experiences to name just a few, can be learned best outside the classroom.

Understanding what job experiences develop the competencies of future leaders provides organizations with important direction for creating (job assignment-driven) learning experiences that will round out future leaders and close critical gaps. The tools to accelerate learning on the job, or experience-based development, are increasingly robust and better understood:

- identification of key, high-leverage learning experiences;
- selection and staffing processes that consider development opportunities as placement criteria as well as performance;
- temporary assignments with clear learning objectives;
- job and assignment sequencing for accelerated development;
- learning contracts with focused learning objectives tied to job experiences;
- cross-functional task force or committee assignments that broaden and deepen perspective on emerging issues;
- mentoring or coaching from those who have already learned from their own personal experiences things that will be required of future leaders;
- attendance at meetings outside of core responsibilities;
- ad hoc project assignments.

Too often, conventional wisdom and practice is to always put the person in the job who already knows how to do it, usually because they have already done it before. Organizations that use experience to develop their leaders consider both development and performance as placement criteria. The challenge becomes identifying what are the best developmental experiences, and making sure the right people are given those experiences at the right time.

The best practices in leadership development generally leverage both classroom and experience-based development. Innovations in both approaches have created a much more powerful, integrated system for developing leadership, and a broader range of alternatives to meet leadership development needs.

Innovative classroom learning initiatives

Traditionally, development is usually thought of as formal development experiences in corporate training facilities and universities where the newest and best thinking is taught and shared with the students.

Improvements in formal development experiences continue to strengthen the transfer of learning and real world relevance through design, technology, and innovation. Technology has brought virtual classrooms and learning teams together from around the world. Sophisticated computer simulations enable teams to dig much deeper into case studies and play different roles in the analytical and problem-solving phases of learning.

Organizations are increasingly investing more time and money in executive or leadership development. Their facilities are widely recognized for not only providing quality management and executive development, but shaping and managing their organization's culture, and creating new innovations in classroom learning.

Leadership development "pipelines" or pathways have been clearly defined with specific leadership requirements at several key "passages" within the organization (Charan et al. 2001). Six typical passages have been identified that in turn characterize important transitions that characterize the various sets of leadership skill requirements of large global organizations.

Each transition indicates a significant shift in the knowledge, skills, and abilities individuals must master to be successful at that level to transition from one stage to another:

329

1.　managing self to managing others;
2.　managing others to managing managers;
3.　managing managers to functional manager;
4.　functional manager to business manager;
5.　business manager to group manager;
6.　group manager to enterprise manager.

Each transition requires additional skills, and abilities, some of which can be taught in the class-room, others through experience. Leadership development programs take place at the various levels of the organization through both internally and externally developed and delivered programs.

By far the most important innovations in classroom-based development are new program designs that have increased relevance and value by focusing on business issues that take the classroom into the field. In place of business cases and lectures, participants are formed into ad hoc teams assigned an issue or problem facing the company, and sent out to work the issue onsite. These types of learning initiatives, often referred to as *action learning*, bring the classroom closer to the company's problems, and create a much richer learning experience. Learning is done as teams solve real time business problems. Teams are assigned a specific issue facing the organization. Projects are selected and sponsored by business leaders who participate in defining the issue, provide resources to the team to address the problem, then return at the end of the program to discuss the team's findings and recommended solutions.

In addition, subject matter experts and external experts are often brought in to provide methodologies, problem-solving approaches, or benchmark comparisons. The experts and instructors serve as a resource for new concepts and methods to enhance the learning by doing. Work is coordinated by a learning professional liaison to ensure learning objectives are being met as work is getting done, and reduce administrative requirements of the project.

Action learning also makes participants active partners in the learning process and shifts the focus from passive to hands-on learning. The results of the project are typically presented to the unit management team and senior management. Exposure to senior management creates an opportunity to share the team findings with an authoritative group, creates pressure to put new ideas and concepts to work, and often results in powerful and practical solutions.

In addition to technological innovations, leadership pipelines, and action learning, several new innovations in classroom-based learning characterize the way new training methodologies are used to develop leaders:

- strategy and business-driven curriculum;
- leadership competencies driven;
- management as faculty;
- multiple-session classroom training;
- 360-degree feedback assessments on values and competencies;
- leadership advisory board;
- centralized funding;
- core leadership curriculum with additional electives.

Strategy and business-driven curriculum

Formats such as action learning tackle real time business issues. Leadership development professionals work with senior management to anticipate new areas where business skills and knowledge need to be strengthened and design curriculum focused on those needs.

Leadership competencies driven

Studies of leadership competencies yield an inventory of competencies leaders need today, and in the future. These competencies provide the basis for assessment and development systems throughout the organization. Not only are they helpful to the organization for such things as curriculum development and career planning, but they help individuals map out their personal development plans.

Management as faculty

Business school cases provide interesting discussions and broaden perspectives on issues, which leads to greater knowledge and perspective on a problem. However, key questions for future leaders are: Has anyone done this successfully in our environment?; and What can *we* do to learn from their experience?

Involving senior management in the instruction of future leaders is a powerful approach to sharing information and transferring best practices. Sessions characterized by sharing of ideas and discussion are much more valuable than those characterized by lecturing and presenting. Not only will ideas that are immediately applicable to business challenges be shared, but next-generation leaders will develop increased respect for the wisdom and leadership of those who share their experience, knowledge, and expertise.

Each "manager instructor" should have direct hands-on experience dealing with central issues facing the company, and where necessary, should be supported by professional program developers to ensure their ideas are communicated succinctly and in an understandable and easy to adapt manner (Tichy and DeRose 1995).

Multiple-session classroom training

This reduces the need for large blocks of time while enhancing the ability to address complex and difficult problems. Several group sessions spread out over several months, and often in different locations, provide for better practical application and learning transfer to the real world. Multiple-session learning also significantly increases retention levels of high-potential people who see the investment the company is making in their skills. The level of commitment of multi-session, multiple-location experiences reinforces the investment the organization is making in them, and the sense that learning is the ultimate objective, not getting your ticket punched.

360-degree feedback assessments

360-degree feedback tools are well established as an extremely powerful tool for focusing development and behavior. Valid assessments, aligned with business strategy, and organization-specific leadership competencies, provide focus and motivation to learn new KSAs needed to meet the challenges of the future.

Leadership development advisory boards

These, comprised of senior line executives and learning professionals (both internal and external), are used to provide direction and focus to ensure learning initatives do not stray from key needs or grow stale. They create shared ownership for leadership development effectiveness and enlighten leaders regarding new technologies and approaches to learning.

331

Centralized funding

Core programs that focus on basic building blocks such as key transitions are fully funded so they don't force the geographic or market units to trade off necessary investments in strategic development against tactical training requirements.

Each program or learning initative focuses on a different audience and addresses different levels of leadership development needs. Internally developed and delivered initiatives also focus on the communication and refinement of the key cultural norms and values of the organization as well as learning objectives

Core leadership curriculum

Core leadership development programs form the basis of an organization-wide definition of leadership. These core programs usually focus on typical leadership issues that cut across the organization, and create a richer learning environment. Participants can be drawn from diverse backgrounds and experiences to build networks across the organization, and facilitate communication and innovation. Typical programs include:

- aligning and motivating employees;
- managing in a changing environment;
- increasing teamwork;
- communication;
- matrix management.

To supplement the core leadership curriculum, business units also create elective programs to address real time issues facing various geographies or markets.

Innovations in experience-based learning

Innovations in on-the-job learning initiatives have also created powerful tools to strengthen and accelerate leadership development:

- new diagnostics have been developed to inventory individual experiences (Hatch and Kizilos 2000);
- tools have been designed to identify key developmental experiences (Hatch and Kizilos 1998);
- analytical tools have been developed to deepen understanding of the lessons, skills, and perspectives gleaned from experience (Bly and Kizilos 2007);
- lessons from various developmental experiences have been documented and catalogued (Eichinger and Lombardo 1990; Lombardo and Eichinger 1989);
- systems are in place to assign potential leaders to the experiences they need, when they need them.

Determining the right stuff

In addition to competency-based analyses to determine leadership requirements as discussed earlier, leadership development professionals ask their best leaders what on-the-job learning experiences have been most valuable to them in their careers and where they got that experience. By identifying key learning experiences, organizations determine which experiences future leaders need to have to get the best development.

For example, through numerous studies, several highly developmental experiences have been identified for general managers:

- managing front line performers;
- early P&L (profit and loss) responsibility;
- balancing HQ and field perspectives;
- facing serious adversity (e.g., competition, natural disasters);
- business or new market start-ups;
- managing a turnaround situation;
- managing a large operation.

Through better development planning and job mapping, organizations are able to reduce the time required to develop new leaders, and increase time in position to promote stability and accountability.

Furthermore, rather than fast-track talent quickly through a large number of jobs requiring moderately more scope and responsibility over the course of ten to fifteen years, organizations look to identify those key high-impact experiences where the most experience occurs, and reduce the speed (short tenure) and number of assignments high potentials experience to a smaller, more productive set.

Identifying talent

Most of a company's future leadership team is already part of the organization. They are the talented – "best and the brightest" – individuals that were hired by the organization years ago. They have been working and contributing to the organization in a wide variety of roles and responsibilities, each experience adding to their knowledge, perspective, vision, and drive for the future and ability to lead effectively.

More importantly, they are eager to continue to grow and develop into the challenging roles of the future. They are the assets that the organization has already invested in; they have proven their loyalty, their tenacity, their acumen and most importantly, their ability to learn. They are excited about the company or organization's future and are ready to drive for results and grow or improve the organization's performance to unprecedented levels.

Nevertheless, organizations tend to know very little about the job experiences and accomplishments of even their best talent. Knowledge is typically limited to job titles and time in position with no explanatory descriptions or experiential insight. Managers tend to emphasize their own direct experience with the individual's recent assignments, and frequently are unaware of valuable experiences the person may have had in previous positions, ad hoc assignments, or project work within the company. If the individual was hired by another manager, their previous work experience is also most likely completely unknown beyond what organizations they might have worked in.

Historically, when there are insufficient numbers of next-generation leaders in the pipeline to meet business requirements, hiring managers and Human Resources depend on the overview of the prospective candidate's past experiences to determine their talent and skills. By reviewing the candidate's resumé, as well as their responses to enquiries about what they learned in those positions, interviewers look for predictors of the individual's potential and fit with the company's leadership requirements.

Tools and technologies to inventory experiences and capture lessons learned are an emerging part of new talent management systems. Even without the new tools and systems, leaders intuitively look for patterns of performance and experience that indicate that the individual has leadership potential, and a proven track-record of accomplishment. Technologies to inventory experiences and lessons learned not only help identify talent, they also serve to educate individuals as to what lessons must be learned to succeed, and where they are most likely to find them.

Identifying developmental experiences

People learn from all kinds of experiences, but in order to leverage learning experiences that make successful leaders, experiences with the highest developmental value need to be identified. To identify key development experiences for future leaders, focus groups, archival analysis, and structured interviews are used. Interviews with top-performing leaders are conducted to determine their most developmental experiences and how they relate to the current and future leadership requirements. In-depth studies of their past assignments, accomplishments, and how they get things done deepen the understanding of the lessons learned from each experience.

The results of these and other analyses provide an emerging view of what specific experiences relate to high performance, what lessons are learned from those experiences, how those lessons build knowledge, perspective and skills, and which leadership competencies drive sustained high performance. Bly and Kizilos (2007) researched how experience-based analyses also help teach people to think about their experiences as learning opportunities and to maximize the development they receive from them. See Figure 19.2.

Once experiences have been identified, they can be communicated and shared not only to highlight lessons learned but inspire aspiring leaders and high potentials to focus more on the lessons learned in their own experiences that prepare them for greater responsibilities (Bly and Kizilos 2007).

Most importantly, developmental experiences and the lessons learnt are used to build development plans that prepare individuals for future responsibilities and alert them to potential lessons that are aligned with leadership profiles and the competencies required for future leadership

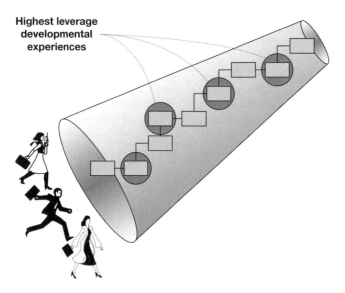

Figure 19.2 Highest leverage developmental experiences

positions. They also facilitate coaching and mentoring from experienced leaders by making it easier for them to talk about what types of knowledge and experiences high potentials should seek.

Getting the right experience

The most important requirement for effective learning through experience is to assign the right individuals to the most valuable developmental experiences, when they can best learn from that experience. Internal staffing within an organization managed by HR is a dramatically under-utilized tool. As the developmental value of key experiences has become known, HR partnering with line management works to ensure that high potentials and next-generation leaders are given priority for those experiences.

High-development jobs are always in demand not only for their developmental value, but because they are almost always key performance jobs as well. Because key jobs are highly competitive, few in number, and do not come up as often as needed to develop talent, organizations have looked for ways to increase the number of developmental opportunities, or change the nature of the assignment.

Once the central learning elements of a job are understood, leadership development professionals work to identify similar learning elements in other jobs or ad hoc assignments. Often similar developmental learning can take place through temporary job assignments that are often more ubiquitous, present less of a risk, do not require a job change, and as a result are much easier to accommodate.

For example, experience running a business or working outside the home company is almost always identified as a key developmental experience for global general managers. However, there are several complicating factors. Expatriate assignments are expensive. They are often disruptive for young families, and the failure rate is high in part because of family issues. Perhaps most importantly, they don't come up that often.

By understanding what key lessons are learned in a typical expatriate experience and how they relate to future leadership requirements, leadership development professionals can search for a series of ad hoc experiences that the person can have outside of their home country on a *temporary* basis rather than waiting for an opening, and moving their family. Everyone wins: less expense, less risk, more frequent, and more learning.

Human resource planning or project staffing tools that inventory open positions and ad hoc projects across the company make it much easier for leadership development professionals to see across organizational boundaries and highlight assignments that are needed for potential leaders. Not only do these processes accelerate learning and development, they help organizations meet staffing requirements for important positions in a cost-effective and efficient manner.

Over a period of many years best practice organizations have fine-tuned their development systems to not only build the talent they need, but to get to know their most talented people, and drive learning across their vast organizations. They have leveraged their learning programs as a powerful management tool to manage change and strengthen organizational competitiveness. Each organization allocates significant human and financial resources to leadership development and feels the investment is time and money well spent.

The result of focus and investment is an integrated system of corporate core events, geographic complementary offerings, and organizational transformational programs (special initiatives) that characterize the state of the art in leadership development. Their programs are driven by business strategy, focused on current and future issues, co-taught/led by company or subject matter experts, and sequenced for development at key transition points in an individual's career.

As organizations learn to capitalize on the learning capacity of experiences within their organizations, integrating them with innovative classroom-based learning, their capacity to develop high-performing leaders increases dramatically.

Talent management

The term "talent management" is relatively new. Fifteen years ago, if you were to use the term most people would have thought you were talking about musical or performing arts talent. Traditionally, talent has referred to a natural ability or aptitude that sets a person apart from the crowd as outstanding or special.

Today talent management (TM) has become a powerful strategic force within organizations in general and HR in particular as businesses, schools, universities, hospitals, governmental agencies and so on plan and prepare to meet their "talent" needs of the future. Usually, the impetus for improved TM has resulted from growth, or demographic shifts. For example, in the 1990s, PepsiCo was growing at a compounded annual growth rate of a little over 12%, which meant that the company was doubling in size every five years, an impressive but not unheard-of accomplishment. What became alarming to the HR leadership team was that PepsiCo, with three of the largest food service franchises in the world, would not only double their sales volume, they would also dramatically increase the size of their workforce.

With over 400,000 employees in over 170 countries, in three different lines of business, senior management began to wonder what it would be like to run a business with nearly one million employees.

- Could the company find the skills they needed, where they needed them, when they needed them, at the cost that PepsiCo could afford to pay?
- Could the employee growth rate be sustained?
- With double and triple digit turnover rates in the food service businesses, where would they find all of those people?
- Would the quality of employees drop?
- Could the company's thirst for talent slow down or stop the company's growth?
- What would be the impact of scope and scale on the performance-driven culture of the company?

Suddenly, Human Resources' role in the company began to take on much greater, more strategic, significance. In the 1990s, few companies wrestled with similar problems. HR, as caretaker of employee relations, benefits, compensation, recruiting, and development was pretty straightforward, and stable. Labor relations and contract negotiations were winding down; healthcare and benefits costs were out of control and getting most of the attention. But in the 1990s, globalization, availability of capital, and most importantly, technological innovation kicked the pace of change into a much faster gear, and HR has never been the same.

Today, many forces are affecting HR's ability to get the talent needed within the organization. Companies are routinely forced into managing the cost side of the business at the expense of growth. General Managers and CEOs are frequently accused of being better skilled at saving their way to meet their business plans than growing their top line. Companies are frequently forced to forgo growth opportunities and acquisitions because they lack the leadership talent to run the resulting businesses. Massive out sourcing and offshoring of work has resulted in the displacement of hundreds of thousands if not millions of jobs. Lay-offs, downsizing, and de-layering have became the tools of managing talent in organizations not as "its most valuable resource" but "its biggest cost."

As the world's pendulum swung wide to the cost side of business, those looking further out into the future began to consider how it was going to swing back. As changes in the way talent was viewed within organizations continued to shift, a few human resource teams began to rethink their paradigms. Just as PepsiCo was confronted with the inevitable consequences of growth, these HR teams began to consider other forces already at work that would begin to reshape the competitive landscape.

For example, in the United States an emerging force for change was a seemingly innocuous demographic study called *Workforce 2000*. *Workforce 2000* was a comprehensive study done by the Hudson Institute that revealed some surprising forecasts about the workforce demographics that US organizations would be facing at the turn of the millennium. As their findings first caught the attention of HR professionals, they wasted no time ringing senior management's bell (Hudson Institute 1987).

Workforce 2000 projections made in 1987:

- US population and workforce growth was slowing – the supply of talent was decreasing;
- the average age in the workforce was going to increase, but pools of young workers would decrease – retirements up, new recruits down – resulting in a widening workforce gap;
- more women would be entering the workforce – pay equity and anti-discrimination issues would likely become more critical;
- by the year 2000, more than 15% of the workforce would be minorities – diversity would play an increasing role;
- immigrants would form a larger part of the increase in the workforce than they had since the influx of the early 1900s; this would result not only in more diverse employees but more diverse customers.

HR teams began to ask more thoughtful and forward-looking questions, and began to think about how they were going to manage their changing workforces . . . how they were going to manage their *talent*. In more general terms, people moved from being thought of mostly as a ubiquitous *liability* or cost, to a scarce *asset* or value.

The forecasts of *Workforce 2000* were met with great concern and analysis. Organizations began to manage their talent focused primarily on the diversity implications of the projections and largely forgot the others. Diversity programs helped organizations focus on all aspects of the talent management chain, but almost exclusively the minority and gender-driven implications of the research.

In the fall of 2001, a second study jolted everyone back to the much broader implications of the *Workforce 2000* study. McKinsey and Company published the results of a five-year in-depth study on how companies manage talent in a book sensationally entitled *The War for Talent* (Michaels et al. 2001).

McKinsey's study not only significantly changed how HR viewed talent within their organization, but also focused the attention of many company leaders on the crucial role talent management would play in the immediate future. The study prescribed several changes companies needed to make in order to succeed in the coming years. From a demographic point of view, similar to *Workforce 2000*, their study predicted that the size of the total workforce from 1998 to 2008 will *grow* 12%, yet the size of the 25–47-year-old demographic segment that supplies companies with future leaders would actually *decline* 6% during the same period, creating a significant talent shortfall, and therefore, a "war for talent."

McKinsey was much more explicit than was *Workforce 2000* in laying out the implications of their findings, including five things that leaders of successful companies were already doing to not only win the "talent war" but make talent a competitive advantage. Their recommendations included:

1. embrace a talent mindset;
2. craft a winning employee value proposition;
3. rebuild the company's recruiting strategy;
4. weave development into the organization;
5. differentiate and affirm their people.

(Michaels et al. 2001)

Each recommendation suggested a new and more integrated way to address talent management than was generally being practiced in organizations at that time.

Hoping to better frame the new and increasingly significant talent management issue, in early 2004 the Conference Board published a white paper written by Lynne Morton (Morton 2004). Morton identified several individual components of talent management that she grouped into the brackets shown in Table 19.2.

Morton's early framework for TM began to describe the range of activities that she logically saw as talent management. Some components have emerged as more significant than others. Recruiting, talent development, and performance management play an increasingly important role as organizations work to meet current and future talent needs. Retention, feedback and measurement, workforce planning, and culture, though important, are not as yet seen as major initiatives as often as the others, but are receiving increasing focus and importance. Even with the wide range of activities identified so far, still more initiatives are likely to emerge as part of the new focus on talent.

For example, McKinsey's Lowell Bryan and Claudia Joyce have enlarged the role talent plays in the future of global business by researching the relationship between talent and creating wealth. They have identified a whole new reason for companies to focus on the management

Table 19.2 Components of talent management

Recruitment	Retention	Professional development	Leadership/ high potential development	Performance management	Feedback/ measurement	Workforce planning
College recruitment	Specific efforts	Professional development systems	Stretch and short-term assignments	Competency profiles	Exit interviews	Forecasting of talent needs and demand
Experienced hires	Total rewards	Assessment centers	High-potential development	Performance management systems	Regular employee surveys	Talent skills development
On-boarding		Learning and training	Executive coaching	Rewards and recognition	Balanced scorecard™	
			Cross-functional and international opportunities			

and disposition of talent in their organizations (Bryan and Joyce 2007). They propose new approaches to managing employees and organizing talent to maximize wealth creation and achieve competitive advantage. Although still in the early stages of development, Bryan and Joyce's work has the potential to encourage CEOs and unit heads to look for talent management innovations and focus their attention more productively on people as a more robust asset than simply focusing on costs.

Just as technology and globalization have created business opportunities that didn't exist before, how talent is defined, acquired, organized, managed, paid, and how expectations are being met have become significant opportunities for innovation and change. New business models and TM approaches are being explored and refined. TM pioneers are creating new paradigms and models that transform how we see the world of talent, creating new tools, processes, and systems: "deploying such devices as talent marketplaces, knowledge marketplaces, formal networks to make intangible assets flow throughout the company, as opposed to going up and down vertical chains of command" (Barsh 2007).

An integrated talent management process

Since Morton's typology almost four years ago, a more integrated view of the emerging focus on talent has emerged, one that enables organizations to increase management focus, manage the changes necessary to better compete for and develop talent, and take a more coordinated and holistic approach. Given that most talent is already part of the organization, and that most promotions, transfers, and assignments are given to people within the company, a new management process is emerging in organizations that are serious about TM.

Management processes are driven chiefly by the finance function. Processes such as the strategic planning process, annual operating plan, and annual budget have become powerful tools to prioritize and allocate resources, focus the organization's attention on important initiatives, set goals and objectives, guide activities and create an ongoing management process

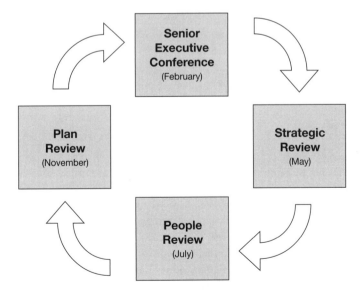

Figure 19.3 The integrated talent management process

to coordinate activities, focus effort, and build capability across the organization in ways that are aligned with the overall direction of the company.

For example, over the last twenty years, the strategic planning process has become a standard management process in nearly all organizations, creating a regular forum for senior management to focus on the future, identify potential competitive advantages, anticipate challenges, and prepare for strategic opportunities that require anticipation and planning.

Management processes by their nature are powerful levers to concentrate the resources and attention of the organization on essential tasks of the organization. They create a defined time and place to discuss key issues, use standardized approaches and guidelines that create a consistent, stable system to communicate, discuss, and decide on important issues facing the organization. In addition, management processes elevate and group together numerous initiatives, projects, and strategies into a single, more integrated effort. They also create common frameworks, models, initiatives, and end products that facilitate communication. They create a common language across the organization, and serve to sanction initiative, resourcefulness, and accountability as they relate to the overall mission of the organization consistent with the processes' purposes.

Just as strategic planning solutions have evolved over the last two decades, talent management processes are evolving in today's organizations, representing the integration or coordination of efforts across most if not all of the TM elements mentioned earlier. Like other management processes, they are being carried out at the corporate, group, and business unit level, and organizations are focusing more and more attention and resources to meet talent management requirements. Elements of talent management processes include:

- annual or semi-annual talent review;
- training and development needs assessments, priorities, and objectives;
- leadership profile identification and maintenance;
- development planning and follow-up;
- job or ad hoc project assignment;
- mentoring and coaching coordination;
- leader-led development initiatives;
- ongoing leadership assessment;
- leadership development budgeting;
- selection for key learning experiences;
- strategic workforce planning;
- talent, skills, and workforce forecasting;
- key skill identification and development;
- external staffing strategies;
- cultural or engagement surveys;
- performance management;
- internal staffing or game planning.

Organizations known for their capacity to attract, retain, and develop superior quality talent have various versions of the talent management process described here. These successful organizations have made TM one of the company's core planning tools. The new process represents the most significant step forward that an organization takes to formalize and elevate the importance of talent management. Through this annual and sometimes biannual process an organization's ability to leverage its talent management capabilities is magnified tenfold.

General Electric's Session C (Welch and Byrne 2001) and PepsiCo's Organization and Human Resource Plan processes (Pearson 1987) are two examples of talent management processes that are key accountabilities of senior management, and have become ingrained in the organization's culture. An illustration of the evolution of TM processes are the changes being made in succession planning. Rather than simply rehearsing "what if" scenarios about who would take over a particular job if the incumbent got hit by the proverbial beer truck, effective talent management processes play a much broader role.

Succession planning has historically focused on having one to three "ready now" candidates for key positions. In contrast, a talent management approach mindful of a wider range of activities will focus on talent pools, building a strong bench of next-generation leaders to be assigned to a wider range of positions, and on a renewal process for building talent in the organization. From a focus on replacements for key positions arrayed beneath boxes in the organization chart, talent management processes concentrate on building talent pools and leadership capability across a much broader array of positions, better positioning organizations in dynamic environments.

The objectives of a typical talent management process could be:

- determine leadership requirements via forecasting, or strategic human resource planning;
- assess leadership, and management, talent across the enterprise using assessment tools focused on performance, potential, past job assignments, and leadership competencies;
- alert business or organization unit heads to shortfalls and talent gaps by function, geography, business unit, and talent pool;
- create human resource plans that address the organization's strategy and change initiatives in a detailed and comprehensive manner;
- identify high potentials as early in their career as possible and develop plans to accelerate their growth;
- assess the organization's progress toward diverse workforce goals in the management levels and identify plans to close gaps;
- identify strategic and scarce skill sets and create plans to close the gap.

Companies that have strong talent strength usually do similar things and have similar methods and approaches. Below are several key elements that make them successful.

High talent standards

Assessment and evaluations follow strict evaluation criteria where potential and performance is differentiated. Sometimes performers are grouped into categories such as "Top 20%, Very High Potential," or "Promotable." They also focus on who the solid players are, and who is in the bottom 10%. The latter are either transferred to a role in which they can succeed, or are moved out of the organization. The top 10–20% are placed in positions where they can be further developed and learn as much as possible.

Talent review sessions

Talent is discussed on a regular basis, at least once a year, at the time of promotion, salary bonus time, and when developmental opportunities present themselves. Individual background and assessment profiles provide each of the members of the review team with a clear, detailed overview of their performance, experiences, leadership competencies, and development plans. Views of individual successes or failures are candidly discussed from several vantage points in a fair and balanced manner.

Lots of early "bets"

Identifying highly talented professionals and future leaders is a numbers game. The earlier in the process the assessment and development begins, the greater the chances are of developing the right people. Rather than focusing on a select few, successful talent management systems stock the development pipeline with as many talented candidates as they can, carefully assessing them and nurturing them as much as possible.

Mentoring

Talented individuals are encouraged to seek out mentors to help guide and teach them. Experienced high performers are encouraged to share their knowledge and experiences with others, coaching and teaching them those things that can't be learned any other way.

Job and project assignments

On-the-job learning is facilitated by identifying and tracking key learning assignments in the organization and ensuring that not only high performers but high-potential talent has an opportunity to have key learning experiences. The focus is shifted from staffing based solely on performance, to performance and learning needs to meet future leadership requirements.

In-depth assessments

In addition to self-assessments by the individual, and management assessments by superiors, selected high potentials and next-generation leaders are assessed using in-depth assessment processes. These assessments create a deep understanding of the individual's strengths, weaknesses, developmental needs, and long-term potential. They are focused largely on feedback from individuals who have worked closely with the candidate over an extended period of time against comprehensive criteria for advancement to very senior level positions within the organization. They include detailed interviews, 360-degree survey assessments and other assessment tools aimed at getting a deep understanding of the individual's capabilities and potential. Sometimes aptitude tests and other measurement tools with appropriate reliability and validity are used.

Winning or performance culture

In addition to the methods and approaches listed above, organizations that are successful in managing their talent often have a winning or performance culture where moderate risk taking, high performance, competition, openness, freedom and flexibility, empowerment, and high standards of achievement are evident. A high performance culture is a high development culture as individuals and organizational units stretch to reach challenging objectives and break performance goals and targets through innovation and hard work.

Effective integrated talent management systems create a common language across the organization to discuss and assess talent. They ensure development plans for individuals are more business issue focused, and career integrated. They strengthen the sense of accountability for talent acquisition and development through consistent involvement of the management team.

Strong talent management solutions foster candid, open dialogue about each individual in the talent pools: who they are, what their development needs are, and how they can be best developed. Discussion, discussion, and discussion lead to greater awareness, deeper understanding, more accurate assessments, and most importantly, ownership of the process. Ram Charan highlights the importance of an integrated talent management system as well as the importance of discussion as a key criterion for a successful talent-building organization (Charan 2005).

An integrated talent management process enables HR to play a proactive role with management in the selection and development of talent. As the keeper of the process, and protector of the data, HR is well positioned to partner with line managers in the diagnostic, review, and solutions stages of the process. By aligning key talent needs, and solutions to business goals and strategies, an integrated process deepens leadership awareness, and focuses scarce resources on key areas. It provides a better (reliable and valid) assessment of talent across the organization that is validated and improved each year.

The process promotes a much clearer understanding of talent gaps and implementation issues, and ties them to specific action plans for the coming year. Development needs are discussed in the context of business and leadership challenges rather than management fads or popular concepts.

Efforts to move talent globally or across organizational silos are strengthened, as the developmental value of such moves is clearly understood as both short- and long-term solutions. Finally, senior management and oversight groups such as a board of directors, regulatory agencies, and other stakeholders have an opportunity to audit an organization's talent management systems and determine if proper priorities are being set, and investments are being made. This access provides a much deeper look into the talent challenges faced by an organization, and a clearer understanding of the organization's talent requirements and resources. Most importantly, they can see what the plans are to resolve talent issues and what is being done to make them more effective.

Conclusions

Even ten years after McKinsey's *War for Talent*, most companies are still unprepared to implement a semblance of its recommendations. Even if there were no demographic shifts, or if HR was given all the resources it asked for to meet its leadership development and talent management accountabilities, the pace of change in today's world still demands that organizations be offensive players in an ever-challenging environment.

Many HR teams still lack the tools, skills, and knowledge to develop the leaders of the future, and manage the talent as we approach a new reality. Furthermore, many lack the confidence of management in their ability to play a key role in this critical issue.

As new technologies, tools, and systems gradually take hold, new roles and responsibilities need to be determined, and strategic HR skills need to be developed. New efforts are bearing fruit, and momentum is beginning to build. HR can't do it all alone. Line managers have learned in the last two decades how to trim a dime or even twenty cents from a dollar, but they have also learned how to survive in a dynamic, fast-changing environment. Now, they must raise their sights and focus on the much more powerful potential sources of competitive advantages described in this chapter.

References

Barsh, J. (2007) Innovative Management: A Conversation with Gary Hamel and Lowell Bryan. *The McKinsey Quarterly*. November.

Blake, R.R., and Mouton, J.S. (1964) *The Managerial Grid*. Houston: Gulf Publishing.

Bly, P., and Kizilos, M. (2007) *Key Developmental Experiences for Thomson Business Leaders*. Thomson corporate manuscript.

Bryan, L. and Joyce, C. (2007) *Mobilizing Minds Creating Wealth From Talent in the 21st Century Organization*. New York: McGraw-Hill.

Burns, J.M. (1978) *Leadership*. New York: Harper Colophon Books.

Charan, R., Drotter, S., and Noel, J. (2001) *The Leadership Pipeline*. San Francisco: Jossey-Bass.

Charan, R. (2005) Ending the CEO Succession Crisis. *Harvard Business Review*, February.

Dychtwald, K., Erickson, T., and Morison, R. (2006) *Workforce Crisis: How to Beat the Coming Shortage of Skills and Talent*. Boston, MA: Harvard Business School Press.

Eichinger, R. and Lombardo, M. (1990) *Twenty-two Ways to Develop Leadership in Staff Managers*. Report No. 144. Greensboro, NC: Center for Creative Leadership.

Hamel, G. (2007) *The Future of Management*. Boston, MA: Harvard Business School Press.

Hatch, D., and Kizilos, M. (1998) *Analysis of Key Developmental Experiences for IT Professionals*. Atlanta: Delta Technology unpublished manuscript.

Hatch, D., and Kizilos, M. (2000) *Online Experience-based Development Diagnostic*. Royal Bank of Canada Financial Group unpublished manuscript.

Hatch, D. and Kizilos, M. (2007) *Key Developmental Experiences for Thomson Business Leaders*. The Thomson Corporation unpublished manuscript.

Hersey, P., and Blanchard, K.H. (1977) *The Management of Organizational Behavior* (3rd. edn). Englewood Cliffs, NJ: Prentice Hall.

Hudson Institute (1987) *Workforce 2000*. Indianapolis: Hudson Institute, Inc.

Kotter, J.P. (1990) *Leading Change*. Boston, MA: Harvard Business School Press.

Lewin, K., Lippitt, R., and White, R.K. (1939) Patterns of Aggressive Behavior in Experimentally Created Social Climates. *Journal of Social Psychology*, 10, 271–301.

Likert, R. (1961). *New Patterns of Management*. New York: McGraw-Hill.

Lindsey, E., Homes, V., and McCall, M.W., Jr. (1987) *Key Events in Executives' Lives*. Technical Report 32. Greensboro, NC: Center for Creative Leadership.

Lombardo, M., and Eichinger, R. (1989) *Eighty-eight Assignments for Development in Place: Enhancing the Developmental Challenge of Existing Jobs*. Report No. 136. Greensboro, NC: Center for Creative Leadership.

McCall, M. W. Jr. (1998) *High Flyers: Developing the Next Generation of Leaders*. Boston, MA: Harvard Business School Press.

McCall, M., Lombardo, M., and Morrison, (1988) *The Lessons of Experience: How Successful Executives Develop on the Job*. New York: Free Press.

Michaels, E., Hanfield-Jones, H., and Axelrod, B. (2001) *The War for Talent*. Cambridge, MA: Harvard Business School Press.

Morton, L. (2004) *Integrated and Integrative Talent Management: A Strategic HR Framework*. New York: The Conference Board.

Pearson, A. E. (1987) Muscle-build the Organization. *Harvard Business Review*, 65(4): 49–55.

Spencer, L., and Spencer, S. (1993) *Competence At Work: Models for Superior Performance*. New York: John Wiley & Sons.

Spreitzer, G., McCall, Jr., M., and Mahoney, J. (1997) Early Identification of International Executives. *Journal of Applied Psychology*, 82(1): 6–29.

Stogdill, R.M. (1974). *Handbook of Leadership: A Survey of the Literature*. New York: Free Press.

Tichy, N., and DeRose, C. (1995) Roger Enrico's Master Class. *Fortune*, November 27: 105–6.

Ulrich, D. and Smallwood, N. (2007) *Leadership Brand: Developing Customer-focused Leaders to Drive Performance and Build Lasting Value*. Boston, MA: Harvard Business School Press.

Welch, J., and Byrne, J. (2001) *Straight From the Gut*. New York: Warner Books.

Yukl, G. (2002) *Leadership in Organizations*. Upper Saddle River, NJ: Prentice Hall.

20

Human resources, organizational resources, and capabilities

Patrick M. Wright and Scott A. Snell

This chapter examines the role of human resources and HR practices in building organizational resources and capabilities. It then discusses how these resources can be integrated at different levels of the firm in building capabilities. The implications for research are then discussed.

In a world characterized by global markets and rapid change, the importance of firms acquiring, developing, and leveraging resources to build capabilities for competitive advantage has become increasingly evident. Because these strategic resources may likely include human capital, and because a firm's people are integral to any capability, researchers have increasingly focused on HR practices as critical levers – or investments – through which firms might build resources and capabilities.

The extant literature on HR and firm performance has fairly well documented the empirical connection between HR practices and various financial measures such as sales growth, profitability, and market value (cf., Delerey and Doty, 1996; Huselid, 1995; Snell and Youndt, 1995; Wright et al., 2003). Even so, there is a recognized gap in the literature that examines the mechanisms through which this relationship occurs. Authors have generally referred to this as the "black box" phenomenon, and have called for more research and theory that improves our understanding of the mechanisms through which HR practices influence organizational performance (Becker and Gerhart, 1996).

A recent stream of thinking in this area has focused on the ways in which HR practices can build the resources (human capital and social capital) that underlie the capabilities of the firm. The purpose of this chapter is to provide some background on the ways in which this connection occurs, the logic that drives the decisions, and the HR practices that may be most useful for an overview of the kinds of resources and capabilities that might be those impacted by HR practices, and through which those practices might impact firm performance. In sum, this chapter will propose that HR practices have their most direct impact on the human capital resources of the firm. These human capital resources are critical to certain kinds of capabilities that firms seek to build, and, if focused strategically, HR practices can influence these capabilities.

The problem with HR and performance research

As previously discussed, an established body of research exists examining the relationship between HR practices and performance. Such research has been conducted at the corporate (e.g., Huselid, 1995), business (e.g., Wright et al., 2003) and plant level (e.g., Youndt et al., 1996). Studies have examined multiple industries (e.g., Guthrie, 2001), a single industry (e.g., MacDuffie, 1995) or even a single corporation (Wright et al., 2003). While the observed effect sizes may differ across studies, qualitative reviews of this literature conclude that in almost all cases HR practices are found to be at least weakly related to performance (Boselie et al., 2005; Wright et al., 2005). This conclusion is supported by a recent meta-analysis concluding that the mean effect size for the HR–performance relationship is approximately .14 (Combs et al., 2006) implying that a one standard deviation increase in the use of high-performance work systems is associated with a 4.6% increase in return on assets.

One major problem with this research is that, while performance is certainly a strategic outcome, the basic tenet of strategic HRM is that HRM systems need to be aligned with the strategy of the business. For instance, Cappelli and Singh (1992) early on suggested that strategic HRM assumed that (a) different strategies require different employee requirements (e.g., skills and behaviors), and (b) different employee requirements are elicited by different HRM systems.

Much subsequent theorizing has attempted to describe the types of alignment one might observe between different firm strategies and HR systems. For instance, Miles and Snow (1994) suggested that firms engaged in prospector (innovation) strategies would focus on rewarding outcomes rather than behaviors, whereas defender firms would be more likely to reward behaviors than outcomes. Many others have suggested frameworks that might indicate how HR systems might differ across different organizational strategies (Delery and Doty, 1996; Schuler and Jackson, 1987; Snell, 1992; Wright and Snell, 1991; Youndt et al., 1996).

In spite of the mass of theorizing, sadly, the empirical research fails to demonstrate consistent support for the "fit" between HR and strategy (Becker and Huselid, 2006). Wright and Sherman (1999) suggested that the failure to find "fit" in the HR–performance relationship most likely stemmed from the focus on measuring generic HRM practices (e.g., pay for performance) rather than the products or targeted outcomes that the practices aimed at eliciting what might differ across strategies. For instance, pay for performance might constitute a basic principle of good HRM, but a firm engaging in innovation might tie pay to new products whereas cost-focused firms might tie pay to cost reduction or cost control. Respondents across those two firms would both report the existence of a pay for performance system, revealing no differences across strategies, when, in fact, differences certainly exist, just at a more molecular level than the measure captures.

While we still believe that the specificity of the measures helps to explain why past research has failed to reveal the "fit" effect, more recently, authors have begun to also question the specificity of strategy measures. A focus on strategic processes and capabilities may be a more specific and therefore productive target for understanding the alignment of HR practices and performance (Becker and Huselid, 2006; Delery and Shaw, 2001; Wright et al., 2001). In order to more deeply explore the role of HR in enhancing organizational capabilities, we will first discuss the Resource-Based View of the firm and its treatment of capabilities.

The Resource-Based View of the firm

The Resource-Based View (RBV) of the firm (Barney, 1991; Wernerfelt, 1984) has become the predominant paradigm driving Strategic Human Resource Management (SHRM) research and thinking (Wright et al., 2001). The RBV has its roots in the work of Penrose who referred to the firm as a "collection of productive resources" (1959: 24). Rubin (1973) was also one of the early researchers who focused on firms as bundles of resources before the formal conceptualization of the RBV by Wernerfelt (1984). Barney (1991) later extrapolated from Wernerfelt, integrating what had become a fragmented literature on the RBV. He presented a formal RBV framework which proposes that firms that possess resources which are valuable, rare, inimitable, and non-substitutable will be able to sustain their competitive advantage over the long term. While the basic framework has not necessarily changed, the applications and examinations of resources have progressed significantly over the past 15 years. In general, the evolution of thinking in this area has been around resources, capabilities, and dynamic capabilities.

A focus on resources

Early RBV work focused, not surprisingly, on resources. Amit and Schoemaker defined resources as

> stocks of available factors that are owned or controlled by the firm. Resources are converted into final products or services by using a wide range of other firm assets and bonding mechanisms such as technology, management information systems, incentive systems, trust between management and labor, and the like. These Resources consist, inter alia, of know how that can be traded (e.g., patents and licences), financial or physical assets (e.g., property, plant, and equipment), human capital, etc.
>
> (1993: 35)

Barney (1991) categorized these resources as being either human, physical, or organizational.

SHRM researchers have taken two broad tracks in utilizing the RBV for research. The primary track that SHRM researchers have taken is to focus on the HR practices themselves; that is, the organizational resources. Lado and Wilson (1994), for example, suggested that because HR practices are complex and path dependent, they could be valuable, rare and costly to imitate; therefore a source of competitive advantage. Most of the empirical research linking HR and firm performance is based on this premise, though few have tested the theory directly (cf., Becker and Gerhart, 1996; Becker and Huselid, 1998; Guthrie, 2001).

The other track taken by SHRM researchers is to focus directly on the people rather than the practices; that is, the human capital. Wright et al. (1994) argued that the larger a firm's human capital pool, the more likely that it would have superior skills and behavior that would be valuable, rare, and costly to imitate. Wright et al. (1995) examined the skills and strategies of NCAA basketball teams, and found some support for the match between skill types and strategies for determining their team's performance.

Similarly, Lepak and Snell (1999, 2002; Lepak et al., 2003) used the RBV to examine the link between valuable and unique human capital and firm performance. In a similar way, researchers such as Hitt et al. (2001), Sherer (1995), and Hatch and Dyer (2004) have demonstrated how firms leverage different forms of human capital to drive firm performance.

Whether the focus is on the HR practices or the human capital itself, much of the SHRM literature has used the RBV to focus on resources as a source of competitive advantage (Wright et al., 2003). However, research by Newbert (2007) suggested that this approach may be missing the mark. In an exhaustive review of research using the RBV, he found that of the 232 empirical examinations of the relationship between resources (not just human) and either competitive advantage or performance, only 85 (37%) were found to be significant. Newbert concluded that "the empirical results seem to suggest that while capabilities and core competencies do indeed contribute significantly to a firm's competitive advantage and/or performance, resources do not" (p. 136).

A focus on capabilities

Over time, strategy researchers have focused more broadly on the *organizational* resources, particularly examining routines and capabilities. And increasingly, the strategy literature has come to equate resources and capabilities so that they "are used interchangeably and refer to the tangible and intangible assets firms use to develop and implement their strategies" (Ray et al., 2004: 24). However, in order to more clearly focus SHRM researchers, we more fully explore the concept of capabilities.

While Penrose (1959) and Rubin (1973) viewed firms as collections of resources, they did not specifically argue that the resources alone would impact a firm's ability to compete. For instance, Penrose argued that resources could only contribute to a firm's ability to compete if they were exploited by the firm. In addition, Rubin stated that "firms must process raw resources to make them useful" (p. 937). Prahalad and Hamel (1990) argued that it was not just static resources, but rather the inimitable skills, technologies, knowledge, etc. with which these resources were deployed that determined the value of those resources. Finally, while Barney's (1991) conceptualization focused on resources, he later noted that such a static view was too narrow. In response to criticism (Priem and Butler, 2001) that the RBV had become static in concept, he stated that "once a firm understands how to use its resources . . . implementation follows almost automatically" as if the actions necessary to exploit the resources were obvious (Barney, 2001: 53). In essence, the focus within much of the strategy literature has evolved from that of resources, to that of capabilities.

According to Amit and Schoemaker, "Capabilities refer to a firm's capacity to deploy resources, usually in combination, using organizational processes, to effect a desired end" (1993: 35). Eisenhardt and Martin described them as a "set of specific and identifiable processes such as product development, strategic decision making, and alliancing" (2000: 1106). In this sense, capabilities can be thought of as information-based tangible or intangible processes that are developed over time through complex interactions among the firm's resources. They can abstractly be conceived of as "intermediate goods" generated by the firm to provide enhanced productivity of its resources, as well as strategic flexibility and protection for its final product or service. Capabilities might be developed in functional areas (e.g., brand management or marketing) or by combining physical, human, and technological resources at the business or corporate level. For instance, firms may build such "corporate capabilities as highly reliable service, repeated process or product innovations, manufacturing flexibility, responsiveness to market trends, and short product development cycles" (Amit and Schoemaker, 1993: 35).

In this sense, the concept of capabilities parallels Porter's (1996) emphasis on value chain analysis. Porter had suggested that each phase in the value chain consisted of a set of activities that the firm engaged in, and that a firm's strategic orientation suggested differential abilities to perform certain activities better than their competitors. For instance, when Dell entered the PC industry, most of the firms in the industry used intermediary distributors as partners to sell and/or deliver computers to corporate clients. Dell's "direct" model circumvented this distribution step in the value chain, as Dell created its "premiere pages" enabling corporate clients to order and receive shipments directly without a distributor taking a commission. In addition, Dell leveraged a superior supply chain management system to control inventories more efficiently than the existing competitors. It was these "activities" (or capabilities) that provided Dell with a lower cost business model that distinguished it from competitors (Dell and Fredman, 1999).

The "capabilities" concept may provide both a more specific and comprehensive frame for the connection between HR and performance. Because capabilities combine processes and resources they can serve as non-tradeable assets which develop and accumulate within the firm (Dierickx and Cool, 1989). It is not just the processes themselves, but the tacit and complex learning that takes place among individuals who execute and improve those processes over time that can distinguish a firm. Such a conceptualization led Prahalad and Hamel (1990) to argue that core competencies, particularly those based in collective learning and knowledge, improve as they are applied.

The focus on capabilities has only recently been addressed in the SHRM literature. Such a focus requires examining human capital resources, not in isolation, but in conjunction with organizational routines, processes, and systems/technologies.

Researchers such as Lepak and Snell (1999, 2003), Delery and Shaw (2003), and Becker and Huselid (2006) have suggested that identifying critical processes, talent pools, and job families helps to more clearly link HR and firm performance.

Becker and Huselid (2006) argue that taking a "capability"-based approach to SHRM leads to a focus on concrete business processes as the intermediate outcome to reflect strategy implementation. In fact, they note that Ray et al. (2004) suggested that business processes "are the way that the competitive potential of a firm's resources and capabilities are realized and deserve study in their own right" (2004: 26). They present a conceptual model in which the market positioning strategy leads to a set of strategic business processes. In their model, each business process requires a different HR system to build the necessary human capital and elicit the required employee behaviors which translate into strategic implementation effectiveness. We agree with the basic tenets, but think that the value chain provides a more comprehensive approach to understanding the differentiated HR systems.

As shown in Figure 20.1, analysis of the value chain identifies the key business processes and activities that underlie a firm's core capabilities.

Certainly, numerous sub-processes take place at each stage in the value chain, but our focus is on those that are most critical in order to deliver an end product or service. Two implications derive from this.

First, examining processes within the value chain suggests that different strategies require superior capabilities at different stages in the value chain. For instance, Dell's operational excellence strategy requires a superior capability in supply chain management relative to PC industry competitors. On the other hand, Ritz Carlton's customer intimacy requires significantly greater capability in customer service relative to its hotel competitors. Thus, the value chain points to the first step in linking HR to strategy by providing a tool for identifying which strategic business processes must be executed in a way superior to competitors.

Second, the value chain analysis provides a tool for identifying the key human capital pools that must be effectively managed in order to build the required capability. Lepak and Snell (1999) were among the first to suggest that different human capital pools require different HR systems. Their framework suggested that the strategic value and uniqueness of the skill sets determine the overall strategic importance of a given human capital pool. Becker and Huselid (2006) suggest that rather than focusing on the skills, a focus on jobs enables a clearer link to business processes. For instance, they argued that computer programming skills may be the same, but the strategic importance of those skills differs between the computer programmer job in strategic software development relative to the computer programmer job in support function.

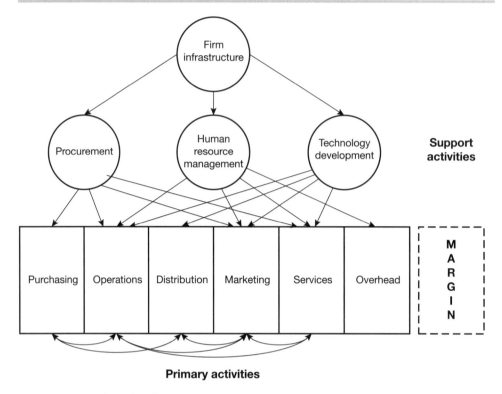

Figure 20.1 Complete value chain

By examining the value chain, one can identify the strategic job families (and consequently skill sets) that are critically paired with the execution of strategic business processes. It is important to note that this does not imply that only one job would be critical to the execution of a particular business process; often these processes require the coordination and cooperation of individuals within two or more jobs.

Once the key human capital pools have been identified, this framework enables the analysis of the skills and behaviors that are required in the execution of the business processes. As Wright and Snell (1998) noted, employee behavior is the most proximal and important HR outcome in the execution of strategy. Business processes require key behaviors of employees, both in the actual execution of the process as well as the tacit and explicit sharing of knowledge in the process of learning.

However, the exhibition of employee behavior entails possessing requisite skills and abilities that must be selected into or developed within employees in the focal jobs. The human capital skills and knowledge encompass the tacit and explicit knowledge necessary for the execution of these processes. Thus, Figure 20.2 illustrates the critical interdependence of business processes, human capital skills and knowledge, and employee behaviors that constitute a capability.

Finally, this analysis leads to the design of the HR system necessary to assure the right number and type of employees required to execute and improve key business processes that underlie core capabilities for drive value creation. Kaplan and Norton (2006), in fact, delineate a measure of "human capital readiness" that calibrates the gap between the human capital requirements relative to the current number of employees who are currently qualified for strategic jobs. This assessment is then used to inform HR investment decisions directed at developing or acquiring skills and abilities of individuals in key jobs, eliciting key behaviors from these individuals, and designing work that provides the requisite level of participation, communication, and knowledge exchange.

This leads into an examination of HR practices. Past research in HR practices has often operationalized the HR system as a single scale of HR practices (Dhatta et al., 2005; Guthrie, 2001) or sometimes an empirically derived multidimensional scale (e.g., Huselid, 1995). However, a number of SHRM researchers have noted that human resource systems can be described along three common dimensions (Appelbaum et al., 2000; Delery, 1998; Dyer and Holder, 1988).

First is the degree of investment in HR practices intended to improve the knowledge, skills, and abilities of the companies' employees. These include recruiting, training, selection, socialization, and any other practice functioning to enhance the workplace competencies of the employees. Such practices seek to build specific relevant skills, or increase the level of those skills among the focal human capital group. With regard to capabilities, this category of practices can aim to ensure that the organization has the skills and skill levels required by those employees key to the execution of business processes.

The second dimension is the degree of investment in HR practices functioning to motivate employee behavior. In general, HR practices can seek to elicit task-related behavior (that is necessary to perform the basic job), encourage employees to exhibit discretionary behavior (i.e., go outside the expected job behaviors to positively impact organizational effectiveness), or to discourage counterproductive behavior (actions that negatively impact the firm such as theft, sabotage, etc.) Practices such as incentive pay plans, performance bonuses, gain sharing, and performance management systems primarily aim at managing employee behavior. Because business processes require certain behaviors of key employee groups, one focus of the HR system has to be on eliciting the positive behaviors and inhibiting the negative ones.

Finally, HR practices function to provide opportunities to participate in substantive decision making regarding work and organizational outcomes. These include such practices as quality circles, suggestion systems, granting discretion and authority on the job, information sharing about the service or production process, and opportunities to communicate with employees and managers in other work groups. This is one area where differentiation may be seen across a variety of business processes. For instance, Starbucks, the coffee retailer, seeks operational excellence in the processes used to make a cup of coffee. Figure 20.2 shows the composition of the value chain in Starbucks Coffee.

A number of training programs within Starbucks teach specific procedures for exactly how much of each ingredient should be used, in what order, etc. In these processes there is little opportunity for employees to deviate from the prescribed behavior. However, in terms of serving customers, Starbucks employees have great latitude to deviate from prescribed behavior, or share ideas and suggestions for certain aspects of the operation.

While the practice can be subcategorized within the AMO framework, Lepak et al. (2003) note that the framework does not preclude overlap among the practices. For instance, training programs may primarily aim at building the requisite skill base, but may also communicate a commitment to the employee that elicits motivation as well. Similarly, participation programs provide opportunity, but may also help build the knowledge and motivation of employees.

In summary, an analysis of capabilities broadens SHRM beyond an exclusive focus on human capital or HR practices as direct or independent resources that drive performance or competitive advantage toward a more comprehensive understanding of how those resources are aligned with processes and technologies. This is consistent with the argument of Mahoney and Pandian (1992) that "[a] firm may achieve rents not because it has better resources, but rather the firm's distinctive competence involves making better use of its resources" (p. 365).

Figure 20.2 Starbucks coffee

	Sourcing and SCM*	Coffee operations	Sourcing and SCM	Regulatory and environment
PROCESS • Cost • Quality • Speed	Procurement	Roasting and blending	Order fulfillment	Conservation 'C.A.F.E.'
SYSTEMS	e-procurement systems	Roasting curves	POS inventory and CRM	Scientific certification system
PEOPLE	• Coffee trader	• Coffee master • Roaster	• Barista • Floater	• Agronomy • Compliance
OBJECTIVE • Competencies • Behavior • Engagement	• Reduce supply chain risk through long-term relations	• Identify house blend combos • Assess sourcing value	• Increase store throughout capacity and fix bottlenecks	• Develop farmer yield capacity • Ensure local development
INVEST	• Experience hire • Technical training • LT incentives	• Job security • Education • Rotation/assign	• Team-based • Time incentives • Share/suggest	• Experience hire • Local knowledge • License/certify • CSR scorecard

* Supply chain management

Dynamic capabilities

While capabilities distinguish a firm positively, over time the capabilities can serve as a constraint as well. For instance, Peteraf suggested,

> These resources can provide both the basis and the direction for the growth of the firm. For example, there may be a natural trajectory embedded in a firm's knowledge base. Current capabilities may both impel and constrain future learning and investment activity.
>
> (1993: 181–2)

Such a concern with the "core rigidity" that may stem from capabilities led to the concept of dynamic capabilities.

Teece and his colleagues defined dynamic capabilities as "the subset of the competencies/ capabilities which allow the firm to create new products and processes and respond to changing market circumstances" (Teece and Pisano, 1994: 541) and later as "the firm's ability to integrate, build, and reconfigure internal and external competencies to address rapidly changing environments" (Teece et al., 1997: 516). Eisenhardt and Martin suggested that dynamic capabilities "are the organizational and strategic routines by which firms achieve new resource configurations as markets emerge, collide, split, evolve, and die" (2000: 1107). Some have argued that even dynamic capabilities can become rigid, impeding a firm's ability to adapt to a changing environment. Our purpose here is not to debate the concept itself, but rather to note that in addition to specific capabilities such as being able to distinguish a firm's value creation strategy at a given point in time, firms often must also find ways to transform or develop new capabilities in the face of environmental change. This has important implications for SHRM.

Milliman et al. (1991) were early authors examining the concept of HR flexibility, exploring it within the multinational HRM environment. Wright and Snell (1998) proposed a more specific and formal conceptualization for exploring HR flexibility, positing that such flexibility consisted of skill flexibility, behavior flexibility, and HR practice flexibility.

Wright and Snell defined the flexibility of employee skills as the "number of potential alternative uses to which employee skills can be applied" (1998: 764) and "how individuals with different skills can be redeployed quickly" (1998: 765).

Flexibility of employee behavior refers to the degree to which employees are able to exhibit adaptable as opposed to routine behaviors. It deals with the extent to which they possess a broad repertoire of behavioral scripts and can adapt those scripts to specific situations.

Flexibility of HR practices refers to the extent to which HR practices can be adapted and/or applied across a variety of situations or sites within the firm, and the speed with which these adaptations can be applied.

Implications of resources, capabilities, and dynamic capabilities for SHRM

The more recent emphasis on aligning HR practices with strategy through a focus on capabilities has some important implications for HR research. First, as Becker and Huselid (2006) noted, while some HR practices are differentiated across jobs within the firm, there may also be some general HR practices or principles that are part of the larger HR architecture. For instance, during the 1990s IBM sought to transform its "entitlement" culture into a "performance-based" culture. Part of this transformation required implementing more

353

performance-based rewards and even shifting employees to cash-balance pension plans to move the risk from the company to the employees. While the specifics may have differed across jobs, the basic principle began to infiltrate the HR systems across all jobs.

Second, the kinds of practices that have been measured in the past seem to be more of the larger HR architecture (e.g., "On average, how many hours of training do employees get per year?" or "What is the average merit increase for a high performer? For a low performer?"). As researchers began to focus more on core jobs (Delery and Doty, 1996; MacDuffie, 1995) the research began to recognize that certain jobs are more central to a firm's success, and that it is the practices in regards to these jobs that may be most important. This was more explicitly recognized by Lepak and Snell's (1999) HR Architecture that articulated a framework for understanding which jobs were most critical. Thus, future research needs to (a) identify the key job(s) within the firm and (b) focus on the HR practices covering those jobs.

Third, identifying the key jobs will likely entail understanding the core capabilities that the firm is attempting to create or exploit. Differing customer strategies require different capabilities within the firm's value chain, and understanding the key capabilities will lead to better identifying the most critical jobs.

Finally, this leads to a more specific set of tools for tying HR to strategy. Past attempts have usually assessed overall HR practices within the firm and sought to see if those practices "fit" with the firm's strategy to determine performance (c.f., Huselid, 1995). However, a more realistic approach suggests that the key to fit is through understanding the core capabilities inherent in implementing the strategies, and the core jobs within those capabilities, and then focusing an effective set of HR practices to maximize the performance of individuals in those key jobs. Thus, alignment of HR and strategy will best be understood in the context of capabilities, and not global fit with strategy.

References

Amit, R. and Schoemaker, P.J.H. 1993. Strategic assets and organizational rent. *Strategic Management Journal*, 14, 33–46.

Appelbaum, E., Bailey, T., Berg, P. and Kallenberg, A.L. 2000. *Manufacturing advantage. Why high-performance work systems pay off.* New York: Cornell University Press.

Barney, J. 1991. Firm resources and sustained competitive advantage. *Journal of Management*, 17(1), 99.

Becker, B. and Gerhart, B. 1996. The impact of human resource management on organizational performance: Progress and prospects. *Academy of Management Journal*, 39(4), 779.

Becker, B.E. and Huselid, M.A. 1998. High performance work systems and firm performance: A synthesis of research and managerial implications. *Research in Personnel and Human Resource Management*, 16, 53–101.

Becker, B. and Huselid, M. 2006. Strategic Human Resources Management: Where do we go from here? *Journal of Management*, 32(6), 898–925.

Boselie, P., Dietz, G. and Boon, C. 2005. Commonalities and contradictions in HRM and performance research. *Human Resource Management Journal*, 15, 67–94.

Capelli, P. and Singh, H. 1992. Integrating strategic human resources and strategic management. In D. Lewin, O.S. Mitchell and P.D. Sherer (Eds), *Research frontiers in industrial relations and human resources* (pp. 165–192). Madison, WI: IRRA.

Combs, J., Ketchen, D., Jr., Hall, A. and Liu, Y. 2006. Do high performance work practices matter? A meta-analysis of their effects on organizatonal performance. *Personnel Psychology*, 59, 501–28.

Datta, D., Guthrie, J. and Wright, P. 2005. Industry as a moderator of the HR–firm performance relationship. *Academy of Management Journal*, 48(1), 135–45.

Delery, J.E. 1998. Issues of fit in strategic human resource management: Implications for research. *Human Resource Management Review*, 8(3), 289.

Delery, J.E. and Doty, D.H. 1996. Modes of theorizing in strategic human resource management: Tests of universalistic, contingency, and configurational performance predictions. *Academy of Management Journal*, 39, 802–35.

Delery, J. and Shaw, J. 2001. The strategic management of people in work organizations: Review, synthesis, and extension. *Research in Personnel and Human Resources Management*, 20, 165–97.

Dell, M. and Fredman, C. 1999. *Direct from Dell: Strategies that revolutionized an industry*. New York: John Wiley.

Dierickx, I. and Cool, K. 1989. Asset stock accumulation and sustainability of competitive advantage. *Management Science*, 35, 1504–11.

Dyer, L. and Holder, G. 1988. A strategic perspective of human resources management. In L. Dyer and G. Holder (Eds), *Human Resources Management: Evolving roles and responsibilities*. Washington, DC: American Society for Personnel Administration.

Eisenhardt, K. and Martin, J. 2000. Dynamic capabilities: What are they? *Strategic Management Journal*, 21, 1105–21.

Guthrie, J. 2001. High involvement work practices, turnover, and productivity: Evidence from New Zealand. *Academy of Management Journal*, 44, 180–92.

Hatch, N. and Dyer, J. 2004. Human capital and learning as a source of sustainable competitive advantage. *Strategic Management Journal*, 25, 1155–78.

Hitt, M., Bierman, L., Shimizu, K. and Kochar, R. 2001. Direct and moderating effects of human capital on the strategy and performance in professional service firms: A resource-based perspective. *Academy of Management Journal*, 44, 13–28.

Huselid, M.A. 1995. The impact of human resource management practices on turnover, productivity, and corporate financial performance. *Academy of Management Journal*, 38, 635–72.

Lado, A.A. and Wilson, M.C. 1994. Human resource systems and sustained competitive advantage: A competency-based perspective. *Academy of Management Review*, 19(4), 699–727.

Lepak, D.P. and Snell, S.A. 1999. The human resource architecture: Toward a theory of human capital development and allocation. *Academy of Management Review*, 24(1), 31–48.

Lepak, D.P. and Snell, S.A. 2002. Examining the human resource architecture: The relationships among human capital, employment, and human resource configurations. *Journal of Management*, 28(4), 517–43.

Lepak, D.P. and Snell, S.A. 2004. Managing the human resource architecture for knowledge-based competition. In S. Jackson, M. Hitt and A. DeNisi (Eds), *Managing knowledge for sustained competitive advantage: Designing strategies for effective Human Resource Management*, SIOP Scientific Frontiers Series, (pp. 127–54). San Francisco: Jossey-Bass.

Lepak, D.P., Takeuchi, R. and Snell, S.A. 2003. Employment flexibility and firm performance: Examining the moderating effects of employment mode, environmental dynamism, and technological intensity. *Journal of Management*, 29(5), 681–705.

MacDuffie, J.P. 1995. Human resource bundles and manufacturing performance: Organizational logic and flexible systems in the world auto industry. *Industrial and Labor Relations Review*, 48, 197–221.

Mahoney, J. and Pandian, J. 1992. Resource-based view within the conversation of strategic management. *Strategic Management Journal*, 13, 363–80.

Miles, R. and Snow, C. 1994. *Fit, failure, and the Hall of Fame*. New York: Free Press.

Milliman, J., Von Glinow, M. and Nathan, M. 1991. Organizational life cycles and strategic international human resource management in multinational companies. *Academy of Management Review*, 16, 318–39.

Newbert, S. 2007. Empirical research on the resource-based view of the firm: An assessment and suggestions for future research. *Strategic Management Journal*, 28(2), 121–46.

Penrose, E. 1959. *A theory of the growth of the firm*. Oxford: Oxford University Press.

Peteraf, M. 1993. The cornerstones of competitive advantage: A resource-based view. *Strategic Management Journal*, 14, 179–91.

Porter, M. 1996. What is strategy? *Harvard Business Review*, 74, 61–78.

Prahalad, C.K. and Hamel, G. 1990. The core competence of the corporation. *Harvard Business Review*, 68(3), 79–91.

Priem, R.L. and Butler, J.E. 2001. Tautology in the resource-based view and the implications of externally determined resource value: Further comments. *Academy of Management Review*, 26, 57–66.

Ray, G., Barney, J. and Muhanna, W. 2004. Capabilities, business processes, and competitive advantage: Choosing the dependent variable in empirical tests of the resource based view. *Strategic Management Journal*, 25, 23–37.

Rubin, P. 1973. The expansion of firms. *Journal of Political Economy*, 84, 936–49.

Schuler, R. S. and Jackson, S. E. 1987. Linking competitive strategies with human resource management practices. *Academy of Management Executive*, 1(3), 207–19.

Sherer, P.D. 1995. Leveraging human assets in law firms: Human capital structures and organizational capability. *Industrial and Labor Relations Review*, 48: 671–91.

Snell, S.A. 1992. A test of control theory in strategic human resource management: The mediating effect of administrative information. *Academy of Management Journal*, 35(2), 292–327.

Snell, S.A. and Youndt, M.A. 1995. Human resource management and firm performance: Testing a contingency model of executive controls. *Journal of Management*, 21(4), 711–37.

Teece, D. and Pisano, G. 1994. The dynamic capabilities of firms: An introduction. *Industrial and Corporate Change*, 3(3), 537–56.

Teece, D.J., Pisano, G. and Shuen, A. 1997. Dynamic capabilities and strategic management. *Strategic Management Journal*, 18(7), 509–33.

Wernerfelt, B. 1984. A resource-based view of the firm. *Strategic Management Journal*, 5(2), 171–80.

Wright, P.M. and Snell, S.A. 1991. Toward an integrated view of strategic human resource management. *Human Resource Management Review*, 1, 203–25.

Wright, P.M. and Snell, S.A. 1998. Toward a unifying framework for exploring fit and flexibility in strategic human resource management. *Academy of Management Review*, 23, 756–72.

Wright, P.M., Dunford, B.B. and Snell, S.A. 2001. Human resources and the resource based view of the firm. *Journal of Management*, 27, 701–21.

Wright, P.M., Gardner, T.M. and Moynihan, L.M. 2003. The impact of HR practices on the performance of business. *Human Resource Management Journal*, 13, 21–36.

Wright, P.M., McMahan, G.C. and McWilliams, A. 1994. Human resources as a source of sustained competitive advantage: A resource-based perspective. *International Journal of Human Resource Management*, 5, 301–26.

Wright, P.M., Smart, D.L. and McMahan, G.C. 1995. Matches between human resources and strategy among NCAA basketball teams. *Academy of Management Journal*, 38, 1052–74.

Wright, P.M., Gardner, T.M., Moynihan, L.M. and Allen, M.R. 2005. The relationship between HR practices and firm performance: Examining causal order. *Personnel Psychology*, 58, 409–46.

21

Options for human capital acquisition

*Mousumi Bhattacharya
and Patrick M. Wright*

With increasing uncertainty over human capital, many firms are relying on alternative employment arrangements that can respond quickly to changes. The predominant theoretical explanations for such arrangements focus on the 'resource-based view' or the 'transactions cost' aspect of these arrangements. An 'options' view explains how firms that face uncertainty over human capital would use alternative employment arrangements like temporary, part-time, contractual workers and internships, or outsource the work. We analyze the 'options' view of alternative employment arrangements and discuss two types of options – skill options and employee options – that create flexibilities as well as growth and learning opportunities. The opportunity cost of not having these options is quantifiable, which makes this approach valuable for human capital acquisition decisions in strategic human resource management.

Firms are using a number of alternative work arrangements such as part-time employment, temporary and contract employment (Cappelli, 1995, 1999a, b), outsourcing and internships to manage the uncertainties associated with human capital. The predominant theoretical explanations for these work arrangements have been the resource-based view (Wright et al., 2001) and the transactions cost theory. The transactions cost explanation maintains that firms would engage in alternative employment arrangements in an attempt to lower costs (Cappelli, 1995, 1999a, b). The resource-based view (RBV) suggests: (a) that organizations use contingent employees to buffer their core employees from the uncertainties of the labor market because they need a committed and cooperative workforce, therefore there would be a higher proportion of contingent employees in establishments with a higher level of internalization (Gramm and Schnell, 2001; Osterman, 1994, 2000); (b) the contingent workforce is hired as needed for specific skills or specialized know-how without investing the time and resources required to develop employee skills for what may be a short-term project or a project deemed to be risky because technological advances may make the investment obsolete; and (c) alternative employment arrangements are used to provide greater strategic focus in the sense that a firm may retain standard, full-time employees only in those areas that it deems its core competencies. However, none of these explanations elaborate *how* the firm can build the flexibilities needed to meet the uncertainties in skills or employment levels.

In this chapter we propose that the real options logic (Bowman and Hurry, 1993; Dixit and Pindyck, 1994; Kogut and Kulatilaka, 2001; McGrath, 1997) provides another explanation for why firms use alternative employment arrangements and *how* they attain flexibility in response to increased uncertainty. Real options are exploratory investments in capabilities that hedge the future (i.e., that allow the firm to change decisions in the future). When uncertainty about skills or employee fit are high, firms would invest in alternative employment arrangements through time-deferred (start with alternative workers, hiring may be done later), sequential (start with alternative workers and then increase scale), path-dependent (knowledge about skill and employee fit increases after employing the alternative workers) decision choices called 'options' (Kogut and Kulatilaka, 2001; Leiblien, 2003). The options part of these arrangements create operational flexibilities such as options to wait (not hiring upfront), defer (hire at a later date) or abandon, i.e., not hiring at all (Trigeorgis, 1996) as well as growth and learning opportunities, i.e., learning difficult skills through alternative work arrangements (Amram and Kulatilaka, 1999; McGrath, 1997; Trigeorgis, 1996). Therefore these human capital options create value for the firm under conditions of high uncertainty and irreversibility of investments (Bowman and Hurry, 1993; Dixit and Pindyck, 1994; Kogut and Kulatilaka, 2001).

For example, in a highly skilled profession such as information technology (IT), a resource-based prescription would be to internalize the skills by direct hiring so that firm-specific valuable, rare and inimitable human capital can be created. However, the real options view would propose that if uncertainty about the skills is high in the sense that the skill sets required of IT professionals change rapidly over time, then it is better to contract out such work to experienced IT professionals so that the flexibility to change the skill sets by changing contractual employees is retained. When a firm hires, it makes some irreversible investments in human capital in the form of recruitment, training and other costs. If the employee skills become obsolete, or if the employee leaves due to high demand for his/her skills, then this investment is lost. Alternatively, little or no training is provided to contractual employees, and they are expected to produce results from day one, so there are no irreversible investments. However the contractual employees may be more expensive than regular employees, therefore he/she would be able to renew the contract only when the returns to the firm are adequate. This example shows that a real options view provides a heuristic decision process contingent upon unveiling of information in the future and therefore provides a rich explanation of the process of human capital acquisition.

The real options view, as applied to human capital acquisition decisions, provides a theoretical framework that explains how operational flexibilities and growth and learning opportunities are created. The resource-based view has been criticized as tautological in the sense that 'valuable' resources explain creation of value, and that the process of value creation is ambiguous (Leiblein, 2003; Priem and Butler, 2001) and discovered 'by luck'. Real options theory addresses these concerns and explains how investments in options (i.e., time-deferred choices) create value by generating operational flexibility (Leiblein, 2003) as well as growth and learning opportunities. This approach is specifically suitable for a 'what if' analysis of future situations and contextual changes, thereby adding a 'dynamic' component to the 'static' predictions of the resource-based view (Priem and Butler, 2001). According to the resource-based view, a firm would strive to acquire valuable human capital upfront so that its current assets are of maximum value. The underlying assumption is that value for firm is created through internalizing the valuable human capital. The real options view, on the other hand, would suggest that if the uncertainty about the future value of human capital is high, the firm is better off by not internalizing the human capital, but engaging in alternative work arrangements, which may or may not be internalized in the future. Here the risk of loss of future value of human capital is minimized by maintaining operational flexibilities – therefore value is created through flexibility. Our explanation sheds light on the question of how managers decide to acquire skills and employees in the presence of uncertainty of demand, supply and returns, so that these can be a source of competitive advantage. Therefore options theory, a heuristic, sequential investment model, helps make sense of how managers find talent and create value for the firm.

The options framework

Options are contractual rights to buy (call) or sell (put) assets (stocks, commodities, foreign currency) in a predetermined price, at a future date, after which they expire. They provide a way to capitalize on the *uncertainty* of asset prices. For example, in the case of call options, if price movement works favorably (i.e., market price becomes higher than the predetermined price), then the option is exercised and positive returns are generated; if not, only the investment in option price is lost. For put options, if the market price goes down, then the option holder profits by selling it at the higher predetermined price. Financial options, therefore, defer the decision to invest in the asset to a future point of time, which reduces the uncertainty about future prices and reduces the loss associated with unfavorable price movements. Another important function of options is to provide *flexibility* for investment decisions. The owner of the option has the choice whether or not to exercise the option. Therefore financial options buy time and flexibility to invest, at the cost of the option price. The distinguishing characteristic of an options approach lies in an individual making investments that confer the ability to select an outcome only if it is favorable.

Real options follow a similar rationale, but the assumptions and nature of options are somewhat different. These are decisions regarding investments in assets that are similar to financial options in spirit but different in many aspects (Amram and Kulatilaka, 1999; Bowman and Hurry, 1993; Dixit and Pindyck, 1994). While financial options are created for financial assets that can easily be valued and are readily tradable in markets, real options are created for real assets (the term 'real' probably implies that these assets are actually used in the production of goods and services), which may not be perfectly tradable; the investments may be *irreversible*, and difficult to put a value on. Creation of real assets may also need non-financial investments like time and effort. As a result real options are not precisely defined, neatly packaged, or traded like financial options: they may be implied or exist implicitly in the resources, capabilities, and processes of the firm (Kogut and Kulatilaka, 2001); they may have invisible components, which makes exact valuation of real options difficult even with the passage of time; they may not be perfectly tradable because of market imperfections and information asymmetries; and they may involve unknown or uncertain expiration dates (McGrath et al., 2004). Real options, unlike their financial counterparts, are rarely backed by legal contracts guaranteeing the holder's rights in precise terms. Most are non-proprietary investment opportunities whose terms are somewhat vague and far from guaranteed. In a few instances a legally enforceable property right such as an oil lease or patent confers a proprietary right similar to that granted by a financial option. Table 21.1 provides a comparison of financial and real options (as well as human capital options discussed later).

Although the primary underlying rationale for real options remains the same as for financial options (i.e., time-deferred investments) the emphasis is also on *growth* (Amram and Kulatilaka, 1999; Trigeorgis, 1996), *operational flexibility* (Bowman and Hurry, 1993), and *learning* (Amram and Kulatilaka, 1999; McGrath, 1997). Timing options create time-deferred investment choices for assets that have high irreversibility (e.g., oil exploration sites, power plants) so that decisions can be made as more familiarity is gained in the future while maintaining preferential access to the asset. Options to defer (Trigeorgis, 1996) and options for staging (Amram and Kulatilaka,

Table 21.1 Comparison of financial, real, and human capital options

Dimension	Financial options	Real options	Human capital options
Underlying assets	Financial securities, e.g., stocks, currency, commodities	Real assets, tangible or intangible, e.g., projects, products, technology, new venture	Skills, employees
Nature of underlying assets	Tangible, perfectly tradable	Tangible with intangible components, partly tradable	Mostly intangible, not tradeable, ownership not transferable, the firm never 'owns' the asset
Value of underlying asset	Underlying security has value	Underlying asset has value	Employees add value through application of their skills
Uncertainties	Price of security varies over time	Value of assets varies over time	Demand and supply of skills vary over time, uncertainty about returns from application of skills, uncertainty about skill-matching and person-matching of employee
Types of options	Calls, puts	Options to defer, wait, abandon, switch, flexibility options, learning options, growth options	Options to defer, wait, abandon, switch, flexibility options, learning options
Use of options	Time-deferred investment choices	Time-deferred investment choices, operational flexibility, growth and learning	Time-deferred investment choices, operational flexibility, learning, switching
Rights under the contract	Right to buy or sell securities at a set price on a future date	Right to further develop, abandon, or switch projects/operations in the future	Uncertain rights
Investment required	Premium to be paid at the time of the contract	Partial investment or extra investment in the current period	May entail extra cost in the current period
Expiration date	Fixed	Varies, can be indefinite	Can be indefinite
Benefits of options	Allow the investor to cover risks and benefit from volatile prices with far less investment	Allow firms to buffer against future loss of value, enables lower sunk cost, create flexibility of investment	Identify valuable human capital, reduce uncertainty of human capital

1999) fall into this category. Growth options (Amram and Kulatilaka, 1999; Trigeorgis, 1996) are limited investments that create future growth opportunities (e.g., projects to develop new markets). Through these options, the firm gains access to the potential upside (new business) while limiting the losses (amount invested in the project) they would otherwise incur from unfavorable outcomes. Similarly, learning options (Amram and Kulatilaka, 1999; McGrath, 1997) are limited investments to test the market or to gain more familiarity because the future returns from these investments are uncertain. Flexibility options create choices for the scale and scope of operation. Options to alter operating scale (Trigeorgis, 1996), options to abandon (Trigeorgis, 1996) or exit options (Amram and Kulatilaka, 1999), and options to switch (Trigeorgis, 1996) belong to this category.

Real options theory is complementary to the resource-based view in explaining the significance of firm resources and capabilities for competitive advantage (Leiblen, 2003). Although the resource-based view highlights how resources and capabilities contribute to firm performance, it does not address the issue of how managers may develop them. Rather it assumes that firms have (somehow) made upfront investments in the processes of creating resources whose eventual value is inherently ambiguous and uncertain (Leiblen, 2003). This gives rise to the notion of resource heterogeneity and resource immobility arising out of history-driven causal ambiguity. Real options theory, on the other hand, explicitly addresses the issue of investment choices for future resources and capabilities. It assumes that managers possess a level of foresight sufficient to enter into contracts (options) that provide implicit or explicit claims on future opportunities (Leiblen, 2003) and analyzes how firms can lay claim to future rent-generating capabilities through investment in these options. Real options theory is similar to the resource-based view in claiming that present resources and capabilities arise out of past investments. However, it goes further in specifying how time-deferred choices and operational flexibilities can add value for investments in irreversible resources and processes with uncertain returns. (Leiblen, 2003). According to Bowman and Hurry (1993), the options framework offers an economic logic for incremental, path-dependent resource investment. In other words it specifically addresses the issue of finding a superior mechanism of resource allocation (McGrath et al., 2004).

Human capital

Human capital, i.e., the knowledge, skills, and abilities embodied in the employees of a firm (Becker, 1993), exhibits many of the characteristics of real assets, as discussed by real options scholars. It provides current as well as future returns for the firm as employees generate value through their knowledge, skills, and competencies that are used for all value-added activities of the firm over a period of time. Investments, in the form of time, money, and effort, are needed to acquire, motivate, and maintain human capital. Many investments in human capital are irreversible because they cannot be taken back from employees or traded in the market. The returns from these investments are uncertain, as employees may not perform as per expectations, or may leave the firm, or the skills may lose value.

However, human capital is different from other real assets in a few ways (see Table 21.1). First, human capital is almost entirely intangible and is difficult to quantify (most measures are 'proxies', e.g., education, experience). The value of human capital lies mostly in its application to other assets, rendering it extremely difficult to dissociate and quantify the value generated by human capital from that produced by other real assets. Second, unlike other forms of asset, a firm never fully 'owns' its human capital. The knowledge, skills, and abilities reside in the people, and are lost when people leave the firm. Therefore there is a unique risk associated with human capital, the risk of capital loss or turnover (i.e., the asset 'walking away'). At the same time this also makes human capital more 'reversible' than other forms of real assets as firms can lay off employees. Third, non-financial investments like time, communication, and leadership constitute a major part of investments that generate returns from human capital through eliciting the commitment and competency of employees over the long run. These, combined with the fact that human capital is almost never tradable in the market, makes management of this form of asset a more difficult task.

Managers must identify and assemble a bundle of human resources that contributes to competitive advantage, a central problem for human capital management of the firm. While both the resource-based view and real options theory address this problem, they provide different, albeit related, rationales. The resource-based view delineates the characteristics that human capital needs to be able to contribute to competitive advantage. They should be valuable enough to enable the firm to create strategies to reduce cost and/or generate greater revenues; and should be rare, difficult to imitate, and non-substitutable so as to put limits for competition (Leiblen, 2003). They should generate more value than when they were acquired, in a causally ambiguous way, so that competition is imperfect in the factor market. Therefore the resource-based view assumes that the process of creating valuable, rare, inimitable, and non-substitutable human capital is causally ambiguous and history-driven so that it cannot be replicated.

The real options theory on the other hand focuses on the creation of decision choices for uncertain and irreversible investments in human capital, so that when the uncertainty is resolved managers can invest optimally. In other words, when the managers are not sure about returns, or when the investments cannot be recouped easily, it is more valuable to wait or to build in flexibilities through options. Although this may cost more initially, the opportunity cost of inflexibility is greater, making the options investment more attractive. Real options theory predicts that time-deferred or flexible investments generate valuable human capital because investments are made after the value-creating potential becomes more apparent. These also create a causal path, which nevertheless is difficult to imitate because of time-dependency as well as the complexity of combinations. Additionally, they make human capital rare and non-substitutable because of continued investments over a long period of time. Consequently, a salient contribution of real options theory is also to capture the value of certain investments that the traditional valuation methods cannot ascertain. For example, as we discuss below, the value of temporary and contingent workers lies not only in cutting cost and creating operational flexibilities, but also in generating valuable 'learning' and knowledge and offering the value of 'waiting' before making commitments of skill acquisition.

Options for human capital acquisition

The real options framework predicts that firms can create valuable human capital by creating options which are time-deferred, sequential decision choices. Kogut and Kulatilaka recognize that 'a real option is the investment in physical and *human assets* that provides the opportunity to respond to future contingent events' (2001: 745, emphasis added). Expanding on this notion, human capital options are defined as investments in the human capital pool of an organization that provides the capability to respond to future contingent events (Bhattacharya and Wright, 2005). These options enable the firm to develop, maintain, and deploy human capital for managing uncertainties and irreversibilities associated with them. Figure 21.1 provides a framework for our discussion.

In order to analyze options for human capital acquisition, we need to discuss the uncertainties and irreversibilities associated with employee skills and employee fit. Uncertainty is

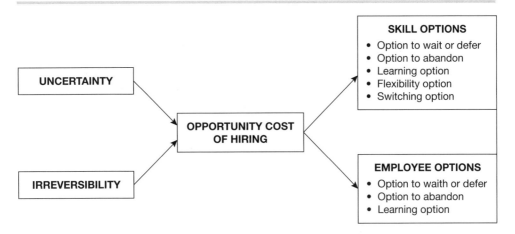

Figure 21.1 Options model for human capital acquisition

inability to predict future and irreversibility is the inability to costlessly revisit an investment or decision (Kogut and Kulatilaka, 2001). Skills constitute human capital and contribute towards firm capabilities. Under traditional HR practices, firms acquire 'skills' by recruiting employees whose skill sets match the job. Under this paradigm, the 'person–job' fit is critical in hiring an employee. However, this approach does not consider contingencies when the nature of the job or the skills required for the job would change. The resource-based view, which purports acquiring valuable, rare, and inimitable human capital, would recommend that firms be 'selective' in recruitment and also consider 'person–organization' fit so that firm-specific complex human capital can be generated. This approach assumes that the firm has sufficient knowledge about the value and rarity of the human capital; however, this may not be the case and the source of value and rarity may change over time. The 'options' view would consider acquisition of skills somewhat differently – it would first evaluate the uncertainties associated with the skills, i.e., how soon or how certainly the demand for the skills is expected to change. Second, it would determine how much irreversible investment in the form of recruitment, training, and other costs is required in order to acquire the skills. If both uncertainties and irreversibilities are high then this view would recommend that the firm waits before internalizing the skills and consider alternative employment arrangements for skill 'options' till the uncertainties are reduced. We will now discuss these skill options in detail.

Skill options

Uncertainty regarding skills has evoked quite some attention in recent years as technological, global, and demographic forces have brought about continuous changes in demand, supply, and returns of skills. Skill acquisition is a major investment decision for human capital because skills, especially highly specialized ones, can be difficult to acquire (Coff, 2002) and cost of labor is a major component of overall cost of goods produced. Although the resource-based view posits that the unique skills and experiences of human capital can give the firm a competitive advantage (Lado and Wilson, 1994), it offers little towards how such skills are acquired. The real options view, on the other hand, provides a process heuristic for understanding the sequential investment choices in skills. This process is highlighted by alternate investment decision choices for skill acquisition, which are, to hire employees and internalize the skills, to use temporary or contractual employees, or to outsource. Although these choices have long been exercised by firms, it is only now that we can explain these through a comprehensive theoretical rationale, which is the real options logic – neither the resource-based view of the firm, nor the transactions cost theory can fully explain why the firm would choose one mode of employment over the other. The resource-based view can explain how valuable skills lead to firm competitive advantage but does not explain the process of value creation; the transaction costs view emphasizes cost savings through alternative arrangements but offers little beyond that.

Hiring is upfront investment in human capital with associated costs of recruitment, subsequent training and benefits, as well as responsibilities for maintaining human capital and obtaining results from them. Most of these investments are irreversible and are lost if the employee is terminated or if the employee leaves. Along with the costs associated with recruitment, the investments made in developing human capital are lost. There may also be substantial exit costs in the form of severance payments to laid-off employees, a declining reputation as a good employer, and/or reduced morale among remaining employees (Matusik and Hill, 1998). The primary uncertainty in hiring is whether the skills acquired can lead to firm capabilities that are valuable, especially for capabilities that require complex or higher level skills. As Quinn and Hilmer (1994) point out, these skills need intensity and dedication that is difficult to achieve if many activities in the value chain are integrated. In other words, efforts to develop too many capabilities may dilute the skill set, especially for high skill categories. If the skills do not produce the desired results then not only the investment is lost, but additional costs of layoffs may be incurred (Brockner, 1988). McElroy et al. (2001) find that layoffs and turnover can have adverse effects on firm performance. Therefore for skills where uncertainty and irreversibility of hiring is high, options for alternative employment arrangements are valuable.

From a real options perspective, use of temporary or contractual employees may have options value. Although temporary or contractual employees can be employed to cut costs (the transactions cost view) or to avoid liability associated with permanent employees, they are also used to meet demand fluctuations (Hippel et al., 1997). Firms can easily alter their scale and scope, and the mix of human capital through alternative work arrangements (Davis-Blake and Uzzi, 1993; Kochan et al., 1994; Matusik and Hill, 1998) because through these work arrangements the firm makes employees a loosely coupled component of the system, thus increasing their recombinability and its own flexibility (Lepak and Snell, 1999). In essence these are flexibility options, i.e., options, to change scale and scope of operation (Bowman and Hurry, 1993). If there is uncertainty about whether a skill requirement will continue in the future, hiring temporary employees creates an 'option to defer' or 'option to wait' till demand is more certain (Foote and Folta, 2002). The option to 'abandon' the skills also exists (Matusik and Hill, 1998) because as future requirements are unveiled, the firm may or may not choose to internalize these skills. If the firm employs contingent work for accumulating and creating knowledge or to get access to specialized skills (Matusik and Hill, 1998), then 'learning' options (Amram and Kulatilaka, 1999; McGrath, 1997) are created. These options have value because of the gain of knowledge in uncertain skill application areas. As McGrath et al. note, 'exploration in uncertain new areas is strongly associated with heterogeneity in resource accumulation, creating the potential for preferential access' (2004: 90). This implies that learning options are the first stepping stones for creating rare, path-dependent, and inimitable human capital through incremental investments.

Although the underlying rationale of human capital acquisition options is similar to real options, there are some important differences (see Table 21.1). First, the firm may or may not get preferential access to the underlying asset, which is the new set of skills. As the firm get familiar with the skills through interaction with temporary workers, they may become more knowledgeable about it, but this is not preferential access in the true sense because the firm cannot lay a claim on the human capital (although in many cases of 'contract to hire', the contractual employee joins the company). Second, it is difficult to determine when these options will expire. The firm may continue to get the work done through temporary employees even if the uncertainties are resolved. Third, options theory leads HR professionals to subcontract and/or hire temporary employees. There are advantages and disadvantages associated with hiring more temporary employees. Options on people may not be the same as financial options since hiring people does not mean capturing their commitment and energy. Unless temporary or contract employees have commitments equal to full time, they may not be as effective.

Nevertheless, the options perspective helps us understand the value of using temporary or contractual workers better (Foote and Folta, 2002). Accordingly we propose:

Proposition 1a: Alternate employment modes like temporary and contractual workers, create flexibility options, options to wait or defer investments in human capital acquisition, options to abandon, as well as options to learn.

However, the question of when to invest in options instead of upfront hiring is much more complex and belies a simple explanation. Scholars have argued that temporary or contractual workers may have less commitment towards the firm (Dyne and Ang, 1998; Hippel et al., 1997), may affect quality of work (Hippel et al., 1997; Kochan et al., 1994; Mallon and Duberlay, 2000; Rousseau and Libuser, 1997), may be more difficult to control and coordinate (Mallon and Duberlay, 2000), may result in less innovation (Zahra and Nielsen, 2002), and may cause dissemination of knowledge outside which could lead to the decay of competencies (Matusik and Hill, 1998). Moreover, the firm may have to pay premium wages to contractual workers and the agency providing the workers may charge extra fees. For example, wages for temporary or contractual workers are higher than for permanent workers in IT (Kunda et al., 2002). Therefore the opportunity costs of hiring vis-à-vis that of options play a role in these decisions. Opportunity costs are investments that will not be made from a given set of scarce resources because they were invested in something else. In other words opportunity costs are returns lost because of forgone investments. Typically they are calculated as the difference between the returns from the investment and its alternatives. Opportunity costs of human capital acquisition choices are difficult to isolate, verify, and validate mathematically. At the same time, they are critical for our discussion of options.

Opportunity costs of hiring depend on the value of flexibility options, options to wait or defer, options to abandon, learning options, and switching options (see Appendix). As Foote and Folta (2002) contend, the value of the options created by temporary and contractual employees depends on the uncertainty and irreversibility of investments associated with hiring permanent employees. In other words options will be more valuable if uncertainty and irreversibility associated with hiring are high. For example, the value of flexibility options (i.e., expand or contract the skill set) is high if uncertainty of demand and supply of skills is high *and* hiring permanent employees involves high irreversible investments in the psychological contract of providing stable employment (Rousseau and Wade-Benzoni, 1994). Options to wait or defer investments in human capital are valuable when there is high uncertainty about continuation of demand for the skill *and* hiring permanent employees involves irreversible investments in recruitment costs and human capital development (e.g., extensive orientation training). Options to abandon are valuable when uncertainty about abandonment of skills is high (e.g., due to escalation of commitment; Adner and Levinthal, 2004) *and* there are high irreversible investments in employment contracts with permanent employees (e.g., due to unionization).

Learning options (through limited investments) are valuable when uncertainty about returns on skill applications is high (e.g., for very specialized skills) *and* irreversible investments for developing skills are high. Finally, value of switching options (i.e., substituting one set of skills with another) is high when uncertainty of returns from specific skills application is high *and* irreversible investments in in-house resources and processes is high.

We have noted that the psychological contract of providing stable employment is one of the irreversible investments in human capital. We feel that this concept merits some discussion. Schein (1980) defines the psychological contract as an unwritten set of expectations operating between every member of an organization and various managers and others in that organization. Robinson et al. (1994) have gone further and argued that the psychological contract involves something stronger than just 'expectations', that what is involved are 'promissory and reciprocal obligations' that are not included in the formal contract of employment. Recent research indicates that breach or non-fulfillment of such contracts affects employee performance and induces turnover (Turnley and Feldman, 1999). Psychological contracts may be difficult to change (Stiles et al., 1997), especially if they are 'relational contracts' (Rousseau and Wade-Benzoni, 1994) characterized as having considerable investment by both employees (company-specific skills, long-term career development) and employers (extensive training). These make them partly irreversible; however, the degree of irreversibility will depend on the organization and nature of work.

Opportunity cost of options represents lost value when temporary or contractual employees are hired instead of permanent employees (see Appendix). Although there is contradictory evidence in this area (Pearce, 1993; Porter, 1995), some findings indicate that temporary or contractual workers may have less commitment towards the firm (Dyne and Ang, 1998; Hippel et al., 1997). Scholars have also cautioned that use of temporary workers may affect quality of work and carry the risk of safety violations (Hippel et al., 1997; Kochan et al., 1994; Mallon and Duberlay, 2000; Rousseau and Libuser, 1997). Others contend that temporary and contractual workers may be more difficult to control and coordinate (Mallon and Duberlay, 2000), may result in less innovation (Zahra and Nielsen, 2002), and may cause dissemination of knowledge outside, leading to the decay of competencies (Matusik and Hill, 1998). All these reduce the value of options and increase their opportunity cost. A firm has to assess these before evaluating the opportunity cost of temporary and contractual workers.

As options become more valuable, the opportunity cost of hiring becomes higher than that of options (i.e., investments in options become more valuable than investments in hiring permanent employees). Therefore firms will invest in flexibility options, options to wait or defer, options to abandon, and learning options through temporary or contractual employees, when the opportunity cost of hiring permanent employees is more than the opportunity cost of hiring temporary or contractual employees – which implies that the firm may lose more in hiring than in creating options (see Appendix).

Proposition 1b: Firms will employ temporary and contractual workers if the opportunity cost of hiring is more than the opportunity cost of creating options.

Outsourcing, which involves contracting the job to an external agency on a recurring basis, is done primarily to offload non-core activities in order to cut costs and improve strategic focus. The skill itself is taken out of the firm and given to another firm (which probably specializes in that area). This is different from employing temporary or contractual employees in two ways: (a) the outsourcing firm is not responsible for getting the work done; and (b) the contracts are often long term and recurring. Outsourcing for cutting costs is explained by the transactions cost perspective, which prescribes efficiency as the criterion for contracting. However, in recent years, firms are outsourcing for other reasons, such as to facilitate rapid organizational change, to launch new strategies, and to reshape company boundaries (Linder, 2004). Many of these represent options. For example, the capability to switch among various choices and adjust quickly to a changing environment is essentially a 'flexibility' option or 'switching' option (Trigeorgis, 1996). The outsourcing firm can achieve this because of less commitment to in-house resources and the ability to switch between firms providing various choices for outsourcing. This capability also allows them to heuristically search for valuable skills and capabilities, although through external agencies. Additionally, the option to abandon is inherent in the decision to outsource, as the firm may choose not to renew the contract. This may be due to non-continuation of the skill, or to search for a better provider.

Therefore we propose:

Proposition 2a: Outsourcing creates flexibility and switching options as well as options to abandon.

However, outsourcing may also have opportunity costs (see Appendix). For example, contracting is a critical issue in outsourcing; if the contract is not flexible there may be little scope for modifying it within the contract period. Managing the vendor is another issue where inefficiencies and inflexibilities may creep in. In fact managing the vendor may become more difficult than managing the firm's own employees because there is little control over the vendor's employees. A third issue is switching vendors. Although this represents flexibility, the switching costs may be high, making the contract or flexibility option inefficient (Barthelemy and Adsit, 2003). Loss of customer satisfaction is another risk associated with outsourced work. Although Gainey and Klaas (2003) did not find evidence that outsourcing of training would lower client satisfaction, in some cases customer satisfaction has been a concern (*Wall Street Journal*, 2003). Finally, perhaps the most important concern is the risk of knowledge dissemination outside and decay of competencies because of the minimal skill involvement of the outsourcing firm (Earl, 1996; Lei and Hitt, 1995). The presence of one or more of these factors increases the opportunity cost of outsourcing vis-à-vis hiring and influences the decision to outsource the skill.

Therefore we propose:

Proposition 2b: Firms will outsource skills if the opportunity cost of hiring is more than the opportunity cost of creating options.

Employee options

Human capital is different from other real assets in one aspect – a firm never owns human capital in the true sense, it resides in employees. In other words there is a dual claim of ownership on human capital. Therefore the employee as an individual plays a significant role in human capital investment decisions, and it is critical that we discuss employees separately along with the uncertainty and irreversibility associated with them.

The uncertainties related to an employee are skill matching (person–job fit) and person matching (person–organization fit). Skill matching is a critical requirement for generating maximum return on investment from recruitment of employees. Although skill tests can determine, to some extent, the proficiency of a candidate, the actual match of skills is revealed only over time as the person works on the job. A mismatch can cost the firm in terms of lost productivity. To avoid this many firms hire interns or part-time employees so that skill levels can be better judged. Especially for highly skilled jobs as in law firms (Hitt et al., 2001; Malos and Campion, 1995) interns work for several years before getting permanent status. Similar practices are followed for faculty jobs in top research universities where tenure is granted only after evidence of skill in research and publishing. Firms requiring creative talent, like advertising agencies or entertainment companies, hire part-time or on test projects before committing work. In essence these are learning options to provide more information on the employee.

Similar concerns exist for person matching, i.e., whether or not the employee fits as a 'person' with the organization. Person–organization (P–O) fit, or the compatibility between people and the organizations in which they work, is key to maintaining the flexible and committed workforce that is necessary in a competitive business environment (Kristof, 1996). Several firms place more emphasis on person–organization fit than a job fit (Bowen et al., 1991). Internships and part-time employment create learning options for these uncertainties too. The firm can 'judge' the fit of an employee with the organization during the period of pre-employment. Clearly, the option to abandon (i.e., terminate) the employee's contract in case of mismatch is available for such work arrangements. Therefore we propose that:

> *Proposition 3a*: Pre-employment appointments such as internships and part-time employment create learning options and options to abandon with respect to employees.

However, these options may also involve some opportunity costs. Although the cost of internships may be minimal (another reason why firms employ them), cost of part-timers may not be so. Firm investments in development of such employees (e.g., training), or firm-specific human capital generated on-the-job (e.g., specific knowledge about a project), can be lost at termination. Additionally, there are long-standing concerns about the performance of such employees (Feldman, 1990), although a recent meta-analysis has shown little difference between full-time and part-time workers on organizational commitment and intention to leave (Thorsteinson, 2003). Taken together, these costs may affect the decision to use such employment arrangements or not.

We propose that firms will create these options when they are more valuable than hiring upfront.

> *Proposition 3b*: Firms will use pre-employment appointments such as internships and part-time employment, if the opportunity cost of hiring is more than the opportunity cost of creating options.

Discussion

The real options approach provides an alternative rationale for value creation in human capital, and is complementary to the resource-based view explanation. According to the logic of real options, firms faced with high uncertainty and irreversibility should invest in time-deferred, contingent alternative work arrangements or 'options', until major uncertainties are resolved. This approach recommends capability development in stages, through sequential path-dependent investments, as well as through pursuit of opportunities with significant upside potential (McGrath et al., 2004). Therefore this view provides a heuristics guidance on how to create valuable, rare, inimitable, and non-substitutable resources, as prescribed by the resource-based view.

We investigate human capital acquisition decisions using the real options framework. We propose that when uncertainty over skills is high, and investments in hiring are significantly irreversible, options to wait, defer or abandon skills, as well as to learn new skills and operate flexibly become more valuable. Greater value of options increases the opportunity cost of hiring upfront, i.e., the cost of not investing in options becomes high. In that case a firm would invest in these options through use of temporary or contractual employees, or by outsourcing the skill altogether. We also discuss how employees, as owners of skills, need to be considered separately for investment decisions in human capital because there may be uncertainty and irreversibility associated with employees as well. In case of high uncertainty over person–job and person–organization 'fit' we propose that firms would use pre-employment arrangements like internships or part-time employment as long as the opportunity cost of doing so is lower than that of hiring.

Our theoretical model, as presented in Figure 21.1 and mathematically represented in the Appendix, throws some light on the 'black box' issue in strategic HRM, i.e., what is the process through which HRM impacts human resources so that valuable, rare, inimitable, and non-substitutable human capital is generated? This question assumes enhanced significance when uncertainty about the returns from the human capital is high; uncertainty about the demand and supply of skills is high; and significant uncertainty about person–job and person–organization 'fit' exists, which has major implications for the firm. If irreversibility of investments in human capital through hiring is also high, then the real options logic suggests that alternative work arrangements like temporary/contractual/part-time workers, interns, or outsourcing of the work may provide managers with the time to let uncertainties reduce and the flexibility to continue or abandon the skills/employee. Additionally, these work arrangements may provide preferential access through learning and generate growth potential. Uncertainty resolution helps managers identify skills and employees that are more valuable to the firm, and create a sequential investment path which is rare and difficult for competitors to imitate. Therefore, options are the stepping stones for valuable, rare, inimitable human capital.

In presenting our model we use the notion of 'opportunity cost' of hiring vis-à-vis that of options and assert that these will affect the decision to invest in options. Opportunity cost of hiring is the returns forgone by *not* investing in options, which we identified as the option value to (1) operate flexibly, (2) wait or defer, (3) abandon, (4) learn, and (5) switch, reduced by the premium to buy the options and the switching costs. Opportunity cost of options consists of returns not generated because work is not done by permanent employees. These are concerns about quality of work, commitment of employees, rate of innovation, loss of control, increased effort in managing alternate employees/contracts, lower customer satisfaction, and decay of competencies through knowledge dissemination outside. We propose that a firm would invest in options only if the opportunity cost of hiring is more than that of options.

One must also consider the interdependence of the options in terms of positive and negative effects. On the upside, we have argued that several options may be present simultaneously in an investment decision like employing temporary workers or outsourcing. The expectation is that these options would complement each other's effects and create synergies that may override the costs. For example, the option to wait on skill acquisition and the option to abandon may together make the opportunity cost of not using temporary employees high, even though such workers may be costlier in terms of remuneration (Kunda et al., 2002). Similarly, flexibility options as well as options to abandon may be present in outsourcing, which makes the opportunity cost of not doing so greater. Therefore 'bundles' of options may provide synergistic benefits to override their costs (Trigeorgis, 1996). However, on the downside, one must recognize that some options may run counter to others. For instance, while the use of contingent workers allows the firm to adjust to changing volumes, contingent workers may not be emotionally bound to the firm in ways that result in the same positive behavioral effects (Dyne and Ang, 1998; Hippel et al., 1997).

369

It is necessary to recognize the significance of the 'exercise' and 'expiration' of options, which is the use of the capabilities generated through options. Financial options, if not exercised within the stipulated date, become non-usable; real options like joint ventures or R&D investments may lose their value after a certain period if their potential is not realized. Human capital options may also lose their value, which means the capabilities may become less useful, if the level or source of uncertainty changes. However, these options may be more durable than either financial options or real options, because capabilities like growth, learning, and flexibilities are fairly generic and not specific to a particular job or skill. For example, in many instances firms keep on employing temporary or contractual workers even though the uncertainty is resolved (Kunda et al., 2002). Therefore, human capital options, in general, can be more sustainable than other types of options. However, we also recognize that some options, like flexibility or switching options, if not exercised, may become non-usable or lose significance due to escalation of commitments (Adner and Levinthal, 2004).

One could argue that what we propose in this chapter are certainly not new contributions to the strategic HRM literature. Firms have implemented a variety of the practices we note for arguably, if at least implicitly, the goals of managing uncertainties. However, past explications of these relationships have usually focused on cost, revenue, or productivity considerations. While decision makers may have implemented practices as piecemeal responses to experienced uncertainty, this has been done without an overall framework for thinking about uncertainty and irreversibility facing the firm's human capital. For the field of HRM to ignore these would result in far less than optimal strategic decision making. Therefore the real options approach is an appropriate 'way of thinking' (Amram and Kulatilaka, 1999) that provides three components which are of great use to managers: creation of capabilities even if they may not be used; contingent decisions based upon unfolding of events; and managing human capital investments proactively.

Future directions and practical implications

We believe that the emphasis on options in human capital raises a number of issues that need further investigation. First, this theoretical framework sets the stage for empirically investigating the relationship between options, uncertainty, and irreversibility associated with human capital. Second, we believe that HR options would have synergistic effects when they act in a 'bundle' as multiple interacting options. Research is needed to analyze the different 'bundles' of options in human capital based on the purpose they serve together. Third, we contend that HR options may manage more than one type of uncertainty. Further research could examine the ways in which these options impact the various forms of uncertainty we have identified.

From the practical point of view, in this fast-changing world, managers are increasingly looking for ways to rationalize their investment decisions in human capital. Our framework assists them in choosing appropriate skill and employee acquisition practices that address particular needs of the organization. This way they would be able to justify the work arrangements they adopt. Our fine-grained analysis of various options goes a step further in explaining how these arrangements may be helpful to them. For example, outsourcing is universally thought of as a cost-reduction practice leading to productivity gains. However, in recent years other benefits from outsourcing, namely rapid change and growth, have been highlighted (Linder, 2004). We discuss these in terms of 'options value' and 'opportunity costs', which may be quantified and therefore of use to managers in making investment choices. By articulating a comprehensive schema for evaluating each option in terms of uncertainty and irreversibility, we provide a viable way to do a judicial cost–benefit analysis for investments in human capital.

In conclusion, we propose that options enable the firm to reduce uncertainty associated with its investments in human capital, which in turn allows managers to generate valuable human capital. We have discussed how firms would evaluate the uncertainty of human capital and irreversibility of investments in hiring to arrive at decisions to invest in options. In doing so we assert that the real options framework addresses the question unresolved in the RBV of value creation, which is: How do firms recognize which resources will be valuable? The options view provides a heuristic process approach of sequential investments through uncertainty resolution to explain value creation in firms.

References

Adner, R., and Levinthal, D. A. 2004. What is *Not* a real option: Considering boundaries for the application of real options to business strategy. *Academy of Management Review*, 29: 74.

Amram, M., and Kulatilaka, N. 1999. Disciplined decisions. *Harvard Business Review*, (Jan–Feb): 95–104.

Barthelemy, J., and Adsit, D. 2003. The seven deadly sins of outsourcing. *Academy of Management Executive*, 17(2): 87.

Becker, G. S. 1993. *Human capital: A theoretical and empirical analysis with special reference to education* (3rd edn). Chicago: University of Chicago Press.

Bhattacharya, M., and Wright, P. M. 2005. Managing human assets in an uncertain world: Applying real option theory to HRM. *International Journal of Human Resource Management*, 16(6): 933–52.

Bowen, D. E., Ledford, G. E., Jr., and Nathan, B. R. 1991. Hiring for the organization, not the job. *Academy of Management Executive*, 5(4): 17.

Bowman, E. H., and Hurry, D. 1993. Strategy through the options lens: An integrated view of resource investments and the incremental-choice process. *Academy of Management Review*, 18: 760–82.

Brockner, J. 1988. The effects of work layoffs on survivors: Research, theory, and practice. In B. M. Staw and L. L. Cummings (Eds), *Research in Organizational Behavior*, 10: 213–55. Greenwich, CT: JAI Press.

Cappelli, P. 1995. Rethinking employment. *British Journal of Industrial Relations*, 33: 563–602.

——. 1999a. *The New Deal at work*. Boston, MA: Harvard Business Press.

——. 1999b. Career jobs are dead. *California Management Review*, 42: 146–67.

Coff, R. W. 2002. Human capital, shared expertise, and the likelihood of impasse in corporate acquisitions. *Journal of Management*, 28: 107–28.

Davis-Blake, A., and Uzzi, B. 1993. Determinants of employment externalization: A study of temporary workers and independent contractors. *Administrative Science Quarterly*, 38: 195–223.

Dixit, A., and Pindyck, R. 1994. *Investment under uncertainty*. Princeton, NJ: Princeton University Press.

Dyne, L. V., and Ang, S. 1998. Organizational citizenship behavior of contingent workers in Singapore. *Academy of Management Journal*, 41: 692.

Earl, M. J. 1996. The risks of outsourcing IT. *Sloan Management Review*, 37(3): 26.

Feldman, D. C. 1990. Reconceptualizing the nature and consequences of part-time work. *Academy of Management Review*, 15: 103–12.

Foote, D. A., and Folta, T. B. 2002. Temporary workers as real options. *Human Resource Management Review*, 12: 579.

Gainey, T. W., and Klaas, B. S. 2003. The outsourcing of training and development: Factors impacting client satisfaction. *Journal of Management*, 29: 207.

Gramm, C. L., and Schnell, J. F. 2001. The use of flexible staffing arrangements in core production jobs. *Industrial and Labor Relations Review*, 54: 245–58.

Hippel, C. V., Mangum, S. L., Greenberger, D. B., Heneman, R. L., and Skoglind, J. D. 1997. Temporary employment: Can organizations and employees both win? *Academy of Management Executive*, 11: 93.

Hitt, M. A., Bierman, L., Shimizu, K., and Kochhar, R. 2001. Direct and moderating effects of human capital on strategy and performance in professional service firms: A resource-based perspective. *Academy of Management Journal*, 44: 13–28.

Kochan, T. A., Smith, M., Wells, J. C., and Rebitzer, J. B. 1994. Human resource strategies and contingent workers: The case of safety and health in the petrochemical industry. *Human Resource Management*, 33: 55.

Kogut, B., and Kulatilaka, N. 2001. Capabilities as real options. *Organization Science*, 12: 744–58.

Kristof, A. L. 1996. Person–organization fit: An integrative review of its conceptualizations, measurement, and implications. *Personnel Psychology*, 49: 1–49.

Kunda, G., Barley, S. R., and Evans, J. 2002. Why do contractors contract? The experience of highly skilled technical professionals in a contingent labor market. *Industrial and Labor Relations Review*, 55: 234.

Lado, A. A., and Wilson, M. C. 1994. Human resource systems and sustained competitive advantage: A competency based perspective. *Academy of Management Review*, 19: 699–727.

Lei, David, and Hitt, M. A. 1995. Strategic restructuring and outsourcing: The effect of mergers and acquisitions and LBOs on building firm skills and capabilities. *Journal of Management*, 21: 835.

Leiblen, M. J. 2003. The choice of organizational governance form and performance: Predictions from transactions cost, resource-based, and real options theories. *Journal of Management*, 29: 903.

Lepak, D. P., and Snell, S. 1999. The human resource architecture: Toward a theory of human capital allocation and development. *Academy of Management Review*, 24: 31–48.

Linder, J. C. 2004. Transformational outsourcing. *MIT Sloan Management Review*, 45(2): 52–8.

Mallon, N., and Duberlay, J. 2000. Managers and professionals in the contingent workforce. *Human Resource Management Journal*, 10: 33.

Malos, S. B., and Campion, M. 1995. An options based model of career mobility in professional service firms. *Academy of Management Review*, 20: 611–44.

Matusik, S. F., and Hill, C. W. 1998. The utilization of contingent work, knowledge creation, and competitive advantage. *Academy of Management Review*, 23: 680–97.

McElroy, J. C., Morrow, P. C., and Rude, S. N. 2001. Turnover and organizational performance: A comparative analysis of the effects of voluntary, involuntary, and reduction-in-force turnover. *Journal of Applied Psychology*, 86: 1294.

McGrath, R. G. 1997. A real options logic for initiating technology positioning investments. *Academy of Management Review*, 22: 974–96.

McGrath, R. G., Ferrier, W. J., and Mendelow, A. L. 2004. Real options as engines of choice and heterogeneity. *Academy of Management Review*, 29: 86–101.

Osterman, P. 1994. How common is workplace transformation and who adopts it? *Industrial and Labor Relations Review*, 47(2): 173–88.

Osterman, P. 2000. Work reorganization in an era of restructuring: Trends in diffusion and effects on employees welfare. *Industrial and Labor Relations Review*, 53(2): 179–96.

Pearce, J. L. 1993. Toward an organizational behavior of contract laborers: Their psychological involvement and effects on employee co-workers. *Academy of Management Journal*, 36: 1082–96.

Porter, G. 1995. Attitude differences between regular and contract employees of nursing departments. Paper presented at the annual meeting of the *Academy of Management*, Vancouver.

Priem, R. L. and Butler, J. E. 2001. Is the resource-based view a useful perspective for strategic management research? *Academy of Management Review*, 26: 22–40.

Quinn, J. B., and Hilmer, F. G. 1994. Strategic outsourcing. *MIT Sloan Management Review*, 35: 43.

Robinson, S. L., Kratz, M. S., and Rousseau, D. M. 1994. Changing obligations and the psychological contract: A longitudinal study. *Academy of Management Journal*, 37: 137–52.

Rousseau, D. M., and Libuser, C. 1997. Contingent workers in high risk environments. *California Management Review*, 39: 103.

Rousseau, D. M., and Wade-Benzoni, K. A. 1994. Linking strategy and human resource practices: How employee and customer contracts are created. *Human Resource Management*, 33: 463–90.

Schein, E. H. 1980. *Organizational psychology*, 3rd edn. Englewood Cliffs, NJ: Prentice-Hall.

Stiles, P., Gratton, L., Truss, C., Hope-Hailey, V., and McGovern, P. 1997. Performance management and the psychological contract. *Human Resource Management Journal*, 7: 57.

Thorsteinson, T. J. 2003. Job attitudes of part-time vs. full-time workers: A meta-analytic review. *Journal of Occupational and Organizational Psychology*, 76: 151.

Trigeorgis, L. 1996. *Real options: Managerial flexibility and strategy in resource allocation.* Cambridge, MA: MIT Press.

Turnley, W. H., and Feldman, D. C. 1999. The impact of psychological contract violations on exit, voice, loyalty, and neglect. *Human Relations*, 52: 895.

Wall Street Journal. 2003. Technology Brief – Dell Inc.: Corporate support calls. Nov 24: 1.

Wright, P. M., Dunford, B. B., and Snell, S. A. 2001. Human resources and the resource-based view of the firm. *Journal of Management*, 27: 701–21.

Zahra, S. A., and Nielsen, A. P. 2002. Sources of capabilities, integration and technology commercialization. *Strategic Management Journal*, 23: 377.

Appendix

I. Opportunity cost of hiring = x + w + a + l + s − p − sc

'*x*' is option value of *flexibility* = *f* (uncertainty of demand for *and* supply of skill; irreversible investments in psychological contracts with permanent employees)

'*w*' is option value to *wait or defer* = *f* (uncertainty of continued demand for skills; irreversible investments in hiring and developing human capital)

'*a*' is option value to *abandon* = *f* (uncertainty of skill abandonment; irreversible investments in employment contracts with permanent employees)

'*l*' is option value to *learn* = *f* (uncertainty of returns from skills application; irreversible investments in developing skills)

'*s*' is option value to *switch* = *f* (uncertainty of returns from specific skills application, irreversible investments in in-house resources and processes)

'*p*' is *premium* for options = cost of temporary/contractual/outsource vendor workers − cost of permanent workers

'*sc*' is *switching* cost of flexibility options = cost of switching temporary/contractual/outsource vendor workers

II. Opportunity cost of options = q + m + i + n + e + cs + k

'*q*' is the difference in *quality* of work between permanent and temporary/contractual/outsource vendor workers

'*m*' is the difference in *commitment* between permanent and temporary/contractual/outsource vendor workers

'*i*' is the difference in *innovation* between permanent and temporary/contractual/outsource vendor workers

'*n*' is the difference in *control* between permanent and temporary/contractual/outsource vendor workers '*e*' is the difference in *effort* in managing permanent employees and temporary/contractual/outsource vendor workers

'*cs*' is the difference in *customer satisfaction* between permanent and temporary/contractual/outsource vendor workers

'*k*' is the risk of *knowledge dissemination* outside through permanent and temporary/contractual/outsource vendor workers

Part 8

Changing contexts

This section describes the changing contexts of HR. Strategic HRM, while growing prodigiously over the past three decades, has largely been based on research and theorizing with regard to large domestic companies. Much of the research on HR and performance such as Huselid (1995), Delery and Doty (1996), and Guthrie (2001) has used domestic samples, which, while they may contain global companies, are all generated from home country headquarters. This work, while valuable, tells us little about small, entrepreneurial firms, nor about how large global firms are seeking to manage successfully across boundaries. In addition, it is obvious that the world continues to change, and research based on samples that are 15 to 20 years old may not be perfectly applicable to either the world firms face today, or the one they will face in the future. This section seeks to shed light on these omitted topics.

The first chapter in this section, by Tamara Erickson, presents a compelling case for the fact that HR faces a new world. She argues that the future landscape differs greatly from the present one, and that "many corporations today continue to operate according to a model that was shaped in the early twentieth century." In what ways is this landscape different? First, she describes the changing workforce. This workforce will present a skill shortage, in large part due to fewer entrants into the workforce in almost all industrialized countries. In addition, those entering tend to have different value systems and are highly diverse. Technological changes will also contribute to this changing landscape. It enables firms to collect, store, and employ information through so-called "Web 2.0" internet-related technologies such as networking sites, wikis, and folksonomies. Internet connections for companies and individuals will become ubiquitous, always-on broadband, and provide instant access to almost anything via new search technologies. In this world, she proposes "Next-Generation Enterprises" which are collaborative, informed, technologically adept, and skilled at ongoing experimentation. These new organizations will create new fundamentals for managing the workforce such as the transformation of traditional career paths, the near ending of retirement, and performance management processes that provide frequent peer-based feedback. She suggests that over the coming decade, HR will "come to bear primary responsibility for managing the talent required by the business" and concludes by describing how HR can build transformation capability.

This very different landscape described by Erickson provides an introduction to Molloy, Tansky, and Heneman's chapter on SHRM and entrepreneurship. Substantial research has been conducted regarding what constitutes "best" HRM practices and their impact on firm performance. However, much of this work has been conducted on large multinational firms, and the authors argue that it is not perfectly applicable to small, entrepreneurial firms, in particular, because of the uniqueness of their product markets. They propose that "the 'entrepreneurial' constructs provided here emphasize that what entrepreneurs 'do' is establish new firms in conditions in which resources are scarce and pressures to quickly commercialize the innovation and earn profits are intense." They then argue that the conditions at the time of founding create lasting blueprints regarding characteristics such as structure, human resource systems, and performance. Thus, they seek to explain the different founding conditions that might create such imprints, and focus on the growth intentions of the founder, and the nature of the entrepreneurial opportunity. Many entrepreneurial firms are founded with the goal of simply providing income or an opportunity to earn money from a hobby such as running a ski resort. Other founders hope to grow quickly in order to either go public or sell the firm for a considerable profit. Regarding the entrepreneurial opportunities, they discuss discovery opportunities as ones that are risky, but for which the service offerings are similar to those of other firms, thus enabling them to be better able to project market demand. Creation opportunities, on the other hand, do not exist until the entrepreneur creates them. They then juxtapose these two dimensions to describe the unique HRM system challenges or strategies that are likely under each of the proposed conditions and conclude by discussing some of the research implications of their typology.

While entrepreneurial firms face unique environments because of their small size, multinational firms face unique environments because of their gargantuan size and global reach. In the chapter by Beechler and Baltzley the authors begin by discussing the challenges that CEOs see their global strategies as creating with regard to finding leaders who can manage the complexity inherent in them. They then trace the history of research in this area, focusing on expatriate managers to global managers, to global leaders. They present a "Global Leadership Framework" defining global leadership as "the process of influencing individuals, groups, and organizations (inside and outside the boundaries of the global organization) representing diverse cultural/political/institutional systems to contribute towards the achievement of the global organization's goals." They describe the elements that differentiate global leaders from domestic leaders in terms of knowledge and skills, intellect, and personality/style. They then conclude by describing how firms can seek to develop global leadership through talent management.

The changing landscape created by new demographics and new technology, the uniqueness of entrepreneurial firms, the control/coordination challenges faced by global firms, and the need for global firms to develop a new generation of global leaders all provide an important foundation for understanding the strategic management of human resources.

22

The changing context for HR

Tamara J. Erickson

Introduction

As the nature of organizations has changed over the past century, from early industrial models to the highly complex communities evolving today, the associated roles and responsibilities of Human Resources have changed as well. The purpose of this chapter is to explore current changes that are creating a new context for HR, with a focus on those driven by demographics and technology.

Together, radically new demographic patterns and a newly functional global information network are challenging every aspect of how corporations operate – none more significantly than the role and responsibilities of the Human Resources function. Over the next decade, changes in workforce demographics, worker expectations, and the technological infrastructure available to employers and employees alike will reshape the corporate landscape in profound ways. The pool of workers will be chronologically older in most of the world and, in many countries, will lag in size behind expected labor demands and lack the skills required for the fastest growing segments of the economy. This increasingly diverse workforce will also hold highly disparate ideas about the value of work in their lives and the goals they hope to achieve through employment.

The world's technology infrastructure has advanced dramatically, even over the last decade. Today, corporations can reasonably expect ubiquitous, low-cost connectivity among operations around the globe. The rapidly evolving capabilities will drive the costs of communication and coordination toward zero and push toward increasingly horizontal organizations, networked and porous, with open information flows among workers in a wide variety of relationships – employees, as well as contractors, outsourcers, and collaborators.

Although the landscape is changing, many corporations today continue to operate according to a model that was shaped in the early twentieth century – hierarchical structures, rigid job designs, unilateral employment relationships, and cascading decision-making that is at odds with the values of many segments of the workforce and fails to leverage the capabilities of the new technology. To adjust to the seismic shifts in the workforce and take full advantage of the benefits of the rapidly evolving technologies, corporations will need to turn essentially inside out and upside down – creating organizations that are horizontally networked and able to tap the wisdom and knowledge from multiple, widely dispersed sources.

For many corporate leaders and human resource professionals broadly, this new environment will represent a sharp departure from even the recent past. In the last decades, corporations have responded to the problems posed by vigorous global competition by striving to cut costs and find efficiencies wherever possible. Through the top-down actions of downsizing, rightsizing, outsourcing, and re-engineering, most corporations squeezed increased productivity out of their workers and their systems. While great savings have resulted from these efforts, they have also conditioned many corporate executives inside and outside of the Human Resources department in approaches that are ill matched to the leadership challenges of the twenty-first century.

Human resource professionals today face exciting opportunities for unprecedented leadership – helping their business partners understand the looming impact and potential of these global demographic and technological developments and guiding their corporations in developing a sound approach to securing the talent needed for business success.

This chapter will explore the nature of the changes that are underway, how they are reshaping the context in which HR will operate over the upcoming years, and the resultant requirements for HR success.

The changing workforce: scarce talent, shifting values, and growing diversity

The twenty-first century workforce will be significantly different than the workforce of the past century in multiple key dimensions.

Limited in availability

Decades of slowing birth rates are catching up with the workforce in many countries around the world. For the last several decades birth rates have fallen around much of the world. As a result, for the foreseeable future, the workforce will grow slowly or even decline in size in most developed markets and in many emerging economies, as well.

In the United States, the workforce is forecast to grow by only a fraction of a percentage point a year for most of the first half of the century – just 2 to 3 percent per decade from now through 2030 and then increase to 3 to 4 percent each decade through 2050. By comparison, the rates in the United States have been 12 to 15 percent per decade for most of the second half of the twentieth century.

The change will be even more dramatic in many countries in Europe. Europe's working-age population will actually *decline* in size over future decades. The population of traditional working age (in this case, defined as between 15 and 64) in the 25 countries that make up the European Union (EU25) is expected to change from 307 million in 2004 to 255 million in 2050 – a decline of 52 million workers, representing 20 percent of today's workforce.

On a global basis, relatively few countries today have birth rates above replacement levels, key to having a growing population of younger individuals. Countries whose population under 25 is actually declining this decade are as wide-ranging as Argentina, Austria, Belgium, Brazil, China, Japan, Korea, Singapore, Sweden, Thailand, Trinidad and Tobago, and Turkey. India remains one of the few major countries with birth rates significantly above replacement. There, the challenge becomes the provision of educational opportunities that will allow the population to participate in a global economy.

Meanwhile, economic growth has continued throughout most of the world. As a result, a gap is beginning to appear between the number of jobs and the number of people available to fill those jobs. Going forward, the shortage of skilled workers is expected to grow in industry after industry, region after region, throughout the country and around most of the world.

Chronologically older

Lower birthrates mean that the composition of the workforce will also shift, with the overall mix becoming progressively older. Individuals over the age of 55 will represent larger proportions of the workforce. A declining number of mid-career workers, slow or declining growth in the number of younger workers, and a rapid increase in the number of older workers are found in most countries around the world. Fueled by ever-longer life spans and lower birth rates, older workers will continue to grow as a portion of the global labor pool throughout the century.

The proportion of over-55 workers in the United States will increase from 11 percent in 2000 to 20 percent in 2015. But this pattern is not unique to the United States. Workforces throughout Europe, Russia, China, Japan, Australia, New Zealand, and Latin America will age substantially over the next several decades. India, the Middle East and Africa stand out as some of the few major areas around the world with a distinctly different pattern. In India and the Middle East the continuation of birth rates above replacement levels means that these countries will see growth across all age cohorts until at least 2020. Low life expectancies in Africa mean that this area will continue to be predominantly composed of younger individuals.

Lacking key skills required to meet business needs

A serious skill mismatch will add to the potential for a future workforce crisis. The education and capabilities of new entrants to the workforce are not a good fit for the knowledge worker jobs that corporations are increasingly creating this century. Key skill sets will unquestionably be in critically short supply in many countries around the world. The workforce in the United States and Europe will not – and in many instances, already does not – have the optimum mix of talent needed by today's knowledge-intensive industries. The mismatch between skills available and skills in demand is particularly acute in engineering and science, although the shortage is spreading to college-educated individuals in general. We are on the brink of critical shortages in a number of skill areas.

Over the next decade, only 30 percent of Americans are expected to hold college degrees when they turn 30 (today, the figure is even lower – 26 percent). At the same time, the number of jobs being created based on college-level skills is increasing – some estimate that as many as two-thirds of the new jobs created in the United States over the next decade will be designed for workers with a college education.

Europe is also facing widening shortages in many key skill sets. For example, in the category of advanced technology skills, the number of unfilled job openings across Europe as a whole is expected to double in just three years, going from 8 percent in 2005 to 16 percent in 2008. In some countries, the sense of being at a tipping point is even more palpable: Spain, for example, is expected to go from a shortage of 7 percent in 2005 to nearly 16 percent in 2008, Germany from 6 percent to 18 percent, and France from 6 percent to 12 percent. In the space of three years, many European countries will experience a rapid increase in the number of job openings that go unfilled as the scarcity of highly qualified talent grows.

Global

In part as a result of labor and talent shortages and in part to take advantage of cost arbitrage or market-based opportunities, off shoring or "smart shoring" of work will continue to grow, as will competition for imported talent. By mid-century, most corporations will encompass a wide variety of global talent sourcing arrangements.

Profoundly disengaged from "work"

Many employees today seem to be searching for "more" than they are able to draw from their work experience. Mid-life's pivotal point today is more often than not a reflection on the impact of one's life on the world. As employees reach whatever milestone triggers a sense of middle age, more and more are reprioritizing to live up to the idealistic values formed as youth. Increasingly, employees are asking whether the paths they have taken are indeed consistent with the values they formed earlier in life. Coupled with a general disillusionment with corporate life, many workers are emotionally pulling away – detaching from work, and depriving businesses of immeasurable energy, innovation, and drive. Around the world, on average, only approximately 20 percent of the workforce is currently significantly engaged in work.

Highly diverse

The workforce in the twenty-first century will be diverse in virtually every conventional dimension – race, gender, age, religion and cultural identity. It will also be populated by individuals with widely differing values and assumptions about work itself. These divergent attitudes toward work will be among the most important forms of workplace diversity this century, challenging employers to find innovative ways to understand and respond to disparate needs.

Some of the shifting views on the role of work are reflected in the generational cohorts. The following is, granted, an oversimplification, but it illustrates the significant variety in how different individuals view "work:"

- to many older workers, born of Depression-era parents and becoming teens in booming post-World War II economies, work is a way to gain financial security and the material rewards money provides;
- to many who were born in the post-war baby boom and became teens during the rebellious years of the 1960s and 1970s, work is an arena in which to compete, as they have throughout their lives, for a spot among the crowded field of other boomers;
- to young adults, whose teen experiences were likely to have included major social change – women entering the workforce, skyrocketing divorce rates and widespread unemployment – work is one way to gain the skills required for lifelong self-reliance.

The newest generation entering the workforce represents, perhaps, the most significant shift in both views and habits. For those in their mid-twenties and younger, work is one, but only one, element of a satisfying life. It is an important part of a life, not a life in itself.

This group is also the first cohort to enter the workforce with "unconsciously competent" technology skills. Many do not remember the first time they logged on to a computer. They have literally grown up using technology as an integral part of how they get things done. As a result, without even trying, these new entrants to the workforce are bringing innovative perspectives to the workplace, valuable for companies who are open to tapping and experimenting with these fresh ideas. Some of these divergent perspectives coming into the workplace include:

- Asynchronous lives: Growing up on TiVo, young workers today prefer to do almost any activity on their own time. They are generally astonished at older workers' need to get everyone together on a conference call or in a physical meeting in order to discuss an issue, since they hold their discussion on social networking sites.
- Coordination, rather than planning: Young workers are comfortable making spontaneous arrangements. They find limited value in creating elaborate plans and are comfortable re-adjusting on an ongoing basis.
- Solving problems and performing tasks collaboratively: Many young workers learned to work in teams in elementary school and prefer working in ways that allow them to network and learn from others in the corporation. The new tools of Web 2.0 – such as wikis, social networks, and blogs – are, in essence, technological enhancements of collaborative working groups.
- Selecting and using technology in ways that make their lives easier: Unlike older workers who often feel that technology has encroached into their personal lives – and resent the intrusion – young workers are skilled at managing the technology in ways that they find helpful and freeing, rather than a source of stress.
- Finding new uses for technology that are "good enough": Young workers are adept at trying technologies in new ways to "invent" entirely new functions. Youth developed the approach of texting on phones and turned the camera, via the camera phone, from a method of documentation into an entirely new mode of instant communication.
- Reliance on reputation rather than hierarchy: This generation depends on reputation as a source of authority and knows how to build their own – a critical skill for digital interactions.
- Knowing how to be physically alone, and yet connected: Young workers are comfortable being physically alone, yet feeling completely connected to a community that they may never actually see.
- "Owning" the technology, redrawing the line between institutional and personal: Young employees express an overwhelming preference for using their "own" hardware and software for work. Their personal technology is as intimate and useful to them as wallets and purses are to their parents. Soon the concept of corporations supplying computers or cell phones will be as outdated as the clothing allowances of the 1950s or company calculators of the 1970s. All tomorrow's employees will ask is that business "beams them in."

Taken together, new views and shifting habits represent a major challenge for corporations – and HR leaders. Employees will increasingly demand that work accommodate their lives, rather than, as they did in the past, make substantial efforts to accommodate their lives to work. Older workers now want to devote a part of their energies to idealistic goals. Younger cohorts have an inherent reluctance for institutional affiliation, and a tendency to prefer independent relationships – more flexible arrangements and greater choice, customized careers and individual development plans, exposure to senior mentors and new, interactive forms of performance feedback. Workers in this century will be increasingly articulate in demanding work relationships with corporations that allow them to retain the degree of control and flexibility required to pursue other activities equally successfully. Fortunately, although the rapidly evolving technology adds to the complexity, it also increases the range of possible options for action.

Technology and the nature of work

While the characteristics of the workforce are changing, so too significant advances in technology are redefining the way our businesses operate. Within the past decade, a number of significant technology-driven changes have laid the foundation for a fundamentally new way of operating.

The types of technology advances and the related social changes – and their implications for organizations – include:

- The nature of information exchange among companies: Gone are the days of sharing only episodic transactional information. Companies now collect, store, and employ non-transactional information, such as conversations, wisdom and knowledge, through a new generation of so-called "Web 2.0" Internet-related technologies – such as social networking sites, wikis, and folksonomies.
- Business models for software: The need to engage in massive, time-consuming "buy" decisions and implementation processes in order to have access to the desired software capabilities through ownership has disappeared; it has been replaced by the ability to "rent" software using a "Software as a Service" model, allowing rapid, low-risk use. Technology disappears as a barrier to the execution of virtually any strategy or experimental idea.
- Data leverage within companies: From the frustration of having literally hundreds of individual databases, each maintained with separate, incompatible software applications, has emerged an unprecedented ability to merge data across different systems. The widespread use of XML (Extensible Markup Language) allows data linkage and the creation of new processes and insight through business analytics.
- Access to the Internet for both businesses and individuals: Connections in most parts of the world have moved, or soon will, from spotty and slow to nearly ubiquitous, always-on broadband.
- Search technology: Finding what you're looking for has gone from nearly impossible to the ease and usefulness created through Google's advanced algorithmic breakthrough and the competing frenzy of innovation by Yahoo!, Microsoft, and Amazon.
- Attitude regarding privacy: No longer do individuals assume the right to be left alone and to control who has data on their activities. Today most do not expect control over data collection and accept the idea that no one is anonymous or obscure – although they do expect to retain some control over who uses data on their activities and how it is used.
- User sophistication: Consumers who weren't accustomed to operating online, didn't trust e-commerce and had no idea how or why to form online communities, have learned to buy things over the Internet comfortably and with abandon and are enthusiastically participating in online communities.
- Maturation of online advertising: Marketers who didn't understand online ads and had no sound model for placing the right ads on the right websites have turned Internet advertising as a multi-billion-dollar-a-year medium with the advent of Google's AdSense and Yahoo! Search Marketing Solutions.

These elements of technological and closely related social change allow businesses to operate in very different ways today than they have even as recently as ten years ago. These advances serve to reinforce the desires of individual workers – encouraging greater personal flexibility, autonomy and participation. They also enable organizations and Human Resources leaders to respond in increasingly creative and effective ways.

The next-generation enterprise

The shifting demographics and evolving technology are combining to create very different types of organizations. The momentum behind the evolution is straightforward: people probably would have always preferred to work in an environment that offered greater choice and personal autonomy; technology now allows it. The realities of today's competitive and financial environment add pressure to change.

By the quarter-century, most corporations will operate as what my colleagues and I have termed *Next-Generation Enterprises*: intensely collaborative, continually informed, technologically adept, and skilled at ongoing experimentation. Rather than rigid boundaries, these organizations will operate as connected communities encompassing a wide variety of partners and contractor relationships. They will tap regional "hot spots" around the world – nodes of connectivity, talent, and infrastructure. Work will increasingly be done anywhere, anytime, rather than in fixed locations on 9-to-5 schedules. Companies will adopt flexible relationships and continual active connections to attract both talented employees and loyal customers.

The shifts in how corporations operate will include:

- Fundamental orientation: Corporations will turn from vertical orientation and pre-determined relationships, to horizontal, collaborative and networked – a loose, ad hoc web.
- Source of authority: Leadership will require reputation-based influence rather than position-based authority. Workers will increasingly turn to individuals they know and trust (friends, mentors, even contacts outside the company) for guidance, based on the individual's reputation in the specific area of question, rather than necessarily to the person who holds the seemingly relevant position.
- Information flows and access: Workers will tap open flows from multiple, reliable sources on the Web and "anywhere." Corporations will find approaches to move away from currently tightly controlled access, while still addressing concerns regarding security and/or privacy.
- Collective activity: Team-based work will increasingly depend on ongoing coordination with frequent adjustments – "always" in touch – more than long-term planning, with the significant investments in scheduling calls and meetings that it often entails.

These trends will change many aspects of how organizations function, creating a new context for human resource policies and practices. For example, companies will increasingly shift from top-down direction and episodic strategic planning events to rapid waves of near-term experimental initiatives, brought into focus by a shared view of a company's long-term strategic direction. Growth will increasingly emerge from the creativity and innovation that comes from this bottom-up collaboration – driven by engaged employees, partners, and even customers. HR will play a key role in the integral organizational transformation.

The technology will create highly efficient markets, continuing the unrelenting pressure on corporations for increased levels of productivity. The easy availability of inexpensive coordination technology will make the relationship between business and consumers even more efficient and threaten any firm whose business model contains inefficiencies. Consumers will find it easier to collect information, compare prices, and select multiple providers based on the core competencies of each, placing pressure on corporations to offer extraordinary customer experiences as a basis of competition. Again, HR will be central to the change, by strengthening the links between employee engagement and customer satisfaction.

383

Networked technology will facilitate the unbundling of integrated corporations, leading to smaller, more focused companies, specialized around core competencies. Coordination-intense, networked organizational structures will allow firms to adjust continuously to changing requirements for different combinations of skills and resources and challenge human resources to tap a flexible talent pool through multiple work arrangements.

Technology will allow organizations to conduct their governance processes in fundamentally different ways. As it becomes both economically and logistically feasible to obtain input from a large number of people, opinion polling and even democratic elections will come into the workplace. Market-based mechanisms allowing individuals to make their own mutual agreements, as contractors and freelancers around specific projects, will be commonplace within several decades. Forecasting based on input from multiple close-to-the market sources, rather than lofty centralized groups, will develop, based on information-gathering mechanisms similar to betting. These shifts will require higher levels of business understanding and engagement throughout the workforce.

These advances will both reinforce and enable the desires of individual workers, allowing greater personal flexibility, autonomy, and input. And, they will recreate the context for managing, expand the role for human resources and shake the bedrock of many of today's HR practices.

New fundamentals for managing the workforce

The new fundamentals for Human Resources will include the following:

The population served

HR will no longer work exclusively or even, in many instances, primarily with "employees." The types of relationships that the corporation will have with the people who perform work on its behalf will encompass a wide range – contractors, freelancers, small company specialists, outsourcers, and many others. Increasingly, HR's brief will extend to assembling the talent broadly required to get the work done.

The presumed link between age and role

Entry-level positions will no longer be necessarily filled by the young. As a result of this extended lifetime of work, individuals will enter and exit the workforce at multiple times throughout their lives, in many cases pursuing multiple careers. Older workers will accept "entry"-level jobs as ways into new lines of work or flexible options suited to a preferred lifestyle. HR needs to rethink recruiting and development practices, recruiting for talent at multiple points in an individual's life cycle and ensuring that development investments are tied to individual ambitions, rather than age.

The direction and shape of a career path

Rather than the cliff-shaped career paths of the past century in which individuals ascended on an ever-upward path toward ever-greater "success," twenty-first century careers need to become bell-shaped. HR needs to create a career deceleration phase for employees in their fifties through their eighties that will parallel the career development phase of the twenties through forties. After achieving peak levels of responsibility on one's mid-career, individuals will be able

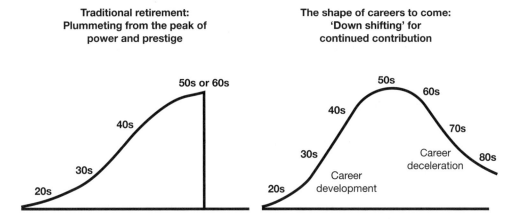

Figure 22.1 Shifts in retirement patterns

to continue to contribute to businesses in legitimate and respected, although less intense, ways. (See Figure 22.1.) Few people want to work as hard as they are at 50 for another 20 or 30 years – but many people say that they would like to continue working if suitable roles were available. Given the looming talent shortages, companies need to create these roles.

Routine retirement

The extended life of workers will also augur the end of "retirement" as we know it – an abrupt end to work that occurs at a specific, common age for most individuals. Over this century, HR needs to retire the concept, replacing it with a more flexible view of work, intermingled with periods of leisure throughout all of adulthood. Already, 34 percent of all U.S. workers say they *never* plan to retire. The better educated and more engaged the employee, the more likely he or she will want to work long past the traditional retirement age. As an added benefit to employers and governments, working longer will reduce the strain (and the expectation) of providing retirement pensions and other retirement benefits to their employees.

Job design

Jobs must be redesigned to accommodate short tenures per role. The time required to get "up to speed" to perform a specific function well needs to be shortened to the extent possible, perhaps through the use of just-in-time technology-based training, easily interchangeable systems, well-structured and effective mentoring, or other means. This is necessary to accommodate younger workers' desire for frequent rotations and also to support the rapid growth in cyclic work arrangements. Already, 49 percent of U.S. workers who plan to work after 65 say that they would prefer cyclical arrangements (periods of full-time employment interspersed with periods of leisure) over more conventional part-time employment. This new model will increasingly become the norm for many workers as talented individuals operate as "intellectual mercenaries" assembled by projects over the Web, as needed.

Definition of individual roles

A corollary of the changes in job design will be that roles will increasingly be scoped and compensated according to the task performed – rather than by the time invested as they commonly are now. The distinction between "full" or "part-time" positions will give way to differentiation in the complexity of the task assigned. The idea of putting in "face time" with the boss as a proof of commitment will diminish, as workers put in only enough time to get the specific task done.

The concept of "promotion" and the basis for increased compensation

Most HR policies are based on the premise that the workforce is shaped like a pyramid – with a small number of older workers, a medium number of mid-career workers, and many young people. This indeed was the shape of the workforce in most countries throughout the twentieth century. As a result, we developed career paths based on promoting people "up" – both to provide variety (something new and interesting to do) and increased compensation.

Today the workforce is not pyramidal in shape (it is more like a diamond, with a large middle group) and it is rapidly evolving into a rectangle, with nearly the same number of workers at each major life stage. Going forward, HR's existing approach to promotion will not be mathematically possible. There will not be enough upward positions possible to provide the workforce with sufficient numbers of opportunities for variety, learning or increased compensation – particularly as the generational cohorts become more eager for frequent change and less willing to remain in one position for extended periods of time.

As a result, one of the most pressing issues for HR is to reshape approaches to compensation, promotion, and career path design to provide lateral opportunities. That is, companies must tie variety, recognition, learning, and compensation to lateral moves. We must learn to reward people for breadth, rather than (only) vertical responsibility within the firm. Individualized paths should be chosen to maximize learning, growth, and challenge.

The approach to performance assessment

HR needs to revise the approach to performance management within the corporation in two ways. First, the pace needs to change – young workers today want and expect fast and frequent feedback – daily interaction, ongoing input, "instant" response. Once per year sit-down reviews are an anachronism of the past.

Second, as it becomes more important for companies to operate in a collaborative way, it will be increasingly necessary to incorporate peer-based feedback mechanisms. Our research shows unequivocally that executives outside a group cannot accurately evaluate the collaborative dynamics within a team.

The role of corporations in education

Corporations are in the education business – that is, they need to be prepared to play an active role in creating a workforce with the skills and capabilities required for today's economy. The current educational patterns will not produce a workforce matched to today's business needs. Whether through formal in-company training, sponsored attendance at external programs, apprenticeships and/or increased mentoring, companies will need to help workers gain the necessary knowledge and abilities.

In the case of younger workers, HR executives will discover that the preferred patterns of personal learning will follow fundamentally different patterns than for their elders. Rather than linear learning from authoritative sources, younger workers tend to learn through a process termed *bricolage* – pulling pieces of information from a variety of sources and piecing them together. This preference, along with the shift to a more collaborative culture, will heighten the importance of mentoring within a firm's development repertoire.

The process of selection

One additional implication of the shortage of candidates with education degrees matched to companies' hiring preferences is that educational credentials can no longer be used as they are today as the primary proxy for preparedness and potential. HR needs to develop new ways of screening candidates to find those with the promise and capabilities they seek.

The bedrock principle guiding human resource decisions

Perhaps the most dramatic challenge for HR leaders is to shift the human resource paradigm from a focus on "equality," played out by treating everyone the same, to "fair, but customized," reflecting different arrangements suited to individual needs and preferences. There is no question that individuals with widely differing values and assumptions about work itself populate the workforce. Creating higher engagement levels is all about recognizing individual strengths, needs, preferences, and values. HR leaders must create more flexible approaches to the "deal" between employers and employees and new and more democratic forms of corporate organizations.

Happily, technology has advanced to the point where it will be possible for corporations to shape dramatically different relationships with employees. Like the "cafeteria-style" benefits offerings of the 1990s, interactions between the corporation and its employees will become more flexible and individualized. As supply tightens, individuals will have greater leverage. Over the upcoming decades, instead of equal treatment for all workers, customized "deals" will be the norm.

The opportunity for HR: managers of talent

The shifting demographics and technologies of today are setting a chain reaction of change in motion: enabling corporations that operate in different ways, necessitating a rethink of human resource practices that have become the norm during the last half-century, changing the role of human resource professionals within the business, and finally, shifting the environment that HR helps to engender.

Over the next decade, human resources (or whatever the function comes to be called) will come to bear *primary* responsibility for *managing* the talent required by the business. Not for "talent management" in a passive sense, as in supplying practices and guidance for others, but increasingly with an active, "line"-like responsibility to provide the business with agile, engaged and capable talent "on-demand" – when and where needed – and with the skills and behaviors the organization requires. Thus HR will be integrally involved in creating an environment that builds customer service levels, innovation, efficiency, collaboration, and learning throughout the business.

As the workforce composition shifts predominantly to knowledge workers in a diverse array of work arrangements – some part-time, some cyclical, some employees, some contract-based – individuals will have little need for "managers" in the traditional sense – but they will need a home base. As the complexity of the workforce grows, so does the need to juggle a wide variety of individuals, with diverse preferences and needs, and a dizzying array of relationships. Increasingly, traditional line managers will be happy to pass on the challenge of keeping track of such a complicated talent pool to another function, in exchange for the promise of "on-demand" talent to meet operating needs.

Before long, the responsibility for managing talent will rest with HR, which will in essence become the "home base" for the corporation's workforce – attracting, tracking, developing and orchestrating this complex talent corps. HR will function like staffing managers in professional service firms today or talent agencies in the film industry, while operating managers remain responsible for overseeing the on-the-job deployment of the talent, much as a director might be today in the film industry. Traditional managers will set direction and run the team of employees who have been assigned to the task or division at that moment in time and guiding the on-the-job development experiences.

In this new role, HR will be judged on the quality, engagement, and "readiness" of the talent the business needs, as well as the creation of a work environment rich in the attributes of innovation and collaboration.

The transformation challenge: a new human resource capability

HR's growing role within the corporation and new responsibilities will require an additional set of skills in addition to those of the traditional human resource function. Increasingly, capabilities will include the following.

Strategic thinking, particularly scenario development and options analysis

As the workplace changes in dramatic ways, HR leaders will need to take the lead in providing thoughtful "what if" perspectives on the business's talent challenges. HR executives must be able to create a long-term workforce strategy that addresses uncertainties related to future needs and counter-intuitive sources of talent. Skill in contemporary strategy formulation and scenario planning will be essential to guiding the firm through the uncertainties and options ahead.

Finance and business acumen, including a sophisticated understanding of return on investment analysis

Companies must invest to build the cadre of talent required and the HR executive must serve as both architect and custodian for these assets. This requires creativity to engineer the development of key components of human capital – social, emotional, and intellectual – in non-traditional ways. HR must develop and use sophisticated comparative metrics addressing any intangible benefits, such as tacit knowledge and development opportunities, as part of their overall scorecard evaluations.

Process design capabilities and skill with metrics

Today, HR executives must design their operations for world-class execution – creating operating models to deliver human resource services through efficient, flexible processes, at the necessary service levels, whether within the firm, or through outsourced relationships. This requires a sophisticated skill in "end-to-end" or "stream of service" process design, and adept use of metrics, including performance metrics aligned with specific business outcomes, value metrics reflecting both objective results and the value perceived by process customers, and health metrics indicating how well the process is being maintained and improved.

Marketing and branding savvy

Improving engagement – finding ways to encourage individuals to invest more psychic energy in work – is the single most powerful lever that most corporations have to improve productivity. After decades of downsizing, rightsizing, and re-engineering, most corporations have virtually exhausted their ability to squeeze increased productivity out of the system through top-down pressure. The opportunity today is to raise workers' engagement with work – to tap into the creativity and passion of the workforce. To maximize engagement, HR executives will have to develop strong marketing capabilities: world-class skills in survey research, segmentation, "brand" management, targeting, and communication strategies.

Ability to create environments supporting collaboration and innovation

Corporations of the future will shift from a culture of competition to one of collaboration. In a world where value must be created through innovation, one that is flattened by ubiquitous communication technology, where resources are coupled flexibly as needed, cooperation becomes *the* most critical organization capability. HR leaders must become experts in the foundations of collaboration and innovation, as well as masters of cultural change – able to diagnose the specific weaknesses in their organization, and design appropriate interventions.

Taken together, these shifts represent a significant transformation challenge for the human resource function – and the requirement for new skills in its leadership.

The changing context of work shaped by recent developments in demographics and technology will be profound. Traditional HR practices will be uprooted. Those HR executives who wait to carve out a new strategic role for HR departments not only put their own careers in jeopardy, but they also undermine the future success of the corporations they work for. But for those who see the change coming, success could be extremely rewarding. By demonstrating the contributions that HR can make to the prosperity of the entire firm, HR executives will find themselves in positions that are far more creative and open-ended than ever before. They will become key participants in the flattened, dynamic, networked, and global corporations of the future.

References

BSG Concours (2007) "Boardroom Imperative: Next Generation Enterprises," BSG Alliance, Inc.

Concours Group and Age Wave (2007) *The New Employee/Employer Equation.* Concours Group and Towers Perrin (2007–8) *Towers Perrin Global Workforce Study: 2007–2008.*

Dychtwald, Ken, Tamara J. Erickson, and Robert Morison (2006) *Workforce Crisis: How to Avoid the Coming Shortage of Skills and Talent* (Boston: Harvard Business School Press).

Gratton, Lynda and Tamara J. Erickson (2007) "Eight Ways to Build Collaborative Teams," *Harvard Business Review,* November, 85(11): 100–9.

IDC (2005) *Networking Skills in Europe: Will an increasing shortage hamper competitiveness in the global market?* IDC White Paper, sponsored by Cisco Systems.

Employment Policy Foundation (2002) *The Seventh Annual Workplace Report, Challenges Facing the American Workplace, Summary of Findings* (Washington, DC: Employment Policy Foundation).

Eurostat (2005) "Population Projections 2004–2050," press release, April 8.

Re.sults Project YE (2007) *Engaging Today's Young Employees: Strategies for the Millennials.* The Concours Institute.

U.S. Census Bureau International Data Base.

23

Research at the intersection of Strategic Human Resource Management and entrepreneurship

Janice C. Molloy, Judith W. Tansky
and Robert L. Heneman

In the last decade there have been regular appeals for research at the intersection of the Strategic Human Resource Management (HRM) and entrepreneurship fields (e.g., Baron 2003; Katz et al. 2000; Tansky & Heneman 2003). Such research is in its infancy (Aldrich & Ruef 2006; Goswami et al. 2006), and although specific studies in this field of inquiry have strengths, the overall body of research has been described as fragmented, incoherent, and atheoretical (Cardon & Stevens 2004; Heneman et al. 2000).

Such descriptions often characterize emerging fields as scholars struggle to establish common theoretical and empirical ground (Weick 1995). Indeed, these descriptions characterized strategic HRM research just 15 years ago, when it too was in its infancy (Wright & McMahan 1992). Since then, although challenges persist, the strategic HRM field has grown into a legitimate field of inquiry. Scholars now draw on common theories from the strategy literature (e.g., Wright & McMahan 1992), scholarly debates are enabled by shared language (e.g., Gerhart et al. 2000; Huselid & Becker 2000), and our understanding of HRM in established firms has grown (Becker & Huselid 2006; Bowen & Ostroff 2004). Moreover, not only have strategic HRM scholars created their own body of literature, but they have also made reciprocal contributions to the strategic management literature from which they draw (Barney and Wright (1998), for example, clarified how human capital resources may underlie competitive advantage).

Reflecting on the strategic HRM field's evolution raises some questions: What will be said 15 years from now about the study of HRM in entrepreneurial contexts? Will such research draw on theories used in the entrepreneurship literature? Will conceptual frameworks exist to identify patterns in this research? And, most importantly, will this research further our understanding of HRM in entrepreneurial contexts in a way that ultimately advances both entrepreneurship and strategic HRM theories?

The reality is that, like the entrepreneurial firms we study, continued study of strategic HRM in entrepreneurial settings is anything but certain. For this research to flourish, scholars must develop and test theories that accurately explain and predict the ways in which vital performance outcomes in entrepreneurial firms are related to people management practices and entrepreneurial firm characteristics. However, although the entities studied under the umbrella of "entrepreneurship" show tremendous diversity, current HRM research treats "entrepreneurial firms" as a colossal population of homogeneous organizations (Aldrich & Ruef 2006). Yet treating entrepreneurial firms as homogeneous curtails examination of extant research (e.g., potential meta-analyses) as well as development of theory that accurately explains variations in entrepreneurial phenomena – both of which are essential to the field's legitimacy.

Given the implications of entrepreneurial firm heterogeneity for theory development, the purpose of this chapter is to describe dimensions that distinguish between types of entrepreneurial organizations and identify the implications of such dimensions for HRM in entrepreneurial contexts. First, formal definitions of entrepreneurs and entrepreneurial firms are provided and characteristics currently thought to distinguish entrepreneurial firms from established firms are discussed. Next, a typology is developed that provides a starting point for scholars to identify patterns underlying extant research and clarify the contributions and boundary conditions of future research. The sketch also provides a starting point for a contingency theory of HRM in entrepreneurial contexts that explains and predicts how the relationship between specific patterns of people management practices and entrepreneurial outcomes is moderated by entrepreneurial firm type. Such a theory would have the potential to not only legitimize the study of HRM in entrepreneurial contexts, but also contribute to the broader entrepreneurship and strategic HRM literatures.

Defining the entrepreneurship landscape

The entrepreneurship literature has been plagued by a lack of clear definitions and theoretical assumptions (Aldrich & Martinez 2006). Such variation may be expected given the wide range of activities and traits that have been described as "entrepreneurial," the multidisciplinary nature of entrepreneurship research, the intermixing of research on small- and medium-sized businesses with research on organizational founding, and the complexities inherent to the emergence and maturation of firms.

Entrepreneurs and entrepreneurial firms

There are numerous definitions of entrepreneurs and the enterprises entrepreneurs create. Although these definitions vary in detail, they share a common root in the French verb *entreprendre* (to undertake). The term *enterprise* emerged about 1400 A.D. and was commonly used to refer to an "undertaking of bold and arduous nature" (Casson 1982).

An entrepreneur is defined here as one who undertakes the creation of a viable business through commercialization of a new and untried technology, product, and/or process innovation while both (a) assuming the risk of the enterprise and (b) investing considerable time and energy on behalf of the enterprise (Ireland et al. 2001).[1] In terms of defining the entrepreneurial enterprise, one could argue that an entrepreneurial firm cannot exist without at least one entrepreneur (Aldrich & Martinez 2001). Moreover, entrepreneurial firms are for-profit organizations whose short-term survival is uncertain, that face resource scarcity and earn limited or no revenues while the innovation is being commercialized (Aldrich & Ruef 2006). In short, entrepreneurial firms endure intense internal, external, and time pressures during founding – pressures that constantly batter founding attempts and threaten the firm's very survival (Shane & Venkataraman 2000).

Implications

Although seemingly immaterial, these definitions have important implications for the contours of entrepreneurial constructs. For example, in terms of the entrepreneur construct, a point of confusion is sometimes the differentiation, if any, between inventors and entrepreneurs. The above definitions suggest that although inventors are likely to invest significant time and energy in pursuit of the innovation, unless the inventor pursues commercialization of the innovation and assumes the risk of such a venture, the individual is not an entrepreneur. As such, inventors may be employed by both established and entrepreneurial firms.

Similarly, established firms sometimes engage in "intrapreneurship," "corporate venturing," or "corporate entrepreneurship" initiatives to create or facilitate organizational cultures that support innovation (Hayton 2005). Corporate entrepreneurship is a property of organizational culture and refers to a strategic orientation a firm takes to renew and regenerate products, processes, services, strategies, or the organization itself (Covin & Miles 1999; Kanter 1985). Corporate entrepreneurship enables an existing firm to discover, create, and exploit highly profitable market opportunities. For the purposes of this chapter, those involved in corporate entrepreneurship are not considered entrepreneurs, nor are firms involved in corporate entrepreneurship considered entrepreneurial firms. Such firms use revenue from existing products to fund their innovations; their inventors do not personally assume the venture's risk or funding; and these firms' resource endowments are not consistent with conditions (i.e., resource scarcity) that nascent entrepreneurs face. As defined here, the risk entrepreneurs personally assume extends well beyond that assumed by employees of corporations engaged in innovation or corporate entrepreneurship.

Indeed, research finds that many nascent entrepreneurs invest (or put at risk) their life savings and incur enormous personal debt to fund start-up costs (Reynolds 2000). Entrepreneurs also devote their time and energy to the firm, and consistent with our definition, this investment is likely full-time. As such, entrepreneurs' investments are undoubtedly high-stakes investments. Entrepreneurs typically bear the full wealth effects of their actions, whether a net income or loss. Entrepreneurial firms also do not have the support corporate product-development employees have (e.g., the ability to leverage existing financial planning and information systems, administrative support staff).

In sum, the "entrepreneurial" constructs provided here emphasize that what entrepreneurs "do" is establish new firms in conditions in which resources are scarce and pressures to quickly commercialize the innovation and earn profits are intense. While an inventor may be an entrepreneur, the two terms are not synonymous.[2] Moreover, with the indications that entrepreneurial ventures are for-profit and that entrepreneurs assume the risk associated with their enterprise, one would surmise that entrepreneurial firms are privately held entities (Shane 2003). The section that follows describes current conceptions of the distinctions between entrepreneurial and established firms.

Superficial dimensions

To operationalize the entrepreneurial firm construct described above, researchers often focus on correlates of entrepreneurial firms. Examples of such correlates include the number of employees (e.g., fewer than 500), age (e.g., less than ten years since founding), and revenues beneath a certain threshold (e.g., < $50M) (Acs & Armington 1998; Aldrich & Fiol 1994). However, although characteristics such as number of employees, age, or revenues may serve as proxies for identification of entrepreneurial firms, these characteristics are superficial indicators. Such indicators lend themselves to black-and-white depictions of entrepreneurial firms, but the extent to which the proxies reflect the underlying nature of the construct remains unclear, and construct validation studies are the exception rather than the rule in entrepreneurship, as the characteristics measured are believed to represent objective features of organizations.

More specifically, with regard to number of employees, for example, scholars would generally agree that firms with 500 or more employees often are not entrepreneurial, nor are firms surviving more than ten years or firms surpassing a certain threshold of sales. However, such independent thresholds are problematic from at least two perspectives. First, such thresholds do not fully reflect the essential nature of entrepreneurial firms as suggested in the definitions presented earlier, nor do such thresholds sufficiently reflect the full range of characteristics consistent with entrepreneurial firms. In addition, such definitions leave unanswered questions such as: Are long-standing successful businesses with fewer than 500 employees that are passed from generation to generation entrepreneurial? What about businesses that have successfully utilized various employment modes such as outsourcing, contract employees, and strategic alliances and therefore have fewer than 500 employees, but substantial revenues – are these firms entrepreneurial? And when do entrepreneurial firms stop being "entrepreneurial?" When they have 501 employees or become ten years old?

Therefore, while such thresholds are commonly used, we argue that they are insufficient (highly likely but not sufficient conditions) for an organization to be considered an entrepreneurial firm. Again, for example, although firms with more than 500 employees are not likely to be entrepreneurial, neither is it certain that firms with fewer than 500 employees are entrepreneurial firms. Therefore, it seems that such thresholds do not isolate the underlying conditions that differentiate the two types of firms; indeed, one could argue that such thresholds isolate the symptoms rather than root causes underlying such differences (Aldrich & Ruef 2006; Baumol 1993). The following section discusses entrepreneurial firm founding conditions, two of which can better isolate the dimensions that underlie differences between entrepreneurial and established firms.

Founding conditions: typology of entrepreneurial firms

That founding conditions influence firm outcomes is often discussed in management literatures (Baum 1996). For example, in the finance literature, analyses of firm performance determinants typically include a "founder's effects" term that represents a collection of unspecified variables (e.g., Hsu 2007). However, far from being a residual variable whose main importance is to aggregate extraneous variance, it is argued here that HRM scholars have much to gain by unpacking founder effects. Founding conditions are recognized in the entrepreneurship, sociology, and strategy literatures as important in shaping firms' survival and potential to gain competitive advantage (e.g., Boeker 1989). Much entrepreneurship research has emphasized that new firms are imprinted at the time of founding with the characteristics of the people and environments that surround the early establishment (e.g., Aldrich & Ruef 2006). Selznick (1957) emphasized the influence of *internal* founding conditions, focusing on the personality and decisions of organizational founders on characteristics of the early organization (including employment relationships) (Selznick also recognized that the decisions of founders are constrained by environmental conditions). Stinchcombe (1965), by contrast, emphasized the influence of *external* or environmental founding conditions, although he stressed an important role for individual founders in the process of creating diversity among organizations. External founding factors include the market stage of the initial environment (early, growth, maturity) (Bamford et al. 2000; Eisenhardt & Schoonhoven 1996), population density (number of competitors) (Carroll & Hannan 1989), and dynamics between the firm and potential customers, suppliers, and competitors (Porter 1985).

Together, Selznick's (1957) and Stinchcombe's (1965) views are known as the organizational imprinting hypothesis (Romanelli 1991). Stinchcombe (1965: 153) stated the hypothesis most clearly when he wrote:

> The organizational inventions that can be made at a particular time in history depend upon the social technology available to them at the time . . . Then, both because they can function effectively with those organizational forms, and because the forms tend to become institutionalized, the basic structure of the organization tends to remain relatively stable.

Research has gone on to show that imprinting has lasting effects on such organizational characteristics as the firm's strategies (Boeker 1988, 1989); structure (Stinchcombe 1965); human resource systems (Baron et al. 1998); and performance (Eisenhardt & Schoonhoven 1990). Moreover, decisions made at founding have significant influence on organizational culture and firm scope (Aldrich & Ruef 2006).

An example: HRM blueprints

Baron et al. (1999) examined founding conditions in their longitudinal study of 170 Silicon Valley high-technology start-ups. They found that the majority of founders had a "blueprint" or conception regarding what employment relations would be like in their firm. These blueprints included dimensions such as the basis of attachment, selection criteria, and nature of coordination and control mechanisms. For example, three dimensions of attachment were detailed: love, or a sense of personal belonging and identification with the firm; work, that is, the opportunity to work at the frontier of technology, and monetary rewards. In this last dimension, the employment relationship was viewed as a simple exchange of labor compensation. The selection criteria dimension of founders' blueprints related to fit. Specifically, Baron, Hannan, and Burton found that founders typically had an interest in maximizing one of three types of fit: current job fit, fit with current work needs (and likelihood to adapt to future needs), and a fit with the organization's culture or values. Finally, the last dimension relates to coordination and control alternatives such as processes involving checks-and-balances, direct oversight, and/or use of controlling through social norms.[3]

Baron and colleagues found that founders' blueprints influenced not only the HRM policies firms pursued initially but also the policies firms had at later points in time. Related research has indicated that HRM policies have strong "inertia" effects and are difficult to change once implemented (e.g., Kalleberg et al. 1996; Snell & Dean 1994). Baron and colleagues' findings are consistent with such research in that ten years later, the majority of firms in their study had HRM programs and policies that were similar to those initially intended.

Entrepreneurial firm typology

The HRM blueprints entrepreneurs have for the firm (e.g., Baron et al. 1999) represent an important founding condition for predicting not only HRM policies but also HRM and firm outcomes. We argue that there are additional fundamental founding conditions that significantly influence both the type of HRM systems firms use and the efficacy of HRM system alternatives and firm performance. Although such conditions are discussed in the entrepreneurship literature, they have been given little if any attention in the HRM arena. Specifically, we suggest that *growth intentions* and the *nature of the entrepreneurial opportunity* are important founding conditions for HRM scholars to examine.

Growth intentions

Although events leading up to the creation of an entrepreneurial firm may be fortuitous, the creation of an entrepreneurial firm is not a chance event; firm creation can be characterized as a form of planned behavior (Ajzen 1991). Underlying the firm formation process are the attitudes, subjective norms, and perceived behavioral controls that shape entrepreneurs' intentions, such as growth-related aspirations or the scale of intended venturing (Cassar 2006; Delmar & Davidsson 1999).

It has been found that entrepreneurs generally have a sense as to whether they would prefer to contain the growth of the firm to provide income for themselves (and perhaps a select group of family members or friends), or whether they intend to instead aggressively pursue growth opportunities and maximize growth and profits (e.g., Birley & Westhead 1994; Cassar 2007; Casson 2006). Understanding these intentions is important, as entrepreneurs' aspirations for growth play a crucial role in the actual growth achieved by ventures (Covin & Slevin 1991; Wiklund & Shepherd 2003). Indeed, many ventures do not achieve substantial growth simply because founders do not intend for them to do so (Davidsson 1989; Kolvereid 1992).

The growth intention construct represents the firm growth the entrepreneur intends to see; in turn, actual growth is typically measured out two and five years from founding (e.g., Shepherd et al. 2007; Wiklund et al. 2003). Although measures of growth are sometimes based on the number of employees desired, the most commonly used measures focus on desired sales revenue. The growth intention construct has a wide continuum of attributes; however, for illustrative purposes, two categories of growth intention are depicted in the typology provided here (see Table 23.1): limited growth and high growth.

Limited growth

Limited-growth firms include firms serving as a "salary substitute" or a "lifestyle basis" for founders. Salary substitute firms are pursued as a form of self-employment. Physicians and dentists have long created such businesses (e.g., U.S. Census Bureau 2002). More recently, Hall (2002) noted a marked increase in individuals pursuing such businesses as an alternative to direct employment; Hall suggested such increase might be due to downsizings and general instability in employment in established firms. Consistent with Hall's research, findings from the Panel Study of Entrepreneurship Dynamics (PSED) also note a significant increase in "salary substitute" firms, especially in the domain of professional services such as information systems, accounting, and human resource management (Reynolds 2000).

In contrast to salary substitute firms, "lifestyle" firms allow the entrepreneur to pursue a hobby or interest (Hitt & Ireland 2003) while being compensated for their efforts (i.e., while "being paid to play"). Examples of such firms may include a bed-and-breakfast business run by owners pursuing a retirement dream, or a ski and snowboard shop run by a ski aficionado. It has been suggested that there has been an increase in lifestyle businesses throughout the world over the past ten years (Kaufman 2005), especially as initiated by those reaching retirement or pursuing a job to bridge between working full-time and full retirement (Reynolds 2000).

From a HRM perspective, firms interested in low growth would want to use external employment modes (rather than hire employees directly) to handle seasonal fluctuations in demand. Such employment support may come through the use of contract labor, formal alliances with other organizations, or informal "bartering" arrangements with other entrepreneurs. PSED data suggest that the vast majority of firms for which the entrepreneur does not intend growth do not take on employees and, as such, do not develop formal HRM policies (Reynolds 2000).

High growth

High-growth firms are defined here as those who seek to fully maximize profits, firm scope, and market share. Such firms often have year-over-year growth of 20 percent for the first five

Table 23.1 Founding conditions: typology of entrepreneurial enterprises

Nature of entrepreneurial opportunity

		Discovery	Creation
Growth Intentions	Limited growth	Incremental shift in an existing concept pursued to provide self-employment (or employment to a small group) (e.g., mom-and-pop restaurant)	A novel and untried concept pursued to provide self-employment (or employment to a small group) (e.g., computer software development)
		Entrepreneur does not intend to grow firm beyond the entrepreneur's managerial capacity	Entrepreneur does not intend to grow firm beyond the entrepreneur's managerial capacity
		Firm established for continued private ownership	To extract value, entrepreneur may sell patent and/or technology rights
	High growth	Incremental shift in an existing concept pursued to maximize market share and profits (e.g., deli intended to expand into chain of delis or franchise)	A novel and untried concept pursued to maximize market share and profits (e.g., Henry Ford's auto)
		Firm positioned as an acquisition target or for initial public offering to acquire capital required for growth	Firm positioned as an acquisition target or for initial public offering to acquire capital required for growth

or more years of business (Aldrich & Ruef 2006). Such firms can vary widely, from Silicon Valley Internet start-ups to franchised restaurant chains. In order to pursue a high-growth strategy, the entrepreneur is likely to found the firm with the intention of either selling (i.e., positioning the firm as a lucrative acquisition target) or "going public" (Barney 2007; Camp & Sexton 1992; Kogut 1991). Why are these "end-game" options likely to be considered at founding? The significant capital needed to fund rapid growth requires outside capital. The critical consideration is the need for the firm to grow quickly in order to fully exploit the market opportunity before rivals do so or before substitute products and services are commercialized. In order to accomplish such rapid growth such firms often acquire venture capital funding to assist with the start-up phase.

Given the importance of early imprints, founders with a high-growth strategy need to pursue such a strategy decisively. Thus, from a HRM perspective, entrepreneurs with high-growth intentions will want to have a clear "HRM blueprint" such as those examined and detailed by Baron et al. (1999). Indeed, such HRM blueprints may be expected by venture capitalists as a condition of funding; venture capitalist firms have been known to require and provide HRM strategy support to founders given the crucial role of human capital in high-growth ventures (e.g., Cyr et al. 2000; Welbourne et al. 1999). The human capital demands of high-growth firms are pressing, and it is in such settings that rapidly deployed hiring and ramp-up processes are most likely utilized (Carter et al. 1996).

Nature of entrepreneurial opportunity

The *nature of the entrepreneurial opportunity* is another characteristic of the founding conditions of entrepreneurial firms. In the entrepreneurship literature there is growing interest in examining such entrepreneurial opportunities, or the characteristics of the market need and profit opportunity that the entrepreneur intends to serve and exploit (Eckhardt & Shane 2003; McMullen et al. 2007). One could argue that the field of entrepreneurship has traditionally been based on the assumption that entrepreneurs differ from non-entrepreneurs in that entrepreneurs are more "alert" to or able to see opportunities to make profits and create sustainable businesses (c.f., Casson 2006; Shane 2000). In such views, however, the opportunities that entrepreneurs exploit "exist." That is, entrepreneurs do not need to take action to *create* entrepreneurial opportunities; instead, entrepreneurs simply need to *discover* already-existing entrepreneurial opportunities and take action to exploit them (Gaglio & Katz 2001; Shane 2003; Venkataraman 1997). Given the focus on discovering existing entrepreneurial opportunities, this approach is known as the discovery theory of entrepreneurship.

Alvarez and Barney (2007) challenged this paradigm by asking whether all entrepreneurial opportunities exist, independent of the perceptions and actions of entrepreneurs, or if instead some entrepreneurial opportunities might be *created* by the actions of entrepreneurs. Such questions give rise to a creation theory of entrepreneurship – a logical alternative to discovery theory. Aspects of creation theory have been described by a variety of authors (Alvarez & Barney 2005; Baker & Nelson 2005; Casson 1982; Gartner 1985; Langlois & Cosgel 1993; Loasby 2002; Sarasvathy 2001; Schumpeter 1934). Both discovery and creation theories have important consequences for the HRM approaches required for exploiting entrepreneurial opportunities.

Discovery opportunities

A fundamental difference between discovery and creation theories is the depiction of the initial decision-making context as one of risk vs. uncertainty.[4] Decision-making contexts are risky if, at the time a decision is made, decision makers can collect enough information to anticipate both the possible outcomes associated with the decision along with the probability of each of those outcomes (Alvarez & Barney 2007; Knight 1921). Such information may be obtained through marketing research, secondary research, or mathematical modeling. But for a founding context to be considered risky, the entrepreneur must know or be able to acquire the information needed to project market demand for the product or service.

Firms whose initial decision-making contexts are characterized by risk are those businesses that pursue product and service offerings that are similar to those provided by other firms. Examples include businesses such as restaurants, for which the demand for dining within an area may be estimated using marketing research and population data. Indeed, most entrepreneurial firms can be characterized as discovery firms. Such businesses typically have the benefit of modeling their business plans and intentions after similar businesses within the same industry or geography.

From a HRM perspective, entrepreneurial firms pursuing discovery opportunities provide a fertile ground in which to apply the well-developed HRM and industrial/organizational psychology research on staffing, appraisal and rewards, and training and development. In such companies, "new" jobs can be modeled on jobs in similar businesses, perhaps using benchmarking or information networks that provide job descriptions and specifications such as the Finland Ministry of Labour (http://www.mol.fi/mol/en/index.jsp) or the U.S. Department of Labor's National Center for O★NET Development (http://online.onetcenter.org/) (e.g., Farr 2004). Along similar lines, staffing needs can be projected using marketing research and benchmarking data. Given that demand can be projected, a context is provided in which incentive structures involving quality and quantity can be established. Finally, given that other businesses have pursued somewhat similar opportunities and a portion of the knowledge and skills employees need are likely tacit knowledge, there may not be the need to internally house all training and development design and delivery.

Creation opportunities

In contrast to those entrepreneurial opportunities that characterize discovery theory, in creation theory entrepreneurial opportunities do not exist until the entrepreneur creates them. Examples of creation opportunities include the high-tech businesses studied by Baron, Hannan, and Burton (1996, 1999). Indeed, Internet companies founded during the 1990s serve as good examples of creation entrepreneurial firms. Hotmail's development of web-based email and Amazon's development of online bookselling – both of which were unknown frontiers at the time – would be examples of the pursuit of creation opportunities. Creation firms are often high-tech firms that commercialize competency-destroying technologies and typify Schumpeter's (1939) views of entrepreneurial firms as growth engines that bring forth progress and new industries.

Unlike discovery opportunities in which risk characterizes the decision-making context, creation opportunities are characterized by uncertainty. That is, in creation contexts, at the point a decision is made about whether or not to create the opportunity, there is no information available to determine the possible outcomes associated with the opportunity or the probability that such outcomes will occur. Moreover, in principle it is impossible to collect all of the information needed to convert an uncertain decision-making setting into a risky one, the best efforts of entrepreneurs notwithstanding. In terms of creation theory the inability to estimate the probability distributions associated with decisions does not depend on the limited time that entrepreneurs have to collect information about a new opportunity, nor does such inability depend on the ability of potential entrepreneurs to analyze the information they have collected. Rather, under uncertainty, even entrepreneurs with a great deal of time and unusual analytical abilities will be unable to estimate the relevant probability distributions (Dunning et al. 2004; Miller 2007), as the information required to estimate these distributions simply has not yet been created.

A good example of the difficulty that firms have acquiring the data they need to determine possible outcomes involves Amazon, the online book retailer. Although marketing research was attempted at the time of Amazon's launch, the consumers surveyed could not relate to Amazon's significant shift in the book-purchasing model, and the limited marketing research that Amazon attempted suggested that the firm would not succeed as individuals would not be willing to purchase books online. That consumers may be unable to provide accurate information simply because they do not understand the full experience the firm is attempting to create is characteristic of creation firms.

An example of a creation firm that evolved into an enterprise quite different from that which was originally intended is the Ice Hotel in Sweden. In this case, the entrepreneur, Yngve Bergkvist, was a former lumberjack who built an organization that would support his passion for creating ice sculptures; with the help of a few employees, he showed his sculptures in a traveling exhibit. Although the exhibit was often well attended, because temperatures had to remain frigid in order to maintain the integrity of the sculptures, people typically rushed through the exhibit and were not willing to pay the premium ticket prices associated with a venue that would allow them to carefully examine and enjoy the show. As a solution to this problem, the firm housed the sculptures in an igloo with seating; eventually a bar was added; and eventually the firm grew into a hotel chain. At the time of the firm's inception neither Mr. Bergkvist nor his original employees expected the company to grow into a hotel (and hotels require very different jobs, skill sets, and training from those required to operate a traveling exhibit). Moreover, early marketing research suggested that a hotel with furniture made of ice (including beds) would not be attractive or successful. Yet today the Ice Hotel is thriving (Bergkvist 2007).

The HRM challenges associated with creation opportunities are significant. Given the lack of availability of market demand information and the difficulty in projecting the evolution of the product, it is difficult, if not impossible, to define jobs and conduct job analyses, which are the cornerstone of the HRM process. Also, given the uncertainties related to market demand and timing, the challenges associated with the development of incentive and reward programs that motivate employees while not expropriating profits are potentially intractable. These and other HRM implications are discussed in the following section.

Implications For Strategic Human Resource Management

As suggested above, the growth intention and entrepreneurial opportunity dimensions detailed in the entrepreneurial firm typology provided here (see Table 23.1) have important implications for strategic HRM in entrepreneurial settings. However, before discussing these implications further, it is important to consider the lens through which HRM in entrepreneurial settings may be examined. It has been argued that HRM scholars examining entrepreneurial firms with the same lens used to study established firms will emerge disheartened, for they will not see much "HRM" through this lens (Barrett & Mayson 2007; Katz et al. 2000). For example, the formalized HRM practices characteristic of high-performance work systems (e.g., Huselid 1995) tend not to be found in entrepreneurial settings (e.g., Cardon & Stevens 2004; Marlow 2006; Tansky & Heneman 2003, 2006).

However, we believe the study of strategic HRM in entrepreneurial settings offers unique and interesting research opportunities. In entrepreneurial settings, general managers typically deal with the HRM implications of their strategies and make some of what we would argue are among the most strategic of decisions – making employment mode decisions (e.g., Klaas et al. 2005a; Lepak & Snell 1999, 2002) while unencumbered by history, precedent, or concern about disrupting existing employment relationships. As such, we believe that those strategic HRM scholars interested in seeing how employment relationships form (from both the firm and employee perspectives) will find entrepreneurial firms a rich context for research. Similarly, although we know that HRM practices tend to persist, we have little understanding of the processes through which HRM evolves from the HRM blueprint (c.f., Baron et al. 1999) (if one exists) to actual HRM practices. Those interested in understanding differences between "intended" HRM practices and strategies and the realities employees experience will find entrepreneurial settings equally engaging. With these considerations in mind, we discuss the HRM implications of our entrepreneurial firm typology, beginning with a discussion of HRM in discovery contexts.

Discovery contexts

Whether or not entrepreneurial opportunities are discovered or created has important implications for entrepreneurial actions, including HRM. For example, if opportunities exist as objective phenomena, then the task of ambitious entrepreneurs is to discover opportunities – using whatever data collection techniques exist – and then exploit them all as quickly as possible, before another entrepreneur does so. Likewise, growth intentions have important implications for staffing, appraisal and rewards, as well as training and development.

High growth

HRM theories and research in the mainstream management and industrial/organizational psychology literatures are highly applicable to high-growth discovery contexts. As suggested earlier, firms exploiting discovery opportunities benefit from their ideas having been implemented previously in at least some form and, as such, can duplicate models used in other businesses (or presented in textbooks). Indeed, one proposition is that entrepreneurs find that "traditional" HRM "best practices" (which are based in part on internal labor markets and enduring employment relationships) (e.g., Huselid 1994) fit well in high-growth discovery businesses. Internal labor markets provide a mechanism to address both firm staffing issues as well as rewards. In addition, the promotion opportunities underlying the internal labor market hierarchy are likely viewed as credible (i.e., employees will probably perceive that there will be higher level jobs and movement between jobs given the firm's expansion). In summary, although an empirical question, high-growth firms in discovery contexts are likely well served by the staffing, appraisal and rewards, and training and development practices traditionally studied in HRM and industrial/organizational psychology.

High-growth discovery contexts provide fertile terrain for the examination of both traditional HRM theories as well as entrepreneurship theories. For example, Edith Penrose (1959) (whose theory of the firm focused on why capitalist economies typically have many firms instead of few, very large, diversified firms) suggested that firm growth is restricted by the firm's stock of human capital. Specifically, Penrose argued that in order to grow, firms require managers fully versed in the firm's strategy, philosophies, and internal systems – individuals who can pursue and manage growth initiatives in a manner consistent with what founders would desire. It is the lack of experienced managerial talent (i.e., "middle managers" with firm-specific skills regarding policies, practice, and firm strategies) that Penrose suggested may limit growth. Although the "Penrose effect" has been studied in the entrepreneurship and international business literatures (e.g., Gander 1991; Tan & Mahoney 2005), perhaps HRM scholars, with their measurement expertise in employment relationships and staffing, may test the effect in alternative ways, thereby contributing to the entrepreneurship, strategy, and strategic HRM literatures. The typology in Table 23.1 provides HRM scholars with guidance as to where they may want to target such research initiatives – for example, firms pursuing limited growth are not likely to endure Penrose effects, and as such, sampling frames attempting to establish Penrose effects that include limited-growth firms would have confounded results.

Low growth

In contrast to high-growth discovery firms, firms pursuing discovery opportunities who also plan to curtail growth will not likely find HRM "best practices" or the content of HRM textbooks to be particularly helpful. Indeed, low-growth discovery firms may find some traditional staffing practices such as the use of customized selection tests to be ineffective, as such practices are associated with the maintenance of high staff levels, and such staff levels are not required in small firms. However, although low-growth firms will probably have few employees, founders do need to manage staffing fluctuations caused by increases in demand through employment modes such as outsourcing, contract labor, and alliances (Lepak & Snell 1999). Such options provide the firm flexibility for managing demand without the burden of maintaining employment relationships throughout economic cycles.

As suggested here, given that low-growth firms probably have limited staff levels (and limited hierarchies), such firms probably do not have internal labor markets. Thus, well-defined job roles, promotion opportunities, and career paths with defined training and development opportunities likely do not exist in such firms. In turn, the lack of an internal labor market may lead to certain HRM challenges. That is, employees may become disheartened regarding the lack of promotion or training and development opportunities – thus, the lack of an internal labor market may lead to difficulty attracting and retaining employees. Indeed, if individuals seeking employment desire promotion opportunities and surmise that such opportunities are not possible due to the firm's business strategy, individuals would need to either (a) be willing to accept a position in which advancement, if any, is unclear and career paths are neither explicitly communicated nor implied, or (b) eschew employment opportunities with low-growth entrepreneurial firms, pursuing employment at companies that offer a clear career path.

Creation contexts

It is in creation contexts that we believe HRM becomes most interesting. As described earlier, it is in creation contexts – in which the firm both creates and fills a previously non-existent market need – that firms lack the information necessary to determine the possible outcomes associated with the opportunity or the probability that such outcomes will occur. Thus, creation-based firms are most likely to have emergent (rather than intended) strategies. As such, given the fluid nature of emergent strategies, founders are not able to identify the role behaviors expected of employees; indeed, the conditions necessary to effectively implement traditional HRM practices (e.g., Wright & Snell 1998) do not exist. This suggests that it is unclear to what extent the often-studied HRM "best practices" are applicable in creation contexts. The uncertainty characterizing creation contexts has important implications for staffing, appraisal and rewards, and training and development in creation firms.

High growth

Silicon Valley start-ups (e.g., Yahoo, PayPal, Hotmail, CraigsList, Firefox, Google) are prototypical examples of high-growth creation firms. As suggested above, the uncertain contexts of creation firms mean that entrepreneurs need to hire without the benefit of job analyses, systematic planning of compensation and benefits, or information regarding the potential for promotion opportunities within the firm. For example, if an entrepreneur knows she wants to commercialize a product, but neither she nor her employees has specialized knowledge of the processes required to develop the product, how is the firm to develop specific, measurable, achievable, and results-oriented goals? Such conditions are theoretically problematic, as employment relationships of any type (whether these involve "direct hires" or external "contract employees") are based on the need to balance the contributions–inducements exchange (Barnard 1938; March & Simon 1958). When required contributions cannot be identified, it is unclear how the firm is to provide inducements that compensate the individual adequately without also "overpaying" him or her. While these challenges are present for any creation firm with employees, these issues are especially problematic in high-growth firms simply because high-growth firms need to develop employment relationships with many employees.[5]

High-growth creation-based firms also face challenges with training and development, as in creation contexts the knowledge that is most significant for the firm's continued growth is being created through the idiosyncratic and path-dependent process the firm is using to grow and survive. Indeed, founders' and employees' "blind variations" (i.e., choices that are not purposeful but that may prove fruitful) and the path-dependent nature of the knowledge that is developed mean that a significant portion of knowledge is likely to be tacit, which limits the firm's ability to "scale up" and train new employees in a time-efficient way. Indeed, it may well be that creation firms' employees are uncertain as to which specific choices along the development path have contributed to their product or service's unique attributes. Such training challenges would not be as significant in low-growth firms, where there are not as many employees to train and the firm is not continually hiring new employees.

Low growth

Given that low-growth creation firms do not intend to take on employees and are most likely developed simply to provide employment for the founder (and perhaps a select group of additional individuals), the HRM challenges facing such firms are not as significant as those facing high-growth creation firms. Given the limited impact of HRM issues for such firms, one central challenge for firms with more than one founder becomes a concern with founding team dynamics.[6] There is a burgeoning research in this area, including work on the internal dynamics among founding team members (e.g., Balkin & Swift 2006; Beckman & Burton forthcoming) as well as the impact of team members' social networks (e.g., Collins & Clark 2003) on the firm. Internal dynamics would include topics such as addition of new members, conflict management and interpersonal fallouts, and shifting of decision rights over time. Examples of "external" social network dynamics include the influence of team members' social capital on the firm's ability to both acquire resources (e.g., funding) and maintain them (e.g., scarcity of resources following an employment "honeymoon" period may hinder employees' productivity or cause them to want to leave the firm). External dynamics (e.g., the breadth and depth of team members' relationships with potential buyers) also impact the firm's ability to secure initial sales and successfully launch innovations into the marketplace. For a summary of extant research on founding teams and the challenges facing creation firms with limited growth intentions, see Aldrich and Ruef (2006).

Discussion

As stated in the beginning of this chapter, there have been regular appeals for research at the intersection of the strategic HRM and entrepreneurship fields in the last decade (e.g., Baron 2003; Katz et al. 2000; Tansky & Heneman 2004). At one time, such calls for research would have been considered paradoxical. How could entrepreneurial firms, which were not large enough to have HR departments and not likely to have formalized HR practices, engage in HRM? However, during the last five years it has become clear that entrepreneurs seldom act alone when exploiting market opportunities. During this same time, conceptualizations of HRM have expanded to include a broad view of the ways that managers access and coordinate the human capital needed to formulate and implement strategies (e.g., Collins & Allen 2006; Klaas et al. 2005; Lepak et al. 2003). Indeed, the fundamental decisions entrepreneurs make about whether to hire or contract human capital may be among the most strategic HRM challenges organizations face (Hayton 2004).

There are certainly examples of exemplary research on the unique aspects of entrepreneurial firms; and such research provides a much-needed foundation for legitimization of the study of HRM in entrepreneurial settings (e.g., Baron et al. 1999; Beckman & Burton forthcoming; Cardon & Stevens 2004; Collins & Allen 2006; Collins & Smith 2006; Jack et al. 2006). On the other hand, much of the work in this area has drawn upon HRM theories and practices that are based upon established firm settings. Indeed, McLarty (1999: 198) suggests that the assumption in HRM is that "small firms are embryonic large firms." Moreover, when the unique features of entrepreneurial firms *are* considered, research has focused mostly on these firms' broad aggregate attributes, such as size and age (Tansky & Heneman 2003; Williamson 2000). More often than not, the application of HRM theories and practices to entrepreneurial settings fails to take into consideration the unique contexts that differentiate entrepreneurial firms both from established firms and from each other. Movement towards recognizing the complexity and variation that abounds in new venture creation is important both for the field of entrepreneurship as a whole and for HRM in entrepreneurial firms in particular. In this chapter we have outlined a framework to differentiate entrepreneurial firms in terms of founders' growth intentions and the nature of the entrepreneurial opportunity, which provides scholars one way to ground theoretical and empirical HRM research within the entrepreneurship literature and arrive at a more nuanced understanding of HRM in entrepreneurial contexts.

What about strategic HRM scholars who do not focus on entrepreneurial firms or who currently may have little interest in entrepreneurial firms? Why might these scholars find research on HRM in entrepreneurial firms of interest? Even if scholars have no specific interest in entrepreneurial firms, we believe examining HRM in emerging organizations yields significant benefits to the strategic HRM field as a whole. First, issues of generalizability and external validity arise when theory and research are based exclusively on the experiences of relatively large, long-lived organizations, as is true in the domain of HRM and strategic HRM. To date, there is simply much more information available about the HR practices and performance of established enterprises than there is about the HR practices and performance of entrepreneurial firms, and many have thus sought to derive theory and insights by examining the characteristics of established companies – companies that have been successful over long periods of time. While such research can be illuminating, it can have drawbacks. For example, the danger in drawing inferences from long-lived or seemingly successful organizations is that one typically lacks information on the enterprises that have failed over the same period.

Entrepreneurial firms also provide a window through which to examine the evolution of HRM practices, functions, and executive roles. Such an opportunity is not afforded in established contexts. We know little about the transitions firms make from the ad hoc handling of HRM tasks to more formal practices, and given that HRM practices demonstrate inertia (Kalleberg et al. 1996; Kaufman 2004; Snell & Dean 1992), creating a path-dependent character of employment relations, research on HRM in entrepreneurial firms is likely to illuminate our understanding of HRM in both entrepreneurial and established firms. Given the importance of crafting HRM policies that are closely aligned with the organizational context and that display strong internal consistency, examining the birth and early evolution of HRM practices in new organizations can provide important insights into the determinants of enduring HRM policies and practices (e.g., Collins & Allen 2006).

Conclusion

This chapter provided a sketch of the next frontier of HRM research in entrepreneurial contexts. We argue that this frontier emerges when one considers the following. Some of the most interesting questions in this area arise when focusing not on the *entrepreneurial firm* but rather on the *market opportunities that underlie entrepreneurial firms*. Indeed, we argue that research examining market opportunity characteristics and the entrepreneur's intentions for a firm's growth may yield insights regarding not only HRM in entrepreneurial firms but also HRM in general, and strategic HRM in particular. Such research involves a focus on the theoretical assumptions underlying HRM in entrepreneurial and established settings, rather than a contrasting of the superficial characteristics of entrepreneurial vs. established firms.

Despite the recent research that has enriched our understanding of HRM in entrepreneurial contexts, with few exceptions current studies present little or no framing in terms of entrepreneurship or strategic HRM theories. This lack of connection between the entrepreneurship literature, along with the lack of integration across HRM functional areas, hinders acceptance of HRM in entrepreneurial contexts as a legitimate field of inquiry. Ultimately, it may be possible to build a contingency theory of HRM by linking a typology of entrepreneurial firms with specific people-management practices. That is, there may be certain sets of people-management practices that are interconnected and logically consistent that enable the exploitation of certain types of entrepreneurial opportunities, and different configurations of people-management practices that enable the exploitation of other opportunities. As suggested earlier, such a contingency theory has the potential to contribute not only to the study of HRM in entrepreneurial firms but also to the broader entrepreneurship and strategic HRM literatures.

Notes

1 Entrepreneurship scholars have long examined ways in which entrepreneurs are systematically different than nonentrepreneurs; however, results from such research are mixed (e.g., Busenitz & Barney 1997; Collins et al. 2004; Low & MacMillan 1988). Hisrich et al. (2007) provide a detailed discussion of the state of this research.

2 This discussion highlights that to date there is no nomological network that frames entrepreneurs and entrepreneurial firms within a conceptual space, defining relationships among similar and different constructs. Such clarification of constructs and relationships highlights an important priority for future research.

3 Baron and colleagues identified five common combinations of the three blueprint dimensions identified in their study; these five HRM systems are detailed in Baron et al. (2001).

4 Although conditions of risk and uncertainty are often used interchangeably in the entrepreneurship (Shane 2003) and strategic management (Balakrishnan & Wernerfelt 1986; Wernerfelt & Karnani 1987) literatures, these terms have distinct meanings (Knight 1921).

5 Livingston (2007) provides detailed interviews with founders who describe the HRM challenges associated with high-growth creation firms.

6 Obviously, founding team dynamics concern any firm with more than one founder.

References

Acs, Z. and Armington, C. (1998) "Longitudinal Establishment and Enterprise Microdata (LEEM) Documentation," Washington, DC: U.S. Bureau of the Census, Center for Economic Studies, Discussion: 98–109.

Ajzen, I. (1991) "The theory of planned behavior," *Organizational Behavior and Human Decision Processes*, 50(2): 179–212.

Aldrich, H. and Fiol, C. (1994) "Fools rush in? The institutional context of industry creation," *Academy of Management Review*, 19(4): 645–670.

Aldrich, H. and Martinez, M. (2001) "Many are called, but few are chosen: An evolutionary perspective for the study of entrepreneurship," *Entrepreneurship: Theory & Practice*, 25(4): 41–57.

—— (2006) "Entrepreneurship as social construction: A multilevel evolutionary approach," in J. Zoltan and D. Audretsch (eds) *Handbook of Entrepreneurship Research: An interdisciplinary survey and introduction*, New York: Springer.

Aldrich, H. and Ruef, M. (2006) *Organizations Evolving*, 2nd edn, Thousand Oaks, CA: Sage.

Alvarez, S. and Barney, J. (2005) "How do entrepreneurs organize firms under conditions of uncertainty?", *Journal of Management*, 31(5): 776–793.

—— (2007) "Discovery and creation: Alternative theories of entrepreneurial action," *Strategic Entrepreneurship Journal*, 1(1): 1–13.

Baker, T. and Nelson, R. (2005) "Creating something from nothing: Resource construction through entrepreneurial bricolage," *Administrative Science Quarterly*, 50: 329–366.

Balakrishnan, S. and Wernerfelt, B. (1986) "Technical change, competition and vertical integration," *Strategic Management Journal*, 7(4): 347–360.

Balkin, D. and Swift, M. (2006) "Top management team compensation in high-growth technology ventures," *Human Resource Management Review*, 16(1): 1–11.

Bamford, C., Dean, T. and McDougall, P. (2000) "An examination of the impact of initial founding conditions and decisions upon the performance of new bank start-ups," *Journal of Business Venturing*, 15: 253–277.

Barnard, C. I. (1938) *The Functions of the Executive*, Cambridge, MA: Harvard University Press.

Barney, J. (2007) "Positioning of high-growth firms," e-mail (November 7).

Barney, J. and Wright, P. (1998) "On becoming a strategic partner: The role of human resources in gaining competitive advantage," *Human Resource Management*, 37(1): 31–46.

Baron, J., Burton, D. and Hannah, M. (1996) "The road taken: The origins and evolution of employment systems in high-tech firms," *Industrial and Corporate Change*, 5(2): 239–275.

—— (1998) "Engineering bureaucracy: The genesis of formal policies, positions, and structures in high-technology firms," *The Journal of Law, Economics, and Organization*, 15: 1–41.

Baron, J., Hannan, M. and Burton, D. (1999) "Building the iron cage: Determinants of managerial intensity in the early years of organizations," *American Sociological Review*, 64: 527–547.

—— (2001) "Labor pains: Change in organizational models and employee turnover in young, high-tech firms," *The American Journal of Sociology*, 106(4): 960–1012.

Baron, R. (2003) "Editorial: Human resource management and entrepreneurship: Some reciprocal benefits of closer links," *Human Resource Management Review*, 13: 253–256.

Barrett, R. and Mayson, S. (2007) "Human resource management in growing small firms," *Journal of Small Business and Enterprise Development*, 14(2): 307–320.

Baum, J. (1996) "Organizational ecology," in S. Clegg, C. Hardy and W. Nord (eds) *Handbook of Organization Studies*, Thousand Oaks, CA: Sage.

Baumol, W. (1993) "Formal entrepreneurship theory in economics: existence and bounds," *Journal of Business Venturing*, 8: 197–201.

Becker, B. and Huselid, M. (2006) "Strategic human resources management: Where do we go from here?," *Journal of Management*, 32: 898–925.

Beckman, C. and Burton, M. (forthcoming) "Founding the future: Path-dependence in the evolution of top management teams from funding to IPO," *Organization Science*.

Bergkvist, Y. (2007) "Ice Hotel history," e-mail (November 9).

Birley, S. and Westhead, P. (1994) "A taxonomy of business start-up reasons and their impact on firm growth and size," *Journal of Business Venturing*, 9(1): 7–31.

Boeker, W. (1988) "Organizational origins: Entrepreneurial and environmental imprinting at the time of founding," in G. R. Carroll (ed.) *Ecological Models of Organization*, Cambridge: Ballinger.

—— (1989) "Strategic change: The effects of founding and history," *Academy of Management Journal*, 32(3): 485–488.

Bowen, D. and Ostroff, C. (2004) "Understanding HRM-firm performance linkages: The role of the 'strength' of the HRM system," *Academy of Management Review*, 29(2): 203–221.

Busenitz, L. and Barney, J. (1997) "Differences between entrepreneurs and managers in large organizations: Biases and heuristics in strategic decision-making," *Journal of Business Venturing*, 12(1): 9–30.

Camp, S. and Sexton, D. (1992) "Trends in venture capital investment: Implications for high-technology firms," *Journal of Small Business Management*, 30(3): 11–19.

Cardon, M. and Stevens, C. (2004) "Managing human resources in small organizations: What do we know?," *Human Resource Management Review*, 14: 295–323.

Carroll, G. and Hannan, M. (1989) "Density delay in the evolution of organizational populations: A model and five empirical tests," *Administrative Science Quarterly*, 34: 411–430.

Carter, N., Gartner, W. and Reynolds, P. (1996) "Exploring start-up event sequences," *Journal of Business Venturing*, 11(3): 151–166.

Cassar, G. (2006) "Entrepreneur opportunity costs and intended venture growth," *Journal of Business Venturing*, 21(5): 610–632.

—— (2007) "Money, money, money? A longitudinal investigation of entrepreneur career reasons, growth preferences and achieved growth," *Entrepreneurship*, 19(1): 89.

Casson, M. (1982) *The Entrepreneur: An Economic Theory*, Oxford: Edward Elgar.

—— (2006) *The Oxford Handbook of Entrepreneurship*, Oxford: Oxford University Press.

Collins, C. and Allen, M. (2006) *Research Reports (1–5) of the Cornell University/Gevity Institute Study's Working Paper Series*, Cornell University Center for Advanced Human Resource Studies.

Collins, C. and Clark, K. (2003) "Strategic human resource practices, top management team social networks, and firm performance: The role of human resource practices in creating organizational competitive advantage," *Academy of Management Journal*, 46: 740–751.

Collins, C. and Smith, K. (2006) "Knowledge exchange and combination: The role of human resource practices in the performance of high-technology firms," *Academy of Management Review*, 49: 544–560.

Collins, C., Hanges, P. and Locke, E. (2004) "The relationship of achievement motivation to entrepreneurial behavior: A meta-analysis," *Human Performance*, 17(1): 95–117.

Covin, J. and Miles, M. (1999) "Corporate entrepreneurship and the pursuit of competitive advantage," *Entrepreneurship Theory & Practice*, 23(3): 47–63.

Covin, J. and Slevin, D. (1991) "A conceptual model of entrepreneurship as business behavior," *Entrepreneurship Theory & Practice*, 16(1): 7–25.

Cyr, L., Johnson, D. and Welbourne, T. (2000) "Human resources in initial public offering firms: Do venture capitalists make a difference?," *Entrepreneurship: Theory & Practice*, 25(1): 77–92.

Davidsson, P. (1989) "Entrepreneurship and after? A study of growth willingness in small firms," *Journal of Business Venturing*, 4(3): 211–226.

Delmar, F. and Davidsson, P. (1999) "Firm size expectations of nascent entrepreneurs," *Frontiers of Entrepreneurship Research 1999*, Wellesley, MA: Babson College.

Dunning, D., Heath, C. and Suls, J. (2004) "Flawed self-assessment," *Psychological Sciences in the Public Interest*, 5(3): 69–106.

Eckhardt, J. and Shane, S. (2003) "Opportunities and entrepreneurship," *Journal of Management*, 29(3), 333–349.

Eisenhardt, K. and Schoonhoven, C. (1990) "Organizational growth: Linking founding team, strategy, environment, and growth among U.S. semiconductor ventures, 1978–1988," *Administrative Science Quarterly*, 35 (3): 504–529.

—— (1996) "Resource-based view of strategic alliance formation: Strategic and social explanations in entrepreneurial firms," *Organization Science*, 7(2): 136–150.

Farr, M. (2004) *O*NET Dictionary of Occupational Titles*, 3rd edn, Indianapolis, IN: Jist.

Gaglio, C. and Katz, J. (2001) "The psychological basis of opportunity identification: Entrepreneurial alertness," *Small Business Economics*, 16(2): 95.

Gander, J. (1991) "Managerial intensity, firm size and growth," *Managerial and Decision Economics*, 12(3): 261–266.

Gartner, W. (1985) "A conceptual framework for describing the phenomenon of new venture creation," *Academy of Management Review*, 10: 696–706.

Gerhart, B., Wright, P. and McMahan, G. (2000) "Measurement error in research on the human resources and firm performance relationship: Further evidence and analysis," *Personnel Psychology*, 53(4): 855–872.

Goswami, R., McMahan, G. and Wright, P. (2006) "Toward an understanding of strategic human resource management in entrepreneurial firms: Opportunities for research and action," in J. Tansky and R. Heneman (eds) *Human Resource Strategies for the High-growth Entrepreneurial Firm*, Greenwich, CT: Information Age.

Hall, D. (2002) *Careers in and out of Organizations*, Thousand Oaks, CA: Sage.

Hayton, J. (2004) "Strategic human capital management in SMEs: An empirical study of entrepreneurial performance," *Human Resource Management*, 42(4): 375–391.

—— (2005) "Promoting corporate entrepreneurship through human resource management practices: A review of empirical research," *Human Resource Management Review*, 15(1): 21–41.

Heneman, R., Tansky, J. and Camp, S. (2000) "Human resource management practices in small and medium-sized enterprises: Unanswered questions and future research perspectives," *Entrepreneurship: Theory & Practice*, 25(1): 11–27.

Hisrich, R., Langan-Fox, J. and Grant, S. L. (2007) "Entrepreneurship research and practice: A call to action for psychology," *American Psychologist*, 62: 575–589.

Hitt, M.A. and Ireland, R.D. (2003) "The essence of strategic leadership: Managing human and social capital," *Journal of Leadership and Organization Studies*, 9(1): 3–14.

Hsu, D. (2007) "Experienced entrepreneurial founders, organizational capital, and venture capital funding," *Research Policy*, 36(5): 722–741.

Huselid, M. (1994) "The impact of environmental volatility on human resource planning and strategic human resource management," *Human Resource Planning*, 16(3): 35–51.

—— (1995) "The impact of human resource management practices on turnover, productivity, and corporate financial performance," *Academy of Management Journal*, 38(3): 635–672.

Huselid, M. and Becker, B. (2000) "Comment on 'Measurement error in research on human resources and firm performance: How much error is there and how does it influence effect size estimates?' by Gerhart, Wright, McMahan, and Snell," *Personnel Psychology*, 53(4): 835–854.

Ireland, R., Hitt, M., Camp, S. and Sexton, D. (2001) "Integrating entrepreneurship and strategic management action to create firm wealth," *Academy of Management Executive*, 15(1): 49–63.

Jack, S., Hyman, J. and Osborne, F. (2006) "Small entrepreneurial ventures culture, change and the impact on HRM: A critical review," *Human Resource Management Review*, 16(4): 456–466.

Kalleberg, A., Knoke, D., Marsden, P. and Spaeth, J. (1996) *Organizations in America: Analyzing their Structures and Human Resource Practices Based on the National Organizations Study*, Thousand Oaks, CA: Sage.

Kanter, R. (1985) "Supporting innovation and venture development in established companies," *Journal of Business Venturing*, 1(1): 47–61.

Katz, J., Aldrich, H., Welbourne, T. and Williams, P. (2000) "Guest editor's comments: Special issue on human resource management and the SME: Toward a new synthesis," *Entrepreneurship Theory & Practice*, 25: 7–11.

Kaufman, B. (2004) *Theoretical Perspectives on Employment Relationships*, Ithaca, NY: Industrial Relations Press.

—— (2005) *Theoretical Perspectives on Work and the Employment Relationship*, Champaign-Urbana, IL: Industrial Relations Research Association.

Klaas, B., Gainey, T., McClendon, J. and Yang, H. (2005) "Professional employer organizations and their impact on client satisfaction with human resource outcomes: A field study of human resource outsourcing in small and medium enterprises," *Journal of Management*, 31(2): 234–254.

Klaas, B., Hyeuksueng, Y., Gainey, T. and McClendon, J. (2005) "HR in the small business enterprise: Assessing the impact of PEO utilization," *Human Resource Management*, 44(4): 433–448.

Knight, F. (1921) *Risk, Uncertainty and Profit*, New York: Houghton Mifflin.

Kogut, B. (1991) "Joint ventures and the option to expand and acquire," *Management Science*, 37: 19–33.

Kolvereid, L. (1992) "Growth aspirations among Norwegian entrepreneurs," *Journal of Business Venturing*, 7(3): 209–222.

Langlois, R. and Cosgel, M. (1993) "Frank Knight on risk, uncertainty, and the firm: A new interpretation," *Economic Inquiry*, 31(3): 456–465.

Lepak, D. and Snell, S. (1999) "The human resource architecture: Toward a theory of human capital allocation and development," *Academy of Management Review*, 24: 31–48.

—— (2002) "Examining the human resource architecture: The relationships among human capital, employment, and human resource configurations," *Journal of Management*, 28: 517–543.

Lepak, D., Takeuchi, R. and Snell, S. (2003) "Employment flexibility and firm performance: Examining the interaction effect of employment mode, environmental dynamism, and technological intensity," *Journal of Management*, 29: 681–703.

Livingston, J. (2007) *Founders At Work: Stories of Startups' Early Days*, Berkeley, CA: Apress.

Loasby, B. (2002) "The organizational basis of cognition and the cognitive basis of organization," in M. Augier and J. March (eds) *The Economics of Choice, Change and Organization: Essays in Memory of Richard M. Cyert*, Cheltenham, UK: Edward Elgar.

Low, M. and MacMillan, I. (1988) "Entrepreneurship: Past research and future challenges," *Journal of Management*, 14(2): 139–161.

McLarty, R. (1999) "The skills development needs of SMEs and focus on graduate skills application," *Journal of Applied Management Studies*, 8(1): 103–112.

McMullen, J., Plummer, L. and Zoltan, J. (2007) "What is an entrepreneurial opportunity?," *Small Business Economics*, 28: 273–283.

March, J. G. and Simon, H. A. (1958) *Organizations*, New York: Wiley.

Marlow, S. (2006) "Human resource management in smaller firms: A contradiction in terms?," *Human Resource Management Review*, 16(4): 467–477.

Miller, K. (2007) "Risk and rationality in entrepreneurial processes," *Strategic Entrepreneurship Journal*, 1(1): 42–54.

Penrose, E. (1959) *The Theory of the Growth of the Firm*, New York: Wiley.

Porter, M. (1985) *Competitive Advantage: Creating and Sustaining Superior Performance*, New York: Free Press.

Reynolds, P. (2000) "National panel study of U.S. business startups: Background and methodology," in J. Katz (ed.) *Databases for the Study of Entrepreneurship*, New York: Elsevier.

Romanelli, E. (1991) "The evolution of new organizational forms," *Annual Review of Sociology*, 17: 79–103.

Sarasvathy, S. (2001) "Causation and effectuation: Toward a theoretical shift from economic inevitability to entrepreneurial contingency," *Academy of Management Review*, 26(2): 243–258.

Schumpeter, J. (1934) *Theory of Economic Development: An Inquiry into Profits, Capital, Credit, Interest and the Business Cycle*, Cambridge, MA: Harvard University Press.

—— (1939) *Business Cycles. A Theoretical, Historical, and Statistical Analysis of the Capitalist Process*, New York and London: McGraw-Hill.

Selznick, P. (1957) *Leadership in Administration*, New York: Harper & Row.

Shane, S. (2000) "Prior knowledge and the discovery of entrepreneurial opportunities," *Organization Science*, 11(4): 448–470.

—— (2003) *A General Theory of Entrepreneurship: The Individual–Opportunity Nexus*, Northampton, MA: Edward Elgar.

Shane, S. and Venkataraman, S. (2000) "The promise of entrepreneurship as a field of research," *Academy of Management Review*, 25(1): 217–230.

Shepherd, D., McMullen, J. and Jennings, P. (2007) "The formation of opportunity beliefs: Overcoming ignorance and reducing doubt," *Strategic Entrepreneurship Journal*, 1(1): 36–49.

Snell, S. and Dean, J. Jr. (1992) "Integrated manufacturing and human resource management: A human capital perspective," *The Academy of Management Journal*, 35(3): 467–504.

—— (1994) "Strategic compensation for integrated manufacturing: The moderating effects of job and organizational inertia," *Academy of Management Journal*, 37: 1109–1140.

Stinchcombe, A. (1965) "Social structure and organizations," in J. G. March (ed.) *Handbook of Organizations*, Chicago: Rand McNally.

Tan, C. and Mahoney, J. (2005) "Examining the Penrose effect in an international business context: The dynamics of Japanese firm growth in US industries," *Managerial and Decision Economics*, 26(2): 113–127.

Tansky, J. and Heneman, R. (2003) "Guest editor's note: Introduction to the special issue on human resource management in SMEs: A call for more research," *Human Resource Management*, 42(4): 299–302.

—— (2006) *Human Resource Strategies for the High-growth Entrepreneurial Firm*, Greenwich, CT: Information Age Publishing.

U.S. Census Bureau (2002) *Guide to the Economic Census*, Washington, DC: U.S. Census Bureau.

Venkataraman, S. (1997) "The distinctive domain of entrepreneurship research: An editor's perspective," in J. Katz and R. Brockhaus (eds) *Advances in Entrepreneurship, Firm Emergence, and Growth*, Greenwich, CT: JAI Press.

Wernerfelt, B. and Karnani, A. (1987) "Competitive strategy under uncertainty," *Strategic Management Journal*, 8(2): 187–194.

Weick, K. (1995) *Sensemaking in Organizations*, Thousand Oaks, CA: Sage.

Wiklund, J. and Shepherd, D. (2003) "Aspiring for and achieving growth: The moderating role of resources and opportunities," *Journal of Management Studies*, 40(8): 1919–1941.

Wiklund, J., Davidsson, P. and Delmar, F. (2003) "What do they think and feel about growth? An expectancy-value approach to small business managers' attitudes toward growth," *Entrepreneurship Theory & Practice*, 27(3): 247–270.

Williamson, I. O. (2000) "Employer legitimacy and recruitment success in small businesses," *Entrepreneurship: Theory & Practice*, 25(1): 27–43.

Wright, P. and McMahan, G. (1992) "Alternative theoretical perspectives on strategic human resource management," *Journal of Management*, 18: 295–320.

Wright, P. and Snell, S. (1998) "Toward a unifying framework of exploring fit and flexibility in strategic human resource management," *Academy of Management Review*, 23(4): 756–772.

24

Identifying and developing Global Leaders

Schon Beechler and Dennis Baltzley

Introduction

Companies have rapidly globalized to take advantage of growth opportunities in international markets and to capture supply opportunities in diverse locations. Reflecting this trend, global foreign direct investment figures grew by 29% to $916 billion in 2005, following a 27% increase in 2004 (PwC, 2007). The dynamic international business environment provides unprecedented opportunities as well as formidable challenges because globalization is a manifestation of complexity (Lane et al., 2004). As Klaus Schwab, Founder and Executive Chairman of Davos, notes: "We are living in an increasingly schizophrenic world where economies are booming and global signs are promising but underneath are economic, political, and social risks as well as imbalances and inconsistencies" (World Economic Forum, 2007).

In their ninth and tenth Annual Global CEO Surveys of over 1,400 CEOs, PriceWaterhouseCoopers report that over 70% of CEOs believe complexity in their organizations is higher than it was three years ago and that complexity is an inevitable aspect of business (PwC, 2006: 32–3). In addition, globalization is a force of disorderly transition, driven by internet-enabled technology and new financial and market opportunities, no longer realized through a "one-size-fits-all model" (PwC, 2007: 1). Finally, this report concludes:

> Whether through the adoption of new, potentially collaborative approaches to assessing and mitigating risk, or through the integration of new organizational capabilities for managing a geographically and culturally diverse organization, the impact of globalization on the demands on business leaders is profound.
>
> (PwC, 2007: 7)

To compete and win in this global context, CEOs increasingly identify the need to find "global citizens" – people who can view business with a truly global mindset and who are flexible and adaptable enough to deal with complexity and uncertainty. It will not be technology platforms, systems, or processes that create sustainable value in this world; it is people, with their inherent complexity and flexibility, who will enable firms to meet the global competitive challenges successfully (Bartlett and Ghoshal, 1989; Evans et al., 2002; Levy et al., 2007a; Pucik et al., 1992). As Morrison (2000: 119) suggests, this drives a virtuous circle:

As companies rely more and more on global strategies, they require a greater number of global leaders. This tie between strategy and leadership is essentially a two-way street: the more companies pursue global strategies, the more global leaders they need; and the more global leaders companies have, the more they pursue global strategies. That the world has an ever-greater need for global leaders is consistent with the increased globalization of competition over the past two decades.

Despite the clear demands on business leaders and the need for increasing supplies of Global Leaders, companies are simply unable to find and develop the Global Leaders that they need. For example, in their study of international companies over 15 years ago Adler and Bartholomew (1992) declared that most companies were unable to implement their global strategies due to a lack of Global Leadership. In 2006 the situation had not improved. A global survey by Mercer Delta of 223 senior executives from large corporations across 17 industrial sectors in 44 countries predicts that within the next five years, 50% of senior managers in the Fortune 500 will retire, leaving a huge leadership gap to be filled.

The demand for Global Leaders has (and will continue to) outstrip the available supply. In addition, this demand has raced ahead of our knowledge regarding what actually distinguishes Global Leaders from other leaders and managers and how to select and develop them. To help address this gap, this chapter provides an overview of what we know about global leadership and distinguishes it from previous work in cross-cultural management, diversity, and studies of expatriates and global managers. We then offer a definition and model of global leadership that we believe is differentiated from domestic or "local" leadership. Finally, we suggest strategies for selection and development of Global Leaders.

Global leaders in the literature

The notion of "Global Leadership" first appeared in the literature in the 1960s and 1970s to describe a company's *market position* but it wasn't until the end of the 1980s that the term "global" was being applied to executives themselves and to individual jobs (McCall and Hollenbeck, 2002). Until then, the focus had been on expatriates rather than on Global Leaders. In fact, in many places today the old "expatriate mindset" persists. For example, a recent report on developing Global Leaders from The Conference Board is subtitled *Enhancing competencies and accelerating the expatriate experience* (Kramer, 2005), reflecting an American bias that leadership development is focused squarely on American executives traveling from the home country to manage and lead overseas operations.

The following section traces the development of research on Global Leadership, summarizing the major approaches and conclusions from the literature and then offers an integrated model of Global Leadership. We draw on research that has progressed along three largely independent paths: management research on expatriates, work on cross-cultural management and leadership, and the newer field of diversity and inclusiveness.

Expatriate managers

The term "expatriate manager," sometimes also referred to as an international manager, is defined as an executive in a leadership position that involves international assignments. The individual is defined as a function of his or her location, vis-à-vis the company headquarters. There are a large number of studies on expatriates, most of which have focused on the issue of selecting managers for international assignments and the competencies that they should possess. In addition, because of the high failure rates and the costs involved with sending expatriates overseas, many writers have focused on human resource practices that can help companies select, develop and retain competent expatriate managers (Pucik and Saba, 1998).

Hays' (1974) article on expatriate competencies is one of the earliest writings in this area and focuses on the different roles that expatriates play. He categorizes expatriates into four types: the *structure reproducer* who is responsible for reproducing a structure from another part of the organization in a foreign subsidiary; the *technical troubleshooter* who is sent overseas to analyze and solve a technical problem; the *operational expatriate* who is placed in a well-defined position in an ongoing business overseas; and the *chief executive officer* who oversees and directs a foreign operation (Hays, 1974).

While early writings highlight expatriate roles, most of the subsequent research on expatriates focuses on competencies, a term that was introduced by McClelland in 1973 that came into use in the early 1980s to describe the group of skills, attitudes, values, and personal traits that were considered essential to performing a specific task (Boyatzis, 1982; Briscoe and Hall, 1999). In their influential expatriate adjustment model, Black, Mendenhall and Oddou (1991) focus on three sets of expatriate competencies: perception management, relationship management and self-management. Perception management is based on how individuals perceive people who are different from them, their mental flexibility when confronted with cultural differences, their tendency to make rapid rather than thoughtful judgments about differences, their ability to manage perceptions, and their natural curiosity. Relationship management includes interest in relationships, interpersonal engagement, emotional sensitivity, self-awareness and behavioral flexibility. And finally, self-management includes optimism, self-confidence, self-identify, emotional resilience, non-stress tendency, stress management and interest flexibility (Bird, 2008; Black et al., 1991).

McCall (1992) focuses on expatriates' ability to learn from experience and identifies curiosity about how things work, having a sense of adventure, demonstrating readiness and hardiness toward learning, a bias toward action, responsibility for learning and change, respecting differences among people, seeking and using feedback, and showing consistent growth over time as the most critical competencies for success.

Complementing McCall's work, Black, Morrison and Gregersen (1999) find in their research that successful expatriates have a drive to communicate with local people in their new country and don't give up easily if early attempts fail or embarrass them. In addition, successful expatriates are both enthusiastic and extroverted in conversation and not afraid to try out their new language skills and establish social ties not just with fellow expatriates but with local residents. They exhibit cultural flexibility and are willing to experiment with different customs, have a cosmopolitan mindset and intuitively understand that different cultural norms have value and meaning to those who practice them. Finally, a collaborative negotiation style is a critical competence for successful expatriates.

In contrast to the above research on interpersonal competencies, Rothwell (1992) focuses on the expatriate's knowledge in his competency framework: general knowledge about the world and global economy; national information about conditions in a specific country; and business understanding of strategy, process and leadership style. While a thorough review of the literature is outside of the scope of this chapter, the subsequent voluminous research on expatriates identifies a large number of skills, characteristics, and competencies. In their recent review, Mendenhall and Osland identified no less than 61 competencies in the literature (Mendenhall, 2006).

From expatriate managers to global managers

In the late 1980s and early 1990s, the focus in the international business literature shifted from expatriates to global managers. This shift paralleled changes in the strategy and structure of many multinational companies from HQ-dominated entities to more global or transnational corporations (Bartlett and Ghoshal, 1989). As companies moved from strategies focused either on local responsiveness or global integration, to more complex global or transnational strategies involving both global integration and local differentiation, the nature of many positions within the organization changed, as well as the characteristics of managers needed to resolve the complex and potentially paradoxical challenges embedded in the global environment.

In the early 1990s Tichy (1992) identified these individuals as "globalists," who have a global mindset and can conceptualize complex geopolitical and cultural forces as they impact business. These globalists also have the energy, skills and talents to be global networkers, possess Global Leadership skills and behaviors such as the ability to build effective cross-cultural teams, and skills as global change agents. Similarly, Adler and Bartholomew (1992) contrast the behaviors and competencies required by expatriate and transnational (global) managers (see Table 24.1) by focusing on the degree of cultural and organizational complexity faced by these two groups of managers over the course of their careers.

Brake (1997), in his thorough and complex model which captures much of the earlier research on expatriates, identifies three clusters of Global Leadership competencies: relationship management (including change agentry, community building, conflict management and negotiation, cross-cultural communication and influencing), business acumen (depth of field

Table 24.1 Differences between expatriate and global managers

	Expatriate manager	Transnational manager
Global perspective	Focuses on a single foreign country and on managing relationships between HQs and that country	Understands worldwide business environment from a global perspective
Local responsiveness	Becomes an expert on one culture	Must learn about many foreign cultures' perspectives, tastes, trends, technologies, and approaches to conducting business
Synergistic learning	Works with and coaches people in each foreign culture separately or sequentially	Works with and learns from people from many cultures simultaneously
	Integrates foreigners into the HQ's national organizational culture	Creates a culturally synergistic organizational environment
Transition and adaptation	Adapts to living in a foreign culture	Adapts to living in many foreign cultures
Cross-cultural interaction	Uses cross-cultural interaction skills primarily on foreign assignments	Uses cross-cultural skills on a daily basis throughout his/her career
Collaboration	Interacts with colleagues from within clearly defined hierarchies of structural and cultural dominance and subordination	Interacts with foreign colleagues as equals
Foreign experience	Expatriation or inpatriation primarily to get the job done	Transpatriation for career and organization development

Source: Adler and Bartholomew, 1992.

413

which demonstrates a willingness and ability to switch perspectives, entrepreneurial spirit, professional expertise, stakeholder orientation, and total organizational astuteness) and personal effectiveness (accountability, curiosity and learning, improvisation, maturity, thinking agility).

While many competency models for global managers focus on what these managers do, Barham and his colleagues (Barham and Aantala, 1994; Wills and Barham, 1994) identify two complementary sets of competencies based on interviews with 60 senior international executives: "doing" competencies and "being" competencies. "Doing" competencies include championing international strategy, operating as cross-border coach and coordinator, acting as intercultural mediator and change agent, and managing performance effectiveness for international business. "Being" competencies include cognitive complexity (the ability to see multiple dimensions in a situation and identify relationships between those different dimensions); emotional energy (the ability to deal with stressful conditions); and psychological maturity (strong curiosity that drives learning; willingness to apply a large amount of psychological energy to understand the complexity of a situation; and strong personal morality).

From global managers to global leaders

In the mid- to late 1990s, a gradual shift of focus from expatriates and global managers to Global Leadership occurred in both the academic and practitioner literatures. Researchers across this field, as well as those in cross-cultural (Hampden-Turner and Trompenaars, 1997; Harris et al., 2004) and early diversity research began to expand their purview outside of a "home country" mindset to considering multiple perspectives. By the early 2000s, these three fields began to converge and highlight common themes.

One of the earliest and most influential writers to focus on Global Leadership was Stephen Rhinesmith (1995, 1996) who identifies a set of 24 competencies related to three main responsibilities of Global Leaders: strategy and structure, corporate culture, and people. Rhinesmith picked up on earlier work (e.g., Perlmutter, 1969; Tichy, 1992) to highlight the important role of a global mindset to Global Leadership. A global mindset, Rhinesmith (1993: 24) argues, is

> a way of being rather than a set of skills. It is an orientation of the world that allows one to see certain things that others do not. A global mindset means the ability to scan the world from a broad perspective, always looking for unexpected trends and opportunities that may constitute a threat or opportunity to achieve personal, professional or organizational objectives.

Rhinesmith contrasts a global mindset with a traditional "domestic" mindset, as shown in Table 24.2 below.

Table 24.2 Traditional and global mindsets

	Traditional mindset	Global mindset
Strategy/structure	Specialize Prioritize	Drive for broader picture Balance contradictions
Corporate culture	Manage job Control results	Engage process Flow with change
Structure	Process	Flexibility
People	Manage self Learn domestically	Value diversity Learn globally

Source: Rhinesmith, 1996.

As highlighted by our review thus far, the number of choices and lists of what it takes to be effective as a Global Leader can seem infinite. We have seen specific examples of aggregated lists that range from 120 to over 200 "vital" competencies. McCall and Hollenbeck (2002) provide, we believe, a comprehensive categorization derived from interviews with 101 highly effective global executives from 36 countries who worked for 16 global companies. In their research McCall and Hollenbeck do not focus on the business skills required to do well in an international posting, as these are considered a basic requirement. Rather, they focus on the experiences that prepare a person for Global Leadership challenges, the characteristics needed to excel in an executive job (see Table 24.3).

Cross-cultural leadership and management research

As the research from expatriates to Global Leadership was evolving, a largely independent body of research was focusing on cultural differences in leadership (for reviews see Bass, 1990; Dorfman, 2004; Gelfand et al., 2007; House et al., 1997; Peterson and Hunt, 1997; Smith and Peterson, 1988). A number of authors make the argument that culture influences leadership: growing up in a particular culture, leaders develop and internalize the cultural values and practices of the culture and learn, over time, desirable and undesirable modes of behavior. For example, Smith et al. (2002) demonstrate that the extent that managers rely on formal rules and supervisors for guidance is related to their cultural background. Rahim and Magner (1996) also find that leaders in individualistic cultures tend to put more emphasis on coercive power, and Geletkanycz (1997) shows that executives' adherence to existing strategy is related to their cultural background in terms of individualism, uncertainty avoidance, and power distance.

Culture also impacts the context of the relationship between the leader and followers (Yukl, 2006). Cultural norms influence the way people in a society relate to each other and, as such, influence the type and content of relationships in general. In addition, another important impact of culture on leadership is through its impact on the implicit leadership theories of the members of the culture (House et al., 2004; Javidan and Carl, 2004, 2005). In his comprehensive review

Table 24.3 Competencies of the global executive

Open-minded and flexible in thought and tactics: The person is able to live and work in a variety of settings with different types of people and is willing and able to listen to other people, approaches, and ideas.

Cultural interest and sensitivity: The person respects other cultures, people, and points of view; is not arrogant or judgmental; is curious about other people and how they live and work; is interested in differences; enjoys social competency; gets along well with others; is empathic.

Able to deal with complexity: The person considers many variables in solving a problem; is comfortable with ambiguity and patient in evolving issues; can make decisions in the face of uncertainty; can see patterns and connections; and is willing to take risks.

Resilient, resourceful, optimistic, and energetic: The person responds to a challenge; is not discouraged by adversity; is self-reliant and creative; sees the positive side of things; has a high level of physical and emotional energy; is able to deal with stress.

Honesty and integrity: Authentic, consistent, the person engenders trust.

Stable personal life: The person has developed and maintains stress-resistant personal arrangements, usually family, that support a commitment to work.

Value-added technical or business skills: The person has technical, managerial, or other expertise sufficient to provide his or her credibility.

Source: McCall and Hollenbeck, 2002.

of almost 400 studies, Triandis (1994) concludes that the cultural value orientations in a country will determine the optimum leadership profile for that country. While there are some universal attributes of management systems, each distinct culture may have a distinct management style that is both moderated and directly influenced by culture.

This conclusion is supported by results from the large-scale GLOBE research program (House et al., 2004) which shows that members of a culture tend to develop a common implicit theory of leadership which is a set of attributes, expectations, and criteria to assess their leaders. The closer the fit between a leader's actions and attributes and the group's implicit criteria, the more the leader is accepted by the members.

The cross-cultural research summarized above provides valuable insight into the context within which a Global Leader must operate. Quite separate from his/her own competency/skillset, the Global Leader must understand (and be able to operate in) the specific contexts that different cultures present.

Diversity and inclusiveness research

In addition to research on Global Leaders and cross-cultural leadership, work on diversity and inclusiveness has received a great deal of attention in the past eight to ten years because of the intuitive value it brings to business. The business case for diversity has two parts. First, the world's markets require diversity – increasing diversity in the world's workforce and customer base demands that organizations mirror that mix, or at least respond to it in some meaningful way. Second, organizations which establish this diversity of talent, and manage it well (i.e., creating an inclusive environment to tap into the full range of creativity and problem solving in this diverse population), gain a competitive advantage (Hicks-Clark and Iles, 2000).

Originally, the research and writing in the field of diversity was defined by the American conceptualization of diversity, which focuses on differences in identity, primarily ethnicity, disability, age, gender, and sexual orientation. Today, diversity is transitioning to a field where practitioners teach and practice a broader, more global, view of diversity that includes differences in thought and style, more aligned to a cross-cultural view. This broader approach has been influenced by European and Eastern practitioners who pushed the thinking in cross-cultural writing and research toward this more integrated diversity orientation. In Europe for example, leaders face cross-border opportunities on a daily basis where they are confronted with cultural and contextual differences as a natural part of their careers. In the USA on the other hand, the field developed largely as a response to the dismantling of affirmative action (Gilbert et al., 1999).

The field of diversity yields insights about the critical requirement for Global Leaders to have capabilities in areas of diversity to be successful in a global context. These insights focus on three areas:

1. The importance of relationships with people very different to the leader;
2. The ability to understand and effectively lead across different contexts (emphasis on cross-border);
3. The ability to critically examine one's own assumptions as a leader and change, a requirement for a high level of self-insight and adaptation.

Below we briefly review each of these areas to highlight elements in the field that inform the emerging picture of Global Leadership requirements.

The first area focuses on the critical importance of relationships with people very different than the leader, an area that is highlighted across the different fields related to global business and global leadership. Beyond the integration of different people into a collective, an organization that seeks out differences, and values them, can translate those differences into competitive advantage (Cox, 1991). The application to Global Leaders is a direct translation. Their ability to proactively build relationships and work with teams of very different people leads directly to value creation that ranges from attraction of talent and insights into markets, to more thorough critical analysis for problem solving and increased creativity/innovation (Cox and Blake, 1991).

The second area, having the ability to understand and effectively lead across different contextual elements, applies to every leader as they face challenges in cross-functional and cross-industry contexts. More complex and less well understood are the additions of cross-cultural contextual complexity or overlays (e.g., one author recently found himself in a position of helping American and Dutch engineers working with Indian service companies in a joint venture to provide service to clients in Saudi Arabia). Many organizations expend great effort and resources in diversity efforts typically focused on area #1 above, trying to create diverse environments to promote diverse thinking. However, that alone does not create real diversity: the addition of understanding several different contexts, across borders, is also required.

A domestic leader can perform effectively using broadly applicable rules (within one context). For example, historically (and in many religions) we understand the concept of the "Golden Rule" (Carroll, 1990). That is, if you want to be treated fairly, treat others fairly. This serves as a foundational belief that can guide everything from the parameters that dictate a leader's analysis of a situation, to the actual decision-making process. Yet, a Global Leader must have a more sophisticated understanding of the cultural elements, as well as their interpretation, and understand the different situations in which they find themselves.

These first two areas are important, but not sufficient for Global Leadership. In fact, these first two areas may even dilute the attention needed to attend to the most important factor – something within the leader must also change to create a diverse mindset. The third and perhaps most important element is the leader's capability to face his or her own assumptions and biases.

There has been a great deal written about this topic in areas from psychology (changing belief structures) to cross-cultural training (shifting mindset). However, an instructive and highly applied area of the literature is found in how educators are being prepared to teach the topic of diversity.

There are several obvious requirements for educators. They must have cultural knowledge different from their own, and from that knowledge, build "inter-cultural competence," changing one's mono-cultural understanding to an appreciation of diverse cultural perspectives (Bennett, 1995; Key, 2000). When effective, this results in a shift in mindset predicated on insight into one's own cultural identity (Bennett, 1995; Melnick and Zeichner, 1995). Not surprisingly, "field experience" repeatedly surfaces as one of the most important aspects of acquiring both cross-border knowledge and personal insight on one's biases and assumptions (Moore, 1999). The implication is clear for leaders – they must work through their tightly held stereotypical beliefs. They have to get outside their home country to learn, to gain insight into themselves.

Using this literature review to triangulate the common themes, and our applied experience with several large multinational organizations, we turn now to describe our Global Leadership framework and point of view about what differentiates a Global Leader from a domestic leader.

Global Leadership framework

What is Global Leadership and what distinguishes it from "domestic" leadership?

Just because an executive is in charge of a global organization does not mean that he or she is an effective Global Leader (Beechler and Javidan, 2007). Global Leadership starts with understanding and insight into a country's society – its social structures, institutions, and demographics. This understanding must extend to business-relevant issues such as a country's legal, regulatory, and economic structures. It is important to note that Global Leadership, by definition, involves influence by the leader over those who are very different from the Global Leader – from their cultural background to their view of the world. By contrast, a domestic leader grows up in, and knows deeply, one country (their home country) and may integrate some elements of experiences in other countries into their understanding, usually from frequent visits or short assignments.

> How has globalization changed leadership? Doing strategic planning, you now have more pieces on the chessboard to play with. You have the possibility of having your programming done in India. You have the opportunity to recruit trained nurses out of the Philippines. You can't limit yourself by thinking local and thinking linearly. As you think about what you need to do for the future of your organization, the opportunity now is to think internationally and to think in nonlinear ways.
>
> (George Halvorson, Chairman and CEO,
> Kaiser Permanente, quoted in PwC, 2007: 41)

Our definition of and point of view on Global Leadership

While Global Leadership often goes undefined in the literature, in this chapter when we talk about *Global Leadership* we refer to the process of leading across national and cultural borders where one encounters all the wonderful complexities of different cultural, social, legal, regulatory and economic systems. Following Beechler and Javidan (2007), we define Global Leadership as *the process of influencing individuals, groups, and organizations (inside and outside the boundaries of the global organization) representing diverse cultural/political/institutional systems to contribute toward the achievement of the global organization's goals.* This definition has two underlying pillars that reveal our point of view on Global Leadership:

1. *Global Leadership is a process* – not a single competency added to a domestic leader's skill portfolio. As a process, our view of Global Leadership extends beyond a leader's personal skills, to the relationships the leader holds with the people around him/her in a global context.
2. *What knowledge a Global Leader integrates and how they integrate it, are fundamentally different* for a Global Leader than for a domestic leader. Global Leaders must acquire new knowledge about the different contexts in which they work. In addition, the way they use knowledge and information to analyze a situation and act happens from a broader set of choices, and at a higher level of complexity. Increased capacity and the ability to handle increased complexity are the hallmarks of Global Leadership. Each of these foundation concepts is described in more detail below.

Global Leadership as a process (What effective Global Leaders do)

Like everyone, a Global Leader has an anchor in their own culture and societal context; they are grounded in certain values and points of view on a range of topics. At the same time, a Global Leader, through experiences in multiple and varying contexts, has a more unrestricted field of view and is able to see the same landscape through a number of different lenses. They have a distance and perspective across a range of value sets and societal issues that transforms how they see their own values, sense of identity, and of course, their view of the world. Importantly, they also have a different level of understanding of others' views of the world. This results in a leadership decision-making process that is very different to that used by domestic leaders. To illustrate this point, we use Bird and Osland's (2004) information-processing model that moves through three distinct phases to get to leadership action (see Figure 24.1).

We use this model to illustrate two points. First, on the surface, this model applies to both global and domestic leadership, but how a Global Leader works their way around the cycle is very different than what a domestic leader does. Second, human resources professionals and educational institutions often focus primarily on the final section of the cycle – the ability to act differently – or what we would recognize as skill or competency-building activities. No one would question the importance of building skills, yet we suggest it is only 33% of the model, and if focused on exclusively, will miss the mark. If, for example, the challenges that a business faces are largely like the challenges it has faced in the past, then it would make perfect sense to focus on the last arrow exclusively when selecting and evaluating Global Leaders. The analysis, decoding, and choices leaders have to make are known, and the leaders are experienced in those challenges. Therefore, in selection/placement decisions, Human Resources would focus on leaders' past behaviors (through interviews), and some relevant testing to evaluate style to ensure a good fit with the culture of the company. If, however, the business is facing challenges that are different today than in the past, and/or unclear in the future, then focusing on skill building alone will not produce effective leaders. If we don't understand the earlier parts of the cycle – how leaders analyze, decode, and select a course of action – we are unlikely to get a different outcome from our leaders in the future than the ones they know how to deliver today. Leadership, and especially Global Leadership, is a process – the process of how Global Leaders think – and how these leaders think through decisions defines what they can "see."

Figure 24.1 Information-processing model for leaders

Adapted from Bird and Osland, 2004.

1. How you see it and decode it

How individuals grow up and develop as professionals has an impact on their level of success in the future. Individuals integrate experience and skill building to refine their mental models and judgments. This can be a source of blind spots. The more successful individuals are, in specific contexts, the more difficult it is for them to interrogate and question their mental models, making it nearly impossible to see their own biases clearly. This plays out at the individual and organizational level time and time again. For example, GE, an extremely sophisticated and global company, made a series of missteps in its growth strategy in Europe only to be stopped by the European Union's anti-competition policies. In another example, the police department of New York City realized that they were unknowingly training their officers to behave in a racist way by, paradoxically, using one standard of training applied across cultures and ethnic groups. Officers were trained in academy courses to "see" the aversion of eye contact as a non-verbal cue indicating deception when talking with potential suspects. Yet, in a Hispanic culture, a lack of eye contact is often a sign of respect for authority. Global Leaders have the capability to see many different perspectives and views, even when contradictory. They are able to see what is important from complex data and decode it accurately for meaning.

2. Identify the appropriate action

In addition to decoding information accurately, a Global Leader is able to identify the appropriate behavioral response for a given situation. Consider the earlier example of the NY City Police. What do I do if I think the driver I pulled over is lying? What if I think the driver is showing respect? Rather than having a single interpretation of an event and an immediate response, a Global Leader chooses from a broader behavioral repertoire than a domestic leader. This range of choices is based both on their skills, which are built across borders, and the integration of their experiences from different cultural contexts. A broader analysis and the experience gained over time leads to a broader set of choices for the leader to consider. This simple interaction of citizen and law enforcement officer proceeds very differently depending both on how the authority figure decodes the information they can see, and the menu of choices they believe is available upon which they should act.

3. Take action

Once a situation has been decoded and a course of action has been selected, the leader acts. This represents the skill or competence of the leader to behave in the intended way. This sounds straightforward and simple, yet how many of us have been absolutely clear on what was required but at the time of execution, it doesn't turn out as we planned? Coming back to our earlier example, imagine that the police officer has just completed new training on behavioral cues and has stopped a Hispanic male for questioning. Although the suspect is averting his gaze, the officer understands from his/her training that this does not necessarily mean that the Hispanic male is lying, but is probably showing respect. Let's also assume the police officer had strong socialization from youth that a lack of eye contact is a sign of weakness and dishonesty and has been working under the assumptions of his/her prior training for several years. What happens? It's not so clear that the new knowledge can over-ride years of socialization and applied training easily. The knowing and the doing still require a mix of behavioral flexibility and discipline to act appropriately. The lesson here is that Global Leaders live in the cross-border complexity and experience, integrate it into a broader behavioral repertoire, and then possess a greater breadth of skills to a domestic leader, to act on this "knowing."

To summarize, strong domestic or "local" leaders follow this same information-processing model; however, the number of choices to sort through in the field of data, and the complexity of the processing task remains small compared to those used by Global Leaders. Global Leaders need a broad way of thinking, often referred to as a "global mindset," which influences how they perceive situations, analyze them, and understand what is happening (de-coding). They also need to have the knowledge, experience, and the contextual understanding to decide what is the right course of action. Finally, effective Global Leaders have a complex and flexible behavioral repertoire to act appropriately in a given global context. In the next section we explore the characteristics of Global Leaders that help to predict their ability to both think and act globally.

The "top 11" elements that differentiate Global Leaders from domestic leaders

We identified the recurring themes which consistently differentiate Global Leaders from domestic leaders and identified eleven characteristics or skills that can be represented in three categories: Intellectual, Psychological, and Knowledge/skills.[1] From research and our experience we know that these characteristics are not orthogonal – they tend to blend across categories in different ways as shown in the Venn diagram below (see Figure 24.2).

In introducing this model we have three initial observations: First, there are two consistent themes across the three components: capacity and complexity. Second, in the Psychological and Intellectual areas, Global Leaders are different from their domestic counterparts in the degree to which they possess capacity and complexity. And third, in the area of Knowledge and skills,

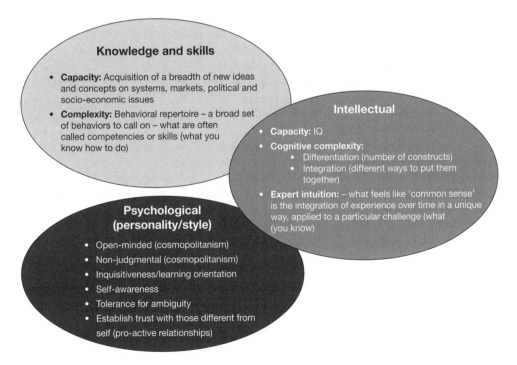

Figure 24.2 Characteristics of Global Leaders

it is not just a difference in degree but also a difference in kind – Global Leaders must acquire new knowledge and skills that are not required of a domestic leader. Each of these areas is described below.

Knowledge and skills

A leader must acquire a broad range of knowledge across very different topics and contexts to be a Global Leader – across cultures, politics, socio-economic conditions, history and inter-relations. The breadth and often also the depth of their knowledge and skills must be greater than those needed for domestic leaders. Second, with regard to complexity, Global Leaders need to have a broader set of behaviors to call on, what we normally call skills or competencies. They must have skills that are contextually appropriate for a broader range of situations or, in other words, they must demonstrate greater behavioral complexity and flexibility.

Behavioral flexibility has been defined as "the ability to act out a cognitively complex strategy by playing multiple, even competing, roles in a highly integrated and complementary way" (Hooijberg and Quinn, 1992: 164). In short, leaders have to be able to act decisively in the face of uncertainty and complexity that would paralyze most people. Behavioral flexibility involves two components – *behavioral repertoire*, the number of leadership roles a manager can use effectively, and *behavioral differentiation*, the ability to use a particular role differently, depending on the situation (Hooijberg et al., 1997). Global Leaders work in an increasingly complex environment and need to balance multiple and often contradictory objectives in order to generate superior corporate performance. These leaders need behavioral flexibility to use competencies and behaviors from different and conflicting models of behavior.

Intellectual

The first component under intellectual capabilities is the need for IQ (capacity). Global Leaders need to be very smart, but that is not enough. High intelligence has to be tempered with a high degree of cognitive complexity in order to deal with the business complexity and cultural complexity inherent in global work (Levy et al., 2007a; McCall and Hollenbeck, 2002).

Cognitive complexity consists of two dimensions: differentiation and integration. Differentiation is the number of constructs or dimensions used to describe a domain while integration refers to the number of links among the differentiated constructs. People who are more cognitively complex can simultaneously hold and apply several valid but competing and complementary interpretations of a domain or situation. Cognitive complexity is also associated with the capacity to balance contradiction, ambiguities, and trade-offs and with the ability to manage dualities or paradoxes (Levy et al., 2007a). Global Leaders must be able to put these concepts together in different ways in order to understand the implications and interaction effects on decisions they could make.

In addition to intelligence and cognitive complexity, Global Leaders are characterized by expert intuition or what many would call "common sense." Global Leaders can quickly determine whether a situation is typical or atypical, based on their previous experience. Rather than comparing alternative courses of action, they may intuitively know what goals are plausible, what solutions are relevant, what they can expect to happen, and which actions would be typical. Next, Global Leaders evaluate the chosen action using mental simulation – both seeing past events and imagining how the action would work. If the mental simulation appears to be successful, they implement the course of action (Osland and Bird, 2006). This expert intuition, also sometimes referred to as learning agility, results from how the leader has integrated their unique experience and learning over their career to bring smart pragmatic solutions to bear on problems in ways they often can't articulate, but which, nonetheless, are good judgments that result in effective action.

Psychological

All leaders need healthy psychological attributes, yet there are areas where a domestic leader can be at a threshold level of attainment where Global Leaders must have high levels. For example, all leaders need to be self-aware, yet Global Leaders must have a greater degree of self-awareness to enable them to understand how they are not only perceived within their home environmental context, but also in diverse contexts by many different others. While there are scores of psychological characteristics that have been identified in the expatriate, cross-cultural and global leadership literatures (see e.g., Bird and Osland, 2004; Gregersen et al., 1998; Osland and Bird, 2006; Osland et al., 2006), the psychological characteristics that seem to truly differentiate Global Leaders from others include the following:

- open-mindedness (cosmopolitanism);
- non-judgmentalness (cosmopolitanism);
- inquisitiveness/learning orientation;
- self-awareness;
- tolerance for ambiguity;
- ability to establish trust with those different from self (proactive relationships).

Self-awareness is important because an absence of self-insight is the single most critical derailer for senior leaders (Dotlich and Cairo, 2003). Global Leaders need to understand their own strengths and weaknesses, their emotions, and their impact on others in order to effectively lead in a global context. The further leaders move up the hierarchy, the less feedback they receive. If they cannot proactively get this feedback or cannot remain open to applying it to gain insight, they will always be at a disadvantage, leading in a vacuum and role modeling poor leadership skills. In addition, Global Leaders need to be open-minded and non-judgmental simply to see the complexity of the information before them and to utilize it effectively to make good decisions.

In addition, Spreitzer et al. (1997) find that individuals who are more likely to succeed as international executives manifest inquisitiveness and that it motivates them to enjoy the process of learning. Inquisitiveness and having a learning orientation has been identified by a number of authors as one of the most important characteristics of successful Global Leaders (e.g., Black, 2006; Black et al., 1999; Dalton and Wilson, 1998; Gregersen, 2007). Inquisitiveness in Global Leaders refers to a deep curiosity about other peoples and cultures. It is an interest in what makes people similar and what makes them different, as well as an interest in how other people live and work.

> Inquisitiveness is the fuel that keeps global leaders marching ahead, spanning boundaries, and managing differences. Rather than being exhausted by all the differences in time zones, languages, laws, and politics, global leaders are intrigued by them. The differences and the learning opportunities they provide invigorate rather than exhaust successful global leaders.
> (Black, 2006: 183)

Tolerance for ambiguity is another important psychological trait because ambiguity in a global business world is constant. A Global Leader will never have all the data or enough data to make thorough, sound decisions. They must love ambiguity and relish the opportunity that ambiguity provides to make progress where others are paralyzed. From their perspective, the lack of clarity means that more possibilities exist and more avenues to success are open: "This open road coupled with the fuel of inquisitiveness leads successful global leaders to embrace ambiguity as an opportunity to grow, learn, create, discover, build, reinvent, and revitalize" (Black, 2006: 194).

Lastly, as we know from the research in the diversity field, being able to establish trust and proactively build relationships with those different from the self is a critical capability for Global Leaders who must work with a large network of individuals from different cultural and national backgrounds in order to accomplish the goals of the organization. Global Leaders need to influence individuals, teams and organizations from different parts of the world to help achieve their organizations' objectives. They need to do this without relying on traditional lines of authority.

In the preceding sections of this chapter we have described the range of research and provided an organizing framework that we believe represents the core areas that differentiate Global Leaders from domestic leaders. In the following section we discuss the implications for talent decisions, selection, and development of Global Leaders.

Global Leadership through talent management

As described in the opening pages of this chapter, talent management has steadily risen in importance and is now an urgent and pressing issue in every multinational company. In fact, most multinational companies the authors work with have executive committees who schedule entirely separate meetings to talk only about talent and people issues and at the top of that list are two questions: Where do we find Global Leaders (and relatedly, *future* Global Leaders)? And; How do we accelerate the development of the ones we have? (Duke Corporate Education annual CLO roundtable, 2007). The business case for having strong Global Leaders is clear. As noted by Araoz, a senior partner of top executive search firm Egon Zehnder with over 20 years' experience: "dealing with executive search consultants from 62 offices worldwide, I have consistently found that mastering great people decisions is the absolutely indispensable requisite for successful performance, all around the world" (Araoz, 2007: 44). Araoz further notes that when looking over thousands of assessments and people decisions globally, most companies are not that great at it, and consistently "miss" in at least a third of their decisions (Araoz, 2007).

The Corporate Leadership Council's research shows that getting the talent management right on a global scale has clear retention and bottom-line benefits (Corporate Leadership Council, 2007). First, when a company can focus to create and deliver a clear, competitive value proposition to prospective employees, an organization can increase its access to candidates in the market by more than 50%, with an ancillary benefit of improving the commitment of current employees by up to 29%. Second, effective execution of talent development contributes to profitability directly, with as much as a 15.4% advantage in shareholder return. For any organization to succeed in a global context, they must have strong talent management systems – that is, identify talent early, attend to the experience set they are getting, ensure they are applying what they learn to other situations, and develop them broadly.

This brings us to a significant quandary for managers today: given the nascent state of the Global Leadership literature, how can any organization expect to select and grow global talent consistently? Currently, firms take their best shot at what they believe will predict success across borders and execute against it. Typically they will select/place people based on the applicant's past experience in a different context/country (usually limited to one or two markets), and some judgment about elements in what we label the Psychological factor (i.e., open-mindedness, ability to establish trust, natural curiosity). The framework provided in this chapter can help focus the organization on three critical areas, not simply the psychological attributes, and can therefore enhance the ability to select and place even more successful Global Leaders.

Our model provides a second observation for developing Global Leaders from this model. In reviewing the characteristics of Global Leaders, one observes that many of the elements develop slowly over time either through experience that is integrated and applied to other situations or slow changes in the characteristics of personality. This observation has four practical implications for organizations:

1. Talent management for Global Leaders starts at hire, selecting candidates with the necessary intellectual and psychological profiles that they can build on through experience. That is, they must build a broad base of experience to integrate into an evolving "global" expert intuition, and from that, a broad behavioral repertoire.

2. Generally, higher levels of the Intellectual and Psychological attributes identified in our model are necessary for Global Leaders. However, if companies are successful in #1 above, efforts to coach and develop this talent may shift from "closing gaps" in skills where there is a shortfall, to "managing overused strengths" in areas where people were selected to be strong. That is, they will now have a sufficiently high level of a characteristic that will come with its own unique blind spots and development challenges. Consider the leader with considerably high IQ and expert intuition who has a great capacity for cognitive complexity – who always arrives at an answer well before everyone else, has mentally explored all the options, and is impatiently wondering why it is taking everyone else so long. They have the capabilities to be an effective Global Leader but only if they have an equal amount of self-insight and ability to establish a high degree of trust so as to not disable their team's decision making or condition them to become dependent on the leader.

3. All is not lost for executives who are successful capable leaders domestically! We do not imply that strong domestic leaders cannot be successful in a global context, but suggest that organizations who do not attend to the 11 areas identified in our framework may be over-confident in the probability of their success. At a minimum, leaders should do a personal self-assessment, or alternatively have an honest discussion with a coach to gain insight into areas where they are strong and where they may expect difficulties or roadblocks in a global role.

    How leaders begin their global journey is critical because it will be a fundamental personal challenge when they embark on becoming a Global Leader:

    It is the crossing of cultural lines that is an assault on the identity of the person. When the task becomes managing differences of country, culture, language, and values, the assumptions we make about ourselves and other people are brought into question. Effective executive performance when crossing country and cultural borders often demands a kind of transformation of who we are and how we see ourselves.

    (McCall and Hollenbeck, 2002: 22)

4. Perhaps the most interesting implication involves how domestic job assignments can help groom Global Leaders. In our review of the literature we quickly came to the conclusion that highly complex roles in a domestic setting (multiple and diverse markets, channels, moves) mimic many of the conditions and challenges a Global Leader

425

faces (without the knowledge acquisition requirement). That is, these jobs require higher levels of Psychological and Intellectual capabilities. To the extent that "local" assignments have these critical elements is the extent to which these leaders will be better prepared to compete and succeed globally.

Specific recommendations for selection and development of Global Leaders

In addition to the implications for talent management systems, our Global Leadership framework leads to recommendations in selecting and developing leaders. The first recommendation for both selection and development derives from implication #4 above: The probability of a leader's success is higher if a company can select someone with experience from, or place someone to develop into, a domestic role with several highly complex elements. In addition, we have a number of other recommendations.

Selection (and placement)

Selection begins with the leader's psychological and intellectual capabilities. The six psychological elements must all be present in the applicants (or placement candidates) and these must be core strengths for early success of the leader. We believe that at the heart of the psychological elements, the first three (open-minded; non-judgmental; inquisitive) are the core. With those in place, an applicant could, through successive professional assignments and with high motivation, grow their capabilities in self-awareness, tolerance for ambiguity, and the proactive establishment of trust with individuals very different from the self. Gaining a valid and reliable picture of these skills can be achieved through on-the-job observation where possible (and an interview with supervisors when not possible), in-depth background interviews, and psychological testing.

Regarding the intellectual elements, it has become less popular in the past several years to discuss using IQ in selection, with the emergence of concepts like Emotional Intelligence (Goleman, 1996). However, IQ remains a stable predictor of success. Considering the three areas of intellectual capability (IQ; cognitive complexity; expert intuition), we suggest that the first two, IQ and cognitive complexity, are the more critical in selection situations, while "expert intuition" may be learned over time, through successive sets of achievements in business outcomes. The caution is that expert intuition or "street smarts" is the ability to know "what will work" to get pragmatic solutions in place. In considering selection methods to get a valid picture of these elements, we recommend some form of multi-method process. Using interviews alone will not be sufficient as they may not differentiate well between the "good" and the "great" applicants. A good interviewer may find an absence of capability, for example, in cognitive complexity, yet interviewees with some skills can look very skilled when able to cite their best examples and experiences. For this reason we recommend the addition of relevant IQ testing and for critical positions, some type of simulations or role plays that place the applicant in a complex situation where they must formulate a pragmatic way forward under time pressure.

Finally, in Knowledge and skills, there is the acquisition of new ideas and concepts across the range of social, cultural, political, and legal issues. In assessing a candidate's knowledge, we suggest simple resumé reviews and behavioral interviewing. It is also the easiest of the three areas to grow someone's skills. Finding applicants who have the broad set of behavioral skills or competencies to call on which can be determined from interviews is critical. Again, candidates who are otherwise strong can learn this breadth in behavioral repertoire over successive assignments or projects with very different contextual settings and teams.

Developing Global Leaders

As noted earlier, development of Global Leaders begins at selection. The first step is a two-part formula. A leader must first understand their strengths and weaknesses (gain insight), and then have the motivation and interest to change in critical areas. Insight is gained through many methods other than cumulative experience. Psychological testing to understand one's own style and approach to people and situations, 360-degree tools to see how others perceive the leader, and a coaching or mentoring relationship where sufficient trust is present for honest feedback to both be given, and accepted. One hopes the periodic reviews between supervisor and staff can serve as the foundation for these conversations.

We recommend six things for the practitioner to consider in developing a Global Leader's skills once a good assessment is in place and some measure of self-insight has been achieved:

1. Get out of your home country

A deep understanding of several countries can begin with reading and conversations. Curiosity and education will take a leader well along this journey, and yet there is no substitute for being in a country (more than a few weeks or a month for industrial tourism) to acculturate to the differences and "feel" the contrasts and similarity.

2. Identify the mentors in the organization who exemplify the characteristics of Global Leaders

Deliberately find opportunities for them to spend time with key leaders who are developing into Global Leaders. While there is some controversy on the topic of "matching" mentors and mentees, allowing a pool of mentors and "mentees" to self-select into pairings yields good results.

3. Build skills in managing strengths

If the selection process for Global Leadership characteristics is strong, an organization's development model for these leaders will shift from primarily strengthening areas of weakness, to one of managing areas of strength. Helping people with high levels of capabilities in different areas means helping them see the line they can cross in using that capability "too much." This has implications for the coaching and feedback models used throughout companies.

4. Think two to three assignments ahead

The time horizon for developing Global Leaders must be significantly longer than for domestic leaders. While the press for time is great for developing skills month to month and year to year, many of the high-value integrative skills that high-performing Global Leaders need will come over successive assignments.

5. Vary the assignments

For some organizations this may be counter-intuitive. They may operate from the view: "We invested in this leader's development and now they are over the learning curve and we want to give them similar assignments and challenges to hone their skills and extract value for the business." We respectfully suggest this is a domestic or expatriate mindset and will not build

427

Global Leaders who are broadly capable wherever they operate. The assignments must be complex and they should vary in a number of areas from type of business challenge to type of cross-border challenge.

6. Periodic explicit integration of learning

Related to #4 and #5 above, a great deal of value can be realized at the end of every assignment or project. The organization must focus the leader on the deliberate integration and application of learning to other situations in a concrete way to accelerate their effectiveness. Often organizations that work hard to get #4 and #5 in place fail to establish this integrative mechanism at the end.

There are many specific recommendations that can be written about each of the 11 characteristics described in the model. Overall, we return to the concepts of capacity and complexity reflected in each element of the model. Ensure that developmental efforts incorporate a challenging level of complexity and require leaders to stretch their current capacity. As we noted at the opening of this chapter "globalization is a manifestation of complexity" and it is not slowing down or going away. The ability of organizations and their leaders to recognize and embrace the needed characteristics to be truly Global Leaders will be directly related to their success in this complex arena of globally competitive business. We encourage you to apply these concepts to existing structures and processes in your organization or a client's organization.

Acknowledgements

A number of the ideas in this chapter originated in co-authored articles, chapters, and conversations with Mansour Javidan, Anne-valérie Ohlsson, Paul Evans, Hal Gregersen, Allan Bird, Joyce Osland, Orly Levy, Sully Taylor, Nakiye Boyacigiller, Mark Mendenhall, Vladimir Pucik, and Karine Jaffredo. All of their intellectual contributions to this chapter are gratefully acknowledged.

Note

1 We have not included the characteristics of honesty and integrity, nor basic technical knowledge in our framework. These characteristics are necessary for all leaders, global and local, and are therefore taken as givens in our conceptualization.

References

Adler, N. and Bartholomew, S. 1992. "Managing globally competent people." *Academy of Management Executive*, 6(3): 52–65.

Araoz, C.F. 2007. *Great People Decisions: Why they matter so much, why they are so hard, and how you can master them*. New Jersey: John Wiley & Sons.

Barham, K. and Aantala, B. 1994. "Competencies for the pan-European manager." In P. Kirkbride (Ed.), *Human Resource Management in Europe: Perspectives for the 1990s*. London: Routledge.

Bartlett, C.A. and Ghoshal, S. 1989. *Managing Across Borders: The transnational solution*. Boston: Harvard Business School Press.

Bass, B.M. 1990. *Bass and Stogdill's Handbook of Leadership: Theory, research, and managerial applications* (3rd edn). New York: Free Press.

Beechler, S. and Javidan, M. 2007. "Leading with a global mindset." In M. Javidan, R. Steers and M. Hitt (Eds), *Advances in International Management: Special issue on global mindset*, 19: 131–69.

Bennett, C.I. 1995. *Comprehensive Multicultural Education Theory and Practice* (3rd edn). Boston: Allyn and Bacon.

Bird, A. 2008. "Assessing global leadership competencies." In M.E. Mendenhall, J.S. Osland, A. Bird, G.R. Oddou, and M.L. Maznevski, *Global Leadership: Research, practice, and development*. New York: Routledge.

Bird, A. and Osland, J. 2004. "Global competencies: An introduction." In H. Lane, M. Maznevski, M. Mendenhall, and J. McNett (Eds), *The Handbook of Global Management: A guide to managing complexity*. Malden, MA: Blackwell Publishing.

Black, S. 2006. "The mindset of Global Leaders: Inquisitiveness and duality." *Advances in Global Leadership*, 4: 183–202.

Black, S. and Gregersen, H. 1999. "The right way to manage expats." *Harvard Business Review*, March/April: 52–62.

Black, S., Mendenhall, M., and Oddou, G. 1991. "A comprehensive model of international adjustment: An integration of multiple theoretical perspectives." *The Academy of Management Review*, 12(2): 291–317.

Black, S., Morrison, A., and Gregersen, H. 1999. *Global Explorers: The next generation of leaders*. New York: Routledge.

Boyatzis, R.E. 1982. *The Competent Manager: A model for effective performance*. New York: John Wiley & Sons.

Brake, T. 1997. *The Global Leader: Critical factors for creating the world class organization*. Chicago: Richard D. Irwin.

Briscoe, J.P. and Hall, D.T. 1999. "Grooming and picking leaders using competency frameworks: Do they work?" *Organizational Dynamics* (autumn): 37–51.

Carroll, A. 1990. "Principles of business ethics: Their role in decision making and an initial consensus." *Management Decisions*, 28: 24–9.

Corporate Leadership Council. 2007. *Improving Talent Management Outcomes*. Washington, DC and London: Corporate Leadership Council. Available at: www.corporateleadershipcouncil.org (accessed January 2008).

Cox, T.H. 1991. "The multicultural organization." *Academy of Management Executive*, 5: 34–47.

Cox, T.H. and Blake, S. 1991. "Managing cultural diversity: Implications for organizational competitiveness." *Academy of Management Executive*, 5: 45–56.

Dalton, M. and Wilson, M. 1998. "Antecedents of effectiveness in a group of Arab expatriates: The role of personality and learning." Paper presented at the 24th International Congress of Applied Psychology. San Francisco, CA, August.

Dorfman, P. 2004. "International and cross cultural leadership research." In B.J. Punnett and O. Shenkar (Eds), *Handbook for International Management Research*, 8(4): 265–355. Ann Arbor, MI: University of Michigan Press.

Dorfman, P., Hanges, P., and Brodbeck, F. 2004. "Leadership and culture variation: The identification of culturally endorsed leadership profiles." In R.J. House, P.J. Hanges, M. Javidan, P.W. Dorfman and V. Gupta (Eds), *Leadership, Culture, and Organizations: The GLOBE study of 62 societies*. Thousand Oaks, CA: Sage.

Dotlich, D.L. and Cairo, P.C. 2003. *Why CEOs Fail: The 11 behaviors that can derail your climb to the top – and how to manage them*. San Francisco: Jossey Bass.

Evans, P., Pucik, V. and Barsoux, J. 2002. *The Global Challenge: Frameworks for international human resource management*. Boston: McGraw-Hill/Irwin Pub.

Furuya, N. 2006. *Repatriation Management Effectiveness: A mechanism for developing global competencies through a comprehensive process of repatriation*. Unpublished dissertation. University of Tsukuba, Japan.

Geletkanycz, M.A. 1997. "The salience of culture's consequences: The effects of cultural values on top executive commitment to status quo." *Strategic Management Journal*, 18: 615–34.

Gelfand, M., Erez, M., and Aycan, Z. 2007. "Cross-cultural organizational behavior." *Annual Review of Psychology*, 58: 479–514.

Gilbert, J.A., Stead, B.A., and Ivancevich, J.M. 1999. "Diversity management: A new organizational paradigm." *Journal of Business Ethics*, 21: 61–76.

Goleman, D. 1996. *Emotional Intelligence: Why it can matter more than IQ*. New York: Bantam Books.

Gregersen, H. 2007. "Global leader curiosity." Presentation at the Academy of Management Annual Conference, Atlanta, GA, August.

Gregersen, H., Morrison, A., and Black, J.S. 1998. "Developing leaders for the global frontier." *Sloan Management Review*, 40: 21–32.

Hampden-Turner, C. and Trompenaars, F. 1997. *Riding the Waves of Culture: Understanding diversity in global business*. London: Nicholas Brealey Publishing.

Harris, P., Moran, R., and Moran, S. 2004. *Managing Cultural Differences: Global leadership strategies for the twenty-first century* (6th edn). Oxford: Elsevier Butterworth-Heinemann.

Hays, R. 1974. "Expatriate selection: Insuring success and avoiding failure." *Journal of International Business Studies*, 5(1): 25–37.

Hicks-Clark, D. and Iles, P. 2000. "Climate for diversity and its effects on career and organisational attitudes and perceptions." *Personnel Review*, 29: 324–45.

Hooijberg, R. and Quinn, R.E. 1992. *Behavioral Complexity and the Development of Effective Managers*. Westport: Quorum Books.

Hooijberg, R., Hunt, J.G., and Dodge, G.E. 1997. "Leadership complexity and development of the Leaderplex Model." *Journal of Management*, 23(3): 375–408.

House, R.J., Wright, N.S., & Aditya, R.N. 1997. "Cross-cultural research on organizational leadership: A critical analysis and a proposed theory." In P.C. Earley and M. Erez (Eds), *New Perspectives in International Industrial/Organizational Psychology*. San Francisco: The New Lexington Press.

House, R.J., Hanges, P.J., Javidan, M., Dorfman, P., and Gupta, V. 2004. *Culture, Leadership, and Organizations: The GLOBE study of 62 societies*. Thousand Oaks, CA: Sage Publications.

Javidan, M. and Carl, D. 2004. "East meets West: Searching for the etic in leadership." *Journal of Management Studies*, 41(4): 665–91.

Javidan, M. and Carl, D. 2005. "Leadership across cultures: A study of Canadian and Taiwanese executives." *Management International Review*, 45(1): 23–44.

Key, S.G. 2000. "Applications of 'multiculturalism' demonstrated by elementary preservice science teachers." Paper presented at the Annual Meeting of the American Educational Research Association, New Orleans, LA (ERIC Document Reproduction Service No. ED 444937).

Kramer, R. 2005. *Developing Global Leaders: Enhancing competencies and accelerating the expatriate experience*. New York: The Conference Board.

Lane, H., Maznevski, M., and Mendenhall, M. 2004. "Globalization: Hercules meets Buddha." In Lane, Maznevski, Mendenhall, and McNett (Eds), *The Blackwell Handbook of Global Management: A guide to managing complexity*. Malden, MA: Blackwell Publishing.

Levy, O., Beechler, S., Taylor, S., and Boyacigiller, N. 2007. "What we talk about when we talk about global mindset." *Journal of International Business Studies*, 38(2): 231–58.

McCall, M. 1992. "Identifying leadership potential in future international executives: Developing a concept." ICEDR Working Paper 92-01, ICEDR, Massachusetts.

McCall, M. and Hollenbeck, G. 2002. *Developing Global Executives: The lessons of international experience*. Boston, MA: Harvard Business School Press.

Melnick, S.L. and Zeichner, K.M. 1995. *Teacher Education for Cultural Diversity: Enhancing the capacity of teacher education institutions to address diversity issues*. Report no. NCRTL-RR-95-4. East Lansing, MI: National Center for Research on Teacher Learning.

Mendenhall, M. 2006. "The elusive, yet critical challenge of developing global leaders." *European Management Journal*, 24(6): 422–49.

Moore, C. 1999. *Teacher Thinking and Student Diversity* (ERIC Document Reproduction Services No. ED 429947). East Lansing, MI: National Center for Research on Teacher Learning.

Osland, J. and Bird, A. 2006. "Global leaders as experts." *Advances in Global Leadership*, 4: 123–42.

Osland, J.S., Bird, A., Osland, A., and Mendenhall, M. 2006. "Developing global leadership capabilities and global mindset: A review." In G. Stahl and I. Bjorkman (Eds), *Handbook of Research in International Human Resource Management*. Northampton, MA: Edward Elgar.

Perlmutter, H. 1969. "The tortuous evolution of the multinational corporation." *Columbia Journal of World Business*, 4(1): 9–18.

Peterson, M.F. and Hunt, J.G. 1997. "International perspectives on international leadership." *Leadership Quarterly*, 8(3): 203–31.

PriceWaterhouseCoopers. 2006. *The 10th Annual Global CEO Survey*. New York: PwC.

PriceWaterhouseCoopers. 2007. *The 11th Annual Global CEO Survey*. New York: PwC.

Pucik, V. and Saba, T. 1998. "Selecting and developing the global versus the expatriate manager: A review of the state-of-the art." *Human Resource Planning*, 21(4): 40–54.

Pucik, V., Tichy, N., and Barnett, C. (Eds) 1992. *Globalizing Management: Creating and leading the competitive organization*. New York: John Wiley & Sons.

Rahim, M.A. and Magner, N.R. 1996. "Confirmatory factor analysis of the bases of leader power: First-order factor model and its invariance across groups." *Multivariate Behavioral Research*, 31(4), 495–516.

Rhinesmith, S. 1993. "A manager's guide to globalization: Six keys to success in a changing world." Alexandria, VA: American Society for Training and Development.

Rhinesmith, S. 1995. "Open the door to a global mindset." *Training and Development*, May: 35–43.

Rhinesmith, S. 1996. *A Manager's Guide to Globalization: Six skills for success in a changing world*. New York: McGraw Hill.

Rothwell, S. 1992. "The development of the international manager." *Personnel Management*, 24(1): 33–5.

Smith, P.B. and Peterson, M.F. 1988. *Leadership, Organizations and Culture: An event management model*. London: Sage.

Smith, P.B., Peterson, M.F., and Schwartz, S.H. 2002. "Cultural values, source of guidance, and their relevance to managerial behavior: A 47-nation study." *Journal of Cross-Cultural Psychology*, 33(2), 188–208.

Spreitzer, G., McCall, M., Jr., and Mahoney, J. 1997. "Early identification of international executive potential." *Journal of Applied Psychology*, 82: 6–29.

Tichy, N. 1992. "Global development." In V. Pucik, N. Tichy and C. Barnett (Eds), *Globalizing Management: Creating and leading the competitive organization*. New York: John Wiley & Sons.

Triandis, H.C. 1994. "Cross-cultural industrial and organizational psychology." In H.C. Triandis, M. Dunnette, and L.M. Hough (Eds), *Handbook of Industrial and Organizational Psychology* (Vol. 4). Palo Alto, CA: Consulting Psychologist Press.

Wills, S. and Barham, K. 1994. "Being an international manager." *European Management Journal*, 12(1): 49–58.

World Economic Forum. 2007. *Annual Meeting 2007: Shaping the global agenda: The shifting power equation*. Davos, Switzerland, January 24–28.

Yukl, G. 2006. *Leadership in Organizations* (6th edn). Upper Saddle River, NJ: Pearson Prentice Hall.

Part 9

Regions

Previous chapters have frequently referred to the impact that globalization has had on organizations and HR functions. Certainly, many firms have implemented strategies of global labor arbitrage, locating operation where they are able to minimize labor costs. This certainly has led to increased growth in the developing world. This section discusses developments in three areas – India, China, and Africa – that have become targets of foreign investment.

In Chapter 25, Pawan Budhwar focuses on the challenges in managing human resources in India. From the vantage point of those of us who live in the US or Europe, so many multinationals have rushed into this market and the country seems to be experiencing so much growth that we may begin to think of India as just barely behind the West in its management practices. However, Budhwar's analysis of India's history, culture, and institutional structures makes it clear how different it is. He describes how India's culture constrains how HRM can be practiced within Indian firms, and then how the entrance of large non-Indian multinationals with their western HRM practices is beginning to create a two-tiered system of HRM across these different types of organizations. He describes the HRM challenges facing India, including the recently appearing skill shortage. For instance, by 2008 the BPO sector is expected to fall short by 262,000 people. This chapter presents a realistic view of the upcoming constraints that will challenge India's ability to maintain its recent growth.

Chapter 26 focuses on China. Fang Lee Cooke begins by describing the major forms of ownership that exist in China, focusing primarily on state-owned enterprises (SOEs), joint ventures and multinationals, and privately owned enterprises (POEs). She then presents a coherent comparison of the distinctive types of HRM practices that seem to characterize each. She describes how three growing HR issues – performance management, enterprise culture management, and learning organizations – are all evolving, largely as Western-based practices with minor Chinese twists. Finally, she covers the legislative environment, and the impact of unions and the degree of protection afforded to disadvantaged groups such as women and rural workers.

Finally, Frank Horwitz takes on the unenviable task of trying to describe HRM challenges in Africa. The challenge here is that Africa is such a large and diverse continent, ranging from the Arab north to the mostly Christian south, with some 2,000 different ethno-cultural communities, that to talk about HRM in Africa would require volumes. However, he rises to the challenge and describes how Western HRM practices are being diffused across the continent, but with an African cultural influence. He describes talent management and diversity challenges in this environment. He discusses the development of unions, and calls for a more collaborative approach in order for African firms to compete in the marketplace. Finally, he describes the tragic impact that HIV/AIDS is having on the workforce across Africa. This pandemic is ravaging the nation, and while heartbreaking at a social level, it is creating a major challenge to firms seeking to fill their workforces.

India, China, and Africa are areas into which many multinationals are moving, and for those of us in the West, they seem like distant spots on a map that may differ from our environments, but only in minor ways. These chapters, on the one hand, show that there does seem to be a convergence of global best practices in HRM, albeit with minor local variations. On the other hand, they describe worlds quite different from what many of us are used to, and in some cases, ones that we have difficulty in comprehending.

25

Managing Human Resources in India

Pawan S. Budhwar

Introduction: the Indian context

This chapter is structured around three themes: the socio-economic profile of India; developments in Indian human resource management (HRM); and the challenges facing the HRM function in India. In order to better understand the context-specific nature of HRM, this first section presents information on the historical, socio-cultural and economic context of India.

India is a sovereign, socialist, secular and democratic republic, comprising twenty-eight states and seven union territories. It occupies a strategic location in south Asia for international trade. It borders Bangladesh, Bhutan and Burma in the east, China in the north and northeast, Pakistan in the west and northwest and Sri Lanka in the south. The Indian peninsula is surrounded by the Bay of Bengal in the southeast, the Indian Ocean in the south and the Arabian Sea in the southwest and by the great Himalayas in the north and northeast. With an area of 3.3 million km², India is the second largest country in Asia and the seventh largest in the world (Budhwar, 2001).

As per the census of 2001, the total population of the country is 1,027 million (making India the second most populous country in the world, after China) which includes 531.28 million males and 495.73 million females. India's share of the world population is 16.7 percent. The literacy rate among the population for seven years and above for the country stands at 65.38 percent (75.85 percent males and 54.16 percent females). The density of population (per km²) is 324 and the sex ratio (females per 1,000 males) is 933. The total workforce in the country is approximately 397 million, out of which nearly 92 percent or more are engaged in the activities of the unorganized sector (including the so-called informal sector) and remaining 8 percent of the workforce is employed in the organized sector. Sixty percent of the workforce is engaged in agriculture and the remaining 40 percent in the non-agriculture sector. Of the non-agriculture sector employment, the unorganized workforce is 82 percent and the remaining 18 percent belongs to the organized segment. Only about 12 to 15 percent of the total workforce in the country is estimated to fall into the category of wage/salary employment. Such employees constitute 6 percent of the workforce in the rural areas and about 40 per cent of the workforce in the urban areas. It is estimated that only about 5 percent of the workforce in the age group of 20 to 24 years has acquired some kind of a formal vocational training. Despite such dismal statistics, India manages to have the largest pool of scientific and technical personnel in the world. The technical education system produces over 200,000 engineering/ technical graduates annually all trained in English, providing one of India's real strengths (see Datt and Sundram, 2006).

India is a strong multi-cultural society with six main religious groups: Hindus (83.2 percent), Muslims (11 percent), Sikhs (2 percent), Christians (2 percent), Jains and Buddhists (less than 1 percent). India has over 3,000 castes, 179 languages and 544 dialects. The constitution recognizes sixteen languages, 'Hindi' and English being the two official languages. India has one of the largest English-speaking populations in the Asia-Pacific region. Though rich in culture and natural resources, India currently faces a number of problems: political and religious instability; ever-increasing levels of population; unemployment and poverty; inadequacy and shortage of skills; corruption in government offices; castism; a low per capita income; poor infrastructure; instability of output in agriculture and related sectors; slow privatization of the bloated public sector; lack of adequate intellectual property protection; red tapism; excessive workforce; unsatisfactory levels of productivity; slow progress with the next generation of reforms; and an increasing gap between rich and poor.

In 1950 the government set up the Planning Commission to formulate national plans. Since then a 'mixed economy' approach (emphasizing both private and public enterprise) has been adopted. This had the effect of reducing both entrepreneurship and global competitiveness – both necessary for national growth. Economic planning is mainly carried out through the five-year plans and industrial policies. Presently, the tenth five-year plan (2002–7) and the industrial policy of 1991 are in progress. Despite the formalities of planning, the Indian economy reached its worst in 1991. It witnessed a double-digit rate of inflation, decelerated industrial production, fiscal indiscipline, a very high ratio of borrowing to the GNP (both internal and external) and a dismally low level of foreign exchange reserves. Foreign reserves had become so low that they were barely sufficient to meet the cost of three weeks' imports. The Indian government was forced to pledge gold to the Bank of England to meet the country's foreign exchange requirements. The World Bank and the IMF agreed to bail out India on the condition that it changed to a 'free market economy' from a regulated regime. To meet the challenges, the government announced a series of economic policies beginning with the devaluation of the rupee, followed by a new industrial policy and fiscal and trade policies. A number of reforms were made in the public sector, trade and exchange policy, the banking sector and foreign investment was liberalized.

Since these reforms, the economy has responded positively and per the forecasts of the World Bank, by 2020, India could become the world's fourth largest economy. In the last few years the state control and ownership of the economy have been reduced, bold steps have been taken to correct the fiscal imbalance, to bring about structural adjustments and to attract foreign direct investment. Substantial reforms have been made in the telecommunications, financial and shipping sectors, as well as in direct tax and industrial policy. Significant reforms have already been initiated in the insurance sector by the present government. As a result of such reforms, India has now become the second most attractive emerging market (after China) for foreign firms. Approximately 20,000 multinational firms are now operating in India and many more are expected to do so. However, India still has a long way to go before it can compete fully with some of the more economically advanced Asian nations.

Undoubtedly, the liberalization of the Indian economy has on the one hand created serious competition for Indian firms from international firms, but on the other has also created opportunities for them to learn, refine, develop and further professionalize mechanisms regarding the effective and efficient management of their human resources. In the present Indian competitive context where firms are adopting strategies of continuous growth via strategic alliances, rightsizing, diversification and internationalization, HRM issues have become more important then ever. Such developments have significant implications for the Indian HR function as it is under severe pressure to bring about large-scale structural changes and develop a domestic workforce which is capable of taking on the challenges thrown up by the new economic environment. In such conditions the performance of the HR function has become more important than ever (Saini and Budhwar, 2004). The next section highlights the historical developments in Indian HRM and also discusses the main factors determining HRM policies and practices in the Indian context.

Developments in Indian HRM

The origins of the human resource function in India go back to the 1920s when it was a concern for labour welfare in factories. The Trade Union Act of 1926 gave formal recognition to workers' unions. The Royal Commission of 1932 recommended the appointment of labour officers and the Factories Act of 1948 laid down the duties and qualifications of labour welfare officers. All these developments formed the foundation of the present HR function in India (Balasubramanian, 1994, 1995) and in some ways paralleled the initial developments of the British HR function, as provisions similar to those provided by Cadbury in Britain were provided by the Tata group in India in the early 1920s.

After independence, in the 1950s, two professional bodies emerged: the Indian Institute of Personnel Management (IIPM), a counterpart of the Institute of Personnel Management in the United Kingdom, was formed in Calcutta, and the National Institute of Labour Management (NILM) in Bombay. In the 1960s, the personnel function began to expand beyond the welfare aspect with the three areas of Labour Welfare, Industrial Relations and Personnel Administration developing as the constituent roles for the emerging profession (Budhwar, 2004). In the 1970s, the thrust of personnel function shifted towards greater organizational 'efficiency', and by the 1980s it began to use and focus on terms and issues such as HRM and Human Resource Development (HRD). The IIPM and NILM merged in 1980 to form the National Institute of Personnel Management (NIPM) at Bombay. A similar event took place in Britain in 1994 when the IPM and the Institute of Training and Development merged to form the Institute of Personnel and Development (IPD). Thus, we see that the status of the personnel function in India has changed over the decades. The HR debate in India in the late 1990s was quite similar to the one which was dominant in the Western literature in the 1980s, which contained arguments about the difference between personnel management and HRM and HRD and the relabelling of job titles from personnel manager to HRD executive (see Budhwar, 2000). The rapidly changing business context strongly influences the nature of Indian HRM function.

In order to better understand the nature of Indian HRM in the present dynamic environment it is important to examine its key determinants. Considering India's unique socio-economic context, one can expect the main determinants of Indian HRM policies and practices to be different from those in other countries (or at least the logic surrounding the same to be unique to the Indian context). Next an overview regarding the main determinants of Indian HRM is provided. The existing literature highlights that national factors (such as national culture, institutions, business environment and industry sector), contingent variables (such as age, size, nature, life-cycle stage of the organization) and business strategies significantly dictate the nature of HRM policies and practices of a given set-up (see Budhwar and Sparrow, 2002a; Budhwar and Debrah, 2001). Some scholars (such as Budhwar and Sparrow, 1997, 1998) have conducted research to highlight the prominent determinants of HRM in India.

Determinants of HRM in India

From the analysis of the existing literature, a mixed picture is emerging regarding the main factors influencing HRM in India. For example, there is a significant difference in the nature of HRM policies and practices in local/national versus multinational firms. Also, there is an emerging distinction between HRM in new sectors such as the information technology enabled services (ITeS), business process outsourcing (BPO) and call centres and traditional manufacturing sector. Initially, information related to the nature of HRM and its main determinants in local/national organizations is presented and later on information about the emerging patterns of HRM systems in both foreign firms operating in India and firms in the new sectors is shared.

As highlighted above, India is a very diverse society, which is reflected in its patterns of life, styles of living, land tenure systems, occupational pursuits, inheritance and succession rules. An analysis of Hofstede's (1991) ranking of India on his four initial dimensions of power distance, uncertainty avoidance, individualism and masculinity reveal that India stands relatively high on power distance and uncertainty avoidance and relatively low on individualism and masculinity. Budhwar and Sparrow (1998, 2002b), investigating the influence of national factors on HRM policies and practices in 137 Indian local firms, revealed the influence of national culture on HRM, mainly along Hofstede's dimensions. For example, the relative high-power distance score for India implies that managers and subordinates accept their relative positions in the organizational hierarchy and operate from these fixed positions. Such a set-up allows the managers to misuse their positional power due to different pressures (such as political, caste, group and bureaucratic), as obedience is due to the holder of the position not on a rational basis, but simply by virtue of the authority inherent in that status. This creates a culture of sycophancy, inequality and apathy, triggered by a feudalistic outlook by employers and a strong backing of political parties by unions. This logic influences their thinking about most HRM practices. A possible explanation for such behaviour can be traced to the traditional hierarchical social structure of India, which has always emphasized respect for superiors, whether elders, teachers or superiors at work, i.e., the nature of Hinduism evidenced by the caste and social system (Sahay and Walsham, 1997).

Relatively high uncertainty avoidance implies an unwillingness to take risks and accept organizational change. Accordingly, people tend to easily accept that uncertainty is inherent in life and take each day as it comes. It is understandable to have such behaviour in a country with a high rate of poverty, unemployment, corruption in government offices, political instability, castism, low per-capita income, prone to natural and man-made disasters and with an increasing gap between rich and poor. In order to reduce uncertainty at the workplace, the HR function places more emphasis on training and development and career development. The element of uncertainty forces Indian managers to take calculative risks, which means that people value job security and stability. This has implications for the recruitment function.

The relatively low individualism implies that family and group attainments take precedence over work outcomes (Sharma, 1984). This may be changing rapidly in the metropolitan areas, where there is an increased emphasis on individualism at the managerial level and collectivism at the shop-floor level. The emphasis on collectivism for the lower level of employees is mainly dictated by the strong trade unions. As mentioned above, a strong interference by social relations, caste and religion dynamics at the workplace is still observable in Indian organizations (Sahay and Walsham, 1997).

The relatively low masculinity implies that employees' orientation is towards personalized relationships rather than towards performance. Indian male managers appear to exercise their superiority and assertiveness over their female employees by expressing their reluctance to recruit them irrespective of their performance during the recruitment process. Such behaviour is based on the cultural roles of men and women in the traditional Indian society where women are expected to devote themselves to internal household affairs and men are required to work outside to provide the economic maintenance of their households (Budhwar and Sparrow, 2002b).

Amongst the various national institutions, the influence of national labour laws is clearly evident on Indian HRM policies and practices, especially in local/national organizations (see Saini and Budhwar, 2004). This is understandable as there are over 150 state and central laws in India which govern various aspects of HRM at the enterprise level. Some of the main legislation which dictates terms and conditions at the workplace includes the Industrial Disputes Act 1947, the Trade Unions Act 1926 and the Industrial Employment (Standing Orders) Act 1946. Unfortunately, while there is a proliferation of legislation, the implementation is weak (Venkata Ratnam, 1996). Apart from legislation, unions also significantly influence HRM policies in India. Traditionally, they are known for their antagonistic nature, which is mainly due to the strong political support they have and the existence of pro-labour laws. Further, there also seems to be an impact by the vocational and training set-up of India on its HRM policies and practices. For example, a number of institutes such as the Indian Society for Training and Development and the HRD Academy were initiated in the 1980s. These and many similar bodies emphasize vocational training in India, especially to combat the pressures thrown up by foreign competition.

To summarize, Indian societal culture has had a lasting impact on most HR functions, such as staffing, promotions, communication, leadership, motivation and control. Staffing for top managerial positions within Indian organizations (especially in the private sector) is generally restricted by familial, communal and political considerations. Authority in Indian organizations is likely to remain one-sided, with subordinates leaning heavily on their superiors for advice and directions. Motivational tools in Indian organizations are more likely to be social, interpersonal and even spiritual (see Sparrow and Budhwar, 1997).

However, as discussed above, it is also true that the economic liberalization in India has resulted in stiff competition for national firms from overseas operators. As a result, the number of business alliances has significantly increased in India. Also, the rapid developments in information technology have implications for functions such as recruitment, training and development and performance appraisals. In the new economic environment Indian managers perceive the aim of their HRM function has been expanded to focus on the increase of productivity, reduction of costs and tackling over-manning whilst generating employment, improvement in quality, and reduction in voluntary and involuntary absenteeism (Saini and Budhwar, 2004).

One clear outcome of such changes is the increased focus on the development of human resources. In the majority of local/national Indian firms, HRD is the dominating term used to denote personnel function. The primary reason for an emphasis on the HRD function in India is directly related to the liberalization of the economy. This also has direct implications for HR function in India as it is required to develop a domestic workforce capable of taking on the challenges thrown up by the new economic environment. To improve organizational performance and to tackle such challenges, both Indian academics and practitioners have advocated the adoption of the concept of HRD (see Sparrow and Budhwar, 1997). This was further supported by the formation of the 'HRD Network' in the early 1990s which now has a large membership of academics and HRM and other managers; it symbolizes the need to debate HR interventions and sharpen the abilities of HR professionals. This network has aroused tremendous sensitivity for the need for HRD in particular and for HRM in general (Saini and Budhwar, 2004).

The literature also suggests that the nature of HR function is gradually changing and becoming proactive. An earlier analysis (see Budhwar and Sparrow, 1997) showed that around

439

50 percent of 137 Indian firms practise a high level of integration of HRM in their corporate strategy and suggest an increasing trend in this regard. Indian interviewees report a low level of devolvement of responsibility for HRM to line managers. However, the practice of HRD emphasizes the development of line managers to make them more responsible. Despite the strong presence of HRD function in Indian organizations, this does not seem to be taking place. There can be two possible reasons for this. First, research shows that Indian managers prefer centralized decision making, use limited delegation and practise tight control (see Sparrow and Budhwar, 1997). Second, this could be attributed to the lack of confidence of senior managers in line managers or an absence of adequate training or unwillingness of senior managers to share decision-making power with line managers (Budhwar and Sparrow, 2002b).

It is questionable whether the above account is also valid for both foreign firms and firms in the new sectors which are rapidly becoming dominant business sectors in India such as the ITeS, BPOs and call centres. The emerging evidence suggests quite a different picture to the one portrayed above. Budhwar et al. (2006a, b) explored the pattern of HRM systems emerging in the BPO/call centres operating in India. Their investigation is based on over fifty firms, both Indian and overseas, and used a mixed methodology, involving both qualitative in-depth interviews and questionnaire surveys. They found a prevalence of highly structured, formal and rationalized HRM policies and practices which seems to be the norm for this sector. The recruitment process is detailed and every effort is made to attain the most suitable candidate. The selection procedures ensure objectivity prevails (achieving which is a big challenge in the Indian socio-cultural context). A strong emphasis is laid on training and development of all employees, especially at the entry level. The performance management systems are strongly data-driven, which results in transparency and objectivity for assessing rewards and benefits. It is interesting to see a more or less complete absence of unions in this sector (their creation is now strongly muted). The career system is being refined and developed in this sector, but a lot needs to be done for the shop-floor-level employee. Despite such professional systems, the sector is facing serious problems with skill shortages, recruitment and retention. To a great extent these problems are due to the strong growth of this sector and the nature of work in it. Irrespective of such issues, it is fascinating to observe that in a country like India where the above-discussed socio-cultural aspects of its society and unions significantly influence HRM policies and practices; organizations operating in this sector are able to develop and practise highly rationalized HRM systems (see also Raman et al., 2007).

The BPO/call centre sector is not an exception in this regard; research by Budhwar and Bjorkman (2003) in 76 foreign companies operating in India reveals a similar picture. These sample firms are from a variety of sectors and are of different ownerships (for example, 100 percent owned subsidiaries; joint ventures or strategic alliances). It is interesting to discover that the majority of firms in this research are successfully adopting 'globally standardized' HRM policies and practices in their Indian operations, with slight modifications. This is clearly valid for recruitment and selection, training and development, employee communication, and the successful adoption of the parent company's culture. Perhaps foreign firms struggle more to adopt a globally standardized approach to performance management and compensation. Indeed in the latter case it is understandable, and with performance management systems, the socio-cultural aspects of the Indian society make it very difficult to allow rationalization of such systems. Nevertheless, after initial resistance from Indian employees, many MNCs are able to refine these systems as well (see also Bjorkman and Budhwar, 2007).

In both of the above cases – the BPOs and foreign firms – unlike the Indian local firms, Indian socio-cultural, legal and unionized context does not seem to be significantly determining HRM policies and practices. Instead, it seems that factors and variables such as firms' ownership, industrial sector, dynamic business environment, organization's philosophy, an increased emphasis on customer satisfaction, quality enhancement and market forces are proving to be the key determinants of HRM systems. Also, there is strong evidence that HR is playing a more strategic role in both the foreign firms operating in India and in the BPO sector. HR is not only represented at the board level, but is also involved from the outset in corporate strategy and is known to be proactive in nature (see also Bjorkman and Budhwar, 2007; Raman et al., 2007). What does all this mean?

A few things can be deduced from this analysis. First, a whole range of factors and variables significantly influence HRM in the Indian set-up. Second, their impact tends to vary from sector to sector and with the ownership of the firm. Third, irrespective of socio-cultural context, if the top management wishes, they can certainly successfully adopt formal, structured and rationalized HRM systems in the Indian set-up, especially in the modern services sector which tend to recruit literate employees. Indeed, they will have to overcome initial and strong resistance from various stakeholders such as employees with a traditional mind-set and unions apart from others. This will also necessitate reorienting management systems and processes, and undertaking programmes of attitudinal change. These include mixed bags of harder measures as well as attempts towards greater professionalism for HR empowerment. Fourth, as with most macro-level changes, it will be a major challenge for traditional Indian HR function to modernize itself, due to India's strong socio-cultural traditions. The next section further raises other core challenges for the Indian HRM function.

Challenges facing HRM in India

The discussion above highlighted how the socio-cultural set-up of India to a great extent dictates HRM policies and practices in many local and national firms. In such firms, HRM still plays the traditional role of 'gate-keeper' and 'record-keeper'. Professionalization of the HRM department might not be a priority of these firms; managers might also not be ready to devolve responsibilities to line managers. No matter what exactly the reason might be behind the continued existence of such traditional HR roles, the passive mind-set of management about their personnel function (i.e., their lassitude in further developing their HR functions) is a key one (Budhwar and Sparrow, 2002b). Despite the pressures created by the new economic environment such changes are slow and are proving to be a major challenge for the HR field in India.

Along the same lines, the existing evidence (see Budhwar and Sparrow, 1997, 2002b) reveals that HRM is not playing a strategic role in many Indian national firms. This is evidenced by a low representation of the personnel function at board level, few organizations having devised formal corporate HR strategies. A few do consult their personnel function from the outset; many involve personnel during the implementation of their corporate strategy. On the other hand, it seems that Indian firms are still witnessing less devolvement of responsibility for HRM to line managers. The existence of such practices poses serious challenges for the HR managers and should encourage them to adopt a more strategic approach.

Another key challenge before the Indian HRM function is to get strong support from unions and work in partnership with them. Much like unions were in the UK in the 1970s and 1980s (i.e., playing a less supportive role), unions in India are still very antagonistic, less supportive and strongly influenced by the agenda of political parties supporting them (Venkata Ratnam, 2001). Although the membership of unions is gradually declining in India, there is a strong need to reform the existing Trade Unions Act of 1926, whose provisions are obviously dated. It is interesting to observe that the booming BPO sector has so far managed to operate more or less union-free. Nevertheless, as the sector is maturing, there are signs of entry by the unions in some BPOs. It is hoped that unlike most other traditional sectors, unions in this sector (as and when they fully enter it) will play a supportive role. This will be a big challenge for all concerned as somehow the petty interests of political parties supporting unions tend to overwhelm the real issues affecting both the employees and employers (Mishra, 2001). In this regard, there is also a strong need to initiate new mechanisms for 'worker participation'. Until now, the provisions of the Industrial Disputes Act of 1948 in the form of 'works committees' have been one of the main mechanisms for workers' participation in India. Unfortunately, this is also not fully functional.

Apart from the IDA, most of the more than 50 central labour laws and over 100 state laws need modifications as they are rigid and not suitable for the present business context. For HR departments it is a big challenge to implement the provisions of these dated legislations, which do not help to improve productivity or create flexibility at the workplace. Further, the existing labour laws have different applicability in terms of industries and employees covered; also, different sets of administrative mechanisms and dispute-resolving quasi-judicial bodies have been created under various acts. Such complexities pose serious challenges for HR managers to fully follow the provisions of Indian labour legislation. It is then not surprising to see a lack of implementation of the same. It is also interesting to observe that the majority of the foreign firms operating in India are not too bothered about Indian labour legislation, as their HRM systems are already well advanced and easily fulfil the provisions of the minimum standards legislation (see Budhwar and Bjorkman, 2003).

In the rapidly growing Indian economy, a further key challenge before the Indian HR professionals is to attract, attain and retain key HR talent. This is more valid for some of the booming sectors such as the ITeS and BPO/call centres. A recent analysis (see Budhwar et al., 2006b) shows that by 2008, the BPO sector is expected to fall short by roughly 262,000 people, despite the regular turnaround of approximately three million graduates trained by Indian universities each year. However, the gap between abilities and skills is increasing substantially. For example, by 2009, the BPO sector will need around 160,000 people with different European languages; the projection is that India can only produce around 40,000. The majority of the educational and vocational training institutes in India are run by the government (although the number of private training institutions is increasing rapidly) and the performance of the existing state-regulated vocational training system in the country is far from satisfactory. In this regard, India can learn from countries such as Singapore who have excelled in developing their competitive performance through enforcing comprehensive needs-driven schemes of skill development (Debrah et al., 2000).

Perhaps the most challenging problem experienced by the HR function in the ITeS and the BPO industries is the ever-increasing attrition rates and retention of talent. Indeed, HR professionals are developing new initiatives in this regard, but the strong job market and infancy of these sectors (along with other factors) are not allowing such initiatives to fully control such problems (for more details see Budhwar et al., 2006a). In many small and local BPOs the facilities provided to employees are not comparable to the more renowned names in the sector. Employees in such organizations complain about issues related to health, provision of low wages, and non-payment of bonuses and many benefits given by market leaders. In the competitive market it is then a big challenge for the HR function to look after their employees in the absence of sufficient resources.

The existing literature also highlights the existence of unique internal labour markets (ILMs) in the majority of traditional local and national Indian firms, which are based on social relations, political affiliations, political contacts, caste, religion and economic power (see Budhwar and Khatri, 2001). However, this is not the case in most foreign firms and BPO organizations operating in India (see Budhwar et al., 2006b). Although it poses a serious challenge for HR managers in local/national Indian firms to pursue more rationalized HRM practices and build strong ILMs (which should solely emphasize performance and be less influenced by these social, economic, religious and political factors), nevertheless, considering that it is possible to do in the Indian context (e.g., in the BPO sector), serious efforts should be made in this regard to adopt these practices in other sectors in India.

Unlike China and many other East Asian countries, India still lacks a research culture and it is very challenging to get access to companies for conducting research. In the present competitive business environment radical changes are taking place, and it is difficult to keep track of so many changes. The new economic environment presents a number of threats to local firms; it also offers many opportunities to learn, collaborate and change to suit the new context. To make the best use of the existing conditions, Indian firms need to encourage research and analysis and be open to share key findings. HR departments can play an important role in this regard by not only providing access for research but also initiating investigation of key issues in the present economic context. Such initiatives are now being pursued by a number of IT and software firms. Also, there seems to be a significant gap regarding established HRM systems between MNCs and Indian local firms. Platforms like the HRD Network provide opportunities to share the best HR practices. Unfortunately, due to the lack of support for such HR initiatives in many local Indian firms (e.g., towards upgrading the status of HR), the best use is not made of such great opportunities and this understandably frustrates the concerned HR professionals.

Considering the above developments, in the global business context, a paradigm shift in the mindsets of individuals is needed and many of the established norms and work preferences need to be challenged and modified. For example, Indians have traditionally shown a strong preference to work in a reputable public sector organization and go for firms which offer lifelong employment. The emerging norm of organizational life is rapidly moving towards performance-based systems. Given that the Indian worker has traditionally either preferred a secure employment in the sluggish public sector or has been hostile to the exploitative practices of the family-run private enterprises, the move to performance-based systems in a traditional society like India poses serious challenges for the HR function. Again the key learning for local Indian firms is available from MNCs operating in India which are successful in adopting performance-based systems and have set useful benchmarks for others to follow.

At present, a large number of foreign nationals are going to India on different assignments. These can be categorized as expatriates, self-initiated expatriates (for example, a number of call centre employees) or self-initiated repatriates (i.e., non-resident Indians settled abroad are now returning to India). Indian HR managers are not used to managing such diverse kinds of employees. Also, it seems that neither the government nor organizations have clear policies and practices to ensure a smooth adjustment of such employees in the dynamic Indian context. This can be seen both as a serious challenge as well as an opportunity for the Indian HR function to make its mark by developing useful procedures to facilitate the stay of foreign nationals in India.

Another important phenomenon emerging within the Indian context is that of the increased number of strategic alliances (mergers and acquisitions) being developed within India between Indian firms, between foreign and Indian firms, or between foreign firms operating in India. Indeed such alliances have serious implications for HRM; however, the existing research does highlight that it is mostly at the implementation stage that HR is involved during the creation of such alliances. The literature also highlights that the success of such alliances can be significantly improved if HR is involved at the initial phase of creation of these alliances (see Evans et al., 2002). In a set-up like India where HR is known to play a reactive role, it then becomes a big challenge for the HR function to play a proactive and strategic role during the creation of various strategic alliances between firms.

Finally, another important development in the world of business is the growth of multinational companies from emerging markets like India and China. At present, there is no information regarding the kinds of HRM systems being developed by Indian multinational firms to successfully operate in overseas markets. Literature based on Western and Japanese MNCs provides ample information regarding the key role of HR in the efficient management of local subsidiaries. It is safe to assume that Indian HR professionals working in Indian MNCs face strong challenges to develop relevant HRM systems for their overseas subsidiaries.

Conclusion

This chapter highlighted the state of HR in India and its embeddedness in the country's historical, socio-cultural and economic context. The analysis shows that there is a remarkable progress towards the professionalization of the HRM departments in the new business sectors. To a great extent this can be attributed to the liberalization of the Indian economy and to the progressive policies brought along and pursued by the MNCs and professionally managed Indian organizations, including some of the public sector enterprises.

The analysis also reveals that a mixture of factors and variables influence HRM policies and practices in the Indian context. To a great extent it depends on the type of industrial sector (modern services or traditional manufacturing) and ownership (Indian or foreign) of the firms. The attitude towards the contribution HR can make in business success is changing in general, hence the increased emphasis on HRD. Nevertheless, the HR function faces a number of serious problems that adversely influence it. These include the less supportive roles of unions, tackling the dated and rigid Indian labour legislation, lack of a vision for skill and competency development, the traditional mindsets of employers, and the inability of the government to take bold decisions which can increase the pace of the next generation of economic and industrial relations related reforms.

The analysis also highlighted a number of challenges facing the HRM function in the Indian context. These include the need to change the traditional role played by Indian HRM to a more strategic and proactive role. To achieve this there is a need to further align HRM with business needs and strategies. There are also serious challenges for the Indian HR function as it moves to altogether new areas of strategic alliances and Indian multinationals. Despite such challenges, the present business context also provides a number of opportunities for the HR function to make its mark. The time is very appropriate in this regard as most firms and employers have now realized that the management of their human resources is an important aspect of management if they are to continuously improve their performance.

The information provided in this chapter is useful from different perspectives. For example, it helps to build academic contributions on HRM in general and on Indian HRM in particular. It also has a number of key messages for practitioners regarding what determines HRM in the Indian context and how they can build their HRM systems so as to suit the need of the present dynamic business environment. Hopefully, it also helps to break down existing stereotypes regarding the passive image about Indian HRM, and provides plenty of material for serious consideration by policy makers regarding the challenges they face.

Acknowledgement

The author thanks Professor Debi Saini for his useful comments on an earlier version of this chapter.

References

Balasubramanian, A. G. (1994) Evolution of Personnel Function in India: A Re-examination, Part 1. *Management and Labour Studies*, 19 (4): 196–210.

Balasubramanian, A. G. (1995) Evolution of Personnel Function in India: A Re-examination, Part II. *Management and Labour Studies*, 20 (1): 5–14.

Bjorkman, I. and Budhwar, P. (2007) When in Rome . . .? Human Resource Management and the Performance of Foreign Firms Operating in India. *Employee Relations*, 29 (6): 595–610.

Budhwar, P. (2000) Indian and British Personnel Specialists' Understanding of the Dynamics of Their Function: An Empirical Study. *International Business Review*, 9 (6): 727–53.

Budhwar, P. (2001) Doing Business in India. *Thunderbird International Business Review*, 43 (4), 549–68.

Budhwar, P. (2004) HRM in India. In P. Budhwar and Y. Debrah (Eds) *HRM in Developing Countries*. London: Routledge, 75–90.

Budhwar, P. and Bjorkman, I. (2003) A Corporate Perspective on the Management of Human Resources in Foreign Firms Operating in India. *2003 International HRM Conference*, 4–6 June 2003, Limerick, Ireland.

Budhwar, P. and Debrah, Y. (2001) Rethinking Comparative and Cross-national Human Resource Management Research. *The International Journal of Human Resource Management*, 12 (3): 497–515.

Budhwar, P. and Khatri, P. (2001) HRM in Context: The Applicability of HRM Models in India. *International Journal of Cross Cultural Management*, 1 (3): 333–56.

Budhwar, P. and Sparrow, P. (1997) Evaluating Levels of Strategic Integration and Devolvement of Human Resource Management in India. *The International Journal of Human Resource Management*, 8 (4): 476–94.

Budhwar, P. and Sparrow, P. (1998) Factors Determining Cross-national Human Resource Management Practices: A Study of India and Britain. *Management International Review*, 38, Special Issue 2, 105–21.

Budhwar, P. and Sparrow, P. (2002a) An Integrative Framework for Determining Cross-national Human Resource Management Practices. *Human Resource Management Review*, 12 (3): 377–403.

Budhwar, P. and Sparrow, P. (2002b) Strategic HRM through the Cultural Looking Glass: Mapping Cognitions of British and Indian HRM Managers. *Organization Studies*, 23 (4): 599–638.

Budhwar, P., Luthar, H. and Bhatnagar, J. (2006a) Dynamics of HRM Systems in BPOs Operating in India. *Journal of Labor Research*, 27 (3): 339–60.

Budhwar, P., Varma, A., Singh, V. and Dhar, R. (2006b) HRM Systems of Indian Call Centres: An Exploratory Study. *The International Journal of Human Resource Management*, 17 (5): 881–97.

Datt, R. and Sundharam, K. P. H. (2006) *Indian Economy*. New Delhi: S. Chand and Company.

Debrah, Y., McGovern, I. and Budhwar, P. (2000) Complementarity or Competition: The Development of Human Resources in a Growth Triangle. *The International Journal of Human Resource Management*, 11 (2): 314–35.

Evans, P., Pucik. V. and Barsoux, J-L. (2002) *The Global Challenge: Frameworks for International Human Resource Management*. New York: McGraw Hill.

Hofstede, G. (1991) *Cultures' Consequences: Software of the Mind*. London: McGraw-Hill.

Mishra, L. (2001) *Economy & Labour*. New Delhi: Manak Publications.

Raman, S. R., Budhwar, P. and Balasubramanian, G. (2007) People Management Issues in Indian KPOs. *Employee Relations*, 29 (6): 696–710.

Sahay, S. and Walsham, G. (1997) Social Structure and Managerial Agency in India. *Organisation Studies*, 18: 415–44.

Saini, D. and Budhwar, P. (2004) Human Resource Management in India. In P. Budhwar (Ed.) *Managing Human Resources in Asia-Pacific.* London: Routledge, 113–39.

Sharma, I. J. (1984) The Culture Context of Indian Managers. *Management and Labour Studies,* 9 (2): 72–80.

Sparrow, P. and Budhwar, P. (1997) Competition and Change: Mapping the Indian HRM Recipe Against World-wide Patterns. *Journal of World Business,* 32 (3): 224–42.

Venkata Ratnam, C. S. (1996) *Industrial Relations in Indian States.* New Delhi: Global Business Press.

Venkata Ratnam, C. S. (2001) *Globalization and Labour–Management Relations: Dynamics of Change.* New Delhi: Response.

26

HRM in China

Fang Lee Cooke

Introduction

The approach to managing human resources has changed significantly in China over the last twenty-five years, as its transformation from a state-planned economy to a market-oriented economy continues. There is now a substantial body of literature that has captured the key characteristics of traditional HRM, or more precisely, personnel management, in China during the planned economy period and what fundamental changes have been taking place (e.g. Child, 1996; Cooke, 2005; Selmer, 1998; Warner, 1999, 2005). This chapter does not intend to review this body of literature at length. Instead, it focuses on some of the new developments in HR practices and critically assesses the likely impacts of these practices on organizations as well as employees. In addition, key issues related to employment regulations and workers' representation are reviewed.

This chapter consists of three main sections. The first provides an overview of the employment and HRM characteristics in China based on different ownership forms. These include, for example, the public sector, state-owned enterprises (SOEs), domestic privately owned enterprises, and multinational corporations (MNCs). China is a vast transitional economy that spreads across a wide spectrum. Firms of different ownership forms and business nature are likely to operate in considerably different product and labour market conditions and are consequently likely to adopt different approaches to HRM. It is therefore necessary to adopt a nuanced approach to explore the differences in HR practices across firms of different ownership forms and to understand what constraints and opportunities they may experience. The second section examines developments in a number of HR practices and evaluates the extent to which they differ from the Western approach. These include: performance management, enterprise culture management, and learning organization and innovation initiatives. The third section focuses on the employment legislation and labour relations aspect of HRM. It investigates the extent to which labour laws are effective in protecting workers' interests, what voice mechanisms are in place for workers' representation, and what HR initiatives are in place, if any, in managing equal opportunities and workforce diversity at the workplace level.

Major characteristics of employment and HRM in different ownership forms

The structure of employment in China has experienced fundamental changes since the mid-1980s. Perhaps the most significant change is the drastic reduction of state sector employment that has been accompanied by the emergence and expansion of a variety of ownership forms and the rapid growth of employment outside the state sector, including foreign-funded firms, domestic privately owned enterprises (POEs), self-employed businesses, and township and village enterprises (see Table 26.1). Although the state had been the predominant employer, providing employment to nearly 80 per cent of all urban employees until the end of the 1970s, it only provided employment to less than a quarter of the urban workers employed by the end of 2005 (see Table 26.1). This is a consequence of the decade-long downsizing and privatization of state-owned enterprises as part of the state sector restructuring programme. For those who remain employed in the state sector, the nature of their employment relations with their state employer has changed considerably, with marketization and a general reduction in the provision of workplace welfare benefits as the main features that are convergent to that experienced by the rest of the labour force in the country.

HRM practices are influenced by a number of national, industrial, organizational and individual factors (Boxall and Purcell, 2003). The effect of contingent factors is arguably more prominent across different types of business ownership in China because of the markedly different institutional environment under which these businesses operate (Cooke, 2005; Tsui et al., 2006). Table 26.2 summarizes some of the key characteristics and differences of HR practices across different ownership forms. For example, state-owned enterprises in general have a much longer company history and a strong tradition of socialist values that is reflected in their management practices. They have established company procedures and clear lines of control in the management structure, often driven down from the higher authority. Organizational leaders have less discretion in management decisions (Child, 1996; Tsui et al., 2006; Xin et al., 2002). SOEs have a relatively high level of workplace welfare provisions, although this has declined since the 1990s as part of the state sector reform. They have an espoused policy of trade union involvement and employee participation in enterprise decision making and management. In addition, they have high levels of trade union recognition and membership, although the effectiveness of the trade union has been questioned (Chan, 1998; Clarke, 2005; Ng and Warner, 1998; Taylor et al., 2003; White, 1996).

By contrast, prestigious MNCs and international joint ventures (JVs) have a much shorter company history. The majority of them have only been established since the 1980s when China opened up its state-planned economy. They tend to have more autonomy in managing their own business. Compared with SOEs and privately owned Chinese firms, they have more resources and a higher level of technology capacity and are more innovation-driven. Wage levels are generally higher in these firms and so is the level of training provision (Cooke, 2005). They are more able to recruit and retain well-qualified employees than Chinese-owned firms. However, compared with the state sector, there is a much lower level of recognition and influence of the trade union. They take a cautious approach to collective negotiation for fear of the wider implications for other subsidiaries of the MNC outside China and there is a relatively low level of employee participation and union involvement in decision making. Human resource policies are more established and performance-oriented in these firms than those in SOEs. A higher proportion of managers in these firms than those in other ownership forms have been educated in the West, and hence are more receptive to Western management theories and practices.

Table 26.1 Employment statistics by ownership in urban and rural areas in China* (figures in million persons)

Ownership	1978	1980	1985	1990	1995	1998	2000	2002	2005
Total	**401.52**	**423.61**	**498.73**	**647.49**	**680.65**	**706.37**	**720.85**	**737.40**	**758.25**
Number of urban employed persons	95.14	105.25	128.08	166.16	190.93	206.78	231.51	247.80	273.31
State-owned units	74.51	80.19	89.90	103.46	112.61	90.58	81.02	71.63	64.88
Collectively owned units	20.48	24.25	33.24	35.49	31.47	19.63	14.99	11.22	8.10
Cooperative units	–	–	–	–	–	1.36	1.55	1.61	1.88
Joint-ownership units	–	–	0.38	0.96	0.53	0.48	0.42	0.45	0.45
Limited liability corporations	–	–	–	–	–	4.84	6.87	10.83	17.50
Share holding corporations ltd.	–	–	–	–	3.17	4.10	4.57	5.38	6.99
Private enterprises	–	–	–	0.57	4.85	9.73	12.68	19.99	34.58
Units with funds from Hong Kong, Macao and Taiwan	–	–	–	0.04	2.72	2.94	3.10	3.67	5.57
Foreign-funded units	–	–	0.06	0.62	2.41	2.93	3.32	3.91	6.88
Self-employed individuals	0.15	0.81	4.50	6.14	15.60	22.59	21.36	22.69	27.78
Number of rural employed persons	306.38	318.36	370.65	472.93	488.54	492.79	489.34	489.60	484.94
Township and village enterprises	28.27	30.00	69.79	92.65	128.62	125.37	128.20	132.88	142.72
Private enterprises	–	–	–	1.13	4.71	7.37	11.39	14.11	23.66
Self-employed individuals	–	–	–	14.91	30.54	38.55	29.34	24.74	21.23

Source: adapted from China Statistical Yearbook, 2003, pp. 126–7; China Statistical Yearbook, 2006, p. 125.

*Since 1990, data on economically active population, the total employed persons and the subtotal of employed persons in urban and rural areas have been adjusted in accordance with the data obtained from the 5th National Population Census. As a result, the sum of the data by region, by ownership or by sector is not equal to the total (original note from China Statistical Yearbook, 2003, p. 123).

Table 26.2 Key characteristics of HRM in different ownership forms

HR practices	Government and civil service organizations	State-owned enterprises	Privately owned enterprises	Prestigious MNCs and joint ventures
Job security	Relatively high	Continuous downsizing and privatization	Fixed-term contract employment the norm	Relatively high
Performance management	Hard as well as 'soft' criteria Performance outcome more difficult to measure Performance outcome linked to promotion and annual bonus Emphasis of moral behaviour and loyalty to the Party Egalitarianism	Performance management becoming more widely adopted due to pressure of competition Performance outcome closely linked to financial reward Some emphasis of behavioural norms in performance assessment Egalitarianism	Relatively easier to conduct appraisal due to more specific purpose and measurable criteria Performance criteria productivity oriented Performance appraisal outcome closely linked to financial reward	A more comprehensive approach to performance management Performance outcome linked to reward as well as training and development needs
Financial reward and benefits	Pay level determined by the state Relatively good welfare provision	Pay determination influenced by the state but largely determined by management at workplace level Diminishing welfare provision	Performance-related pay widely adopted Limited welfare provision	Relatively high wage level compared with other sectors A variety of welfare provision

Training and development	Relatively high level of training and development, with a heavy focus on political studies Workforce generally well educated	Skill training mainly available to professional and managerial staff and technical workers Workforce reasonably well educated	Relatively low level of skill training and career opportunity in comparison with other ownership forms Workforce less well educated compared with other ownership forms	Relatively high level of skills training and more opportunities for career development Workforce generally very well educated Ability to attract and retain talent as 'employers of choice'
Organizational culture management	Very cautious adaptation of Western practices due to sectoral and ideological differences	Welfare and relational management-oriented Heavily influenced by socialist and Chinese cultural values	Performance as well as relational management-oriented Influenced by Chinese cultural values as well as Western practices	Performance and procedural management-oriented Heavily influenced by Western practices
Labour relations	Harmonious Little role for trade unions due to lack of identification with unionism from the employees	Rising level of labour disputes as a result of reform Relatively high level of union recognition, but trade unions mainly playing a welfare role	Relatively high level of labour disputes Low level of union recognition due to persistent management resistance	Relatively low level of labour disputes Low level of union recognition, partnership approach adopted where union is recognized

Privately owned Chinese enterprises have been a major source of employment and economic growth in the last twenty years. This is despite the fact that the majority of them are relatively small compared with SOEs and MNCs. POEs tend to have stronger adaptability to market trends because of their relatively simple product structure and technology. They are highly profit driven and therefore more adventurous and opportunistic. These businesses tend to have a more flexible utilization of human resources. The level of union recognition is generally low, with weak bargaining power from the workers and a high level of management/ owner prerogative. Workplace welfare provisions are limited and formal HR policies are often absent. Nevertheless, there are signs that a number of top-performing POEs are beginning to see the importance of strategic management of human resources to gain competitive advantage. They tend to adopt a high-commitment model of HRM that emphasizes employee training and development, cultivation of innovativeness, performance-related reward to incentivize individual performance, promotion by competence, and extensive employee welfare provision (Cooke, 2008a; Liu and Xu, 2004).

New developments in HR practices

Since the turn of the twenty-first century, the notion of HRM has gained much popularity in China. Performance management, team building, organizational culture management, employee involvement, knowledge management, and learning organization are amongst the growing number of HR initiatives that feature regularly in management writings and corporate HR policy statements. These initiatives are often promoted as advanced Western HR techniques, although some of them have long existed in China in primitive forms. In this section, we will examine the implementation of three of these initiatives – performance management, organizational culture management, and learning organization.

Performance management

Since the 1990s, performance appraisal systems have been more widely and systematically adopted by organizations than in the past.[1] For example, Björkman and Lu's (1999) study of 72 foreign-invested enterprises in China found that nearly half of them had adapted their Western performance appraisal system to suit the Chinese culture. Ding et al.'s (1997: 611) study of 158 foreign-invested enterprises in southern China showed that 'regular evaluation of individual employee performance and setting employee pay levels based on individual performance have become organizational norms'. They also found that workers were receptive to individually oriented performance measurement and reward in order to maximize their income. Lindholm's (1999) survey of 604 Chinese managerial and professional employees from MNCs in China found that they were satisfied with the Western-style performance management system adopted in their company. They particularly liked the developmental approach in the system and were keen to participate in setting their performance objectives and receiving formal performance feedback. It must be noted that prestigious MNCs in China are attractive to those who have strong career aspirations and desire development opportunities. Bai and Bennington's (2005) more recent study of SOEs in the coal mining industry revealed that as a result of increasing pressure from intensified market competition, SOEs were utilizing modern performance appraisal measures as effective tools to enhance their management efficiency and productivity. Their study showed that whilst differences from Western performance appraisal practices persist, significant changes were taking place in performance appraisal practices in China that depart from the traditional form. Performance management has also become a top priority in the management of government and civil service organizations since the mid-1990s, as part of the state's broader initiative of reforming its civil service function. Many municipal governments have adopted a 'management by objective' scheme in which performance targets are cascaded down from each level and reviewed on an annual basis (Cooke, 2008b).

Whilst sharing some similarities, the performance management system applied to ordinary employees tends to differ from that for professional/managerial staff. These differences become even more marked between enterprises and government/civil service organizations. Generally speaking, performance appraisal for ordinary workers was mainly about linking their productivity and level of responsibility with their wage and bonuses in order to motivate them to work towards the organizational goals. This is in spite of the fact that an employee's moral behaviour continues to be part of the appraisal in many SOEs. By contrast, results of performance appraisals for professional and managerial staff, particularly those in government and civil service organizations, are often linked to annual bonuses and promotion. The state also has a much more hands-on role in designing the performance indicators for government officials and civil servants. Broadly speaking, performance appraisals for ordinary employees in enterprises tend to be held on a more regular basis than for government officials and civil servants. This is mainly because the outcome of the former is often directly linked to the appraisee's financial reward and job security. Appraisal methods used for ordinary employees in enterprises are also simpler, and occur mainly between the supervisor and the individual being appraised. By comparison, annual performance appraisal is the norm in government and civil service organizations. The performance appraisal procedure adopted is more sophisticated. It normally involves the initial self-appraisal, followed by a peer appraisal discussion meeting held collectively in the department as an act of democracy, and concluded with the department leader's comments in the annual review form.

Performance appraisal is perhaps one of the HRM practices that display the most enduring influence of Chinese culture. It has been widely noted that the Chinese culture respects seniority and hierarchy, values social harmony, and adopts an egalitarian approach to distribution (Hofstede, 1991; Takahara, 1992; Yu, 1998). Similarly, egalitarianism has long been recognized as a unique Chinese societal culture and continues to be used by some as a yardstick of fairness and equity in rewards, especially in the distribution of bonuses. Since performance appraisal in China is often narrowly related to financial reward and promotion instead of training and development needs, these Chinese norms play a particularly influential role throughout the appraisal stages. The Chinese cultural norm of modesty and self-discipline (Bailey et al., 1997) is also reflected in the appraisal system because self-evaluation and criticism often forms part of the appraisal process and content, particularly in government and civil service organizations. However, it must be pointed out that changes in cultural outlook are taking place in China. For example, Bai and Bennington's (2005) study revealed that the Chinese cultural values did not impede the implementation of individual performance-related reward schemes, suggesting that the new materialism has overtaken traditional cultural forces. The implementation of a performance management system in China encounters a number of pitfalls and challenges. Some of them are universal, others accentuated by Chinese cultural values. These include, for example, lack of a strategic HRM mindset, insufficient understanding of and managerial competence for performance management, performance appraisal seen as a formality, and intervention of subjectivity in performance appraisals.

In general, the traditional performance appraisal system in China is reward driven and tends to focus on the person and behavioural performance, whereas the performance appraisal system promoted in Western HRM literature takes a developmental approach and focuses on the alignment between individual performance and organizational goals. Nevertheless, recent studies on performance appraisal practices in China have detected a discernible trend that an increasing number of Chinese organizations are adopting a Western-style performance management system. Whilst a total transfer of Western practices is not found, or indeed possible, a unique blending of both modernizing and traditional forces is at play in shaping the new performance management practices (Bailey et al., 1997). The continuing trend of adaptation of Western performance management practices is likely to lead to further behavioural changes in Chinese managers and employees that depart from traditional Chinese cultural norms exhibited in the Chinese-style performance appraisal system.

Organizational culture management

Organizational culture management, often known as 'enterprise culture building', is another HR initiative that is being promoted in China as a new import of Western HR technique. The practice of enterprise culture building is in fact nothing new. As Chan (1995) observed, many so-called 'Japanese management techniques' adopted by Chinese enterprises, such as morning briefings, had existed in China during the state-planned economy period. Cooke's (2008c) analysis of 82 case study reports of companies that have adopted the enterprise culture management (ECM) initiative revealed that ECM activities can be categorized into six broad types. They are: 'employee welfare', 'employee entertainment', 'productivity enhancement', 'enterprise external relationship/image', 'enterprise procedures and rules' and 'employee development'. *Employee welfare* focuses on the material welfare and physical well-being of employees. *Employee entertainment* includes a series of workplace entertainment provisions, such as sports events, arts competitions, theatrical performances, etc. to satisfy a higher level of needs. These activities are aimed to enhance the employees' quality of life in order to retain and motivate them. Some enterprises also have a more sophisticated agenda in the provision of these activities – to influence the ideological development of employees so that they conform to the enterprise's cultural value. *Productivity enhancement* activities include quality improvement schemes (e.g., ISO 9000), problem-solving teams, innovation, employee involvement and suggestion schemes, continuous improvement of plant and production processes, and customer care initiatives. Skill and craftsmanship competitions, quality and productivity competitions, and technical collaborations are promoted in order to raise the skill level and productivity of employees as well as the quality standard of products. *Enterprise external relationship/image* activities are designed to project a desired external image of management style, employees' behaviour, product and service quality, and ultimately the image and reputation of the enterprise. These are achieved through a range of deliberate enterprise image-building activities including participation in local public events and competitions, charity functions, sponsorships and donations, trade fairs and exhibitions, media publicity, and collaboration with other enterprises. Enterprises also invest heavily in enhancing the physical layout of the workplace through uniform, badge, logo, modern construction, trendy refurbishment and well-maintained gardens. They are essentially corporate branding activities that are also aimed to enhance the employees' identification with and commitment to the company. *Enterprise procedures and rules* are implemented mainly through the systemization of workplace procedures and specifications of behavioural norms at the workplace. The objective of these procedures and rules is to ensure that employees' behaviour conforms to the enterprise's regulations and that the responsibilities of each individual are clearly defined. Some companies are well aware of the fact that this represents a hard approach to eliciting required employee behaviour and that this approach needs to be coupled with a softer approach to gain the acceptance of employees. There are two aspects to *employee development*. One is the development of technical skills and educational standards of the employees. These are usually carried out through skill training to enable employees to raise their skill levels and general educational courses to enhance their educational qualification level. The other is the development of employees' ideological thinking. This is usually achieved by setting role models, moral teaching of the socialist and enterprise values, and enterprise history education for new employees. It is believed that these measures will enhance the consciousness of the workers and shape their ideology to be in line with that promoted by the socialist state and the enterprise.

Productivity enhancement and employee development are the two major foci of enterprises in their culture management, particularly in quality enhancement, innovation, customer care and skill upgrading of employees. This suggests that productivity and quality rather than employee welfare are the primary concern of enterprises. In addition, the content of enterprise culture in SOEs, particularly in the employee care and welfare aspects, carries strong traces of their historical background as socialist enterprises. In comparison, MNCs and JVs focus far more on productivity enhancement and company procedures than on other types of enterprise culture activities.

Research evidence suggests that the content of organizational culture in China is more strongly influenced by the Chinese cultural values than by the Western values in general, but the degree of influence of each may vary depending on the institutional and cultural environment both the organizational leader and the company are subject to (Cooke, 2008c; Xin et al., 2002). The concept of ECM seems to have taken on different interpretations and manifestations of its meaning. Taken together, enterprise culture in China appears to be a complex and multi-layered social system that places more emphasis on relationship building than performance outcome. It may be a set of traditional values rediscovered and modified to suit current needs. It may be politicized as socialist moral teaching and prescribed as the espoused ideology of those in control. It may be seen as equivalent to enterprise management practices and HRM and promoted as an effective management strategy. It may be adopted as a superficial fashion due to isomorphic effect and has no real impact on the organization's performance enhancement. Whilst the substantive components of enterprise culture reflect distinct characteristics of Chinese societal values and tradition, the adoption of enterprise culture initiatives in China seems to share the same approach to that in Western societies. That is, the conceptualization of culture appears to be functionalist, normative, and instrumentally biased (Schein, 1989) in which 'culture is seen as a pattern of basic assumption that has "proved" to be valid for a group coping with problems of external adaptation and internal integration' (Alvesson, 1995: 28). What remains unknown is the extent to which the Chinese workers identify themselves with the organizational culture management initiatives and what impact they may have on the workers.

Developing a learning organization and an innovative workforce

China is suffering from a worsening skill shortage, in part because of its unprecedented rapid economic development but also because of its insufficient investment in enterprise training and inadequate provision of vocational training. The shortage of skilled workers has become a bottleneck in the manufacturing industry. Similarly, the lack of managerial talent has been widely noted to have negative effects on China's economic development (e.g. Child, 1996; Chwee, 1999; Ralston et al., 1997; Smith and Wang, 1997; Zhang et al., 2004). Many enterprises ignore the importance of investment in human capital and do not invest sufficiently in training. According to a survey conducted by the Ministry of Labour and Insurance on enterprises in 40 cities, the overall investment in enterprise training was reported by the employers to be 1.4 per cent of the total wage bill, slightly below the state requirement of 1.5 per cent which is already lower than the 2–4 per cent level in developed countries. Nearly 60 per cent of the employers reported that less than 20 per cent of the investment was actually spent on the training of skilled workers (Mo, 2004). The same survey also showed that at least 30 per cent of the enterprises paid only lip service to employee education and training, with an annual training budget of less than US$2 per person.

Nevertheless, in the last two decades, considerable amounts of efforts and resources have been invested in the training and development of managerial and professional workers by the state (Cooke, 2005). One of the more recent initiatives is the *chuangzheng* initiative: 'to build' ('*chuang*') a learning organization, to be ('*zheng*') a 'knowledge worker'. It is a high-profile, nation-wide and state-led initiative launched in December 2003 to promote learning, skill enhancement and innovation (*Workers' Daily*, 19 October 2004). Enterprises are encouraged to adopt a wide variety of forms of learning, including self-study, technological innovation, skills and performance contests, on-the-job training and problem-solving teams. It is hoped that these mechanisms will provide a learning environment to motivate employees to acquire new knowledge and skills (*Workers' Daily*, 19 October 2004). These activities share two similar characteristics: to raise employees' skill level through training and competition, and to harness employees' innovative ideas through participation and suggestion schemes. The objective is to increase productivity and organizational competitiveness. This has resulted in a renewed enthusiasm in skill competitions and employee participation schemes in innovations in enterprises.

Many of the 'learning organization' practices adopted have actually long existed in SOEs in China. For example, the promotion of 'role models' has been a favourite approach adopted by the Chinese socialist state to convey its ideology and behavioural norms. Skill and craftsmanship competition has long been part of the enterprise life in SOEs dating back to the early 1950s as an important means to boost workforce morale and to raise the level of skills and productivity during the early period of economic development of socialist China. There has long been a culture of employee involvement (e.g. suggestion schemes and problem-solving teams) in larger and aspiring SOEs in the improvization and innovation of production technology and production process. More broadly, continuous learning and self-development has for centuries been regarded as a virtue in the Chinese culture which has inspired people to undertake learning activities after they have completed their formal education and beyond their workplace requirement.

However, the notion of a 'learning organization' is a new import of Western management philosophy and technique. To some extent, the prescriptive and unitary approach to learning organizations matches the traditional, paternalistic and unitarist Chinese management style in which employees are expected to treat the company as their family (Cooke, 2005). The modelling of 'learning organizations' adopted by Chinese organizations suggests that they see 'learning organization' as 'learning at work' where individuals learn at work on a continuous basis rather than through formalized courses. They also assume a 'learning climate' perspective in which a 'learning organization' is one that facilitates its employees to learn and to develop themselves through a supportive environment. This is in line with the second and third of Ortenblad's (2002) four typologies of learning organizations. However, the unitarist approach typical of the Chinese management style carries a strong element of coerciveness and simplicity in which commitment, compliance and malleability of employee behaviour are taken for granted. While participation and empowerment are key elements of a learning organization, the Chinese management style and culture may not be conducive to 'ownership' or 'empowerment' (Elsey and Leung, 2004). Despite the fact that task forces and problem-solving teams have long existed in SOEs to tackle specific technological and production problems and to undertake workplace innovations, these are largely elite teams that consist of a small number of highly motivated and skilled persons. There is no evidence that employee involvement en masse is a commonly adopted practice at workplaces. Whilst the state-driven *chuangzheng* learning initiative has undoubtedly encouraged an increasing number of organizations to adopt the notion of learning organization, there is a danger that companies are just following it as a management fashion without a proper understanding of what it really means for them. Whether lifelong learning and creativity is now embedded at the workplace remains debatable.

Nonetheless, the 'learning organization' initiative represents another step forward by Chinese management towards a more systematic approach to human resource management and innovation. It is an example of Chinese management's readiness to adopt Western management techniques, at least in name if not in practice. An important management implication is that a more informed and strategic approach is needed when designing and implementing the learning organization initiative. In other words, the initiative has to be part of the business strategy. Adequate support systems, both technical and psychological, have to be in place to facilitate learning and knowledge management. This requires organizational leaders to be more strategic, a requirement that may be challenging for the Chinese managers because management competence is considered relatively low in China, especially at the strategic level.

Employment regulations and employee representation

The landscape of employment relations in China has experienced significant changes over the last two decades, with a proliferation of categories of workers with different needs and expectations that are 'neither represented nor often officially recognized' (Howell, 1998: 153). In light of the diversification of ownership forms, the rapid growth of the private sector, the emergent labour market, and the rising number of unemployed and laid-off workers, the state has issued a series of employment-related regulations in order to regulate the labour market and to offer a level of employment protection to workers. As a result, the majority of the employment regulations in China have been issued in the last twenty years. Major labour regulations include: the Labour Law of China (1995) which provides the main framework of employment regulations; the Trade Union Law (1950, amended 2001) which sets out the scope of responsibilities of the trade unions; the Provisions Concerning the Administration of the Labour Market (2000) which sets out the basic principles for the governance of the labour market; and the Labour Contract Law (2008) which provides more employment protections to workers, particularly in job security and payment. Other regulations include: a series of gender-related regulations in order to improve gender equality in employment; the minimum wage regulations issued in 1993; training regulations; and the 'Temporary Provision for Collective Wage Negotiation' issued by the Ministry of Labour and Social Security at the end of 2000. In addition, each sector (e.g. the civil service, foreign firms, and joint ventures) is issued sector-specific regulations.

These regulations in principle set out the minimum labour standards and provide a legal framework under which labour disputes can be resolved. For instance, all employers are now required by the Labour Law of China (1995) and the Labour Contract Law (2008) to sign an employment contract with their workers, by adapting a standardized employment contract provided by the local labour authority. Employers are required to specify in the contract any other clauses that are not included in the standardized contract. The contract also specifies the employment rights for workers concerning unfair dismissal, and whistleblowing on employers' malpractices. Since the mid-1990s, enterprises have been encouraged by the state to establish a legally binding collective negotiation system, an area in which trade unions are expected to play an important part. It has been argued that collective negotiation is the kind of industrial relations that the Chinese government and the All-China Federation of Trade Unions (ACFTU) have hoped for – 'one that is regulated by collective bargaining without being confrontational, and without politically independent unionism' (Chan, 1998: 124). However, the legislative impact on collective labour protection remains controversial. It has been argued that the Labour Law of China places emphasis on individual labour relations instead of collective relations (Cheng, 2004) and that the collective negotiation system promoted by the state since the mid-1990s proves to be largely a meaningless paper exercise that offers little real protection to the workers (Clarke et al., 2004). In the process of achieving a collective contract, there is rarely any real negotiation with little substantive content listed in the contract (Taylor et al., 2003).

One unique feature of China's burgeoning economic development has been the extensive participation of the rural migrant workers, who make up over 46 per cent of the workforce in the manufacturing and service sectors (*Workers' Daily*, 9 November 2004). Rural migrant workers are the largest and most needy social group requiring labour protection in the urban area but are the least unionized. How to organize and represent the rural migrant workers to protect their rights and interests has become a pressing issue and a focal point in the political and social policy agenda in China. Despite their indispensable contribution to China's urbanization and rapid economic development, rural migrant workers enjoy very few labour rights, and where rights exist, they tend not to be actively enforced (Cooke, 2005). As a result, the vast majority of the migrant workers work and live under very poor conditions (Chan, 2001; Gallaghar, 2005; Ngai and Smith, 2007; Xu, 2000). ACFTU's response to the growing force of migrant labour has been through various stages from the initial exclusion to accommodation and more recent attempts at organization and representation. Due to persistent resistance from the employers, grassroot trade unions have not been able to establish a presence in the majority of the sites where rural migrant workers are employed. Grassroot unions' lack of political power and professional competence also contributes to their perceived inefficacy in improving employment terms and conditions and ultimately workers' disinterest in workplace unionism. As a result, distant expansion, i.e. operating outside workplaces, remains the main channel for trade unions to reach workers, with packages of services (e.g. job market information and legal support) as inducements to attract members.

Women workers represent another disadvantaged group in the labour market. China has one of the highest women's employment participation rates in the world. More than 38 per cent of its full-time workforce in urban units are women. The majority of them work full-time, including those with childcare responsibilities. A series of regulations and administrative policies have been introduced by the state since 1949 in order to protect women's employment rights. These provisions have made significant impacts on improving women's employment and career prospects. However, the continuous advancement of women in their education and professional/managerial careers has not yet led to genuine equality between men and women. This is despite the fact that China has achieved possibly greater gender equality than industrial capitalist societies (Stockman et al., 1995). At the management level, a much smaller proportion of women than men are in leadership positions or in the professional and technical personnel category. For example, only 0.7 per cent of women worked as heads of organizations in 2004, compared with 2.5 per cent of men who did so. Only 5.7 per cent of women were in the professional technical personnel category whereas 8.4 per cent of men were in this category. Discriminatory practices exist in recruitment, job allocation, training, promotion, redundancy and retirement, in part as a result of the slack enforcement of employment laws (Cooke, 2005). Few organizations have an equal opportunity policy and a career development policy in place as part of their HR policy.

The demographic characteristics of the disadvantaged groups in the labour market and the HR environment of China have different implications for MNCs. On the one hand, exploitative employment practices are rampant in labour-intensive foreign-funded (including Hong Kong and Taiwan funded) sweatshop factories. They have had the highest share of labour disputes, disproportionate to their share in employment, and the number of cases has risen sharply throughout the 1990s (Cooke, 2005). On the other hand, prestigious MNCs, though a small but growing number in China, may encounter barriers in their attempt to implement a progressive global HR policy, such as equal opportunities, or managing workforce diversity and inclusiveness initiatives. In Western countries, issues related to the diversity of the workforce may include gender, race, ethnicity, religion, age, disability, immigration status, social class, political association, marital status and sexual orientation. Many of these differences are accepted by Western society and protected by law and company policy. By contrast, the concept of managing diversity is relatively new to China; many employing organizations may never have heard of the phrase. Inequality at the workplace and in society generally is often accepted and unchallenged. This gives rise to different needs and focus in managing workforce diversity. For example, discrimination against (rural) migrant workers in China is widespread both in policy and in informal practice. One of the key issues in managing diversity in China is therefore the harmonization of groups of workers from different geographical areas, particularly across the rural–urban divide. Equally, where MNCs outsource their recruitment function to local recruitment agency firms, which is an increasingly common practice of MNCs, the MNCs' corporate attempt to uphold a gender equality policy may be circumvented by the local outsourcing provider's discriminatory practices, informed by a local social attitude in which women are deemed less productive than men due to their family commitment.

Summary

This chapter has provided an overview of the key aspects of HRM in China. Given space constraints and the significant differences in HRM across regions, sectors and ownership forms in a vast economy that spans a wide spectrum, massive simplification is inevitable and important areas remain uncovered. It is clear that radical changes have taken place in the country's business and employment environment, resulting in a rising level of management–labour disputes on the one hand, and a widespread adoption/adaptation of Western HRM practices on the other. These imports are indicative of Chinese management's quest for effective management tools and their desire to be seen as modern and connected with the world. The danger is that these Western practices are often embraced uncritically as new techniques and 'holy grails', while in fact some variations of them have long existed in China and the implementation of these techniques, (e.g. performance management), suffers similar problems to those in the West. Nevertheless, it is evident that Chinese employees in enterprises are becoming more receptive towards performance-oriented rewards and welcome career development opportunities through the implementation of a performance management system. Research evidence on organizational culture management also suggests that paternalism is a unique feature in Chinese firms' approach to HRM, with typical Chinese cultural values that emphasize unification, integrity, harmonization, moral teaching and role model setting. At the same time, they also adopt a normative approach that focuses on procedures and impartiality – indicating a break away from nepotism in principle.

In short, there is no doubt that the approach to and substance of HRM have changed considerably in the last two decades. HRM is receiving more, albeit still insufficient, attention from organizational leaders as a key to enhancing organizational competitiveness. However, the majority of organizations have yet to adopt a strategic approach to HRM to gain sustainable competitive advantage. Many organizations still lack a well-designed HR strategy that forms an integral part of the business strategy. How to retain talent and incentivize performance of key employees remain two key challenges to organizations, with pay rises and promotion appearing to be the main solution commonly adopted that is only partially effective. The HR department remains primarily an administrative department instead of being a strategic partner of the business. The majority of HR personnel have not received professional HR training. HR degree qualification courses only started to emerge in the twenty-first century, although the development in this area is rapid. Furthermore, there is a need for a serious debate, informed by research studies, amongst academics and practitioners in China as to how Western HRM practices can be best applied to the Chinese context, and how China can develop its own set of HRM practices that combines the strengths of the East and West in a way that is appropriate for its institutional and cultural environment.

Note

1 See Zhu and Dowling (1998) for a more detailed overview of performance management system in China.

References

Alvesson, M. (1995), *Cultural Perspectives on Organizations*, Cambridge: Cambridge University Press.
Bai, X. and Bennington, L. (2005), 'Performance appraisal in the Chinese state-owned coal industry', *International Journal of Business Performance Management*, 7, 3, pp. 275–87.
Bailey, J., Chen, C. and Dou, S. (1997), 'Conceptions of self and performance-related feedback in the US, Japan and China', *Journal of International Business Studies*, 28, 3, pp. 605–25.
Björkman, I. and Lu, Y. (1999), 'A corporate perspective on the management of human resources in China', *Journal of World Business*, 34, 1, pp. 16–25.
Boxall, P. and Purcell, J. (2003), *Strategy and Human Resource Management*, Basingstoke: Palgrave Macmillan.
Chan, A. (1995), 'Chinese enterprise reforms: Convergence with the Japanese model?', *Industrial and Corporate Change*, 4, 2, pp. 449–70.
Chan, A. (1998), 'Labour regulations in foreign-funded ventures, Chinese trade unions, and the prospects for collective bargaining', in O'Leary, G. (ed.), *Adjusting to Capitalism: Chinese Workers and the State*, New York: M. E. Sharpe, pp. 122–49.
Chan, A. (2001), *China's Workers under Assault: The Exploitation of Labour in a Globalising Economy*, New York: M. E. Sharpe.
Cheng, Y. Y. (2004), 'The development of labour disputes and the regulation of industrial relations in China', *The International Journal of Comparative Labour Law and Industrial Relations*, 20, 2, pp. 277–95.
Child, J. (1996), *Management in China during the Age of Reform*, Cambridge: Cambridge University Press, paperback edition.
China Statistical Yearbook (2003), Beijing: China Statistics Publishing House.
China Statistical Yearbook (2006), Beijing: China Statistics Publishing House.
Chwee, W. (1999), 'Individual and organisational learning of Chinese executives at Compaq China', *Advances in Developing Human Resources*, 4, pp. 69–82.
Clarke, S., Lee, C. H. and Li, Q. (2004), 'Collective consultation and industrial relations in China', *British Journal of Industrial Relations*, 42, 2, pp. 235–54.
Clarke, S. (2005), 'Post-socialist trade unions: China and Russia', *Industrial Relations Journal*, 36, 1, pp. 2–18.
Cooke, F. L. (2005), *HRM, Work and Employment in China*, London: Routledge.
Cooke, F. L. (2008a), *Competition, Strategy and Human Resource in China*, Basingstoke: Palgrave Macmillan.
Cooke, F. L. (2008b), 'Performance management systems in China', in Varma, A. and Budhwar, P. (eds.), *Performance Management Systems around the Globe*, London: Routledge.
Cooke, F. L. (2008c), 'Enterprise culture management in China: What is in the "tool kit"?' *Management and Organization Review*, 4, 2, pp. 291–314.

Ding, D., Field, D. and Akhtar, S. (1997), 'An empirical study of human resource management policies and practices in foreign-invested enterprises in China: The case of Shenzhen Special Economic Zone', *International Journal of Human Resource Management*, 8, 5, pp. 595–613.

Elsey, B. and Leung, J. (2004), 'Changing the work behaviour of Chinese employees using organisational learning', *The Journal of Workplace Learning*, 16, 3, pp. 167–78.

Gallagher, M. (2005), *Contagious Capitalism: Globalisation and the Politics of Labour in China*, Princeton: Princeton University Press.

Hofstede, G. (1991), *Cultures and Organizations: Software of the Mind*, Berkshire: McGraw-Hill Book Company.

Howell, J. (1998), 'Trade unions in China: The challenge of foreign capital', in O'Leary, G. (ed.), *Adjusting to Capitalism: Chinese Workers and the State*, New York: M. E. Sharpe, pp. 150–72.

Lindholm, N. (1999), 'Performance management in MNC subsidiaries in China: A study of host-country managers and professionals', *Asia Pacific Journal of Human Resources*, 37, 3, pp. 18–35.

Liu, Y. Q. and Xu, Z. X. (2004), *Report on the Competitiveness of Non-state-owned Enterprises No. 1: Competitive Quality and Competitiveness Index*, Beijing: Social Sciences Academic Press.

Mo, R. (2004), 'Shortages of rural migrant labour and skilled workers in the context of labour market over-supply', in Yu, X., Lu, X.Y., Li, P. L., Huang, P. and Lu, J. H. (eds.), *Analysis and Forecast on China's Social Development (2005)*, Beijing: Social Sciences Academic Press, pp. 260–72.

Ng, S. H. and Warner, M. (1998), *China's Trade Unions and Management*, London: Macmillan.

Ngai, P. and Smith, C. (2007), 'Putting transnational labour process in its place: The dormitory labour regime in post-socialist China', *Work, Employment and Society*, 21, 1, pp. 47–65.

Ortenblad, A. (2002), 'A typology of the idea of learning organisation', *Management Learning*, 33, 2, pp. 213–30.

Ralston, D., Holt, D., Terpstra, R. and Cheng, Y. K. (1997), 'The impact of national culture and economic ideology on managerial work values: A study of the United States, Russia, Japan and China', *Journal of International Business Studies*, 28, 1, pp. 177–207.

Schein, E. (1989), *Organizational Culture and Leadership*, San Francisco, CA: Jossey-Bass.

Selmer, J. (ed.) (1998), *International Management in China: Cross-cultural Issues*, London: Routledge.

Smith, P. and Wang, Z. M. (1997), 'Leadership, decision-making and cultural context: Event management within Chinese joint ventures', *Leadership Quarterly*, 8, 4, pp. 413–31.

Stockman, N., Bonney, N. and Sheng, X. (1995), *Women's Work in East and West: The Dual Burden of Employment and Family Life*, London: UCL Press.

Takahara, A. (1992), *The Politics of Wage Policy in Post-revolutionary China*, London: Macmillan.

Taylor, B., Chang, K. and Li, Q. (2003), *Industrial Relations in China*, Cheltenham: Edward Elgar.

Tsui, A., Zhang, Z., Wang, H., Xin, K. and Wu, J. (2006), 'Unpacking the relationship between CEO leadership behavior and organizational culture', *The Leadership Quarterly*, 17, 2, pp. 113–37.

Warner, M. (ed.) (1999), *China's Managerial Revolution*, London: Frank Cass.

Warner, M. (ed.) (2005), *Human Resource Management in China Revisited*, London: Routledge.

White, G. (1996), 'Chinese trade unions in the transition from Socialism: Towards corporatism or civil society?', *British Journal of Industrial Relations* 34, 3, pp. 433–57.

Workers' Daily, 19 October 2004.

Workers' Daily, 9 November 2004.

Xin, K., Tsui, A., Wang, H., Zhang, Z. and Chen, W. (2002), 'Corporate culture in state-owned enterprises: An indicative analysis of dimensions and influences', in Tsui, A. and Lau, C. M. (eds.), *The Management of Enterprises in the People's Republic of China*, London: Kluwer Academic Press, pp. 415–41.

Xu, F. (2000), *Women Migrant Workers in China's Economic Reform*, New York: Macmillan.

Yu, K. C. (1998), 'Chinese employees' perceptions of distributive fairness', in Francesco, A. M. and Gold, B. A. (eds.), *International Organisational Behavior*, New Jersey: Prentice Hall, pp. 302–13.

Zhang, D., Zhang, Z. and Yang, B. (2004), 'Learning organisation in mainland China: Empirical research on its applications to Chinese state-owned enterprises', *International Journal of Training and Development*, 8, 4, pp. 258–73.

Zhu, C. and Dowling, P. (1998), 'Performance appraisal in China', in Selmer, J. (ed.), *International Management in China: Cross-cultural Issues*, London: Routledge, pp. 115–36.

461

27

Managing human resources in Africa

Emergent market challenges

Frank M. Horwitz

Introduction

Other than in South African firms and some multinational energy firms, managing people strategically in Africa is a rare but insistent need. This chapter explores emergent strategic human resource management (SHRM) themes considering (1) the extent to which good HRM practice is converging on the continent, (2) HRM implications of structural adjustment programs, (3) cross-cultural issues in HRM, (4) diffusion of HRM, (5) cultural and managerial styles, (6) employment relations, and (7) the HR implications of HIV/AIDS.

SHRM research concentrates on the West and the East, initially on comparative Japanese studies and more recently on international HRM (IHRM) issues in China and India. The debate on HRM in Africa has languished somewhere between these two geographical spaces. This is understandable given that Africa was once dubbed the 'hopeless continent' (*The Economist* 2001). There is also a paucity of published work on SHRM in transitional economies (Horwitz et al. 2006, Zupan and Kase 2005). This chapter provides a comparative overview of HRM in the African context, drawing conclusions about the enabling role of multinational corporations (MNCs) in SHRM. Positively, there is more work on economic development, trade and foreign aid and increasingly now on human capital issues. This signals some significant priorities for Africa: around socio-economic development, employment creation, skills development and the eradication of poverty (Kamoche et al. 2004: 1–2).

Sweeping 'Afro-pessimistic' generalizations about the continent ignore unique features of each country. The diversity of Africa cuts across many dimensions. Ethnically, with some 2,000 different ethno-cultural communities it is wrong to assume homogeneity within specific countries. Notwithstanding this cultural diversity, a principal division of Africa into two can be made: sub-Saharan Africa with its multiplicity of African cultures, and the northern countries which are predominantly Arabic (Carmichael and Rijamampianina 2006). Sub-Saharan Africa is also largely Christian with indigenous, strongly collectivist and masculine (in a Hofsteden (1991) sense) and humanistic (versus instrumental) African cultural precepts such as Ubuntu, a notion that selfhood is a function of relations and identity with others (Jackson 2004, Mbigi 2000). However, with modernity, economic development and growth and increased urbanization, there is evidence of a shift towards stronger individualism and instrumental values. Diversity in Africa is not only based on race or culture but also on religious, linguistic and sub-cultural features. The legacy influence of former colonial regimes on language and culture remains pertinent to organizational behaviour and managerial practices. Institutional and cultural factors may also influence the extent of convergence or divergence in these practices (Wright et al. 2005).

Today the stereotype of Africa as a 'lost continent' is becoming increasingly misplaced, though most countries still have massive human resource and other development challenges (Kamoche et al. 2004: xvi). Until recently Africa attracted less than 2 percent of the world's FDI and of this four countries including South Africa, Nigeria and Egypt attracted most of it (Luiz 2006). Yet Africa is experiencing the highest GDP growth, of 5.2 percent, in its history (Naidoo 2006). Whilst lower than the huge inflow of foreign direct investment (FDI) to China, the latter country signed 14 agreements worth US$1.9 billion for projects in infrastructure, telecommunications and other fields with African countries in 2006, with two-way trade expected to reach US$50 billion, a five-fold increase since 2000 (*Argus* 2006a). China, with an interest in Africa's raw materials such as coal and oil, has become the largest foreign investor in Africa in the past five years. A deal to build a US$8.3 billion railway line in oil-rich Nigeria has been announced together with joint Chinese-African exploration of energy development. China has cancelled US$10 billion in bilateral debt forgiveness with African countries. Trade tariff reduction and training and development programs as well as further infrastructural development are part of regular policy-level talks between China and African governments including South Africa, Angola and Nigeria. Africa in 2006 also attained the largest increase in tourism growth at 10.6 percent, making it the highest growth region in the world for tourism. Sub-Saharan Africa in spite of its poverty may begin to see some relief in this regard with a 12.6 percent rise in tourism in 2006 (*Argus* 2006b).

Strategically the question is whether the continent is beginning to experience a turn-around and, importantly, what HR challenges need to be addressed. Most poignant is whether African countries including the more developed South Africa have the skills capacity and appropriate HRM strategies to meet the challenge of higher economic growth and global competitiveness. African countries including South Africa, its largest economy, still lag behind other leading emergent markets such as Brazil and China regarding FDI. Nonetheless all 94 US-based emergent market mutual funds have stakes in South African companies, making it a destination of choice given its relative stability and steady economic growth (Lynch 2006). Key to sustaining and improving this is the extent to which political democratization, the rule of law, institution building and HRM development are speeded up. There are positive signs with fewer conflicts over the past five years, though HIV/AIDS and corruption especially in sub-Saharan African countries retard economic growth, human resource development and organizational capacity building.

Human resource aspects of structural adjustment programs

Many emerging economies in Africa were by the early 1990s under one form or another of structural adjustment program (SAP), comprising policy measures to find effective solutions to macroeconomic problems. The problems generally include a lack of self-reliant growth and development, low productivity and stagflation, imbalance of payments, external debts, and government budget deficits. The SAPs have often been prescribed by the Bretton Woods institutions (the International Monetary Fund and the World Bank), on whom crisis-laden economies depend for development credit and finance (Matanmi 2000: 100). The prescriptions usually comprised the following: devaluation, removal of subsidies on basic commodities, reduction of government expenditure, labor market reforms, reduction of trade protection, and increased incentives for the traditional sector (agriculture and mining). These measures have so far not jolted many countries into clear signs of possible recovery. Matanmi concludes that the effects of SAPs on employment relations and HRM have been unfavorable. These include union membership decline, lower formal employment, increasing casual and unprotected, insecure employment. There is a vital need for institution building in African countries to strengthen HRM and employment relations systems and practices. This underlines arguably the most important strategic challenges facing Africa – human resource development, building managerial capacity, investing in training and development and sound human resource management practices.

There is a need for practical HR initiatives aligned with organizational strategies focusing on building organizational and work commitment, workplace cooperation, HRM practices and service delivery and HR strategies for attracting, motivating and retaining talent. The alignment between these issues and performance outcomes is necessary for international competitiveness in African organizations. Proactive organizational responses to the competitive pressures emanating from globalization and the changes in the employment relationship have occurred (Aryee et al. 2004). Human resource issues in emergent economies include the 'inappropriate use of foreign models, over-reliance on particularistic practices driven by local institutional and legislative regimes, lack of transparency in decision-making, and concern with procedural and transactional HRM rather than strategic focus' (Kamoche et al. 2004: xvii).

Cross-cultural diffusion of HRM practice

'African management is cross-cultural management' (Jackson 2004: 16).

An enduring theme in emergent market HRM is the appropriateness of Western management principles and practices. There are challenges to MNCs and local firms which adopt practices with little consideration for their suitability or relevance (Horwitz 2006, Kamoche 2000, Kamoche et al. 2004, Nzelibe 1986, Seddon 1985). Ahiauzu (1986: 54) argues that an indigenous African thought-system reflects a high degree of harmony between an individual and society, use of symbolism to make sense of the world, and a strong emphasis on family and immediate community. The importance of family is seen in the network of interrelationships, extended family and mutual obligations not unlike Confucian 'guanxi' network relations in east Asian cultures. This has led some authors like Maruyama (1984) and Mbigi (2000) to propose an epistemological shift away from predominant Western management theories to alternative ones based on African perspectives. These include cultural diversity as a potential source of mutual win–win cooperation, an integrated/common vision on what constitutes 'objective' truth, the mental connectedness the worker shares with group members, and the idea that the individual assumes a relational existence and identity whose *raison d'être* is located within his/her community.

Human resource strategies need therefore to be firm-specific. Though the African notion of 'ubuntu' is not widespread in all parts of modern Africa, some view it as a basis for fostering an Afrocentric managerial culture with aligned HRM practices (Jackson 2004, Mbigi 2000). The notion of 'ubuntu' literally translated means 'I am who I am through others'; this in contrast to the Western tenet of 'cogito ergo sum' – 'I think therefore I am'. It is this contrasting of a form of communal humanism with individualism and instrumentalism, which has a normative appeal for advocates of an African economic and cultural renaissance. However, a desired future vision and current empirical reality should not be confused.

Adapting strategic HRM in Africa

Although Western managerial practices have prevailed for decades in African countries there is an increase in southern and east African firms adopting Japanese and east Asian practices (Faull 2000, Horwitz et al. 2002, Keenan 2000). These include lean manufacturing, just-in-time methods and other operations management measures to reduce product defects, stock holdings, inventory and waste. Quality and productivity improvement measures have sought to benchmark international standards in South African hospitality MNCs, the Sun International and Protea Groups. These measures have increased in the manufacturing sector where firms have introduced kaizen, kanban methods, Nissan-type green areas, Total Quality Management (TQM) and quality improvement teams. Increasingly, the ideas of lean thinking have gained currency in African firms such as Bell Equipment, Nampak Management Services, South African Breweries (SABMiller), Shatterprufe Windscreens, Sasol Polymers, GK Engineering and Joel Goldmine. The motivation for these measures is primarily productivity and work process improvement. However, the adoption of east Asian work practices is seen by some as unworkable, arguing that Japanese work philosophies are rooted in a different cultural context and therefore cannot be copied in African countries (Keenan 2000: 26). Diffusion thus requires eclecticism and sensitivity to the African context (Horwitz et al. 2004).

African workplace practices are more collectivist than individualist, often with strong masculine and patriarchal cultures. Human resource practices such as team working based on group and collective behavior and norms operate effectively, especially if reward systems are designed for group or team performance and performance management objectives. These issues reflect important concerns about the way people are managed in Africa and impediments managers have to overcome before HRM can come of age. Multinational corporations in Africa through their local managers are increasingly adopting contemporary management ideas and HRM practices. The latter concern the strategic contribution of HRM to organizational strategies and performance. SHRM is increasingly seen as a business alignment process potentially contributing to better performance outcomes and competitive advantage (Schuler and Jackson 1999). Given the nature of African society, which is variously characterized by collective decision-making considerations and extended family, adaptation of HRM practices is expected to contribute to achieving organization objectives. Managers often have to satisfy many stakeholders with conflicting interests. These realities suggest that the prescription and more importantly, the application of standard management tools cannot always be expected to work.

Up to a third of formal sector employees work in parastatal or government-linked organizations in many African countries. Here there is often insufficient procedural discipline and under-developed HRM. However, managers in Africa generally recognize the need to apply practices that are effective, developmental, and appropriate. But adoption of HR practices does not exist in a vacuum. It is important to understand social and institutional circumstances within which managers operate, the challenges they face, and how they respond to these. As mentioned earlier, this underlines the need to understand the African context and indigenous thought systems. Jackson (2004: 18) argues that in Africa there are often paradoxical value systems – Western instrumental and individualist versus humanistic systems often found in tribal and rural communities. A collective orientation can enable team-based practices and group incentive systems. A disadvantage in some countries may be a high degree of group conformism and sometimes nepotism in hiring, promotion decisions and practices. In sum this has led some authors like Mangaliso (2001) to propose a shift away from the predominant Western management theories to alternative ones based on African perspectives.

465

Managerial styles, culture and high performance HRM

Cultural context factors may also limit or assist the adoption of Western or east Asian practices such as performance-related pay and merit promotion, where, in the latter, deference to seniority, service and age remain important where family control of large enterprises remains strong (e.g. Malawian firms in Africa). South Africa would permit greater flexibility in adopting performance appraisal, merit pay and promotion, and financial incentive schemes. Yet within a country and national cultural context, variation between MNC and local firm propensity to adopt strategic HR practices occurs (Horwitz and Smith 1998: 590). This study found that MNCs in South Africa used numerical forms of flexibility, such as outsourcing and subcontracting to a larger extent than South African-owned firms. However, MNC influence may extend beyond HRM. In Engen (SA) its Malaysian shareholder had for some time key Malaysian staff members in the South African operation's strategic planning department responsible for charting the future direction of the company. This supports the proposition that MNC influence on global integration and work practice standardization reveals cross-cultural convergence of HRM practices within MNCs through adoption of 'best global practice', compared with a higher degree of divergence in local firms.

Cutting across cultural dimensions is an emergent black middle class which has begun to occupy decision-making roles. Class mobility is likely to have an impact on managerial culture and inform strategic choices about appropriate organizational culture, business and HRM practices in the African context (Horwitz 2002). Organization and national culture in many African countries reflect considerable diversity and pluralism. The advent of democracy, especially in South Africa, and the 'glasnost' effect of global competition begs the ongoing question as to the inevitability of SHRM convergence and global hegemony of 'best practice' over local exigencies. In practice, hybrid or 'crossvergent' models appear more likely (Ward et al. 1999).

Managerial styles in many African countries reflect both Western values based on individualism, meritocracy and an authoritarian legacy of apartheid and colonialism. These are often rooted in high masculinity cultures (Hofstede 1991). Indigenous models of leadership and organization, emphasizing the notion of 'ubuntu' or humaneness, group decision making, and interdependence, struggle to assert themselves in the face of a converging global business orthodoxy (Mbigi 2000). These notions may be similar in concept to the Confucian emphasis on family and social cohesion. Investment in southern Africa by east Asian firms and local interest in Japanese work methods has occurred, and as discussed earlier there is increased experimentation with Japanese work methods such as self-directed teams, employee empowerment through task-level participation and multi-skilling in southern African firms such as Cashbuild, Toyota (SA) and the Plate Glass Group (Horwitz and Townshend 1993).

Semi-autonomous teams are an example of a collective orientation to motivation and work design. This is more of a feature of Japanese and European organizations than the individualism of Anglo-Saxon countries. However, these practices tend to be more successful in restructured organizations where authority and responsibility are devolved to well-trained and informed work groups. There is anecdotal and case study evidence of these forms of functional flexibility emerging in the African context in firms such as Pick n Pay Retailers and SA Nylon Spinners. However, these practices are less common (under 10 percent) in relation to use of numerical flexibility such as downsizing and outsourcing, and temporal flexibility types such as part-time, temporary and casual, short-term work (Allan et al. 2001, Brosnan et al. 2000). Practices such as work flexibility, multi-skilling and performance-based pay have become more important in several African countries. Horwitz et al. (2002) found a degree of adoption of high-performance work practices like team-based systems based on cultural precepts such as 'ubuntu'. Practices from Asian countries such as Japan and China are being increasingly diffused into more developed and investment-attracting African countries.

Patterns of diffusion

The diffusion of HR practices shows an uneven pattern in degree of adoption and actual modification/adaptation for successful implementation. Some are adopted 'as is', or with some modification, or comprehensively redesigned to suit local conditions. SHRM research in Africa needs to move beyond descriptive evaluation of the extent and type of HR diffusion, and convergence/divergence debate, to a more rigorous evaluation of processes affecting success or failure in HR diffusion. Hybrid HR strategies occur in nomenclature, design, content and implementation processes. In South Africa, indigenous African terms are now being given to adapted east Asian practices, often in preference to using Japanese terminology; for example, the Zulu term 'Indaba' groups for TQM teams or 'sebenza' problem-solving teams. 'Indaba' refers to 'debate in groups'; 'sebenza' means work or workplace. Horwitz and Smith (1998: 590–8) found that although consultation and employee involvement occurred in introducing these practices, MNCs were more likely than local firms to involve employees in both design and implementation processes.

In the southern African context, 'as is' adoption is rarely effective and some or extensive modification occurs. This underlines the need for sensitivity to local circumstances and support for the notion of 'integrative crossvergence' (Ward et al. 1999). For example, where performance-based pay and variable pay are introduced, these tend to be work group or team-based schemes rather than individually based. Malaysian and Taiwanese firms in Africa have also implemented home-based policies and practices. In the latter case, however, managerial practices are somewhat traditional, based on low labor cost/cost-reduction methods, and cannot be considered 'high performance'. There is evidence of reverse diffusion. SABMiller's jointly owned breweries in Poland have successfully implemented best operating practices and management know-how on systems, process and technology based on Japanese practices and its experience in emergent economies, and South African indigenous restaurants in Singapore draw on home-country practices. Similarly, the South African-based consultant firm Competitive Capabilities (CCI), using Japanese world class manufacturing and operations methodologies and building on its African experience, has extended these precepts into its work in Australia and Singapore. Identical HRM practices cannot be transferred intact.

There is also relatively recent expansion of firms from Africa to east Asia. SABMiller is, for example, the second largest beer company in China. Burgeoning South African MNCs such as SABMiller (beer), MTN International (ICT), Nando's (fast foods) and Sasol (synthetic fuels) also show evidence of varying degrees of cross-cultural diffusion and convergence of their African-based hybrid managerial practices into their international operations (Horwitz et al. 2006, Wocke et al. 2007). Understanding the notion of gaining competitive and performance leverage from local contextual factors, such as cultural diversity and local skills supply, is important. De Cieri and Dowling (1998) stress the importance of considering, at the micro-level, the life-cycle stage of the organization and intangible endogenous factors such as a firm's experience in international business and the headquarters' international orientation. More research is also needed on comparative practice diffusion, including the relative impact of European, United States and East Asian MNCs on HRM practices in African countries. Culture and institutional and regulatory factors are pertinent. It is important to move beyond descriptive cross-cultural analysis by examining the actual nature of changing patterns of adoption of HR practices and the type and degree of hybridization.

Talent management and diversity

Migrancy and the flight of knowledge workers from Africa or between African countries is becoming critical as more African countries seek to attract, develop and retain key skills to grow their economies and compete both domestically and globally. In Africa, the main labor-receiving countries are Botswana, Mauritius and South Africa. An allied issue is the widespread move towards labor market flexibility and an increase in subcontracting and outsourcing as work is externalized. The casualization of the labor market is increasing even in countries with more regulated legal regimes such as South Africa. Numerical and temporal flexibility and even pay flexibility have a profound effect on employment security, the psychological contract and workplace arrangements. Talent management research in South African shows that professionals in knowledge-intensive firms rate opportunity to plan and control their own work, challenging and stimulating work, sound workplace relations, work–life balance, and personal development and growth more highly than remuneration (Horwitz et al. 2004, 2006). Good working conditions, career opportunities and competitive pay are vital. For example, well-trained nurses have been lost to hospitals in Britain and Dubai resulting in serious shortages in South African hospitals. Engineering and occupational therapy skills are being lost as better opportunities occur abroad. Estimates are that between 3,000 and 6,000 engineers, technologists and technicians are required in South Africa over the next five years (*Argus* Oct 25, 2004: 14). Budget constraints together with poor HRM practices, and in some instances poor application and unintended consequences of employment equity measures, have made retention problematic. Yet these problems are reversible with progressive policies, implementation of good HR practices and leadership commitment. Retention of needed talent such as knowledge workers requires organizations to create a challenging and stimulating work environment, allowing knowledge workers more influence in planning and organizing their work, more active engagement of knowledge workers, providing opportunities for personal growth and development, ensuring flexible and competitive remuneration, offering stretching and interesting assignments or projects and a culture which encourages strong and supportive peer relations (Horwitz et al. 2003, Sutherland 2006).

An important allied theme is diversity management. It is erroneous to assume homogeneity within specific countries too, since many African countries have diverse ethno-cultural communities (Kamoche et al. 2004: xvi). In countries like Zambia and Ghana with extensive privatization of state-owned enterprises (SOEs), the HRM landscape has been reshaped in significant and enduring ways. Many Zambian SOEs, for instance, have been bought by South African companies, whose managers apply employment practices based on those of the parent company. The southern African region (in particular Botswana and South Africa) has emerged as a catchment area for talent from other parts of Africa, in particular East and Central Africa. African countries variously have their own policies of localization or Africanization, and in some countries like Zambia, Zambianization. South Africa has employment equity legislation and a recent strong focus on broad-based Black Economic Empowerment (BEE) to enhance share ownership and other forms of employee empowerment. Industry charters are developed, setting targets for BEE in sectors such as insurance, mining, oil and energy. The basis of these policies is to redress employment skills and access to managerial, professional and economic opportunities by groups previously denied these opportunities. In South Africa the constitution permits policies aimed at redress of unfair discrimination based on race, culture and ethnicity and gender.

The effects of ethnicity are not well documented regarding impacts on employment relations in Africa (Nyambegera and Almhdie, 2004). Managerial styles, HRM practices and preferences for particular types of conflict resolution may be mediated by ethnic factors, including the degree of cultural ethnocentrism, and tolerance or intolerance of diversity. Firm-level employment practices in some countries like Kenya and South Africa have in some sectors reflected preferences for particular ethnic groups or family members of an ethnic group. Post-independence governments have promoted policies variously referred to do Africanization, localization and employment equity. These are similar in intent to affirmative action (USA) and equal opportunity legislation (UK) and require designated employers employing over a speci-fied number of historically disadvantaged employees, in some cases minority groups and in others majority groups (for example, in Namibia and South Africa), to set targets and timetables for improving diversity and representation of the workforce at all levels. Employers are also required to remove unfair discrimination practices, for example, in recruitment and selection and promotion policies, and in the case of South Africa, to submit an annual report to the Department of Labour indicating progress on these objectives. In South Africa too, in terms of the Employment Equity Act (1998), trade unions have to be consulted by employers on the latter's employment equity plans. In most African countries where such policies and practices occur, they focus on setting affirmative action representation targets or quotas, timetables for attaining these, proactive recruitment and selection to meet diversity targets and review of employment practices regarding potentially unfair discriminatory aspects. These tend to focus on numerical change to enhance representation at all levels of an organization. Qualitative changes in workplace attitudes, institutional culture, and leadership styles are however equally important. More organizations have diversity training aimed largely at promoting cross-cultural understanding and tolerance, though these have been criticized as unwittingly promoting cultural stereotypes.

Employment relations

The regulatory context of employment relations in Africa varies considerably. Positively, more employment relations systems on the continent are adopting International Labour Organization (ILO) conventions. There are many challenges facing workers as well as managers in Africa today. Forced to open their markets as part of World Bank and IMF structural adjustment programs (SAPs) and finding many foreign markets closed to their products, organizations have borne the brunt of globalization, resulting in plant closures and higher unemployment. In the worst cases countries like Somalia have been so ravaged by war that they have no real economy, failing to function as modern nation states. However, there are more democratically elected governments in Africa today than fifteen years ago. Matanmi (2000) summarizes the major elements of employment relations in emergent or transitional economies as having elements of colonial impact, nationalism, post-colonial states and crises of development; influenced by structural adjustment programs; coping with the democratic challenge; and handling the emergent demands of social partnership (Matanmi 2000: 95–6).

Employment relations regimes are relatively new and evolving. The International Labour Organisation (ILO), for example, has a number of advisors working with African governments to establish employment relations systems, legislative frameworks, collective bargaining and dispute resolution systems based on ILO conventions. Since its launch in 2000, the ILO Project based in Pretoria has made considerable progress in initiatives to strengthen social dialogue in six SADC countries – South Africa, Namibia, Lesotho, Botswana, Swaziland and Zimbabwe; this by seeking to create tripartite forums and designing employment relations and dispute resolution systems (Anstey 2004: 59). As emergent economies, many African countries show uneven patterns of development and under-development, with low average per-capita national income, low living standards and poorly developed social welfare. In HR terms African countries are not monolithic. The contiguous sub-Saharan African countries differ in levels of infrastructural development or acquisition for expanding wage-employment and industrial sectors. Unevenness in this regard widens when comparing regional faster growing and more rapidly industrializing South Africa with other African countries like Ethiopia (Matanmi 2000: 96). Political independence expanded wage-employment sectors (largely public, but also private sectors), creating legislative frameworks legitimizing trade union rights to varying degrees.

The role of government in African HRM varies from state control in formally socialist states such as Ethiopia and Mozambique, to state direction in countries like Zambia, to a strong legislative framework permitting more voluntarist systems such as in South Africa and Namibia. Under colonialism or apartheid, trade union movements could be characterized, in part, as social movements often mobilizing workers against an existing political regime. South Africa was a good example of this. Leadership development emerged from trade union movements to subsequently assume prominent political and business leadership roles following democracy. But when government becomes hegemonic, for reasons of ineptitude or malfeasance, labor policies are sometimes inconsistent and unenforced (Fashoyin 2000). In Nigeria, the degree of robustness of labor rights has been a function of dispositions of successive national governments from colonialism to the present era of protracted military dictatorship. In some African countries public policy on employment relations has reflected the state's tendency for taking complex industrial and labor relations decisions by fiat (for example, wage determination in the public sector, with often serious inflationary consequences), rather than allowing employment relations institutions that do exist, to operate independently. Yet a culture of collective relations has endured in the private sector, with collective agreements/contracts being negotiated at either industry or enterprise levels where a union has significant representation. Strong independent unions negotiate wages and employment conditions in some African countries, notably South Africa which has well-developed dispute resolution mechanisms such as mediation and arbitration, with the reference of certain disputes such as unfair labor practices to the labor court. The Commission for Conciliation, Mediation and Arbitration (CCMA) or bargaining councils, deal with unfair dismissal and mutual interest wage disputes. This helps to regulate and channel conflict into constructive resolution, though the ready accessibility of the CCMA does involve managers sometimes having to spend considerable time and effort in conflict resolution, with no administration cost to an employee who wishes to lodge a dispute.

Since the 1980s an increasing number of enterprises in Africa have taken a more accommodating approach to providing a voice for workers. Thus, what the future portends for employment relations is how to balance the organizational interests of the workers with the commitment to corporate effectiveness and competitiveness (Fashoyin 2000: 173). There are pressures for significant change through democratization and good governance. The New Partnership for African Development (NEPAD) is a political initiative taken by African governments to foster democracy, economic development and poverty alleviation on the continent. It has a peer review mechanism to exert pressure on governments whose actions fail to meet its normative requirements.

The emergence of seemingly powerful industrial unions in critical sectors of certain countries has occurred – for example, Ghana, Nigeria and Zimbabwe – and has also influenced the proliferation of employers' associations and federations. Many African economies are experiencing a transition from large and often overstaffed public corporations to enterprises which are more publicly accountable and private firms which have to compete globally and be profitable (Jackson 2002: 999). The employment relations impact of multinational companies such as Johnson & Johnson, most oil MNCs, such as Shell and BP, foreign subsidiaries and joint-venture organizations is important. Organizations in this latter category occur in all sectors, particularly in manufacturing, textiles and automobile assembly. Several African nations subscribe to ILO conventions on freedom of association and the right to collective bargaining. However, implementation is often not strongly supported. Trade unions are sometimes restricted in the scope of their activities due both to the limited spread of wage or paid employment and to unfavorable state policies which impede their ability to effectively use bargaining machinery. Considering an often authoritarian/paternalistic style of management, collective bargaining does not always receive the approval of management (Fashoyin 2000: 172–3). Through the ILO's 'Improve your Business project', employer associations have helped members to address the business and management problems of small enterprises, for example, in Ghana (Aryee 2004: 130). Downsizing in the public sector, the traditional bastion of unionism, has led to a decline in union density in many countries.

In Africa the HRM and employment relations agenda will have to increasingly concern itself not only with managerial–working class relations, but with a growing and socially excluded underclass. Traditional trade union contestation and power-conflict models may be inappropriate as are traditional distributive forms of collective bargaining based on an adversarial tradition. In Africa, union and employer strategies will need to increasingly focus on human resource development. Joint collaboration in the workplace will be vital for effective competition in the marketplace.

Workplace implications of HIV/AIDS

The HIV/AIDS pandemic is a global problem and has the potential to derail any gains in productivity in sub-Saharan African organizations in the last two decades (Kamoche et al. 2004: 187–8). It is estimated that over 28 million people in Africa are living with HIV and in some countries 30 percent of the adult population are infected with the virus (UNAIDS 2002). Labor productivity has fallen up to 50 percent in countries hardest-hit. There are serious implications for the workplace. These include increased absenteeism, skills provision and training impacts, retarding of career and succession planning and long-term sick leave. Governments have not always made concerted enough attempts to tackle the spread of the disease. This has put an onus on employers, with many such as AngloGold Ashanti implementing policies and programs to address the adverse input on their workforce and communities. It is estimated that by 2020, over 25 percent of the workforce may be lost to AIDS in the most severely affected countries. In Zambia, for instance, it is estimated that nearly two-thirds of mortality of managers is attributable to AIDS. In Kenya, AIDS accounts for up to three out of four deaths in the police force (UNAIDS 2002). In much of sub-Saharan Africa the delivery of essential services is under threat as trained and skilled staff succumb to the disease.

Hence the HR response of organizations and workers to the HIV/AIDS pandemic in African is crucial in maintaining organizational sustainability. There is a critical need, which some firms such as AngloGold Ashanti have developed, for workplace HIV/AIDS policies and programs. The workplace is a vital educational opportunity in promoting preventive measures and their benefits to employees, though many organizations are either ignorant or not convinced of the deleterious impacts of the disease on their employees, erosion of skills and the organization's operations. A small number of studies have been done assessing workplace HIV/AIDS programs and business responses in the African region (Baruch and Clancy 2000). Most have focused mainly on South Africa, Tanzania, Uganda and Botswana and are usually conducted by trade unions and non-governmental organizations. A study in Ghana showed that employers knew little about the effects on their organizations. Generally employers have regarded HIV prevention as the responsibility of individuals, their families and governments (Ankomah and Debrah 2001). Although most employers would consider the development and implementation of HIV/AIDS policies, they tend to be more supportive of policies dealing with its legal aspects such as unfair discrimination, pre-employment testing and dismissals, than preventive programs (Ankomah and Debrah 2001). Such views are pertinent in the context of efforts of UNAIDS to use the workplace for promoting non-discrimination towards people with HIV/AIDS. Similarly, the Council of the Southern African Development Committee (SADC) has approved a regional code aimed at guiding employers, employees, and government on economically sustainable and humane ways of responding to HIV/AIDS in the workplace. This remains a key HR issue affecting talent development, retention of key skills and organizational sustainability in Africa.

Conclusions

Managing people strategically in Africa has become more important given the increased globalization of markets, including labour markets, positive economic growth on the continent, increased foreign direct investment, especially by China, and the mostly adverse impact of World Bank and IMF economic structural adjustment programs (SAPs) on formal employment security in many African countries (with exceptions such as South Africa and Libya). Liberalized economies with privatization and deregulatory measures have seen a drop in formal employment and deterioration of labor standards. Whilst there is some evidence of a concomitant rise in employment relations institutions such as collective bargaining and dispute resolution, as democratization occurs, strong independent trade unions not linked to the state or employers are exceptions. Positively however, tripartite corporatist engagement is not uncommon, for example, in South Africa.

A second theme is that of HIV/AIDS, which especially in sub-Saharan Africa has a devastating impact on employment, employment and health care costs and union membership decline. HIV/AIDS also has a deleterious effect on absenteeism, training, career and succession planning, with adverse effects on state and union negotiated medical schemes. A third theme is significant change in labor market policy and structures with both the state and employers in many countries, either promoting or turning a blind eye to ineffective monitoring at legislative protective and collective agreements, as increased cost reduction and flexibility is sought, with a consequent deterioration in employment standards, social protection and rising casualization in labor markets. Examples include the decline of regional centralized bargaining structures in the building and construction industry in South Africa.

Bahadur (2004) notes a relationship between the African Growth and Opportunity Act (AGOA) and sweat-shop conditions. Much of this investment has been by Asian multinationals supplying retailers in other parts of Africa, and particularly by the United States. AGOA is a United States Act passed in 2000, offering preferential access for certain African exports. It reflects a philosophical shift in the USA's approach to Africa stemming from a policy of 'trade not aid' (Bahadur 2004: 39). At present 37 sub-Saharan African countries qualify to export to the USA under AGOA. One result is a switching of Malawian exports previously destined predominantly for South Africa, to the USA. In a number of cases working conditions have deteriorated, for example, increased overtime of up to 27 hours weekly in Lesotho, repression of trade union rights and little enforcement of labor laws. With high unemployment in sub-Saharan Africa, the bargaining power of unions in this sector is compromised. In South Africa, over 40,000 retrenchments have occurred in the clothing industry, a result largely of cheap imports from lower cost producers in Asia. A well-organized and soundly led union, the South African Clothing and Textile Workers Union (Sactwu) has struggled to fight this trend but has recently persuaded government to successfully negotiate some import restrictions on Chinese clothing to try and preserve jobs.

These industry examples reflect the increasingly precarious nature of employment and flexible labor markets in many African countries. This is important for HRM. Even in South Africa, arguably with a strongly protective Labour Relations Act (1995) institutionalized Labour Court, and Statutory Conciliation Mediation and Arbitration Commission, as well as minimum standards legislation in the form of the Basic Conditions of Employment Act (1997) and arguably the strongest union movement on the continent, precarious, non-standard work has increased while formal standard work has declined. Kalula (2003) argues in this regard that labor laws in southern Africa do not take into account the social realities of countries in the region, with their changing labor markets. He submits that labor law reflects Western models, 'borrowing and bending' legal reforms seeking adherence to ILO standards, sometimes transplanting inappropriate legal precepts focusing on formal sector standard employment, ignoring the bigger reality of a dramatically increasing informal sector. He states that 'the vast majority are left out', arguing that

> labour law is a sharp instrument of social policy. Labour market regulation must strive to influence work beyond the formal sector narrowly defined. Mutual rights and obligations in the workplace remain important, but employment law must be part of an agenda for alleviating poverty
>
> (Kalula 2003: 57)

and developing human capital for the continent.

The benign neglect of HRM in Africa is in part a reflection of the poor economic performance of African countries in the global economy, and the paucity of internationally published work emanating from the continent; this is in comparison with a much richer east Asian HRM research tradition by both east Asian-based and Western HRM and organizational culture researchers. Yet why, in Anglo-Saxon Western and in some emergent economies, have best practices been so uncritically applied by practitioners and academics alike without properly considering contextual issues? One cautions against mindless 'groupthink' which cannot offer competitive differentiation. Lessons can be learned from previous efforts to transfer management practices in order that managers might adopt a more eclectic approach and that researchers approach this emergent field with an open mind.

References

Ahiauzu, A.I. (1986). 'The African thought-system and work behavior'. *International Studies of Management and Organization*, 16(2): 37–58.

Allan, C., Brosnan, P., Horwitz, F.M. and Walsh, P. (2001). 'From standard to non-standard employment'. *International Journal of Manpower*, 22(8): 748–63.

Ankomah, A.K. and Debrah, Y. (2001). 'HIV/AIDS prevention in the workplace: Some evidence from Ghana'. Invited paper, Conference at the Postgraduate Institute of Health, University of Teeside, United Kingdom.

Anstey, M. (2004). 'African renaissance – implications for labour relations'. *South African Journal of Labour Relations*, 28(1): 59.

Argus Newspaper (2004). October 25: 14.

Argus Newspaper (2006a). November 6: 7.

Argus Newspaper (2006b). November 7: 16.

Aryee, S. (2004). 'HRM in Ghana'. In Kamoche, K. et al. (eds), *Managing Human Resources in Africa*, London: Routledge, 121–34.

Bahadur, A. (2004). 'Taking the devil's rope – AGOA'. *South African Labour Bulletin*, 28(1): 39–42.

Baruch, Y. and Clancey, P. (2000). 'Managing AIDS in Africa: HRM challenges in Tanzania'. *International Journal of Human Resource Management*, 11(4): 789–809.

Brosnan, P., Horwitz, F.M., Walsh, P. and Allan, C. (2000). 'Workplace flexibility – perspectives from the Southern Hemisphere'. *South African Journal of Business Management*, 2(3): 1–8.

Carmichael, T. and Rijamampianina, R. (2006). Managing diversity in Africa'. In Luiz, J. (ed.), *Managing Business in Africa*, Cape Town: Oxford University Press, 164–73.

De Cieri, H. and Dowling, P.J. (1998). 'Strategic human resource management in multinational enterprises'. Adapted from Schuler, R.S., Dowling, P.J. and De Cieri, H. 1993. 'An integrative framework of strategic international human resource management'. *Journal of Management*, 19: 419–59.

Fashoyin, T. (2000). 'Management in Africa'. In Warner, M. (ed.), *Management in Emergent Countries*, London: Thompson Learning, 169–75.

Faull, N. (2000). *The Manufacturing Round Table project*, Graduate School of Business, University of Cape Town.

Hofstede, G. (1991). *Cultures and Organizations: Software of the mind*, London: McGraw-Hill.

Horwitz, F.M. (2002). 'Management in South Africa.' In Warner, M. (ed.), *Management in Emergent Countries*, London: Thompson Learning: 214–27.

Horwitz, F.M. and Smith, D.A. (1998). 'Flexible work practices and human resource management: A comparison of South African and foreign-owned companies'. *International Journal of Human Resource Management*, 9(4): 690–7.

Horwitz, F.M. and Townshend, M. (1993). 'Elements in participation, teamwork and flexibility'. *International Journal of Human Resource Management*, 4(4): 17–29.

Horwitz, F.M., Chan, T.H. and Quazi, H.A. (2003). '"Finders, keepers": Attracting, motivating and retaining knowledge eorkers'. *Human Resource Management Journal*, 13(4): 23–44.

Horwitz, F.M., Kamoche, K. and Chew, I. (2002). 'Looking East: Diffusing high performance work practices in the southern Afro-Asian context'. *International Journal of Human Resource Management*, 13(7): 1019–41.

Horwitz, F.M., Nkomo, S. and Rajah, M. (2004). 'HRM in South Africa'. In Kamoche, K., et al. (eds), *Managing Human Resources in Africa*, London: Routledge, 1–17.

Horwitz, F.M., Chan, T.H., Quazi, H.A., Nonkwelo, C., Roditi, D. and van Eck, P. (2006). 'Human resource strategies for managing knowledge workers: an Afro-Asian comparative analysis'. *International Journal of Human Resource Management*, 17(5): 775–811.

ILO (1997). *World Labour Report 1997–98. Industrial relations, democracy and social stability*, Geneva: ILO.

Jackson, T. (2002). 'Reframing human resource management in Africa'. *International Journal of Human Resource Management*, 13(7): 998–1018.

Jackson, T. (2004). *Management and Change in Africa*, London: Routledge, 16–18.

Kalula, E. (2003). 'Labour laws need a dash of reality'. *South African Labour Bulletin*, 27(4): 56–9.

Kamoche, K., Debrah, Y., Horwitz, F.M. and Muuka, G. (eds) (2004). *Managing Human Resources in Africa*, London: Routledge, 1–18, 183–90.

Keenan, T. (2000). 'You can never be too rich or too lean'. *Finance Week*, October: 26–7.

Luiz, J. (ed.) (2006). *Managing Business in Africa*. Cape Town: Oxford University Press, 4–6, 131–50.

Lynch, D. (2006). 'South African government tries to unlock the economy'. *USA Today*, October 27: 25.

Mangaliso, M.P. (2001). 'Building competitive advantage from ubuntu: Management lessons from Africa'. *Academy of Management Executive*, 15(3): 23–32.

Maruyama, M. (1984). 'Alternative concepts of management: insights from Asia and Africa'. *Asia Pacific Journal of Management*, January: 100–111.

Matanmi, S. (2000). 'Industrial relations in emergent countries'. In Warner, M. (ed.), *Management in Emergent Countries, International Encyclopaedia of Business and Management,* London: Thompson Learning, 95–104.

Mbigi, L. (2000). 'Making the African renaissance globally competitive'. *People Dynamics,* 18(11): 16–21.

Naidoo, S. (2006). 'Beijing in major bid to woo Africa'. *Sunday Times,* November 5: 7.

Nyambegera, S.M. and Almhdie, A. (2004). 'HRM in Libya'. In Kamoche, K. et al. (eds), *Managing Human Resources in Africa,* London: Routledge, 169–81.

Nzelibe, C.O. (1986). 'The evolution of African management thought'. *International Studies of Management and Organization,* 16(2): 6–16.

Schuler, R.S. and Jackson, S.E. (eds) (1999). *Strategic Human Resource Management,* Oxford: Blackwell.

Seddon, J.W. (1985). 'The development and indigenization of third world business: African perspectives in the workplace'. In Hammond, V. (ed.), *Current Research in Management,* London: Francis Pinter.

Sutherland, M. (2006). 'How do senior people attract and keep staff? The role of HR in South Africa'. *MBA.COZA,* April 2: 3.

The Economist (2001). 'Africa the hopeless continent'. *The Economist,* May 29: 1–2.

UNAIDS (2002). 'UNAIDS releases new data on impact of AIDS in Africa'. Press release, Geneva, June 25.

Ward, S., Pearson, C., Entrekin, L. and Winzar, H. (1999). 'The fit between cultural values and countries: Is there evidence of globalization, nationalism, or crossvergence?' *International Journal of Management,* 16(4): 466–73.

Wocke, A., Bendixen, M. and Rijamampianina, R. (2007). 'Building flexibility into multi-national human resource strategy: A study of four South African multi-national enterprises'. *International Journal of Human Resource Management,* 18(5): 834–40.

Wright, P.M., Snell, S.A. and Dyer, L. (2005). 'New models of strategic HRM in a global context'. *International Journal of Human Resource Management,* 16(6): 875–81.

Zupan, N. and Kase, R. (2005). 'Strategic human resource management in European transitional economies'. *International Journal of Human Resource Management,* 16(6): 882–905.

Part 10

Performance outcomes

Probably one of the biggest differences between US and European HR thought leaders has to do with their foundational assumptions regarding the relative priority of the various stakeholders to the organization. Researchers in the US tend to take for granted that the prime if indeed not the overwhelming purpose of the managers of a firm is to increase shareholder wealth. But many European researchers and practitioners alternatively seem to recognize the equal, or almost equal, importance of other stakeholders and other interests. This final section illustrates these differing perspectives.

Richard Beatty opens the section, making a strong case for HR's need to focus almost entirely on impacting the economic value of the firm. He begins by briefly tracing the history of HR from pure administration to the need today to be a strategic player. He suggests that too many HR practitioners get led astray by the latest fad or fashion dominating the management or HR literature, and fail to recognize the need to thoroughly analyze their business to identify the customer value created, the key talent roles that are most critical to building that customer value, and how HR can continue to build talent in those roles. Beatty concludes by emphasizing the importance of developing HR metrics that are tied to business outcomes, rather than just the metrics that are easiest to measure.

In Chapter 29 Les Worrall and Cary Cooper introduce additional evaluative criteria. They trace a number of the large-scale organizational changes that are gripping most industries such as outsourcing, reengineering, offshoring, etc. They believe the employees in the organizations undergoing such changes suffer immensely and to determine if they are correct, they report data from 840 managers in UK firms. Their data suggest that while director-level executives do not see many problems, the managers and employees further down the implementation scale incur the brunt of the impact. For example, more than 60 percent of the managers reported sometimes or often experiencing constant fatigue, sleep loss or muscular tension, with a large percentage also reporting anger, headaches, mood swings, and irritability. They state that "Most managers, excluding directors, feel that this change is not being well managed, that it is being used cynically to make the assets sweat, and that it is having undermining effects on employee motivation, morale, loyalty, and sense of job security." This leads them to conclude finally that "We need to put more humanity back into the workplace."

Between the shareholder and the employee comes an additional stakeholder in organizations: the customer. David Bowen and S. Douglas Pugh's chapter (Chapter 30) focuses on linking

477

HRM to customer outcomes. They begin by providing a conceptual model for how strategy translates into HRM practices which influence the climate and employee behaviors that lead to customer satisfaction. They then discuss the research that supports the different stages in this linkage model. Interestingly, this chapter inadvertently seems to provide some reconciliation of the previous two chapters. Bowen and Pugh argue strongly that a climate for service to the customer is impossible without first building a climate for supporting employees. Finally, they describe the implications of this model and research for how HRM systems can be fully leveraged to influence customer loyalty.

This section therefore makes more explicit some of the underlying assumptions that have been represented throughout this book. Organizations exist in competitive environments, and because employees are such a large component of expense, managing them well is a prerequisite to financial success. However, what constitutes managing them well? What evaluative criterion should be taken into account? From one perspective it seems to be that we invest in them only insofar as such investment will pay off for customers and/or shareholders. When competitive costs force the closure of plants or movement of work to lower wage countries, then this is simply part of the basic mode of competition. On the other hand, from a different perspective, while competition cannot be ignored, neither can employees, society, or the environment. From this vantage point, many of the current organizational changes only create short-term advantages which are not sustainable in the long term. The challenge for HR is to seek the balance; a strategy that creates both temporary and sustainable advantages through effective management of the workforce; one that provides fair returns to shareholders but also treats employees fairly; one that keeps costs competitive and wages livable. This is a challenge that is immense, dynamic, and enduring.

28

HRM, the workforce, and the creation of economic value

Richard W. Beatty

For the last decade the HRM profession in the United States (practitioner and academic alike) has lamented that it does not get the respect it deserves. One remedy was a call to turn the HR professionals into *strategic* partners (Ulrich, 1997; Ulrich & Brockbank, 2005). In practice, the term became a call to arms. Practitioners sought a seat at the strategic planning table while proposing catchphrases such as "employer of choice," "best practices," "employee engagement," and capability building. By and large, they tended to remain internally focused, forging cooperative working relationships with the employees and executives *within* the firm, often defining line management as HR's customer.

As firms faced intensified, global competitive environments, and outsourcing of many traditional HR roles occurred, we upped the ante by asserting that if the HR function was to justify its existence, it must become a strategic *player* (Beatty & Schneier, 1995; Ulrich & Beatty, 2002). This meant that HR had to alter its perspective and focus externally on firm success (with customers and investors), and how HR could contribute to that success. We called for the re-examination and re-evaluation of every HR practice to determine how it contributes to firm success and survival. More importantly, we urged HR practitioners to heed the empirical evidence demonstrating the relationship between HR practices and firm success (Huselid & Becker, 1995).

Some even questioned whether the HR profession was a profession. Our answer is that it should be, just like medicine, where professional practice is both an art and a science, evidence-based with hypotheses subject to rigorous testing. This is easier said than done, since the parentage of the academic discipline is multifaceted (as opposed to, say, engineering, accounting, etc.). Moreover, HR practitioners often come from a variety of educational and firm backgrounds. The result has been little convergence of training or purpose, a failure to agree on what should be measured, and testing hypotheses seldom linked to business results.

Becoming "strategic players" requires definition. First, "strategic." The textbook definition of strategy in business is how the firm creates its competitive advantage in order to differentiate itself and win in the marketplace. HR's primary focus should be the strategy of the business: identifying and understanding the firm's desired competitive advantage, the strategic capabilities (or core competencies) required to create its competitive advantages, the strategic positions within capabilities, and the strategic players within strategic positions that directly contribute to firm success. In the strategic context, HR should be focused on that work and those individuals who enable the firm to: (1) influence the customer's perception of value, (2) charge its desired price, and/or (3) produce at its desired cost. Second, "player." A player is an individual who contributes strategic value. What advantage can the HR profession bring to business strategy? It must demonstrate that it can score on the business scorecard. Its metrics must demonstrate how the HR function directly impacts the firm's business success. For example, metrics which show an overall decrease in employee turnover are not strategic. Metrics which demonstrate increased retention of "A" players in strategic positions and exiting of under-performing employees are strategic. The deliverable of HR is thus a workforce that impacts economic and customer value.

No business function – manufacturing, finance, logistics or distribution – operates without metrics of input and output. HR has always been far more focused on *what* it does than what it *delivers* that impacts economic and customer value. To become a strategic player, the HR function must meet the challenge to think first like any business leader – to build a sustainable wealth-creating firm. The domain of HR is to deliver a workforce that adds customer and economic value to the firm focusing on the role of the workforce, the role of HR, and how the workforce impacts value creation.

The art of the HR profession, both for practitioners and academics, is to recognize how radically and rapidly the business environment around them changes. Most firms face constant new competitors, operating in unfamiliar terrain, outsourcing a function, building plants in another country, or learning how to operate in foreign culture.

How does HR contribute to ever-changing environments to impact the bottom line? By first understanding that managers have more influence over the workforce than does HR. Thus HR should focus its efforts on how to better utilize line managers to create value through the workforce, just as a Chief Finance Officer attempts to influence line managers to strategically utilize financial resources to create value for the firm. HR must therefore clarify leadership's responsibilities and accountabilities for practices considered part of the traditional HR "tool kit" – employee selection, performance management, development, rewards, communication, and work design. Thus line managers must do "HR work" to add values and be held accountable for the success of their workforce.

At issue: HR as a profession and HR professionals

A brief history of the HR function in the United States shows that in the nineteenth century it was nonexistent. Hiring was haphazard, based on friendship and affinity groups. At the bottom of the organization, the biggest bully often became a supervisor, and selected workers based on whim. As firms became more complex and their relationship with employees more complex, regularized and rationalized, a bureaucracy grew. As a bureaucracy with a vague mission, the purpose of the HR function changed. Following World War II in the prosperous United States, HR often became a refuge for underperforming employees. Following the cultural changes in the United States with its focus on equality of opportunity, the focus of the function became meeting governmental regulations, taking on an enforcement role as the "HR police." In many of his salient works, Dave Ulrich called for a deeper understanding of the role of the HR function. The function was to expand beyond its traditional roles, and focus on executing strategy and change management and become a "partner" within the firm.

As firms are increasingly competing *with* brainware and *for* talent, it was vital for HR to move beyond partnering to become strategic *players* – on the field, in the game, and with the ability to score on the scorecard of the business. Transitioning the function to the player role has been difficult. Bound by HR's historic mission, to become more efficient at transaction processing, serving as social worker or policeman, HR metrics remained primarily focused on administrative efficiency and employee advocacy (e.g., job satisfaction, employee turnover, and cost per employee). In a fast-moving, globally competitive environment, such metrics are misguided, because becoming "world class" on these dimensions does not produce a world-class workforce or, more importantly, extraordinary firm performance.

If the HR function is to become a strategic player and relevant in the global competition, it must focus on three strategies: business strategy, workforce strategy, and HR strategy (Huselid et al., 2005). Business strategy should determine HR metrics which enable interventions which successfully deliver the firm's strategy. Clearly, employee satisfaction correlated with reduced employee turnover is misguided. Firms need to know *who* is thrilled with the firm and who is leaving. Is the firm losing its key talent and retaining its underperformers, or vice versa? What HR needs are *strategic* metrics that can impact workforce decision-making, thereby delivering greater customer and economic value. Thus the role of HR metrics must be reconsidered, driven by strategic resource allocation, and used for strategic workforce decision-making.

Further attempts by HR to become relevant were to develop competency models (either provided by consultants or developed by HR professionals) for line managers to improve their workforce management skills. Such efforts raised questions for line managers about the contribution of the HR profession as a discipline. The link between such competencies and customer and economic value has not been demonstrated. These models often centered around aspects of "leader likeability," as opposed to how the workforce should be managed to create customer and economic value.

On the other hand, when HR's focus is on how HR practices can maximize customer and economic value, it is speaking the same language as line managers. When the HR function can demonstrate that it can impact strategic value, it stands to be taken far more seriously. If HR wants to join the firm's strategic planning game, it must bring ways of impacting customer and economic value to the table and score on the business scorecard.

HR's failure

There is recent evidence of the failure of HR to serve many major firms. Wal-Mart, DuPont, GlaxoSmithKline, Novartis, BT, Tata Consultancy Services, among others, have named as heads of HR individuals with little or no background in Human Resources. The corollary is that few, if any, move from the HR function to become heads of manufacturing, engineering, finance, supply chain, and so on. What is missing is a professional domain that has the professional rigor to change its mind-set, how it uses resources, and what value the function is to deliver.

HR's mind-set change requires thinking like the leader of a business first and foremost. But it is not enough to know and understand the business; the HR professional must think like a strategist and understand how to impact the business scorecard, by impacting the behavior of a workforce that creates customer and process outcomes that lead to financial outcomes by asking questions such as:

■ What work in the firm adds value (i.e., customer or economic value)?
■ What work does the firm need more (or less) of?
■ What can HR do to ensure that work of less or no strategic value is eliminated)?
■ What work should be initiated to add strategic value?
■ How should value-adding work processes be structured?

We must not only question the mind-set of the profession but also how the profession can influence the mind-set of the firm. Focusing a firm's culture adds value, but just wishing to be a strategic player is asking for justification without efficacy. The HR function must demonstrate its value to *deserve* a seat at the table. Until it can demonstrate why it belongs, it will receive little respect.

Best practices on HR's tendency to "keep up with the Joneses," in the hope that if it adopts the catchphrase de jure, it will earn respect. HR is often more comfortable with the respect of fellow HR professionals, rather than with the criticism raised by astute business strategists. Comforted by campaigns such as employer of choice, employee engagement, and so on, HR has given little thought as to whether these create value, as is shown in Figure 28.1. The focus that we need to bring is not HR employee satisfaction, but value-creating behavior that makes a difference – not mission statements, visions, or values, puffery that has little efficacy once the ink has dried. If such expectations had meaning, they would be inspected in performance appraisals, selection, and reward systems, training programs and so on in an attempt to impact the firm's success. Even if the language found its way into the traditional HR tools, there is no point in creating expectations if those expectations are not inspected and firm leaders are not held accountable for making these admonitions a reality.

Value-creating workforce management transition ...

Equality → Equity

Engagement → Employee strategic focus

Employer of choice → Employee of choice

Entitlement → Earned increases

Employment for a lifetime → Employability

Figure 28.1 Leading the workforce management transition

Second, the mind-set of HR needs to regard the workforce as a resource, one which must be systematically allocated, measured, and managed like any other. Firms have systems for the allocation, measurement and management of other resources, which provide consequences for those who effectively or ineffectively manage them. What is the system for the workforce? Figure 28.2 is an example in which financial resources, material resources, information and time, each have their own system — a budget for financial resources, supply chain for material resources, data analytics for information technology, and schedules for time. What is the system to manage the workforce? Firms must have systems by which they can hold line managers accountable for the workforce (just as we hold them accountable for other resources). This is where the HR function has a critical role to play.

Finally, HR professionals must create customer and economic value. If HR is to be invited to the strategic planning party, its deliverable must be considered strategic. We must impact the strategy of the firm. In the business context, this means HR must deliver a strategic workforce that creates customer and economic value by influencing the customer's perception of the value of the product or service the firm is offering in the marketplace; enabling the firm to charge its desired price, and/or enabling the firm to produce at its desired cost. By this definition, the HR function must ask how it creates value and how it can best utilize its tools and practices to further enhance value creation. This is critical to firm survival, for the workforce in many firms is its largest expenditure. For HR to impact the value-creation process, considerable time, effort and energy must be devoted to understanding the firm's strategic capabilities (i.e., core competencies) and how HR can impact the workforce that creates customer and economic value. Once the HR function understands how customer and economic value are created, it can identify and focus on those *strategic* positions within the strategic capabilities that make a difference in the firm's strategic success.

Business strategy is about differentiation on the outside; the resource allocation systems differentiate on the inside (e.g., financial resources, material resources, information, and time). How do we differentiate with the workforce? What are the criteria for that differentiation? What is the accountability system to measure how well the strategic allocation of the workforce has been realized? The answer to these questions requires profound changes in the way we look at the HR profession and HR practices, and dramatically influences the delivery of a workforce that can substantially impact the value creation of firms. HR can no longer act like lemmings, subscribing to every viral slogan that infects the HR community, but must understand where and how value is created and focus the workforce upon strategic value creation. This will mean differentiating within the workforce and requires HR professionals to become business professionals first and HR professionals second.

For many, this is a challenge. Many HR practitioners never entered the profession to become a business leader. Far too many entered to work with people, a noble aspiration in a social worker or in the clergy, but counterproductive in the current business environment. The *raison d'être* of the firm is to create customer and economic value. That is how firms serve society, and that is how the HR function should serve the firm. Global competition is forcing this issue ever more and will continue to eliminate non-value-added work from organizations as firms become more sophisticated about how precious resources are best utilized.

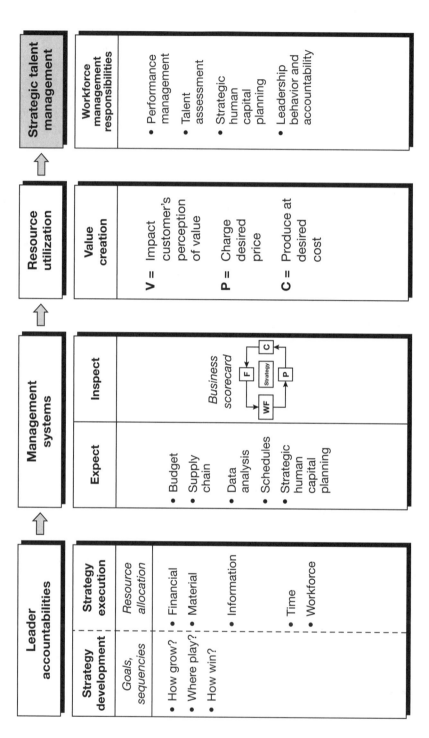

Figure 28.2 The strategic context of workforce management systems

HR's future

This approach advocates a substantially different perspective for looking at HR. HR professionals need to address value creation through workforce management in terms of the strategic focus of the workforce, as well as strategic talent management. This is how HR can impact the workforce and subsequently the success of the firm's strategy. How HR does this is the challenge, but it is critical to understand what this entails. A focus upon value creation requires asking:

- What is strategic value in my firm?
- Where is strategic value created in my firm?
- Does our workforce understand where and how customer and economic value is created?
- What roles or positions create customer and economic value in my firm?
- Who are the incumbents in these roles and how effective are they?
- How will we find or build emerging talent to serve in these roles?

The mission of HR and the metrics associated with this mission will also require asking different questions. For example, What do we want our workforce to understand? How do we know they understand it? This is the strategic focus of the workforce and requires answers to such questions as:

- Who are our customers?
- Which customers are our profitable core, which are "stretch" customers, who are "problem" customers?
- How well are we doing with each customer subset?
- Which customers do we need to give priority or less attention to?
- Do we understand how we add value to be even more successful with our customers in the future?
- What is our level of profitability?
- What work creates strategic value?
- What work destroys wealth?

These are not the traditional questions HR asks. It is not the traditional mission/vision/value issues, but rather forces HR to focus from the outside-in and the reality of the marketplace, to provide the critical HR and workforce understanding that creating value is the only way a firm survives, and that job security depends on customer security. Without customer security there is no job security for any employee in any firm. HR professionals should therefore adopt an economic/market-oriented perspective and seek to provide the workforce with answers.

HR's mission and metrics: understanding, ability, doing and delivering

The mission of HR is to influence the workforce in four major areas, all of which have metrics implications. Focusing on these four areas simplifies and clarifies the mission of the HR function:

1. What do we want our workforce to *understand*?
2. What *abilities* do we want our workforce to have that create customer and economic value?
3. What do we want our workforce to be able to *do* (behaviors based on the workforce's understanding of value creation) to create the value expected?
4. How do we assess how well HR *delivers* a successful workforce with the right understanding, abilities, and behavior?

The answers to these questions are critical. Metrics can be designed for each, enabling HR to have a profound impact on the strategic success of any firm. Very simply, HR can measure what its workforce understands about value creation, what abilities it has that create value, whether it has behaved in ways that create value, and the magnitude of the value created. These are the HR metrics challenges for today's, *not* tomorrow's organizations.

Conclusion and summary

In summary, we urge rethinking the role of HR in the context of the firm's strategy – the role the function must have in delivering a workforce that creates customer and economic value. Otherwise, why have an HR function? Many aspects of HR are transactional, and many of those transactions can and are being outsourced. The real question is: How can HR focus on the creation of strategic value through the firm's workforce in ways that create customer and economic value? If we can understand, design, and deliver ways to do so, the HR profession can have a profound impact on the firm's scorecard, add value and build HR leaders able to build workforces with the strategic understanding and capability of creating the value which sustains the firm's existence.

The above approach may differ from the European approach to HR, because it focuses first on the creation of customer value as the primary mission of firms in serving society, and second on the "superordinate" goal of creating wealth because it is the only way of funding the firm's future strategic initiatives. In fact, a broad-based stakeholder approach usually damages employees in communities it purports to help because it may not generate enough wealth to sustain the firm and/or causes the firm to divert new investments to more efficient economies and firms that best use their earnings on initiative which expand job creation and subsequent employment.

References

Beatty, R.W. and Schneier, C.E. (1997) "New HR roles to impact organizational performance: from 'partners' to 'players' ", *Human Resource Management*, 36(3): 2–20.

Becker, B. and Gerhart, B. (1996) "The impact of human resource management on organizational performance: Progress and prospects", *The Academy of Management Journal*, 39(4): 779–801.

Huselid, M.A. and Becker, B.E. (1997) "The impact of high performance work systems, implementation effectiveness and alignment with strategy on shareholder wealth", *Academy of Management Best Papers Proceedings*, 144–148.

Huselid, M.A., Becker, B.E. and Beatty, R.W. (2005) *The Workforce Scorecard: Managing Human Capital to Execute Strategy*. Boston: Harvard Business School Press.

Ulrich, D. (1997) *Human Resource Champions*. Cambridge, MA: Harvard Business School Press.

Ulrich, D. and Brockbank, W. (2005) *The HR Value Proposition*. Cambridge, MA: Harvard Business School Press.

29

The effect of organizational change on managers' experience of their working lives

Les Worrall and Cary L. Cooper

Introduction

It is undeniable that the last twenty years have seen huge changes in organizational and family life with change in these two domains being inextricably linked as embodied in debates around the work–life balance. The purpose of this chapter is to explore the effects these changes have had on how workers, and particularly managers in larger organizations, perceive their working lives. Rose (2005) has recently drawn attention to what he terms the "despondency thesis" which he has developed from his review of several recent studies that have taken stock of the affective states of UK workers. He cites the recent publications from the Economic and Social Research Council's Future of Work programme, which have revealed a substantial decline in job satisfaction in the UK, and he also cites the Work Foundation which has found that UK workers have become far more critical of their employers and more likely to voice their dissatisfactions with their reward and their working conditions. Other research has revealed that work intensification and declining task discretion have accounted for the observed decline in job satisfaction in the UK (Green and Tsitsianis, 2005). Madeleine Bunting (2004) has also contributed to the debate around the despondency thesis in her book on "willing slaves" where she discusses issues such as work–life balance and the effect of poor job design on employees' health and well-being. Our own research (Worrall and Cooper, 2006) based solely on UK managers has also contributed to the despondency thesis in that we found that managers' physical and psychological well-being have been negatively affected by their sense of not being in control in the workplace; by the effect of a growing architecture and technology of surveillance embedded in performance management regimes; and by their sense of work overload. As Rifkin (1995, cited in Nolan and Wood, 2003) identified, in an era of considerable economic and organizational change "No group is being harder hit than management". The dimensions to be explored include primarily managers' sense of their physical and psychological well-being, though we will examine the effects of different types of organizational change on workers' sense of job security, morale, motivation and loyalty.

This chapter is divided into four main sections. In the first section the objective is to discuss briefly our view of how the despondency thesis has emerged by exploring how the changing environment in which business organizations operate has led to both the intensification (working harder) and extensification (working longer) of work (Burchell et al., 2002) and how a number of strategic human resource management instruments may have exacerbated the effects of increasing work overload. In the second section, the aim is to paint a picture of the scale and nature of organizational change in the UK and to assess its effects on managers using data from a study conducted for the Chartered Management Institute, funded by the Health and Safety Executive, in 2006. In the third section, we will use data derived from the study to gain some insights into the perceived effect of various organizational stressors on managers' physical and psychological well-being. We shall conclude with some observations about the implications of our findings for the design, development and implementation of human resource management strategies.

Organizational change in the UK and its effect on patterns of work

There is a considerable business strategy literature that discusses the nature of the complex relationship between an organization and the environment in which it operates. The adherents and proponents of structural contingency theory (Donaldson, 2001) would argue that the internal configuration of an organization is defined by the demands of the environment in which it operates, implying that organizations need to change continually if they are to maintain a degree of fit with their environments. Resource-based theorists argue that a firm will only survive if it first defines its distinctive competencies and then structures itself around those competencies discarding any activity that it defines as non-core (Prahalad and Hamel, 1990). This tendency to define the core business of the organization has led many to discard functions that are considered non-core and that someone else can do better and more cheaply. Increasingly, in the rhetoric that surrounds the "knowledge economy", the capacity of an organization to develop new knowledge is seen as the path organizations must tread if they are to develop products and services that are non-imitable thus leading to sustainable competitive advantage. These strategic panaceas have become surrounded by a panoply of managerial tools and techniques needed for their implementation.

However, in our view, the world of business strategy and strategic management, with its host of rhetoric-laden technologies designed to bring about goal-directed organizational change, seems to bear little resemblance to the reality of organizational change that has been experienced by most workers (Worrall et al., 2000). Our consistent findings (from 1997 to 2006) have revealed that organizational change in the UK has been perceived to be driven primarily by strategies and tactics geared far more to improving productivity by *cost reduction* than to improving the competitive basis of an organization by innovation, new product and new market development (Worrall and Cooper, 2006). It is our view that there has been a continuing trend over the last decade for employers to develop labour handling strategies that have led to the more intensive use of labour. This they have achieved by modifying the labour process to reduce task discretion and by increasing control and surveillance through performance management regimes. Delayering, redundancy and offshoring, which have led to significant "headcount culls", have been used, ostensibly, in the interests of improving competitiveness and productivity by taking out costs. Under this ethos employees are seen as costs to be cut, not as assets to be nurtured and developed (Cascio, 2002).

There has been a significant growth in interest in the "high-performance work organization" or "high-commitment management systems" emphasizing bundles of interlinked strategic HRM practices (MacDuffie, 1995; Purcell et al., 2003) designed to increase empowerment, enhance employee skills and raise motivation which the proponents of these practices (Appelbaum and Berg, 2001 cited in White et al., 2003) argue are in the interest of both employers (who gain from improved productivity) and employees (who gain from acquiring improved skills, higher levels of job satisfaction and increased job security). However, research by White and his colleagues (2003) provides clear "quantitative and qualitative evidence" (p. 178) that "employees do not always benefit from high performance work practices" (p. 191) given that these practices involve the implementation of performance management regimes and other control and surveillance regimes that serve to intensify the work effort, increase pressure upon workers, sharpen employee accountability and contribute to the creation of what White et al. describe as "negative job-to-home spillovers" (p. 181). Burchell et al. (2002) describe this phenomenon as "work extensification". White et al. (2003, p. 192) warn us that "If these practices continue to diffuse, they will lead to further work intensification and the creation of more severe pressure on home life". Clearly, these high-performance regimes seem to be predicated on a unitaristic view of organizations that is, perhaps, a view only held by naïve managers and the management consultants that peddle their wares to them. Despite what the business strategists and management consultants seem to think, it is much more difficult for any large organization to align all stakeholders than is often suggested.

A review of the human resources literature, in our view, exposes what we feel is a critical deficiency: inadequate attention has been paid to the political economy of organizational change. The UK is characterized by an active Stock Market and the growth of the institutional investor, often in the form of pension funds, has been marked by an increased emphasis on the generation of short-term shareholder value. Froud et al. (2000a, b) have written extensively about the way that organizations are increasingly being managed to meet short-term financial objectives that tend to crowd out long-term human resource development objectives. Williams (2000) has argued that the primacy of shareholder value maximization has changed business priorities and behaviours and that it has been used to legitimize corporate restructuring and downsizing. He has argued that the quest for short-term value maximization has created a "more carnivorous type of capitalism" (Williams, 2000, p. 1) often involving downsizing and an increased willingness to "sweat out labour" (p. 6). To quote Studs Terkel, "Bob Cratchit may still be hanging on but Scrooge has been replaced by the conglomerate" (Terkel, 1972, p. xiv). Labour has been seen as "the first casualty" of shareholder value maximization-driven restructuring (Froud et al., 2000a, p. 771) with a prevailing view that "the more redundancies, the better for shareholders" (p. 776). Jones (2002) has argued that corporate restructuring, often in the form of headcount culls, have been little more than cynical signalling mechanisms to the market designed to boost share prices and there is a large volume of evidence (see Collett, 2002) that shows that share prices often increase after the announcement of large headcount culls or mergers where post-merger headcount reductions are seen as inevitable.

While the public sector does not have shareholders, it does have other forms of stakeholder that are keen to see change. A plethora of central government legislation since the late 1970s has focused on reinventing government (Osborne and Gaebler, 1992) by outsourcing services and exposing government services to competition and market forces. Clarke and Newman (1997) commented that this process of public sector "marketization" was accompanied by a process of "managerialization" and the creation of a "new public management" (Ferlie et al., 1996) heavily dependent on performance management systems which, some would argue, have been put in place to "name and shame" poor performers. Recent research has revealed declining levels of task discretion in public sector professionals (Gallie et al., 2004). Others have argued that the managerialization of the public sector has been designed to shift power from "the professionals" to "the managers" (Kirkpatrick and Ackroyd, 2003) and to "whip the professionals into shape" (Bolton, 2004; Pollitt, 1993) so that the public sector can be run on "sound business principles" (Boyne, 2002).

The "modernization agenda" in the public sector has resulted in reduced staffing, work intensification, the growth of performance monitoring regimes and control architectures (Richardson et al., 2005), a shift in power from professionals to managers (Mather et al., 2007) and reduced "worker discretion" (Grugulis et al., 2003; Rainbird et al., 2004, p. 94). Felstead et al. (2004) have identified a decrease in the proportion of public sector workers feeling that they have choice over the way they do their job and workers feeling that they have less influence over how hard they work. In essence, Felstead and others have found that change in the public sector designed to "take out costs" and improve efficiency has resulted in the intensification and degradation of work, increased work overload, a deterioration in work–life balance and less job involvement for many public sector workers. Our own research has identified that the key stressors for public sector managers included the unmanageability of work, work overload, persistent organizational change, having little control over key aspects of their job, over-zealous performance monitoring and low levels of job involvement (Worrall and Cooper, 2006).

The clear driver for change in both the private and public sector has been cost reduction (Worrall and Cooper, 2006) with change having been enacted through the redefinition of organizational labour handling strategies and the redesign of the employment relationship and the creation of more flexible forms of employment (Gallie et al., 1998). Merger and acquisition activity has been rife in the UK: many building societies, for example, have been demutualized and have subsequently been taken over, and several large accountancy practices and management consultancies have merged. Downsizing, delayering and redundancy programmes have been used to reduce headcounts prior to and after merger and acquisition activity. Organizational boundaries have been redefined by outsourcing, developing networks and partnerships and, in the public sector, by developing shared service agreements between local authorities. Other tactics have involved shifting production to lower wage economies (offshoring); deploying new technology and substituting technology for labour; and "down-scoping" (i.e. focusing in on a narrower set of functions and products). In addition to these substantive changes, many organizations have also put in place culture change programmes which can, cynically, be interpreted as attitudinal and behaviour modification programmes to educate workers to expect less from the employing organization, particularly in their conditions of employment such as reduced pension entitlements and a heightened sense of job insecurity (Burchell et al., 2002; Worrall et al., 2000). While we have identified that there are many possible forms of change, it is important not to see these as unrelated single-strand change initiatives. It has become increasingly common for several change projects to run simultaneously within organizations as organizational change has become more multi-dimensional. We have argued (Worrall and Cooper, 2006) that these persistent and more complex patterns of change have had a substantially greater impact on employees as organizational structures, processes, boundaries, cultures, roles and performance expectations have changed simultaneously and, occasionally, in contradictory ways (Cascio, 2005).

Having developed a framework for understanding why and how organizations change, we now turn to examining what effects these changes have had on managers' perceptions of organizational life, their sense of well-being, their behaviours in the workplace and in the way they manage the boundary between their working lives and their non-working lives. Our task in the following section will be to quantify the scale and dimensionality of organizational change, before going on to assess the effects of these changes on managers.

The scale and nature of organizational change and its effect on managers' perceptions of their organization as a place to work

In 2005–6, the Health and Safety Executive (through the Workplace Health Connect Initiative[1]) funded a national study into the effects of organizational change on UK managers. The study was conducted in conjunction with the Chartered Management Institute (Worrall and Cooper, 2006) as their membership database was used as a sampling frame. The survey was conducted as part of our longitudinal "Quality of Working Life" project that began in 1997 (Worrall and Cooper, 1997). The questionnaire was Internet-based and circulated to 10,000 members of the Institute; 1,642 completed questionnaires were returned (a response rate of 16.4%). The questionnaire was addressed to individual members of the Institute and not focused on specific organizations. As with all questionnaires of this type, there are concerns about the representativeness of the sample; these issues are discussed in depth in Worrall and Cooper, 2006. The analysis presented here is based on 840 managers working in PLCs (261 cases), private limited companies (185 cases) and public sector organizations (394 cases) employing over 250 people. Large firms (employing 250 plus) have been selected as they have well-developed internal labour markets and to ensure a degree of comparability between these three types of organization.

Findings about the scale and nature of organizational change

According to our data set, organizational change has achieved epidemic proportions in the UK and has increased since the late 1990s. Not only has the volume of change increased, so too has its complexity as managers now tend to be confronted by more forms of change concurrently than when our research began in 1997. As shown in Table 29.1, in 2006, over 75% of managers had experienced a cost-reduction programme in their organization in the last year with over 64% having experienced culture change programmes and the use of short-term contract staff to replace discarded workers who had been employed on full-time contracts.

Our findings reveal the extent to which change of different types has permeated different types of organization. In line with our assumptions about the effect of financialization, redundancies, outsourcing, delayering and offshoring were more pronounced in PLCs than in private

Table 29.1 The incidence of organizational change by type of organization (percentage of managers citing)

Form of change	Private limited company	PLC	Public sector	All
Cost-reduction programme	65.5	71.3	82.3	75.3
Culture change programme	52.1	60.1	73.5	64.7
Use of short-term contract staff	58.2	65.7	66.6	64.5
Expansion into new markets	57.2	46.3	n/a	52.1
Redundancies	46.4	51.1	37.0	43.4
Outsourcing	30.4	41.4	27.2	32.2
Delayering	25.8	33.6	25.3	27.9
Merger	14.4	18.7	16.2	16.6
Offshoring	11.3	23.5	n/a	10.3
Average number of types of change experienced concurrently	3.04	3.65	3.30*	

* The average for the public sector is calculated using a lower base than for the two other types of organization as public sector organizations are not able to expand into new markets nor did any engage in offshoring.

limited companies (many of which were family-owned businesses or other owner-managed businesses). Interestingly, managers in private limited companies were more likely to report that their companies had expanded into new markets than were managers in PLCs, and offshoring was much less pronounced in private limited companies than in PLCs. We feel this is consistent with private limited companies taking more of a long-term, developmental and benign view of the need for organizational change than PLCs. The public sector was characterized by a high proportion of managers reporting cost reduction, culture change and the increased use of contract staff. The proportion of managers citing redundancies, outsourcing and delayering was generally lower than the levels experienced in PLCs indicating, perhaps, that higher levels of unionization may have made public sector workers more difficult to "get rid of".

The effects of change on managers' perceptions of their organization as a place to work

The implementation of change to bring about "high-performance work organizations" is often based on the assumption that both the employer and the employee benefit from change. But, our findings reveal that the majority of managerial employees had negative views of the effects of change. Over 52% of managers felt that change had led to increased accountability, 70% felt it had reduced their morale, 63% reported a lower sense of job security, 60% felt that their level of motivation had been reduced and 57% felt that both employee well-being and loyalty had been reduced. Slightly more felt that employee participation had decreased (34%) than felt it had increased (33%) but more felt that the effect of change had been to slow down decision-making (44%) than to increase it (22%). Interestingly, a clear majority felt that the effect of change had been to cause the organization to lose key skills and experience (57% agreed that they had been lost while 20% did not). Given that the majority of change was predicated on improving productivity and profitability, it was disconcerting to note that only about 37% agreed that organizational change had led to productivity and profitability gains. The perceived effects of change were worst in the public sector. While 60% of managers in private limited companies reported that change reduced their morale, this increased to 64% in PLCs and to 78% among managers in the public sector. Public sector managers were far more likely to feel that change had negatively affected employee well-being (63%) than managers in the two other sectors (54% in PLCs and 48% in private limited companies). Not surprisingly, absenteeism levels were much higher in the public sector than in PLCs and in private limited companies (4.5 days per head were lost on average in the public sector in the last year compared to 2.7 days in PLCs and 1.6 days in private limited companies). The more benign approach to change in private limited companies seemed to have manifested itself in significantly lower levels of absence, but relatively high levels of absenteeism in the public sector may reflect higher levels of morbidity or the more lax administration of absence management control systems.

The directors of organizations were far more positive about the effects of change than were senior, middle and junior managers. The differences in the perceptions of directors of the effect of change on managers' working lives compared to other levels of manager were considerable: for example, directors' views about the effect of organizational change on organizational productivity and profitability, on workplace loyalty, motivation and morale were significantly different – and more favourable – from those of even senior managers (see Worrall and Cooper, 2004). Directors were significantly more likely to think that change had resulted in increased profitability, productivity, flexibility and accountability, and significantly less likely to think that change had had negative effects on morale, loyalty, motivation, job security and employee well-being. The dissonance in the perceptions of directors compared to all other levels of manager (including senior managers) calls into question the unitaristic view of organizations on which the move to high-performance work organizations seems to be predicated.

Work extensification, work–life balance and negative job-to-home spillover

In the last few years, there has been a considerable volume of work published on work extensification and the work–life balance. We see work–life imbalance occurring when the labour supply preferences of workers do not match with the working hours demands of employers. Our earlier research (Worrall and Cooper, 1997) reveals that the majority of managers rationalize their long working hours using terms such as "it is the only way to deal with workload", "it is part of my organization's culture", and "it is expected by my employer"; it is clear that the overwhelming majority of managers, particularly the more junior managers, do not work long hours through choice. Indeed, Green and Tsitsianis (2005, p. 410) found that "There is an increasing preponderance of workers who wish to work fewer hours". Many organizations now have "family-friendly" or work–life balance initiatives in place despite the well-known fact that Britain has a "long hours culture" and that workers in the UK work the longest hours in the European Union (Nolan and Wood, 2003). While many organizations have work–life balance policies in place, White et al. (2003, p. 179) argue that these are "little more than an aspiration for the majority (of employers)".

The average manager in our 2006 study claimed to work 1.6 hours over contract per day: in a working week this amounts to an additional day in excess of contract and over the working year of 200 days, this amounts to an additional 43 days. The average manager lost 3.3 days per year in sickness absence and this implies that for each day's absence, the average manager supplied over 13 "free" days to their employer. Over 41% of managers claimed to work more than two hours per day over contract (50.3% in private limited companies, 42.1% in PLCs and 36.8% in the public sector). Directors were much more likely to claim that they worked more than two hours per day over their contract hours (75.0%) than senior managers (53.5%), middle managers (36.6%) and junior managers (17.9%).

Managers, particularly directors and senior managers, were clearly working well over their contract hours: they were asked what effect this was having on various aspects of their working and non-working lives. Substantial proportions of managers reported that working long hours had injurious effects particularly on their relationships with their children, their social life, their relationship with the spouse or partner and on their health (see Table 29.2). Interestingly, while directors tended to work the longest hours, they rated the impact of working long hours on these areas less than all other managers. While 51.2% of junior managers felt that working long hours injuriously affected their morale, this declined to 32.7% for directors. The equivalent figures for the effect of working long hours on productivity were 53.1% and 33.9%. In these two cases, there was a negative association between hours worked over contract and the perceived impact of working these long hours.

The analysis reveals that there is a strong spillover effect of working long hours into managers' non-working lives. Not only do long hours lead to tiredness in the workplace, they also contribute strongly to reducing the quality of managers' relationships with their children and partners, to managers' ill-health and to reducing the quality of managers' social lives which in turn reduces their ability to rest and recuperate from the exigencies of their working lives. Our findings strongly echo those of White et al. (2003) who have argued that existing policy and practice in the realm of work–life balance and the creation of the family-friendly organization look "feeble" and that "systems of workplace regulation are failing to cope" (p. 192) with

Table 29.2 The effect of long working hours by level in the organization (percentage citing that working long hours has a negative effect)

Level	Effect on morale	Effect on productivity	Relationship with spouse or partner[1]	Relationship with children[2]	Relationship with colleagues	Effect on social life	Effect on health
Director	32.7	33.9	55.3	65.8	34.4	67.8	50.8
Senior manager	33.7	43.2	64.9	72.7	35.3	68.9	58.6
Middle manager	43.1	51.0	65.8	73.4	37.3	64.6	59.0
Junior manager	51.2	53.1	66.4	74.2	44.8	67.4	67.2
All managers	40.4	47.3	63.6	72.5	37.6	66.7	59.7

Notes

[1] Includes only those managers who had a partner/spouse
[2] Includes only those managers who had dependent children

the more "carnivorous form of capitalism" that Williams (2003) has identified and with the constant flow of modernizing legislation that is being inflicted upon the public sector (Local Government Employers' Organisation, undated).

Managers' physical and psychological health: effects and outcomes

Our 2006 study was funded by the Health and Safety Executive specifically to explore how issues such as organizational change, managers' control over their pace of work, task discretion and work overload affected managers' physical and psychological well-being. To achieve this we used a previously validated organizational analysis tool known as ASSET[2] to assess the relationship between the presence of symptoms of ill-health among managers and a set of stressors. The incidence of ill-health symptoms is shown in Table 29.3.

Almost 60% of managers reported that they had sometimes or often experienced constant tiredness, sleep loss or muscular tension with substantial proportions reporting having experienced becoming angry, having headaches, constant irritability and mood swings. Managers in the public sector scored highest on sixteen of the seventeen measures. The analysis reveals that a significant proportion of managers had sometimes or often experienced symptoms of ill-health with one in six public sector managers claiming to have experienced panic or anxiety attacks and one in three sometimes or often having felt unable to cope.

The stressor items used in ASSET and the percentage of managers agreeing with each item (which was measured using a six-point scale) are shown in Table 29.4. The most salient items were: having to deal with difficult customers; work interfering with home and personal life; not having enough time to do the job well; a concern about pay and benefits; and, managers working longer hours than they would choose to. About one in four respondents indicated that they did not enjoy their job and about one in seven saw their job as dull and repetitive. Over 30% of managers in PLCs claimed not to enjoy their job and over 40% of managers felt that their job was adversely affecting their health.

While the levels of these measures are interesting in themselves, the key issue is to explore the relationship between these measures and managers' physical and psychological health.

Table 29.3 The percentage of managers citing that they have "sometimes" or "often" experienced various ill-health symptoms

Symptom	Private limited company	PLC	Public sector	All
Constant tiredness	62.7	56.9	60.5	59.8
Insomnia – sleep loss	54.2	54.5	61.9	57.9
Muscular tension/aches and pains	53.1	53.1	61.5	57.1
Lack of appetite or over-eating	51.1	43.4	48.3	47.4
Feeling or becoming angry too easily	44.7	44.7	49.2	46.8
Headaches	48.3	38.4	51.7	46.8
Having difficulty concentrating	38.8	38.3	43.2	40.7
Indigestion or heartburn	40.7	35.7	43.5	40.5
Loss of sense of humour	28.8	34.4	35.8	33.8
Constant irritability	30.9	31.5	36.1	33.5
Mood swings	29.8	29.9	34.1	31.9
Feeling unable to cope	21.3	24.8	33.3	28.0
Avoiding contact with other people	26.8	24.8	28.6	27.0
Unable to listen to other people	19.6	21.7	25.5	23.0
Difficulty in making decisions	14.5	18.4	26.8	21.5
Feeling nauseous or being sick	14.5	13.0	19.4	16.4
Panic or anxiety attacks	7.8	14.2	17.8	14.5

Table 29.4 Percentage of managers agreeing with each statement

Stressor	Private limited company	PLC	Public sector	All
I have to deal with difficult customers/clients	60.9	65.2	75.1	68.9
My work interferes with my home and personal life	68.2	64.6	59.7	63.1
I do not have enough time to do my job as well as I would like	53.1	54.2	60.6	56.9
My pay/benefits are not as good as other people doing similar work	50.6	54.8	59.6	56.1
I work longer hours than I choose or want to	51.7	55.9	52.6	53.4
My performance at work is closely monitored	49.7	50.6	52.1	51.1
My organization is constantly changing for change's sake	36.1	44.8	60.8	50.4
I have little control over many aspects of my job	44.4	50.8	50.1	49.1
I am given unmanageable workloads	36.2	45.1	45.9	43.5
I am not involved in decisions affecting my job	37.4	40.5	42.6	40.8
My job is adversely affecting my health	38.5	43.0	39.7	40.5
I may be doing the same job for the next five to ten years	39.1	33.7	41.4	38.5
I am set unrealistic objectives	27.4	39.8	34.2	34.4
I spend too much time travelling in my job	36.9	39.3	25.4	32.3
The technology in my job has overloaded me	25.0	31.3	32.3	30.4
I have little or no influence over my performance targets	23.6	32.8	29.2	29.1
I work unsocial hours	25.6	29.9	23.2	25.8
I do not enjoy my job	19.7	30.6	23.2	24.7
My ideas or suggestions are never taken into account	19.8	23.1	22.9	22.3
My physical working conditions are unpleasant	15.7	17.8	24.6	20.5
My job involves the risk of actual physical violence	6.7	5.2	27.3	15.9
My work is dull and repetitive	11.8	15.8	13.9	14.0

To this end, the seventeen symptoms were collapsed into two composite measures: one to assess managers' physical health and one to assess their psychological health. Using factor analysis, the stressors were collapsed into six factors. The correlation matrix between the two well-being outcome measures and the six symptoms composite measures is shown in Table 29.5.

The correlation matrix reveals that there were very strong associations between the psychological health measure and managers' sense of control over their job, their work–life balance and job overload. In order to explore the associations in more detail, a correlation analysis revealed that the psychological health measure was strongly related to the following individual items:

- My job is adversely affecting my health;
- I am given unmanageable workloads;
- My work interferes with my home and personal life;
- I have little control over many aspects of my job;
- I do not have enough time to do my job as well as I would like;
- I do not enjoy my job;
- I work longer hours than I choose or want to;
- I am not involved in decisions affecting my job;
- I am set unrealistic objectives;
- My ideas or suggestions are never taken into account;
- I have little or no influence over my performance targets;
- My organization is constantly changing for change's sake;
- The technology in my job has overloaded me.

Managers who had experienced the psychological symptoms most intensively were particularly concerned about the manageability of their workloads, having unreasonable objectives and little influence over the performance targets that affected them, having little control over aspects of their job, not having enough time to do their jobs as they would like to and their jobs having an impact on their life outside work.

Given our earlier concerns about work intensification, we see the strong relationship between job overload and both physical and psychological health as very significant, as we a rgue that further intensification – which is a clear outcome of cost reduction strategies – can only lead to the further deterioration of managers' health. Additionally, the rise of more powerful forms of overt and covert surveillance in the workplace through instruments such as

Table 29.5 Correlations between physical and psychological health and stressors

	Physical health	Psycho-logical health	Work–life balance	Control over job	Job design aspects	Health effect of job	Reward	Job over-load
Physical health	1.000							
Psychological health	0.708	1.000						
Work–life balance	0.365	0.420	1.000					
Control over job	0.404	0.475	0.381	1.000				
Job design aspects	0.385	0.388	0.368	0.587	1.000			
Health effect of job	0.541	0.598	0.542	0.478	0.392	1.000		
Reward	0.255	0.233	0.251	0.301	0.348	0.290	1.000	
Job overload	0.463	0.530	0.552	0.590	0.542	0.663	0.371	1.000

All correlations are significant at the 0.01 level.

performance management systems can only serve to increase managers' sense of being watched and controlled. We are concerned that further increases in workplace control strategies can only serve to reduce managers' health particularly if they feel that they are not consulted about the setting of targets and that the targets and objectives they are expected to achieve are unreasonable and unattainable. As Nolan and Wood (2003, p. 173) remarked, "command-and-control systems are very much in evidence in Anglo-Saxon economies, and probably more widely than ever". To reinforce the concerns raised by White et al. (2003), we clearly have grounds to be concerned about increasing levels of surveillance, control and work overload in the workplace that seem to be a consequence of the enthusiastic adoption of performance management systems in which workers are saddled with undeliverable objectives over which they have little or no control.

Managers were asked to indicate what effect the ill-health symptoms they had experienced in the last three months had had on them. The largest impacts were cited as reduced productivity, a reduced sense of self-efficacy and decreased workplace morale. However, of the managers who had experienced various symptoms, very few managers had reduced their hours, changed their role in the organization or sought medical advice or other guidance. Despite a large proportion of managers experiencing several symptoms, sometimes acutely, it appears that the normal response was to carry on – "business as usual". Perhaps Madeleine Bunting's description of workers as "willing slaves" is appropriate and perhaps understandable given the financial constraints and strictures that affect many workers in today's highly indebted society where the average person is, if one includes mortgages, in debt to the tune of £52,800. Recent estimates indicate that there were between seven and nine million people in the UK in November 2006 with "a serious debt problem" (UK personal debt statistics: http://www.creditaction.org.uk/debtstats.htm).

Conclusions

Our study findings contribute to what Rose (2005) labelled the "despondency thesis". We are not alone in contributing to a body of literature and a series of academic and political debates that identify serious dysfunctions in organizations and in the way that work is being restructured to meet the interests of what Williams (2002) has labelled a more "carnivorous form of capitalism" where the short-term interests of shareholder value maximization crowd out longer term considerations. Hence, organizational developments that are focused on skills development, increased workplace democracy and business development through innovation tend to be neglected. Our research has revealed that there is a fixation in the UK with cost reduction, redundancy, delayering, the substitution of existing workers with agency workers and workers on short-term contracts and with offshoring both jobs and functions to low wage economies.

While we see this as the reality of organizational change, the management literature is conversely replete with depictions of "high-performance work systems" and "high-commitment work practices". These we regard as cynical and rhetorical devices designed to obfuscate what is really happening in large organizations in the UK. The rhetoric of the high-performance workplace does not sit well with the large volume of literature that has revealed declining job satisfaction across the UK, declining levels of task discretion in the public sector and the demise of well-established employee benefits such as final salary pension schemes.

Our research has revealed that managers in the UK are experiencing high and increasing levels of disaffection as a result of persistent and increasingly multi-stranded organizational change. Most managers, excluding directors, feel that this change is not being well managed, that it is being used cynically to "make the assets sweat" and that it is having undermining effects on employee motivation, morale, loyalty and sense of job security. Change has not only intensified the wage-effort equation, it has also extensified work as managers now feel that the only way they can cope with the volume of work is to work long hours, as working long hours is now seen as an integral part of the organization's culture. These pressures are further exacerbated by growing levels of personal debt which mean that large swathes of the workforce could not take the risk of losing their jobs, having become "willing slaves" to use Madeleine Bunting's phrase.

A substantial proportion of workers have reported that they have experienced ill-health symptoms, some of which may be considered relatively trivial in the short term, but which can become compounded in the long term as the effect on workers' social lives increasingly prevents them from resting and recuperating. More intensive work and more surveillance and control in the workplace are clearly correlated with the increased incidence of these symptoms. Perhaps more important is that managers have come to feel increasingly disenfranchised and not in control of their own labour process: they feel that the targets they have to achieve are not only unrealistic but that they are not consulted in the setting of these targets and they also feel that their views are not taken into consideration more generally in an increasingly command-and-control managerial ethos. Of particular concern is the public sector in the UK where morale is remarkably low and where over 60% of workers feel that their organization is just changing for change's sake. In our discussions with senior managers across the public sector the phrase "initiative fatigue" is very often used as one set of central government fiats follows another, often before the previous raft of change initiatives has had time to take effect.

As Green and Tsitsiansis (2005, p. 424) argue, these trends in the UK are not an inevitable consequence of contemporary economic and technological change; rather, they suggest, they are a consequence of "particular institutions and managerial practices" prevalent in this country. The rise of fad-ridden managerialism in the UK is, we feel, a clear contributory factor here. The view of several authors that a new managerial class has been created and inserted within the public sector to whip the professionals into shape by reducing their task discretion is indicative of the creation of institutional structures based on generating conflict and low reciprocal trust. Our research indicates a need to rethink the way that organizations are managed in the UK.

There is a need to develop policies that balance short-term competitive pressures against the need to take a longer term view and to develop HR strategies that focus more on trust, involvement and organizational democracy. The fact that we have identified such a difference in opinion between directors and other managers seems to indicate an "us and them" division. Directors can award themselves massive salary rises well above those of other workers and give themselves generous share-options at a time when they are removing final salary pension schemes, having headcount culls and creating regimes of surveillance and control where workers feel that they have no other option than to work longer and harder. To echo Terkel's work of over thirty years ago, work remains a search for "daily meaning as well as daily bread, for recognition as well as for cash, for astonishment rather than torpor" as workers seek "a meaning to their work well over and beyond the reward of the paycheck" (Terkel, 1972, p. xi). We need to put more humanity back into the workplace.

Notes

1   http://www.hse.gov.uk/workplacehealth/index.htm.
2   ASSET is a proprietary organizational analysis tool developed by Robertson Cooper Ltd. Details about the tool and its structure are available at http://www.robertsoncooper.com/products/Asset.aspx.

References

Appelbaum, E. and Berg, P. (2001) High performance work systems and labor market structures. In I. Berg and A.L. Kallenberg (eds), *Sourcebook of Labor Markets*. New York: Kluwer Academic/Plenum Publishers.

Bolton, S. (2004) A simple matter of control? NHS hospital nurses and new management. *Journal of Management Studies*, 41(2), 317–333.

Boyne, G. (2002) Public and private management: what's the difference? *Journal of Management Studies*, 39(1), 97–122.

Bunting, M. (2004) *Willing Slaves: How the Overwork Culture is Ruling Our Lives*. London: HarperCollins.

Burchell, B., Lapido, D. and Wilkinson, F. (2002) *Job Insecurity and Work Intensification*. London: Routledge.

Cascio, W.F. (2002) Responsible restructuring: Seeing employees as assets, not costs. *Ivey Business Journal*, 68(2), 1–5.

Cascio, W.F. (2005) Strategies for responsible restructuring. *Academy of Management Executive*, 19(4), 39–50.

Clarke, J. and Newman, J. (1997) *The Managerial State: Power, Politics and Ideology in the Remaking of Social Welfare*. London: Sage.

Collett, N. (2002) Reactions of the International Stock Exchange to company employment announcements: redundancies and new jobs. *Journal of Business Finance & Accounting*, 29 (9 & 10), 1181–1208.

Donaldson, L. (2001) *The Contingency Theory of Organizations*. London: Sage.

Felstead, A., Gallie, D., and Green, F. (2004) Job complexity and task discretion: tracking the direction of skills at work in Britain. In C. Warhurst, I. Grugulis, I. and E. Keep (eds) *The Skills that Matter* (pp. 148–169). London: Palgrave.

Ferlie, F., Ashburner, L., Fitzgerald, L., and Pettigrew, A. (1996) *The New Public Management in Action*. Oxford: Oxford University Press.

Froud, J., Haslam, C., Johal, S., and Williams, K. (2000a) Shareholder value and financialization: consultancy promises, management moves. *Economy and Society*, 29(1), 80–110.

Froud, J., Haslam, C., Johal, S., and Williams K. (2000b) Restructuring for shareholder value and its implications for labour. *Cambridge Journal of Economics*, 24(6), 771–797.

Gallie, D., Felstead, A., and Green, F. (2004) Changing patterns of task discretion in Britain. *Work, Employment and Society*, 18(2), 243–266.

Gallie, D., White, M., Tomlinson, M., and Cheng, Y. (1998) *Restructuring the Employment Relationship*. Oxford: Oxford University Press.

Green, F. and Tsitsianis, N. (2005) An investigation of national trends in job satisfaction in Britain and Germany. *British Journal of Industrial Relations*, 43(3), 401–429.

Grugulis, I., Vincent, S. and Hebson, G. (2003) The future of professional work? The rise of the 'Network Form' and the decline of discretion. *Human Resource Management Journal*, 13(2), 30–44.

Jones, M.T. (2002) Globalization and organizational restructuring: a strategic perspective. *Thunderbird International Business Review*, 44(3), 325–351.

Kirkpatrick, I. and Ackroyd, S. (2003) Transforming the professional archetype? The new managerialism in UK social services. *Public Management Review*, 5(4), 511–531.

Local Government Employers' Organisation (undated) *Making Sense of Change: Saying Goodbye to Initiative Fatigue*. London: I&DeA, http://www.idea-knowledge.gov.uk/idk/aio/4450597.

MacDuffie, J.P. (1995) Human resource bundles and manufacturing performance: organizational logic and flexible production systems in the world auto industry. *Industrial and Labor Relations Review*, 48(2), 197–221.

Mather, K., Worrall, L. and Seifert, R. (2007) Reforming further education: the changing labour process for college lecturers. *Personnel Review*, 36(1), 109–127.

Nolan, P. and Wood, S. (2003) Mapping the future of work. *British Journal of Industrial Relations*, 41(2), 165–174.

Osborne, D. and Gaebler, T. (1992) *Reinventing Government: How the Entrepreneurial Spirit is Transforming the Public Sector*. Boston: Addison-Wesley.

Pollitt., C. (1993) *Managerialism and the Public Services: Cuts or Cultural Change in the 1990s?* Oxford: Blackwell.

Prahalad, C.K. and Hamel, G. (1990) The core competence of the corporation. *Harvard Business Review*, 68(3), 79–91.

Purcell, J., Kinnie, N., Hutchinson, S., Rayton, B., and Swart, J. (2003) *Understanding the People and Performance Link: Unlocking the Black Box.* London: Chartered Institute of Personnel and Development.

Rainbird, H., Munro, A., and Holly, L. (2004) Exploring the concept of employer demand for skills and qualifications: case studies from the public sector. In C. Warhurst, I. Grugulis and E. Keep (eds), *The Skills that Matter* (pp. 91–108). Basinstoke: Palgrave Macmillan.

Richardson, M., Tailyb, S., Danford, A., Stewart, P., and Upchurch, M. (2005) Best value and workplace partnership in local government. *Personnel Review*, 34(6), 713–728.

Rifkin, J. (1995) *The End of Work: The Decline of the Global Labour Force and the Dawn of the Post-market Era.* New York: Putnam.

Rose, M. (2005) Job satisfaction in Britain: coping with complexity. *British Journal of Industrial Relations*, 43(3), 455–467.

Terkel, S. (1972) *Working.* New York: The New Press.

White, M., Hill, S., McGovern, P., Mills, C., and Smeaton, D. (2003) "High performance" management practices, working hours and work–life balance. *British Journal of Industrial Relations*, 41(2), 175–195.

Williams, K. (2000) From shareholder value to present day capitalism. *Economy and Society*, 29(1), 1–12.

Williams, S. (2003) Conflict in the colleges: industrial relations in further education since incorporation. *Journal of Further and Higher Education*, 27(3), 307–317.

Worrall, L. and Cooper, C.L. (1997) *The quality of working life: the 1997 survey of managers' experiences.* Chartered Management Institute Research Report. London: Chartered Management Institute. (Repeated in 1998, 1999 and 2001.)

Worrall, L. and Cooper, C.L. (2004) Managers' hierarchies and perceptions: a study of UK managers. *Journal of Managerial Psychology*, 19(1), 41–67.

Worrall, L. and Cooper, C.L. (2006) *The Quality of Working Life: Managers' Health and Wellbeing.* London: Chartered Management Institute.

Worrall, L., Cooper, C.L., and Campbell, F.K. (2000) Perpetual change and employment instability: the new reality for UK managers. *Work, Employment and Society*, 14(4), 647–668.

Worrall, L., Cooper, C.L., and Parkes, C. (2004) The impact of organisational change on the experiences and perceptions of UK managers from 1997–2000. *European Journal of Work and Organizational Psychology*, 13(2), 139–163.

30

Linking human resource management and customer outcomes

David E. Bowen and S. Douglas Pugh

Linking human resource management and customer outcomes

How do a firm's human resource management (HRM) practices affect customer outcomes? We answer this question by examining the linkages across business strategy, employees' perceptions of their human resource management practices, the organizational climates that are shaped considerably by these HRM perceptions, and customer outcomes such as satisfaction, quality perceptions, loyalty, and even profitability.

Consistent with a *strategic* human resource management (SHRM) perspective, the links in the chain begin with business strategy, i.e. leadership's crafted formula for how to win in the marketplace (see Figure 30.1). A common premise of SHRM is that organizations must horizontally align their HRM practices toward their strategic goal and that practices must complement one another for successful strategy implementation (e.g. Schuler & Jackson 1987; Wright & Snell 1991). To drive the remaining linkages, it is essential that HRM professionals can deliver an "HR value proposition" (Ulrich & Brockbank 2005) for each of its key stakeholders – employees, managers, customers, and shareholders. Value is delivered when the work of HRM professionals helps those stakeholders reach their goals, e.g. contribute positively to employee and customer satisfaction. In order for HRM to be of value to customers, HRM professionals must begin with a line of sight to the marketplace (Ulrich & Brockbank 2005), a prerequisite for becoming a true strategic partner.

Despite widespread acceptance that HRM contributes to firm performance, the question has remained as to what "intermediate linkages" drive the connection (Ferris et al. 1998: 394). We describe how an organization's practices, particularly HRM, can create "strong climates" (Bowen & Ostroff 2004; Schneider et al. 2002) which clearly signal to employees what strategic goals are important and how they are expected to behave consistently with them.[1] In turn, we draw upon the growing body of "linkage research," pioneered and continued by Schneider and his colleagues (e.g., Schneider et al. 1980; Schneider & Bowen 1985; Schneider et al. 2005), and also popularly known in the form of the "service profit chain" (Heskett et al. 1997), which reveals that what employees experience in their work worlds is associated with the experiences they provide for customers, and that these experiences translate into important customer outcomes (see Pugh et al. (2002), Schneider & White (2004) for reviews), even linking to profitability.

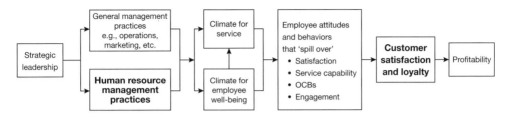

Figure 30.1 A model linking HRM practices and customer outcomes in services

We begin by describing the forces that have contributed to HRM professionals taking customer linkages more seriously. Next, we overview the emergence of thinking and research on the linkages between employee perceptions of their workworld and customer outcomes, and the role of HRM practices in creating those linkages. Then we describe our linkage model (Figure 30.1). The focus is on *service* employees and customers since that is where most linkage research has been conducted. However, this is still a broad focus, since 80 percent of U.S. employees are employed in the service sector (Ford & Bowen, 2008). Additionally, numerous "goods-producing" firms have been increasingly shifting to a services emphasis, with GE generating 70 percent of its revenues from services and IBM 50 percent, as just two examples. Our discussion will also highlight some of the HRM practices in selection, training, and so on, that appear to link to customer satisfaction.

We close by summarizing how HRM needs to be managed strategically, contingently, scientifically, and cross-functionally in order to best link HRM practices and customer outcomes. The discussion throughout is based upon a mix of theory, research and applied examples – the mix we think should guide both HR professionals and scholars as they attempt to understand and manage the HRM–customer relationship.

Assessing management practices from a *customer* perspective

Organizational/management scholars have a long history of failing to examine organizational dynamics and even outcomes through the eyes of customers. This lack of attention to customer outcomes was well captured by Danet (1981) years back when she observed that organization theorists have viewed organizations from the top looking down (management's perspective) and the inside looking around (employees' perspective) but rarely from the outside looking in (which would include the customer's perspective). The customer's absence in the management field is still largely true today, as indicated by how seldom the "customer" appears in management and organizational behavior textbooks and journal articles in our field (Ford & Bowen, 2008).

These general conclusions about not viewing management practices from the customers' perspective have been true of HRM practices, historically, as well. As Schneider (1994) observed, HRM has tended to adhere to an industrial revolution–oriented model with an almost exclusive focus on performance against internally set and internally relevant standards. Effectiveness criteria for HRM practices such as selection have been dominated by internal standards such as employee attendance or number of products and services produced, not against external standards such as customer perceptions of quality.

Forces that encourage a customer focus in HRM

The TQM Movement

In 1987, Congress established the Malcolm Baldridge Quality Award which energized the advancement of the Total Quality Management Movement (TQM). The first and foremost principle of TQM is customer focus; that the central objective of a firm's management practices, such as HRM, to improve quality, is to satisfy customers. The primary endgame of TQM was to improve quality for external customers, but TQM practices were also to be applied to internal customers, such as line managers, and employees.

In short, TQM helped foster thinking and practice about the linkages between internal management practices and customer outcomes. Indeed, TQM proponents advocated viewing organizations not as closed, self-contained systems, but instead as open systems (Bowen & Waldman 1999) not unlike the idea of boundaryless organizations (Ashkenas et al. 1995). This more open view, inclusive of the customer, has been reinforced with the advent of multidimensional assessments of effectiveness such as the "Balanced Scorecard" (Kaplan & Norton 1992).

An emphasis on "customer literacy" in HR professionals

To be able to "score" well on customer criteria, HRM professionals must possess "customer literacy" (Ulrich & Brockbank 2005). This starts with HR professionals really knowing their organization's customers and their buying criteria. They must have their target customers clearly in mind, and what valued and unique benefits they hope to obtain. What bundle of low-cost, personalized service, innovation, product features, etc. drives customer attraction and retention? Only if HRM professionals are customer literate can they then effectively work through the process of specifying the employee behaviors necessary to deliver those benefits, and the HRM practices necessary to enable and reward those behaviors. The goal is to build a strong linkage between the HRM value proposition and the customers' value proposition (Ulrich & Brockbank 2005).

The growth of services

Many services are still labor intensive in their delivery and often that delivery occurs in real-time encounters with customers. Consequently, employees are often close to their customers, both physically and psychologically (Parkington & Schneider 1979) which allows the organization's climate to "show" not only to employees, but to customers as well (Schneider et al. 1980). HRM practices shape organizational climates that employees perceive as customer-oriented, or not.

Real-time encounters between employees and customers means that quality control cannot be exercised via supervision that can "stop production" in-progress or error detection techniques that can remove defects even before they reach the consumer. Instead, in services, quality control is very much a HRM activity (Bowen & Schneider 1988). HRM activities help get the right people in place and make sure they have the appropriate skills via selection and training. Service and sales reps out in the field with customers cannot be subject to direct, personal supervision; quality control must come from HRM practices in hiring and training.

The rise of an employee branding perspective

Employee branding is the process by which employees internalize the desired brand image and are motivated to project that image to customers and other stakeholders (Miles & Mangold

2004). Brand image refers to the conceptualization that an organization wants its customers to have of it – the set of benefits that customers would obtain by doing business with the company. A number of authors have recently positioned employees as the "living brand" (Bendapudi and Bendapudi 2005) or focused on "employee branding" (Miles & Mangold 2004) with the message of generating a bond between the employees and the brand, which in turn forges loyalty between customers and the brand and company. This requires that the firm sends many messages to employees that embed the meaning and core values of the brand within employees. HRM practices that signal the company's priorities and competitive positioning are an important source. Companies that have been mentioned as effective in doing so include the typical service role models such as Southwest Airlines and Ritz-Carlton, but employee branding has also been described in other firms such QuikTrip and Wawa-run convenience stores.

The emergence of research on the linkages between how employees experience their workplace and customer outcomes

The conceptual and empirical origins of what would become linkage research, as labeled by Wiley (1996), are to be found some 25 years ago when Schneider, Parkington and Buxton (1980) asked front-line bank employees about a number of aspects of organizational functioning, such as personnel support, managerial functions, and equipment support, that had emerged from interviews with employees suggesting to them that service in the bank branch was important. They found that what front-line employees in bank branches reported about service climate predicted with statistically significant accuracy the satisfaction of the customers at the branches. The relationships between the employee service climate dimensions and customer perceptions of service quality suggested that the things employees experienced in the workplace (for example, a lack of management support of service delivery) impacts customers' service experiences.

The above 1980 results were then replicated and extended by Schneider and Bowen (1985) who found that dimensions of customer perceptions of service quality were positively related to employees' perceptions of a number of HRM dimensions. They concluded that service organizations in which employees have positive perceptions of human resource practices will be those in which employees can devote their energies to serving customers. That is, when employees perceive that their organization uses rewards to let them know when they have done good work, creates work conditions that facilitate their ability to perform, helps them with career progression, provides orientation and training for new assignments, and the like – i.e., their own needs have been met – they are then more able to concentrate on meeting the needs of their customers – what the authors labeled a "spillover effect." In sum, the same set of human resource management practices helped satisfy two stakeholders, employees *and* customers, essentially linking the "value propositions" of both.

Building upon this, the "service-profit chain" further developed the organizational practices that forge these employee–customer linkages and extended them to their economic consequences (Heskett et al. 1994; Heskett et al. 1997) In the service profit chain, customers' service experiences are linked directly to employees, specifically, employee productivity, which is in turn affected by employees' service capability. Service capability is an employee's ability, authority, and latitude to meet customer needs. Employee satisfaction and loyalty drive service capability, and satisfaction are determined by a number of factors all related to the internal quality of work-life employees experience. The front-end of the chain begins with the operating strategy and service delivery system (also labeled "internal service quality"), which includes HRM elements such as job design, decision-making latitude, selection and development, rewards and recognition, and providing training so that employees have the tools to serve customers. These HRM elements contribute to employee service capability and, ultimately, customer satisfaction and organizational performance. Additional research has repeatedly confirmed that HRM practices help frame climate perceptions and how, in turn, employees then relate to customers (Pugh et al. 2002; Rogg et al. 2001).

Disney theme parks are a good applied and well-known example of such a chain in practice. First, Disney invests considerable energy in selecting the right person for the job even for their part-time park employees. By "right," this refers to particular characteristics of education, physical features, grooming, and appearance (physically fit, attractive, conservatively groomed college students). Second, they invest in training. While some of this training involves technical aspects of the job, a very large part involves teaching the norms, language, roles, and scripted emotional expressions necessary to produce an outstanding experience for the customer (Van Maanen 1991). As a service, Disney is fundamentally selling an experience to customers, and that experience cannot be controlled and monitored by management as could the production of a car or TV set. The shape of the experience is largely at the discretion of the employees, and the climate and culture of Disney shape the employee behaviors.

As the Disney example illustrates, the experiences employees are having at work are going to show to the customers with whom they interact. We now cover this in more depth in our linkage model that follows.

A model of the linkages between HRM practices and customer outcomes

Strategic leadership

As shown in Figure 30.1, which builds upon the preceding linkage research, our model begins with strategic leadership from the top, but also leadership *throughout* the organization. Recalling our discussion of "customer literacy," what is the customer's value proposition? How can the firm link to that in crafting its hoped-for winning formula in the marketplace? The answers to these strategic leadership questions should then drive efforts through HRM practices to create "strong" organizational climates, in which employees *share* an understanding of strategic goals and what is expected of them.

These statements about building the linkage between strategy and organizational climates in which employees have shared perceptions is only prescriptive! Often, employees are not as clear on these linkages as management assumes. In fact, one of the key assumptions of linkage research is that if you want to find out how the strategy is working in *reality*, not theory, ask front-line employees, e.g., climate surveys and their perceptions of customer outcomes, to discover how the strategy is really playing out (Macey & Schneider 2006).

Management practices and climate formation: the "strength" of the HRM system

Employees form climate perceptions from how they see the organization carrying out its day-to-day business, and the goals the organizations appear to be pursuing (Schneider & White 2004). Employee perceptions of management practices, both general and HRM-focused, are important.

The "strength" of the HRM system is a critical factor in determining whether strong organizational climates are created that signal to employees what is important to management, and rewarded in the organization (Bowen & Ostroff 2004). This refers to the characteristics of how HRM practices operate as an overall *system*. HRM strength is found in system characteristics such as: "agreement among principal HRM decision makers" as to the strategic HRM message to convey; "consistent HRM messages," e.g., practices that all send the same strategic signal; "validity," practices that accomplish what they are supposed to; and "instrumentality," employees see favorable consequences, a compelling value proposition, for behaving consistent with signals. HRM practices, in the form of a "strong" HRM system, together with other management practices, influence the creation of two interrelated organizational climates relevant to customer outcomes.

Climate for service

Organizational climate is typically conceptualized, and managed, around a specific strategic objective, e.g., innovation, safety, service, as opposed to its being treated as a set of shared employee perceptions of management practices, in general (e.g., Schneider 2000). That is, there is a climate *for* some type of strategic referent, as opposed to climate as some generic, global shared set of employee perceptions. Our focus is on the *climate for service* (which, itself, can assume different climate *for* refinements, depending upon the customers' value propositions) referring to employees' shared perceptions of the practices, procedures, and behaviors that are rewarded, supported, and expected by the organization with regard to customer service and customer service quality (Schneider et al. 1998). When employees perceive an abundance of cues from a setting's management practices that highlight service quality, they are experiencing a climate for service.

What general management practices can contribute to a climate for service? As one example, Schneider and Bowen (1985) found that a climate for service emerged via management practices in the areas of: (a) logistics, e.g., the availability of equipment, supplies, tools to deliver service; (b) systems support, e.g., marketing, operations, etc.; (c) efforts to retain customers; and (d) general managerial behavior, such as planning, coordinating, and establishing goals and routines to serve customers. Later work has focused on similar themes; for example, Schneider et al. (1998) found that work facilitation and inter-departmental service directly contributed to overall service climate, and Johnson (1996) found that information seeking, training, and rewards and recognition were the major themes that contributed to service climate and, through climate, to customer satisfaction.

Climate for employee well-being

Managers in pursuit of service quality and customer satisfaction need to create two different, but interrelated climates: a climate for service and also a climate for employee well-being, which is a climate focused on meeting the needs of employees (Schneider & Bowen 1993). As indicated by the arrow upward from climate for well-being to climate for service, the climate for employee well-being is an important foundation on which a climate for service can be built. Employees need to feel that their own needs have been met before they can truly focus on meeting the needs of others, e.g., customers. Similar findings have been shown by Borucki and Burke (1999), who found that employee climate perceptions could be classified into two categories: management concern for customers (equivalent to service climate) and concern for employees (equivalent to climate for well-being). *Both* of these climates contributed to sales personnel service performance.

These two climates are interrelated. Work facilitation, assessed as an HRM dimension in Schneider and Bowen (1985), is a dimension that also correlated significantly with climate for service. Although interrelated, it is important to state again that they are still different – they are only moderately intercorrelated, and emerge as distinct factors (Borucki & Burke 1999). As such, they involve different organizational dynamics, and both climates are necessary to fully drive subsequent linkages toward customer outcomes. HRM professionals must design practices to support employees both in their general roles as organizational members as well as in their specific roles as service providers.

HRM practices that link to climate for service and customer outcomes

The HRM practices we highlight next are those that have demonstrated some effectiveness in influencing customer satisfaction. Again, the "validity" of HRM practices contributes to the strength of the HRM system and its ability to create a strong climate. Here are some approaches to various HRM practices that appear to send all the right "signals" about a climate for service and create the service capabilities necessary to satisfy customers.

Selection

Heskett and colleagues (1997) stress that the best service companies hire for attitudes, not skills. More fully, the focus should be on hiring for positive attitudes toward customer service, with training complementing this hiring. Recent research suggests that this attitude can be measured effectively through personality-based measures of customer orientation (Frei & McDaniel 1998; Ones & Viswesraran 2001; Ones et al. 2005). Ones and colleagues have described customer orientation as a compound personality trait, containing elements of the "Big 5" personality factors. Most important, they have shown that customer orientation significantly predicts not only managerial ratings of performance, but also other dimensions of performance including counterproductive workplace behavior. Moreover, customer orientation measures add incremental validity beyond the effects of cognitive ability.

Another aspect of service-oriented selection has become known as the preferred employer in an industry – which builds a more favorable selection ratio to find those employees who fit well the needs of the targeted market segment. As Zeithaml, Bitner and Gremler (2006) report, Rosenbluth International, a corporate travel agency, has acquired such a reputation, likely owing to President Hal Rosenbluth's philosophy, "We don't believe the customer can come first unless our people come first. If our people don't come first, then they're not free to focus on our clients; they are worried about other kinds of things." This point of view reinforces another service management maxim "Treat Your Employees the Way You Would Like Them to Treat Customers."

Another approach that builds linkages is found at Southwest Airlines which often includes frequent flying customers as part of the interviewer panel screening applicants for flight attendant positions. Strategically, Southwest strives to differentiate itself in the marketplace by being a fast, fun, and loving airline. Customers have the best sense of what that competitive edge looks like in flight attendant behavior, so they are afforded a voice in hiring. And this certainly also leverages customer loyalty to the airline.

Employee performance measurement

"What gets measured gets done," so it would seem that having customers provide feedback on employee performance would inform management whether employees are living the brand

and whether the climate for a particular type of service is strong enough to influence desired employee behaviors. Customers, then, could be included as raters in a 360-degree appraisal process (Waldman & Bowen 1998). Given employee concerns about the validity of surprise customer appraisals, one middle course used with some frequency is to alert both employees and customers that the service encounter is being monitored, e.g., "being recorded for quality purposes" (Schneider & White 2004).

Customers could be allowed to view the employee appraisal form to see if the behaviors and outcomes align with their own expectations (Ulrich & Brockbank 2005). Also, customer and service quality criteria should be included upward through the organization, from supervisors to senior managers. Sometimes there is a tendency to emphasize customer care criteria only for front-line employees (Schneider et al. 2005b).

Training

Training can deliver value to both employees and customers. Salanova et al. (2005), for example, found that training impacted service climate directly, and also had an impact on employee engagement. Liao and Chuang (2004) found in a sample of 25 restaurants that manager rankings of the extent to which service-related elements were emphasized in training (e.g., providing quick service, introducing customers to menu items and ingredients, being sensitive to customers' individual needs and wants) were significantly associated with employee perceptions of service climate. Again, employees form perceptions of what is important to the organization based on the signals they receive in training.

General Electric links employee and customer value propositions by inviting certain customers to attend training programs being run at Crotonville – for employees (Ulrich & Brockbank 2005). For example, leadership development programs on change management may include both executives and customer representatives, leveraging HRM practices to create strategic unity between otherwise internal and external stakeholders.

Employee reports about what they know of customer perceptions, attitudes, preferences, and the like should help frame the content of training programs. Linkage surveys can be used to ask employees where they need the development of skills and abilities to better serve customers, and the connections between these responses and customer outcomes suggest that employees can accurately identify training needs (Schneider & White 2004). And this customer-driven training content should be used in training and development throughout organizational levels, not just at the front-line (Schneider et al. 2005a).

Finally, this closeness between employees suggests that employees need to be trained in the skills necessary to perform "emotional labor" – i.e., how to deal with the ongoing press of customer demands and angry customers. Many training programs still focus on technical or interpersonal skills necessary to be effective with other *internal* members of the organization.

Rewards and recognition

Service climate is defined as perceptions of what is *rewarded*, supported, and expected with regard to service delivery, and as such, reward systems are powerful communications of what is important to management. If management says that quality service is important, but rewards quantity over quality, employee service climate perceptions will reflect what behaviors are actually rewarded, not what behaviors management says are important. Unfortunately, the "folly of rewarding A, while hoping for B" (Kerr 1975) appears to be a common malady in services.

Many leading companies tie aspects of compensation to customer satisfaction metrics. For example, at PeopleSoft, the performance evaluations of account managers are based on customer satisfaction and customers' ability to use the company's software (Webber & Row 1997). Johnson (1996) found that employee perceptions that the organization rewarded and recognized employees who provide superior service and take a personal interest in solving customer problems contributed significantly to service climate, and this dimension was strongly related to customer satisfaction.

Another example is offering customers the opportunity to reward employees whom they view as deserving. At least one airline provides some of its best, frequent-flying customers $50 coupons on which they can write an employee's name, sign it, and return it to be given to the employee (Ulrich & Brockbank 2005).

Employee empowerment

Empowerment is often recommended as an effective management practice for delivering service quality and satisfying customers. Empowerment has been defined as sharing with employees: more decision-making power and autonomy; information on strategy, business plans, competitor information, customer data; skills and knowledge via training in understanding business information, effective teamwork skills, customer complaint management; and rewards based upon performance (Bowen & Lawler 1992, 1995). Empowerment, then, requires more of an HRM investment in employees than the low-cost, production-line approach to service delivery as found in fast-food, convenience stores, in which customer expectations are simple and stable, and technology is routine. The added HRM investment from empowering employees delivers a return with more complex services in less predictable environments such as airline travel and consulting.

Seeking customer information for the design of HRM practices

Many of the HRM practices we have mentioned require seeking out information from customers and feeding that information back to employees. A highly consistent finding across linkage research is that organizations which develop strong service climates and deliver excellent customer service actively seek out information about customers *and* relate that information back to employees.

Unfortunately, customer data are often overcollected and underutilized (Schneider & Bowen 1995). Many organizations collect customer information, but the act of providing that information to employees to enhance service performance communicates the importance of service delivery to top management. Unfortunately, the task of collecting and using customer information is often associated with units or functions in the organization other than Human Resources, but it should not be. HR *should* have a role in the strategic management of this information because of its powerful signaling function in the design of HRM practices.

Linking climate and customer outcomes: the spillover effect

Of the many possible employee attitudes and behaviors that might spill over to affect customer outcomes, the most frequently mentioned are employee satisfaction and service capability-based behaviors (from the service-profit chain). We will focus on two others that are more recent in receiving attention. One is a set of behaviors, organizational citizenship behaviors (OCBs), including employee displays of altruism, courtesy, sportsmanship, conscientiousness, and civic virtue that can enhance customer satisfaction and loyalty. The other is employee engagement.

Organizational citizenship behaviors

When employees are treated fairly, they, in turn, are more likely to display organizational citizenship behaviors (OCBs) toward customers, resulting in their satisfaction (Bowen et al. 1999; Masterson 2001; Maxham & Netemeyer 2003). Fair treatment of employees can consist of many aspects, such as supervisor displays of interactional fairness, e.g., communicating respectfully with employees, that can drive employee displays of OCBs (Cropanzano et al. 2007). Fair treatment can also be evidenced by HRM practices which employees perceive as fair. The idea that employees evaluate HRM practices is based on a "user reactions" perspective on HR, which advocates that *internal* customer satisfaction, i.e., employees' own evaluation of how they feel treated by HRM practices, should be included among technical criteria, such as reliability and validity that dominate assessments of HR effectiveness (Cardy & Dobbins 1994; Gilliland 1993). Examples of fair HRM would include designing and conducting performance appraisals with input from employees and communicating ratings to employees in a timely manner; in rewards, setting salaries internally equitably among employees in the organization and, if any inequities are necessary, explaining why to employees.

Employee engagement

A recent perspective that is generating great enthusiasm in the academic and applied literatures and in-practice is employee engagement (Harter et al. 2002; Macey & Schneider, 2008; Salanova et al. 2005; Schneider et al. 2005). Engagement moves beyond traditional ideas of job satisfaction in that it has a strong affective tone suggesting passion for the work and organization, involvement of the self, absorption in the work, and a high degree of energy. Unique to the idea of engagement is vigor: feelings of physical strength, cognitive liveliness, and emotional energy that employees tie directly to the work and workplace (Shirom 2003). Engaged employees also demonstrate behaviors including organizational citizenship, role expansion, and initiative, all of which serve organizational goals (Macey & Schneider 2008).

As a newer construct, there is debate over engagement as to where it fits into a linkage model connecting the organization, employees, and customers (see Macey & Schneider, 2008), but research leaves little doubt that engagement affects outcomes important to the organization (Harter et al. 2002; Salanova et al. 2005). Salanova et al. (2005), for example, view engagement as a motivational state that is directly influenced by organizational resources. They developed their measure of organizational resources through a grounded theory method of front-line service employees, and identified three categories with direct bearing on HRM issues: training, job autonomy, and technology. In their model, engagement, along with organizational resources, predict service climate, and service climate directly impacts employee performance as rated by customers. As such, engagement is cast by Salanova and colleagues as similar to the foundation issues (Schneider et al. 1998) that need to be present for a climate for service to develop. What does seem clear from the research is that engagement attitudes and behaviors begin with an organization that provides resources and leadership, and these behaviors spill over to customers, affecting employee perceptions of the quality of service provided and customer loyalty (Salanova et al. 2005). Harter and colleagues (2003), for example, report that in a study of more than 7,000 business units, there was a mean difference of 2.9 percent in ratings of customer loyalty between those units in the lowest quartile on employee engagement and the units in the highest quartile. The revenue impact of that 2.9 percent difference between units with lower and higher levels of employee engagement will of course depend on factors such as the type of service, size of business unit, and sales per customer, but the impact of a 2.9 percent gain in customer loyalty is probably substantial for many service organizations.

Customer outcomes . . . and profitability

It is now very well established in the literature that an organization's service climate matters: it is related to various indicators of customer attitudes including customer satisfaction, perceptions of service quality, ratings of service employee performance, and customer loyalty (see Pugh et al. (2002) for a review). Most service climate research studies end the story there, using research in marketing and consumer behavior to make the point that these customer outcomes matter because they, particularly customer loyalty, ultimately have a positive impact on organizational profitability. This is a compelling argument because the evidence is indeed there that customer satisfaction drives customer loyalty and ultimately organizational profitability (Heskett et al. 1997). But, it is interesting that the body of research tying service climate to organizational financial performance is relatively sparse (note, however, that there is a larger body of linkage research tying more general attitudes such as employee satisfaction or morale, rather than service climate, to organizational financial performance, e.g., Harter et al. 2002).

The linkage between customer satisfaction and financial performance is complex, to say the least. Although there are a few studies linking service climate to organizational financial performance (e.g., Borucki & Burke 1999; Schneider et al. (2005) on unit sales) there are other studies showing counterintuitive negative relationships between employee and customer perceptions and financial performance (Wiley 1996). Busy stores, for example, may often perform financially well but have lower customer satisfaction. What we are best able to conclude, however, is that service climate impacts customer satisfaction, and to the extent customer satisfaction is important to an organization, service climate is a lever that can be used to influence it with favorable returns on organizational performance, across various measures and time.

Final thoughts on linking HRM and customer outcomes

We close with four overarching perspectives on how to manage the relationship between HRM practices and customer outcomes. Connecting to customer outcomes is leveraged in these four areas.

Strategically

Sharpen strategic focus

One message that sometimes comes out of the strategic HRM literature is simply that organizations should "do HRM better" (Schneider & White 2004). That is, the advice is rather generic: good organizations do a good job at strategically selecting, training, and rewarding. But with HRM being *strategic*, it suggests that some HRM practices should be better suited to particular organizational purposes than others. In order for climate for service to set in motion the strongest linkages to employee behavior and customer outcomes, the strategic focus should be sharpened from just generic service to a more market-segmented climate for certain types of service. For example, a low-cost business strategy geared to customer expectations of low-frill, standardized service offerings at a Red Roof Inn obviously requires a different mix of HRM practices to create a climate for that type of service versus that of a Four Seasons. An obvious point, perhaps, but one that should not obscure the less obvious notion of strategically designing internal HRM practices to focus on *your* customers' value proposition.

Compete on intangibles

HRM professionals and HRM practices can help build organizational climates and shape employee behaviors that customers view as valuable and rare, and competitors view as difficult to copy. This is the *sustainable* competitive advantage of the pantheon of service role models such as Southwest Airlines, Toyota and Lexus dealerships, and Four Seasons hotels around the world. HRM can build *relationships* within the firm, and between the firm and its customers, built on emotional ties, trust, and fairness linking to customer loyalty and even profits (Bowen et al. 1999; Ulrich & Brockbank 2005).

Create high-performing customers as a competitive advantage

Involve customers as partners in designing and co-producing the services they consume; stay involved with them in the ongoing co-creation of value. Customers help co-produce many services from simple examples of ATM or online banking to business-to-business examples of business customers helping to co-design, operate, and maintain information systems with firms such as EDS. To accomplish this is difficult, and thus difficult for competitors to copy. To do so, firms must work with their customers as important human resources of the firm (Bettencourt et al. 2002; Bowen 1986; Tax et al. 2006). Creating high-performance customers requires selecting customers to work with who possess the necessary competencies, training them in how to perform as expected, and rewarding them for doing so.

Contingently

Determine the conditions under which climate linkages are the strongest

Before HRM professionals dedicate resources to building service climates, they should assess where and when service climate will be strongly linked to customer outcomes. Here are some research-based insights on relevant conditions.

CUSTOMER CONTACT

The core argument in the service climate literature is that service climate is important because of the physical and psychological closeness of employees and customers (Parkington & Schneider 1979). But what of organizations where there is less physical and psychological contact? Increasingly, some organizations are moving to take the human element out of service delivery (e.g., ATMs, kiosks at airports). Where there is less contact, does service climate become less relevant for shaping customer attitudes? A study by Dietz et al. (2004) suggests that the answer is yes. In their study, they found typical positive relationships between service climate and customer satisfaction, but they found that these associations were significantly weaker in bank branches characterized by lower levels of customer contact. This implies that the employees who have the greatest degree of customer contact should be the ones with the best information about customers and the organizational practices that affect them. These employees should be the primary focus of survey efforts.

FREQUENT SHOPPERS

In one study it was found that in a video rental chain, frequent customers valued high-quality service interactions (Kendall & Barker 1999). For these customers, employee perceptions of service climate affected customer satisfaction (these were the customers who expected high-quantity and quality interactions with employees). Low-volume customers (occasional renters), on the other hand, were primarily interested in price, not employee expertise. Their satisfaction was not related to employee attitudes.

STORE PACE

Several studies have shown that when stores are busy, customers expect employees to focus on the core aspects of service delivery, and their expectations for pleasant emotional displays by employees are less (Rafaeli 1989; Rafaeli & Sutton 1990). These authors found that training to increase friendly service at checkout in convenience stores correlated negatively with store profits. Also, in busy retail environments, aggregated employee perceptions of their work environment were more weakly related to customer satisfaction than in more slow-paced environments (Goldberg-Siderman et al., unpublished manuscript).

OTHER BOUNDARY CONDITIONS? DIRECTIONS FOR FUTURE RESEARCH

What are the dynamics and strengths of the linkages among HRM practices, climate, and customer outcomes in firm–customer relationships other than B2C services? For example, certainly, there is psychological closeness in B2B settings between firm reps and firm agents/buyers – how do the linkages operate in such settings? This question has not received serious research attention.

Scientifically

Invest in HRM practices based on data – not on intuition or trend chasing

Linkage research should be used by practitioners to discover the important drivers of customer satisfaction, in their own unique strategic and organizational context (e.g., Macey & Schneider 2006; Wiley & Campbell 2006). These drivers provide valuable information for how to predict and improve customer satisfaction. By validating HRM practices against *external* customer criteria, it becomes possible to make informed choices about which HRM practices to emphasize the most in pursuit of customer satisfaction. Data-driven linkage research searches not just for correlations between HRM practices and customer outcomes, but for the most *important* correlations. For example, which HRM investments, e.g., upgrades to selection or training, will yield the highest return on a variety of customer outcomes of interest? And statistically significant linkage data support reliance upon employees as valid reporters of how customers perceive the "internal" organizational climate and customer perceptions of service quality.

Consider "new" performance data to utilize

Many business performance measures are capital based and, consequently, inadequate for assessing the unique economics of people-businesses (Barber & Strack 2005). These authors emphasize the need to focus on factors such as how employees create value directly for customers. Therefore, economic profit is more appropriately calculated using a people rather than a capital denominator as is used in economic value added (EVA) or cash value added (CVA).

Cross-functionally

Avoid the "HR Trap"

Senior management must not mistakenly think that if they take care of employees, and have the right HRM mix, customer satisfaction will follow – and if it does not, employees are to blame.

Customer satisfaction requires marketing making attractive customer value propositions, management setting reasonable prices, operations creating service delivery systems that allow both employees and customers to accomplish what they are trying to do. Effective service requires a seamless, integrated approach across different organizational functions with which the customer interacts. As a final word, HRM links most fully and positively to customer outcomes when HRM professionals partner with their colleagues in other functions to implement business strategies that create value for stakeholders, both internal *and* external.

Note

1. We should note that there has been some discussion in the academic literature on the differences between the constructs of climate and culture (e.g., Dennison 1996). Climate is generally regarded as the perceptions of organizational imperatives, as captured by what is rewarded, supported, and expected in the organization, whereas culture refers to the "deeper" beliefs and values that underlie these practices. For our purposes, we are focusing mainly on climate – and the HRM practices that shape employees' perceptions of them – but both ideas capture the notion of what is important, valued, and rewarded in the organization.

References

Ashkenas, R., Ulrich, D., Jick, T. & Kerr, S. (1995). *The Boundaryless Organization: Breaking the Chains of Organizational Structure*. San Francisco, CA: Jossey-Bass.

Barber, F. & Strack, R. (2005). The surprising economics of a 'people business'. *Harvard Business Review*, June, 81–90.

Bendapudi, N. & Bendapudi, V. (2005). Creating the living brand. *Harvard Business Review*, May, 1–7.

Bettencourt, L., Ostrom, A.L, Brown, S.W. & Roundtree, R.I. (2002). Client co-production in knowledge intensive business services. *California Management Review*, 44(4), 100–28.

Borucki, C.C. & Burke, M.J. (1999). An examination of service-related antecedents to retail store performance. *Journal of Organizational Behavior*, 20, 943–62.

Bowen, D.E. (1986). Managing customers as human resources in service organizations. *Human Resource Management*, 25, 371–83.

Bowen, D.E. & Lawler, E.E. (1992). Total quality-oriented human resource management. *Organizational Dynamics*, 20, 29–41.

Bowen, D.E. & Lawler, E.E. (1995). Empowering service employees. *Sloane Management Review*, 36, 73–84.

Bowen, D.E. & Ostroff, C. (2004). Understanding HRM–firm performance linkages: The role of 'strength' of the HRM system. *Academy of Management Review*, 29, 203–21.

Bowen, D.E. & Schneider, B. (1988). Services marketing and management: Implications for organizational behavior. *Research in Organizational Behavior*, 10, 43–80.

Bowen, D.E. & Waldman, D.A. (1999). Customer-driven employee performance. In D.R. Ilgen & E.A. Pulakos (Eds), *The Changing Nature of Performance: Implications for Staffing, Motivation, and Development* (pp. 154–91). San Francisco, CA: Jossey-Bass.

Bowen, D.E., Gilliland, S.W. & Folger, R. (1999). HRM and service fairness: How being fair with employees spills over to customers. *Organizational Dynamics*, 27, 7–24.

Cardy, R.L. & Dobbins, G.H. (1994). *Performance Appraisal: Alternative Perspectives*. Cincinnati, OH: South-Western.

Cropanzano, R., Bowen, D.E. & Gilliland, S.W. (2007). The management of organizational justice. *Academy of Management Perspectives*, 21(4), 34–48.

Danet, B. (1981). Client-organization relationships. In P.C. Nystrom & W.H. Starbuck (Eds), *Handbook of Organizational Design* (pp. 382–428). New York: Oxford University Press.

Dennison, D.R. (1996). What is the difference between organizational culture and organizational climate? A native's point of view on a decade of paradigm wars. *Academy of Management Review*, 21, 619–54.

Dietz, J., Pugh, S.D. & Wiley, J.W. (2004). Service climate effects on customer attitudes: An examination of boundary conditions. *Academy of Management Journal*, 47, 81–92.

Ferris, G.R., Arthur, M.M. & Berkson, H.M. (1998). Toward a social context theory of the human resource management–organization effectiveness relationship. *Human Resource Management Review*, 8, 235–64.

Ford, R. & Bowen, D.E. (2008). Service-dominant management education: It's about time. *Academy of Management Learning & Education*, 7, 224–243.

Frei, R.L. & McDaniel, M.A. (1998). Validity of customer service measures in personnel selection: A review of criterion and construct evidence. *Human Performance*, 11, 1–27.

Gilliland, S.W. (1993). The perceived fairness of selection systems: An organizational justice perspective. *Academy of Management Review*, 18, 694–734.

Goldberg-Siderman, L., Grandey, A. & Pugh, S.D. (undated). *Linking Leader Behavior to Employee Attitudes to Customer Service Outcomes: Business-Unit-Level Mechanisms and Constraints*. Unpublished manuscript.

Harter, J.K., Schmidt, F.L. & Hayes, T.L. (2002). Business-unit-level relationship between employee satisfaction, employee engagement, and business outcomes: A meta-analysis. *Journal of Applied Psychology*, 87, 268–79.

Harter, J.K., Schmidt, F.L. & Keyes, C.L. (2003). Well-being in the workplace and its relationship to business outcomes: A review of the Gallup studies. In C.L. Keyes & J. Haidt (Eds), *Flourishing: The Positive Person and the Good Life* (pp. 205–24). Washington, D.C.: American Psychological Association.

Heskett, J.L., Sasser, W.E., Jr. & Schlesinger, L.A. (1997). *The Service Profit Chain*. New York: The Free Press.

Heskett, J.L., Jones, T.O., Loveman, G.W., Sasser, W.E., Jr. & Schlesinger, L.A. (1994). Putting the service–profit chain to work. *Harvard Business Review*, March–April, 164–74.

Johnson, J.W. (1996). Linking employee perceptions of service climate to customer satisfaction. *Personnel Psychology*, 49, 831–51.

Kaplan, R.S. & Norton, D.P. (1992). The balanced scorecard – Measures that drive performance. *Harvard Business Review*, 70(1), 71–9.

Kendall, S.D. & Barker, L. (1999). When does service matter? Linking employee service emphasis to customer satisfaction within heavy, lapsed, and light customer segments. Paper presented as part of a symposium at the 14th Annual Conference of the Society of Industrial and Organizational Psychology, Atlanta, GA.

Kerr, S. (1975). On the folly of rewarding A, while hoping for B. *Academy of Management Journal*, 18, 769–83.

Liao, H. & Chuang, A. (2004). A multilevel investigation of factors influencing employee service performance and customer outcomes. *Academy of Management Journal*, 47, 41–58.

Macey, W.H. & Schneider, B. (2006). Employee experiences and customer satisfaction: Toward a framework for survey design with a focus on service climate. In A.I. Kraut (Ed.), *Getting Action from Organizational Surveys* (pp. 53–75). San Francisco, CA: Jossey-Bass.

Macey, W.H. & Schneider, B. (2008). The meaning of Employee Engagement. *Industrial and Organizational Psychology: Perspectives on Science and Practice*.

Masterson, S.S. (2001). A trickle-down model of organizational justice: Relating employees' and customers' perceptions of and reactions to fairness. *Journal of Applied Psychology*, 86, 594–604.

Maxham, J.G. III & Netemeyer, R.G. (2003). Firms reap what they sow: The effects of shared values and perceived organizational justice on customers' evaluations of complaint handling. *Journal of Marketing*, 67, 46–62.

Miles, S.J. & Mangold, G. (2004). A conceptualization of the employee branding process. *Journal of Relationship Marketing*, 3, 65–87.

Ones, D.S. & Viswesvaran, C. (2001). Integrity tests and other criterion-focused occupational personality scales (COPS) used in personnel selection. *International Journal of Selection and Assessment*, 9, 31–39.

Ones, D.S., Viswesvaran, C. & Dilchert, S. (2005). Personality at work: Raising awareness and correcting misconceptions. *Human Performance*, 18, 389–404.

Parkington, J.P. & Schneider, B. (1979). Some correlates of experienced job stress: A boundary role study. *Academy of Management Journal*, 22, 270–81.

Pugh, S.D., Dietz, J., Wiley, J.W. & Brooks, S.M. (2002). Driving service effectiveness through employee–customer linkages. *Academy of Management Executive*, 16, 73–84.

Rafaeli, A. (1989). When cashiers meet customers: An analysis of the role of supermarket cashiers. *Academy of Management Journal*, 32, 245–73.

Rafaeli, A. & Sutton, R.I. (1990). Busy stores and demanding customers: How do they affect the display of positive emotion? *Academy of Management Journal*, 33, 623–37.

Rogg, K.L., Schmidt, D.B., Shull, C. & Schmitt, N. (2001). Human resource practices, organizational climate, and customer satisfaction. *Journal of Management*, 27, 431–49.

Salanova, M., Agut, S. & Peiro, J.M. (2005). Linking organizational resources and work engagement to employee performance and customer loyalty: The mediation of service climate. *Journal of Applied Psychology*, 90, 1217–27.

Schneider, B. (1994). HRM – a service perspective: Toward a customer-focused HRM. *International Journal of Service Industry Management*, 5, 64–76.

Schneider, B. (2000). The psychological life of organizations. In N.M. Ashkanasy, C.P.M. Wilderson & M.F. Peterson (Eds), *Handbook of Organizational Culture and Climate* (pp. 17–21). Thousand Oaks, CA: Sage.

Schneider, B. & Bowen, D.E. (1985). Employee and customer perceptions of service in banks. *Journal of Applied Psychology*, 70, 423–33.

Schneider, B. & Bowen, D.E. (1993). The service organization: Human resources management is crucial. *Organizational Dynamics*, 21, 39–52.

Schneideer, B. & Bowen, D.E. (1995). *Winning the Service Game*. Boston, MA: Harvard Business School Press.

Schneider, B. & White, S.S. (2004). *Service Quality: Research Perspectives*. Thousand Oaks, CA: Sage.

Schneider, B., Macey, W.H. & Young, S.A. (2005). The climate for service: A review of the construct and implications for achieving CLV goals. *Journal of Relationship Marketing*, 3, 111–32.

Schneider, B., Macey, W.H. and Young, S.A. (2005). Corporate service intelligence. *Technical Report/Newsletter*. Rolling Meadows, IL: Valtera Corporation.

Schneider, B., Parkington, J.J. & Buxton, V.M. (1980). Employee and customer perceptions of service in banks. *Administrative Science Quarterly*, 25, 252–67.

Schneider, B., Salvaggio, A.N. & Subirats, M. (2002). Climate strength: A new direction for climate research. *Journal of Applied Psychology*, 87(2), 220–9.

Schneider, B., White, S.S. & Paul, M.C. (1998). Linking service climate and customer perceptions of service quality: Tests of a causal model. *Journal of Applied Psychology*, 83, 150–63.

Schneider, B., Ehrhart, M.G., Mayer, D.M., Saltz, J.L. & Niles-Jolly, K. (2005). Understanding organization–customer links in service settings. *Academy of Management Journal*, 48, 1017–32.

Schuler, R.S. & Jackson, S.E. (1987). Linking competitive strategies and human resource management practices. *Academy of Management Executive*, 1(3), 207–19.

Shirom, A. (2003). Feeling vigorous at work? The construct of vigor and the study of positive affect in organizations. In D. Ganster & P.L. Perrewe (Eds), *Research in Organizational Stress and Well-being* (Vol. 3, pp. 135–65). Greenwich, CN: JAI Press.

Tax, S.S., Colgate, M. & Bowen, D.E. (2006). How to prevent your customers from failing. *Sloan Management Review*, 47, 30–8.

Ulrich, D. & Brockbank, W. (2005). *The HR Value Proposition*. Boston, MA: Harvard Business School Press.

Van Maanen, J. (1991). The smile factory: Work at Disneyland. In P.J. Frost, L. Moore, M. Louis, C. Lundberg & J. Martin (Eds), *Reframing Organizational Culture*. Beverly Hills, CA: Sage Publications.

Waldman, D.A. & Bowen, D.E. (1998). The acceptability of 360 degree appraisals: A customer–supplier relationship perspective. *Human Resource Management*, 37, 117–31.

Webber, A.M. & Row, H. (1997). Four who know how: Best-practice answers to the four key customer service questions. *Fast Company*, October, 130–1.

Wiley, J.W. (1996). Linking survey data to the bottom line. In A.I. Kraut (Ed.), *Organizational Surveys: Tools for Assessment and Change* (pp. 330–59). San Francisco, CA: Jossey-Bass.

Wiley, J.W. & Campbell, B.C. (2006). Using linkage research to drive high performance: A case study in organizational development. In A. Kraut (Ed.), *Getting Action from Organizational Surveys: New Concepts, Technologies, and Applications*. San Francisco, CA: Jossey-Bass.

Wright, P.M. & Snell, S.A. (1991). Toward an integrative view of strategic human resource management. *Human Resource Management Review*, 1, 203–25.

Zeithaml, V.A., Bitner, M.J. & Gremler, D.D. (2006). *Services Marketing: Integrating Customer Focus Across the Firm* (4th edn). New York: McGraw-Hill Companies.

Index

Aantala, B., 414
Abrahamson, E., 152
Ackers, P., 47
Ackroyd, S., 42, 490
Acs, Z., 392
Adler, N., 411
Adler, P., 93, 99
Adner, R., 365
Africa Context, 462–473
    Adapting strategic HRM, 465
    Employment relations 469–471
    Patterns of diffusion, 467
    Talent Management and Diversity, 468–469
African Growth and Opportunity Act (AGOA), 472
Ahiauzu, A.I., 464
Aiken, M., 211
Ajzen, I., 395
Alavi, M., 271
Aldrich, H., 390–394, 397, 402
Alexander, J., 247
Allan, C., 466
Allen, M., 403, 404
All-China Federation of Trade Unions (ACFTU), 457, 458
Allstate Corporation, 36–37
Almhdie, A., 468
Alternative dispute resolution (ADR), 88
Altschuld, J., 265
Alvarez, S., 397, 398
Alvesson, M., 63, 455
Amabile, T.M., 255
Amit, R., 347
Amram, M., 358, 359, 361, 364, 370
Ankomah, K.A., 472
Ang, S., 365, 366, 369
Appelbaum, E., 351, 489
Araoz, C.F., 424

Ashkenas, R., 504
Argus Newspaper, 463, 468
Armington, C., 392
Aryee, S., 464, 471
Atwater, L., 248
Autocratic recruitment model, 213–214, 221

Bach, S., 40
Bacon, N., 41,
Badham, R., 154, 158, 162
Bagley, C.E., 71, 72, 83
Bahadur, A., 472
Bai, X., 452, 453
Bailey, J., 453, 454
Baker, T., 397
Baldwin, T., 272
Balkin, D., 235, 402
Baltzley, D., 410
Bamford, C., 393
Bandura, A., 248
Barber, A.E., 209
Barber, F., 514
Barham, K., 414
Barker, L., 513
Barnard, C. I., 402
Barney, J., 311, 346, 390, 397, 398
Barney, J.B., 236–237, 262
Baron, J.N., 211, 213, 214, 218–219, 390, 394, 397–398, 400, 403
Baron, R., 403
Barrett, R., 399
Barsh, J., 339
Bartholomew, S., 411
Bartlett, C.A., 410, 413
Baruch, Y., 471
Bass, B.M., 415
Bassi, L., 269, 275
Batt, R., 228

Baum, J., 393
Baumol, W., 393
Beatty, C.A., 152, 279
Beatty, R.W., 479
Becker, B., 235, 237, 277, 345, 353, 390
Becker, G.S., 83, 361, 479
Beckman, C., 402, 403
Bedrick, D., 168
Beechler, S., 83, 410, 418
Beer, M., 233–234
Belcourt, M., 274
Bendapudi, N., 505
Bendapudi, V., 505
Bennet, N., 239
Bennett, C.I., 417
Bennington, L., 452, 453
Bennis, W., 145
Berg, I., 489
Bergeron, B., 187
Bergkvist, Y., 399
Berkowitz, P.M., 86
Bettencourt, L., 513
Bettis, R.A., 133
Bhattacharya, M., 362
Bird, A., 412, 419, 422, 423
Birley, S., 395
Bishop, J., 239
Bitner, M.J., 508
Bjorkman, I., 440, 441, 442, 452
Black Economic Empowerment (BEE), 468
Black, S.E., 117, 412, 423, 424
Blake, S., 417
Blanchard, K.H., 323,
Blanpain, R., 72, 78, 85
Blinder, A., 111, 112, 113
Bloom, N., 120
Bly, P., 332, 334
Boeker, W., 393, 394
Bolton, S., 490
Borucki, C.C., 507–508, 512
Bossidy, L., 142
Boudreau, J.W., 23, 28, 32, 35–36
Bowen, D., 60, 61
Bowen, D.E., 368, 390, 502–508, 510–511, 513
Bowman, E.H., 357–358, 361, 364
Boxall, P., 47, 448
Boyatzis, R., 167, 412
Boyle, E., 103
Boyne, G., 490
Brinkley, I., 107, 109
Briscoe, J.P., 412
Brockbank, W., 168, 182, 188, 299, 303, 504, 509–510, 513
Brockner, J., 364
Bronfenbrenner, K., 113
Brosnan, P., 466
Broughton, A., 198
Brown, A., 119

Brown, K., 270
Bryan, L., 324, 338, 339
Bryson, A., 43
BT, 481
Buchanan, D., 124, 154, 158, 162
Buckingham, M., 143
Budhwar, P., 433, 435, 437, 438, 439, 440, 441, 442, 443
Bunting, M., 488, 498, 499
Burchell, B., 488, 490
Burck, C., 142
Bureacracy, 91–3, 100
Bureaucratic recruitment, 214–216, 221
Burke, M.J., 507–508, 512
Burns, T., 213
Burton, D., 398
Burton, M., 402, 403
Business knowledge and performance, 178–179
Business processing outsourcing (BPO), 438, 440–443
Business Processing Reengineering (BPR), 95–97
Butler, J.E., 358
Buxton, V. M., 505
Byrne J., 340

Cadsby, C.B., 231
Cairo, P.C., 423
Caldwell, R., 150–152
Calori, R., 130
Camp, S., 397
Campbell, B.C., 514
Campbell, J.P., 226
Campion, M., 87, 368
Cannon, M.D., 233–234
Capability-building, 317, 318
Capex, 28
Capital markets, 115
Capitalism, 110, 115, 118, 121,
Cappelli, P., 346, 357
Cardinal Health, 141
Cardon, M., 390, 399, 403
Cardy, R.L., 511
Carl, D., 415
Carliner, S., 267
Carmichael, T., 462
Carpenter, M.A., 230
Carroll, A., 417
Carroll, G., 393
Carter, N., 397
Cascio, W.F., 22, 489, 491
Cassar, G., 395
Casson, M., 391, 395, 397
Centre for Effective Organisation, 18, 19
Chan, A., 448, 454, 457, 458
Chang, H-J., 112
Change agent, 151
Charan, R., 142, 329, 343
Cheng, Y.Y., 458

Child, J., 447–448, 455
China Context 447–460
    Characteristics of employment and HRM,
      448–452
    Employment regulations and employee
      representation, 457–459
    New developments in HR, 452–457
Choi, J.T, 236
Christensen, R., 183
Chuang, J., 509
Chwee, W., 455
CIPD, 299–300
Clancy, P., 471
Clark, K., 402
Clarke, J., 490
Clarke, S., 448, 458
Classroom-based learning, 329–330
Clegg, S., 58, 101
CMS (critical management studies), 54
Coats, D., 107, 109, 115
Coff, R.W., 363
Coffman, C., 143
Colbert, A.E., 22–23
Collaborative teams, 285, 286, 287, 288, 291
    challenges and risks, 288–290
    practices of, 292–296
Collett, N., 490
Collins, C., 209, 211, 402–404
Collins, D., 153
Collins, J., 137, 145, 209
Colquitt, J., 271
Combs, J., 277, 346
Commission for Conciliation, Meditation and
    Arbitration (CCMA), 470
Commitment recruitment model, 214, 218–221
Cook, M.E., 191
Cooke, F.L., 447–448, 452, 453, 454, 455, 456,
    459
Cooper, C.L., 41, 42, 488–489, 491, 492, 493,
    494
Cornell, C., 267
Corporate Leadership Council, 424
Corporate Social Responsibility, 49
Corporate strategy, 93
Cosgel, M., 397
Cothrell, J., 271
Counterbalancing risks, 290–292
Courpasson, D., 92
Covin, J., 392, 395
Cox, T.H., 417
Coyle-Shapiro, J.L.M., 41
Cropanzano, R., 511
Crowdsourcing, 19
Custom and practice, 44
Customer outcomes, 502–514
Cyr, L., 397

Dalton, M, 423

Danet, B., 503
Datta, D., 280
Davenport, R., 264
Davidow, W.H., 102
Davidsson, P., 395
Davis-Blake, A., 364
Dawson, P., 153–154
De Cieri, H., 467
Dean, J. Jr., 394, 404
Debrah, P., 437, 442
Debrah, Y., 471
Decision framework, 23–25, 32, 37
Decision science, 17, 19, 20, 23
Delery, J.E., 277–279, 345, 351
Dell, M., 348–349
Delmar, F., 395
DeLong, D., 270
Deming, W.E., 238
Department of Trade and Industry (DTI), 118,
    119
DeRose, C., 331
Dhatta, D., 351
Dietz, J., 513
DiMaggio, P.J., 82
DiMaggio, P.W., 127
Ding, D., 452
Disney, 137
Dixit, A., 357, 358, 359
Dobbin, F., 82
Dobbins, G.H., 511
Dohm, A., 209
Domestic mindset table, 414
Donaldson, L., 489
Dorfman, P., 415
Dotlich, D., 271, 423
Doty, D.H, 277–279, 345
Dowling, P.J., 236, 467
Drucker, P.F., 247,
Dual labour market, 8,
Duberlay, J., 365, 366
Dunning, D., 399
DuPont, 481
Durkheim E., 41
Dutton, J.E., 160
Dweck, C.S., 249
Dyer, L., 351
Dyne, L.V., 365–366, 369

Eckhardt, J., 397
Edelman, E.B., 85
Edwards, P., 41–44, 48, 49
Edwards, R., 91
Egon Zehnder, 424
Egri, C.P., 154
Eichinger, R., 325, 332
Eisenhardt, K., 353, 393, 394
Elfring, T., 102
Ellig, B.R., 235

Elsey, B., 456
Employees:
    and employers, 15, 43, 46, 71, 81, 85, 87–88,
        119, 173, 177, 217, 260, 366, 402, 442, 456
    and compensation, 206, 442
    and complexities, 212
    and local managers, 7
    and performance management, 206, 368, 369,
        465
    and redundancies, 489
    and rights, 74, 76–78, 81, 177, 318, 442
    and risk-taking, 217
    Discretionary energy, 9, 119
    Expectations from, 41–42, 87, 116, 258, 336
    Network of relationships, 5, 87, 115, 118, 120,
        144, 147, 218–220, 287, 293– 295, 393, 402,
        438, 465
    Options, 367–374
    Value proposition, 9
Employment Equity Act, 469
Employment practices liability (EPL) 87–88
Enterprise Culture Management (ECM), 454,
    455
Entrepreneurship landscape, 391–393, 399
Erickson, T., 377
Esping-Anderson, G., 114
Essential evolution, 17
European Union (UN), 76–77
Evans, P., 410, 444
Expatriate managers, 411, 412, 413, 414

Fahey, I., 133
Fahey, W., 270
Family Medical Leave Act (FMLA), 73
Fang, M., 236
Fannie Mae, 138
Faraj, S., 271
Farr, M., 398
Farrell, L., 37
Fashoyin, T., 470, 471
Faull, N., 465
Feldman, D.C., 366, 368
Felstead, A., 491
Fenn, D., 268
Fenton-O'Creevy, M., 117
Ferlie, E., 95, 490
Ferris , G.R., 158, 502
Fiol, C., 392
Florkowski, G.W., 71, 74, 79, 83–84, 86
Folta, T.B., 365
Foote, D.A., 365
Forbath, T., 97–98
Ford, J.K., 263, 265–266, 272, 274
Ford, R., 503
Foucault, M., 16, 58
Fournier, V., 54
Frank, R., 114
Frankel, L.P., 162

Freeman, J., 236
Freeman, R.B., 43, 111
Frei, R.L., 508
Friedman, T., 111
Frost, P.J., 154
Froud, J., 490
Fuller, S., 85

Gaebler, T., 490
Gaglio, C., 397
Gainey, T., 267
Galbraith, J.R., 94, 183, 211
Gallaghar, M., 458
Gallie, G., 115, 118, 490
Gallup Organisation, The, 300, 302–303, 307
Gander, J., 401
Gartner, W., 397
Gavino, M., 143
GE, 503
Gehart, B., 224–226, 228–233, 235–238
Geletkanycz, M.A., 415
Gelfand, M., 415
Gerhart, B., 345
Ghoshal, S., 269–270, 273, 410, 413
Gibbons, R., 238
Gilbert, J.A., 416
Giles, W.F., 248
Gilliland, S.W., 511
GlaxoSmithKline, 481
Globalisation, 43, 110–111, 113–114, 118, 120,
    255, 321, 339
    and organizational change 7, 141
Global Diversity, 416
Global Executive Table, 415
Global High-Tech company case study,
    256–260
Glyn, A., 114
Godard, J., 116
Goldstein, I., 266, 272–273
Goleman, D., 145, 426
Gooderham, P.N., 85
Gordon, J.R.M., 152
Goswami, R., 390
Gouldner, A.W., 42
Gramm, C.L., 357
Green, F., 42, 47, 119, 488, 494, 498
Greenberg, J., 248
Greenwood, R., 127
Gregerson, H., 412, 423
Gremler, D.D, 508
Grey, C., 42, 54
Grimes, A., 52
Grimshaw, D., 48
Gross Domestic Product (GDP) 109
Grugulis, I., 491
Guest, D.E., 41–42, 47, 57, 157
Gustafson, D.H., 153
Guthrie, J., 346, 351

Hackman, J. R., 306, 307
Hage, J., 211, 213, 217
Hagerman, J.L., 73, 87
Hall, D., 395, 412
Hamel, G., 92–93, 103, 145, 147, 324, 489
Hammer, M., 95–97
Hampden-Turner, C., 414
Handy, C., 106
Hannan, M.T., 236, 393, 398
Harcourt, M., 83
Harcourt, S., 83
Harley, B., 42
Harris, M.M., 248
Harris, P., 267, 414
Harrison, D.A., 231
Harter, J.K., 302, 511, 512
Hatch, N., 347
Hatch, D., 332
HayGroup, 238
Hays, R., 412
Hayton, J., 277, 392, 403
HC Bridge Framework, 26
Helin, S., 87
Heneman, R., 390, 399, 403
Herriot, P., 41
Hersey, P., 323
Heskett, J.L., 129, 141, 143, 502, 508, 512
Heslett, S., 262
Heslin, P.A., 249,
Hicks-Clark, D., 416
Hierarchy, 93, 96, 99–100
Hill, C.W., 364, 365, 366
Hill, S., 115
Hilmer, F.G., 364
Hinings, 127
Hippel, C.V., 364–366, 369
Hirst, P., 110
Hitt, M.A., 368, 395
Hofstede, G., 236, 255, 438, 453, 466
Holder, G., 351
Hollenbeck, G., 411, 415, 425
Holton, E., 273
Hoojiberg, R., 422
Horwitz, F.M., 462, 464–468
House, R.J., 415, 416
Howell, J., 457
Hsu, D., 393
Hudson Institute, 337
Hughes, R., 279
Hulsink, W., 102
Human capital, 4, 6, 8, 9, 87, 111, 142, 222, 350, 358, 361–370, 397
Human Resource Management (HRM)
    Competency Study, 168–169, 172–173, 175, 178–179
    Commitment model of, 7, 139
    Corporate Social Responsibility Impact on, 15
    Cross-cultural diffusion of, 464

Focus and vision of, 138, 141–143, 145
Future of, 484–85
Implications of, 399–403
Integration within and between, 46
Legal environment of, 71–72, 75, 78, 81–82, 84, 86
Organisational structure, 175, 205, 398
Practice topics of (HRM-P), 8–11, 56, 61–64, 400
Strategy, 21, 52, 70, 123, 125–127, 137, 170, 171, 206, 350, 370, 390, 403
Styles and culture, 466–467
Technology of, 179
Theories and practices, 11, 22, 43, 47, 73, 83, 85–86, 116–117, 139, 144, 167, 171, 205–206, 213, 218, 296, 351, 363, 390, 400, 403–404, 440, 489
Value creation of, 138, 140, 143, 146–147
Weaknesses of, 41
HR professionals, 10–11, 47, 72, 74, 79, 80, 84–87, 124, 141–142, 145–147, 251, 256, 260, 365, 390–391, 393, 401, 403–404, 480–484,
    Strategic contributions of, 169–179
Hunt, J.G., 415
Hunter, L.W., 228
Hunter, M., 158
Huntley, R., 255
Hurry, D., 357–358, 361, 364,
Huselid, M.A., 154–155, 265, 277–279, 346, 351, 353, 390, 399, 400, 481
Hutton, H.R., 152
Hutton, W., 112, 113
Hyman, R., 46

Ibarra, H., 158
IBM, 503
Iles, P., 416
Iles, V., 153
India Context, 435–444
    Challenges, 441–444
    Determinants, 438–441
Indian Institute of Personnel Management (IIPM), 437
Industrial Disputes Act (IDA), 442
Industrial Relations (IR), 40–41, 43–47, 49
Information processing, 211–212
Innovation, 100, 103
Innovative classroom learning initiatives, 329–332
Intagliata, J., 167
Internal Labour Markets (ILMs), 442, 443
International Labour Organization (ILO), 74–75, 79, 469, 473
International Labour Standards, (ILS), 74
Involvement moves, 160
Ipe, M., 271
Ireland, R., 391, 395

Jack, S., 403
Jackson, R., 66
Jackson, S.E., 151, 346, 465
Jackson, T., 462, 464–465, 470
Janssens, M, 53
Javidan, M., 415, 418
Jenkins, C., 106
Johnson, G., 130, 266
Johnson, H.T., 24, 33
Johnson, J.W., 507, 510
Johnson, R., 156
Jones, F., 114
Jones, M.T., 490
Joyce, C., 324, 338, 339

Kahn, W.A., 300
Kaiser Permanente, 418
Kalleberg, A., 394, 404
Kalula, E., 473
Kamoche, K., 462–464, 468, 471
Kang, S., 270
Kanter, R., 392
Kaplan, R.S., 141, 142, 247, 350, 504
Karreman, D., 65
Katz, H.C., 236
Katz, J., 390, 397, 399, 403
Kaufman, B.E., 40, 49, 395, 404
Kaufman, R.T., 235, 265
Keenan, T., 465
Kelly, E., 82
Kelly, J., 41
Kendall, S.D., 513
Kenny, J., 168
Kerr, S., 509
Kersley, B., 117, 118
Ketels, C., 130
Ketter, P., 299
Key, S.G., 417
Khatri, P., 443
Kidwell, R.E., 239
King, Z., 54, 157
Kirkman, B.L., 95
Kirkpatrick, I., 490
Kirn, S. 141
Kizilos M., 332, 334
Klaas, B., 267, 400, 403
Klimoski, R.J., 249
Kluger, A.N., 248
Knight, F., 398
Knowledge economy, 131–132
Knowledge management, 42
Knowledge, skills and abilities (KSAs), 211–212, 221, 322, 326, 329, 331, 361, 426
Kochan, T.A., 364, 365
Kogut, B., 357–359 362–63, 397
Kolb, D., 167
Kolvereid, L., 395
Kotter, J.P, 153, 323,

Kozlowski, S., 275, 280
Kraiger, K., 262–263
Kramer, R., 411
Kristof, A.L., 368
Kruse, D.L., 235
Kulatilaka, N., 357, 358, 359, 361, 362, 363, 364, 370
Kunda, G., 365, 369, 370

Labor knowledge, 179
Labor law, 72, 74, 77, 147
    Of China, 457–458
    Workplace and employment law, 72–74, 76–78, 80, 84–86
Labour markets, 69, 106–108, 113–115, 120, 209, 401
Lado, A.A., 347, 363
LaFasto, F., 144
Lam, S., 83
Lampel, J., 127
Lane, H., 410
Langlois, R., 397
Larson, C., 144
Latham, G.P., 248, 254
Lawler, E.E., 18, 32, 183, 188, 190–191, 225–226, 233, 510
Lawrence, P.R., 211
Layard R., 107, 119,
Lazear, E.P., 230, 238
Leadership
    Development model, 324–325
    Evolution of, 322–323
    Framework, 418–421
    Global, 411, 413–417, 419–423, 425
    Information processing model, 419
    Selection and development of, 426–428
    The challenge of, 321–322
Legge, K., 43, 46, 49, 53, 56, 158
Leiblien, M.J., 358, 361, 362
Leidner. D., 271
Leigh, D., 265
Lepak, D.P., 127, 211, 264, 278–279, 351, 364, 400–401, 403
Lepsinger, R., 265
Leung, J., 456
Lev, B. 140, 145
Levinthal, D.A., 365
Levy, O., 410, 422
Lewin, K., 322,
Liao, H., 509
Libuser, C., 365
Lievens, F., 266
Likert, R., 323
Linder, J.C., 370
Lindholm, N., 452
Lindsey, E., et al, 325
Lippitt, G., 168
Littler, C.R., 92

Liu, Y.Q., 452
Loasby, B., 397
Locke, E.A., 248, 254
Lombardo, M., 325, 332,
London, M., 245, 249, 263
Lord, R.G., 254
Lorsch, J.W., 211
Losey, M., 167
Lossey, M., 18
Lu, Y., 452
Luce, S., 113
Lucia, A., 265
Luiz, J., 463
Luthans, F., 302
Lynch, D., 463
Lynch, L., 117

Mabe, P.A., 248
Mabey, C.D., 46
MacCormack, A., 97–98
MacDuffie, J.P., 489
Macey, W.H., 313, 506, 511, 514
Magner, N.R., 415
Maher, K.J., 254
Mahoney, J., 351, 401
Mallon, N., 365, 366
Malone, M.S., 102
Malos, S.B., 368
Management by Objectives (MBO), 247
Management Process, 340
Mangaliso, M.P., 465
Mangold, G., 504–505
March, J.G., 160, 212, 402
Marketing, 17, 159
Markides, C., 131
Marlow, S., 399
Marmot, L., 107, 118, 119
Marquardt, M., 271
Martin, J., 353
Martinez, M., 391
Maruyama, M., 464
Maslow, A.H., 226
Masterson, S.S., 511
Matanmi, S., 463, 464
Mather, K., 491
Matusik, S.F., 85, 364, 365, 366
Maxham, J.G., 511
Mayer, M., 149–150, 157
Mayson, S., 399
Mbigi, L., 462, 464, 466
McCall, M., 324–328, 411, 412, 415, 425
McCauley, C., 262
McClelland, D., 167, 412
McCullough, M., 168
McDaniel, M.A., 508
McElroy, J.C., 364
McEvily, A., 95
McGrath, R.G., 357–359, 361, 364, 368

McLagan, P., 167, 168
McLarty, R., 403
McMullen, J., 397
McMurrer, D., 275
McNulty, T., 95
McRae, K., 190
Measurement systems, 177
Melnick, S.L., 417
Mendenhall, M., 412
Mercer Consulting, 127
Metrics and measurement, 486
Michaels, E., 337, 338
Miles, M, 392
Miles, R., 279, 346
Miles, S.J., 504–505
Milkovich, G.T., 224–225, 229, 232, 237–238
Miller, K., 399
Milliman, J., 353
Minimum wage, 69, 107, 114
Mintzberg, H., 127
Mishra, L., 442
Mo, R., 456
Mone, E.M., 245, 249
Moore, C., 417
Morris, J.T., 236
Morrison, A., 412
Mowday, R.T., 302
Muir, D.M., 83
Muller-Bonanni, T., 86
Multinational Corporations (MNCs), 447, 448, 452, 455, 458–459, 462
Multinational Enterprises (MNE), 74, 76, 79–85, 285
Murphy, K.J., 237
Mutanmi, S., 469

Nadler, L., 168
Nahapiet, J., 269–270, 273
Naidoo, S., 463
Napier, S., 83
Narayanan, V.K., 133
Nath, S., 83, 84
National Institute of Labour Management, (NILM), 437
National institute of Personnel Management, (NIPM), 437
Nelson, R., 397
Netemeyer, J.G., 511
New Partnership for African Development (NEPAD), 470
Newbert, S., 347
Newman, J.M, 224, 490
Next Generation Enterprise, 383
Ng, S.H., 448
Ngai, P., 458
Nielson, A.P., 365, 366
Noe, R., 264, 267, 274
Noel, J., 271

Nohria, N., 85
Nokia, 286, 295, 486
Nolan, P., 488, 494, 498
North American Agreement on Labor
    Co-operation (NAALC), 77
North American Free Trade Agreement
    (NAFTA), 77, 79
Norton, D.P., 141, 142, 350, 504
Novartis, 481
Nyambegera, S.M., 468
Nzelibe, C.O., 464,

O'Connor, E., 217
Oakes, K., 267
Occupational change, 110, 120
Oddou, G., 412
Odiorne, G.S., 247
Offshoring, 113
Oldham, G.R., 306
Olsen, J.P., 160, 238
Ones, D.S., 508
Options framework, 359–361
Organisation Development (OD), 174–175, 256,
    258, 259
Organisational change, 488–499
Organisational Citizenship Behaviours (OCB),
    510–511
Organisational structures, 211–213
Organization of Economic Cooperation and
    Development (OECD), 70, 76, 108–109,
    113–114
Ortenblad, A., 456
Osborne, D., 490
Osland, J., 412, 419, 422, 423
Osterman, P., 228, 357
Ostroff, C., 60, 61, 265–266, 390, 502, 507
Outsourcing, 98–99

Packaging moves, 160
Palley, T., 113
Pandian, J., 351
Panel Study of Entrepreneurship Dynamics
    (PSED), 395
Parkington, J.P., 504–505, 513
Patterson, M.G., 155
Pearce, J.L., 366
Pearson, A.E., 28, 340
Pemberton, C., 41
Penrose, E., 347, 400
Perception management, 412
Performance improvement strategies, 251
Performance Management Cycle, 246
Performance management programs, 252, 255
Performance Management, 177, 206, 245,
    248–249, 259–260
Performance yield curve, 34–35
Perlmutter, H., 414
Peteraf, M., 353

Peterson, M.F., 415
Petty, M.M., 238
Pfeffer, J., 117, 155, 157, 159, 226, 238
Philips, A., 152
Pinder, C.C., 31
Pindyck, R., 357, 358, 359
Pisano, G., 353
Polanyi, M., 268
Pollitt, C., 490
Pollock, R., 276
Polzer, J.T., 248
Poole, M.S., 153
Porras, J., 137
Porter, G., 366
Porter, M., 130, 139, 142, 393
Posthuma, R., 87
Powell, W., 82, 127
Pralahad, C.K., 92–93, 103, 133, 147, 349, 489
Price Waterhouse Coopers (PwC), 410, 418
Priem, R.L., 348, 358
Pritchard, R.D., 226
Privately owned enterprises (POEs), 433, 448,
    452
Process moves, 160
Professional recruitment model, 214, 219–221
Pucik, V., 410, 412
Pugh, S.D., 502, 506, 512
Purcell, J., 47, 448, 489
Putnam, R., 5, 118

Quinn, J.B., 364
Quinn, R., 141, 422

Rafaeli, A., 514
Raghuram, S., 279
Rahim, M.A., 415
Rainbird, H., 491
Rajagopolan, N., 235
Ralston, D., 455
Raman, S.R., 440, 441
Ray, G., 348
Reagons, R., 95
Recruitment and selection, 209–215, 218–220,
    222
Reed, M., 92
Reilly, P., 183, 188, 198
Relationship management, 412
Resource-based view (RBV), 357
Retirement, 385
Return on investment (ROI), 246
Reuter, 287
Reward systems, 177–178
Reynolds, P., 392, 395
Rhinesmith, S., 414
Richardson, M., 491
Rifkin, J., 106, 488
Rijamampianina, R., 462
Riketta, M., 302

Ringdal, K., 85
Risk management, 88, 296
Ritz Carlton, 349
Robinson, S.L., 366
Roehling, M.V., 72, 73, 85, 87
Rogers, J., 43
Rogg, K.L., 506
Romanelli, E., 393
Rose, M., 488, 498
Rosen, B., 95
Rosenzweig, P.M., 85
Rothwell, S., 412
Rottenberg, S., 225
Rouiller, J., 266, 272–273
Rousseau, D.M., 41, 365, 366
Row, H., 510
Royal Bank of Scotland, 285–286, 291, 292
Rubery, J., 48
Rubin, P., 348
Rucci, A. J., 123–124, 141, 143, 145
Ruef, M., 390–391, 393–394, 397, 402
Ruggles, R., 269
Ryans, S.L., 209, 225–226, 228–229, 231–232,
    234–235, 237, 239

Saba, T., 412
Sabiru-Perez, M., 87
Sahay, S., 438
Saini, D., 439
Saks, A., 274, 300, 302
Salaman, G., 103, 135
Salanova, M., 511
Salas, E., 275
Sallie-Dosunmu, M., 266
Sanchez, J., 266
Sandstrom, J., 87
Sarasvathy, S., 397
Sarnin, A.,130
Sasser, E., 129
Sasser, W., 141
Schein, E.H., 366, 455
Schlesinger, L.E., 129
Schneider, B., 313, 503–508, 510–514
Schneider, S.C., 135
Schneier, C.E., 479
Schnell, J.F., 357
Schon, D.A., 131, 134, 152
Schoonhoven, C., 393, 394
Schoonover, S., 167
Schroeder, R.G., 22
Schuler, R.S., 62, 151, 346, 465, 502
Schumpeter, J., 110, 397, 398
Scott-Jackson, W., 191
Sears Roebuck, 141
Seddon, J.W., 464
Self-management, 412
Selmer, J., 447
Selznick, P., 393

Sen, A., 11, 113
Sena, J., 271
Sennett, R., 115, 118
Sessa, V.I., 263, 249
Sexton, D., 397
Shane, S., 391–392, 395, 397
Shani, A., 271
Sharma, I.J., 438
Shaw, J.D., 235
Shaw, K., 300
Shepherd, D., 395
Sherer, P.D., 347
Sherman, B., 106
Shippmann, J., 265
Shirom, A., 300
Shoemaker, P.A., 347
Simon, H.A., 212, 402
Singh, V., 158
Sisson, K., 40, 46, 117
Skinner, W., 18
Slevin, D., 395
Smallwood, N., 141, 182, 195, 324,
Smith, C., 458
Smith, D.A., 467
Smith, K., 209, 211, 403
Smith, P.B., 415, 455
Smither, J.W., 249, 254
Snell, S.A, 127, 211, 264, 278–279, 345, 350, 353,
    364, 400–401, 404
Snow, C., 279, 346
Social capital, 5, 118, 402
Society for Human Resource Management, 266
Sonenshein, S., 161
South African Clothing and Textile Workers
    Union (SACTWU), 473
South African Development Committee (SADC),
    472
Sparrow, P., 41, 42, 437, 438, 439, 440, 441
Spencer, L., 167, 327
Spencer, S., 167, 327
Spender, J.C., 133
Spreitzer, G., 328, 423
Staeyert, C., 53
Staff management, 4
Staffing models, 205, 210
Stalker, G.M., 213
Stamoulis, J., 249
Starbuck, W., 272
Starbucks, 351–352
State-owned enterprises (SOEs), 433, 447–448,
    453, 455, 456, 468
Steel, P., 248
Steffy, B., 52
Stevens, C., 390, 399, 403
Stiglitz, J., 114
Stiles, P., 366
Stinchcombe, A., 100, 393, 394
Stjernberg, T., 152

Stockman, N., 458
Stogdill R.M., 322
Storey, J., 40, 46, 53, 95, 103, 123, 150–152
Strack, R., 514
Strategic Human Resource Management
(SHRM), 3, 5–6, 69, 70, 83, 93, 137, 221,
351, 353
Strategic Performance Management (SPM) 247,
250–251, 255
Structural Adjustment Programmes (SAPs),
463–464, 469, 472
Subunits, 212–213, 215–219, 221, 222
Suhadolnik, D., 167, 168
Supply chain management, 100
Sutherland, K., 153
Sutherland, M., 468
Sutton, R.I., 117, 514
Swift, M., 402

Takahara, A., 453
Talent decisions, 23, 35, 37
Talent Management (TM), 336, 338, 339, 340,
341, 387–388
Talent market, 17, 20
Talent resources, 26
Talent segmentation, 35–36
Talentship, 19, 25, 31
Tamkin, P., 188, 198
Tan, C., 401
Tannenbaum, S., 262–263, 266, 275–276, 278
Tansky, J., 390, 399, 403
Tata Consultancy Services, 481
Tax, S.S., 513
Taylor, B., 448
Taylor, M.S., 42, 209
Taylor, R., 118
Taylor, S., 83
Teece, D.J, 132, 353
Tekleab, A.G., 42
Temporary Help Agencies (THA), 82
Terkel, S., 490, 498
Thompson, G., 110
Thompson, J.D., 211, 212
Thomson, P., 42, 48
Thorsteinson, T.J., 368
Tichy, N., 331, 413, 414
Tobin, D.R., 269
Total Quality Management (TQM), 22, 45, 49,
465, 467, 504
Townshend, M., 466
Tracey, J., 266, 272–273
Trade blocs, 77–78, 84
Trade unions, 109, 112, 114–115, 117, 120, 458
Training programs, 174–175, 258
Trevor, C.O., 231–232, 238
Triandis, H.C., 416
Trigeorgis, L., 358–359, 361
Trompenaars, F., 414

Tsitsianis, N., 488, 494, 498
Tsui, A., 448
Turnley, W.H., 366
Tyson, S., 150

Ulrich, D., 141, 150–151, 165, 167–168, 182,
187–188, 195, 299, 303, 324, 429, 480, 502,
504, 509–510, 513
Unemployment, 107, 109
United Nations Global Compact, 75
Uzzi, B., 364

Valentin, V.K., 133
Value-chain scoreboard, 141, 350
Van Buren, M., 270, 275
Van deVen, A., 130, 153
Van Maanen, J., 506
Vandewalle, B., 249
Venkata Ratnam, C.S., 439, 441
Venkataraman, S., 391, 397
Viswesvaran, C., 508

Wade-Benzoni, K.A., 365, 366
Wajcman, J., 41–42, 49
Waldman, D.A., 504, 509
Wall, T., 116, 117
Wal-Mart, 481
Walsham, G., 438
Wang, Z.M., 455
Ward, S., 466, 467
Warner, M., 447, 448
Wasko, M., 271
Waters, K.W., 85
Watson, T.J., 61, 158
Web 2.0, 382
Webber, A.M., 510
Weick, K., 212, 217
Weiss, A., 239
Welbourne, T.M., 277, 309, 312, 311–312, 397
Welch, J., 92, 340
Wernerfelt, B., 346
West, M.A., 156
Westfield, E., 88
Westhead, P., 395
White, G., 448
White, M., 115, 489, 490, 494, 498
White, S.S., 506, 509, 512
Whittington, R., 149–150, 157, 162
Wick, C., 276
Wigdor, A., 237
Wiklund, J., 395
Wiley, J.W., 512, 514
Wilkinson, A., 47
Williams, R., 271
Williams, S., 490, 494, 498
Williams, T., 183, 1980
Williamson, I.O., 403
Wills, S., 414

Wilson, M.C., 363, 423
Wiseman, R.M., 235
Witkin, B., 265
Wocke, A., 467
Wolf, M., 110, 115, 118
Wood, R., 248
Wood, S., 116, 117, 275–276, 488, 494, 498
Workers' Daily newspaper, 456, 458
Workplace implications of HIV/AIDS,
    471–472
World Economic Forum, 410
Worrall, L., 488–489, 491, 492, 493, 494
Wright, P.M., 235, 237, 345, 350, 353, 362,
    390, 401, 463
Wright, P.W., 72, 73, 84, 85

Xin, K., 448, 455
XML, 382
Xu, F., 458

Yahoo!, 382
Yelon, S.L., 274
Youndt, M.A., 345, 346
Yu, K.C., 453

Zahra, S.A., 365, 366
Zaleznik, A., 145
Zamutto, R., 217,
Zanko, M., 157
Zeickner, K.M., 417
Zeithaml, V.A., 508